Robert M. La Follette

THE MACMILLAN COMPANY
NEW YORK · CHICAGO
DALLAS · ATLANTA · SAN FRANCISCO

THE MACMILLAN COMPANY
OF CANADA, LIMITED
TORONTO

Robert M. LaFollette

JUNE 14, 1855—JUNE 18, 1925

CHAPTERS I-XXVI BY

BELLE CASE LA FOLLETTE

AND

CHAPTERS XXVII-LXXII BY

FOLA LA FOLLETTE

In Two Volumes

Volume II

THE MACMILLAN COMPANY *New York* · 1953

First Printing

Printed in the United States of America

70836

DEC 15 1953

Contents

Volume II

vi   *Contents*

Illustrations

Volume II

Cartoons and Facsimiles

Volume II

CHAPTER XLVI

A Campaign to Maintain
Constitutional Rights

The Sixty-fifth Congress remained in extra session from April 2 until October 6, 1917. It was not until late in October, after Congress had adjourned, that the first American shot was fired in the trenches of Europe. But it was during this session that the Administration's war program was formulated in legislation and approved by Congress. Steffens had understood what Bob's role was to be when he wrote shortly after the Armed Ship bill filibuster predicting that Bob would "be fighting all the reactionary measures proposed under the shadow of war" and would "be beaten in most of them."[1] Bob also received many letters from people who did not agree with him on the war issue but admired his courage and begged him to raise his voice "during the War to prevent graft and the robbing of natural resources."[2]

Bob was a member of the important Senate Finance Committee and thus had a direct responsibility as to the methods for financing the war. The Administration's first war measure was a bond issue calling for $7,000,000,000, which was described on the Senate floor as the greatest that had "ever been proposed in this or in any other country in the world."[3] It passed the House without a dissenting vote and was unanimously approved by the Senate at a single sitting on April 17, just fifteen days after war had been declared. The bill provided for large credits to the Allies and for Army and Navy supplies. Bob did not approve of the loan to the Allies or of the method of financing the war by bond issues. He did not believe that vast sums should be appropriated without any budget or any guarantee as to how the money was to be spent. But he voted for the bill because he could not vote against the loan without also voting against the supplies for the Army and Navy.[4]

Hastily framed legislation was rushed through Congress with little time for consideration. Immediately after the bond bill passed, the Senate took up the so-called Espionage bill. Bob thought this was the worst legislative crime of the war because it menaced freedom of the press, freedom of speech, freedom of assembly, freedom from unwarranted search and seizure, and other rights which had been won by generations of struggle and sacrifice. The popularly accepted title of "Espionage" bill led many uninformed people to assume it was directed solely against enemy spies and therefore to interpret any opposition as "unpatriotic." It was, in fact, an omnibus bill containing provisions on various subjects and giving the President extraordinary powers. The Senate Judiciary Committee refused to hold hearings on the bill, but when it came up in the Senate the debate centered upon the first amendment to the Constitution, which forbids Congress to enact any law "abridging the freedom of speech or of the press, or the right of the people peaceably to assemble and to petition the Government for a redress of grievances." It raised the question as to whether the war powers of the Government gave a general power to disregard the Constitution and delegate vast powers to the Executive. Those supporting the bill argued that Congress should "trust" the President. Throughout the debate Bob supported every amendment which sought to prevent drastic restrictions of free speech, free press, and free assembly.

As originally drafted by the Department of Justice and submitted to the Senate by the Judiciary Committee, the bill provided for a strict censorship of the press through a board created and controlled by the President. The *New York Times* denounced this provision as "a tyrannous measure" reminiscent of "abhorrent Prussian despotism."[5] The American Newspaper Publishers Association condemned it,[6] and the metropolitan press of the country joined in protesting it. Bob voted for an amendment eliminating this provision which passed 39 to 38.[7] The President sought unsuccessfully to have this censorship provision restored in the House, declaring this authority was "necessary for the protection of the Nation."[8]

Widespread newspaper protest undoubtedly defeated the provision giving the President power to appoint a board to censor the press. But they had not campaigned against other provisions restricting freedom of speech, assembly, and press which passed by large majorities. Bob was especially concerned about a provision enlarging the powers of postoffice officials and thus permitting them to suppress publications through arbitrary denial of mailing rights. When the bill passed the Senate, Bob was one of six Senators who voted against it. Under this "Espionage" law, rendered more severe by amendments adopted June 16, 1918, the Department of Justice arrested, indicted, and convicted hundreds of people for the exercise of rights guaranteed them under the Constitution. Within six months an attempt was made to apply one of the provisions of this law to Bob.

Bob also opposed the Conscription bill which came before the Senate while the Espionage bill was still pending. In the House enough Democratic leaders opposed conscription to make it appear for a time as if the Military Affairs Committee might defy Administration pressure and present a majority report in favor of raising a volunteer army before resorting to the draft.[9] Speaker Clark and Representative Dent, Democratic chairman of the committee, both denounced the draft bill on the floor of the House.[10] But in the Senate a majority of the Military Affairs Committee favored the Conscription bill as drafted by the War Department, although a minority report was made advocating the raising of troops by the volunteer system before resorting to conscription.[11]

Debate on the bill began in the Senate on April 21, and was limited under a unanimous-consent agreement to vote upon it on April 28.[12] Bob offered an amendment calling for an advisory referendum to allow the people of the United States to register their opinion on an issue which affected them so profoundly.[13] He was unable to obtain the floor to speak for his amendment until eleven thirty on the night of April 27, when he presented his argument against conscription for about two hours and twenty minutes in the first prepared speech he had delivered since the declaration of war.[14] Word had been passed around that the Senate would adjourn. Therefore, at that hour, the galleries were practically deserted and there were very few Senators on the floor. Belle, who was in the family gallery, thought that he was in his best mood and that "if he had been talking to an immense audience he could not have been more effective."[15]

In opening his argument against the bill, Bob declared that it clothed one man with power, acting through his agents appointed by him, to enter at will every home in our country and violently lay hold of one million of our finest and strongest boys, ranging in age from nineteen to twenty-six years, and deport them across the seas to a foreign land more than three thousand miles away, requiring them under penalty of death if they refused, to wound and kill other young boys like themselves toward whom they felt no hostility. For such action, under the conditions at that time he maintained there was "no precedent in all our history" or "in the history of any people making the slightest claim to freedom."[16]

Bob declared it was a travesty upon legislation for supporters of the bill to try to drive it through Congress by arguing that it was a measure in the interest of democracy. It had come to the Senate "straight from the secret committee room, without an opportunity having been granted to the public to know its terms, much less to discuss them." In all his years of experience in the House and Senate, he said he had never "heard so much democracy preached and so little practiced as during the last few months. . . . We should remember that the momentous issues with which we are dealing to-day, and have been dealing during the last few weeks, have not been directly in issue in any election." Therefore, he argued, there should be an advisory vote on the Conscription bill which could be taken under the amendment he offered without setting up any new machinery or delaying war plans. He maintained that if we were afraid to rely upon volunteer soldiers, "we might better reexamine the reasons for our entering into the war than abolish volunteers and substitute for them men dragged into the ranks by draft." Contrasting what had been done by other governments he said that "under the law Germany's colonial troops can only be enlisted for overseas service upon their voluntary application," and the "English law as to the overseas service of men obtained through her colonies is the same . . . after almost three years of war Canada has not even considered the draft."[17]

Under the Constitution of the United States, Bob declared there was no authority for drafting an army to be sent across the seas to foreign lands, and supported his contention by reading from Daniel Webster's argument on a Conscription bill proposed in 1814.[18] He also charged that the autocratic character of the 1917 Conscription bill, drafted by the War Department, was a deadly peril to democracy which held the menace of a permanent military power and the Prussianizing of the United States.

In closing he pleaded that we should use our influence and power to bring about a just and durable peace. Quoting at some length from the President's "peace without victory" speech, he commented that it had rarely been "given to one man to speak so movingly to a listening world," and noted free Russia's recent response in a declaration that its object was not the domination of other nations but "to establish a durable peace on the rights of nations to decide their own destiny."[19]

Among the few people in the gallery that night were Art Young of the *Masses* staff, Mrs. Harriet P. Thomas, secretary of the Woman's Peace Party, and Arthur Garfield Hays, a prominent New York lawyer. Although Hays disagreed with Bob's views on conscription, he listened to the entire speech, and wrote afterward that he had "seldom been more moved by eloquence" or more impressed by the courage of a man who dared "express himself squarely in spite of opprobrium—and insult."[20]

Soon after Bob finished speaking, the Senate recessed until the next morning. Although he did not get to bed until three o'clock, he was on the Senate floor again that afternoon, voting for amendments to increase the maximum age limit of the draft. He also offered his amendment extending the rights of conscientious objectors and providing for tribunals to pass upon claims for exemption. It was based upon an English statute which had been adopted after a year and a half of war. When his amendment came to a vote, he asked for the yeas and nays, but not enough Senators seconded his request to secure a roll call. Therefore his amendment giving conscientious objectors in this country the same rights they were allowed in England was rejected without putting Senators on record as he had hoped.[21]

As a substitute for the Conscription bill, Bob later offered an amendment which called for the raising of an army of 500,000 by voluntary enlistment while the issue of conscription was being referred to the people for an advisory vote. The Senate clerk had just finished reading Bob's substitute when the French Mission, led by Marshal Joffre and former Premier Viviani, entered the Chamber. The Senate rose and applauded enthusiastically. During a brief recess Senators were presented to the distinguished guests. Viviani made a short, eloquent speech, and Joffre was greeted with rounds of applause when he responded to calls for an address by saying, "I do not speak English. *Vive les États-Unis!*"

From the family gallery Belle watched the enthusiastic reception with interest, observed the sturdy figure of Joffre in the gay French uniform, and decided he was undoubtedly a lovable person. But she wrote the children that during the ceremonies she kept thinking, "how different where the poor fellows are fighting. How can we forget what this demonstration means, what this mission is for?"[22]

When the French Mission had been escorted from the Chamber, Bob spoke briefly for his substitute amendment. It was defeated 64 to 4, Gore, Gronna, and Vardaman being the only Senators who voted with Bob.[23] There had been a good many Senators present during Bob's speech, and Belle noted that they listened attentively. She thought, however, that Norris made a "very lame explanation of why he could not vote for it."[24] The volunteer plan for raising troops had been rejected by both Senate and House. When the final text of the Conscription bill came from the Conference Committee, it was adopted in the Senate by 65 to 8. Gore, Gronna, Hardwick, Kirby, Norris, Stone, and Trammell joined Bob in voting against it. Vardaman was paired, but announced that he would have voted against it.[25] The next day the President signed the bill and announced for the first time that American troops would be sent overseas. In proclaiming June 5 as registration day for all men between the ages of twenty-one to thirty-one, Wilson stated that the draft was "in no sense a conscription of the unwilling" but rather a "selection from a nation that has volunteered in mass."[26]

Bob differed fundamentally with this opinion. His correspondence and reports coming to him from many sources in different parts of the country convinced him that the President's statement was an unjustified assumption based upon wishful thinking. In a subsequent debate Bob expressed the opinion, which he held to the end of his life, that the law drafting men for overseas service in foreign lands was unconstitutional, un-American, undemocratic, and should never have been passed.[27] He believed that the Supreme Court had correctly interpreted the Constitution ninety years before when it declared that the President's power to call out the state militia was limited to cases of actual invasion or insurrection.[28] He did not waver in this conviction when the Supreme Court reversed its previous decision a few months after the passage of the Conscription bill and sustained the Government's right to draft men in the state militia and elsewhere for service in foreign lands.[29]

It was Bob's profound conviction that a democracy ought never to enter upon a war it could not prosecute by volunteers. He frankly told the Senate that he intended to fight for the repeal of the Conscription law.[30] But he knew this could not be accomplished by merely introducing bills and making speeches about them if they were to be buried in the *Congressional Record*, thus giving hostile newspapers the opportunity to misrepresent the issues and blacken the characters of those who raised them. Therefore he sent out by mail the speeches he made, the amendments he offered; and the roll call votes he forced whenever he could get enough Senators to second his request were all parts of a clearly defined plan to take these issues to the people of the United States just as he had done in Wisconsin.

At the next national elections he intended to organize campaigns in the different States for the election of Congressmen and Senators on a specific platform. In a letter to Gilbert Roe he outlined the three issues that he considered especially important: (1) repealing the draft law; (2) that it is the *right* and the duty of *Congress* to determine upon the motives, the cause, and the objects of any war when it commences, or at *any time* during the *progress* of its existence; (3) that no more bonds should be issued, and that henceforth all moneys for war purposes should be raised by taxing war profits and surplus incomes.[31]

Bob recognized that a fund to carry on the campaign was essential, and had been encouraged by the interested response of Amos Pinchot, Rudolph Spreckels, Edwin Borchard, Gilson Gardner, and other friends in different parts of the country who shared his conviction as to its importance. Bob was also working on a plan to organize small agencies in different communities in each State where, quietly by word of mouth, directions could be given and appeals made for contributions. Then, when sufficient funds had been collected and everything was ready, those organizing the movement were to come out and make an open stand on their Constitutional rights in a campaign to elect Senators and Representatives on the platform Bob had outlined.[32]

Several Members of the House and a number of Senators were

cooperating in preparing mailing lists for their States. The president of one of the farm organizations had given Bob the names of good men who would take care of at least a dozen States. Since March 4 Bob, Jr., had been going through the letters received in his father's office, classifying them by States and making selected lists of names from the best of them. This gave a tentative list for every State, and he had drafted a letter to go out to these men. When responses came from those willing to undertake work in their States, they were to be furnished with blanks to fill out by precincts—ten good names to a precinct. In this way Bob was certain effective lists could rapidly be built up in each State.[33]

Thousands of copies of Bob's speeches had been sent out. The response had been unprecedented. The office force could not keep up with the correspondence, and Bob was obliged to employ extra people. In June he wrote Gilbert Roe that he needed stenographic and clerical help: "Postage bills and printing bills have to be met. My salary this month was not enough into $400 to meet current living expense & life insurance. Next month it will be worse because interest falls due on my mortgage [on the farm]. Sometimes it looks mighty black. I would give it all up and go to farming if I could quit but I can't quit when there is more to fight for and more to fight against than ever before since I entered public life."[34]

As a part of his campaign to carry these issues directly to the people, Bob made the most of the only medium open to him at the time. In *La Follette's Magazine* he published articles by Gilbert Roe, Hannis Taylor, Elizabeth Glendower Evans, and others dealing with the issues of free speech, free press, and conscription. In the June issue he devoted three pages to a signed editorial on the right of American citizens to discuss the issues of the war and the right of Congress to shape the war policy. Clearly stating that it was the citizen's duty to obey a law until it was repealed or declared unconstitutional, he insisted that the citizen had the inalienable right to fight both in the courts and at the ballot box what he deemed an obnoxious law or a wrongful public policy. In concluding this editorial he said: "American citizens have the right to begin a campaign tomorrow to elect United States Senators and Members of the House of Representatives who will represent them in securing the repeal of obnoxious laws, in declaring the definite objects for which this war is prosecuted and the conditions upon which it can be terminated at an early hour with honor and credit to the nation. God reigns and constitutional rights will be maintained. This is still the Government of the people."[35] The sale of this issue of *La Follette's Magazine* was so great that they had to reprint twice to supply the newsstand demands.

Subscriptions and letters commending the editorial swamped the clerical force in the *La Follette's Magazine* office at Madison. Bob, Jr., who was handling the correspondence in his father's office, wrote his mother that he thought it was vitally important to do all in our power to remove the inhibitions from the people. "The right kind of sentiment is seething and boiling under the surface. It is evident here even among the senators and the report from every source thru out the country is amazing and encouraging. They are talking and thinking but not out loud because of fear of persecution. The gag removed they will make themselves felt and heard in no uncertain way."[36]

In the Senate, Bob himself noted "a gradual disappearance of all that bravado and swashbuckling which marked the first weeks following the declaration of war—a gradual lengthening of faces—hats not so much on one side." He thought "the awful seriousness of the thing" was beginning to soak in and that many of those who had rushed things expected "the President had some big concealed plan by which *peace* with a glory that would exalt him before all other Presidents, was to be achieved in a few weeks." Bob also reported to the family that "The old vets from the South drop a good many remarks about the war which the newspapers dont print."[37]

The President's signature made the Espionage law effective on June 15. The suppression of many Socialist newspapers soon followed. Bob received new complaints almost every day, and thought that his own magazine might be suppressed at any time. Shortly after the publication of the June issue, Borah congratulated him on his editorial defining the constitutional rights of citizens in wartime, and expressed the hope that *La Follette's Magazine* would be denied the mails, as he thought this action would make the case against the Administration so strong that the issue could be taken up in Congress. Early in July Morris Hillquit, Clarence S. Darrow, Seymour Stedman, Frank P. Walsh, Amos Pinchot, Roger N. Baldwin, and others appeared before the Department of Justice to protest against the suppression of Socialist newspapers through the

denial of mail privileges. But they got no relief. They reported to
Bob that they had been given an ultimatum to "Cut-out war criticism or stay out of the mails."[38] Bob arranged appointments for
them to see Borah, Johnson, Norris, Reed, and other Senators he
thought might be willing to help. In different parts of the country
people were being arrested and imprisoned for discussing public
questions. Appeals for help came to Bob from the families of those
concerned or from public-spirited men and women who believed
that the constitutional right of free speech and free press should be
preserved even in time of war. Knowledge of many flagrant violations of constitutional rights also came to Bob through Gilbert
Roe, who was giving a great deal of his time to defending incon-
spicuous people in New York who had been illegally imprisoned.[39]

While the Espionage and Conscription bills were being debated
in the Senate, Bob had also been working on the Revenue bill trying
to secure a just distribution of the heavy taxes necessary to finance
the war. He believed the money should not be raised by bond issues
but by taxation on a pay-as-you-go principle with the burdens distributed in proportion to ability to pay. He and many others had
expected the President to support this policy. The press had generally interpreted the President's phrasing of his statement regarding the need for adequate credits to the Government as favoring a
pay-as-you-go taxation policy when he addressed Congress and
asked for a declaration of war on April 2.[40] The War Revenue bill,
hastily framed under Administration pressure, had passed the House
on May 23 and remained before the Senate Finance Committee for
ten weeks in continuous daily sessions until it came up in the Senate
on August 10. It called for over $2,000,000,000 and was the largest
revenue bill Congress had ever considered, although the $7,000,000,-
000 bond issue had already been authorized and was being sold as
the first Liberty loan.

Bob attended the daily sessions of the Finance Committee, where
representatives of great business interests protested provisions
adopted by the House and sought to prevent taxes on the big in-
dustries, especially excess profits taxes.[41] He wrote that the best
features of the House bill were being stricken out, and forms of
taxation substituted which allowed those who were best able to pay
"to escape or to have their burdens greatly lightened."[42] On the
days when the Senate was not in session, he said they wrangled "in

committee from 10 in the morning till 5:30 at night on the Tax bill" and that every day made it a worse bill for the masses, and lightened the load on wealth.[43] He decided to make a minority report. The day the Senate Committee adopted the final draft of the War Revenue bill, he made a strong argument for his minority report and got the votes of two other Members, Thomas and Gore.[44] Soon after this report was presented to the Senate, Gore overheard Penrose say to another Senator, "If we don't watch out La Follette's amendments will make this God damned war unpopular."[45]

The minority report was the first move in Bob's fight to modify and improve the Committee bill. He also planned to offer a series of amendments. Although aware that most of them would be defeated, he hoped to get some through and also to put Senators on record through roll call votes. After getting all that he could through amendments, he intended to offer a substitute bill simplifying the taxation plan and putting the burdens chiefly upon surplus incomes and war profits.

Even before the minority report was published, the press was commenting on what it called "La Follette's bill." The Oregon *Journal* described it as paying "for the war out of excess war profits, taking no more bread out of the mouths of the poor and stripping none of the scant clothing from their backs."[46] In an editorial signed by Mark Sullivan, *Collier's Weekly* commented favorably on it as "a piece of pioneering work which commands the respect even of persons who, politically, do not like him," and predicted it might turn out that no man in Congress would "have made so useful a contribution to the conduct of the war as the one who most stubbornly resisted our entering it."[47]

The majority report was finally presented to the Senate on August 6, and a large printing ordered. Bob then obtained an agreement for an equal printing of the minority report,[48] which was submitted on August 14.[49] He was surprised and pleased to find that the Washington *Star* printed an excellent digest of it and that it received publicity in many newspapers.[50] Two weeks later minority reports were sent out from his office in envelopes bearing Senator Gore's frank to every county clerk in the United States, and subsequently many more were distributed in response to requests from different parts of the country.[51] Bob thought the newspaper vilification after the Armed Ship bill filibuster might lead many people to drop an envelope bearing his own signature in the wastebasket without looking at the content.[52]

The debate on the War Revenue bill was opened by Senator Simmons, chairman of the Finance Committee, on August 10, and continued steadily for thirty days. Bob attended the sessions constantly, entered into the running debate frequently, and on seven different days presented his principal arguments. Throughout most of this period Gilbert Roe was in Washington assisting him. Night after night they returned to the office, staying until two o'clock in the morning, drafting amendments, working with experts from the Treasury Department assigned at Bob's request, and assembling data to be used on the Senate floor. Through the generosity of Amos Pinchot, Bob also had the help of an economic and statistical expert.

His first general attack upon the bill was made on August 21, when he declared it was a part of the history of all great wars that wealth had "demanded the minimum of taxation and the maximum of loans." He charged that the $2,000,000,000 bill was unsound; that the committee itself admitted the measure would raise only a small fraction of the first year's war expenditures; that it would necessitate issuing billions of dollars' worth of bonds. This policy he condemned as unsound because bonds found their way into the hands of the wealthy, and bond issues merely mortgaged the many for the benefit of the few.[53] Leading economists of the world from Hume, Adam Smith, Ricardo, and John Stuart Mill, down to those of our own time had, he said, with few exceptions, strongly contended that every war should be wholly financed by taxation on the pay-as-you-go principle. He called attention to a petition presented to Congress soon after the declaration of the present war, signed by over three hundred leading American economists, advocating that it be financed solely by taxation.[54]

Bob maintained that an equitable distribution of all further taxation was especially important since the war had already laid a tax of 50 to 100 per cent upon every man, woman, and child in the higher cost of all the necessities of life. In simple human terms he summarized his creed for war taxation: "So long as there is an income to be found in the country so large that it yields to its possessor a surplus over and above what he needs for the comfort or even luxuries of life for himself and family, I am in favor of taking such portion of that surplus income by taxation as the Government needs for war purposes, and if it needs it all I am in favor of taking it all before we take one penny from the slender income of the man who receives only enough to provide himself and family with the bare necessaries of life. So long as a man can be found who is making 'war profits'—that is, profits due to war in excess of normal profits —I am in favor of taking such portion of those profits by taxation as the Government needs for war purposes, and if it needs them all, I am in favor of taking them all before one penny is added by taxation to the burden of the man already staggering under the load of high prices caused by the war. . . .

"Surely, sir, it is not too much to ask that they be relieved of the burdens of war taxation until those who profit by the war and those who live in luxury and security in spite of the war have contributed a substantial portion of their surplus. That, sir, is what the minority of this committee demands. It is all that they demand."[55]

The newspapers reported that Bob's speech had caused uneasiness among the supporters of the Committee bill who had hoped it would go through with only perfunctory debate. The speech had been widely reported, and they feared the effect it would have on the country. The Washington correspondent of the conservative *Boston Evening Transcript* said in his dispatch, "La Follette goes to the root of the whole question of war taxation. . . . The sober and exhaustive presentation of his case by La Follette, despite his dramatic delivery, made a great impression upon the Senate."[56] The next day the income-tax part of the bill came up, and the advocates of a higher tax on wealth won the first skirmish when the schedule of the committee was rejected.

Bob then submitted his substitute amendment for the entire schedule of income-tax rates. It provided for a graduated tax of from 1 per cent to 50 per cent.[57] For three-quarters of an hour he discussed his plan, comparing it with the Committee bill and the British income tax.[58] That night supporters of the Committee bill were sufficiently alarmed to hold a conference and send out telegrams calling absent Senators back to Washington to help defeat Bob's amendment.[59] The following day Simmons spoke for about an hour and a half against Bob's substitute amendment and made a bitter personal attack upon him, practically charging that it had been offered in order to make the war a failure and embarrass the

Administration.[60] Bob replied in a two-hour speech, explaining his plan and stating that he knew no body of men in the country who favored paying all the expenses of the war by taxation "excepting about 350 of the greatest economists in America." Among these he said he knew of only one who had opposed the declaration of war against Germany. Yet the chairman of the Finance Committee had put under suspicion the loyalty of every one of these university professors who was devoting himself strictly to the ideals and principles of the science which he had made his life work. This, Bob added, was the lot of everyone who did not accept the majority report.[61] When Bob's amendment came to a vote, it was supported by virtually all the progressive Republicans and ten Democrats who broke away from the Administration. But the conservative bipartisan alliance was strong enough to defeat it 58 to 21.[62]

When it came to the war-profits section of the bill, Simmons, on behalf of the Finance Committee, reported a change in the Committee bill which nearly doubled the revenue from war profits.[63] By a series of questions Bob brought out that Simmons had denounced this proposal when he first made the majority report.[64] This belated revision was generally recognized as a partial concession to the minority "radicals."[65] But every subsequent attempt to increase the tax on war profits failed.

Borah brought out the fact that France was about to levy an 80 per cent tax on war profits, and that England had already raised the war-profits tax to this figure.[66] The next day, however, when Johnson offered an amendment providing for the same tax on American war profits, United States Senators defeated it 62 to 17.[67] This vote was interpreted as meaning that all similar proposals were probably doomed. But Bob immediately introduced his amendment calling for a 72 per cent tax on war profits and made a three-hour speech[68] which received the close attention of "the ten to twenty" Senators who remained in the Senate Chamber on that hot Saturday afternoon.[69]

The following Monday Bob continued his attack on the bill by pointing out its failure to tax sufficiently the huge profits of the large corporations during the war years. At one point in his argument Simmons interrupted to charge him with attempting to "hoodwink" the Senate. A sharp verbal clash followed, and Bob refused to yield further on the ground that a Senator who made such an accusation had forfeited his right to make that request. Simmons at first attempted to withdraw the offensive remark, and then later refused to do so.[70] Bob offered three different proposals for a tax on war profits, trying first for 70 per cent, then for 65 per cent and finally for 60 per cent.[71] All three were defeated.

The next day Bob, Jr., wrote his mother that "Dad gave them hell yesterday for two or three hours and then Borah got in for about an hour. It makes a splendid record to go to the people with and as I figure it when they win this sort of a fight they lose. . . . We have been at it night and day. . . . Daddy is fine in spirit and well in health I think altho of course he is bone tired. Uncle Gil is a great comfort."[72]

On the same day that Bob had offered an amendment to increase the tax on war profits, Theodore Roosevelt was speaking at a county fair in New York State urging a graduated tax on war profits as heavy as Great Britain's.[73] A Western newspaper commented editorially that "The spectacle of the gallant Colonel fighting shoulder to shoulder with his arch-enemy La Follette in a good cause is delightful. The lion and the lamb have lain down together, or at least enlisted in the same war."[74]

On the final day of the debate, Bob submitted a complete substitute for the entire Committee bill. His substitute raised the tax on individual incomes so that it would have yielded $162,000,000 more. It fixed a rate identical with the British 80 per cent tax on war profits, which would have raised $994,000,000 more from war profits than the Committee bill. It also eliminated all consumption taxes except those on liquor and cigars.[75] After explaining his substitute bill, Bob read into the *Congressional Record* the roll call votes on the different amendments which had been offered to the income-tax and war-profits provisions of the Committee bill. When questioned as to his purpose in doing this, Bob replied that he wished to collect in one connected statement the record that had been made by the United States Senate on this bill, as he thought it would "make wholesome and interesting reading for the people of this country."[76] Bob's substitute bill was defeated 65 to 15,[77] and later that same day the War Revenue bill was passed 69 to 4, only Borah, Gronna, and Norris joining Bob in voting against it.[78]

Although this was the largest tax bill Congress had ever passed, it proved inadequate and was soon being condemned by some of the newspapers which had excoriated Bob and the minority for criticizing it.[79] That minority, organized and led by Bob, had, however, forced an increase of $498,000,000 in war profits and an increase of $64,000,000 in income taxes. They had also forced abandonment of the proposed taxes on tea, coffee, cocoa, and sugar, thereby relieving the public of $158,500,000 in direct-consumption taxes, including a proposed increase on letter postage.[80] But the minority had been defeated in its effort to pay the major portion of the cost of the war by taxation. It was passed on to future generations through bond issues. An editorial, written by former Senator Bristow of Kansas for his newspaper, the *Salina Journal*, predicted that the fight made at Washington by a small group of Senators for an equitable tax on war profits would be an issue in many States in the next campaign. Commending the speeches made by Johnson and Borah, he noted that "La Follette in a great speech that lasted for three hours graphically portrayed the infamy of the legislation. . . . These senators, in as righteous a cause as was ever championed by free men, lost and, when they lost, wrong triumphed. The *Journal* enquires, where was Mr. Wilson while these men were making such a gallant fight for human rights?"[81]

Bob's fight to amend the bill and increase the tax on war profits was widely noted in the press. Although most of the newspaper editorials branded him as a traitor seeking to "obstruct" the war program, the news reports of the Senate debate brought so many letters requesting copies of his speeches and the minority report that he had to get extra help to take care of the mail.

Commenting months later on the defeat of the minority, Bob wrote: "Oh, for one plainly spoken word from the Chief Magistrate of this country in favor of the highest tax on incomes and war profits in that crucial time! It would have won the day for just taxation, reduced measurably the size of the loans, the bond sales, checked inflation, and halted the increase in prices on the necessaries of life at a time when they are well nigh intolerable. But alas, that word was not spoken. The President was silent."[82]

A year after the War Revenue bill had passed the House, the President appeared before Congress to ask for urgently needed additional revenues. He then advocated principles of taxation similar to those which Bob and the small minority group had fought for. Wilson denounced the raising of funds by large bond issues as unsound, and declared that it was necessary to turn to war profits, incomes and luxuries for additional taxes.[82] On the front page of *La Follette's Magazine*, in his leading editorial, Bob quoted from this "trenchant address" which had, he said, "heartened and encouraged every student of War Finance." In another editorial in this same issue he commented that it was unfortunate for the country that the President had not addressed Congress ten months before in support of such a tax. With a pen pointed by ironic recollections of the hearings before the Senate Finance Committee and the minority fight to amend the War Revenue bill, he wrote under the title of "Standing Back Of The President," "Now all of you profiteering 'patriots' who have bawled yourselves hoarse about 'standing back of the President' get into line and support his recommendation for 'additional taxes on war profits, incomes and luxuries.' "[84]

While the Senate had been voting by large majorities against Bob's amendments to increase taxes on war profits, the first drafted soldiers were being sent to training camps under the Conscription Act. Patriotic demonstrations were held in different cities. As soldiers marched to the trains, flags waved, bands played, and crowds lined the streets to cheer them. At the Nation's Capital on September 4, the Senate recessed early to join in a parade down Pennsylvania Avenue with the drafted men of the District of Columbia. Bob did not march in the parade, and some newspapers insinuated that his absence was due to lack of patriotism. The fact was that he had stayed in his office in the Capitol to work on an amendment which would increase by $50 a month the pay of all American soldiers sent to serve in foreign countries. As he looked out the window and saw the Senators going to join the parade, he turned to his son Bob, Jr., telling him that he was drafting the amendment and predicting that when it was introduced, "Those gentlemen in their plug hats will vote against it."[85] Seventy-five of them did three days later.

The amendment Bob had drafted while the Senators were marching in the parade had been introduced at his request by Senator Hardwick.[86] It provided that the funds for the additional $50 a month to soldiers serving abroad should be raised by increasing the tax rate on incomes over $25,000. After heated debate in which John Sharp Williams denounced Hardwick as a traitor seeking to undermine the spirit of the troops, the only Senators who voted for the amendment were Hardwick, Gronna, Reed, Vardaman, and Bob.[87] Three days after the defeat of the amendment, Bob expressed his feeling about the charges which had been made in the Senate against Hardwick. On the Senate floor Bob, Jr., his young son, listened to this speech and shared the indignation his father revealed when he exclaimed: "Shame upon this country! Shame upon anybody who votes against giving as much to the men whom we are to send to wallow in the mire and blood of the trenches in a foreign country as Canada gives to her troops in that same service! . . . In God's name, is a man to be arraigned here as a traitor who would put the troops of this great country at least in something approaching as good a position as the troops of Canada? . . . When men with an income of $25,000, and from that up to those with incomes of from one to ten million dollars, can not give out of such incomes 10 per cent to provide this tax to put our soldiers not just on a par with Canada, but on a little better basis than Canada, Mr. President, I can not understand it. I can not understand the spirit which prevailed in the Senate when an amendment of that kind was offered here and is derided and denounced as disloyal. It seems to me that every Senator should have risen in his place and that this amendment should have been adopted by the unanimous vote of this body."[88]

Reading about the defeat of his amendment in the Madison papers, Belle wrote Bob that she thought the fight he had been putting up for the conscription of wealth was splendid. "They may vote you down," she said, "but like so many propositions which you have advocated that are essentially right and simple and plain for the folks to see and understand it makes a record and creates opinion that cannot be resisted."[89]

Twenty-five years later, during another world war, their son, Bob, Jr., then Senator from Wisconsin, addressed the Senate on the same subject, and through skillful and persistent parliamentary strategy finally succeeded in getting an amendment passed by a roll call vote which increased the base pay of American soldiers serving in foreign countries to $50 a month.[90]

CHAPTER XLVII

Bob's Resolution for a Declaration
of Our War Aims by Congress

Throughout the spring and summer of 1917, Bob had followed events in Europe as reported in the newspapers and interpreted by friends who had confidential sources of information. He shared the opinion of many liberals in the United States, England, and Europe who feared that secret agreements existed among the Allies which, unless publicly abrogated, would be a menace to a peace in accord with the high standards set by President Wilson in his peace without victory speech. Having entered the war, Bob thought it was our obligation to use the power and influence of the United States to bring about a just and enduring peace. He was convinced that one of the first steps toward that goal was an early declaration of our war aims. Unless an educational campaign were carried on to set reasonable limitations and define right policies for bringing this country out of the war in a just and honorable way, he believed the United States might be dragged through years of war to establish imperialism and exploit the weaker nations.[1]

After nearly three years of fighting, neither the Allies nor the Central Powers had achieved a decisive military victory. The Russian Revolution in March, 1917, had introduced a new and uncertain element. From the time we entered the war, Bob had steadily utilized every opportunity to help direct the thought of the American people toward a constructive and enduring peace based upon the principles he had publicly endorsed immediately after the President's "peace without victory" speech on January 22, 1917. Three months later, on the Senate floor, Bob quoted from Wilson's speech and called attention to the encouraging fact that on April 9 one

749

of the Allies, Russia, "in the very throes of her new birth," had proclaimed her adherence to certain principles Wilson had declared were fundamental to any enduring peace.[2]

Shortly after this, Philip Snowden introduced a resolution in the House of Commons welcoming the declaration of the new democratic government of Russia and calling upon the British Democracy to join the Allies in restating the Allies' terms in conformity with the Russian declaration.[3] Although it was voted down, the agitation for a statement of war aims was given an additional impetus when the Provisional Government issued another statement on May 19. It declared that Russian foreign policy would openly undertake the aim of obtaining in the shortest possible time a universal peace based neither on dominion of other nations nor on seizure of their territories, but a peace without annexations or indemnities on a basis of the self-determination of nations.[4] A few days later Lord Robert Cecil, Minister of the Blockade, stated in the House of Commons that all imperialist aims, based on force or conquest, were completely absent from the British purpose and that the most recent declaration of the reconstituted Government of Russia was in complete harmony with this policy.[5]

These reports and an announcement in the New York *World* that the President had sent a note to the Russian Provisional Government outlining the attitude of this country on the major issues of the war made Bob feel that it was important Congress should assert its proper authority and declare the war aims of the United States.[6] He believed the introduction of a resolution in Congress would stimulate thought and help to unite a constructive public opinion in this and other countries. Through David Thompson, Frederic C. Howe, Andrew Furuseth, Steffens, and Lady Barlow, who was a frequent guest at the La Follette home, Bob had followed the activity of the British Labour Party and the English Liberals in the Union of Democratic Control who had been carrying on a campaign for a restatement of Allied war aims in harmony with the principles expressed in President Wilson's January 22 speech and in the Russian declaration. Although Bob did not know it at this time, the Executive Committee of the Union of Democratic Control had written the President urging him to take action to bring about a restatement of Allied war aims along these lines. The letter was signed by J. Ramsay MacDonald, Charles Trevelyan, Arthur Ponsonby, E. D. Morel, Norman Angell, Philip Snowden, F. W. Pethick-Lawrence, J. A. Hobson, Charles Roden Buxton, F. W. Jowett, Irene Cooper Willis, and H. M. Swanwick.[7] This appeal was sent to the President through Colonel House, who was not in accord with its purpose and did not give it to Wilson until several weeks later.[8]

The Russian proclamation also stimulated the demand for a clear-cut declaration of both Allied and American war aims. Even the conservative *Springfield Daily Republican* was troubled with "doubts in regard to British imperial aims" and was urging that Great Britain and her Allies should formulate more clearly "a program of disinterested action for the common good which will satisfy Russia and the United States."[9] In Chicago, New York, and other cities committees were formed, mass meetings arranged, and resolutions passed calling upon Congress for a statement of our peace terms. On Sunday afternoon, May 27, four thousand people occupied every available seat in the Chicago Auditorium, and a thousand were turned away. Robert M. Lovett, dean of the University of Chicago, presided and delivered the keynote address. The principal speeches were made by Seymour Stedman, former Socialist candidate for governor, Mary McDowell of the University of Chicago Settlement, Reverend Fred A. Moore, pastor of the Universalist Church, and Arthur Fisher, son of Walter Fisher who had been Secretary of the Interior under President Taft. Among those who occupied seats on the platform were Jane Addams of Hull House and Jenkin Lloyd Jones, editor of *Unity* and founder of Abraham Lincoln Centre.[10] Although this meeting was sanctioned by some of Chicago's distinguished citizens, the intolerance which accompanies war expressed itself the next night when a crowd gathered opposite Dean Lovett's home and hanged him in effigy for his participation in an effort to secure a declaration of our war aims.[11]

In New York a series of six conferences was organized by the People's Council of America, which was composed of men and women from various cities who represented many different shades of opinion on social and economic questions. David Starr Jordan, former president of Leland Stanford University, was the treasurer. This series was designated as the First Conference for Democracy and Terms of Peace and culminated in a meeting at Madison Square Garden where the audience was variously estimated as between twelve and fifteen thousand. Dr. Judah L. Magnes presided, and addresses were delivered by David Starr Jordan, Jenkin Lloyd Jones, Morris Hillquit, and others. Among those who were most active in organizing the conferences were Louis P. Lochner and Professor Emily Green Balch of Wellesley, who received the Nobel prize for work in behalf of peace many years later.[12] Resolutions were passed urging Congress to declare our war aims. A copy was sent to each Member of Congress. Subsequently similar conferences were held in Chicago, and the People's Council issued a call for delegates to meet at a convention in Minneapolis in September.[13] But Governor J. A. A. Burnquist of Minnesota issued a proclamation forbidding the holding of the convention.[14] When Lochner telegraphed the President protesting in the name of the People's Council, Wilson attached a memorandum to the telegram for his secretary to the effect that he knew of no ground for his interference with the proclamation of the governor of Minnesota.[15] Twenty-one days earlier the President had received a communication from the Philadelphia branch of the People's Council protesting the Post Office Department's action in excluding certain newspapers from the mails. In referring this to Postmaster General Burleson to handle as he deemed best, Wilson said that he did not even know what the People's Council of America was.[16]

Late in June Bob received a note saying that Steffens would soon be in Washington, and he awaited his friend's report on the Russian situation with intense interest. The fact that Steffens had gone with Crane had given him an exceptional opportunity to learn a great deal in a brief period. Crane had many friends in the Provisional Government. He had long been known as "a friend of Russia," and his appointment in May by the President to the Russian Diplomatic Mission had been welcomed. They had sailed from New York on the same steamer which carried Trotsky as a steerage passenger. Trotsky had been taken off the ship at Halifax and detained. But Crane and Steffens reached Petrograd without difficulty and were among the first outsiders to enter Russia after the revolution.[17]

Steffens arrived in Washington on June 25, and that night he, Bob, and Bob, Jr., dined together on the roof garden of the Powhatan Hotel. In his extraordinarily vivid way, Steffens, who was a remarkable reporter, told them of what was happening in Russia. Bob, Jr., in a letter to the family at Madison wrote: "We had a most interesting evening, as you may all guess. I am sending you under separate cover, some little paragraphs which I wrote to help me remember some of the things that he told us. From it, with your knowledge of Mr. Steffens and the way he tells the story, and by the aid of your imagination, you may be able to get some sort of a picture of what the Russian revolution means to the world."[18] These "little paragraphs" typed on scratch paper that had yellowed with time were found many years later in Phil's desk at Madison.

Steffens told them that the Russians were convinced there was "something rotten in the secret treaties between the Allies," and that until these were cleared up they would not fight. He said a million Russian soldiers had left the German front and returned home after fraternizing for a month with German soldiers. On their return they reported that the German soldiers thought they were fighting for the same thing that Russia was. The Vice Premier of the Provisional Government, Alexander Kerenski, who was at that time in Steffens' opinion the "most popular man in Russia," was "trying his best to make Free Russia fight" but expected to fail.[19] Kerenski thought, however, that there was one person who could answer these German charges and destroy this belief in the minds of the Russian peasants. He believed that if President Wilson would call a public conference in some conspicuous place and abrogate the secret treaties it would then be possible to persuade the Russian troops to return to the front and continue fighting the Germans. Ambassador Francis and Crane shared this opinion, and had urged Steffens to take Kerenski's message to the President.[20]

Late in the afternoon of the day following his talk with Bob, Steffens called on the President at the White House. Cables from Petrograd had prepared the way for his visit. He also brought letters from Crane and Ambassador Francis. As he delivered his important verbal message from Kerenski about the secret treaties, the President listened in thoughtful silence. When Steffens had finished, Wilson answered, as if thinking out loud: "I know nothing of those treaties, you know. That makes it difficult for me to do what Kerenski and Governor Francis ask. If we had such a treaty ourselves, if we were a party to their making, then I could say to our allies, 'Let us abrogate our treaties.' That would be easy, human, diplomatic, polite. But having no such treaty and having no knowledge of those treaties, I would have to say, 'Here, gentlemen, do you meet openly before the world and tear up those secret treaties of yours!'—No, that is hard. That I cannot very well do." The President did not, of course, say what his answer to Kerenski would be. But he was evidently disturbed by the problem that had been presented, and asked many acute questions about Russia which Steffens answered as best he could.[21]

After his talk with the President, Steffens went to Bob's office and dictated a memorandum of the conversation to Grace Lynch, one of Bob's secretaries.[22] Then he saw Bob and told him all about his talk with the President.[23] This report, which seemed to indicate that Wilson did not intend to take any action in regard to the secret treaties, intensified Bob's feeling that it was vitally important Congress should declare our war aims to make it clear that the United States was not bound by any secret commitments the Allies had made. He believed that such power as we had must be utilized while the Allies needed us. If we waited until the war was over and victory won, he thought it would be too late to impose upon imperial-minded governments the high standards Wilson had set forth in his "peace without victory" speech.

A few weeks later the German Reichstag adopted a resolution declaring that Germany sought "a peace of mutual agreements and the enduring reconciliation of peoples."[24] It had been adopted on July 19, following a political upheaval in Germany which brought a change of chancellors. A few days later, J. Ramsay MacDonald moved in the British House of Commons that the German resolution expressed the principles of Great Britain and called upon the Allied Governments to "restate their peace terms." It was rejected by a vote of 148 to 19.[25] *

On that same day Senator Borah stated in the Senate that he thought "we ought to say in as clear terms as possible just what America demands as a prerequisite of peace."[26] The *New York Times* gave the Senator a sharp editorial spanking for his speech,[27] although the National Editorial Association had recently adopted resolutions urging President Wilson to obtain from the Allies a definite statement of their war aims.[28]

The day after Borah's speech, Bob wrote his family that Amos

* This resolution also contained the statement that the freedom of the seas must be secured.

Pinchot had been in Washington "to help along a declaration of war purposes" and had so written the President. He added that Crystal Eastman and Charles Hallinan had also called to see him about it the day before; that they all wanted a resolution introduced, but wanted it done by someone "who had voted for *war*" and would try Johnson, Borah, and others.[29]

About a week later Senator Stone read to the Senate a letter from the American Union Against Militarism asking him, as chairman of the Senate Foreign Relations Committee, to introduce a resolution which would enable the Senate to state its ideas of the proper basis for peace negotiations. Stone stated that he hoped to speak on the subject soon. The letter was signed by Amos Pinchot, Lillian D. Wald, L. Hollingsworth Wood, Max Eastman, John Haynes Holmes, Roger N. Baldwin, Alice Lewisohn, Norman M. Thomas, Charles T. Hallinan, John L. Elliot, and Crystal Eastman.[30]

Earlier in the summer a resolution and speech calling for a declaration of war aims by Congress had been prepared by another Democratic Senator, Owen of Oklahoma. Owen submitted them to Secretary Lansing, who forwarded them to the President with the suggestion that Wilson see the Senator. Lansing expressed the fear that any resolution of this kind might precipitate debate which would give those hostile to the President an opportunity to criticize his declaration of principles as to our purposes in the war and cause serious differences with our co-belligerents. The President saw Owen the following evening.[31] The resolution was not presented.

Reports were filtering through to Bob by uncensored channels from Russia and other countries which led him to think that "the masses on the other side" would not stand for war much longer. Similar reports from more official sources were current in the Senate. Early in August Senator Smoot told Bob "in whispers" that he "had it 'straight' from French officers just over that France would break into revolution in spite of ev[e]rything soon." Bob, in a letter to his family, commented that it would be a wholesome thing for the world "if the people *quit* ev[e]rywhere & forced all the belligerent governments to arrange peace terms."[32]

It seemed to Bob, and to many others who were receiving uncensored information from unofficial sources, that a situation had developed in Europe where an immediate repudiation of the imperialistic secret treaties and a public declaration of specific democratic war aims by the Congress of the United States might unite the peoples of Europe in forcing their governments to declare objectives which would lead to an early and enduring peace. He also thought this was the surest way to weaken the German military party, since it could not then effectively misrepresent our purposes to the German people. It was with this purpose and in this faith that Bob himself worked on a statement of these aims and also sought the help of Edwin Borchard and Gilbert Roe in drafting the resolution he introduced on August 11.

In the preamble to his resolution Bob cited the proposals advanced in other countries which he believed furnished a basis for ending the war. With these proposals he linked the recent official declarations, disavowing purposes of conquest, which had been made by responsible spokesmen for the British, German, and American governments. He referred also to the secret treaties among the Allies, the terms of which were unknown to the people. The resolution affirmed the Constitutional rights of Congress "to determine and to declare definitely" the war aims of the United States; it disavowed on the part of Congress the continuation of the war for purposes of territorial annexations or indemnities; it favored the creation of a common fund by all belligerents for the restoration of devastated regions; it called for a public restatement of the Allied peace terms. Bob asked to have the resolution read and placed upon the table to be called up by him.[33]

Immediately after this, Senator King of Utah introduced another resolution demanding a vanquished Germany and declaring the United States would not make peace until the purposes and principles set out by the President in his war message to Congress had been acknowledged and accomplished. King explained that he had introduced his resolution because "of the untimely talk of peace" and "the resolution submitted by the distinguished Senator from Wisconsin."[34]

Bob's resolution brought a storm of criticism. Its assertion of the rights of Congress was unwelcome to the Administration. Its proposal that all belligerents contribute to the restoration of war-damaged areas appeared to shock the press. The editorial and cartoon comment was generally bitter and in many instances scurrilous. The New York *World* denounced it as "pro-German,"[35] while it was blasted on the Pacific Coast as a "Made in Germany proposal."³⁶ In Bob's home town the *Wisconsin State Journal*, edited by his former admirer and friend Richard Lloyd Jones, declared it was designed "to defend, comfort and help the greatest criminal the world has ever known."³⁷ When Belle had read the resolution, published in this same paper as a news dispatch a few days before the editorial was written, she telegraphed Bob that it seemed "to strike the keynote of an aggressive and determined effort to secure a rational basis for settlement of the awful conflict. I am sure it expresses the desire and judgment of a suffering war exhausted world[.] No word can express my gratitude and satisfaction."³⁸

During the next few days prominent Senators in both parties publicly denounced Bob's resolution and predicted its defeat. Senator New of Indiana, former chairman of the Republican National Committee, was reported to have said to a newspaper correspondent, who interviewed him in the Senate lobby, that La Follette had "put himself, by his attitude in the Senate, outside the pale of the party."³⁹ Senator Atlee Pomerene, a Democratic member of the Foreign Relations Committee, who had formerly been a great admirer of Bob's, now told a Washington correspondent that "sympathizers of the Kaiser, the slackers, and the I.W.W.'s" were "the only ones who would support such a resolution as that offered by Senator La Follette," and that Congress was in no mood now "for this character of trifling with the integrity of America."⁴⁰ A reliable diary entry made three days after Bob introduced his resolution records that "Senator Gore, who was supposed to be asleep in the Senate cloakroom, heard John Sharp Williams and [Senator] Martin talking about expelling" La Follette "for offering his Peace Resolution."⁴¹

On the same day that Bob had introduced his resolution, Secretary Lansing announced that no passports would be issued to Americans desiring to attend the Socialist Conference at Stockholm, where Russian, French, German, and English delegates were planning to meet in an effort to bring about a restatement of war aims by their governments which would lead to peace negotiations. Leading Liberals and Members of the Labour Party in England were so amazed at this action and so disappointed at the President's failure to respond to the appeals to use his influence toward bringing about a restatement of Allied war aims that Ramsay MacDonald wrote a long memorandum summarizing their feeling to William H. Buckler, American Special Agent of the State Department at London, for the benefit of the President and Colonel House.[42]

On August 15 Senator Sherman of Illinois offered a resolution specifying certain war objectives which should be embodied in any peace treaty made at the end of the war.[43] Immediately after this, Senator J. Hamilton Lewis offered a resolution to leave all peace propositions to the President.[44] This was interpreted as an Administration move to suppress further discussion in Congress of the United States war aims, for it was known that Lewis had seen Wilson on August 6 and had told reporters afterward that the President felt the time was not ripe for peace talk; that the country would hear from him when conditions called for him "to take Congress and the people into his confidence."[45]

A Washington dispatch to the *New York Times* reported that after a talk with the President on August 16, Senator King of Utah had conferred with other Senate leaders and a plan had been made to kill the La Follette resolution and prevent adoption of any resolution calling upon the President to define the war aims of the United States or suggesting any policy for him to follow in dealing with Germany.[46] Another dispatch reported that it had been arranged to force executive sessions and close the doors if any Senator began a speech on war aims or peace negotiations.[47]

While these plans were being made in private conferences to prevent any open discussion of war aims in Congress, an appeal was issued by Pope Benedict for peace negotiations. The press carried it on August 14, and Bob published the text in the August issue of *La Follette's Magazine*. This appeal suggested as basic principles for peace: disarmament, a neutral ocean, foregoing of indemnities, restitution of occupied territory, and territorial adjustments.[48] The New York *World*, which had denounced Bob's resolution as pro-German, now expressed the opinion that the President would "make the gravest of mistakes if he neglects this opportunity to define in detail the aims and objects of the United States in this war and state concrete terms on which peace can be made."[49] The Allies decided to leave the task of replying to the Pope's note to the President.[50]

The President, without consulting his Cabinet,[51] replied on August 27, rejecting the Pope's proposal for immediate negotiations.

He disavowed, so far as the United States was concerned, any wish for punitive damages, dismemberment of empires, or establishment of "selfish and exclusive economic leagues." But the substance of the reply was a refusal to treat with Germany, to "take the word of the present rulers of Germany as a guarantee of anything that is to endure."[52]

Bob's resolution continued to slumber "on the table" while invective was hurled at him from coast to coast. For the mere assertion of the right of Congress to declare the purposes and objects of the war in the form of a resolution to be considered and discussed Bob had, as he said later on the Senate floor, "been denounced throughout this broad land as a traitor" to his country.[53]

Among those who made the most virulent denunciations of Bob was Charles Edward Russell, a former friend, who had been appointed by the President as a member of the Russian Mission headed by Elihu Root. Returning to the United States early in August, Russell launched his first blast in an interview the day after Bob had introduced his resolution by declaring, "Every pacifist in this country that goes about prattling of peace, every Congressman that introduces a peace resolution, every Senator that is playing the German game, is doing far more harm to the United States, to the cause of democracy, to the ideals of his country, than a million German soldiers on the battle line can do."[54] Although Bob's name was not mentioned, the *New York Times* readily identified him the next day in an editorial quoting Russell's final phrase and commenting, "One can imagine how Senator La Follette's eyes glisten as he reads that. More harm 'than a million German soldiers on the battle line'! This is better than he dreamed."[55]

When the Russian Mission was formally welcomed at a meeting at the Union League Club in New York, Elihu Root denounced pro-German traitors in and out of Congress, and Russell again delivered another vile, anonymous diatribe which was widely reported as an attack on La Follette. Describing the "disloyal Senator" as a "traitor in disguise" who "goes to the Senate of the United States to do the dirty work of the Kaiser," he said he wished he could have taken him by the throat, dragged him to Petrograd and placed him in the Field of Mars on a Sunday afternoon to see German agents going from crowd to crowd repeating his words of treason and quoting what he had said in the Senate when he introduced "a resolution demanding that the Allies state their terms."[56] In other speeches and in signed syndicated articles Russell continued to make similar accusations, apparently attributing to Bob every untoward event in Russia. When the Russian city of Riga fell to the Germans, Russell told an audience in Minneapolis that it had not been taken by von Hindenburg and German troops. "Riga was taken by La Follette, Gronna, and Bill Stone." Exhorting them to action he said: "You don't have to sit still and let La Follette betray you. Get out your petitions and have him and his companions thrown out, as they should be. They have no more right in Congress than Benedict Arnold has in Heaven. They are the most awful traitors that ever betrayed any people."[57]

The return of the Russian Mission was news, and the denunciations of its members were reported from coast to coast. In San Francisco Steffens read the reports of the Union League Club meeting and wrote Bob: "Of course I see what you are doing and I see the effects. Rage is developing, the war rage which is the I.W.W. spirit of force raised to the nth power. Root expressed it yesterday. Russell, too. That is not a sentiment to be criticised. That is war insanity. They know it in Europe. It is as dangerous as madness and as unapproachable to reason. Doctors, not statesmen, must deal with it. The place for it is in the trenches and not behind, but in front of the guns. At home, inactive, on the platform, it is something to look out for. I don't mean that it is to be feared, but it must be allowed for and reckoned with. Be very patient, Bob."[58]

CHAPTER XLVIII

A Campaign to Expel La Follette
from the Senate

The attacks upon Bob because of his resolution calling for a declaration of war aims by Congress were still reverberating in the newspapers when he made his final argument in the Senate on September 10, 1917, advocating a just taxation measure to finance the war. That same day he received an invitation to speak in St. Paul, Minnesota, on September 20, at the closing session of a three-day conference called by the Nonpartisan League to discuss the high cost of living. The League was composed chiefly of Northwestern farmers, pioneering men and women who had known winters without fuel, repeated failures of crops from drought, and low prices in abundant years because they were helpless against the unfair practices of the grain combines, milling interests, and great railroads. For years Bob had spoken throughout the Northwestern States. He knew these people and their problems. As early as 1906 he had introduced a resolution to investigate the grain-elevator trust[1] and had been interested in the Nonpartisan League since it first came into being.

In December, 1915, he had spoken in the vast auditorium in St. Paul to seven thousand farmers who had come together under the magnetic leadership of George Loftus to protest against conditions which later brought forth the Nonpartisan League and a cooperative grain elevator, owned and operated by the farmers. During that same winter the North Dakota legislature had refused to provide for a state-owned terminal grain elevator which had been authorized in a referendum vote on a constitutional amendment. The League had adopted a program calling for state-owned terminal grain elevators and flour mills and for the public ownership of the rail-roads and other public utilities. In 1916 it had elected Lynn J. Frazier governor of North Dakota and had carried that normally Republican State for Wilson. Upon the death of Congressman Helgesen of North Dakota soon after the declaration of war, the League had elected John M. Baer, a native of Wisconsin, to fill the vacancy. The farmers' revolt in the Northwest had begun to attract notice in the East. A national Nonpartisan League had been formed with headquarters in St. Paul, and organizers were being sent into eight other States to prepare for the 1918 primaries and elections.

Although the League had opposed entry into the European War, the leaders had pledged loyal support to the Government after the declaration was passed. Following enactment of the Conscription bill, the League had declared for conscription of wealth by taxation and called upon the President for a specific declaration of the peace terms of the United States. The position of the League on a number of recent issues in Congress was therefore similar in many respects to that taken by Bob.

The invitation to speak at the League's St. Paul Conference was signed by James Manahan, a loyal friend who had been elected Congressman at large from Minnesota in 1912, and William Lemke, later to serve as Representative from North Dakota. Bob was very tired and loath to undertake any additional burdens, but felt that he could not refuse if the legislative situation permitted him to leave Washington. On September 17 the War Revenue bill went to conference. As this meant the Senate would hold only nominal sessions for a week, he decided to go, although there had been no time to prepare a special speech for the occasion. Late that afternoon he left for St. Paul, stopped off at Madison between trains, and insisted Belle go with him. From Washington Bob, Jr., had already telegraphed urging her to go because he knew she would be such a help and comfort to his father, who always dreaded making a speech which he had not had time to prepare carefully.[2]

Bob and Belle arrived in St. Paul on September 19, the morning of the second day of the conference. He was somewhat disturbed to learn that the previous evening Senator Borah had talked about the pending War Revenue bill in detail. This was the subject Bob himself had decided to discuss when he found that it was impossible to prepare a special speech before leaving Washington. Because of

Borah's address, it suddenly seemed necessary to change his plan. After talking the situation over with Belle, he decided to shut himself up in his room at the Hotel Frederic for the next thirty-four hours and whip into shape a speech he had drafted but had not yet had an opportunity to deliver in the Senate in connection with his war-aims resolution. He had brought material from Washington which he had been gathering for some time. It was based upon careful research as to historical and legal precedents upholding the constitutional right of free speech and the right and duty of Congress to declare the objects and purposes of the war.

Bob was scheduled to speak at nine the following night. His completed speech as written for this occasion was typed and ready for him about six thirty that evening. When James Manahan and William Lemke called at his hotel, he gave it to them to read. It dealt with the importance of solving constructively certain problems created by the war, and the constitutional rights of American citizens to express their opinions freely and thus participate in shaping decisions as to how their Government should solve them. Subsequently the text of this speech became a major part of his October 6, 1917, address, which many consider one of the finest speeches Bob ever delivered in the Senate. But Manahan and Lemke, two men who usually had great courage, were afraid to have Bob deliver this speech that night. The conference had been misrepresented in the newspapers and harassed by secret service men to such a degree that they feared a speech on this subject might cause trouble and bring further attacks upon their organization. Belle frankly expressed her indignation at this timidity[3] and urged Bob to refuse to address the conference at all unless he delivered his speech exactly as prepared. Bob offered to withdraw from the program, but Manahan and Lemke were distressed at what this would mean to the closing meeting of the conference. They pled so effectively that he was finally persuaded to go to the auditorium and speak extemporaneously—if only for a few minutes.[4]

When they arrived at the auditorium, the evening meeting had begun. For blocks the streets were packed with throngs who could not enter the hall. It was reported that fifteen thousand people had gathered to hear Bob speak. Ten thousand men and women occupied all the seats on the main floor and in the vast galleries that reached almost to the roof. As Bob slowly made his way through the crowded aisles to the platform, the audience rose spontaneously, cheering again and again, as they gave him one of the greatest ovations he had ever received. When Manahan sensed the enthusiasm of the audience, he clapped Bob on the back and said, "Go ahead, Bob; make your speech!" But this renewal of Manahan's habitual courage came too late. Bob had left his manuscript at the hotel, and taken with him only a few notes on the Revenue bill, which he intended to discuss briefly.

The demonstration continued for five minutes after Bob reached the platform. He looked out upon an audience composed largely of farmers from the Northwestern States and wage earners from Minneapolis and St. Paul. It was the first public meeting at which he had appeared since the 1916 campaign in Wisconsin. For six months the press had hurled denunciations upon him while he fought his losing battles in the hostile atmosphere of the Senate Chamber at Washington. But in the great auditorium at St. Paul ten thousand men and women gave proof that they had understood his purpose and had kept their faith in him.

Bob had been told that secret service agents were scattered throughout the hall, and he knew that as the leader of the opposition to the President's war policies in Congress he must expect hostile interruptions from hecklers undoubtedly sent for that purpose.[5] He had to speak extemporaneously, without any written manuscript to refute possible misquotation. But fortunately three stenographic reporters were present who took down his speech. One was the official reporter of the conference, another was there for the Minnesota Commission of Public Safety, and the third for the Department of Justice. Thus three stenographic records were made of this extemporaneous talk which became one of the least read and most criticized speeches ever delivered by a United States Senator. The false quotations sent out in the press dispatches that night, together with the libelous interpretations and misrepresentations in many papers throughout the country, initiated what became an organized campaign for his expulsion from the Senate and subjected him to months of vilification as a traitor to his country. But that night none could foresee this when the audience sang "America," and Governor Frazier introduced him.

The great crowd remained standing, applauding, cheering, and waving flags as Bob stepped to the front of the platform. Although deeply moved by the friendly greeting of the audience, he began his talk in clear, deliberate tones which reached to every corner of the auditorium. Touching first upon the theme of representative government, which he intended to use as an approach to a discussion of the War Revenue bill, he said: "Mr. President, Ladies and Gentlemen: It is needless for me to say anything about the importance of this conference conducted under the auspices of the Nonpartisan League. It speaks for itself. It is a nonpartisan league" formed because "political parties have failed to give the people of this country real representative government." Cheers and applause broke in, and then he went on to ask: "What is representative government? Every man or woman in this audience who stood up here to-night when you sang that glorious anthem, 'My Country 'Tis of Thee,' answers that question. What was it for which men died in 1776? It was that the Government established by their valor and their devotion and their sacrifice, sealed with their blood, should be a real representative government. . . . A government that represents all the people."[6]

He sketched the historical background of the struggle for representative government in the Northwest, recalling the early Granger movement of the seventies which had tried to grapple with the corporate power of the great railroads and "restore representative government to the people of that day." This early Granger movement was "the result of the logical thinking of the farmer as he followed his plow"; the Nonpartisan League was "but another crop of the seeding of that time," and contained "the seeds of a great social and political advancement."[7] Out of his own early experience in Wisconsin, Bob brought a message of encouragement which this audience understood. "Twenty years ago this very season," he said, "at a little farmers' gathering in Ferndale, Wis., I opened the fight against corporate power in that State. I was denounced then as the nonpartisan league has been denounced now. . . . What was the kernel, what was the center of thought of the little speech that I delivered on that day? It was only this: That the corporations in Wisconsin were not paying their fair share of the taxes and that they ought to be made to pay up, just as the farmers and owners of homes! That was all. But that was considered 'treason.' Just as some things are denounced as disloyal to-day. But, fellow citizens, I didn't stop then and I won't stop now." He went on to say that recently in the Senate and in the Committee on Finance he had been fighting for the same principles he had advocated "down at the Ferndale picnic in Wisconsin 20 years ago."[8]

From the beginning of his speech the audience was responsive, frequently applauding, cheering, and laughing in appreciation of something Bob said or implied by his inflection or expression. They were familiar with his work in Wisconsin and in the Senate; many had often heard him speak, and felt they knew him personally. After he had been talking only a few minutes, friendly voices began to interpolate comments of agreement such as, "Yes," "Good," "Go ahead," "We don't take the *Tribune*, Bob," "Nor the *Journal*, either," "We know it, Bob." As he approached a discussion of possible methods for financing the war, around which he intended to focus his extemporaneous talk, he frankly said that he had not been in favor of going into the war. This statement was greeted by cheers and applause. Lest he be misunderstood, he added: "I don't mean to say that we hadn't suffered grievances; we had—at the hands of Germany. Serious grievances!" Voices from the audience broke in shouting, "Yes." "You bet!" Then Bob went on to complete his thought: "We had cause for complaint. They had interfered with the right of American citizens to travel upon the high seas—on ships loaded with munitions for Great Britain."

Quickly silencing the laughter and cheers which followed this sentence, he said: "I would not be understood as saying that we didn't have grievances. We did. . . . We had a right, a technical right, to ship the munitions, and the American citizens have a technical right to ride on those vessels. I was not in favor of the riding on them, because it seemed to me that the consequences resulting from any destruction of life that might occur would be so awful—" Here a voice shouted, "Yellow!" This was the first hostile interruption. Bob asked, "What did you say?" The voice repeated the one word "Yellow!" Turning in the direction from which the epithet came, Bob retorted, "Any man who says that in an audience where he can conceal his identity is yellow himself." From many parts of the huge auditorium came angry cries: "Put him out!" "Put him out!" Above these cries Bob's voice rang out: "Sit down everybody. I don't want any of that in an audience where I am speaking. All I want is order. I will take care of everybody that interrupts if you will just give me the chance." Bob's quick command of the situation instantly changed the angry mood of the crowd to cheers. As these subsided he continued, "I say this, that the comparatively small privilege of the right of an American citizen to ride on a munition-loaded ship, flying a foreign flag, is too small to involve this Government in the loss of millions and millions of lives." A voice broke in to ask, "Where is the yellow guy now?" Laughter and cheers followed with calls for order as Bob went on to say: "Now, fellow-citizens, I didn't believe that we should have gone into this war for that poor privilege. The right of an American citizen to travel upon a foreign vessel loaded with munitions of war. Because—" For the second time a hostile voice interrupted to call out, "How about the *Lusitania*?" Bob replied, "Wait just a minute," and, amid cheers and applause, finished stating his position: "Because a foreign vessel loaded with munitions of war is technically foreign territory and an American citizen takes his life in his own hands, just as much as he would if he were on the territory of France and camped in the neighborhood of an arsenal!" Bob then stated briefly why he had opposed the Armed Ship bill, and went on to say that before entering a war a country ought to consider the terrific cost and what it had at stake. If all a country had at stake were loans made by the House of Morgan to foreign governments, and the profits munition makers might earn by shipping their products to foreign countries these "ought to be weighed not in a common hay scale but in an apothecaries' scale."

After thus completing his interrupted argument, he then turned to answer the heckler's question about the *Lusitania* in a statement which later stirred up heated controversy: "Four days before the *Lusitania* sailed," he said, "President Wilson was warned in person by Secretary of State Bryan, that the *Lusitania* had 6,000,000 rounds of ammunition on board, besides explosives; and that the passengers who proposed to sail on that vessel were sailing in violation of a statute of this country: that no passenger shall sail or travel upon a railroad train or upon a vessel which carries dangerous explosives.* And Secretary Bryan appealed to President Wilson to stop passengers from sailing on the *Lusitania*. I am giving you some history that probably has not been given you here before.

"So, I say," he recapitulated after cheers had interrupted, "that

---

* This was not a literal statement of the Passenger Act of 1882, but his phrasing conveyed the spirit of the law.

the grievances that carried this country into war, into a war the limits of which, as to the loss of life, and the burdens, financial burdens, that shall be laid upon us, can not be calculated by any man—I say that the conditions that carried us into that war needed to be weighed carefully. For I enunciate no new doctrine. I say what Daniel Webster said when the Mexican War was on at full tilt— that it is the right of the people of this country to determine for themselves whether there has been a sufficient grievance for the people to incur all of the burdens and risks that go with the entrance into war."[9]

Requesting the audience to let him have all the time because he must soon catch a train, he went on to discuss the theme he had been leading up to when the hostile interruptions had diverted him. "We are in a war," he said. "We have got to finance it. How shall we do it?" Briefly touching upon the mistakes made in past wars, he presented his argument for the method, recommended by 350 leading economists, of imposing taxes upon surplus incomes, war profits, and other sources of revenue "so that we should pay as we go." He criticized the Administration for approving, and Congress for passing, a bill which levied only 31 per cent, on the average, upon war profiteers. The main portion of his speech was given to the subject of war taxation and to his opening discussion of the Granger movement and the Nonpartisan League as expressions of the struggle for representative government.

Toward the end of his speech he told the audience that the present Congress had failed to fulfill its responsibility as the legislative branch of the Government; that under the Constitution Congress had the right to determine the objects and purposes of every war in which the United States was engaged. In closing he said that if Henry Clay, Daniel Webster, Abraham Lincoln, and the men of that time "understood the Constitution and the rights of the people, you, the humblest one of you, have the right to discuss freely the question of whether this war might not be terminated with honor to the Government and the awful slaughter be discontinued."[10]

As Bob finished, the audience rose to give him an ovation. Manahan, Townley, and other leaders of the Nonpartisan League rushed forward to congratulate him. Governor Frazier, who presided at the meeting, said that not a single comment came to him that night after Bob finished his speech to indicate that anything had been said to which the slightest objection could be made.[11]

To both Bob and Belle the understanding response of this great audience to his discussion of the important issues before Congress had been heartening. As they drove to the station, he turned to her and said, "Now, Belle, aren't you glad we stayed." They took the train that night with a feeling of deep satisfaction that the trip had been worth while in spite of all the strain it had meant for Bob. The next morning they arrived in Madison and drove immediately to the farm, where they spent a serene and quiet day. As always, Bob was intensely interested in the place, inspected the fields, barn, dairy herd, horses, and ponies. He was delighted at finding the barn and barnyard "clean enough [to] eat in," and especially pleased to learn that under Belle's careful supervision the milk had been brought up to such a high standard that it was being recommended by the doctors.[12] Not until the following day were either of them aware of what had happened after they left St. Paul.

While the train carried them to Madison, an Associated Press dispatch had been telegraphed from St. Paul to more than a thousand newspapers. Under glaring headlines this dispatch spread from coast to coast the next morning an absolutely false report directly quoting Bob as having said in his speech at St. Paul, "We had no grievance against Germany." Whereas the stenographic records showed he had actually said that we had serious grievances against Germany.[13] Many months later the Associated Press apologized for this inaccurate quotation, but precisely how it occurred has never been adequately explained. According to Frederick Roy Martin, their assistant general manager, the Associated Press did not have a staff reporter covering the Nonpartisan League Conference. They were depending upon a reporter for the *St. Paul Pioneer Press*, a newspaper which had long been hostile to Bob and the progressive movement in Wisconsin, as well as to the Nonpartisan League. On the night Bob spoke, the St. Paul editor of the Associated Press had obtained shortly before 2 A.M., a duplicate copy of the account of the meeting written by the *St. Paul Pioneer Press* reporter. This was sent out without waiting for it to be edited and revised by the author.[14] There was, however, a strange discrepancy in the duplicate accounts as printed the following day. The *St. Paul Pioneer Press* was equally hostile in its general interpretation of the meeting, but it quoted Bob as having said, "We had grievances."[15] This discrepancy was never explained by the Associated Press. Their dispatch from St. Paul had also further misrepresented Bob as having declared that the sinking of the *Lusitania* was justified; that the loans of the Morgans and the profits of the munitions makers were the only stake we had in the war. The meeting was described as noisy and disorderly, with the implication that the audience was a crowd of disloyal ruffians. In addition to all this falsification, there was nothing to indicate that Bob himself had not undertaken to discuss the causes of the war; that such references as he made to them had been in response to questions from hecklers; nor that the principal part of his speech had been a discussion of the pending Revenue bill and how best to finance the war. The *New York Times* headlined the St. Paul dispatch, "La Follette Defends Lusitania Sinking," quoted him as saying, "We had no grievance against Germany," and in an editorial comment on the speakers at the Nonpartisan League Conference called Bob and Gronna "chartered libertines of sedition."[16] These false and garbled news reports of Bob's St. Paul speech brought vituperation, invective, and abuse in editorials, cartoons, and public addresses. From coast to coast he was denounced in terms similar to those used by the editor of a Western newspaper who described him as "the most sinister, forbidding figure in latter-day American history. His very name has come to spell sedition and speak treason. . . . his hand wickedly raised against his country."[17]

Two days after Bob's speech at St. Paul, Governor Burnquist, head of the Minnesota Public Safety Commission, ordered an investigation for evidence of sedition and joined in the general denunciation by announcing that Bob's arrest, indictment under the Espionage Act, and return to the State for trial were being considered.[18] At the secret hearings held by the Public Safety Commission, officials of the Nonpartisan League were questioned. Among those who were summoned was the new president, A. C. Townley. After a severe grilling in the terrifying atmosphere that prevailed, he was so intimidated that he repudiated the St. Paul speech and stated that he regarded Bob's views on the war as "seditious and disloyal."[19] After a few days of these secret hearings, the Minnesota Public Safety Commission adopted a resolution charging Bob with making a speech of a "disloyal and seditious nature" and petitioning the Senate to expel him.[20] A United Press dispatch reported that the resolution had been signed by Governor Burnquist and the attorney general of Minnesota, Lyndon Smith.[21] Subsequently a letter from James Manahan to Gilbert Roe stated that the attorney general had not signed the resolution and that he thought "there was not a line in the speech that could by any reasonable construction be held to be in the slightest degree disloyal, seditious, or treasonable."[22]

Among those who took the lead in hurling scathing epithets at Bob in public speeches was Theodore Roosevelt. The colonel was on a speaking tour at this time, addressing daily mass meetings arranged under the auspices of the National Security League. This League, which contributed to his expenses,[23] was a self-constituted body, backed by great wealth, and headed by prominent men. Many of its members were leaders in financial organizations and industrial corporations with large international interests. The activities of the National Security League during the war were subsequently investigated by a Congressional committee of the House of Representatives, and excoriated as being those of "men seeking partisan ends, and undertaking to hide their self-interest beneath the cloak of public service and national good."[24] Previously, certain prominent members had publicly denounced Bob for his war-aims resolution and his fight to finance the war by taxation rather than bond issues. The day after Bob's St. Paul speech, Roosevelt was in Chicago. When asked by newspaper men, "What about La Follette?" he answered: "I haven't read his latest speech. I don't have to. I know that La Follette, in these times, outshines the arch copperheads of Civil War days. I may say that La Follette is the Grand American neo-copperhead."[25] A few days later, in a speech at Kansas City, Missouri, Roosevelt characterized him as the worst enemy democracy has alive today, a sinister enemy of democracy, and "at the moment loyally serving one country—Germany." Here too the colonel made his first specific public suggestion for Bob's expulsion from the Senate when he said, "If I were this minute a member of the Senate I would be ashamed to sit in that body until I found some way of depriving Senator La Follette of his seat in that chamber."[26] Before a mass meeting in Chicago he declared La Follette's proper place was in the German Reichstag, not in the Senate where he was "a cause for shame and humiliation to every worthy American." The mass meeting promptly adopted resolutions prepared by the National Security League condemning "Senator La Follette for his public utterances against the government and the vigorous prosecution of this war, and as an unfaithful and disloyal official, unworthy longer to represent the loyal and devoted citizens of America."[27] Similar denunciations were followed by similar resolutions at mass meetings in other cities, including one at Racine, Wisconsin.[28] In St. Paul, from the same platform where Bob had spoken eight days before, Roosevelt dubbed him one of the "Huns within our gates," and expressed a fervent desire to send him and his "shadow huns" as a "free gift to the Kaiser," naming Gronna and Congressman Lundeen of Minnesota as the "shadow huns."[29] In Minneapolis he found the new epithets of "microbe" and "lesser microbe" to apply to them.[30] Soon after his return from this trip, Roosevelt wrote Lodge that he had been in Wisconsin and elsewhere "on a little missionary tour" in the interest of La Follette.[31]

Without resorting to the invective of his former friend Theodore Roosevelt, former President Taft appealed to a Unitarian church conference to "stamp on all proposals of peace as ill-advised or seditious,"[32] and later condemned Bob for his inaccurately reported statement at St. Paul about "technical rights" by saying that a Senator's use of such terms "shocks one's deepest feelings."[33] In a family letter Bob's daughter ironically commented, "Democracy is certainly making great gains in this country these days," adding that "T. R. is proving a noble spokesman too. At last he and W. H. Taft are in agreement. It must be a great comfort to them both."[34]

Roosevelt's demand for Bob's expulsion from the Senate was echoed in the East by Nicholas Murray Butler, president of Columbia University, in a speech before the annual convention of the American Bankers Association. Calling for immediate action, he was greeted with applause when he declared, "why you might just as well put poison in the food of every American boy that goes to his transport as to permit that man [La Follette] to talk as he does." He also asserted that no single act would go so far in shortening the war as the removal of La Follette.[35]

While this tornado of denunciation was still in its early stage, Bob and Belle left Madison by train for Toledo, Ohio, where he was to speak on Sunday afternoon, September 23. The meeting, which had been arranged before he left Washington, was under the auspices of an independent church, organized by the Reverend H. J. Hahn, after he had been driven from his own church because of his anti-war stand. Hahn acted as chairman of the meeting. Many years later he still remembered vividly the almost incredible war hysteria which then pervaded the city. "Vigilante groups dominated Toledo, hounded, horsewhipped, and tarred and feathered war-resisters who dared whisper their convictions." The hotels were so fearful of mob violence that he had difficulty in getting a room for Bob. Finally one was secured on the condition that "it be veiled in secrecy." When Bob and Belle arrived he was given a batch of letters. He looked them over and then, with a grim smile, handed them to Hahn. They contained threats of violence if he dared to speak in Toledo. Hahn asked, "What shall we do about it?" Without hesitation Bob replied, "Why go ahead with the meeting, of course."[36]

Fearing violence, the authorities had made elaborate preparations for the mass meeting, which was held in Toledo's largest auditorium. Twenty-five men in uniform, and a dozen plain-clothes men were on guard with five secret service men who came from Cleveland to assist. As a "safety" measure the use of the galleries had been prohibited, but the lower floor was filled to its capacity of 2,800 long before Bob arrived.[37] Hundreds had been refused admission, and outside excited masses of men and women surged through the streets surrounding the building. As Bob and Hahn arrived at a side door, the police stopped them and sought to discourage his appearance, but Bob insisted upon entering the auditorium.[38] In an atmosphere so tense that it seemed as if almost anything might happen, he delivered his speech from the typewritten manuscript he had prepared for the St. Paul conference. The tension in the auditorium soon eased, for it was evident that the large audience was with him and that no hostile groups would dare to break up the meeting as the authorities had feared.

In this two-and-a-half-hour speech he made his first public statement of the thought and purpose which had led him to introduce his resolution calling upon Congress for a declaration of war aims. The audience of almost three thousand men and women followed him with close attention, expressing their enthusiastic approval by frequent applause, and giving him an ovation when he concluded just as his audience had done in St. Paul three days earlier. But throughout the Toledo meeting there had not been a single hostile interruption nor an unpleasant incident. A local reporter seemed surprised that his speech contained "no special cause for offence," and that he made "no reference to or defense of the sinking of the Lusitania" but spoke "chiefly on the right of the people 'who bear the burdens of war' to discuss the war and the terms on which peace should be made."[39]

This was the last public address Bob made outside the Senate during the war period. From Toledo he returned to Washington, and Belle went back to the farm at Madison. Three days later she wrote to Netha Roe: "The St. Paul and Toledo meetings were wonderful beyond imagination and description. They satisfied me as nothing other than the experience of being there could—how the American people—the working people and the farmers are thinking and feeling."[40]

Bob arrived in Washington from Toledo on the morning of September 25 by a train which was two hours late. From the station he drove directly to the house, where he cleaned up, had breakfast, and then went to the Senate. That evening Bob, Jr., wrote his mother that it had done him and Gilbert Roe "lots of good to have the story of the two meetings in detail," and that he was so glad she had gone to both meetings, as "it must have been like a refreshing breeze on an August day to really see how the people, or at least thirteen thousand of them, felt on the issue."[41]

During his Toledo speech Bob had availed himself of his first opportunity to deny publicly the inaccurate reports of his St. Paul speech. He had walked over to the edge of the platform nearest the press tables and had directly addressed the newspaper correspondents, telling them that his speech at St. Paul was "being deliberately misquoted throughout the country."[42] His statement was carried by the press but was probably seen by comparatively few people, as most newspapers did not give it the startling headlines and front-page space which had been allotted to the false quotations and misrepresentations of the St. Paul Associated Press dispatch. The *St. Paul Pioneer Press* carried Bob's statement at Toledo as a dispatch sent by the Associated Press from that city.[43] But the Associated Press did not investigate the accuracy of its report of the St. Paul speech until eight months later. Then, when hearings before a Senate committee had made it front-page news, they admitted the error and claimed to have learned for the first time that the accuracy of its account had been challenged.[44]

In the first possible issue of *La Follette's Magazine*, Bob utilized his only other available medium for refuting the false statements attributed to him. Prominently printed in a boxed form under the heading "What Sen. La Follette said and what Newspapers say he said," were quotations from several leading newspapers and one from the *Literary Digest*, all reporting that he had said we had no grievance against Germany. Then followed the accurate quotation from the certified transcript of the official stenographer clearly showing that he had actually stated we had serious grievances against Germany.[45] However, even this citation of the stenographic record received practically no attention from the press, and many people, including some of his friends, continued to blame him long after the event because they thought he had remained silent under grave, false accusations.[46]

It happened that the day after Bob's speech at St. Paul, Secretary Lansing had given to the press the text of a message sent to Berlin in January, 1917, by Ambassador von Bernstorff asking authority to expend $50,000 through an unnamed organization to influence Congress. The message was played up in sensational headlines the following day and stirred the country. The implications of the story as given out aroused resentment in Congress and brought demands for an investigation. Congressman Heflin of Alabama made a speech in the House referring to the message and declaring that he could name thirteen or fourteen Members who had "acted in a suspicious manner."[47] In the press he was reported to have also made charges that certain Members of Congress had actually been receiving money from German sources. When his statements were indignantly challenged by his colleagues and the names of the men accused were demanded during a session of the House Rules Committee, he said that he would like to have a thorough investigation of the organizations which had endorsed certain bills of Representatives Mason, Britten, and Baer and Senator La Follette.[48] When reporters went to Bob's office, he refused to make any public answer to this scurrilous innuendo, but he commented privately to his family that Heflin had "made a lot of fool statements in a speech before the House Rules Committee."[49] After stirring up this hornets' nest, Lansing advised against a Congressional investigation and emphatically declared that the von Bernstorff message did not reflect upon any Member of Congress.[50] A few days later the State Department gave out a statement that there was no evidence connecting any of them with German propaganda, and the subject was dropped.[51] But the Heflin charges, although not credited in Congress, had been widely publicized. Garbled versions continued to circulate and undoubtedly contributed to the whispered slander that Bob had received fabulous sums of money from the German Government.

Upon his return to Washington, Bob had found that the persistent misrepresentation of his St. Paul speech had "stirred up lots of feeling" against him. Although he remarked humorously to his family that Roosevelt's attacks had aroused some resentment among the Democrats because they probably wanted "to do all the cussing themselves," he was fully aware that a serious situation had been created. In order to be prepared for whatever might happen, he telegraphed Manahan to send on at once a certified transcript of the official stenographer's report of his St. Paul speech. He also saw the newspaper correspondent who had informed him of Bryan's personal appeal to the President to stop passengers from sailing on the *Lusitania* because of the ship's cargo of ammunition. Bob was assured that in spite of the nation-wide attacks upon him, this man was willing at any time to testify under oath as to the accuracy of the information he had given. In the first letter Bob wrote to Belle after his return, he said: "The feeling against me at this time is very bitter in administration circles—I have no doubt. It seems strange that it could be so when I have been so careful to keep within the bounds of legitimate discussion & have in fact never been critical of the administration. Well goodnight beloved ones. We will all go the straight course—truly loyal to our own country our constitution and our flag with all it means."[52]

Two days later, on September 29, the resolution of the Minnesota Public Safety Commission, in the form of a petition asking for Bob's expulsion, was presented to the Senate by Senator Kellogg of Minnesota. In accord with the customary procedure in presenting petitions, it was not read aloud, but was immediately referred to the Committee on Privileges and Elections.[53] A few moments later Bob, who had been attending a meeting of the Finance Committee, came on the floor and went to his seat. Apparently he did not know what had happened, and at first other Senators also seemed unaware that anything unusual had occurred. As the news spread, however, a press correspondent in the gallery noted that Senators gathered in groups in the rear of the Chamber while Bob, entirely isolated, sat reading a letter at his seat on the aisle in the first row.[54] A few minutes later the Senate went into executive session. When newspaper correspondents pressed Bob for a statement, he declined to comment.[55]

That night he telegraphed Belle that the petition for his expulsion had been introduced and referred to the committee but that no resolution had been introduced by any Senator. "I do not expect one will be offered but look for other petitions to come in[.] the war traders are making a campaign of it and the old tory crowd think it a good opportunity. . . . your council [sic] would be great help but want you to be where ever it will be easiest for you."[56]

Only three days after the resolution calling for his expulsion from the Senate was introduced, Bob made a twenty-minute speech sharply criticizing the Conference Report on the War Revenue bill as still violating every principle which should control the financing of a war.[57] Afterward, Senator King of Utah told Bob he had said just the things King himself wished to say. Later King came up to him again, put his arm around Bob, and said, "I can't see how you can take the view you do of this war, but I want to tell you I'm for you, old man." That same day a Democratic Senator, Hollis of New Hampshire, gave Bob a copy of his St. Paul speech as printed by the Committee on Privileges and Elections and told him confidentially that "it was a damned good speech."[58]

As Bob had expected, the petitions for his expulsion and impeachment continued to come. The Executives Club of Toledo went so far as to telegraph a resolution to President Wilson and to Governor Cox of Ohio asking that La Follette be deported.[59] Public-safety commissions, chambers of commerce, merchants' and manufacturers' associations, Rotary and Kiwanis clubs, Councils of Defense, the National Security League, and Grand Army veterans joined in demanding his expulsion. Printed petitions were circulated in different States, including Wisconsin. There, as elsewhere, the reactionary elements made the most of the opportunity that false newspaper reports had given them. From towns in Bob's own State came petitions headed and circulated by his bitterest political enemies. In this strange company appeared the names of some of his former supporters and lifelong friends. A huge mass meeting had been arranged in Madison on October 3 for Secretary of the Treasury McAdoo, who was entertained at dinner and introduced by Governor Philipp.

Special trains brought bankers and distinguished citizens from every section of the State. Before the meeting that night, thousands of people lined the sidewalks from the capitol square along State Street and University Avenue to watch the parade in McAdoo's honor, headed by the university band. Those who had often gathered along this same route to cheer Bob now saw illuminated box transparencies held aloft which bore such slogans as: "La Follette misrepresents Wisconsin! GET HIM OUT!" "Copperheads bite you in the heel! LOOK OUT!" "La Follette is one of only a few SLACKERS IN WISCONSIN!" "We are at war and Bob is against our own boys!"[60] The following morning the *Madison Democrat* commented in an editorial, "Secretary McAdoo will now be able to take back to Washington the information that the Wisconsin capital, home of Senator La Follette, is thoroughly loyal despite the evil impression which may have been created."[61]

Although Belle found it hard to leave Phil and Mary alone in the hostile atmosphere which pervaded Madison, she felt that Bob needed her even more, and had taken the train for Washington the day before this parade. On her arrival she found that while the newspaper headlines were reporting the demands for Bob's expulsion from the Senate, obscure dispatches on inside pages and Bob's own correspondence recorded the fact that many men and women throughout the country had not been misled by the false reports of his St. Paul speech. Without a dissenting vote delegates to the California State Federation of Labor adopted a resolution at Sacramento expressing confidence in Bob's "integrity and loyalty" and asking for him the right to express the views "of an intelligent minority."[62] A letter to Belle from Alice Brandeis expressed her own feeling and that of her husband, Louis D. Brandeis, when she wrote: "I can't tell you how shocked we are & outraged too, by these recent attacks on the Senator—it is almost incredible that such things should come to pass—his long, long years of utmost service his loyalty, his devotion all forgotten. It makes my blood boil, Belle & I can't at the same time feel aught but very sad that we should have reached such a stage as this."[63]

CHAPTER XLIX

Freedom of Speech in Time of War

As the petitions for Bob's expulsion came in day after day, they were referred to the Committee on Privileges and Elections, which was composed of fifteen Senators. Although Bob did not know it at the time, Senator Kellogg, a member of the committee, called at the State Department on Tuesday, October 2, and left a memorandum requesting information regarding statements Bob had made about Bryan and the *Lusitania* in his St. Paul speech.[1] The newspapers reported that on that same day Bryan saw the President and Secretaries Baker and Daniels.[2] The next morning the committee met and discussed procedure relative to the resolution of the Minnesota Commission of Public Safety calling for La Follette's expulsion, which Kellogg had presented to the Senate.[3] That same day Bryan telephoned Bob at his office and indicated he would publicly deny the statement that he knew the *Lusitania*'s cargo contained ammunition and had informed the President before the ship sailed urging that passengers be warned.[4] Two young secretaries who were in the office listened in on an extension telephone without Bob's knowledge. One of them recalls that the tone of the conversation was cordial, but that Bob expressed confidence in the source of his information and suggested that Bryan might be mistaken in his recollection.[5] Bob communicated at once with the man who had been the authority for his statements, and told him Bryan would probably deny the facts as stated. This man, whom Bob had known for many years, said he would be willing to testify under oath, and wrote a letter to Bob recapitulating what he had previously told him.[6]

On the afternoon of October 3, Secretary Lansing telephoned Kellogg that a careful search had been made of the State Department records, and that they had "no information such as is stated by Senator La Follette in his speech." Lansing added that he had talked on the telephone with Bryan, who "said he knew nothing about any ammunition on board the vessel until three or four days after the *Lusitania* had been sunk."[7]

The next morning the Committee on Privileges and Elections held its second meeting "to consider further what, if any action it should take relative to petitions asking the Senate to institute proceedings looking to the expulsion from the Senate of Honorable Robert M. La Follette." Eleven members were present, with Chairman Pomerene presiding. Petitions from the Rotary Club and the Sidney Post Number 41, G.A.R. of Ithaca, New York, and a letter from W. E. D. Stokes of New York City, demanding La Follette's expulsion, were read and discussed. Senator Walsh moved that the committee had jurisdiction to consider these and other petitions. The motion was agreed to without a roll call.[8] That afternoon Walsh saw the President.[9]

That evening Belle wrote Phil and Mary: "It has been a rather anxious day. The Committee did not take any action on the petitions that were before them. But we understand there was some heated discussion as to what they have a right to do." She warned them that a statement their father had made at St. Paul might be denied, but that his authority stood back of it, and that she hoped this might result in closing the controversy. "Otherwise it will be another sensation. There is much in the newspapers of the time that is corroborative in its nature. . . . Cousin Will is standing behind papa in true La Follette fashion so do they all. We owe them our gratitude. Be careful what you say to others but keep Auntie & Uncle posted."[10]

The day that Belle wrote this letter, their father was condemned in the Assembly Chamber of the state capitol by the annual Conference of the City Superintendents of Wisconsin Schools. The state superintendent of schools was Charles P. Cary, who had long been hostile to Bob. At one of the sessions, "without any previous notice or announcement, the Superintendent of City Schools at Ripon, A. F. Cook, stepped to the platform" and read a long resolution of denunciation which concluded by declaring that "we heartily disapprove and repudiate any and all of the seditious utterances of said Robert M. La Follette as being absolutely unrepresentative of the people of Wisconsin and respectfully petition the United States Senate to promptly expel him and thus give the people of Wisconsin the right to hold up their heads without shame." What followed has been recorded by Nicholas Gunderson, then superintendent of the Prairie du Chien schools: "On a rising vote, I found myself the only person seated. Amid jeers and boos, the chairman asked if the vote couldn't be made unanimous. I then stood up and said, 'Robert M. La Follette has championed the cause of the common people for too many years for me now, on the spur of the moment, to vote for his expulsion from the United States Senate. I vote *"No"* on that resolution. . . . At the close of the meeting, Mrs. Mary D. Bradford, Superintendent of the Kenosha Schools, said to me, 'Mr. Gunderson, I am proud of you. Many would have liked to have voted with you, but we didn't dare to.'"[11] The Madison newspapers did not report Gunderson's protest against the resolution, but the action of the conference was widely noted in the press.

That same day La Follette was hanged in effigy at Sheboygan, Wisconsin.[12] On the morning of October 5, the committee met again in Washington. The press reported that at its secret session the committee decided to confine the investigation to La Follette, and that a preliminary investigation would be conducted by a subcommittee of five which would limit the inquiry solely to the accuracy of the statement of facts in the St. Paul speech, and that Bryan would be called to testify. The newspapers also stated that the committee's decision was unanimous, but noted that two Senators had opposed the inquiry. Senator William H. King of Utah was quoted as saying there was "nothing seditious or to warrant expulsion in the speech." Senator James A. Reed of Missouri was reported as stating that neither the speech nor other statements nor actions of Senator La Follette warranted drastic action.[13]

Bob was not officially informed as to the action of the committee, but the minutes of the meeting show that Ollie James moved that Chairman Pomerene appoint a subcommittee of five, the chairman to be ex officio chairman, "to investigate the accuracy of the report of the speech delivered by the Honorable Robert M. La Follette, a United States Senator from the State of Wisconsin, September 20th, 1917," and "to investigate the accuracy of the statements made by the said Honorable Robert M. La Follette in said speech; and to report its findings to the full committee the first day of the next regular session of the Congress in December 1917." The motion was agreed to without a roll call, and Pomerene named Senators Ollie M. James, Thomas J. Walsh, William P. Dillingham, and Albert B. Fall to serve as the subcommittee.[14] That same day Chairman Pomerene submitted to the Senate a resolution authorizing the committee or a subcommittee to conduct an investigation and report to the Senate. It did not mention Bob's name. The Senate went into executive session to consider the resolution, and therefore the *Congressional Record* merely states that it was passed by unanimous consent.[15] Later in the afternoon a messenger delivered to Bob, Jr., at his father's office in the Capitol, a letter from Pomerene, addressed to his father, and a copy of the St. Paul speech which had been sent to Senator Kellogg by the Minnesota Commission of Public Safety. The letter asked if this was a correct copy of the speech and, if not, requested Bob to state wherein it was not correct and to give the committee a correct statement thereof.[16] Bob read it and immediately wrote Pomerene that the copy submitted was not correct; that he would not then undertake to state wherein it was incorrect, but would furnish a correct copy as soon as he could secure an accurate transcript.[17]

When Pomerene's letter arrived on Friday afternoon, Bob was in his office working on a speech announced for the following day. Newspapers reported that under an informal agreement he would begin a three-hour speech when the Senate met at ten o'clock on Saturday.[18] It was a fact that he had entered into an agreement to limit his speech to about three hours because this seemed the only way he could be certain of obtaining the floor before Congress adjourned.[19] A resolution fixing the hour of adjournment for three o'clock on Saturday afternoon had been adopted by the House[20] and was lying on the Vice President's desk awaiting Senate action. Everyone assumed that Bob intended to discuss his St. Paul speech and the disloyalty charges that had been made against him. The newspapers correctly predicted that the Senate leaders would allow the House resolution to lie upon the Vice President's desk until Bob finished.[21] This strategy assured them an opportunity to reply and also made it possible to prevent him from answering their attacks. A dramatic session was anticipated, as it was known that Kellogg and other Senators were preparing to answer him.

On Saturday morning the newspapers reported that Bryan had

publicly declared: "I read a statement which purported to have been made by Senator La Follette in a speech in Minnesota to the effect that four days before the sinking of the *Lusitania* I had notified the President that there was ammunition on board the vessel. When I passed through Washington last Wednesday I notified the State Department and also Senator La Follette that the Senator had been misinformed, and that I had not known until after the sinking of the *Lusitania* that it carried ammunition in its cargo."[22]

Before the Senate convened that morning, the galleries were filled, and long lines of men and women stood in the corridors waiting for any seat which might be vacated. Gilbert Roe, Belle, and her son-in-law, George Middleton, had arrived early and were in the family gallery. At ten o'clock, when Vice President Marshall called the Senate to order, nearly every seat on the floor was occupied. During the morning hour petitions demanding Bob's expulsion from the Senate were presented by Senators Sheppard of Texas, Smith of Maryland, and Poindexter of Washington. The one from Colfax, Washington, a town near the home of Congressman William L. La Follette, was accompanied by a letter asking for Bob's impeachment.[23]

When Bob entered the Chamber, the crowds in the gallery leaned forward. A reporter noted that he "appeared composed" as he walked slowly down the aisle, followed by a page who carried books and documents.[24] After the Senate had transacted some routine business, Bob rose to a question of personal privilege and obtained the floor. Standing at his desk in the front row of the center aisle, he read his address from manuscript. His manner was neither excited nor repressed. There was no sense of oratory or climax. Listening intently, Belle, who was always an exacting critic, thought his mood throughout fitted perfectly what he had to say. Although intense, he was natural, and there "was no consciousness of anything personal at stake." To her and to others who shared his conviction as to the importance of free speech in time of war as in peace, he was upholding a great basic constitutional right which was being violated in a way that threatened, "if allowed to go unchallenged to destroy our free institutions."[25]

Early in his speech Bob referred to a mass of clippings piled up on his desk. These represented, he said, only a small part of the accumulation clipped from the daily press which accused him and other Senators, who had opposed American entry into the war, of "the highest crimes of which any man can be guilty—treason and disloyalty," without any suggestion that evidence existed to support the accusations. To show the extent to which fundamental principles of the law were being violated, Bob read a clipping he had just received which quoted the charge made to a grand jury by a Federal Judge in Texas. This Judge, after naming Bob, Stone, Hardwick, Vardaman, Gronna, and Gore, was reported to have stated to the jury: "If I had a wish, I would wish that you men had jurisdiction to return bills of indictment against these men. . . . I have a conviction, as strong as life, that this country should stand them up against an adobe wall to-morrow and give them what they deserve. If any man deserves death, it is a traitor. I wish that I could pay for the ammunition . . ."[26] *

This clipping had been sent to Bob by a Federal Judge in North Dakota, Justice Charles F. Amidon, who had written on the margin that "the conduct of this judge might very properly be the subject of an investigation." Bob also read a letter from Judge Amidon, who wrote: "It is a time when all the spirits of evil are turned loose. The Kaisers of high finance, who have been developing hatred of you for a generation because you have fought against them and for the common good, see this opportunity to turn the war patriotism into an engine of attack. They are using it everywhere, and it is a day when lovers of democracy, not only in the world, but here in the United States, need to go apart on the mountain and spend the night in fasting and prayer. I still have faith that the forces of good on this earth will be found to be greater than the forces of evil, but we all need resolution. I hope you will have the grace to keep your center of gravity on the inside of you and to keep a spirit that is unclouded by hatred. It is a time for the words, 'with malice toward none and charity for all.' "[27]

Following the reading of this letter, Bob made his only reference to the accusations against him. "I am aware," he said, "that in pursuance of this general campaign of vilification and attempted intimidation, requests from various individuals and certain organizations have been submitted to the Senate for my expulsion from

* The *Madison Democrat* had printed this statement of the Texas Judge in a special boxed story on the front page.

this body, and that such requests have been referred to and considered by one of the committees of the Senate.

"If I alone had been made the victim of these attacks, I should not take one moment of the Senate's time for their consideration, and I believe that other Senators who have been unjustly and unfairly assailed, as I have been, hold the same attitude upon this that I do. *'Neither the clamor of the mob nor the voice of power will ever turn me by the breadth of a hair from the course I mark out for myself, guided by such knowledge as I can obtain and controlled and directed by a solemn conviction of right and duty.'* "

Charging that the war party was seeking to intimidate not only members of Congress, he went on to describe the terrorizing of honest, law-abiding citizens by public officials, the invasion of their homes and the violation of their constitutional rights in the recent hysterical effort to coerce public opinion and suppress discussion. Although he recognized that war inevitably imposed certain restrictions upon citizens, he maintained that *"the right to control their own Government according to constitutional forms is not one of the rights that the citizens of this country are called upon to surrender in time of war.*

"Rather in time of war the citizen must be more alert to the preservation of his right to control his Government. He must be most watchful of the encroachment of the military upon the civil power. . . . More than all, the citizen and his representative in Congress in time of war must maintain his right of free speech. . . . I am contending . . . for the great fundamental right of the sovereign people of this country to make their voice heard and have that voice heeded upon the great questions arising out of this war, including not only how the war shall be prosecuted but the conditions upon which it may be terminated with a due regard for the rights and the honor of this Nation and the interests of humanity.

"I am contending for this right because the exercise of it is necessary to the welfare, to the existence, of this Government, to the successful conduct of this war, and to a peace which shall be enduring and for the best interest of this country."[28]

He argued that although what is popularly called "the Government" consists of the members of Congress and the President, in fact back of them is always "the controlling sovereign power of the people, and when the people can make their will known, the faithful officer will obey that will. . . . How can that popular will express itself between elections except by meetings, by speeches, by publications, by petitions, and by addresses to the representatives of the people? Any man who seeks to set a limit upon those rights, whether in war or peace, aims a blow at the most vital part of our Government. . . . And before this great fundamental right every other must, if necessary, give way, for in no other manner can representative government be preserved."[29]

Standing at his desk, from which he seldom moved during this address, he read his closely reasoned argument as he might have presented a case to the Supreme Court. He cited precedents supporting the principle of freedom of discussion during previous wars. For an hour and a half he read excerpts from speeches made during the Mexican War by Lincoln, Sumner, Clay, Corwin, and Webster severely criticizing President Polk and the prosecution of a war to undisclosed ends. He showed that in the midst of war they had arraigned the President and asserted the power of Congress to shape the war policy. He maintained that every representative in Congress and every American citizen had the same right in respect to this war and that the arguments of Lincoln, Sumner, Clay, and Webster were potent so long as the Constitution remained the law of the land.[30]

After reading excerpts from Sumner's speech at Tremont Temple in Boston during the Mexican War, Bob contrasted it with a recent address in which Secretary of the Treasury McAdoo was reported to have declared, "America intends that those well-meaning but misguided people who talk inopportunely of peace . . . shall be silenced" and "that every pacifist speech in this country made at this inopportune and improper time is in effect traitorous."[31] Pointing to a statue on the wall of the Senate Chamber, Bob said: "In these times we had better turn the marble bust of Charles Sumner to the wall. It ill becomes those who tamely surrender the right of free speech to look upon that strong, noble, patriotic face."[32]

After giving many American precedents for freedom of speech in wartime, Bob cited John Bright's opposition to the Crimean War, quoted from Lloyd George, who had opposed the Boer War, and read excerpts from the historic protests of the Duke of Grafton, Edmund Burke, Charles James Fox, and Lord Chatham against the policy of George III, while the American colonies were still fighting for independence.

These quotations from some of the leading statesmen of England were made, he said, "to show that the principle of free speech was no new doctrine born of the Constitution of the United States," but "a heritage of English-speaking peoples, which has been won by incalculable sacrifice, and which they must preserve so long as they hope to live as free men." In a clear, quiet voice, without fear of contradiction, he said, "there has never been a time for more than a century and a half when the right of free speech and free press and the right of the people to peaceably assemble for public discussion have been so violated among English-speaking people as they are violated to-day throughout the United States."[33]

Bob went on to discuss the constitutional right and duty of Congress to determine the purposes and objects of the war which Congress itself had declared. He reminded his colleagues of the fact that for the mere assertion of this right in the form of a resolution introduced on August 11, 1917, to be considered and discussed by the Senate, he had been denounced throughout the United States as a traitor to his country. Expressing his profound conviction that the war could have been avoided if "Congress had exercised its constitutional power to influence and direct the foreign policy of this country," he maintained the framers of the Constitution knew "that to give one man that power meant danger to the rights and liberties of the people. They knew that it mattered not whether you call the man king or emperor, czar or president, to put into his hands the power of making war or peace meant despotism. . . . They placed the entire control of this subject in the hands of the Congress. . . . The only power relating to war with which the Executive was intrusted was that of acting as Commander in Chief of the Army and Navy and of the militia when called into actual service. This provision is found in section 2, Article II, and is as follows: 'The President shall be Commander in Chief of the Army and Navy of the United States and of the militia of the several States when called into the actual service of the United States.' Here is found the sum total of the President's war powers. After the Army is raised he becomes the General in Command. His function is purely military."[34]

Through specific quotations and citations he showed that Congress had at various times exercised its right to express an opinion on foreign questions both in war and in peace, and that there was an unbroken line of precedents upon this subject down to the time of the present Administration. The House of Representatives had in 1848 gone so far as to pass a resolution declaring that President Polk had begun the war with Mexico unnecessarily and unconstitutionally. "And yet to-day," Bob said, "merely suggesting a possible disagreement with the administration on any measure submitted, or the offering of amendments to increase the tax upon incomes, or on war profits, is 'treason to our country and an effort to serve the enemy.'" Recalling the fact that the President had "asked the German people to speak for themselves," Bob asked the Senators: "Why should not the American people voice their convictions through their chosen representatives in Congress? . . . Have the people no intelligent contribution to make to the solution of the problems of this war? I believe that they have, and that in this matter, as in so many others, they may be wiser than their leaders, and that if left free to discuss the issues of the war they will find the correct settlement of these issues. . . . Common honesty and fair dealing with the people of this country and with the nations by whose side we are fighting, as well as a sound military policy at home, requires the fullest and freest discussion before the people of every issue involved in this great war and that a plain and specific declaration of our purposes in the war be speedily made by the Congress of the United States."[35]

As Bob finished his speech, Belle felt profoundly satisfied. Nothing he had ever done seemed to her of such tremendous value, and if the Senate had voted to expel him at the close of his address she would have felt it worth while.[36] Throughout his address the galleries and floor had remained crowded. A large majority of the Senators had given him continuous and respectful attention,[37] and he had been interrupted only once for a question. When he concluded a spontaneous outburst of applause swept the galleries and continued as Senator Kellogg of Minnesota rose and addressed the Chair. It persisted until the Vice President warned spectators that applause was against the rule and the galleries would be cleared if a repetition occurred. The Senate then passed the resolution to adjourn at three o'clock as the newspapers had predicted. Immediately after this, Kellogg, who had already obtained the floor, proceeded, as previously planned, to attack the St. Paul speech. Quoting two paragraphs from the version made for the Minnesota Public Safety Commission, he called attention to Bryan's denial in the morning newspapers of Bob's statement that Bryan knew the *Lusitania* carried ammunition and had warned the President. At some length he maintained that Bob's statement was not "a question of free speech" but "of an erroneous statement of facts," which tended "to aid and encourage the enemy and to cast dishonor and discredit upon this Nation."[38] While Kellogg was speaking, Bob sat quietly at his desk making a few notes of points he intended to answer if he could obtain the floor.

As soon as Kellogg finished, Senator Robinson of Arkansas rose from a seat near the front of the Chamber across the aisle from Bob and began a long tirade in which he used what the United Press correspondent described as "the most unrestrained language that ever has been heard in the Senate."[39] In a speech which covers five pages of the *Congressional Record* he hurled one insult after another at Bob. Declaring that the greater portion of the address Bob had just delivered was directed "to the quotation of mere platitudinous utterances by great men of the past," Robinson turned toward Bob and shouted: "I say to you that while I can not find language within the rules of the Senate to appropriately characterize the sentiments uttered on this floor this morning by the Senator from Wisconsin, if I entertained those sentiments I would not think I had the right to retain a seat on the floor of the United States Senate. I would apply to the Kaiser for a seat in the Bundesrath." A tense silence followed this outburst. Men and women in the crowded galleries were shocked to complete quiet, and Senators sat mute. Robinson went on to arraign Bob for his resolution calling upon Congress to declare our war aims, and for his St. Paul speech, mentioning a huge sum of money the German Government had spent in propaganda, and charging that Bob had "lent himself, his great talents and his services, to the promulgation of the ideas, theories, and desires of the Kaiser." Becoming more vehement as he went on, Robinson shouted: "Those who would betray their flag and their country, and those who are foolish enough not to know their duty, had better get to cover. There is no compromise on this issue. There are only two sides to this conflict—Germanism and Americanism; the Kaiser or the President."[40]

Throughout this attack Bob sat at his desk, occasionally taking
notes. As the denunciation became more virulent and personal, he
half turned his chair so that he directly faced the speaker. Robinson
moved toward him, shaking his fist. Bob eyed him coolly. As Robinson reached the climax of his attack, he violated the Senate custom
of addressing a colleague in the third person. Bob kept a steady
gaze upon him. Robinson moved closer, pointing at Bob and shouting: "I want to know where you stand. I heard every word of the
speech of the Senator from Wisconsin, and I do not know where
he stands. I read his speech as reported from St. Paul, and I do
not know from it where he stands. The American people are
wondering where he stands. . . . You had the right to question the
wisdom of the war, if in your honest judgment you doubted it, but
when Congress passed the declaration of war, then, instead of going
about the country and leaving your place on the floor of the Senate,
where duty calls you, instead of going over the country, stirring up
sedition, and gathering together the discontented elements of the
country and seeking to inflame them against your flag, your country,
and your President; by God, you ought to stand here and support
the flag and the President and help bring victory to American
arms!"[41]

Among the Senators who had expected to reply to Bob was Ollie
James of Kentucky, who refrained because he had been appointed
to the subcommittee which was to investigate the St. Paul speech.[42]
However, another member of the subcommittee, Albert B. Fall of
New Mexico, felt no impropriety in acting as both judge and
prosecutor. Immediately after Robinson concluded, Fall obtained
the floor. During his denunciation he said that the statements Bob
was reported to have made might properly have been made in the
Senate but not elsewhere. When made as they were, he declared,
"no more dangerous doctrine has been preached, no more insidi-
ously dangerous utterance has been heard from any source, in my
judgment, than that of the Senator from Wisconsin made at Minneapolis. [sic]" After developing this argument at some length and
protesting his "kindly feeling" for the Senator from Wisconsin, he
proceeded to distort a quotation from the St. Paul speech[43] and
implied that one subject for investigation might be Bob's criticism
of the War Revenue bill. At this point Fall yielded to Senator
Chamberlain, who asked and secured consent for the confirmation
of certain nominations. Other business was also transacted.[44]

Bob saw that the hands of the clock were nearing the hour set for adjournment. He had taken notes during the speeches of Kellogg and Robinson which had given him the first authoritative indication as to the specific parts of his St. Paul speech the subcommittee intended to investigate.* In his desk he had documents substantiating statements made at St. Paul, and he wished to reply at once to the false charges made in the Senate that afternoon. When Fall rose and addressed the Chair to obtain the floor and continue his speech, Bob also rose and addressed the Chair. But the Vice President recognized Fall first and then asked if the Senator from New Mexico yielded to the Senator from Wisconsin.[45] Although Fall had previously yielded to Bob once for a question, he now refused. Bob then asked to be allowed to make a very brief statement, and without further objection was permitted to say: "The accuracy of a statement which I made in the speech at St. Paul has been questioned here. I had expected that I would have an opportunity to say a few words in conclusion of this debate, and at that time I had expected to be given a chance to lay before the Senate and the country the authority upon which I made the statement. I thank the Senator for giving me the opportunity to say that I shall have to avail myself of some other means of communicating the facts to the public."[46]

Senator Fall continued to exercise his right to hold the floor until three o'clock, when Congress adjourned. During the last hour of the debate the President was in his room at the Capitol, with Secretary Lansing, Postmaster General Burleson, and others. The press reported that murmurs of the denunciation of La Follette floated into the room.[47] Throughout the five-hour session the scene in the Senate had been tense, "one of the most dramatic in a generation."[48] The Senators left the Chamber quietly. Senator Vardaman crossed to Bob's desk and spoke to him.[49] Bob went to his office carrying with him the papers he had intended to lay before the Senate had he been permitted to answer the charges hurled at him that afternoon.

A few hours later his son, Bob, Jr., who had listened to the address from the floor, telegraphed to Phil and Mary, "This day was a great triumph most wonderful speech he has ever made."[50]

* These three pages of notes in Bob's handwriting indicate the points he intended to discuss had he been permitted to reply.

CHAPTER L

An Avalanche of Attacks

The day after Congress adjourned, Belle wrote Phil and Mary that she thought the Administration was determined to suppress free speech, and therefore what the Committee did to their father would have no relation to his words or acts but would be decided by how far they felt they could go "without getting a comeback." Whatever happened, she assured them there was nothing to worry about because their father had said that he "could quit and feel that he had rounded out his service when he finished his talk yesterday"; that he was perfectly willing to go back to farming and "sit on a milk stool the rest of his life."[1]

The same day this letter was written the newspaper dispatches indicated that the two Republican Senators from Massachusetts, Lodge and Weeks, would cooperate in every effort to expel Bob from the Senate. Neither had heard his October 6 speech, as both were in Springfield, where Lodge delivered the principal speech to the State Republican Convention. While cheers of approval resounded through the Auditorium, the convention passed without a dissenting vote a resolution condemning La Follette "as a senator of the United States and as an individual, for his attitude and public utterances in the matter of the world war, as of comfort to the common enemy, the imperial German government, and as of marked disloyalty to his country, the United States of America."[2]

This resolution undoubtedly had Lodge's blessing. But he admitted in a letter to Roosevelt that expulsion from the Senate would be more difficult than it might seem to the public because a two-thirds vote was required, and that to try and fail must be avoided, as that would mean a triumph for La Follette.[3] The colonel, who had been clamoring for expulsion, replied that he had never thought

La Follette could be expelled, that in fact he was only 10 per cent worse than Wilson since many of his most evil utterances were almost exact repetitions of things Wilson had said.[4]

A day-by-day coordination of the public denunciations of Bob with the contemporary private correspondence and engagement books of the period now available indicates that a campaign of vilification received encouragement from high places in Washington. At the National Capital and at the state capital in Wisconsin men who were striving to have Bob expelled were especially active on October 9. That afternoon the State and County Councils of Defense held a conference in the Assembly Chamber of the capitol at Madison. The meeting was addressed by Bob's and Belle's classmate, Charles R. Van Hise, president of the university, and Dean H. L. Russell of the College of Agriculture. A resolution was unanimously adopted declaring, "We do condemn the stand taken by Senator La Follette, believing that he is aiding and abetting the enemy, thereby prolonging this fearful struggle at the cost of additional lives and money," and "we do demand the immediate resignation of R. M. La Follette as Senator from the State of Wisconsin to the end that our fair State may no longer be misrepresented in the United States and before the people of the country," and "in the event of his failure to resign we ask the Senate of the United States to preserve its own honor and that of the State of Wisconsin by his expulsion by that honorable body." This resolution was telegraphed to the President, who stated in a memorandum to his secretary that he doubted if it would be wise for him to acknowledge personally resolutions reflecting upon the character of a United States Senator and suggesting that Tumulty acknowledge them with an expression of the President's warm appreciation of the patriotic feeling and purpose they embodied.[5]

The delegates who passed this resolution also sponsored and attended a huge mass meeting that same night at which Madison citizens had been promised "a sensation." It was held in the university gymnasium where Bob had been nominated for his second and third terms as governor. The presiding officer was Magnus Swenson, chairman of the State and County Councils of Defense, who was associated with private water-power enterprises and had long been hostile to Bob and the progressive movement.[6] Governor Philipp, leader of the stalwart Republicans, delivered the principal address. The closing speech was made by Richard Lloyd Jones, editor of the *Wisconsin State Journal*, which had been attacking Bob ever since the President had denounced the little group of "willful men" for preventing passage of the Armed Ship bill. The university regents and President Van Hise were on the platform. Because certain influential delegates had thought the resolutions passed at the afternoon session were not severe enough, a committee had been appointed to frame another for the evening meeting. Among them were Carl Johnson, president of the Gisholt Machine Company in Madison, which manufactured machinery necessary for war purposes, and Richard Lloyd Jones. This resolution, which passed that night by a rising vote without a single protest, charged Bob with "opposing the prosecution of this war," demanded that he do Wisconsin "an honor by forthwith resigning his senatorship," and that if he failed to do so "the United States Senate cleanse itself by expelling him" when Congress convened in December.[7] Magnus Swenson promptly telegraphed this resolution to the President and Senator Pomerene.[8]

That same day two vituperative articles attacking Bob, which had been written for and published in the *Wisconsin State Journal*, were sent with a letter to Pomerene by the author, John M. Olin, a leading lawyer in Madison.[9] When Bob and Belle were students at the university, Olin had been one of their teachers, and later the two men had frequently tested their legal skills in the Wisconsin courts on opposite sides of important cases. Olin had also been attorney for the Stalwarts in 1904, opposing Bob's lawyer, Gilbert E. Roe, when the Republican National Committee had seated the delegates chosen at the stalwart rump convention in the Madison Opera House. But in spite of these legal and political contests, Bob and Olin had always maintained a friendly personal relation and mutual respect. Olin's second article, which attacked Bob's St. Paul speech, had been published on October 8, the night before the mass meeting arranged by the State and County Councils of Defense. It warned people to remember that "this disloyal and traitorous address of Senator La Follette was promptly laid before the Kaiser." In quoting excerpts, torn from their context with the meaning skillfully misinterpreted, Olin stated that these quotations had been taken from a transcript of the La Follette speech which had been "furnished" to him, although he did not disclose who had sent it.[10]

In Washington, on October 8, the subcommittee of five Senators, James, Walsh, Dillingham, Fall, and Chairman Pomerene, met "to consider the subject matter" of letters received from Bryan and Lansing.[11] The next morning Pomerene called at the State Department and talked with Lansing about the La Follette investigation.[12] A letter from Pomerene to Lansing, dated that same day, quoted excerpts from the St. Paul speech, asked for diplomatic correspondence relating to the sinking of the *Lusitania*, and submitted four specific questions relating to it.[13] That afternoon at four thirty Pomerene also saw the President.[14] The next day Bob learned through the newspapers that Pomerene had made these calls to gather material "for examining La Follette's statement that ex-Secretary Bryan, having knowledge of ammunition cargo on board the *Lusitania* when she sailed on her last voyage, urged the President to keep Americans off the ship."[15]

The next morning the *Washington Post* printed what appeared to be an officially inspired report that the President had told Pomerene this statement was false, and that Lansing had assured the Senator the State Department would give the subcommittee all the facts it had regarding the *Lusitania* cargo. This signed story and other similar dispatches sent out from Washington also imputed treasonable intent by asserting that Bob's St. Paul speech had been "an almost exact reproduction" of the German Foreign Minister von Jagow's note of May 28, 1915, and that the German Ambassador, Count von Bernstorff, had been the source of Bob's statement that Bryan had warned the President about the *Lusitania* cargo and had urged him to keep Americans off the ship.[16]

After reading these dispatches, Belle wrote Mary that the committee "was evidently feeding the newspapers stuff"; that her father had been working on the problem of the wisest way to meet the committee—whether to "let them go along in their own way or to ask them for a statement of their charges." She said Gilbert Roe was in Washington "looking up the law," but that there was "no one to confer with among the Senators." The La Follette cousins were "wonderfully sympathetic and kind"; Cousin Will gave them the use of his car most of the time, which made it "so much easier going back and forth to the office."[17]

On the same day this letter was written, Bob had sent Pomerene a printed copy of the transcript of his speech as certified by the official reporter of the St. Paul Conference. In an accompanying letter, printed and bound with the speech, he called attention to the fact that there had been two interruptions from the audience which had been recorded in the *New York Times* and other press reports but were not indicated in this transcript. He also pointed out some important particulars in which it differed from the version the committee had received from the Minnesota Public Safety Commission. If it was the committee's purpose to make an investigation as to any statement of fact in the speech, he requested that the committee advise him what statement was called into question, and in what respect. He also asked the right to question witnesses who might testify and to call his own witnesses. If his right to make the speech was to be considered, he asked an opportunity to be heard in person and by counsel. Toward the end of his two-page letter, he said: "I assume that the wholly false reports sent out by the press generally, to the effect that I have stated in various forms 'We had no grievance,' is receiving no credence from you, since that is contrary to the text of the speech you furnished me. I shall be very glad, however, if your investigation is sufficiently broad to take in an inquiry into the causes which led to the publication generally of these grossly false statements by the press."[18]

Although this entire paragraph of Bob's letter was quoted in the dispatch which the Associated Press correspondent sent out from Washington that day,[19] no correction was elicited from Associated Press officials until seven months later, when on May 23, 1918, the assistant manager sent Pomerene a telegram acknowledging their error.[20] The *Washington Times* reported on the front page that "La Follette claimed important misquotations in press reports and flatly denied he ever said 'we had no grievance' for entering the war."[21] Many other newspapers carried similar reports. The *New York Times* printed his letter to Pomerene, but again misled its readers in the headline which said, "Calls Some Reports False But Tells Committee The New York Times Account of His Speech Was Accurate."[22] The fact was that this newspaper had not only misquoted him as saying "We had no grievance," but had grossly misinterpreted his entire speech by the headlines it had given to two St. Paul dispatches published in different editions the day after the speech. One of these headlines read, "La Follette Defends Lusitania Sinking"; the other proclaimed, "La Follette Faces A Threat Of Arrest."[23]

After receiving Bob's letter of October 11, the subcommittee met that same day and compared the transcripts of the St. Paul speech as submitted by him and by the Minnesota Commission of Public Safety. The following day they met again and agreed upon a reply to La Follette, signed by Pomerene, which stated that the only question the subcommittee was authorized to investigate was the accuracy of the statements in the St. Paul speech. This letter, dated October 12, asked Bob to appear before the subcommittee on October 16 at ten thirty in the morning to inform them "with reference to the accuracy of various statements contained in the speech," but it did not specify what statements were challenged and it also ignored Bob's other requests.[24] Thus in violation of customary legal procedure, he was summoned to appear as the first witness in an investigation looking toward his expulsion without specification of the offense with which he was charged. Bob knew that if he appeared at the hearing under these conditions, it would be possible for the subcommittee to confine the investigation to an attempt to discredit his testimony and then abruptly close the investigation without giving him an opportunity to produce evidence supporting the challenged statements of fact.

After consulting with Belle, Bob, Jr., and Gilbert Roe, who had been spending most of his time in Washington since October 1, Bob sent Pomerene a long letter the next day stating that the procedure was "most extraordinary and wholly unprecedented"; that in refusing to give him a definite statement of the offense with which he was charged and the evidence supporting it the subcommittee was denying him a right accorded to every man called to answer even a misdemeanor. Point by point he reviewed the action of the Committee on Privileges and Elections and the correspondence that had been exchanged.

Noting that the committee had seen fit to act upon a petition and resolution charging him with disloyalty and demanding his expulsion, he reminded them that this grave charge had been heralded far and wide by the press as the trial of a United States Senator for disloyalty. The public had thus been led to believe that the committee was conducting an investigation to determine his guilt or innocence and that upon their finding might be based his ex-

pulsion from the Senate for treason. If this charge were of sufficient importance to be investigated, he maintained it should be
investigated by the procedure which experience had shown was
necessary to fairness and the establishment of truth; namely, to
acquaint the accused of the specific charges and give him the
elementary right to meet the witnesses face to face, hear their
testimony, and question their correctness of memory and accuracy
of statement before producing his testimony. He again demanded
that if the accuracy or truthfulness of any fact stated by him was
denied, "it be denied on sworn testimony or duly verified records."
He also demanded the right "to question the witnesses, and to
investigate the records and all the records bearing upon the issue,"
and said he would thereupon present "verified records and the
testimony of witnesses under oath to support such controverted
statements."[25]

On the evening of the day this letter was delivered to Pomerene,
a Washington newspaper reported that the exact charges against
Senator La Follette "were troubling the committee" and added
that if he insisted they be formulated in strict accordance with the
rules of criminal law, hearings might be delayed.[26] The following
Monday Lansing sent Pomerene photographic copies of the original
and supplemental manifests of the *Lusitania* and a copy of a letter,
dated June 2, 1915, from the Treasury Department.[27] That afternoon a letter from Pomerene was delivered to Bob at his office. It
granted his right to have counsel, to have witnesses subpoenaed in
his behalf, to cross-examine witnesses and inspect any and all documents submitted to the subcommittee. Pomerene stated that the
committee had challenged no assertion in the speech. But he refused
to comply with Bob's request for a bill of particulars, and insisted
that each committee member would feel free to question him on any
portion of his St. Paul speech.[28] Until late that night Bob and Roe
talked over every aspect of the situation. Finally they drafted a
letter to Pomerene and worked out a plan of action which was
carried out the next day.

The subcommittee met in its room on the gallery floor of the
Capitol at ten thirty Tuesday morning. Pomerene was wearing a
Prince Albert coat in honor of the occasion, and the stage was set
for drama. Bob was about ten minutes late because he had understood the hearing was to be held in the Senate Office Building. A

reporter noted that during this interval Senators Pomerene, Dillingham, and Walsh, who were seated at the committee table, assumed a dignified appearance and tried to look unconcerned while they waited.[29] The room was crowded with newspaper correspondents and spectators who anticipated a sensation when Pomerene and Walsh, who were known to be hostile, began to question their Wisconsin colleague.

Bob entered the room alone and bowed to members of the subcommittee, who were obviously relieved at his arrival. Pomerene called him to the witness stand and began the hearing by saying, "Senator La Follette, it was the desire of the committee to interrogate you concerning some of the statements of fact in this speech—" At this point Bob interrupted to state why he had been delayed and then went on to say, "I appear here, Mr. Chairman, to submit to you in the form of a letter, addressed to you as chairman of this subcommittee, all the statement that I deem it proper or necessary for me to make at this time, and I now present that statement." Reaching into his pocket, he took out the letter he and Roe had written, placed it on the table, bowed, and added, "I will say good morning to the committee," and walked briskly out of the room.[30]

Pomerene, taken by surprise, indiscreetly directed the secretary to read the letter aloud. This was precisely what Bob had hoped, because reading it in open session made it possible for him to give it to the press. A reporter, who watched Pomerene, Walsh, and Dillingham during the reading of the letter, commented privately that "they were like three spiders waiting to prey upon a fly, and when the fly got into the web he turned to a bumblebee and they didn't know what to do. Another said they were like a troop of players who had rehearsed their play, set the stage, rung up the curtain, and had another company come on and give the show."[31]

The letter, after answering Pomerene's communication of October 15 point by point, declared Bob had, of course, believed in the accuracy of every statement at the time he made the speech; that he still believed all statements were accurate; that if accorded a fair opportunity to face and cross-examine any and all persons denying the accuracy of statements, he believed he could convince the subcommittee that the statements were accurate. In closing the letter he said he was most anxious for a thorough and complete investigation "to the end that it shall do justice to all participants and shall constitute an honorable precedent when ever so grave a matter as the proposed expulsion of one of its Members shall come before the United States Senate."[32]

When the reading of the four-and-a-half-page letter was finished, Pomerene, Dillingham, and Walsh conferred for a few moments in low tones. The chairman then announced that the subcommittee would go into executive session, and asked the audience to withdraw. An afternoon Washington newspaper reported that after the secret session Pomerene had announced the subcommittee would not hold any more hearings but would obtain information from the State Department and other sources regarding La Follette's assertions, and report to Congress in December.[33]

That same day Pomerene wrote a long letter to Lansing asking him to appear before the subcommittee in the near future to submit diplomatic correspondence and make such statements of fact as would "demonstrate the accuracy or inaccuracy" of La Follette's assertions in his St. Paul speech regarding the *Lusitania* having a cargo of 6,000,000 rounds of ammunition and other explosives and Bryan's appeal to the President to prevent passengers from sailing on the vessel.[34] The next morning, October 17, Pomerene, Walsh, and Dillingham conferred at the State Department with Secretary Lansing and Attorney General Gregory about the La Follette investigation.[35] Bob did not know of this conference, as it was not reported in the press. But that day he received a brief note from Pomerene stating that the subcommittee hearing would be resumed at ten thirty on November 26.[36]

Under the same date as Pomerene's letter of October 17, a dispatch was sent out from Washington which appeared the following morning on the front pages of two New York newspapers, the *Sun* and the *New York Tribune*. Although printed in slightly different form, the false statements and the innuendoes imputing treason were so similar that they seemed to have been inspired by the same source. The *Sun* headlines screamed "La Follette In Attack On Loan." Both stories charged that at a time when patriotic men were trying to get people to buy bonds, La Follette was flooding the country with hundreds of thousands of pamphlets, printed at Government expense, containing his speeches on the War Revenue Act which predicted the failure of the second Liberty Loan and by indirection advised people not to subscribe to it. As evidence pretending to support this charge, both newspapers quoted less than two and a half sentences taken from the middle of a long paragraph of a speech he had made in the Senate on September 7, during the debate on the War Revenue bill, when he was appealing to Senators to vote for one of his amendments placing higher taxes on war profits and surplus incomes. By thus beginning the quotation more than halfway through a long conditional sentence, they had completely distorted the meaning of what he had actually said in the Senate.[37]

But the fact was that neither these quoted sentences nor any part of the September 7 speech had been included among the speeches he had had reprinted from the *Congressional Record* at his own expense and sent out in pamphlet form. The *Sun* also told its readers that information as to what La Follette was doing and the huge orders he had placed with the Government Printing Office "was in the hands of the Senate investigating committee" and was "being investigated by the Government departments charged with the enforcement of the censorship clause in the trading with the enemy act."[38]

Although Bob seldom replied to personal attacks, he felt he could not allow this grave accusation to go unanswered. On October 21 he issued a four-page typewritten answer declaring that certain individuals and newspapers were persistently giving wide circulation to "a mendacious and libelous statement launched a day or so ago by a New York newspaper." Exposing the deliberately deceptive use of the quotation, he charged that the newspaper had knowingly published "a false and libelous statement."[39] He expressed his own opinion and that of many friends in different parts of the country when he asserted that the real motive behind this assault upon him was fear that the distribution of the three pamphlets containing excerpts from his speeches on the War Revenue bill would marshal public opinion to support legislation increasing the tax on wealth when this important issue must inevitably come before Congress at the next session.[40] These pamphlets had in fact been printed at his own expense, he said, and sent out under his frank for this entirely legitimate purpose. "Any effort to suppress free discussion of so momentous and practical a question" was "evidence of an attempt to protect wealth from paying its just share of the burdens of war." His statement closed with the declaration that until the end of the war he would continue to support "the levying of taxes on a sound financial basis."[41]

Brief excerpts from his statement were printed on inside pages of the *Sun* and the *New York Tribune*.[42] But probably few who had read the original attack on the front page ever saw his denial of the accusations. Hostile newspapers in Wisconsin and elsewhere persisted for months in falsely asserting that the Government was paying for the printed pamphlets containing his speeches. Charges were filed with the Wisconsin Council of Defense that he was indirectly, if not deliberately, interfering with the sale of Liberty bonds.[43] This accusation continued to circulate in print and in private correspondence, stimulating scathing editorials and petitions calling for his summary expulsion from the Senate. Late one afternoon, when Bob and Roe came through the outer office on their way home to dinner, Bob stopped a moment to speak to his secretary, Grace Lynch. As he stood beside the desk where she was answering mail, he picked up a bunch of recent resolutions demanding that he resign. After reading a few, he tossed the letters and telegrams on the desk and said with a grim smile, "Tell them we aren't the resigning kind."[44]

The constant barrage of false charges against Bob brought new problems each day which necessitated immediate, time-consuming decisions in addition to the important task of preparing for the Senate investigations. Night after night Bob, Belle, Roe, Bob, Jr., and the two devoted secretaries, John Hannan and Grace Lynch, returned to the office. One of the questions frequently discussed was when and where it might be best to start the libel suits Bob had been planning to bring. To meet the persistent misrepresentations of Bob's position on war legislation, a complete record was prepared of his votes on bills and amendments which Roe subsequently used effectively in a libel suit. While Roe was preparing his brief to present to the committee, Bob was working on a statement of the facts and circumstances relating to his extemporaneous speech at St. Paul which had been grossly misrepresented by Townley, president of the Nonpartisan League, and by Oliver S. Morris, editor of the League's official publication, the *Nonpartisan Leader*. In addition to writing an inaccurate editorial report of Bob's St. Paul speech, Morris had also given a false account in a long letter to

Edward A. Rumely for publication in the New York *Evening Mail*.[45] Bob had read this letter in a clipping someone had sent him. In reply to a friend in St. Paul who had assured him after its publication that the officers of the Nonpartisan League did not sanction the letter,[46] Bob wrote, "In these days of malicious attack Morris' assault was 'just one more,' although it was an especially vindictive and cowardly one, and came with apparent authority and from a direction which makes it all the more hurtful and reprehensible." He added that the Morris letter would have "a select place in a choice collection" he was making.[47]

Bob had also seen the newspaper reports of Townley's testimony before the Minnesota Public Safety Commission[48] and had been informed that Townley and other witnesses would be summoned from St. Paul by the Senate Committee.[49] * Roe therefore retained Charles H. Crownhart to find out about some matters in St. Paul. Belle was assisting Roe in looking up legal precedents and in gathering material which newspaper reports led them to believe might be pertinent to the trend of the investigation. Bob, Jr., was helping with the mail in addition to his many other duties. The intense pressure under which they were all working was recorded in a family letter in which he said that five hours was a comparatively long night's rest, and that he was so tired he could sleep standing "on the toes of one foot." He told his sister Mary that when they got home to Madison she would have no cause to complain about making his bed because he planned to get in it and stay there until it was time to come back again. He added that his father was tired but his spirits were fine and that he was "wonderful in his faith and confidence in the ultimate out come of it all."[50]

Meanwhile Senators Kellogg and Walsh, both members of the Committee on Privileges and Elections, were out in their home States denouncing him to large audiences. At a huge mass meeting in the St. Paul Auditorium on November 15, Kellogg branded Bob's recent speech from the same platform as "one of the greatest

---

* Townley subsequently sent word to Bob that this testimony as taken down by the secretary of the commission was garbled, erroneous, and misleading; that it did not contain a correct statement of his testimony and that he would correct it if called to testify before the Senate Committee (A. C. Townley to R. M. L., Nov. 30, 1917, with enclosure of copy of transcript of Townley's testimony, LFP).

slanders on American patriotism and honor that has ever been made in public."[51] The newspapers announced that the purpose in calling this loyalty meeting and another held in Minneapolis the next day had been "to obliterate completely any stain that might be left from the Nonpartisan league conference where La Follette was the headliner."[52] A telegram from the President to "The Northwest Loyalty Meetings" and the fact that the Assistant Secretary of Agriculture, Carl Vrooman, addressed one of the audiences seemed to give these loyalty meetings and their announced purpose Administration approval.[53]

From the newspapers Bob also learned that in Montana large audiences were responding enthusiastically to attacks made by Senator Thomas J. Walsh upon his St. Paul speech and the position he had taken toward the war and Administration legislation.[54] Although newspaper reports as to the general response to this series of speeches were probably accurate, Bob's correspondence indicates there were thoughtful dissenters in Walsh's audiences. A lawyer who had heard the Senator address the Kalispell Club in Kalispell sent Bob a newspaper report of the speech and wrote that "In view of the fact that he is a member of the senate committee appointed to investigate your St. Paul speech, it seems to me that he is not observing the proprieties in going about the country criticizing your speech.

"You have many friends in this community and we believe we are as patriotic as some who assume to lecture the people on loyalty. In fact, some of us have seen military service in time of war and believe all war questions should be thoroughly discussed without impugning any one's loyalty."[55] This letter was written on the same day that Kellogg was impugning Bob's loyalty at a large mass meeting in St. Paul. Bob and Roe shared this Montana lawyer's opinion as to violation of the proprieties to such an extent that they considered challenging the fitness of Walsh and Kellogg to serve as judges in the Senate investigation.[56]

Although Bob did not know it, Walsh, in preparing for the hearing, had written out in longhand a six-page memorandum entitled "Inquiries La Follette Examination," which included questions as to what evidence La Follette had as to 6,000,000 rounds of ammunition and other explosives on the *Lusitania* and as to Bryan's having communicated these facts to the President and having asked the latter to issue a warning.[57] Also, Walsh and Pomerene had each submitted to the Legislative Reference Service of the Library of Congress a list of questions relating to specific statements in the St. Paul speech.[58] Nevertheless Pomerene persistently refused to inform Bob which portions of the speech were to be challenged. Therefore the only leads Bob and Roe had were the newspaper reports which had repeatedly predicted the hearing would focus on the statement that Bryan knew the *Lusitania* carried munitions and had urged the President to keep Americans off the ship.

At the time the *Lusitania* was torpedoed, a summary of the manifest had been published, and the newspapers had frequently referred to the fact that the vessel had carried contraband and munitions. Senators and Congressmen had commented on it in interviews, and Herman Winter, assistant manager of the Cunard Line, which owned the ship, had been quoted as saying that for years they had been "sending small-arms cartridges abroad in the *Lusitania*."[59] In preparing for the Senate investigation these public comments had been collected from the newspapers, but Roe and Bob thought that the invoices of shippers and the *Lusitania*'s complete manifest would reveal even more than the published summary. Believing the Government had official records which would show that this vessel had been carrying munitions to Great Britain, Bob asked the Treasury Department for a copy of the report made on the *Lusitania* by the Collector of the Port of New York, Dudley Field Malone. He was referred to the State Department, which refused on the ground that the report had become a part of the secret archives.[60]

When Bob was denied access to documents which the newspapers had indicated would be available to the investigating subcommittee, Roe decided to seek elsewhere for the information he thought essential to any fair investigation. He arranged for Bob to talk with Malone, who had been appointed Collector of the Port of New York in 1913 by President Wilson. On Saturday, November 3, Bob, Belle, and Roe left Washington on the midnight train for New York. On Sunday morning Bob and Belle went directly from the train to the apartment of their son-in-law George Middleton and their daughter Fola at 158 Waverly Place. After breakfast Roe came in, and they all waited in some suspense for Malone, who had promised to stop in on his way to speak that afternoon at a meeting in Madison Square Garden, arranged by the non-socialist leagues which had endorsed Morris Hillquit for mayor of New York City. When Malone arrived, Bob expressed his warm appreciation to him for coming. Then, seated in an armchair opposite the open fire, he presented the facts regarding the probable trend of the Senate investigation in so far as he had been able to piece them together from the newspapers and the correspondence with Pomerene. He talked quietly, without tension or gestures, summarizing the incidents briefly but vividly. Malone, seated across the room between the fireplace and the window, leaned forward in his chair, listening with intense interest. When Bob finished his quiet, factual account, Malone, without an instant's hesitation, said he thought it was outrageous to refuse a United States Senator an official document which would aid in his defense, and offered to send Roe a copy of the report he had made to the Treasury Department on his official inspection of the *Lusitania* before the ship's final ill-fated voyage. After some further discussion of the *Lusitania*'s cargo and the probable procedure of the subcommittee, Malone had to leave for the meeting. As he rose to go, Bob placed his left hand on Malone's arm, clasped his right hand and, looking into his eyes, told him with intense feeling how much his courageous offer of help meant. It was evident both men were deeply moved. Malone spoke first, volunteering to come to Washington at any time and testify in support of Bob's statements. He said he would not remain silent and see any man crucified for telling the truth.[61]

Two days later Bob and Roe returned to Washington to continue their preparation for the subcommittee hearing. When they received a copy of Malone's report on the *Lusitania*, it showed that on the final trip the ship had on board at least 5,468 cases of ammunition; it specifically recorded 4,200 cases of metallic cartridges shipped by the Remington Arms-Union Metallic Cartridge Company, consigned to the Remington Arms Company, London, the ultimate consignee being the British Government, and 1,250 cases of shrapnel shipped by G. W. Sheldon & Company for the Bethlehem Steel Company, consigned to the Deputy Director of Ammunition Stores, Woolwich, England. With the report were carbon copies of affidavits signed by members of the "Neutrality Squad" and other officials who had assisted Malone in inspecting the ship.[62] Malone had told Roe that before being called to the witness stand he would try to see if

he could obtain the complete manifest* of the *Lusitania* or access
to it and that he would also go through his files for any correspondence relating to the ship's cargo on this or previous voyages.[63]

Shortly after Bob's return from New York, he started the first of
several contemplated libel suits. This one was for $100,000 against
the Democrat Printing Company and O. D. Brandenburg, president and also editor of the *Madison Democrat*. The action was
filed in the Dane County Circuit Court on November 9 by his
attorneys, Crownhart and Wylie, with Gilbert E. Roe as counsel.
The complaint named eighteen specific counts, including quotations
from editorials and from a speech made by Charles Edward Russell. It also named false reports of Bob's St. Paul speech and
libelous headlines given to news reports about him which were not
in themselves libelous.[64] Although often the target for libelous
attacks in the past, this was the first time Bob had ever brought
suit.

Later he started another suit for $100,000 against the Wisconsin
State Journal Printing Company and Richard Lloyd Jones, pro-
prietor and editor of the *Wisconsin State Journal*.[65] For months
Jones' newspaper had made false charges in editorials and had persistently misrepresented Bob's position on important war legislation. One typical distortion of fact, made in such a way that it
carried a treasonable implication, had been launched in July when
Roe happened to be in Washington, and it had been decided then
to bring a libel suit later. The day after the $640,000,000 aviation
bill had passed the Senate without a dissenting vote, the *Wisconsin
State Journal* had falsely reported that Bob had been the only Senator to vote against it and had thus refused to join Congress in
striking a blow aimed at the Kaiser.[66] Later, during the examination
of Jones in the Superior Court of Dane County, Roe repeatedly
made the point that what Jones had knowledge of and did not
publish was just as important as what he did publish. Under oath
to tell the truth, Jones proved to be an evasive witness suffering

---

* No copy of the complete manifest of the *Lusitania* has been found in
the La Follette papers. A request made in 1938 for access to cargo manifests
of ships sailing from New York in 1915 brought the reply that by Act of
Congress, May 17, 1928, cargo manifests for 1915–1916 had been authorized
to be destroyed (LFP).

from a curious, temporary loss of memory. But by persistent, skillful questioning Roe forced an admission that although Jones had published the fact that Bob had voted against the war resolution, he had suppressed the fact that Bob had voted for the War Appropriation bill and certain other war measures advocated by the Administration.[67]

The day after this examination took place in Madison, a distinguished professor at the University of Wisconsin, Richard T. Ely, wrote the distinguished editor of the *American Review of Reviews*, Albert Shaw, about the libel suit and stated "that the La Follette people are attacking Richard Lloyd Jones and trying to ruin him. They have started a rival paper, called the *Capital Times*, which I regard as a most vicious sheet. . . . Jones was heavily in debt and his creditors presented claims, amounting to $20,000. These, however, fortunately have been taken care of. Now there is a special service that we need, and that is to have the facts gathered together in regard to La Follette's activities in Washington and elsewhere and also concerning the reactions of his activities and speeches in Germany and Russia. I think there can be no doubt that he has been of more help to the Kaiser than a quarter of a million troops." That same day in a similar appeal to Theodore Roosevelt for help "in gathering the facts we want," Ely stated: "This is not a local matter by any means, but one of national significance, and I know this is strongly felt at Washington."[68] Many years later Ely recorded that he had modified his opinion.*

Jones' influence extended far beyond the thirteen thousand circulation his paper then had in Wisconsin. It apparently reached even to the White House, for the President himself had written to express appreciation of the important work he felt Jones was doing.[69] For twenty-three years Jones had been in the newspaper business, and he knew many of the men who were furnishing material to national magazines and periodicals. He had written Charles Edward Russell about coming to Madison to speak and had also

* In 1938 Ely wrote that he did not feel so sure as he had at the time of the World War that "La Follette was wrong and Woodrow Wilson right"; that the experience of trying to make the world safe for democracy had "convinced a great many people that La Follette was right, that Woodrow Wilson was wrong" (Richard T. Ely, *Ground Under Our Feet* [New York, The Macmillan Company, 1938], pp. 217-218).

cooperated in two particularly vicious attacks upon Bob which appeared in the *New York Tribune* during November. Both these articles were written by Samuel Hopkins Adams, whom Jones had known for many years. Adams was a member of a private group of authors, known as the Vigilantes, which had been organized in 1916. He was also a prominent member of the Syndicate Features Division of the official Committee on Public Information, which was headed by the President's appointee, George Creel.[70]

Before publishing his two articles in the *New York Tribune* Adams had spent some time at the Park Hotel in Madison and had seen a great deal of Jones. The article of November 25 was reprinted by Jones in the *Wisconsin State Journal* and subsequently became one of the many counts in the libel suit Bob filed against this newspaper.[71] The article was entitled "Is Wisconsin Against America?" Beneath the title the *New York Tribune* printed a cartoon showing a menacing figure of La Follette forcing a German helmet on the head of a crouching, terrified woman labeled "Wisconsin." Jones did not reproduce the cartoon but he described it vividly.[72] Later, in an examination under oath, he admitted that while Adams was in Madison he had talked with him about the Wisconsin situation and about Senator La Follette. The two malicious articles published in the *New York Tribune* probably reflected the interpretation of Wisconsin, the university, and La Follette that Jones was privately circulating in an even more virulent form wherever his influence reached.[73]

Jones did not publish Adams' first article, which was printed in the *New York Tribune* on November 11, but he advertised it in his newspaper, and this became another count in the libel suit. The article as published in the Sunday *Tribune* contained a caricature of the outline of La Follette's head and face with the German coat of arms in the center, blotting out his features. A large number of these newspapers were sent to a local newsdealer in Madison who was also furnished with cards about twelve by fourteen inches reproducing this caricature and advertising the article. These cards were posted in various places in Madison by the newsdealer, who also placed a two-column advertisement surrounded by a heavy double black border in two issues of the *Wisconsin State Journal*. Crownhart clipped this advertisement and sent it on to Bob with the information that the *New York Tribune* had paid for it, and the legal opinion that the caricature was "a vicious libel per se and recovery would be practically certain."[74] This widely advertised article by Adams was published under the title "Who's Who Against America?" with a subhead in large print naming Robert M. La Follette as the Senator who "Made a Technicality of the Lusitania Crime and Would March to the White House to Tune of 'Die Wacht am Rhine.' "[75]

When Bob had been interrupted during his extemporaneous speech at St. Paul by the question "What about the *Lusitania*?" he had answered spontaneously and honestly, condensing in a few sentences the gist of more detailed information which had come to him from a source he had for many years known to be thoroughly reliable. The substance of his reply that before the *Lusitania* sailed Bryan had warned the President this passenger ship carried explosives and a large amount of ammunition in violation of a United States statute had been given to him by Julius A. Truesdell, a member of the Washington Bureau of the *New York Times* since 1910.

Truesdell was a man of integrity, endowed with exceptional ability and a remarkable memory. He was born in Waukegan, Illinois. His father was clerk of the court and had ridden the circuit with Abraham Lincoln. As a young boy Truesdell had gone to Wisconsin and had earned his way through Beloit College by working on the *Beloit Free Press*. After graduating in 1877, he covered several sessions of the Wisconsin legislature for the *Milwaukee Sentinel*. His intimate association with Bob began in 1884 when Bob was the youngest Member of the House. That same year Truesdell had come to Washington as correspondent for the *St. Paul Pioneer Press* and also for the *Milwaukee Sentinel*, which was then supporting Bob. During these early years the two young men formed a close friendship which endured throughout their lives.

As a representative of the *United States Army and Navy Journal* from 1907 to 1910, Truesdell had acquired a special knowledge of Army and Navy affairs and a wide acquaintance among Government officials. While Bryan was Secretary of State, he had covered the State Department daily for the *New York Times* and the Philadelphia *Public Ledger*. At about the time the United States entered the war in 1917, Truesdell had told Bob what he knew as to Bryan's having warned the President regarding the *Lusitania* cargo. Bob had every reason to credit this information when it came to him, and to the end of his life he believed it was accurate. When Bryan had resigned in June, 1915, it had been generally understood that one of his reasons had been that he differed with the President about allowing passengers to travel on munitions-laden ships.[76] In his Senate speech on April 4, 1917, opposing United States entry into the European War, Bob had referred to the *Lusitania* having a cargo containing 6,000,000 rounds of ammunition destined for the British Army.[77] This statement had not been challenged then or later.

Five months later he had repeated it at St. Paul. When he returned to Washington, Truesdell came to see him at once to say that he did not think the statement about the *Lusitania* and Bryan having warned the President would be denied, but that if it was he would be ready to testify under oath.[78] On October 3 Bryan telephoned Bob that he intended to deny the statement publicly, and also telephoned Lansing that La Follette's statement could be denied.[79] That same day Truesdell wrote Bob a letter summarizing the information he had given him a few months earlier.[80] During the next few weeks, as part of the preparation for the committee hearings, Roe took Truesdell's testimony. As recorded by a confidential secretary in Bob's office, it contains the substance of Truesdell's talk with Bob and many additional details regarding a conversation he had with Bryan, all of which he was willing to give under oath if called to testify before the committee.[81]

The quest for the information Truesdell gave Bob about the *Lusitania* had started on a day in April, 1915, when he and other newspaper men had seen the German Ambassador, Count von Bernstorff, drive up to the east basement door of the State Department in a roadster. The Ambassador entered at this door, and his car remained parked outside for the better part of an hour. When he came out, he passed quickly by the newspaper men and refused to answer questions. This aroused the curiosity of the correspondents, and they immediately began trying to discover the purpose of his visit. Truesdell found out what it had been one evening, soon after the sinking of the *Lusitania*, when he was riding home on the street car with W. J. Dwyer, who for many years published a small newspaper in Washington called the *Bulletin*. Among his associates he was considered "a good news hound and accurate reporter." Truesdell had known Dwyer since 1886. For many years Dwyer had been intimate with Bryan and also knew Mrs. Bryan. To Truesdell the information was therefore authentic when Dwyer said von Bernstorff had gone to the State Department to tell Bryan he knew, through his agents at Bridgeport, that there were munitions on the *Lusitania* and that Bryan ought to put out a warning to prevent Americans from sailing on the ship. Bryan had replied he could not do it because the President had taken all that into his own hands, but that he would get von Bernstorff an audience with the President. Dwyer said von Bernstorff had seen the President, but that Wilson had told him he would not enforce the Passenger Act of 1882.[82]

Subsequently a part of what Dwyer had told Truesdell was corroborated by Bryan himself. Early in June, shortly after Bryan had resigned, Truesdell called at his home to ask about his future plans. During the conversation he learned that Bryan had given out a statement on that point earlier in the day. Truesdell then brought up the subject of the *Lusitania,* asking if before the sinking of the ship Bryan had known of the Passenger Act of 1882 which prohibited passenger vessels crossing the Atlantic from carrying gunpowder, dynamite, and other explosives. Truesdell commented that few people realized the ammunition on the ship amounted to 6,500,000 rounds, and that if the President had enforced the law the lives of the passengers would have been saved. Bryan replied that he had talked all that over with the President before the sailing of the *Lusitania* and that the President felt he could not act under the law.[83]

Bob and Roe both believed that the information which had come to them through Truesdell and Dwyer was accurate, and they intended to call these two men to testify at the hearing scheduled to begin on November 26. Subsequently they received an affidavit which corroborated in substance the recollection of these two men. This testimony came from Judge John M. Becker of Monroe, Wisconsin, a graduate of the University of Wisconsin Law School who had been County Judge of Green County for nineteen years. Becker had known Bryan ever since the campaign of 1896. In the summer of 1916 he had attended a Chautauqua lecture given by Bryan at Freeport, Illinois. The next day he had traveled with Bryan from Freeport to Monroe, Wisconsin. Becker was ready to testify under oath that during their long conversation on the train Bryan had said that previously to the sailing of the *Lusitania* the German Ambassador had informed the State Department that the ship was laden with war munitions and that Bryan had told the President of this fact, urging him to issue a proclamation warning Americans not to sail on the ship, but the President claimed he had no authority to issue such a proclamation.[84] Roe considered this testimony entirely trustworthy as he had a high regard for Becker, whom he had known ever since they had been students at the University Law School.

The Becker affidavit was not received until later. But a detailed study of all the available evidence at this time convinced Roe that Bryan had known that the *Lusitania*, as well as other belligerent ships, had carried munitions and explosives not only on her last voyage but on many previous voyages, and that Bryan had talked with the President about preventing passengers from traveling on vessels carrying such cargoes.[85] Roe therefore hoped the committee would give him an opportunity to examine Bryan. In preparing for the hearing, he dictated fifty specific questions which he intended to ask the former Secretary of State.[86] Two days before the hearing it seemed probable that he would have this opportunity, for the newspapers again reported that Bryan would testify.[87]

Only three days before the hearing, Senator Pomerene had seen the President.[88] A Washington dispatch to the *Milwaukee Sentinel* reported that although Pomerene was exceedingly reticent about the conference, it was "understood that the President indicated to him the attitude of the administration toward the Wisconsin Senator" and that the attitude was known to be that his removal was "not desired because it would give La Follette the opportunity of appearing in the role of a martyr for the cause of free speech." This dispatch also reported that Bryan would be summoned to testify, and that La Follette would stick to his demand "that he be permitted to crossexamine all of the witnesses called by the Committee" and "that he have the right to produce documents from official files in his defense."[89]

On the morning of the hearing, the newspapers stated that the committee expected to complete all the evidence in the La Follette case during the week so as to have its report ready when Congress convened on December 3. They also announced that Secretary Lansing had offered to have witnesses go on the stand to testify regarding the *Lusitania* and to repudiate the allegation that Bryan had told the President the ship carried munitions.[90] Previous news-paper reports and other information Bob and Roe had received led them to expect they might also find Lansing among the array of witnesses in the committee room. They did not know Lansing had written Pomerene a few days before that, after considering the matter and consulting with the President, it seemed "incompatible with the public interest" for him to appear before the committee in connection with the investigation.[91]

On Monday morning, November 26, before going to the hearing, Bob and Roe went to the office. As they were leaving for the committee room, a brief note arrived from Pomerene stating that since Bryan would not be in Washington until the following week the subcommittee had decided to postpone the hearing until a later date to be determined subsequently.[92]

Although Bob was indignant at what he confidentially described as the "spirit of trifling" which the committee had evidenced, he wrote a restrained letter to Pomerene the next day requesting that he be advised at once when the hearing would be held so that his attorney might arrange his work accordingly.[93] On Friday, November 30, Pomerene wrote that he could not give any specific date.[94] But on Saturday afternoon, at four o'clock, Bob received another letter from Pomerene saying Bryan would arrive in Washington that night and he would try to arrange a meeting at two o'clock on Monday, December 3, for the purpose of taking Bryan's testimony. He added that after conferring with Bryan he would communicate further.[95] The meeting was thus tentatively set for the same day Congress was scheduled to convene at noon.

Bob telephoned at once to Roe, who postponed his cases in the New York court. On Sunday, too late to reach Roe, who had already left for Washington, Bob received a telephone message from Pomerene saying Bryan was leaving town that night and there would be no hearing on Monday. Immediately after this telephone message came, Belle wrote Phil and Mary that it was "hard to endure such flippant treatment, but what can one do? We seem to be at the mercy of the mighty power." She added that she did not know what the postponement meant but thought the fact "that Bryan spoke here to-day and that they must have known something about whether he intended to be here tomorrow before they wrote papa

would indicate that Bryan is not *eager* at any rate to appear before
the Committee."[96]

When Congress convened for a brief session on Monday, Bob was
present. After the roll had been called, he announced the death of
Senator Paul O. Husting of Wisconsin and moved that the Senate
adjourn in respect to his memory. That same day Bob replied to
Pomerene's telephone message canceling the subcommittee meeting.
In his letter he suggested it would shorten proceedings and contribute to an early and final disposition of the matter if hearings
could be held before the full committee. He said that he was most
anxious to proceed with the hearings and that his attorney would be
ready at any time except December 10, 11, and 12, when his cases
had been peremptorily set down for hearing as a result of the postponement necessitated by the sudden summons to Washington.[97]

The files of Bob's papers show that on Tuesday, December 4, he
sent copies of the entire correspondence which had passed between
him and Pomerene to at least seven Senators who were members of
the Committee on Privileges and Elections but not members of the
subcommittee. In his covering letter he ventured to hope that they
would find time "to examine and consider" the correspondence
before the next meeting of the full committee which had been called
for December 6.[98] The subcommittee had been instructed to report
when Congress convened, but this was impossible because no hearing had been held. Therefore it now had to secure an extension of
time and authority from the full committee in order to function.
During December four meetings of the full committee were called
and adjourned, ostensibly because it was impossible to secure a
quorum.[99] For months this procedure of postponement continued.

The reasons for this persistent delay were variously interpreted
at the time and later. Bob, Roe, Senator George W. Norris, and
others thought one important factor was Bryan's unwillingness to
testify under oath. Norris also shared their opinion that it was one
thing to give out a denial to the newspapers but quite another to
testify under oath subject to cross-examination and the calling of
witnesses.[100] Dudley Field Malone thought the investigation was
postponed because he was ready to testify to the truth of what Bob
had said about the *Lusitania* cargo.[101] Although Bob never knew it,
Senators Reed and Vardaman, both members of the committee,
agreed to cooperate in forcing postponement by various devices,

including arrangements to prevent a quorum. Their purpose was to postpone action until a time when a more impartial verdict might be had.[102] Early in December 1917, Bob, Jr., wrote Phil and Mary in Madison that he thought the subcommittee was waiting for a cue from somewhere, neither committing itself to going on nor leaving off, but intending to drag it out as long as possible to harass his father and keep him tied up so that he could not work on anything else.[103]

CHAPTER LI

"In the Midst of This Raging
Storm of Hate"

When President Wilson entered the House Chamber of the Capitol at twelve thirty on December 4, 1917, to deliver his annual message to Congress, he was enthusiastically greeted. The galleries and floor were crowded. In the colorful and distinguished audience the officers' uniforms were conspicuous, and it was noted that many women in the galleries were knitting for soldiers. A special section had been reserved on the floor for foreign diplomats. Among them were the French Ambassador Monsieur Jusserand and the British Ambassador Sir Cecil Spring-Rice. Six Justices of the Supreme Court were present. The Senators were also near the front of the Chamber, and Bob had a seat in the center, not far from the rostrum where the President stood. A Washington dispatch to the *Madison Democrat* reported that although the Senators had marched in pairs from the Senate to the House, "La Follette walked alone" because no other Senator would walk with him.[1] Later the scene was interpreted to the British Foreign Secretary, Arthur J. Balfour, by the British Ambassador, who wrote that the sentiment of the Senate was shown by the fact that Senator La Follette "had to walk in alone and sat with two empty chairs on each side of him."[2]

As the President began to read his address from the small type-written pages on the high desk in front of him, the audience listened with intense interest. For days the newspapers and Members of Congress had speculated on the subject of his annual message. But the secret had been carefully guarded, and it was said that not even his Cabinet knew. During the first part of his twenty-three-minute message the President was frequently applauded. He commended the united spirit of the American people in the immediate task of winning the war and said that although he heard men "debate peace who understand neither its nature nor the way in which we may attain it with uplifted eyes and unbroken spirits," he knew they did not speak for the Nation and might "safely be left to strut their uneasy hour and be forgotten." But he added that he thought it was "necessary to say plainly what we here at the seat of action consider the war to be for and what part we mean to play in the settlement of its searching issues." After indicating what must be done before we could consider the war won, he said that when this end was accomplished we would "be free to base peace on generosity and justice, to the exclusion of all selfish claims to advantage even on the part of the victors."[3]

Not until he was more than halfway through his message did the President ask Congress to declare war on Austria-Hungary. A cheer came from a dozen places and swelled to "a mighty shout" that joined with the applause from the floor and galleries where women waved their handkerchiefs. Directly in front of the rostrum where the President stood waiting for the demonstration to subside, Chief Justice White rose with the others who had seats on the floor and turned to view the audience with a beaming smile. Senator Lodge, who was almost directly behind him, "returned the smile and nodded understandingly while he beat the palms of his hands together vigorously like a school boy at play."[4] Many newspaper correspondents noted that "La Follette kept his seat" while Senators around him stood cheering and applauding. The fact that Bob did not participate was commented on in letters written by the British Ambassador and the President's old friend Colonel Edward T. Brown, who was a frequent visitor at the White House.[5] The press interpreted Bob's failure to join in the demonstration as evidence of "disapproval of any measure directed against the Teutonic autocracy" and "resentment of the patriotic outburst."[6]

The real reason for Bob's action was that he still doubted the wisdom of a declaration of war against Austria-Hungary and thought that he probably could not conscientiously vote for it when it came before the Senate. Although the President had elaborated in eloquent phrases his statement that we owed it to ourselves to say we did not wish "in any way to impair or to rearrange the Austro-Hungarian Empire,"[7] Bob thought that broad generalities were not sufficient protection for this country in view of recent disclosures. He was deeply disturbed by the fact that the President had made no specific declaration in respect to the secret agreement of the Allies recently published in the Washington and New York newspapers whereby Italy was to annex Austrian territory and thus make subjects of the Austrian people.[8] That very morning the *New York Tribune* had published a Washington dispatch reporting that the State Department had declined to discuss the publication of the secret treaties and that a high official had intimated "this country might not enter into any definitive discussion and determination respecting their terms until after Germany is beaten."[9]

Bob knew that if he stood up and joined in the applause following the President's request, it would be interpreted as an unqualified endorsement of a declaration of war which he believed might involve this country in the enforcement of the terms of this treaty and prove an obstacle to an early and lasting peace. As it was impossible for Bob to state his position at that moment, he chose what seemed to him the only honest alternative, although aware that it would evoke criticism. Later, when reporters asked his opinion of the President's message he replied, "Any comment of mine will be given on the floor of the Senate."[10] During the next three days Bob drafted a brief speech which he expected to deliver when the resolution for a declaration of war came before the Senate.[11]

From the time this country had entered the war, Bob had feared that unless Congress made a specific declaration of our war aims the United States would become involved in the enforcement of the secret agreements he was certain had previously been entered into among the Allies. His apprehension had increased when Steffens had returned from Russia in June to deliver Kerenski's appeal to the President to abrogate the secret treaties publicly. Bob could not forget Steffens' confidential report of his talk with the President. After the overthrow of Kerenski's Government by the Bolsheviki on November 7, Bob had followed the Russian dispatches closely. Soon after this second revolution he had received confidential information from a source he considered trustworthy that the secret treaties which had been discovered in the Russian archives would soon be published.[12] On November 25, eight days before the President delivered his message to Congress, the *New York Times* and the *New York Tribune* reported that the texts of the Allies' treaties had actually been published in Russia. Although not reported in the press, Secretary Lansing had sent a telegram, on November 30, to the American Minister in Sweden telling him that the State Department had been informed the Bolsheviki Government was publishing secret treaties in Petrograd but that publication in the United States was being held up by the Allies' censor. It also asked the Minister to telegraph the substance of all treaties so far published.[13]* Although Bob did not know about this telegram at the time, he had read that same day a dispatch from London in the Washington *Evening Star* giving the substance of the terms of the treaty whereby Italy entered the war on the side of the Allies. This agreement had been signed on April 26, 1915, and was known as the Treaty of London. Two days before the President delivered his address to Congress, Bob had read a similar dispatch in the *New York Times* which was also carried in the *New York Tribune*. These two newspapers and others had reported that by the terms of this treaty Russia, Great Britain, and France had promised Italy in return for entering the war sweeping annexations of Austrian territory in addition to islands in the Grecian Archipelago and territory in Asia Minor and Africa.[14]

Bob was in the Senate on December 7 when Senator Stone asked unanimous consent for immediate consideration of the joint resolution calling for a declaration of war on Austria-Hungary. No objection was made, and Stone opened the debate with a brief speech for it. Lodge then expressed the hope that it would pass unanimously, and also proposed that similar action be taken immediately against Turkey and Bulgaria. When he finished, Hitchcock began a speech for the resolution by explaining that although he had previously doubted the wisdom of this declaration of war, the President's address had to a large extent overcome his objections. While Hitchcock was speaking it occurred to Bob that "an amendment should be offered which would state that the declaration of war did not make us a party to any of the secret treaties relating to the dismemberment of the Austrian Empire."[15]

He decided that if there was time, he would go to his office in the

---

* Translations of the texts of the secret treaties as they had appeared in the Russian press were sent from Petrograd by the American Ambassador on Dec. 5 and reached the State Department on Dec. 27, 1917 (*Foreign Relations*, 1917, Supplement 2, Vol. I, pp. 493ff.).

Senate Office Building to consult with Belle, Roe, and Bob, Jr., about drafting the amendment. But before leaving the floor, he asked Stone, who was in charge of the resolution, how long the debate would last. Stone told him several Senators were to speak, including Knox and Borah, both members of the Committee on Foreign Relations. On this assurance Bob left the Chamber and took the subway from the Capitol to the Senate Office Building. While he was on the way, the debate ended abruptly. Although Knox was off the floor, the Vice President put the question as to whether the joint resolution should pass, and Stone called for the yeas and nays. The roll-call bell sounded, but Bob did not hear it in the noisy subway. While he was drafting his amendment in his office, Hannan telephoned him that the debate had suddenly ended and that the declaration of war against Austria-Hungary had passed without a dissenting vote.[16]

When this unexpected word came from Hannan, Bob regretted that he had not remained in his seat and voted against the resolution. He returned to the Senate at once and, as soon as he could secure recognition, he stated that he had never dodged any responsibility as a Senator or absented himself from the Senate when any important measure was to be voted upon. After explaining what had happened, he read the amendment he had just drafted. It provided that the United States should assert "its determination not to be bound by, or become a party to, the enforcement of any agreement or agreements heretofore entered into between the allied powers to deprive the Imperial and Royal Government of Austria-Hungary of title to or control of any territory which was a part of the Austro-Hungarian Empire or possessions August 1, 1914." He stated that if this amendment had been added to the joint resolution he would have voted for it as a necessary war measure, but that without this or some similar declaration of our purpose he would have voted against the resolution.[17] Aware that the hostile Madison newspapers would probably misinterpret Bob's absence when the roll was called, Belle wrote Phil and Mary the next morning explaining what had happened and that she and their father thought the United States should renounce the secret treaties not in generalities "like the President's message, but explicitly."[18]

Many newspapers carried headlines implying that Bob had left the Senate floor just in time to dodge the vote. Some, however, reported his explanation, and either quoted or gave the substance of his amendment.[19] Among those which did not carry his explanation was the *Wisconsin State Journal*, which had reprinted the previous day the defamatory article by Samuel Hopkins Adams from the *New York Tribune* of November 27.[20]

A few days after war was declared against Austria-Hungary, the newsstands were selling copies of a well known magazine entitled, for this particular issue, "Traitors' Number," and dedicated chiefly to La Follette. This magazine, established in 1883, and published under the title of *Life*, then occupied a position somewhat similar to the *New Yorker*. This "Traitors' Number" carried on the cover an unsigned, colored cartoon of the Kaiser in the act of pinning an iron cross on La Follette, who was wearing a German military uniform and military boots already covered with iron crosses. On the inside pages were other cartoons. One, entitled "At the Betrayers' Club," showed La Follette being presented by Satan to Tarpeia, Judas, and Benedict Arnold; "The Foul Tackle" depicted La Follette in a football suit, tackling Uncle Sam as he was nearing the goal post of victory; another, entitled "Prosit," showed the Kaiser drinking from a beer mug shaped in the form of La Follette's head. This issue was the culmination of the malicious attacks the magazine had been making for months.[21]

A day or two after the magazine appeared, Bob, Jr., wrote Roe calling attention to the cover cartoon and to certain other specific pages. He said his father thought the magazine files should be gone through, a complaint prepared, and a libel suit filed for at least $250,000, or as much more as Roe thought best. Bob, Jr., added that personally he was "strong for a half million dollars."[22] Roe replied that although he had not yet obtained a complete file, he had found a great deal of libelous material. But he reminded Bob that to date he had hesitated to start actions in New York because he felt uncertain of results there. He also thought it was important not to overload on libel suits as each case would be time-consuming and prevent doing more important things.[23] Bob agreed but thought they should investigate whether service might be secured on a newsdealer as agent who had sold the *Life* magazine in the Eastern Federal Court District of Wisconsin. Bob said the aspect of these attacks which caused him the greatest concern was that "these sweeping broadsides of libel make it very difficult to carry on a successful campaign for just taxation, and also handicap us in doing the vital things necessary to organization work for the approaching election."[24]

When the "Traitors' Number" reached Madison, the editor of the *Wisconsin State Journal* called it to the attention of Bob's constituents by describing the cartoon on the cover, reproaching him for his libel suit against a small-town newspaper like the *Madison Democrat*, and demanding "Why don't you go after *LIFE*, Senator?"[25] The circulation of *Life* was widely distributed, and hostile letters with clippings of the cartoons in this issue were sent to Bob from places as distant as Tampico, Mexico.[26] The magazine also undoubtedly reached many men in the Armed Forces, for in the upper corner of the cover there was the customary "Note to Reader" saying, "After reading this copy place a 1 cent stamp here, hand same to any postal employee and it will be placed in the hands of a soldier or sailor at the front. No wrapping; no address.—A. S. Burleson, Postmaster General."[27] A strong protest against this issue of the magazine was made to the editor, who later published the letter under the satiric title, "Not A Traitor!"[28] The protest was clipped, without the editorial title, and sent to Bob by the man who had written it, William Bross Lloyd, son of Henry Demarest Lloyd, author of *Wealth Against Commonwealth*. For many years Bob had greatly admired the father, and therefore this protest had a special significance. He thought the son was a very brave man to have written it.[29]

On the evening of the day Bob, Jr., had written Roe about bringing a libel suit against *Life*, a meeting was held in Madison at the university gymnasium, where a thousand students and members of the faculty met to form a Loyalty League and sign loyalty resolutions. At the close of the meeting fifteen university students, led by a man from New York, class of 1910, paraded through a biting snowstorm to the lower campus in front of the Library. There they hoisted a dummy which had been prepared in one of the fraternity houses and labeled "Senator La Follette and *The Capital Times*." Touching a match to the figure, this group and some other students who had joined them did an Indian dance as it burned.[30]

Phil had intended to go to the loyalty meeting, but at the last moment changed his plans in response to what may have been a protective telephone call from his French teacher, asking him to help with the rehearsal of a French play. Later he learned about the burning in effigy from an intimate friend. Fearing the family might read exaggerated newspaper accounts and be worried about him, he wrote that night, relaying the report from his friend that one of the professors had known in advance and had encouraged the burning in effigy, but that only a small group of students had actually carried the plan through.[31]

The *Capital Times*, a new Madison newspaper, published for the first time that afternoon, had been burned in effigy with La Follette. For many weeks Charles H. Crownhart, Alfred T. Rogers, Herman Ekern, Michael Olbrich, Gilbert Roe, William T. Evjue, the editor; Fred Holmes, and other friends of Bob's had contributed time and money they could ill afford toward organizing it and providing a meager financial backing. Evjue was a young progressive Republican member of the Wisconsin legislature who had wielded a trenchant pen on the staff of the *Wisconsin State Journal* since 1911 but had recently resigned because he disagreed with its changed policy. The new newspaper had over two thousand subscribers before the first issue, and it was hoped the daily sales would immediately bring it up to 3,500. Soon after it started, however, Crownhart wrote Bob that it was "being boycotted to the limit. If the boys can hold on I am sure they will be alright. However they are not experienced in this game, and it is hard for them to keep up their nerve."[32]

Although the *Capital Times* later became the leading progressive newspaper in the State, this intense hostility and limited funds induced a timid policy at the beginning. This disappointed their progressive friends.[33] Crownhart wrote Bob their political enemies had "the Capital Times boycotted on advertising" and that the management was "coddling along in hopes of getting in. I think they will fail in that way. If they would stand out boldly I believe they can make a field for the paper."[34] Bob replied that he agreed "about the new paper, for they are a good bunch. It would really be good training for them to have to take my medicine for say twenty-four hours."[35]

For some time Crownhart had been carrying on a campaign to counteract the persistent misrepresentation by increasing the circulation of *La Follette's Magazine* in Wisconsin. Beginning in September, he had written a number of advertisements summarizing

Bob's position on several aspects of war legislation but placing particular emphasis on his fight for the taxation of war profits. He placed these in different newspapers which were willing to accept them at regular advertising rates. Some refused. Among those that accepted were the *Wisconsin Farmer*, which had a circulation of 90,000 and *Equity News*, a semiweekly with 14,000 circulation, published in Madison. A list that Crownhart sent Bob showed that by December advertisements had been placed in fifty-four newspapers with a combined circulation of approximately 150,000. These advertisements helped to get some of the facts about Bob's position on financing the war and on other war measures to the people and also brought new subscribers to *La Follette's Magazine*. The response was immediate and encouraging.[36] A letter to Crownhart from Congressman Edward E. Browne written after a visit to his home in Waupaca, Wisconsin, during November is typical of reports from different parts of the State. Browne wrote that at least a dozen people had told him that the quotations from La Follette's speeches in the advertisements of the Waupaca *Republican Post* and farm *Equity* had "put a wholly new light upon his attitude which had been so grossly misrepresented." Browne also reported that the libel suit against the *Madison Democrat* was having "some effect upon public sentiment"; people were beginning "to realize that maybe La Follette has been lied about and quite a strong reaction was setting in."[37]

Crownhart forwarded this letter to Bob early in December. Later in the month he wrote that Governor Philipp's administration men had made a canvass of the State and were scared about the taxation issue. He enclosed a clipping reporting a recent speech which Governor Philipp had made at Waco, Texas, declaring that La Follette's attitude misrepresented Wisconsin and that so long as the war-tax issue periled the issue of patriotism no special senatorial election would be called to choose a successor to Senator Husting. Crownhart closed this letter by saying, "As things are getting brighter ever[y] minute, I can wish you a merry Xmas with some reason to believe you will have one."[38]

Early in December a circular letter, with reprints of advertisements published in *Equity News* and other papers, had been sent to seven thousand voters in Dane County soliciting their subscriptions. The letter summarized the plan Bob advocated for financing the war and also informed the voters that some newspapers in Dane County had "refused ads for *La Follette's.*" One advertisement, reprinted from *Equity News*, stated that when readers of *La Follette's Magazine* studied the figures it had published on the profits of the du Pont powder company, which had one of its plants in Bayfield County, Wisconsin, they might draw their own conclusions as to why the resolutions from that county had condemned La Follette, who had fought to tax this company's war profits 80 per cent to help sustain the war. In preparing this circular Crownhart had the assistance of Fred L. Holmes, an active young progressive Republican who had recently resigned from the staff of the *Wisconsin State Journal* to work for *La Follette's Magazine.*[39]

As this campaign began to produce repercussions, the slanderous attacks from the long-established Madison daily newspapers became more frequent. Shortly after the circular went out to the voters in Dane County, the *Wisconsin State Journal* published a long editorial insinuating that La Follette's position on various war measures had been motivated by traitorous intent and charging him with seeing the war "thru a Prussian periscope" or being "so blinded by his obsession against men who make money in manufacturing war supplies that he becomes a menace to our national welfare."[40]

In the atmosphere pervading the capital city and the University of Wisconsin at this time, an outspoken friend of Bob's needed a seasoned courage such as Crownhart had to meet the challenge of each day as he went about his business in Madison. A few days before Christmas he said in a letter to Bob: "The people here are raising h'l as usual but I think I can detect some improvement. The trouble here in Madison is that our friends are scared stiff. Some day they may warm up."[41]

As the trying year of 1917 ended, Bob received two letters from Madison, both written on December 29. One was three pages in longhand from Crownhart, delivered personally by Herman Ekern, who also reported verbally on the Wisconsin situation, which he had talked over with Crownhart before leaving Madison. Crownhart's letter summarized a recent Madison incident in these three brief sentences: "The night riders are raising Cain here. Last night they fired you from the Madison Club. Am sending [The Madison] Democrat report of it."[42] The other letter, authorized by the board of directors and signed by the secretary, W. N. Parker, read, "Dear Sir: At a meeting of the Board of Directors of this club on December 28, 1917, you were expelled from membership therein on the ground of unpatriotic conduct."[43] Before either letter arrived, however, Bob had learned of his expulsion through the newspapers. On the night of December 28, immediately after the directors took action, the secretary had hurried to the telephone to inform the press.[44] Seven of the nine directors had voted for the resolution; one had been absent. The only vote against it was cast by Bob's law partner, Alfred T. Rogers. Thus the impression was conveyed over the country that Bob's intimate friends who had long been his cronies believed he was a traitor and had cast him out of the club he had frequented for years whenever at home.

The fact was that he had been a member for only two years and had seldom used the club. During a membership drive he had joined at the urgent solicitation of one of the directors who had been his good friend for thirty years. Subsequently he learned that this friend had been intimidated into voting for the expulsion resolution and had deeply regretted his action.[45] Many influential club members were men who had bitterly opposed Bob when he was governor and had continued through the years to fight the progressive legislative program. It was later admitted that the expulsion of La Follette had been persistently urged by Magnus Swenson, Carl Johnson, and his brother Hobart Johnson, all politically hostile to Bob. Crownhart believed these three men were "the headwaters" of the flood of libel that had swept Wisconsin. The club president, F. W. Montgomery, was also president of the Madison Street Railway Company. The resolution for expulsion had been drawn up in the office of the lawyers for the Street Railway Company. At the insistent demand of Swenson and the two Johnsons, a meeting of the board of directors of the Madison Club had been suddenly called on only two or three days' notice.[46] The club by-laws, which required ten days' notice, had thus been violated, as had the stipulation that due notice be given any member against whom expulsion proceedings were to be brought. No notice had been sent to Bob.

This haste and the timing of the meeting for the night of Friday, December 28, were attributed by Roe, Bob, and others to advance information that had been secured about an editorial on "Financing The War" which was to be published the next day in *La Follette's*

Magazine. In this editorial Bob had called attention to the fact that among the firms manufacturing war supplies which should have their excess profits more heavily taxed was the Gisholt Machine Company in Madison that had totaled $3,500,000 in net profits during the two war years as compared with merely nominal profits for previous years. This company was owned by Carl and Hobart Johnson. It was thought they might easily have received confidential advance information about the editorial and have timed the Madison Club expulsion proceedings for release to the press on the same day *La Follette's Magazine* appeared in order "to break the force of the revelations" by distracting attention from themselves.[47]

The magazine was still being printed by the Wisconsin State Journal Printing Company, although Bob had been informed early in November that Richard Lloyd Jones and the other directors had passed a resolution to terminate the contract at the end of the required three months and had also authorized the business manager to say they would prefer to have *La Follette's Magazine* "take this business elsewhere immediately."[48] The material for the December issue, including the editorial, had been in on time, but when publication was later than usual Crownhart had written Bob that the printing was "being delayed by Journal because of rush work."[49] In the same issue of the *Wisconsin State Journal* that reported the expulsion proceedings of the previous night, an editorial commended the action of the board of directors in capital letters as "RIGHT," and predicted it would "have the hearty and enthusiastic support of the members of the club."[50]

The newspaper reports of Bob's expulsion from the Madison Club had appeared after Phil and Mary had arrived in Washington to spend the Christmas holidays with the family. Belle wrote to Bob's sister in Madison that she thought there had been some real rest and relaxation in the vacation, although Phil and Bob, Jr., had been going to work with their father every day except the two holidays and Sunday. "Nothing phases Bob or destroys his faith in the ultimate outcome of all this malign feeling. He is, on the whole in as good health as he has been for some years and everything considered he is wonderfully cheerful. . . . Sometimes I think this ordeal through which we are passing is harder for you and Robert than it is for us. Local matters are especially trying to the nerves whereas we are occupied with things to be done here and the action of the Madison Club is little more than an incident."[51]

Less than two weeks before this "incident," Justice James C. Kerwin of the Wisconsin Supreme Court, who lived in Madison, had become so perturbed at the increasing virulence of the attacks on Bob that he had written a frank, confidential note warning him that after it had been decided war should be declared the people of Wisconsin had "taken a very decided stand in favor of it"; that there had been a great agitation on war matters and a great deal of criticism of his acts. Kerwin suggested, "as a sincere friend for a long time," that although he knew Bob had been charged "by the press and some people with doing many things which you have not done by way of opposing the war policy," it appeared "unwise to take any position hostile to the present policy of this country on the war question."[52]

In a long letter, written early in January, Bob frankly expressed his own feeling at this time and revealed the faith which made it possible for him to live through the experiences of this trying period without permanent inner scars. He began his reply by saying that he knew Kerwin's letter had been prompted by a friendship which had endured since they were boys. "I apprehend," he wrote, "that many times in the long struggle for democracy, which has raged with great bitterness over Wisconsin in the last twenty-five years, that you have questioned the wisdom of my uncompromising attitude, but it warms my heart to believe that it never strained the bond of affection between us or raised a doubt in your mind as to the integrity of my purpose.

"The newspapers and the newborn patriots have the stage now and are filling the public eye and ear with malicious libels and violent denunciation.

"I do not think it strange that all this should make it appear that the '*people*' severely condemn all who in *any way* question 'the propriety of the action taken by Congress and the President.'

"But is it the *people* who are making this raid? Is it not that element directly or indirectly connected with interests which for twenty-five years have denounced me for reasons which we pretty well understood at the time

"I think I can see you shake your big old head and hear you say: 'They may be leading it all, but many of your old time friends are with them.' Perhaps that is true. . . . War is a terribly destructive force, even beyond the limits of the battlefront and the war zones. Its influence involves the whole community. It warps men's judgment, distorts the true standard of patriotism, breeds distrust and suspicion among neighbors, inflames passions, encourages violence, develops abuse of power, tyrannizes over men and women even in the purely social relations of life, and terrifies whole communities into the most abject surrender of every right which is the heritage of free government."

Noting that the Constitution had stood against all the forces which war had "heretofore let loose upon us," he reasoned that "if the Constitution does stand, and if you have registered an oath to support the Constitution as a United States Senator, then one is bound to oppose a plain violation of the letter and spirit of the Constitution by either the President or the Congress—'equally in war and in peace.'" He went on to explain to Kerwin that out of some sixty war measures passed by Congress after war was declared, he had "supported and voted *for all of them except five.*" Listing these five and his affirmative votes on several other important measures which had been misrepresented in certain newspapers, he said, "I think I have been right in every position taken."

With this letter he enclosed a copy of his St. Paul speech. Explaining that it had been extemporaneous and delivered on fifteen minutes' notice, he said, "If I had been charged with making a poor speech, I should at once have entered the plea of guilty," and asked him to, "Read the darned thing, Jim, and then compare anything in it which you think critical as to the beginning of this war, or the President, or the administration, with what Lincoln and Sumner and other statesmen of that time said about the Mexican war and President Polk.

"There is not a disloyal word or thought in the St. Paul speech. And if the Committee even gives me a chance I will show them that I had ample proof to warrant me in making every statement contained in it. . . .

"After the declaration of war I recognized the obligations which a state of war lays upon every citizen.

"But the Constitution still abides. It defines the powers and duties of Congress. It gave Congress every war power, except that it left with the President the right to direct all military operation *in the field.* It gave him no *other war power.*

"This talk of blindly following the President in everything pertaining to war—except as to his conduct of military operation in the field—is blithering idiocy.

"Believe me in all sincerity I want your unsparing criticism, because you are my friend. But I want it on my *acts* not on what the newspapers *say of me.* They never quote what I say, they denounce me as disloyal.

"Now, dear old boy, I am going to send you the St. Paul speech and each of the speeches I have made on the war issues. I know you are busy but since this is the greatest ordeal through which our country has passed in our time and because you *are* my *good* friend, I want you to go through the speeches (St. Paul and all) and then write me again fully and frankly.

"You know me well and you need no assurance from me that you need not soften your criticism to spare my feelings.

"May I say to you that in the midst of this raging storm of hate, I am withal very happy in so far as my own future is concerned. I would not change places with any living man on the record as it stands today."[33]

CHAPTER LII

"History Alone Can Judge Impartially"

Shortly after the Senate met on January 5, 1918, Vice President Marshall announced that he had received a letter from the managing editor of the Vigilantes, "a patriotic, antipacifist, nonpartisan organization of authors, artists, and others, with headquarters at 505 Fifth Avenue, New York City, N.Y., asking the Chair to bring to the attention of the Senate certain inclosed letters of protest against the continuing membership in the highest council of the Nation of Robert M. La Follette." The Vice President stated that in accordance with his recent ruling these letters would be transmitted to the senior Senators of the States in which the writers lived "for such action as the judgment and conscience of the Senators may deem appropriate to be taken."[1]

The Vigilantes were a private group, first organized by a few authors in November, 1916. In an article written in 1918 by Porter Emerson Browne, one of the founders, the organization was said to include more than four hundred American authors, artists, illustrators, publicists, editors, and others who had banded themselves together to fight with pen, brush, and voice "for their country's honor and their country's life." A foreword to the article noted that one of the members who had been a generous contributor to funds for the organization was Theodore Roosevelt. The avowed purpose of the group was to give wide circulation to "the best available type of patriotic publicity" through newspapers and news syndicates.[2] The members volunteered to "write articles, stories, or to draw cartoons, on demand, absolutely without charge, on any subject which the managing editor of the Vigilantes might specify.[3] A study of the contemporary magazines and newspapers indicates that a subject frequently assigned by the managing editor or chosen by members of the Vigilantes for cartoons, articles, and stories was Robert M. La Follette.

The four prominent authors who initiated the organization in 1916 were Hermann Hagedorn, Porter Emerson Browne, Charles Hanson Towne, and Julian Street, who was also a member of the board of trustees of the American Defense Society. At a luncheon at The Players in New York City, they had discussed the idea with S. Stanwood Menken, organizer and president of the National Security League, Thomas Desmond, an engineer "active in politics," and two authors, Cleveland Moffett and Hamlin Garland, both members of the Publicity Committee of the American Defense Society. The project had been greeted with enthusiasm. Subsequently a dinner was arranged, money subscribed, offices rented, and Charles Rosebault, formerly of the New York *Sun*, was made managing editor. Among the authors who immediately volunteered their services were Samuel Hopkins Adams, Gertrude Atherton, George Ade, Rex Beach, Irvin S. Cobb, and Booth Tarkington. The Executive Committee was enlarged to include, in addition to the actual founders, Augustus Thomas, Irvin S. Cobb, Monroe Douglas Robinson, Ellis Parker Butler, Thomas C. Desmond, and Robert J. Wildhack. The first campaign of the Vigilantes had been a series of articles in favor of universal military service.[4] Charles Hanson Towne has recorded that a boiler-plate service of syndicate material was arranged and sent forth from the office. "It was printed everywhere—north, east, south, west. We interviewed millionaires, asking their financial aid, and they opened their checkbooks and wrote checks in three or four figures, handing them to us without a word."[5]

Although Samuel Hopkins Adams, Rupert Hughes, Gertrude Atherton, and certain other individual members of the Vigilantes had previously branded La Follette as a traitor in signed articles and cartoons, the petition and letters to the Vice President record the first instance the author has found of their open attack upon him as an organization. On Sunday, January 6, the day after the Vice President announced he had received the Vigilantes' protest, the *Washington Post* and the *New York Tribune* published excerpts from some of the forty letters they had written. Both newspapers

quoted Meredith Nicholson as having declared "the toleration in
our highest law-making body of a man who speaks the language of
Berlin is an insult to every American soldier and sailor and every
loyal American citizen." Emerson Hough was reported to have described La Follette as "worse than an enemy alien," and Porter
Emerson Browne lamented that the Capitol at Washington tolerated
"so frank, so magnificent a seditionist as the Hon. (God help me!)
Robert M. La Follette."[6] Another author who reiterated his demand
for La Follette's expulsion was Rupert Hughes, who had previously
made a virulent attack in a long article for the *New York Times*.
In this special article he had given his own malicious version of La
Follette's speech at the publishers' dinner in Philadelphia and asserted that the Senator was as much the victim of "distorted mental
machinery" as "thousands of poor crazy folk in padded cells." This
article apparently had the approval of George Creel, chairman of
the Committee on Public Information, for he had taken the trouble
to send it to the President with a note saying he had marked two
passages.[7] Someone in New York had also sent the article to Bob,
who had written across the envelope, "Libel File Important."[8]

The *New York Tribune* dedicated two columns to the Vigilantes'
protest which included excerpts of similar import from the letters
of Lawrence F. Abbott, president of the *Outlook* Company, Gelett
Burgess, Bliss Carman, E. E. Harriman, Wallace Irwin, Burges
Johnson, Julian Street, Augustus Thomas, and Charles Hanson
Towne. It also quoted from the petition which accompanied the
letters, and commented that the Vigilantes had struck at the Senator "at the same time that anti-La Follette sentiment" was "being
organized in his home state" where the Wisconsin Loyalty Legion
hoped "to induce the state to take action censuring him." The
petition declared that although the Vigilantes were "passionately
devoted to the principle of free speech and a free press," La Follette
had "abused both of these with the determined purpose of utilizing
them to the injury of the United States," and that in this crisis
"many privileges must be abridged that the country may survive."
It had long been "notorious," they declared, that La Follette would
"leave no effort untried" which might "interfere with the efficient
prosecution by these United States of the war against autocracy."
The Vigilantes asserted that as writers whose business it was to
keep themselves informed of the sentiment of the country they

The La Follette family in 1910

From left to right, Fola, Bob, Belle, Mary, Phil, and Bob, Jr.

Belle in 1922
Of her, Bob wrote: "She has been my wisest and best counselor."

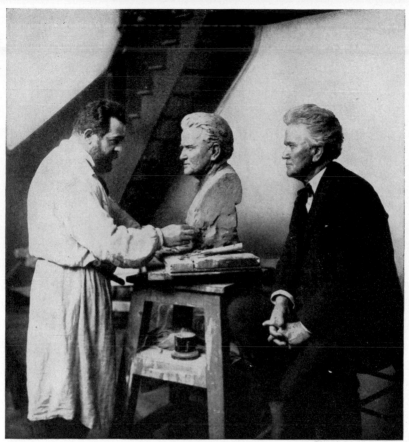

Paris, 1923
Bob in Jo Davidson's studio

Bob and his son Bob, Jr., in Washington, D.C., 1924

St. Louis Post-Dispatch

Bob and his son Phil in St. Louis, October, 1924

could testify "that not a seditious utterance of Senator La Follette has been allowed to lie fallow."[9]

With the powerful weapons of pen and brush, the Vigilantes were an important influence in shaping public opinion. Among the many organizations that appealed to them for help were the American Defense Society, the National Security League, the American Bankers Association, the League to Enforce Peace, and the United States Chamber of Commerce. Undoubtedly many members of the Vigilantes who wrote articles or drew cartoons imputing treason to La Follette, sometimes over their own signatures, sometimes anonymously, believed at the time that they were thus serving the avowed purpose of their organization to give wide circulation to "the best available type of patriotic publicity." Subsequently some of them may have felt as did Irvin S. Cobb, a member of the Executive Committee, who wrote and published over his own signature early in 1918 a short story which, under the thin disguise of fiction, attributed traitorous motivations and acts to La Follette. It was published in the *Saturday Evening Post*, which then had an estimated circulation of nearly two million.[10] Fifteen years later Cobb expressed regret that he had succumbed "to the prevalent hysteria" and had written this piece of propaganda under "the spell of that madness—which we mistook for patriotism." In a letter which he described as a "belated word of contrition" to Bob's family for the injustice he had done to "a far-seeing statesman, a most gallant gentleman and a very great American," Cobb said: "For years I have deeply regretted that I wrote that story, because more and more I have come to realize that the policies which he so courageously advocated, in the face of a then almost nation-wide condemnation, were in the main right policies. We-all were blind, not he. We ran with the herd; he, almost alone, risked his political future and for the moment sacrificed his political popularity, to stand fast by his honest opinions."[11]

Cobb and at least thirteen other prominent authors of the Vigilantes group were also members of the Publicity Committee of the American Defense Society, which had presented to the Committee on Privileges and Elections early in December a brief "prepared by New York lawyers of high standing" to aid in the expulsion of Robert M. La Follette from the Senate. In reporting this the *New York Times* noted that "the Anti-Disloyalty Committee of which

James M. Beck [former Assistant Attorney General] was a one time Chairman and which is now headed by W. H. Gardiner of 2 Rector Street has been collecting evidence against La Follette." The American Defense Society was described as including in its membership "some of the most prominent men of the country."[12]

A letterhead of this organization, carefully preserved among the files of the La Follette papers, lists among the many prominent members of the advisory board and the board of trustees the names of: former President Theodore Roosevelt, former ambassador to France Robert Bacon, at one time a member of J. Pierpont Morgan & Company, who had served as Assistant Secretary of State under Elihu Root; former Ambassador to Germany David Jayne Hill, former Assistant Attorney General James M. Beck, John Grier Hibben, president of Princeton University; Perry Belmont, vice president of the Navy League; William H. Gardiner, formerly associated with the "Proper Bostonian" investment firm of Lee, Higginson & Company; Richard M. Hurd, president of the Lawyers Mortgage Company.[13] Tracing the connections of these and other prominent members of this organization weaves a web of interlocking social and business connections that recalls the list and map of interlocking directorates Bob had presented to the Senate in 1908 during the filibuster against the Aldrich-Vreeland currency bill when he charged that fewer than one hundred men were in control of the country's great business interests.[14] Arrayed against him now, and using every possible device to procure his expulsion from the Senate for disloyalty, were many men who had social or business connections with the powerful special interests he had severely criticized for many years.

Two days before the committee hearing was scheduled, and on the same Sunday morning that the *Washington Post* and the *New York Tribune* carried excerpts from the Vigilantes' letters, another well timed attack appeared. The *New York Herald* published a long unsigned article about the brief which had been submitted by the Anti-Disloyalty Committee of the American Defense Society to aid "in the good work of ousting Senator Robert M. La Follette." Long excerpts were printed under the two-column headline "La Follette's Acts Compared with German Spy Work by American Defense Society."[15] The brief insinuated that Bob was responsible for delaying the investigation, and accused him of abusing his privileges as a Senator "by gratuitously distributing over his frank utterances calculated to incite opposition to the Government of the United States in the prosecution of the war, and to produce disaffection among the people." It cited precedents to show the Senate's power to expel him, and elaborated at great length in legal terms the theme that he was "not loyal to the government of the United States" but was "actually and regardless of his intent 'giving aid and comfort' to the public enemy." The brief was signed by a prominent New York lawyer, Henry Wynans Jessup, of counsel; Richard M. Hurd, chairman of the American Defense Society, and W. H. Gardiner, chairman of its Anti-Disloyalty Committee.

The night before this article appeared, Roe had arrived in Washington to make final preparation for the committee hearing which was scheduled for Tuesday. As usual he was staying at the La Follette home, and it is probable that he and the family read the *New York Herald* article on Sunday morning. Although neither Bob nor his attorney had ever seen the brief, Roe had sent Bob newspaper clippings about it. Early in December, when the *New York Times* reported that the brief had actually been filed with the committee, he had written that he thought these clippings "ought to insure us the right to file a brief in reply before any other steps are taken."[16]

On Tuesday morning, January 8, the same day the committee on Privileges and Elections was to meet, a special Washington dispatch was published in the New York *Sun* under the headline "New Proof Of La Follette's 'Sedition' Filed / American Defense Society Renews Demand For Senator's Expulsion." The report stated that "The apparent disinclination of the Senate Committee on Privileges and Elections to proceed seriously with the investigation of disloyalty charges against Senator La Follette of Wisconsin" had stirred the American Defense Society to file with the Committee on Monday "an attested stenographic report of the speech delivered by La Follette before the Non-Partisan League Convention at St. Paul, Minn., on September 20, 1917," made by a stenographer named Jesse Cary Smith. Scraps of quotations from the speech followed. Sentences and paragraphs were snatched from the context and patched together in a way that maliciously distorted the actual meaning and purpose of the speaker. The excerpts were strung together with inserted phrases which made it seem that this was a digest of the speech from beginning to end. Sometimes omissions were indicated, thus giving an appearance of accuracy. But frequently they were not shown at all.

The attacks of the American Defense Society and the Vigilantes had apparently been carefully timed in relation to the scheduled hearing, but when Tuesday arrived the committee postponed it for the sixth time.[17] That day Roe and Bob decided to send to each member of the committee a clipping of the *New York Herald's* summary of the American Defense Society's brief. To accompany the clipping Bob wrote a letter requesting that if any brief had been filed which the committee felt justified in considering it should be submitted to him at once, and that he be given an opportunity to file a brief in reply. He called attention to the fact that the report of the "so-called brief" insinuated that he had been at fault for the delays in the committee proceedings, and he again asked that a time be fixed to proceed with hearings as speedily as possible. Although for some reason which is not recorded the letter was never sent, his opinion and Roe's were accurately expressed when he wrote, "The pendency of the matter before your Committee furnishes an excuse for libels and defamatory attacks, such as I judge is to be found in the 'brief' referred to, by persons and interests desiring to assail me but who lack the courage to make their attacks without the protection of such privileges as can be claimed for a communication addressed to the Committee."[18]

At noon on January 8, the same day this letter was written, Bob attended a joint session of Congress summoned to hear the President discuss international relations. Congress received only a half-hour's notice of this important address, although he had notified the British Foreign Minister, Balfour, and Prime Minister Lloyd George of his intention on January 5, and had completed his manuscript on Sunday, January 6.[19] Wilson had decided to make this address after a talk with Colonel House on December 18. House, who had recently returned from the Interallied Conference in Paris, had informed the President of his unsuccessful efforts to persuade the Allies to join in "formulating a broad declaration of war aims that would unite the world against Germany," help "to a solution of the Russian problem," and "knit together the best and most unselfish opinions of the world."[20] Before the President had finished writing his address, however, Prime Minister Lloyd George had stated the British war aims in a speech to the Trades Union Congress, made necessary by recent debates in the House of Commons regarding disclosures of the secret treaties and the memorandum of war aims issued by the British Labour Conference.[21]

The failure of the Interallied Conference to restate the war aims of the Allies after the discovery of the secret treaties in the Russian archives had made the "Russian problem" grow more acute day by day.[22] In England the *Manchester Guardian* had begun publication on December 12 of the texts of the secret treaties as released by the Soviet Government. Translations of these texts had been sent from Petrograd by the American Ambassador on December 5, but they did not reach the State Department until December 27.[23] * Five days before they arrived, the Soviet Government had already begun a discussion of peace terms on December 22 at Brest-Litovsk with the German Government. On December 29 the Russian Foreign Minister, Trotsky, had issued an appeal "to the peoples and governments of the Allied Countries" to manifest their readiness to construct peace "on the basis of an entire and complete recognition of the principles of self-determination for all peoples in all states."[24] But before this appeal was made the President had already decided on December 18 that "lacking an inter-Allied manifesto, an address by himself might prove to be the moral turning point of the war. . . ."[25]

Because the notification that Wilson would speak to Congress had been so brief, there were no crowds at the Capitol when he arrived on January 8. Members of the House and Senate had responded to the hurry calls sent out a half-hour earlier, but a reporter noted that five minutes before the President was scheduled to begin his discussion of the international situation the diplomatic gallery was empty.[26] Even the newspaper correspondents apparently arrived too late to observe and record the details that are usually a part of their reports on these important occasions. None seems to have noted whether Bob entered the Chamber alone, where he sat, or what his countenance revealed as he listened to the President

---

* The texts of these secret treaties were not released by the State Department for publication at this time. But translations secured from another source that Bob knew about were published in the *Evening Post* in New York on Jan. 25, 26, and 28, 1918.

deliver his own version of the United States war aims in his historic Fourteen Points address.

The intense interest with which Bob followed Wilson's speech that day can be inferred, however, from the analysis he made of it later and from his own earlier pleas in the Senate for a declaration of war aims. His previous record, his private letters, his public statements, and his subsequent legislative action all indicate how profoundly he must have hoped that time and the final peace conference would prove the accuracy of the President's declaration that "The day of conquest is gone by, so also the day of secret covenants." Bob was in accord with the President's declaration for "Open covenants of peace, openly arrived at," "Absolute freedom of navigation upon the seas, outside territorial waters, alike in peace and in war," limitation of armaments "to the lowest point consistent with domestic safety," and an association of nations based on what the President pronounced as the principle underlying the whole program he had outlined; namely, "the principle of justice to all peoples and nationalities, and their right to live on equal terms of liberty and safety with one another, whether they be strong or weak."[27]

But Bob had grave reservations about the President's suggestions for certain territorial readjustments relating to France and Italy. To him they seemed so dangerously vague that they might commit the United States to years of foreign war to readjust boundary lines of Europe to conform to secret treaties or to "right wrongs" of the past in vain efforts to settle all the complex questions of nationality and race which were the outgrowth of European history.[28]

On the same day Wilson spoke, Bob, Jr., wrote that he thought the President's address was "the first really statesman like document that he or any of the allied diplomats or premiers have rendered," but added with characteristic caution, "if it were not for the fact that he jumps from one extreme to the other one would feel that something really big had been done."[29] The next day Belle wrote Phil and Mary that she thought "the President's last message has great possibilities. But he changes ground so easily that what he says does not have the significance it otherwise would have."[30] In a long editorial for *La Follette's Magazine*, written some days later, Bob commented that it recognized *"the right of the people to know about their own business,—even though that business is* war," and implied *"the right of the people to discuss terms of peace, to express their views on the objects and purposes of the war."* It was, he said, "a belated acknowledgement that war aims should have from the outset been clearly and frankly stated" with "a certainty and definiteness" that would bring them "within the understanding of the plain people who must bear the brunt of the fighting and the weight of the tax bill."[31]

While writing this editorial on peace terms, Bob had also been working on another, entitled "A Statement," which summarized his position on war legislation and the issues growing out of the war. It was never published, but his thought about various aspects of the subject was expressed in letters to several friends. One of these letters was written to James M. Pierce, publisher and editor of the *Wisconsin Farmer*, which had recently printed the advertisements of *La Follette's Magazine* written by Crownhart. With a friendly, understanding letter to Bob, Pierce had enclosed his reply to an irate subscriber who had canceled his subscription and accused Pierce of disloyalty because his paper had carried the advertisements. Bob wrote that the reply was "a rare sermon on real patriotism," and expressed regret that Pierce had been assailed on his account. It was true everywhere, he said, that men who dared to show they were his friends were "being intimidated and punished in innumerable ways." In analyzing the source of some of these attacks, he wrote: "That you or I should have our loyalty to our country questioned is so grotesque, so monstrous that I have never quite been able to believe that a sane mind has ever seriously entertained such a thought. Your record in the Civil War, splendid tribute as it is to your patriotism, was no greater than the loyalty you have shown during all the years of your civil life in which you have fought to make our country a better place for real men and women to live in. After all, that is what a country is for.

"For my part, I think you know without my saying it, that my life has been dedicated to the public service. The record of what I have accomplished in Wisconsin and in the Congress in the interest of the public, modest as it is, will always furnish a sufficient answer to the charge that my devotion to my country's service has been less than the best that was in me. It has happened that my kind of public service has brought me almost from the beginning of my public life into sharp conflict with those you so well describe as

'The American Kaisers of crooked business and corrupt politics.' Autocracy in all its forms has always been peculiarly hateful to me. I early saw that the rule of the people, with all its faults and short-comings, in the long run furnished better government than was attainable in any other way. To maintain that proposition, I have fought scores of political battles. For it I have staked my political life again and again, and whatever small place my record may have in the history of our country will be due to my devotion to that principle. Many of those men that I helped to retire to private life because they stood for the rule of autocracy and the destruction of the people's rights, have now come forth from their burrows of political obscurity and are the loudest declaimers for democracy —in some other country.

"Well, my friend, it is a part of the topsy turvy times that we are 'traitors,' 'disloyal,' and 'partners of the Kaiser,' while the men who have been undermining our government and robbing the people, are the only 'patriots' and friends of the dear old flag. But the storm will pass, reason will return to the people—you see I still believe in democracy and have faith that there remains much more work for us to do."[32]

Two days after Bob wrote this letter to Pierce, his loyalty to his country was questioned in a protest which shocked and hurt him more deeply than the action taken by any other group during the entire war.

On January 14 President Van Hise presided at a University of Wisconsin faculty meeting which made the front page of the *Madison Democrat* the next morning in a special boxed story with heavy, black type headlines announcing "University Professors Protest La Follette's War Attitude And Vote Endorsement Of Wilson."[33] The newspaper report reversed the actual order of procedure and also omitted certain details which would have seemed significant to Bob had he known them. While the meeting was in regular session, with Van Hise presiding, a resolution was presented declaring that the faculty endorsed the President's January 8 message to Congress and pledged enthusiastic support to his "program for securing world peace." It passed unanimously by a rising vote, and a motion was made to telegraph the resolution to the President. This proceeding was mentioned in the minutes. But the minutes did not record the fact that just before the meeting adjourned it was announced that directly after adjournment a memorial would be presented to set the world right on the faculty's attitude toward La Follette. After adjournment Professor William A. Scott stated in presenting this "memorial" that La Folletteism was synonymous with treason, that the university must go on record, and that members of the faculty would be asked to sign. The presentation of this resolution after adjournment prevented any discussion, and thus no one was given an opportunity to take a public stand on it during the faculty meeting.

Two days later Professor Max C. Otto of the philosophy department wrote Van Hise giving his reasons for being unwilling to sign the protest resolution. In this letter, written before he had been asked to sign, Otto said: "It is my conviction that however high-minded the sponsors of the statement of protest may be, and whatever the merits of the case at issue, the procedure adopted is in effect part of the campaign to snuff out such intellectual freedom as still remains to us, and is bound still further to force the surrender of intellectual integrity. The way is thus cleared for the forces most inimical to the ideals which our democracy has espoused before the world.

"Such being my conviction, for me to sign the statement would be to betray my alma mater, my country, and my fellow man. This I am not prepared to do."[34]

To this letter Van Hise replied that the resolution regarding La Follette was not a faculty action but an action which individual members of the faculty might take or not according to their individual convictions.[35] Two days after the faculty meeting, at a regular session of the Board of Regents on January 16, Van Hise made his report on the war activities of the university. That same day Crownhart wrote Bob from Madison saying there was "a very evident conspiracy on here to bring on one thing after another in order to keep the people aroused against you and to influence the action of the United States Senate."[36] Van Hise's report informed the Board of Regents that a statement was being circulated among members of the faculty for signatures to a protest "against those utterances and actions of Senator La Follette which have given aid and comfort to Germany and her allies in the present war" and "deploring his failure loyally to support the government in the prosecution of the war." As given to the newspapers, it also included two letters, obviously written for publication, which had been exchanged between Van Hise and John S. Lord, president of the Wisconsin Alumni Association. On December 26 Lord had written that he would be pleased to have from Van Hise, as president of the university, "a statement of the attitude of the University concerning the policies advocated by Senator La Follette." The following day Van Hise had replied in a brief letter recapitulating the university's support of President Wilson's war policies and ending with the statement, "I strongly believe the policies of Senator La Follette in relation to the war are dangerous to the country."[37]

Van Hise's report and the circulation of the protest among faculty members were the culmination of a series of demands during the preceding four months from various educational groups and certain alumni organizations for La Follette's resignation or expulsion from the Senate. Early in October the president and members of the faculty of the University of Ohio had joined with residents of Athens, Ohio, in a resolution to this effect which had been sent to the Committee on Privileges and Elections.[38] At an annual conference in Madison on October 4 with the state superintendent of schools, Charles P. Cary, the city superintendents of schools had passed a resolution to be sent to President Wilson and the Committee on Privileges and Elections. It repudiated "any and all of the seditious utterances of said Robert M. La Follette," and petitioned the Senate "to promptly expel him and thus give the people of Wisconsin the right to hold up their heads without shame."[39] Later in the month, at a meeting in Eau Claire, the Northwestern Wisconsin Teachers' Association passed with "tremendous applause" a resolution condemning La Follette.[40] On November 3, the same day the Alumni Council met in Madison, the Wisconsin Teachers' Association at their state convention in Milwaukee passed a resolution endorsing Wilson, eulogizing Senator Husting, and declaring that although they remembered La Follette's "staunch and clear-sighted leadership on many momentous occasions in the past," they now deplored that he failed them "in this, the greatest of all crisis. [sic]"[41]

In several cities outside the State, alumni members had been active in efforts to procure his expulsion from the Senate. At a meeting in Minneapolis shortly after his St. Paul speech, a resolution had been unanimously passed and sent to the Committee on Privileges and Elections declaring La Follette had brought "disgrace and humiliation to our great University and to the State which has so signally honored him."[42] Resolutions had subsequently been passed by Wisconsin Alumni Associations in Philadelphia and Chicago.[43] A dispatch from San Francisco telegraphed to the *Wisconsin State Journal* reported that at a dinner in honor of Congressmen Irvine L. Lenroot and John J. Esch of Wisconsin and Professors Richard T. Ely and Chester Lloyd Jones of the University of Wisconsin the members of the Northern California Alumni Association had joined the four guests of honor in speeches denouncing La Follette's attitude.[44]

Some of these resolutions had apparently been inspired by the previous action of the Wisconsin Alumni Board and Council. At a meeting of the Alumni Board in Madison on October 13, a committee of three, including John S. Lord, who lived in Chicago, had been appointed to investigate and report on "what should be done with respect to the speeches and acts of Sen. La Follette, '79." The Alumni Board met again on the morning of November 3, heard the committee's report, and recommended action. That afternoon the committee reported to an Alumni Council meeting. Lord brought word from Chicago that the alumni of that city had considered the matter at several meetings where the discussion was led "with great enthusiasm" by Bishop Samuel Fallows, the distinguished alumnus of the class of '59. They had heartily condemned La Follette and wished they had the power to expel him from both the association and the Senate.[45] Although Lord did not mention it, the bishop, who was a prominent member of the Chicago branch of the National Security League, had previously participated in activities directed toward procuring La Follette's expulsion from the Senate. On September 26, at a huge mass meeting arranged by this organization, with Theodore Roosevelt as the principal speaker, Bishop Fallows had introduced a resolution condemning La Follette for his public utterances and declaring him "an unfaithful and disloyal official, unworthy to represent the loyal and devoted citizens of America."[46]

Lord read to the Alumni Council meeting a long report and a resolution which had been unanimously passed by the alumni group in Chicago demanding that protest should be made by the Alumni

Association of the university "against those utterances of Sen. Robert M. La Follette that tend to discourage or oppose the undertakings of the United States in the world war." In urging passage of a resolution that had been proposed, Lord quoted the remark made by a man who had said he "would rather be Sen[ator] Husting dead in his glory than Sen[ator] La Follette, alive in his shame," and commented that he believed this expressed the feeling of most of the alumni. The resolution, which passed with only two dissenting votes, expressed "the grief and shame" of the alumni at La Follette's "unwise and disloyal utterances giving aid and comfort to the enemy," and denounced "his failure actively and earnestly to support the government in the prosecution of the present war."[47] This resolution was later ordered to be sent to President Wilson with a marked copy of the *Wisconsin Alumni Magazine* giving "complete details" of the proceedings.[48]

One of the votes against the resolution had been cast by J. B. Simpson, a classmate of Bob's and Belle's. This was the genial "Jeff" Simpson who during college days had especially delighted in jests and gay pranks. At the time of the Alumni Council meeting he completely disagreed with Bob's position on the war, but disapproved of the resolution and spoke against it. Recalling to the hostile members of the Alumni Council what Bob had done for the university as governor, "when it was hard up and in bad shape," he declared La Follette had "conferred more honor [on the university] than any other person."[49]

The Wisconsin Alumni Association's condemnation of Bob had proved another effective weapon in the persistent campaign carried on by the *Wisconsin State Journal*, the *Milwaukee Journal*, the *Wisconsin Journal of Education*, and other less public but perhaps more powerful influences working to procure a similar denunciation from the University of Wisconsin. What went on underground can only be inferred. But an editorial in the *Wisconsin Journal of Education* illustrates the type of attack that had been persistently made. The editor of this magazine, which had been founded in 1856, was Willard N. Parker, who was also secretary of the Madison Club. In his editorial Parker stated that although the university had sent many students into the Army and had released several professors for war work, "suspicion still hangs over it, for the reason that its President has not yet openly repudiated the disloyal acts of a few of its graduates." Calling attention to the resolution passed by the Alumni Association condemning La Follette, Parker asked, "Why should not President Van Hise and the Regents do the same?" Although the circulation of this magazine was only 4,500, it reached additional readers. The editorial was reprinted in the *Wisconsin State Journal* and even found its way to the distant page of a newspaper in Helena, Montana, Senator Thomas J. Walsh's home town.[50]

Through the *Wisconsin Alumni Magazine* the resolution passed by the Alumni Council and the Van Hise letter to Lord reached Wisconsin alumni in many different states. The university faculty protest was played up on the front pages of the Madison newspapers but received little publicity in the press outside the State. The original document as deposited at the Wisconsin State Historical Society consisted of twenty-five separate sheets. At the top of all but three pages a typed paragraph stated that the undersigned resident members of the faculty "of the rank of instructor and above, protest against those utterances and actions of Senator Robert M. La Follette which have given aid and comfort to Germany and her allies in the present war; we deplore his failure loyally to support the government in the prosecution of the war. In these respects he has misrepresented us, his constituents." Two additional paragraphs informed the prospective signers that "more than 125 of our colleagues, who might have supported this protest," were "absent from the city in the service of the United States" and that copies of the protest were "to be sent to Senator La Follette and to the press."[51] Beneath this brief statement space had been left for the signatures, which varied from one to thirty-seven on a page.

A certain page records the signatures of two professors who, although they believed the protest justified at the time, later expressed regret at their participation in it. One professor doubtless expressed the feeling of many at that time when he wrote, "We in the University of Wisconsin felt he was pro-German and was siding against his own country." Years later others may have altered their opinions, although not publicly recording the change as did Richard T. Ely and Edward A. Ross.[52] One professor, who subsequently regretted signing the protest, recalled when he saw a photostat of the page with his signature that the original had been

presented to him at the University Club.⁵³ Apparently at least two
pages gathered signatures there, for at the top of another page is an
initialed notation directing that it "be left on desk" at this same
club. Certain faculty members recall that the pages submitted to
them had, so far as they could see, no resolution at the top. Therefore some who signed may have had merely a general impression
that they were putting the university on record as opposing La
Follette's position on the war without being aware of the precise
charges formulated in the resolution.

The contemporary newspaper reports did not describe how the
protest was circulated nor mention that in some instances the requests for signatures were presented to faculty members by heads
of their departments. Nor did the newspapers record the names
of the dozen or less who refused to sign.⁵⁴ Among these was Professor A. R. Hohlfeld, a distinguished Goethe scholar who was
head of the German Department. At the faculty meeting Hohlfeld
had praised President Wilson's message of January 8 to Congress
as a most remarkable document in the history of mankind, expressing hearty accord with the spirit of its program, and voting
for the resolution endorsing it.⁵⁵ Three days after the meeting
Hohlfeld wrote Van Hise stating his position regarding the La
Follette resolution. Bob never saw this letter to Van Hise in which
Hohlfeld said, "In as much as I have not felt able to sign the
resolution of the War Committee in regard to Senator La Follette,
I desire to give to you as president of the University and as chairman of the Committee the reasons for my attitude. Quite aside from
the merits or demerits of Senator La Follette's case, my reasons
are as follows:

"*First.* I deplore the wording of the resolution. Whether so intended by the committee or not, the phrasing is bound to be interpreted by the popular mind as a charge of traitorous conduct, hence,
not only as a criticism of action, but as an assignment of the basest
of motives.

"*Second.* On a charge of such a nature, Senator La Follette's case
is at present in the hands of a committee of the United States
Senate. Until this committee is prepared to report, I must decline to
prejudge his case. I have been fully identified with the latter day
efforts of American university professors to secure for themselves
the right of trial before their peers and of being heard in self-

defense in case that serious charges are raised against them. I should not be true to my convictions if I declined to grant the same rights to a man who in the past has rendered such eminent service to state and nation as has Senator La Follette.

"*Third.* I regret and protest against the inquisitorial method adopted by the War Committee in their desire to have the Faculty go on record in this matter. They have not been satisfied with securing a general Faculty endorsement, but have insisted on every member going on record as an individual, with the provision even, as I understand, that a list of names be given to the press. This amounts to coercion—moral, professional and social coercion of every non-conformist. Such a method of procedure if applied to one question after another, I fear, must undermine that intellectual integrity and freedom of conscience without which there can be no true university life.

"In making these strictures, I do not wish to question the motives of the members of the Committee. I have no doubt that they have been animated, as indeed I am animated, by the desire to serve the best interests of the University, the State, and the Nation."[56]

Hohlfeld received no answer to this letter.

Bob never saw the original document containing 421 signatures of faculty members. He first learned about the circulation of the protest through the newspapers. Several weeks later he received official notification in a letter signed by three members of the faculty committee, professors Frederic L. Paxson, William A. Scott, and George C. Sellery. The letter informed him that the original protest with appended signatures of "almost ninety-three per cent" of the resident members of the faculty had been "deposited in the Library of the State Historical Society at Madison." Enclosed with the letter was a typed list of 399 names of the faculty arranged in alphabetical order beneath a copy of the protest that had been circulated for signatures.[57] The list was incomplete as compared with the document deposited in the Library. But it contained the names of intimate friends, scholars he had admired and championed when their academic freedom was threatened,[58] and close associates through many years in his work for the university and the State. One signature which Bob found it especially hard to believe could have been placed beneath a statement accusing him of disloyalty to his country was that of his intimate friend Charles R. Van Hise, the classmate who had shared with him the teachings and ideals of John Bascom, former president of the university.

Soon after the petition was sent to Bob, and subsequently for several years, inaccurate rumors reverberated through university circles that La Follette was threatening to punish the signers of the protest. One fantastic report of his vindictive plans was apparently believed sufficiently to be perpetuated in the pages of a book by a professor who recorded that La Follette had warned them "he was going to have the entire ninety-two percent of the faculty fired."[59]

At one time when Bob was in Madison, Professor Otto, who had refused to sign the protest, went to talk over the university situation with him because there were rumors that certain professors were to be punished for what they had done to smear his reputation when the situation was most critical in Washington. In a letter recalling this talk, Professor Otto says: "I remember that I argued against getting after any of us on the faculty because that would be inconsistent with his magnificent record in relation to that institution. I was deeply impressed with the positive way in which he had persistently supported education from the lowest schools through the University. I was familiar with that record, for I had had reason to look it up. I shall never forget how he brushed my argument aside. That was the time I saw how his warm eyes could turn to steel, more literally steel than I'd ever seen anything assume that is made of living tissue. He made me see how the issue was not his reputation or any professor's feelings, but the essential principle of public education. It was those who engineered the attack upon him who betrayed education, and if such betrayals were condoned because you feared someone might be hurt or you might lose in standing because you insisted that such betrayers of their trust be brought to book, you were not really defending education but were yourself dragging it down. I got from him then, as I always did, a sense of his *realism* combined with *idealism*. It was impossible to say which belonged in first place. They seemed to be one thing. We discussed the subject for quite a time and the effect upon me was to deepen my appreciation of what a sacred thing he felt public education to be."[60]

The only action Bob ever took, and the only public comment he ever made on the protest of the university faculty, was brought forth five years later by a concurrent resolution which Senator

Henry A. Huber introduced in the Wisconsin senate. The resolution, as introduced on January 19, 1923, proposed the documents signed by the faculty should be turned over by the curator of the State Historical Society to the Superintendent of Public Property, and that he "cause the same to be publicly destroyed by burning." The preamble declared the documents contained "libelous aspersions on the record and character of Robert M. La Follette, Wisconsin's most distinguished citizen," which should be destroyed because many members of the faculty had been induced to sign "under duress and intimidation" and now desired "the wrong, done to Senator La Follette effaced from the public records." As a further reason for burning them, it noted that the people of Wisconsin had recently reelected "Senator La Follette by a majority of three hundred one thousand three hundred sixty-five votes, the largest vote ever given to a public official of this state, strongly endorsing his public record and repudiating his detractors."[61] The resolution was referred to the judiciary committee. There seemed no doubt that it would pass both senate and assembly.

The next day Bob learned from the newspapers that the resolution had been introduced. Later he wrote the following letter to Senator Huber:

"I deeply appreciate the spirit which prompted you to introduce this resolution and the desire on your part to rectify in so far as possible what has seemed to you to be an unfair and libelous attack upon me.

"The signing and promulgation of that resolution by members of the faculty of the University of which I am an alumnus was a source of deep regret and disappointment. Many of them had been life-long friends and associates. Before the experience of the war, I would not have believed that they could bring themselves to impugn my loyalty and devotion to the best interests of this country. However, the support and steadfastness of you and many others gave me great compensation which was a source of strength to me in doing my duty to my state and my country, as it was given to me to see it.

"Time is the great sifter and winnower of truth. The formal destruction of that document cannot change the fact of its existence. I stated many times from the public platform in Wisconsin during the recent campaigns that I would not change my record on the war with any man in the United States Senate. History alone can judge impartially. So far as I am personally concerned, I am well content that this document shall remain as a physical evidence of the hysteria attendant upon the war.

"It seems to me that our energies should be devoted toward bringing our institutions back to the principles upon which they were founded, and which are the true source of our greatness.

"This applies with special significance to the University, and we can perform no greater service toward all our institutions than to see to it that the great University of Wisconsin ever continues that winnowing and sifting by which alone the truth can be found is made a reality and not a fiction."[62]

The *New York Times* conceded that Bob's letter had prevented the burning of the documents. After quoting portions of two paragraphs in an editorial, it stated, "On that platform the Senator deserves the support of all his fellow-alumni, and of everybody else, no matter what may be thought of his war record."[63] The documents remained in the Library of the State Historical Society, where the faculty committee had deposited them on February 2, 1918. But a substitute resolution, introduced by Senator Huber a month after Bob had written him, was passed by the senate 17 to 12 and concurred in by the assembly 81 to 11. It stated, "That the action of those members of the faculty of the University of Wisconsin who caused said documents to be circulated in the university and filed in the historical library, both state institutions, which are and of right should be free from coercive partisan influences, is hereby condemned as unworthy of men employed in Wisconsin's greatest educational institution."[64]

Less than a week after Bob had first learned that faculty members were signing a protest against him, an incident occurred which reflects indirectly how much everything connected with the University of Wisconsin meant to him. On January 19, 1918, Belle was called from the breakfast table to the telephone to receive a telegram from Phil reporting the good news that he had won the joint debate for Athenae, the literary society of which his father had also been a member. The joint debate between Athenae and Hesperia had been one of the most important events in the university's forensic calendar when Bob and Belle were students. Later that morning Belle wrote Phil describing his father's response to the victory: "We had been talking about your joint debate before we came down stairs. When I came back from the phone and told him you had won four out of five, he certainly was a proud and happy man. I am sure you can hear him telling the folks at the table what it meant to win the joint debate—the history of the Athenean Society —the University and all. It would have done your heart good to see how deep down glad he was. After he came up stairs too, he expressed his great satisfaction. I do not think any honor you could have won at the University would mean more to Daddy."[65]

CHAPTER LIII

Ancient Enemies and Former

Friends Unite

On the day that the newspapers had reported the circulation of the university faculty protest, Bob, Jr., had written what he himself characterized as a "bitter epistle" to his brother Phil.[1] He had met all the previous condemnations of his father with extraordinary detachment and objectivity as a part of the day's work. The unusual intensity of his reaction to this episode undoubtedly reflected his intuitive understanding of the deep though silent suffering this particular accusation of disloyalty had caused his father.

For months, Bob, Jr., had been working under intense strain, carrying a heavy load on many fronts. In addition to all his other responsibilities, he had undertaken to write a news letter which was going out to forty-five papers under the title of "The Week In Washington." In the last one, which had been sent off on January 15, he had described arrangements to send out "peace speakers" recently made by George Creel, "chairman of the committee on public information and general 'handyman' around the White House." Creel saw the news letter and wrote a protest reprimanding Bob, Jr., for circulating "rumors." Bob, Jr., drafted a sharp answer, denying the charge, citing sources, and offering, if necessary, to give "additional evidence" which he had not used because he had not wished to embarrass Creel's efforts in this direction.[2] But the reply he drafted was never sent. Before it was finally typed and signed, he suddenly became very ill. On Sunday morning, January 28, he came down to breakfast saying that the house seemed chilly and that he thought he had taken cold during the night because he was too sleepy to close the window when a high wind began to

854

blow. Although he protested that he was not ill, there was a look in his face which made his mother anxious, and she sent for a thermometer. His temperature was 103 2/5. Dr. B. M. Randolph was called, and attended him during the long illness that followed. Dr. Charles Mayo was in Washington, and he came with Dr. Randolph to see him. Throughout the months that brought one crisis after another, the Doctors Mayo gave Bob every counsel that physicians in the research laboratories of the Mayo clinic had in the days when there was no specific treatment known for streptococcic pneumonia.[3]

By the end of January, Bob, Jr., was so seriously ill that in addition to his mother's constant care it became necessary to have two nurses. His father telegraphed to a friend in Madison that an active streptococcic infection had developed, and it had "made more rapid progress within five days than in the same number of weeks in former attack. We must have Doctor Fox, if it is a possibility. Check on magazine account for two fifty. Give him the money and beg him to come and stay a few days. We want him as never before. Dr. Randolph wants him also."[4] During the many months that Bob, Jr., was gravely ill, there were brief intervals of seeming improvement which were followed each time by acute crises accompanied by intense pain. While these sieges were running their cycles, Bob was so apprehensive that he could not sleep. He would slip into his son's room frequently at night to look at the nurse's chart. Throughout the day he stayed at home within immediate call at any moment. He was constantly on the alert for everything that might even briefly lighten the tension of his son's suffering. Any amusing incident or story that he read or heard he would relate to him in his inimitable way, concealing his anxiety beneath his wit and humor as long as he was in his son's room. Each evening Hannan came to the house to report the day's happenings in the Senate and to get Bob's counsel on important matters that no one else could decide.

Shortly before Bob, Jr., had been taken ill, Gilbert Roe had gone to Madison to assist Crownhart and Corrigan in the libel suit against Richard Lloyd Jones. While there he had talked over with Crownhart the two other libel suits and the recent political developments. On his return Roe had stopped off in Washington, where he "went over the whole situation" with Bob. But after this talk he wrote

Crownhart that Bob, Jr.'s, "desperate illness" made it impossible for his father "to get his mind concentrated on this or any other matter." Roe added: "I am afraid the lad is in for a long siege and that the family will be under severe strain for weeks. We will all do the best we can, however, with everything and that is all that is humanly possible."[5] It was in this spirit that these two friends collaborated in helping Bob throughout the devastating months that followed.

The proceedings in the libel suits during January and February, which included the preliminary examinations of Richard Lloyd Jones and three directors of the Madison Club, seemed temporarily to improve the situation in Madison. Crownhart wrote Bob that friends who had previously "been cowed into silence through the activities of the Defense Council and the newspapers" were "becoming more active" and his enemies "less bold."[6] But behind the scenes the latter persistently continued their activities. The day after the first session in Richard Lloyd Jones' examination, the official court reporter wrote to inform the Committee on Privileges and Elections that material regarding the St. Paul speech had been brought out which might be useful in the investigation of "the Wisconsin Senator's disloyalty, treason, etc.," and that counsel had told him it would be "thoroly worked over the next hearing." He also suggested that if a copy of the testimony was desired he would like to know as early as possible.[7]

Although neither Bob nor his attorneys knew it, Jones' counsel, Emerson Ela, wrote three days later to Joseph P. Tumulty to ask whether the President had actually issued the statement regarding "a little group of wilful men" and whether he had intended to convey the idea that La Follette was one of the group. He also asked if it would be possible to take a brief deposition of the President to use at the trial. The letter was submitted to the President, who dictated a memorandum to Tumulty saying he thought it would not be proper for him to make a deposition, but that the attorneys were at liberty to use any statement he had made, and that Ela ought to know Senator La Follette was one of the men to whom he had referred.[8]

Thus the pattern of influences relating to Bob was woven back and forth from Wisconsin to the National Capital. When a special dispatch sent out from Washington was published in the New York

World, known to be a strong Administration newspaper, Roe thought it sufficiently authentic to send on to Bob.[9] The report stated that several attempts to resume the La Follette investigation had failed because it had been impossible to get a quorum but that Pomerene had said he would see this inquiry to a finish before the session was over.[10] On February 4 Governor Philipp, in a speech under the auspices of the County Council of Defense at Watertown, Wisconsin, called upon La Follette to resign and submit his case to a vote of the people. [11]

The governor's challenge captured front-page headlines in the Wisconsin newspapers on the morning of the same day the Committee on Privileges and Elections met in Washington. The proceedings of this meeting were not reported in the press, although a Washington newspaper stated no action had been taken.[12] But a confidential report came to Bob and Roe through Hannan. Senator Reed had made a long argument to the effect that "accepting every statement reported to have been made by Senator La Follette as contained in the speech submitted by the Minnesota Safety Commission or [by] Senator La Follette, that there was nothing to investigate; that there was no offense." But Pomerene and Senator Ollie James had been very insistent that the committee should go on with the investigation. Senator Kenyon favored condemning the speech but said he would not favor doing anything against La Follette. The committee had adjourned, subject to Pomerene's call, with a tentative understanding that the full committee would meet on Friday, February 8. The reports Hannan received from "a very reliable source" all seemed to indicate that the harassing policy of postponement might soon be replaced by action. That same day Hannan wrote Roe, "The Senator believes you should rush the brief so as to have it for use either in the committee or on the floor.[13]

The day before Bob expected the full committee to meet, an alarming crisis developed in Bob, Jr.'s, illness when his temperature shot up to 103 4/5 early in the afternoon. That evening Dr. Randolph decided there was a focus of acute infection. The next morning he brought another physician for consultation. The suspected spot in the pleural cavity was tested by inserting a needle which drew out pus. They advised an immediate operation. In less than an hour Bob, Jr., and his mother and father were at the hospital. His father went with him to the operating room at eleven o'clock and was present while Dr. Mitchell operated. His mother waited in the room until they returned at 12:15. That evening she wrote Fola that Bob, Jr., had stood the operation well and that she thought his father was more composed than he had "been at any time since Bobbie was taken ill. Perhaps we all feel steadied by the hope that this may mean a clearing up of the poison in his system and yet we can not be sure. This experience brings us all close together. I seem to think of you all and long to be helpful to my nestlings in their distress. And I think with horror of all the needless agony of war. How can it go on."[14]

While Bob, Jr., was still critically ill in the hospital, a political contest which had been brewing for months in Wisconsin brought additional anxieties to his father. When Senator Husting died in October, 1917, Bob had been designated one of the honorary pall-bearers and had gone to Wisconsin with Bob, Jr., and the Congressional delegation to attend the funeral. The *New York Times* had published the President's and Bob's tributes in the same issue. It had also predicted that the election of Husting's successor would "test the strength of the La Follette anti-war propaganda in the State" and had reported that leaders of both parties in Washington said the election would have "profound national importance" because it would determine where Wisconsin stood on the nation's war policy.[15] Contemporary correspondence and the President's subsequent direct intervention in the Wisconsin campaign indicate that Wilson and his secretary Joseph Tumulty shared this opinion.[16]

The contest for the Senatorship became national headline news. Soon after Husting's death Governor Philipp had announced that he intended to call a special session of the legislature, and would ask for legislation permitting him to appoint a successor. Bob appealed to progressive citizens irrespective of party to defeat this scheme by "insistently" demanding the right that the progressive 1913 legislature had given them to choose their Senator by ballot.[17] Philipp finally issued a call for the legislature to meet on Tuesday, February 19. On Monday night Philipp let it be known that he would designate Lenroot to fill the unexpired term if granted the appointive power.[18] The *Wisconsin State Journal* promptly declared that if Philipp would bind himself to "place Lenroot in the Senate, the legislature ought to vote that power and vote it without debate or delay."[19] The legislature refused to grant the appointive power, and on February 22 the governor issued a call for a primary on March 19 to be followed by a special election on April 2. Announcements of candidacies followed.

The Democratic nomination was contested by two candidates, Charles McCarthy and Joseph Davies, who resigned as chairman of the Federal Trade Commission to run for the Senate. Victor Berger was the Socialist candidate. Three men came out for the Republican nomination. Former Governor Francis E. McGovern announced his candidacy the morning after the call was issued. Two days later James Thompson, a leading lawyer in the western part of the State, became a candidate on a ten-point platform which included vigorous prosecution of the war, a prompt statement of our war aims by Congress, and a heavy tax on war profits.[20] Thompson had never held any state office but had been elected in 1916 as a La Follette delegate at large to the Republican National Convention.

The day after McGovern's announcement Congressman Lenroot, who was in Washington, had authorized the circulation of his nomination papers during a telephone talk with Richard Lloyd Jones in Madison.[21] A few days later he announced that the sole issue of his campaign would be loyalty to the government.[22] Prominent stalwart Republicans soon followed Governor Philipp's lead in endorsing Lenroot. Men who had long been Lenroot's and Bob's political enemies joined certain progressive Republicans, hostile to Bob since the war, and called a conference to meet in Milwaukee on March 4.[23]

Simultaneously another bitter contest had been taking place in the legislature. At a Republican caucus a stalwart senator, Timothy Burke, president pro tem of the senate, had presented a resolution which "flayed La Follette for disloyalty," but it had been sidetracked by a loyalty resolution which mentioned no names. On the third day of the session Charles D. Rosa, a progressive Republican, introduced a resolution in the assembly which summarized Wisconsin's excellent war record, pledged loyalty and undivided support to the National Government in the prosecution of the war to a successful end, and condemned "as unpatriotic all activities which seek to breed the spirit of disloyalty among the people of our state." After an amendment to censure La Follette had been defeated, this resolution passed the assembly on February 21, by 80 to 11. When it went to the senate that same day, Senator M. W. Perry offered an amendment in the form of an insert which would have made the resolution read, "we condemn as unpatriotic all activities of Senator La Follette and others in congress who seek to breed the spirit of disloyalty among the people of our state." By unanimous consent the resolution and the amendment went over to the Tuesday calendar of the following week.[24] That night Fred Holmes telephoned Bob that the assembly had refused to censure him. He and all the family were happy to have the good news to report to Bob, Jr., on the next day's visit to the hospital.[25]

When the resolution came up on Saturday afternoon in advance of the calendar schedule, Henry A. Huber vigorously opposed the Perry amendment in a speech which took over an hour to read. He reviewed Bob's record in the Senate, citing some sixty specific war measures and amendments La Follette had either voted for or sponsored in support of the war and its financing. Charging that "The truth has been suppressed; his actions misrepresented; words put into his mouth he never uttered, nor even thought," he told the senators that La Follette had in fact "faced ruin of his reputation, accepted disgrace, opprobrium, hatred, and scorn; sacrificed money and friends to be true to his constituency and his convictions."[26]

The senate adjourned that night without voting on the amendment. At the session on Monday the galleries were crowded with men and women who anticipated a dramatic scene. The Perry amendment was withdrawn by unanimous consent, and another substituted which had been offered by Senator Roy P. Wilcox. It condemned "Senator Robert M. La Follette and all others who have failed to see the righteousness of our nation's cause, who have failed to support our government in matters vital to the winning of the war" and denounced "any attitude or utterances of theirs which has tended to incite sedition among the people of our country and to injure Wisconsin's fair name before the free peoples of the world." During the debate that followed six senators attacked the speech Huber had made on Saturday. Some even asserted La Follette had written it. They charged La Follette with treason and inciting to sedition, likened him to Judas Iscariot, Vallandigham, and Benedict Arnold. A senator who was a member of the American Bar Association read a long list of newspapers, persons, and organizations that had condemned him as proof of La Follette's guilt because he had not denied their charges. One senator read a transcript of a stenographic report of the St. Paul speech and quoted Senator Kellogg's denunciation of La Follette delivered in that same city on November 16. Senator Timothy Burke declared that in all the thirty years La Follette had been in public life "no words of patriotism or loyalty have escaped his lips" and that he had become a "sort of a legislative degenerate citizen." Wilcox made the final denunciation, and closed by saying the President "has referred to our senator as the leader of a little group of wilful men, obstructing our government. We must choose, senators, 'Are you for La Follette, or are you for our commander-in-chief, Woodrow Wilson, the president of the United States?' The people of the state of Wisconsin are for the president, and I am sure, senators, that you are." The Wilcox amendment was adopted 22 to 7. Thereupon the loyalty resolution with the amendment was passed 26 to 3 and went back to the assembly where it brought on a bitter fight that recalled the legislative battles of the early progressive movement in Wisconsin.[27] Bob made no public comment on this resolution.[28] But he sent a rush telegram to Roe in New York saying, "Go soon as possible they want and expect you Tuesday night."[29] Roe arrived in Madison as scheduled.

A staff correspondent for the New York *Sun*, who covered the assembly debate on the resolution, telegraphed his newspaper that La Follette was at the "lowest ebb of his career. The State Senate has branded him as a seditionist. Senators, cured of La Folletteism have stood up in their Chamber and called him a traitor and a person no decent man would associate with." As further evidence of La Follette's degradation this correspondent cited the expulsion from the Madison Club and explained that this was "a political and social event which can best be understood in the East if one imagines the Union League Club of New York expelling Charles E. Hughes for disloyalty to the United States," and added that "With one or two exceptions, every newspaper in the State denounces him. He is wabbling, toppling and reeling."[30]

Thus, although Bob was not running for office, he was made an issue in both the primary and election campaigns by the Republicans and the Democrats. On March 1 the *Milwaukee Journal*, which was supporting Davies and following the Administration line, called upon each candidate to declare publicly whether or not he would vote for La Follette's expulsion if elected to the Senate. Davies telegraphed from Washington: "My answer to your question is the same response Paul Husting would have made had he lived today. It is emphatically yes."[31] Charles McCarthy answered, "I would give him a fair hearing, as every man is entitled to, and if he cannot explain satisfactorily his attitude, I would vote without hesitation to expel him at once."[32] McGovern stated, "were I in the Senate now I would stand for his, La Follette's expulsion."[33] James Thompson replied that if elected, he must enter the Senate with a free mind as would a judge or juryman.[34] Lenroot also refused to answer the question as presented by the *Milwaukee Journal.*[35]

While the candidates' answers were appearing in Wisconsin newspapers, front-page headlines were also reporting the bitter battle that had been going on for several days in the assembly over concurring in the Wilcox amendment condemning La Follette. Both sides were fighting with every parliamentary device. A special dispatch sent out from Madison to the New York *World* on March 3 reported that "Attorney Gilbert E. Roe of New York City, former law partner of La Follette and an adroit parliamentarian," had been conferring with members of the assembly and giving them suggestions which might "save the Senator from censure."[36] In a letter from Madison on March 4, Phil told his mother and father that although the issue was still in doubt he thought there was little question that the Wilcox amendment would pass.[37]

That same day the unofficial Republican conference met in Milwaukee to decide whether it would endorse Lenroot or McGovern for United States Senator in the primary. It was composed of 148 invited delegates from 68 different towns and cities, 35 being from Milwaukee. Among these were Senator Timothy Burke and five other senators who had voted for the Wilcox amendment condemning La Follette. An unsuccessful effort was made to require each candidate to declare where he stood on expelling La Follette. A resolution was unanimously passed condemning the war attitude and conduct of La Follette, and a message was sent to Republican members of the assembly requesting them to concur immediately in the loyalty resolution with the Wilcox amendment. The conference endorsed Lenroot as the regular Republican candidate by a vote of 87 to McGovern's 45. It also empowered the chairman,

Willet M. Spooner, son of former Senator John C. Spooner, to name one man in each county to organize supporters for Lenroot.[38]

Thus Lenroot now had the support of Governor Philipp and other old-line Stalwarts who had long been his political enemies. He also had the active support of progressive Republicans who had turned against La Follette and were now joining the Stalwarts in passing resolutions condemning him as disloyal to his country. The leading stalwart newspaper of the State, the *Milwaukee Sentinel*, declared Lenroot the strongest and most eligible Republican candidate, and promised "hearty and unstinted support."[39]

Lenroot's endorsement and the condemnation of La Follette made front-page headlines in newspapers outside the State which also reported that McGovern defied the decision of the conference and refused to withdraw from the race.[40] The New York *Sun* staff correspondent predicted that with Lenroot and McGovern at each other's throats Thompson might capture the Republican nomination.[41] The prospect that a La Follette candidate might win so alarmed Senator Lodge that he telegraphed Roosevelt asking him to urge McGovern to withdraw.[42] The colonel sent a telegram beseeching McGovern in the interest of patriotism to make the great sacrifice of withdrawing in Lenroot's favor so that a united front could be presented to the common enemy of real Americanism and the calamity avoided of letting the fight become a contest between a La Follette man and a Democrat.[43] The day McGovern received this telegram he wrote Roosevelt a long letter impugning Lenroot's loyalty because of his refusal to censure La Follette, and flatly telling the colonel he would not budge an inch to clear the way for Lenroot.[44]

Two days after the Milwaukee conference the newspaper headlines played up the outcome of the battle which had been on for a week in the Wisconsin assembly over the adoption of the loyalty resolution with the Wilcox amendment inserted by the senate.[45] Intermittent sessions had culminated in a continuous session of more than twenty-six hours. Fifteen hours of this time had been under a call of the house to prevent assemblymen from leaving town. Excitement was intense. The galleries and lobby of the capitol were crowded with men and women. On the morning of March 6, after an all-night vigil, three assemblymen spoke in Bob's defense. They were Charles D. Rosa, William T. Evjue, editor of the *Capital*

Times, and Henry Ohl, Jr., a member of the executive board of the Wisconsin Federation of Labor. Ohl declared that "notwithstanding the reports of the newspapers," he did not believe the people of Wisconsin wished to condemn La Follette. He told the assemblymen that during La Follette's St. Paul speech he had been seated on the platform and that when he read the quoted extracts in the press reports he knew the newspapers had "deliberately lied as to what the senator had said."[46]

The longest speech in Bob's defense was made by Evjue. In answer to repeated assertions made in previous speeches that La Follette had never denied the charges published in the press, Evjue called attention to the libel suits Bob had brought against two Madison newspapers and three directors of the Madison Club. Preliminary examinations in the libel suits against these directors and the *Wisconsin State Journal* had been held during the first week of the special session. Thus Evjue was able to make effective use of facts which Bob's attorneys had brought out publicly for the first time through examination under oath of the three directors and Richard Lloyd Jones, editor and owner of the *Wisconsin State Journal.* To this testimony Evjue added certain other information acquired while he was still business manager of that newspaper.

In analyzing the influences brought to bear on the newspaper and on other organizations which had met in Madison and passed resolutions calling for La Follette's expulsion from the Senate, he named names and identified men who had long been La Follette's political enemies. When he had finished his interpretation of the interlocking underground influences he believed chiefly responsible, he told his colleagues that after working ten years on newspapers he knew how these things were manipulated and that he was not going to base his vote "on a case manufactured by the newspapers." In closing he said: "The senior senator and his wife are not interested in the action you people take here today. They have another proposition at Washington that is worrying them a whole lot more at the present time. For the past three or four weeks their son has been at the point of death. They have been at his bedside continually for the past two weeks. Now, I want to tell you people that in view of that, you can take your 'pound of political flesh' if you want to, but I want to tell you that I am not going to be a party to it." After further debate and roll calls on substitute amendments, the loyalty resolution with the Wilcox amendment passed shortly after noon on March 6, by 53 to 32 with 15 senators absent and not voting.[47] The New York *World* quoted the resolution in an editorial entitled "La Follette The Outcast," and commented that since the people who knew La Follette best had passed judgment upon him, "Why should the United States Senate hesitate to deal with the outcast?"[48]

Two days after the resolution passed the assembly, Lenroot opened his campaign in Madison. Among those who sponsored his candidacy by sitting on the platform were Professors John R. Commons and Richard T. Ely, former Governor James O. Davidson, Justice A. J. Vinje of the Wisconsin Supreme Court, John M. Olin, and Richard Lloyd Jones. Former state Senator A. W. Sanborn, Lenroot's campaign manager, introduced him. The meeting was held in the university gymnasium where Lenroot had presided so brilliantly over the Republican State Convention in 1904, when the Stalwarts had bolted to hold their rump convention at the Fuller Opera House. From this same platform, after the hard-fought contest, he had introduced Bob to a cheering crowd of more than two thousand people. On the night of March 8, 1918, Lenroot read a carefully prepared speech which brought forth the greatest demonstration of the entire evening from an audience of some six hundred when he said, "I have been asked whether I condemn Senator La Follette's attitude toward the war. My record in Congress upon the armed neutrality bill, the declaration of war and the conscription act, answers the question for I could not approve his attitude upon those questions without condemning my own. I do not approve of his attitude and I could not support any man who does approve it."[49]

Lenroot ignored McGovern and focused his attack upon his most formidable opponent for the Republican senatorial nomination. Stating he had known Thompson "as a man of high character and ability," he nevertheless described him as "the candidate around whom the enemies of this war are rallying" and charged that "the disloyal support" would be divided between him and the Socialist candidate, Victor Berger. He also expressed regret that within his own party there was any candidate "the disloyal element in our state is willing to support," and questioned Thompson on specific points in his platform.[50]

In a long statement, given out from Madison, Thompson replied to these questions, and reproached Lenroot for having unreservedly condemned La Follette in a speech that "accorded him none of the presumptions of wisdom."[51] The day before this statement was released, Hannan, who had recently arrived in Wisconsin to help in the campaign, wrote Bob that the people he met, including friends and some bitter enemies, were predicting Thompson's nomination and that so far as sentiment was concerned it looked like "an easy win in the primary."[52]

But two days after Hannan sent this report, the situation suddenly took a new turn. The front pages of many newspapers in Wisconsin and elsewhere carried dispatches from Milwaukee announcing that McGovern had withdrawn in favor of Lenroot. The *New York Times* headlines reported McGovern had quit to "Help Beat La Follette Man."[53] Hannan was in Milwaukee at the time, and wrote Bob that immediately after giving the announcement of his withdrawal to the press McGovern went into conference with McCarthy. After more than an hour's talk, the two men "left the hotel arm-in-arm."[54]

On the night that McGovern's withdrawal of his candidacy was given to the newspapers in Milwaukee, Thompson's statement replying to Lenroot's Madison speech and an endorsement of Thompson signed by Bob were given to the press from Madison. Because the release dates were the same, both McGovern's announcement and Thompson's statement were published on March 12. Bob's endorsement appeared the following day. The *Wisconsin State Journal* carried this, and on the same page it also published a statement by Lenroot's campaign manager, former state Senator A. W. Sanborn, declaring the voter must decide whether to vote for "the Thompson-La Follette war stand and to discredit the noble work of American soldiers now in the trenches in France, or for Lenroot and loyal, enthusiastic support of the President in the prosecution of the war to a victorious finish. Lenroot stands for America; Thompson for La Follette."[55]

From this time on, Lenroot's attacks upon Thompson were intensified, and as the primary drew near he became less restrained in his references to Bob. At a meeting in Milwaukee, where Mc-

Govern introduced him and denounced Bob, Lenroot was reported to have said in reply to a question regarding his condemnation of La Follette: "No one regrets more than I do the change that has taken place. I do not gladly engage in this campaign, for it becomes necessary to say the words that patriotism demand should be said. But I want to say to my young friend, that in my long association with Senator La Follette I learned one thing from him because he used to repeat it to me often, and that was that it is the duty of a man to follow wherever his convictions may lead him, irrespective of the consequences. My duty tonight is to my flag and to nobody else . . . it is a source of great regret to me that it becomes necessary to demonstrate at the polls that Wisconsin is loyal to the flag and to the country."[56] A correspondent from the stalwart Republican *Milwaukee Sentinel*, who always had a vitriolic pen for La Follette, traveled with Lenroot and sent in long, detailed reports of his meetings to this newspaper which then had a circulation of about 46,000. Following McGovern's withdrawal, nationally known correspondents began coming into the State from Eastern and Midwestern newspapers.[57] The *New York Times* and the New York *World* published editorials which led the *Milwaukee Sentinel* to burst into headlines telling its readers, "Big Wilson Papers Support Lenroot / New York Times and The World Have Editorials Favoring Him / Eyes of U.S. On State / The Times Says Hindenburg Will Attack In Badger State On March 19."[58]

Few newspapers except the *Capital Times* supported Thompson. Since he made only two speeches during the campaign, the voters had to be reached by several different media. Circulars were sent out to a hundred thousand voters. Advertisements were placed in more than eighty country newspapers and also in many daily newspapers. Crownhart neglected his own campaign for Justice of the Supreme Court to prepare material and to counsel on all moves made in the Thompson campaign. Herman Ekern gave time to these conferences and also put in days telephoning to key people in the State. Lieutenant Governor Edward F. Dithmar, Joseph D. Beck, former member of the Industrial Commission, and others traveled about in the counties where they were best known talking with men on the farms and in the workshops.[59] The generous, loyal response of friends in different parts of the State was heartening to Bob, and he took the good reports to his son at the hospital. Bob had prepared a brief letter on behalf of Thompson to be sent out whenever those in charge of the campaign thought best. It was sent out under the date of March 13 in response to a telegram he received that day from Fred Holmes.[60] The newspapers carried Bob's endorsement on the same day this letter was going into the mails at Washington.

The next day an Associated Press dispatch from Washington reported that Senator Pomerene had called a meeting of the committee for Saturday, March 16, "to resume consideration of the alleged disloyal St. Paul speech of Senator La Follette."[61] But when Saturday arrived, a Washington dispatch reported that the committee had decided upon "Another postponement in the investigation of Senator La Follette's St. Paul speech, to continue while his son is seriously ill."[62]

On Sunday Louis Seibold, who was covering the Wisconsin campaign, sent a dispatch to the New York *World* which may have been intended as an admonition to the committee. Seibold reported that La Follette was "the real, in fact the only, issue in the senatorial primary contest," and predicted that one of the results foreshadowed by the primaries would be a "demand, backed by thousands of men and women in the State, that the Senate waste no further time in expelling La Follette. Justification for such a demand, it is believed, will be found in the letter written by the Senator indorsing his candidate, Thompson, and urging his nomination and election." Seibold described the letter as containing much of the same sort of criticism as La Follette's St. Paul speech which had inspired a demand for his expulsion.[63]

The letter which the *World* reported as justification for expulsion from the Senate actually said: "Dear Friend: I am writing to ask you to take an active interest in support of Mr. James Thompson, candidate for United States Senator. The primary election is called for Tuesday, March 19th. The time is very short and I hope you will use the telephone and every other means at your command to communicate with all your friends. Urge them to go to the polls next Tuesday and vote for Mr. Thompson for United States Senator. The tax dodging profiteers and the war-hogs are trying very hard to defeat him and I want to see them properly rebuked. The way to do it is to give Thompson a big vote."[64]

At 5:36 on the morning of March 20, Hannan telegraphed Bob

from Milwaukee that the result of the primary was in doubt.[65] Early newspaper dispatches had reported that Thompson was leading Lenroot, and these returns inspired the New York *World* to denounce the result of the primary as "a humiliation and a disgrace to the Republican Party of Wisconsin." This editorial was entitled "Is Wisconsin Loyal?" On the same page was a cartoon by Rollin Kirby depicting Wisconsin as a woman looking into a mirror and about to place upon her head a German helmet. Beneath the cartoon were two words, "Loyal? Perhaps."[66] Later in the day it became evident that Lenroot had won. Final returns showed the total Republican vote was 143,958. Thompson received 70,772. Lenroot, who received 73,186, thus became the Republican nominee by 2,414 votes.[67] An editorial in the *Boston Herald* regretted his margin was small but considered him so "stalwart and aggressive in his loyalty" that his victory showed Wisconsin was "still in the Union." It declared that with Lenroot and Davies as candidates, Wisconsin stood redeemed without waiting for the April election, but caustically noted that La Follette was "still in the Senate."[68]

The evening after the primary Belle sent Phil a brief note saying: "Just a word for the mail tonight to tell you that we have not lost our nerve. Dear Daddy feels it keenly and looks upon the result as serious but his spirit is strong and rises to meet the situation. Bobbie and Mary too, are both deeply disappointed but they are well seasoned and able to measure the relative value of things."[69]

When the result of the primary was definitely known, Thompson and many of his supporters, including the *Capital Times*, came out for Lenroot. Various newspaper correspondents noted that after the primary Lenroot ceased his attacks on La Follette and wooed the Thompson vote which had so recently been denounced as disloyal. Before the end of the campaign it became evident that some of Davies' supporters were also angling for these same votes.[70] Bob did not endorse any candidate but the press reported that his signed editorial analyzing the Wisconsin primary helped Lenroot by swinging Thompson votes to him which might otherwise have gone to Berger, the Socialist candidate.[71] In this editorial, which appeared a few days before the election, Bob criticized Berger's platform regarding the war as one that could not be "defended before the American people."[72]

The President had apparently foreseen the outcome of the primary and had made his plans in advance to intervene openly in the election campaign. He had followed what he described as "the critical Senatorial contest in Wisconsin" with anxiety. Four days before the primary he had written an appeal to Vice President Marshall to go into Wisconsin after the primary and campaign for the election of Davies, which he considered of the "utmost importance." He said the attention of the country would naturally be centered upon the election "because of the universal feeling against Senator La Follette" and the question in every patriotic man's mind would be whether Wisconsin was "really loyal to the country in this time of crisis or not." He explained to Marshall that the election of Lenroot would "by no means demonstrate that loyalty" because his own record had been "one of questionable support of the dignity and rights of the country on some test occasions."[73] The day before the primary the President had also written a letter to Davies which was released for publication as soon as the result was definitely known. He thanked Davies for his "steadfast loyalty and patriotism during that trying period before we were thrust into the war," and suggested that it should always be a source of satisfaction to Davies that he had "proved true" when "The McLemore Resolution, the Embargo Issue, and the Armed Neutrality Measure presented the first opportunities to apply the acid test in our country to disclose true loyalty and genuine Americanism."[74]

The President's letter was interpreted throughout the election campaign as intended to reflect upon Lenroot's loyalty, although Wilson had not mentioned his name.[75] Lenroot himself so interpreted it in a speech at Janesville where he called attention to the fact that he had voted for the declaration of war and had supported all of Wilson's subsequent war policies.[76] Since he had also voted for the Armed Neutrality bill,[77] the only "acid tests" on which his "true loyalty and genuine Americanism" could be attacked were his differences of opinion with the President regarding the McLemore resolution in 1916 and the embargo on arms which never came to a vote.

Throughout the campaign the nationally prominent Democrats who came to Wisconsin to speak followed this line and urged the election of Davies as the only candidate whose loyalty was acceptable to the President. Among them was Senator Key Pittman of the

Foreign Relations Committee, who denounced the supporters of the McLemore resolution as having sought to pass a measure that was not only "vicious and disloyal" but also "an usurpation of executive authority," and told Wisconsin voters they had no right to force Lenroot upon their Commander-in-Chief during a war.[78] Responding to the President's appeal for help, Vice President Marshall delivered a widely publicized speech to an immense audience in Madison, where he endorsed Davies. As reported in the newspapers, he also made what was interpreted as a vitriolic attack on the loyalty of Lenroot, La Follette, and all who had supported Thompson, although he did not mention their names. Admonishing Republicans to forego partisanship and thereby save Wisconsin to the Union, he declared: "Your state is under suspicion, you Republicans have made the issue here in Wisconsin. If the vote at the primary is based upon the charges and counter charges which you have made each against the other you are about half for America, half for the Kaiser, and all against Wilson. . . . Having purified the stream in the primary you welcome the sewage to help you over the election. . . . No Republican, as disclosed by the primaries, can be elected to the senate of the United States without receiving votes which in the primary were characterized as 'disloyal votes.' "[79]

During the ensuing days before election, the most bitterly partisan campaign Wisconsin had known in many years swept the State and touched off angry debate in the Senate and House at Washington. The day after Marshall's speech John Sharp Williams aroused the indignation of Republican Senators when he referred to the election in Wisconsin as taking place "between loyalists and disloyalists," and attacked Lenroot's record on war issues, inaccurately charging him with having voted against the Armed Neutrality bill and the declaration of war.[80] Senator Smoot answered him in a speech defending Lenroot's loyalty and criticizing Wilson's letter to Davies, which he said disclosed that the President was "willing to use the prestige of his high office for partisan purposes in time of war."[81]

Williams returned to the attack on Lenroot the next day by reading a long article published in the *Milwaukee Journal*. It quoted excerpts from the *Germania Herald* and various Republican newspapers urging support of Davies and the withdrawal of Lenroot to ensure election of the President's choice. As Williams came upon a hostile reference in an editorial from the Wisconsin *Eau Claire Telegram* to "the Republican Senator who has made most of the trouble," he interrupted his reading to say to his colleagues, "Of course, that refers to the present Senator from Wisconsin, who ought to be expelled from this body."[82] Newspaper headlines from East to West blazoned the report that the expulsion of La Follette had been demanded on the floor of the Senate.[83]

Williams received telegrams and letters commending his speech and urging that La Follette should be kicked out, jailed, or put up against a wall and shot with other traitors and spies.[84] Apparently only one letter, written by a man in Indiana, protested against the attack and suggested that La Follette's position on taxation had long ago incurred the hostility of big business and had something to do with it at present.[85] Williams' answers to these communications reveal that in his public utterances he had restrained the intensity of his fury against La Follette. To a telegram from a man in Tampa, Florida, stating La Follette should be put out of the Senate, branded as a traitor, and that all traitors and spies should be hung, he replied that he agreed.[86] To a man in Missouri who wrote congratulating him on his speech and asking what was the matter with the committee which was investigating La Follette, Williams said he thought they were "afraid,—politically afraid"; that if La Follette got low enough in Wisconsin they would kick him, but if he kept high enough maybe they wouldn't.[87] The day before the Wisconsin election Williams wrote Theodore Roosevelt asking his views on expelling La Follette. He told the colonel they could easily get a majority vote in the Senate, and suggested that if Roosevelt would come out in favor of it they might get the two-thirds vote needed to expel.[88]

In the same issue of the New York *World* that carried Williams' attack on La Follette and Lenroot, a dispatch from Milwaukee reported that Wisconsin newspapers, irrespective of politics, had printed the previous day big display advertisements endorsing Lenroot, signed by thirty-three of the forty-four Republicans in the Senate.[89] An editorial in the *Milwaukee Journal* noted that in Wisconsin Republican politicians were almost "at the point of explosion" over "the partisanship of President Wilson."[90] The *Milwaukee Sentinel*, which was supporting Lenroot, declared: "The lash of insult to the loyalty of republicans of Wisconsin" had "so stung the republican party of the state as to reunite it to a degree that has not been seen for twenty years." Davies, who needed Republican votes to be elected, apparently became alarmed, and protested that party politicians were "trying to whip up old party feeling."[91] In an effort to capture some of these needed votes, the Democrats imported a 1912 Roosevelt "progressive" from Boston, Matthew Hale, who began his speech for Davies in a La Follette stronghold by recalling the founding of the Massachusetts progressive Republican club seven years earlier and telling the voters that "Its idol and its guiding light was La Follette of Wisconsin."[92]

Lenroot was elected by a narrow margin. Bob commented briefly on the result in his magazine, giving the vote for the three contesting candidates, "Lenroot, Republican, 163,983; Davies, Democrat, 148,923; Berger, Socialist, 110,187." He noted that during the primary campaign for the Republican nomination Lenroot had "declared that 'Loyalty' was the only issue between him and his competitors" but that as soon as the primary was over "The 'Loyalty' issue was dropped like a hot poker. Lenroot and likewise Davies, the democratic 'Loyalty' candidate sought the 'traitor' votes of Candidate Thompson with honied unction."[93]

The hardest blow the election brought to Bob was Crownhart's defeat as a candidate for the Supreme Court. This able lawyer and beloved friend had been so generous and self-sacrificing that he had neglected his own campaign to help others. The day after the election Belle wrote Phil that "Daddy stood it better than I could have believed he would. We get so we are prepared for whatever comes. I hope his strength does not fail him later."[94] Knowing Bob would be distressed by his defeat, Crownhart wrote him that same day saying: "Now, Bob, don't spend a moment worrying over this. The water has gone under the mill. There are more interesting days ahead. I am not in the least downcast. I have to work a little harder to make up lost time and money. That is nothing.

"I know the great burden you have to bear and I sympathize with you from the bottom of my heart. Mrs. C[rownhart] joins me in this. I am hoping for better news from Bobbie. Until then I feel there is little use in discussing the political situation here . . . It is not hopeless, and compared with three or four months ago is vastly improved. I don't like to see it slide back and don't think it will."[95]

CHAPTER LIV

The Associated Press Apologizes

Bob, Jr., had been allowed to leave the hospital five weeks after his operation, and plans had been made for him to go away to convalesce. But a few days after his return home, his temperature shot up again, and another crisis developed which lasted for several weeks. The streptococcic infection attacked his face and throat. His eyes were swollen shut, and for five days his throat and tongue were so swollen that it was almost impossible to swallow even liquid nourishment. Bob sent for Dr. Phil Fox, who came from Madison to spend several days with the family. Belle wrote to her son Phil that the visit "was a great blessing as always," but that his brother found "it hard to look forward to another day" because he was "so weary of illness." Two weeks later, when he seemed better, she wrote: "Papa has had almost as hard a time as Bobbie. He has been so wrought up over him He will not go to bed nights and hovers about his room But he will be all right if Bobbie keeps going ahead."[1]

The fact that Bob, Jr., had been critically ill was known to many Senators. John Sharp Williams wrote Roosevelt that everything in the La Follette case must wait until there should not be the slightest appearance of taking advantage of him while he was in domestic trouble. The two men had previously exchanged letters regarding the difficulty of securing the necessary two-thirds majority for La Follette's expulsion which they had both publicly demanded.[2] Roosevelt wrote that the only thing which made him hesitate about further effort for expulsion was that the Wisconsin voters might return La Follette to the Senate. He said he favored the worst possible punishment but thought that, from the standpoint of expediency, a resolution of severe censure might be better, and suggested Williams consult Senators Lodge and Hiram Johnson about it.[5] After showing the Senators Roosevelt's letter, Williams reported that Johnson suggested letting the whole thing lapse, but that he and Lodge were inclined to agree with the colonel that the best thing to do was to try to get a set of resolutions condemning La Follette for his utterances which would be indictable under the Espionage Act if he were not a Senator. Williams insisted, however, that the only argument in favor of a rebuke rather than expulsion was that it would be easier to get since it required only a majority vote.[4] Roosevelt promised that if Williams advocated the resolution he would cordially back it up on the outside.[5]

While this strategy was being discussed by a former President and two prominent Senators, Chairman Pomerene sought out John Hannan to explain that the committee had been waiting for a turn in Bob, Jr.'s, condition before going ahead with the hearings. After expressing sympathy for the Senator and his son, Pomerene said that there was no disposition to crowd the matter but that if Bob, Jr., improved they might plan for a definite date. Hannan immediately wrote a two-page memorandum of the talk, reported it to Bob, and also telephoned to Roe in New York.[6] Roe replied at once that he thought the purpose of the talk "was to put the burden of the delay on the Senator. This, of course, is a damn fraud. There were months of delay when we were seeking a trial before Bobbie was sick at all. Had it not been for the delay then by the Committee, the matter could have been over and disposed of." Roe suggested the kind of letter that should immediately be sent.[7]

The next day Hannan wrote Pomerene that Mr. La Follette had directed him to say that, although deeply appreciating Pomerene's expression of sympathy, he had "at no time requested any delay of the investigation"; that for "eight weeks before his son was taken ill and after the reassembling of Congress" he had been "ready and anxious that the committee take up the investigation, but the committee did not proceed."[8] Pomerene did not reply to this letter.

While waiting for an answer, Roe wrote Hannan "to have copied and to have on hand, the Walsh speech and the Kellogg speech in which they both express opinions upon the questions at issue" so that whenever the case came up Roe could call the speeches to the chairman's attention and thus show the committee the impropriety of having Kellogg and Walsh "take part in passing upon any question upon which they have already formed and expressed positive opinions."[9]

When four days passed without any response, Roe wrote Pomerene that when he had first been retained as attorney he had examined the speech in question and prepared the case, both on the law and the facts, expecting that it would be called for trial and disposed of promptly. He requested that at the earliest possible date he be permitted to submit a motion to the committee that the charges of the Minnesota Commission of Public Safety be dismissed and that the committee promptly so report to the Senate. This letter was accompanied by one from Hannan identifying Roe as Bob's attorney.[10]

These two letters were delivered to Pomerene on April 26, the same day that Roe came to Washington to spend a week working with Bob on the brief. Two weeks passed without any word from the committee.[11] Then Roe repeated his request to Pomerene in another letter which was accompanied by a note from Bob saying, "I heartily approve and endorse the request made by my attorney for a speedy hearing in my case."[12] Late Saturday afternoon, May 11, Hannan gave both letters to Pomerene, who read them hastily and said he would try to get the committee together on Monday or Tuesday to act upon Roe's letter.[13]

On Monday, May 13, Roe learned through the newspapers that a meeting had been called for Wednesday " 'to dispose' of the charges against Senator La Follette." He immediately wrote Pomerene repeating his request to be heard and asking the chairman to explain to the committee that he was in no way challenging their jurisdiction but was asking to be heard on a motion to dismiss the charges.[14] The next day Bob wrote Roe saying the committee would "try to meet" but "How many they will have no one knows—Jim Reed is away for all this week."[15] Reed's absence from Washington was disturbing since they knew from the confidential report received about one of the previous meetings that his presence was important. When the committee met on May 15, Reed was still absent but nine Members were present. They agreed without a roll call to a motion, made by King and seconded by Vardaman, to meet again at the earliest date "mutually satisfactory" for the purpose of hearing Roe.[16]

Bob made every possible effort to have a quorum present. Vardaman telegraphed Reed that the committee was to meet on May 21 "to dispose of the La Follette matter," and asked him to be present.[17] Bob wrote Phil that an argument for the dismissal of the investigation would be made, adding, "Don't know as it will be granted but we have a mighty strong brief for it."[18] Roe arrived in Washington on Sunday to complete the preparation of his argument. He found that Bob, Jr., was undergoing another painful crisis, the second since his return from the hospital.

When the committee met at one o'clock on May 21, ten Senators were present: Dillingham, Fall, Kellogg, Kenyon, King, Sherman, Vardaman, Wolcott, Walsh, and Chairman Pomerene. Bob was at home with his son, who had suffered great distress the previous night. But Hannan was present, and followed the proceedings closely. A special Washington dispatch to the New York *Sun* reported that "On the committee table in front of Chairman Pomerene (Ohio) was a bale of petitions from patriotic organizations and individuals, all over the country, including a bundle bearing Wisconsin signatures and numbering close to 200,000 in which the expulsion of Senator La Follette from the Senate was urged."[19] The petitions from Bob's State had been circulated by the Wisconsin Loyalty Legion and filed with the committee two days after the date for the hearing was reported in the press.[20]

For three hours Roe discussed Bob's St. Paul speech and the Minnesota Commission of Public Safety's petition calling for his expulsion from the Senate "as a teacher of disloyalty and sedition." After stating that he clearly understood the power of the Senate to expel any Senator for cause, or without cause, provided a two-thirds vote could be obtained, he presented his case and cited precedents as if the committee were a court and he was arguing a motion to dismiss because of the insufficiency of the facts alleged. Throughout the entire hearing he steadily maintained that there was nothing in the petition that called for any action by the committee or the Senate except to dismiss it. All the members of the committee were lawyers. Questions were frequently interjected during his review of precedents on expulsion from the Senate and the right of free speech. Many questions were obviously hostile; others seemed impartial efforts to clarify points of law.

While Roe was discussing a question of law from his brief, Kellogg interrupted to read from a recent decision rendered under the

Espionage Act. Later Roe called attention to the fact that the decision in the document from which Kellogg read was not in the *Federal Reporter* but was in a printed document containing cases under the Espionage Act. Picking up a copy of this printed document, which Roe had not seen before the committee hearing, he read the title aloud, thus making it a part of the record: "MEMORANDUM OF INFORMATION SUBMITTED TO THE COMMITTEE ON PRIVILEGES AND ELECTIONS OF THE UNITED STATES SENATE SIXTY-FIFTH CONGRESS SECOND SESSION RELATIVE TO THE RESOLUTIONS FROM THE MINNESOTA COMMISSION OF PUBLIC SAFETY PETITIONING FOR PROCEEDINGS LOOKING TO THE EXPULSION OF SENATOR ROBERT M. LA FOLLETTE, ON ACCOUNT OF A SPEECH DELIVERED BEFORE THE NONPARTISAN LEAGUE, AT ST. PAUL, MINN., ON SEPTEMBER 20, 1917."

Roe told the committee that he had not been furnished with a copy, and asked if one had been furnished to Senator La Follette. Chairman Pomerene replied that the document had been printed and was "open to circulation," adding: "You can have a copy of it any time you desire. If it was not furnished to you it was an oversight."[21] That this had been "an oversight" seemed incredible to Roe and Bob, since all the committee members were lawyers who must have known that failure to submit a document which was practically an opposition brief would have been a violation of fair legal procedure in a court.

Until that day neither Roe nor Bob had ever seen or even heard of this eighty-two-page document. Roe's persistent questioning disclosed that it had been prepared by the Department of Justice at the request of a member of the committee for a compilation of all the cases under the Espionage Act.[22] There was no indication in the document itself as to who had prepared it, but the title page showed it had been "submitted" to the committee and printed by the Government Printing Office. Toward the bottom of the page a line stated it had been "Printed for the use of the Committee on Privileges and Elections," which seemed to give it official sanction. The table of contents, arranged under the four following titles, indicates briefly the intent of the document: "Title I.—Excerpt from the speech of Robert M. La Follette. Title II.—Quotations from recent decisions under war statutes. Title III.—Congressional precedents. Title IV.—Treason defined."[23]

Shortly before the committee adjourned at five o'clock, Roe submitted his brief and requested that it be made a part of the record. That evening, when Roe returned to the La Follette home, he gave Bob a detailed account of the proceedings, including the fact that they had "sprung 'a brief'" which had been "in the Committee room doing its work for months" although neither he nor Bob had ever heard of it until that day.[24]

The next morning the *New York Times* and many other newspapers carried reports of the hearing with quotations from Roe's argument and brief.[25] When the committee met at two o'clock that afternoon, eleven Senators were present: Dillingham, Fall, Kellogg, Kenyon, King, Reed, Thompson, Vardaman, Walsh, and Wolcott, with Pomerene presiding. Before proceeding with his argument, Roe obtained permission to file a supplementary brief in reply to the document which had been prepared by the Department of Justice. He then continued his analysis of the St. Paul speech, paragraph by paragraph, steadily maintaining that it ought to be judged as a whole, including the interruptions from the audience. When Walsh and Kenyon interrupted to insist that Roe interpret the psychological meaning of the "laughter" from the audience as recorded in the transcript of the speech, Reed asked if it would not be a little dangerous "to try a man because somebody in his audience laughed."[26]

The hearing continued for four hours. Senators differed as to which statements or phrases in the speech were the most objectionable. But when Roe came to the paragraphs relating to the last voyage of the *Lusitania* and Bryan's warning to the President that the ship carried explosives and 6,000,000 rounds of ammunition, a barrage of questions interrupted Roe's argument and touched off a prolonged discussion among the Senators. Kellogg challenged any citizen's right to say that the ship carried munitions. Reed retorted that when the ship cleared from New York she was "loaded with munitions." Walsh, although hostile to Bob in most of his questions, declared there was "no doubt in the world that she carried 6,000,-000 rounds of munitions," thus supporting one of the statements Bob had made at St. Paul.[27]

After about two hours Roe informed the committee that he had completed the outline of his argument and added, "I hardly need invite questions, because I know they will be asked me anyhow."[28] From then until adjournment Roe skillfully and calmly answered a steady succession of questions many of which were by implication hostile attacks on La Follette's loyalty. Kellogg, Pomerene, and Walsh were the most persistent in apparently seeking grounds for his expulsion. Kellogg repeatedly referred to the document prepared by the Department of Justice in citing precedents tending to imply that La Follette's intention had been disloyal and that he had violated the Espionage Act. Walsh's questions and comment on various sentences and phrases taken from the St. Paul speech seemed so definitely designed to make this interpretation a part of the record that Reed broke into the discussion. He contended that for the sake of the record certain other excerpts and statements in La Follette's speech should be read in connection with the line of questioning pursued by Walsh. Insisting that the committee ought not to pass on isolated statements, Reed then read pertinent portions of the context of the speech preceding or following the sentences or phrases Walsh had selected.[29]

During the hearing Hannan had slipped out of the committee room for a few moments to telephone Bob. The call had interrupted a letter Bob was writing to Phil. When he returned to his desk, he recorded Hannan's report that "the committee members got into an argument among themselves as to whether ammunition-gunpowder-cartridges &c. were explosives" and that Roe "had to stand by and look on for quite a while." Bob promised to hold the letter for "the latest report," and commented: "Blessed be he who expects little— so I shall not be disappointed no matter what they decide. Its all in a life time and the main thing is to keep your soul clean. Then one can wait patiently for justice." At seven o'clock that evening, after Roe returned, Bob wrote Phil: "Uncle Gil just came. He was before the Committee till 6 o'clock. It was a hot session—Walsh & Pomerene fired a lot of questions. John [Hannan] just phoned me that Gil 'backed them clear off the boards,' answered and questioned and argued till they shut up. They will be against us but they got enough for once. Jim Reed cut loose during the afternoon and kept it up. He supported Gil[']s contention right up to the hilt."[30]

In a letter to Netha Roe the next day, Belle wrote: "I wish you could be here to get the impression of what has been achieved by

Gilbert in the past two days—the result of his thorough understanding and able argument and perfect control. It was a most difficult situation and he so completely mastered it that it seemed a special opportunity created for the purpose of enlightening the Committee and leading them out of the maze. Bob is deeply satisfied and restored in spirit. No words can express my gratitude & Mary & Bobbie & Fola are rejoiced."[31]

Soon after the hearings one committee member, Senator King, went out of his way to comment to Hannan "upon the remarkably good presentation" Roe had made of the case.[32] Many other messages came to Bob through Hannan.[33] One was from the Secretary of the Navy, which Bob recorded in a letter to Phil.[34] That same day Belle wrote that the reaction to Roe's argument had been "favorable far beyond anything we could expect."[35]

The hearings were more widely reported than Bob had dared hope. Many newspapers carried excerpts from Roe's argument and brief. These apparently seemed ominous to the American Defense Society, which had long been demanding La Follette's expulsion. After reading the reports of the first day's hearing, the secretary, P. D. Craig, telegraphed Pomerene asking that before any action was taken the committee give due heed to the brief of their Anti-Disloyalty Committee and stating that if private or public hearings were held they wished to appear.[36] This brief, signed by Henry Wynans Jessup of counsel, had been presented to the committee on December 3, 1917. Excerpts had been published in the press, but the committee had never furnished either Bob or his attorney with a copy.[37]

Some newspapers reported that Roe had called the committee's attention to the fact that among other misrepresentations of the St. Paul speech the *Chicago Daily Tribune,* the *Washington Post,* the *New York Times,* and many other newspapers had completely distorted La Follette's position on the war by quoting him as saying that the United States "had no grievance" against Germany and that every Associated Press dispatch published in the newspapers throughout the country the day after the speech had in substance carried it that way, although the stenographic records proved the Senator had said just the opposite.[38]

Soon after his St. Paul speech Bob had in fact called attention to this particular error. In the next issue of *La Follette's Magazine* he had quoted this phrase correctly from the certified transcript of the official stenographic record and had noted that it had been misquoted in the *Chicago Tribune,* the *Literary Digest,* the *New York Times,* the *Washington Post,* and many other newspapers.[39] A careful check of newspapers in different parts of the country had been made for him by Laura Thompson, sister of David Thompson. She had done the work at night after office hours because she was then Librarian of the Department of Labor.[40] This survey had left no doubt that the newspapers served by the Associated Press had carried the quotation in substantially the same form as the newspapers he mentioned. But he had not specifically named the Associated Press because he could not at that time be certain whether this organization "was responsible for the falsehood" or whether it had been "set afloat in the daily news currents" by one of the other news associations or by newspapers acting independently.[41]

This particular error had also been pointed out in a letter he had written Pomerene on October 11, 1917, which had been reported in many newspapers.[42] That same day the Associated Press had sent a dispatch from Washington to the New York *Evening Post* quoting the portion of Bob's letter which called Pomerene's attention to the fact that the transcript of the speech furnished him by the committee proved he had been falsely quoted as saying "We had no grievance" when he had actually said just the contrary.[43] This and other excerpts from the letter had also been carried in some of the newspapers which had so grossly misrepresented his position on the war through their inaccurate quotation and distortion of his speech.[44] The false quotation, as carried in newspapers served by the Associated Press, had also been cited in the libel suits his lawyers had started in Madison and had been discussed in the preliminary examinations which were reported in the newspapers. But neither his protests nor his libel suits had brought forth any apologies or corrections. Consequently he did not anticipate that any retractions would follow the newspaper reports of the hearings.

Therefore the retraction by the Associated Press came as a surprise to Bob and Roe when they read it in the newspapers two days after Roe had completed his argument before the committee. The apology was in the form of a long telegram to Pomerene from the assistant manager, Frederick Roy Martin, saying the Associated Press had learned for the first time on May 21, 1918, that the accuracy of their account of the St. Paul speech of September 20, 1917, was challenged. Martin stated they had immediately made a thorough investigation which convinced them that they had distributed inaccurately "one important phrase" quoting Senator La Follette as having said, "I wasn't in favor of beginning this war. We had no grievances."[45]

Martin's telegram stated that the investigation showed that the Associated Press had no staff reporter at the meeting, and that their St. Paul editor had transmitted the speech from a duplicate copy of an account written by a reporter for the *St. Paul Pioneer Press*. But Martin could not, or at least did not, explain the puzzling fact that the *St. Paul Pioneer Press* was one of the comparatively few newspapers which quoted La Follette as saying, "I wasn't in favor of beginning the war. We had grievances." Martin's telegram closed with the statement that "The error was regrettable and the Associated Press seizes the first opportunity to do justice to Senator La Follette."[46] Precisely how this error reversing the meaning of this "important phrase" crept into their dispatch and who was responsible for it will probably always remain a mystery.

On the same day that Martin's telegram was published, an editorial in the New York *Evening Post* complimented the Associated Press upon "handsomely and promptly" admitting "its grievous fault in misreporting Senator La Follette." The editorial also noted that "some one slipped the fatal word 'no' into the sentence in the Associated Press report and made it read: 'We had *no* grievances.' Whether this was done maliciously or accidentally will probably never be known, but the fact remains that irreparable injury was done to the Senator, and that a large part of the outcry against him was due to this misstatement in the one thousand newspapers which are served by the Associated Press. Senator La Follette declared at the time that the press had misquoted him, but the matter was never brought to the attention of the Associated Press until Mr. Gilbert E. Roe, his attorney, stated the fact before the Senate Committee of Inquiry on Tuesday. Why the Senator delayed so long is a mystery; but the serious wrong done by this error needs no expatiating. No amount of apology can undo it. The thought that unintentionally so extreme an injustice may be done a public man is one to sober all responsible journalists."[47]

La Follette's Magazine reprinted this editorial with a statement calling attention to the fact that Bob had "immediately publicly denied the correctness of the report of his speech, but the newspapers neglected to make any correction" and that they had "on the contrary continued for months afterward to use the false report as a text upon which to base arguments condemning the Senator and creating public sentiment against him." The statement commented further that "the injustice done the public" was far more serious than the Senator, for if "public men fighting in the interest of the public may be ruined and discredited while the fight is on, the public may lose its fight, and its servants may become intimidated and afraid to make any real fight in its behalf."[48]

The *Evening Post* editorial had been sent to Bob by his son-in-law George Middleton, who wrote that the New York papers had given quite a bit of attention to the Associated Press retraction and that the tendency seemed to be to think the matter was therefore settled.[49] After reading the newspaper reports, Roe also wrote from New York saying he thought they had "fried rather an extensive apology out of the A.P." but that he was sorry he had forgotten to mention in his argument before the committee, as he had intended to do, that he "had started a few libel suits and expected to start a few more. Evidently the A.P. anticipated this."[50] Although Roe may have been mistaken in his opinion as to what finally brought forth the belated apology from the Associated Press, there is a reliable contemporary report recording that "the eye of every client" of the Newspaper Enterprise Association was on the La Follette libel suit against Richard Lloyd Jones and the *Wisconsin State Journal*. Although this suit was not against the Newspaper Enterprise Association, many of the complaints in the case were based upon articles furnished by that organization or the United Press in which they were largely interested.[51]

Some three weeks after the Associated Press apology was published, Robert Scripps, then active head of the Newspaper Enterprise Association, asked for an appointment with Bob before leaving for Europe. As this was not possible, he suggested a talk with Hannan, who went that afternoon to Scripps' office, where he was introduced to John Perry of Cleveland, then general counsel of the Newspaper Enterprise Association and the United Press. After some preliminary talk, Scripps asked whether the Senator intended to press the suit against Jones, whom they would be compelled to defend as a client if the case were forced to trial. He explained that he had been very friendly to La Follette; that he was not in control when the articles listed in the libel suit complaint were sent out; that he wished if possible to arrive at an amicable adjustment of the suit. The attorney then discussed the libel suits and the articles furnished by the United Press and the Newspaper Enterprise Association, including some written by Charles Edward Russell. Hannan had the impression that the attorney was endeavoring to drag him "into a conversation with respect to the merits of the libel suits," and declined to discuss them since this was a matter for the Senator and his attorneys. He promised to report to the Senator what they had said.[52]

As Hannan was leaving the office, he met Negley Cochran, editor of the *Toledo News-Bee* and "one of the king-pins in the Scripps organization." Cochran discussed many things but finally got around to the libel cases and the Russell articles, explaining that Russell "was bugs" and no longer with the organization but was "now with the Creel Bureau" and that "Harry Rickey who was at the head during the time these articles were sent out" was no longer with the organization and was also with the Creel Bureau. That same day Hannan told Bob of his talk with these three men and also sent a detailed report of it in duplicate letters to Roe and Crownhart.[53]

Bob and Roe both thought that these overtures suggesting the possibility of "an amicable adjustment" indicated that the libel suits were already having some effect. From New York Roe wrote that he intended to refer to the Associated Press apology in his reply brief. In a letter accompanying a rough draft of the opening paragraphs, he asked Bob, "Do you think it pinches the Committee too much?"[54] Bob replied, "I have no suggestion to offer except that it is too damn polite." But he left the final decision to Roe by adding, "Anything you do will be right I am sure."[55]

On June 6 Roe submitted his reply brief, analyzing and answering certain cases and precedents in the document prepared by the Department of Justice. He described it as "more likely to mislead than to assist the Committee in arriving at a correct conclusion" because it failed "to apprehend clearly the nature of the present proceeding." He called attention to the fact that the document, as

printed in pamphlet form, did not indicate by whom it had been
prepared or by whom it had been submitted to the committee and
that, lacking sanction from anyone else, it naturally lent itself to
the erroneous impression that it had "in some way the approval or
authority of the Committee." Toward the end of the brief, in discussing the fourth title, "Treason defined," Roe respectfully suggested that the pamphlet ought to "be stricken from the record in
this case," because "If it remains a part of the record with no one
responsible for it except the Committee, then any evil disposed
person may, at any time, now or hereafter, quote from it most unfairly to Senator La Follette but with the apparent approval of the
Committee."[56]

The document prepared by the Department of Justice was not
included in the printed copy of the hearings which contained Roe's
brief, his reply brief, and his argument.[57] Bob, however, carefully
preserved the document as printed in pamphlet form for the use of
the committee by having it bound in book form with the reports of
the hearings.[58]

When Bob read the printed copy of the stenographic report of
these hearings, he felt that he could not let certain pages of that
record stand without protest. It seemed to him that several Senators
had repeatedly implied during their arguments with Roe that his
intent in certain portions of the St. Paul speech had been hostile
to the United States Government and disloyal to his country. He
promptly drafted a two-page letter expressing his protest against
these insinuations of disloyal intent. Then Belle, Hannan, and Bob
made several revisions of the letter. Two versions were submitted
to Roe, and his suggestions were incorporated in a final revision
which was sent on July 3, to Pomerene.[59] Apparently Pomerene
never replied to this letter, and the minutes of the meetings of the
Committee on Privileges and Elections do not record that it was
ever discussed or officially considered.[60]

CHAPTER LV

"Verily Wash Day Is at Hand"

During the months that the disloyalty charges against Bob had been before the Privileges and Elections Committee, he had been beset by harassing financial anxieties. Before his son was taken ill, he had been disturbed by the tone of letters he had received from Madison indicating that an extension of the $14,000 mortgage on his farm might be refused. In a letter early in January, 1918, to his law partner, Alf Rogers, he wrote, "One doesn't know just what to expect these days," and added, "I am sure there are people in my neighborhood who would ruin me financially and beggar my family if the slightest chance offered." His anxiety was intensified by the conviction that after the war a panic would "sweep the world, the like of which has never been seen. *Debts due will be collected.* Loans will be suspended—*borrowing impossible*—property will go down to bed rock. Every man must prepare for the storm *now*—or it will be too late—and very soon I fear." It was time, he said, to reef sails and "nail down every hatch."[1]

After his son became ill, the bills from doctors, nurses, and hospitals had consumed his salary month after month. By the middle of June, Bob, Jr.'s, illness had cost over $3,500. Bob's salary scarcely covered the ordinary living expenses, and he wrote that the $1,000 he had borrowed had "melted away under the withering expense that is literally burning me up." Since he could not earn an additional income on the platform as he had always done, he was also hard-pressed to pay the interest on outstanding notes and on a remnant of $3,800 he had borrowed to meet "a [*La Follette's*] magazine deficiency of several years before." Although he had some paid-up life insurance, other premiums were soon coming due. In a letter written on his sixty-third birthday, he said to Rogers: "If I live until the war is over I will yet go to the lecture platform and earn enough to pay my debts. If I don't the life insurance will just about clean it up." He added that he wished Rogers "could come down for a little visit. It would hearten us up a good bit in these hard days to see you. We are *all very tired.*"

As Bob had anticipated, those who held the $14,000 mortgage on his farm refused to renew it. Application was then made to the Beavers Company for which Herman Ekern was attorney. This company finally granted a mortage of $20,000. The request for the loan was presented to the board of directors by H. W. Adams, who led what he described as "one of the hardest fights we have made on any matter of this sort since I have been on the board, and we cast our first divided vote on record—standing three to two."[2] Rogers forwarded Adams' letter to Bob with a note saying Adams "showed the metal he is made of—he is a good fighter *that boy.*" Rogers also reported that Ekern had "helped a lot."[3] This loan enabled Bob to repay the previous loan with interest due and to deposit in his depleted bank account a check for $5,438.22, which helped toward meeting the heavy expenses he was under during the next few months.

Late in May Phil had written his father that he wished to enter the R.O.T.C. training camp at Fort Sheridan, and he had also asked him to make inquiries about enlisting in the Army or Navy. In one of his letters he said, "If I am to go into the service, I don't want any slacker job."[4] Bob sent Phil the information Hannan had gathered at the Army and Navy Departments and wrote that everybody had been helpful and that this "was especially true of Secretary Daniels and also of Captain now Col. Wilson. Daniels sent me some very dear messages expressing his confidence in me and his emphatic disapproval [of] the attacks which had been made upon me for the last year. He also expressed his deep sympathy with Bobbie."[5] A few days later Phil came to Washington for a brief visit before going to Fort Sheridan, Illinois, where he and his friend Joseph R. Farrington entered the R.O.T.C. for preliminary training. When a reporter sought him out at camp to ask what his father wanted him to do, Phil replied frankly and accurately, "He wants me to do just what *I* feel is right."[6] His father and mother gave this same counsel when Phil came to Washington again in July for two days to consult them about the option of continuing in the service or awaiting the draft.[7]

On the evening that Phil left to return to the camp at Fort Sheridan, he gave Mary a letter for his brother in which he said: "I have just told you good-bye but could not express to you dear old pal what my old heart felt. I didn't want to try because it would have been a miserable failure . . . You have faculties and a personality possessed by one in ten million. If you could only know the hold you have on people's thoughts and affections you would believe me when I say you have an untold future of service to the world of thought and action. But you can never know how deeply my love for you permeates every fibre of my body. . . . Thine to the end of Time's journey."[8] The letter was given to Bob, Jr., the next morning. Later Fola wrote Phil that he "was quite broken up when he read it. He said that he had longed to talk to you the night before but that he was afraid of breaking down & couldn't do it. He said again and again: 'I love Phil so—no one knows what he means to me. All the quarrels we used to have have gone into love. He is such a wonderful boy. He has such a wonderful future before him.' I promised him that I would write and try to tell you what he longed to say and couldn't. Bob was stirred to the depths of that intense nature of his . . . You are bound up in the inmost of his heart, Phil."[9]

Although Bob, Jr., was still so ill that it was necessary to have a night and day nurse, his condition had gradually improved during June. When a record-breaking heat wave descended on Washington in July, Dr. Randolph decided his patient ought to be taken at once to a higher altitude. Bob, Jr., longed for a change, but at first his father feared that the journey would be too great a strain and might cause a relapse. He finally accepted Dr. Randolph's judgment, however, when Dr. Albert J. Ochsner came to make a friendly call on Bob, Jr., and independently gave the same counsel. Fola left immediately to try to find a place in the mountains which met the conditions Dr. Randolph thought essential. After making reservations at the Homestead Hotel in Hot Springs, Virginia, she returned to Washington. On the night of July 20, Bob, Jr., was carried on a litter to the ambulance. His father and one of the nurses rode with him to the train, where Belle, Fola, and the other nurse joined them. Bob's apprehension about the journey was relieved the next morning when they arrived at Hot Springs. As he walked from the train to the hotel beside his son's litter, the tears came to his eyes when he heard Bob, Jr., say: "It's good to see the sky. I'm hungry. I'd like a lamb chop for breakfast."[10]

That afternoon Belle wrote Mary they "were all surprised—Bobbie most of all—at the way he stood the trip."[11] He enjoyed the view from his window, his appetite continued to improve, and he gained strength. They all found the hotel restful and its management perfect. But with two nurses the expense was very heavy. Belle thought if they could find a reasonable cottage Bob himself might be persuaded to take the vacation he so much needed. She also felt that going into the public dining room three times a day was a strain, although he never mentioned it. No unpleasant incident ever occurred during their stay at Hot Springs, but Belle thought that his previous experience on Washington street cars and in other public places made him always aware of the possibility. At her suggestion they began looking for a cottage. When they called on Fola's friend, Mary Johnston, in nearby Warm Springs, she offered to take them into her home with her other paying guests. During their brief visit Mary Johnston expressed her profound admiration for Bob in a way that none of them could ever forget.

Few cottages were vacant at Hot Springs, and all rents were high. But a chance cancellation made a large house near the hotel available at a reduced rate, and they took it for a month. When the lease was signed Bob immediately had word sent to Mary and Mid to join them. By his explicit instruction Mary brought another member of the family, Bud, the English bulldog. In a letter to her absent son Belle said, "With all the beloved family under one roof, the thought of you away is always present[.] When I look around the table or when we are gathered together for any purpose we say 'if only Phil were here.' "[12]

While they were at Hot Springs, Colonel Raymond Robins came from Washington to see Bob. He had recently returned from service with the Red Cross in Russia and wished to tell him about conditions in that country. Bob suggested that the entire family would be interested in hearing him. On four successive days Belle, Fola, Mary, and Mid sat on the secluded veranda, where they followed Robins' vivid narrative while Bob took detailed notes. Bob, Jr., in his wheel chair, listened from a room that gave onto the veranda.

When Bob, Jr., improved enough so that the night nurse was not needed, Bob slept in his son's room and cared for him whenever he wakened, calling the day nurse only when a hypodermic injection was needed to relieve excruciating pain. Dr. Randolph had insisted upon at least a year's convalescence where he could take sun baths and live out of doors. Early in September, Bob, Belle, Mary, and Bob, Jr., who was still unable to walk, left for California. Phil secured leave from camp at Fort Sheridan, met their train at Lafayette, rode with them to Chicago, and carried his brother across the station to the train for the West. They went directly to Pomona, where Bob, Jr., his father, and Mary stayed for a few days at the home of Belle's cousin, Anson Thomas. Belle went to look for a cottage at La Jolla, where, many years before, under the wise guidance of Dr. Fox and herself, Bob had regained his health after a severe illness. Belle wired Bob on September 12 that she had found a place "first month fifty each month thereafter forty five[.] rent of new hair mattress bed two dollars extra."[13] The following Monday they took possession of "Wayside."

Bob had counted on another week with the family to make sure they were well settled. But the much-needed holiday, after the long strain of his son's critical illness, was cut short by two telegrams on September 23 from his secretary. The first informed him that the suffrage leaders claimed "debate [on the Susan B. Anthony amendment] will be continued until arrival if you start immediately." The second, received two hours later, said, "Opposition will not give pair . . . your vote essential."[14] The Susan B. Anthony amendment, which Bob and Belle had always supported, had passed the House and was now the Senate's unfinished business. It might come to a vote at any hour.

Reluctant as he was to leave La Jolla, Bob recognized the value of Belle's "judgment of the importance of returning in time."[15] He took the train for Washington that night. When he left La Jolla, Belle went to the bus with him. They talked of the work ahead, and, as they said goodbye, she counseled him "to pursue a calm and poise that will lift you above personal things."[16] While he was on the train, the newspapers announced that the Senate Committee on Privileges and Elections had decided to postpone further consideration of the charges against him until after the election in November.[17] He arrived in Washington late Saturday afternoon, September

28, to find that a filibuster had held up the vote on the suffrage amendment.

At noon, September 30, 1918, Bob entered the Senate Chamber after eight months' absence. The New York *World* remarked that "his hair had materially whitened, but he seemed fit for the conflict."[18] Many of the Senators greeted him cordially on his return. One was noted by the press galleries to pause conspicuously before Bob's desk in the front row. In a voice that boomed above all, he said, "Glad to see you, Senator. How's the boy?" It was Penrose of Pennsylvania.

That morning Wilson had unexpectedly telephoned majority leader Martin that he would appear before the Senate at 1:00 P.M. to urge the passage of the suffrage resolution. Since 1912 the President had consistently opposed the Federal amendment granting suffrage to women. But in June, 1918, he had reversed his previous position and advocated its passage.[19] The news of the President's arrival at the Capitol, with members of his Cabinet and Mrs. Wilson, had brought crowds to the galleries and a full attendance on the floor. For thirteen minutes Wilson read with great earnestness from his small sheets of paper. As Commander in Chief of the United States armies and fleets he urged passage of the amendment as "vital to the winning of the war and to the energies alike of preparation and of battle."[20]

But this patriotic appeal apparently changed no votes. John Sharp Williams, previously critical of Senators who had opposed the President's requests, remarked, in phrases subsequently revised for the *Record*: "When the President says we can't lick Ludendorff, scare Bulgaria and recognize Palestine because nigger women in Mississippi can't vote, I decline to agree with him."[21] Williams offered an amendment to limit suffrage to white women. Bob voted to table this and all other efforts to modify the suffrage resolution. Twenty Democrats ignored the President's plea. Senator Cummins commented sarcastically, "I very much fear that 'a little group of wilful men' are about to defeat a measure which the President of the United States has declared . . . is vitally necessary for the successful prosecution of the war."[22] The votes of these twenty Democrats combined with the eastern Republicans were enough to defeat the measure. Bob's hurried return had not saved the joint resolution, for on the roll call it proved to be still two votes short of the necessary two-thirds. Bob wrote Belle that it was reported the President was "angry with Democrats for not coming in to help pass the amendment after he had declared that it was necessary as a war measure."[23]

Bob returned to make his home with the La Follette cousins at the 3320 Sixteenth Street house, which, he said, was "a mighty comfortable place to live in—if only we could all be here together."[24] Recalling the meager furnishings of the La Jolla cottage, he wrote the family: "Ev[e]ry night when I 'turn in' it is with a guilty feeling that I get into bed (Bobbies) with de lux[e]-springs and three feet thick of matrass [*sic*] under me. If I had Brian Connors* magic I would send it to you by the 'Good People.' "[25]

He found Washington in the grip of the severe influenza epidemic which was sweeping the country. Although the Senate continued to meet, the galleries were closed to the public as a precaution. Doctors were overwhelmed with calls, and it was difficult to get nurses. Both Cousin Mary La Follette and her daughter Suzanne came down with "flu." Bob helped to care for them and characteristically organized precautionary measures for the entire household.

Deeply concerned lest Phil contract influenza at the crowded camp in Oklahoma, he wrote: "You are in my mind these days when I am here all by myself. You seem a long way off—alone among strangers. Wont you arrange with someone there upon whom I can depend to *wire me* if you should happen to get sick—and *to do it promptly*. You will poo poo this—but do it just for my comfort."[26] In relating this to Belle, Bob commented, "I suppose he told them I was a nervous old boy—but I dont care I wanted it fixed that way."[27] Phil had been transferred from Fort Sheridan to Norman, Oklahoma, after receiving his commission as Second Lieutenant in the Infantry. By communicating the activities of one to another, Bob kept his scattered "Dear Ones" in close touch. For months he wrote every evening, generally after dinner. With a skilled reporter's sense of essential detail he recreated his Washington days in letters to Phil at an Oklahoma Army camp and to the little family on the Pacific coast. "As the immediate events unfold I will keep you informed," he said, "on the unreported matters—which are the controlling things—after all."[28]

* Brian Connor was a friend of Darby O'Gill's, and King of the "Good People."

These long, intimate letters were all written in his own clear script. Many contain his careful copies of important personal communications he sent to others. It had always been his habit to share the day's happenings with the family. When they were separated, he was seldom too tired to continue this life-long custom through letters, for he found it "some satisfaction to visit with you in this way for a little while."[29] In another letter he said: "Ye Gods I wish I could come in and spend the evenings with you. I think of the difference in time between here and there and calculate on 'what you are doing now'—dozens of times a day."[30] He pictured their lives and shared the minutest details in imagination. In Belle's and his children's "family letters" he found comfort. They were, he said, "a home diary and that takes us all into your home life and in a way brings us all together."[31] He revealed a fundamental quality of his relation to his family and intimate friends when he wrote, "what you do—the most trivial things to you are important to me if they are about yourselves."[32]

Throughout his letters there runs the thought for his son's recovery. Although Bob, Jr.'s, general condition was daily improving, his legs, after the many months in bed, continued so contracted that one physician advised an operation. Bob immediately consulted with leading doctors and surgeons in Washington. The consensus was that the safest way to full recovery lay in exercise. It was agony, but in a few months Bob, Jr.'s, systematic efforts made crutches and wheelchair no longer necessary. The continued pain was such, however, that Belle would massage him for hours at night so that he could sleep. When he heard of this, Bob wrote, "Be careful dear heart there are limits—even for you."[33]

Mary was helping Belle with the housework and attending the Bishop School at La Jolla. This had been founded by Miss Ellen Scripps, who, with other friendly neighbors, later did much to make their winter happy. Not long after his return, Bob wrote to Mary, "I know you want a little money of your own to spend now and then and I wont forget you—now and then and oftener when I can. . . . And you are not to measure my love for you by the size of this measly check."[34]

About a week later he received a letter from William Kent with a canceled six months' sight draft for $2,000 which he had borrowed. This letter he sent on to Belle. Kent had written: "I would feel much better to have the inclosed note cleared up. I know the great trouble you have been through and sympathize with you deeply. Please accept the release of the obligation as a proof of my friendship and interest in you."[35]

When Belle learned of this, she wrote: "I am deeply grateful for their generosity and find it lifts a real load off my mind. I have always had an unhappy sense that the debt was one of the *first* we should pay now I feel we can pay it when it is easier to do so than it has yet been. I hope he can be elected to the Senate. He has an outlook and an experience so much broader than most men in public life and Mrs. Kent's influence is the most wholesome and far reaching of any woman I know in Washington."[36]

During the weeks after Bob's return to Washington, he reported to the family the almost daily inquiries about Bob, Jr., from various Senators. He didn't believe "there was *ever* a *Senators* son about the Capitol who had so many friends—black & white high & low—as Bobbie. It isn't any perfunctory thing—they want to know—and they want to *know ev[e]ry day*. They want the latest word. And ev[e]ry one has a good thing to say and a hearty wish for his recovery and return."[37]

Hearing of the reported death of a friend's son, who was in the Army, Bob wrote: "I have been depressed all day. . . . A fine young boy—so vital and full of high spirits! Isn't it horrible that it should have been going on for more than four years—millions and millions of boys, millions and millions of mothers and fathers, brothers & sisters their happiness destroyed their homes desolated—and all for what? How will the peace terms be written—to pay for the slaughter?"[38]

Every item which indicated a step toward peace he sent on to Belle at once—sometimes by wire. On October 6 the German Chancellor, Prince Maximilian, forwarded to President Wilson the text of Germany's peace proposal.[39] That evening Bob wrote: "It really looks as though the end might not be very far off. The papers report peace proposals from the Central Powers—but add the characteristic comment that such proposals are 'coldly received' by the Allies. I heard the other day that Mr. Justice Clark[e] made an address to the American Bar Association the keynote of which was that it must be [a] just peace[—] just to all alike because we have got to live in the same world all together & there could be no lasting peace unless its terms were just. I phoned to his office to get a copy but he had no copy. I am after it and will publish it if I can find it."[40]

As soon as the President's answer to Germany's peace proposal was released, Julius Truesdell brought it in to Bob, who wrote the family that evening: "It is just out & the Bitter Enders are mad because they think it may lead on to peace too soon . . . The subject was brought up in the Senate yesterday a number of Senators making bitter end—knock out speeches. It wasn't very easy to sit it out but I did. Another day will come and I pray it may come soon."[41]

On October 19 Bob wrote: "Another note from the President to Austria today. I think it will be quite satisfactory to the B.E. [Bitter End] people—but nothin[g] can prevent the 'conversations' from reaching a conclusion When people who fight begin to talk it is pretty close to the finish."[42]

Four days later Lincoln Steffens, Fred Howe, and "Andy" Furuseth came to the house and "visited" until midnight. "Steff" had lunched with Bob that afternoon at the Capitol. He was already planning to go to the peace conference, and thought he would "make it all right through Col. House." "Things are hot about the State Dept," Bob wrote that afternoon.[43] After the evening with his three intimate friends, he wrote Phil that Steffens and Howe "had been about the *center* of things during the day or two they have been here. This is all *confidential strictly so*—but there is a *great deal* of feeling springing up between your Uncle Sam and Mr. Jo[h]n Bull regarding the winding up of the game over on the other side. . . . They dont want too much democracy mixed up in this peace affair. If your Uncle Sam fails to get a *permanent democratic* peace for ev[e]rybody big and little with *freedom* of the seas and disarmament to a considerable extent applied to ev[e]rybody on the sea as well as land—then what has he [Wilson] got for his sacrifice and how much has he benefited the world. You can see the complications. But of course you will not discuss *them with anybody*. It isn't supposed to be a *soldiers job*. I am just giving you this glimpse of the cards as they are beginning to fall on the table in a preliminary way that you may have a better understanding as the game goes on."[44]

The following day Bob wrote, "Dispatches from the other side announce the arrival there of Col House He must have been hurried off some ten days ago. There went with him Mr. Achinlos [Gordon Auchincloss]—Solicitor of the State Dept. and Mr. Grew—the latter has been the brains of our ambassidoral [*sic*] aggregation at Berlin for years. I learned to-night that they accompanied House. This is construed to mean[,] taken in connection with House going and the whole situation[,] as making towards a wind up of the big game. . . .

"But *apparently* there is a great stirring among the German people that the thing be ended. Liebknecht's* release from imprisonment and the great popular demonstration given him—flowers and cheers—if truly reported tonight is very significant. If once the flood gates are loosened the Junkers may *all* be swept aside. Eternal justice ought to give the recoil a wide and far sweep.

"The next twenty five years ought to be big with events for masses of mankind. I would like to be permitted to have a part in it."[45]

Although the Senate was in session only about once in three days, and Bob took no part in the running debate, he found himself "rushed all the while,"[46] for the Finance Committee, of which he was a member, was shaping the "Eight Billion Dollar" Revenue bill. "It is," he wrote, "a question of a little more or less here and there. Always changing from the House Bill to the advantage of wealth."[47]

"The committee grinds away all day and ev[e]ry day. It is a regular gab-fest. I do very little of the gabbing— But I did break in today," he told Belle with distinct satisfaction, "and stood up for a five or ten minute speech."[48] His argument concerned an item, put into the bill by the Ways and Means Committee, providing for a bill-drafting bureau, which Bob had advocated for years: "Well, Williams and Hoke Smith & Lodge & Penrose jumped all over it. Nobody said anything & I finally slipped over to [Joseph] Robbinson [*sic*] & gave him a few pointers about the Wis[consin] Drafting Bureau & that several states had them, &c &c. He made

* Karl Liebknecht, one of the few members of the Reichstag who had opposed the Government's war policies. He had been convicted of "war treason" and had been sentenced to a long term of penal servitude.

quite a hot speech for the amendment—you know he always makes a very energetic speech whenever he speaks at all. He mentioned Wisconsin That was enough for Williams & he was quite nasty. I paid no attention to him but spoke for it. . . . The matter went over till tomorrow It will be knocked out of course but anyway I broke the ice & shall go at it again in the morning."[49]

Later he wrote: "I cant tell you how much there is really going to be for me to do here that is worth while. For the present I am under a certain constraint that is very galling."[50] His lawyer, Gilbert Roe, had counseled against extemporaneous speeches while his case was pending. Bob had followed this advice, for he had no quixotic desire to cast himself in the role of a martyr. From bitter experience he knew how casual utterances might be distorted and used toward his expulsion. He believed his most effective service could be rendered by carrying on his work as a Senator. His case, which had now been before the Committee on Privileges and Elections for over a year, still dragged on. Although Roe had moved for dismissal of the charges five months before, no action had been taken.

Since his return several Senators had spoken to him about it, and by late October he was telling the family: "They will have to act on the case as soon as the election is over or drop it altogether. With the war drawing to a certain close it would seem as though there would only be one thing they could do. But one never knows and I dont mean to let it worry me—though I cant feel perfectly free till it is disposed of one way or another."[51]

The elections were soon absorbing Washington. On October 25 Wilson issued a statement to "my fellow countrymen" reminding them that "The congressional elections" were "at hand," and would "occur in the most critical period our country has ever faced or is likely to face in our time." In an appeal which evoked many angry reverberations, he said: "If you have approved of my leadership and wish me to continue to be your unembarrassed spokesman in affairs at home and abroad, I earnestly beg that you will express yourselves unmistakably to that effect by returning a Democratic majority to both the Senate and the House of Representatives. . . . The leaders of the minority in the present Congress have unquestionably been pro-war, but they have been anti-administration. . . . This is no time either for divided counsel or for divided leadership. Unity of command is as necessary now in civil action as it is upon

the field of battle. . . . The return of a Republican majority to
either House of the Congress would, moreover, be interpretative
on the other side of the water as a repudiation of my leadership. . . ."[52]

Senator Smoot, chairman of the Republican Senatorial Committee,
promptly joined with Congressman Fess, chairman of the Republican Congressional Committee, and with Senator Lodge and Congressman Gillette in issuing a sharp party reply to the President. Bob,
recalling Wilson's famous admonition, commented, "Politics 'is adjourned[']—like Hell." With that touch of ironic humor which
the family always enjoyed, he added, "Lodge told me today that he
thought the Rep's would win the next House by 40 majority and
that 'we' have a good chance to get the Senate."[53]

Twenty-four hours later Bob reported: "The political atmosphere
hereabouts has been surcharged with bitterness—since yesterday
late in the day when the President got out his 'appeal.' I think
the Dem. [National] Committee must have thrown the scare into
Wilson to have brought him to the point where he would do it.
Of course there is the other view that he has 'grown' into it in a
perfectly natural way—starting as he did with the view of the Constitution which he had when he brought out his book as late as
1911. All through from 1913 until we got into the war in 1917—
he was taking more & more power to himself over legislation and
reducing Congress to a mere automaton. Since the war the Republicans as well as the Democrats have groveled at his feet and
howled till black in the face about 'standing by the President'
while this war was on. So he might very easily go from one stage
to another until it is easy for him to write: 'This is no time for
divided council [*sic*] or divided leadership. *Unity of command* is
as necessary now in *civil action,* as it is upon the field of battle.'
That goes the limit. If the Republican party had not become a
mere prostitute and camp folower [*sic*] for the last twenty-two
months—there would be a chance for real service."[54]

At the first session of the Senate after Wilson's "appeal,"
the debate crackled with recriminations. Republicans who had without hesitation supported all the President's war measures charged
him with ingratitude and blind partisanship. They reminded him
of the "willful" black sheep in his own party and called his attention to the Democratic party leader in the House, Claude Kitchin,

who had refused to vote for conscription. Bob commented, "I sit back & take some satisfaction in hearing them rail at each other."[55]

The Democrats became alarmed at this criticism, and devised a way to shut off all debate. Each day after the reading of the Journal and the prayer by the Senate Chaplain, Dr. Prettyman, the Senate would immediately adjourn. The verbatim report of the next seven sessions of the Senate fills scarcely seven pages of the *Congressional Record*. In a letter Bob explained the parliamentary procedure by which these "very funny sessions of the Senate" were being held: ". . . they dare not bring up the resolution to adjourn or even a motion to adjourn for three days at a time because either motion is debatable. So as soon as the Journal is read some Democrat at once raises the question of a quorum. The roll call develops the fact that no quorum is present & then nothing is in order but to *adjourn*. . . . which means to the next day at 12 when we go through the same farce. It is quite significant of the fear that possesses the Democrats of having the Wilson appeal discussed with the election right at hand. They are very nervous about the elections anyway—fearful that they will lose control of both houses."[56]

The Administration considered Democratic control of the Senate vital since it would have to ratify any treaty of peace. A Republican victory would mean that Lodge would be chairman of the powerful Foreign Relations Committee. In this uncertainty Congress finally recessed, November 2. Both sides anxiously awaited the election returns.

Until a few days before the election, Bob's letters contain no suggestion that he thought it might also have important results for him. Since no action had been taken on the charges of disloyalty, it was still possible that the Administration might control the Senate by a large majority and be able to force his expulsion. There were some indications, however, that the Senate might be close. On the evening of the day Bob marked his own ballot and posted it to Wisconsin, he speculated more prophetically than he knew on what might happen: "It would be an interesting situation if we got the Senate by *one vote*—wouldn't it. But of course it wont happen that way."[57]

When the election returns came in on November 5, they showed sweeping Republican gains throughout the country, but control of the Senate remained in doubt for several days. The day after election there was a brief session which Bob described in his letter to the family that night: "A handful of Republicans looking grim and yet satisfied. They havent recovered their tempers at what they think was Wilsons unfair appeal. The Democrats—only about a dozen showed up—all looking silly and surprised. They were in a hurry to get away from the Chamber. . . . If Wilson feels like the Democrats look, he already realizes that his jingling rhetoric cannot save him from a rapid decline from this on."

In this letter Bob gave his own interpretation of the Republican victory: "I believe that it simply means that the voters availed [themselves] of the first and only opportunity to hit the war. . . . They had no alternative—and Wilson emphasized the thing by appealing for an endorsement of what he has done. The voter either had to give it or vote the Republican ticket. If the Republicans had been in power and made a record that had agonized and distressed and burdened the people—the voters would have hit the Republicans a swat when the time came to vote."[58]

Two days after election, when it appeared that the Senate would stand 49 Republicans to 47 Democrats, Bob wrote, "A change of one vote would make the Senate a tie and give the Vice President the deciding vote. *That is a very interesting situation*—if it turns out to be a true forecast of the final result. Already both sides are indicating quite a mellowness towards a certain much despised member. What is that quotation? There is something in Holy writ about the stone that was rejected becoming the corner of the edifice."[59] Dillingham, a member of the "Old Guard" and the ranking Republican of the Committee on Privileges and Elections, had chatted with Bob the previous day "and opined that 'this election ought to unite all Republicans.' "[60] Others observed, and still remember, this post-election "mellowness" toward the Wisconsin Senator. When Penrose went over and placed his hand on La Follette's shoulder, calling him "Bob," Senator Swanson leaned over and said to Gore, "They aren't going to expel La Follette from the Senate and the Republicans are going to organize the Senate."[61]

When the outcome of the elections seemed certain, Bob wrote: "It is pretty definitely settled that the Senate will stand 49 Republicans to 47 Democrats. I never drew the long straw before. Just those particular figures if they stand will make a good deal of difference not only with the Committee case but with legislation for the next two years."[62] The following day he said to Phil, "It offers a great opportunity to do a thing now and then for the public good—and the next two years should be *big* with such opportunities." He added that Senator Gore had just telephoned to say, "The New York *World* has an Editorial . . . on 'Battle Bob Controls the Situation in the U.S. Senate.' "[63] The marked clipping of this editorial, entitled "La Follette May Tip Over Senate to Beat Standpats," was preserved, as Bob requested when he enclosed it in a letter to Belle the next day.

A special story from Washington to the New York *World* stated: "The enemies of Senator Robert M. La Follette of Wisconsin have come to a sudden and sickening realization that he can dictate the organization of the Senate of the next Congress. . . . With Mr. La Follette holding the balance of power in the new Senate the investigation of the charge against him becomes more interesting . . . Republicans and Democrats alike will shy at any further delving into the observations of Mr. La Follette. He has become of such vital importance to both parties that he probably will be given painless treatment from all angles."[64]

The *World,* which had so recently denounced Bob, now predicted the legislative possibilities of which he himself was naturally aware: "With but two majority for the Republicans Senator La Follette alone can be an endless source of trouble and worry. He can in effect name his own committee assignments and compel the Republicans to carry out his desires in the matter of reorganization and general legislative policies. In addition, Senators Kenyon, Johnson of California and Capper of Kansas are regarded as strongly inclined to Progressive doctrines. They doubtless will go some distance in the direction of supporting Mr. La Follette. . . . Several of the old Progressive Republican clique that was active in the Senate six years ago are now members. These are Borah, Cummins, Gronna, Jones of Washington, Norris and Poindexter. . . . He will require the aid of but one or two to make his program effective."[65]

Three days after this story appeared, Bob wrote, "Senator Dillingham told me today that he had been against the Committee making any investigation in my case. . . . [he] emphasized the danger of a precedent that would establish the right or practice of the Committee acting on such a communication about a speech made by a

Senator away from or outside the Senate 'when such speech was not seditious.' " Bob remarked, "It seems to be working. Wouldn't wonder if there was real magic in the figures: '49 to 47.' "[66]

As early as November 1, Bob had been told in confidence that an announcement would be made two days later to the effect "that *peace* negotiations or *terms* are *already under discussion with the Germans.*" He was also informed that ". . . Mr. Wilson begins to see that the Allies will go after an imperialistic peace—rather than a permanent democratic peace." He remarked, "Verily wash day is at hand—and some people are getting nervous as to 'just how things are coming out of the wash.' "[67]

Bob was shocked when he read in the newspapers the day after election the text of the document of November 5 on the result of the Allied conference on the armistice.[68] Although signed by Lansing, it was authorized by the President, and revealed that he had agreed to the demand of the Allies that "the freedom of the seas" should be reserved for further discussion at the peace table. This had been point two in the Fourteen Points he had presented to a joint session of Congress in January, 1918. Early in October Germany had requested an armistice on the basis of the Fourteen Points. On October 30, while the Allied conference was still in session, Wilson had cabled authorizing House to say the President could not consent to take part in the negotiation of a peace which did not include the "Freedom of the Seas."[69] But Bob did not know this. He thought Wilson had clearly defined what he meant by "the freedom of the seas" in his address to Congress. Therefore it seemed to Bob that the concession to the Allies for further discussion of one of Wilson's most important terms for the Armistice was an unhappy omen for a just and enduring peace. After reading the report in the newspaper, Bob's indignant reaction was that Wilson thus "surrenders the freedom of the seas—the *very issue* on which he insisted upon our *going to war*. It makes me boil. I dont know when I shall break loose on it but it seems like a base betrayal. He knew of this attitude of England Monday and kept the lid on for fear of its effect on the elections The Washington *Herald* got the news Monday & Monday night it got out an Extra. The Administration got after them quick and surpressed [*sic*] it A few copies got out I have been unable to get one so far."[70]

All Bob's confidential information, his reading of history, and his own experience caused him "to discount very liberally" the press dispatches which still reported "the greatest harmony" in the views of the United States and the Allies. He believed, in a general way, as he wrote to Phil, "that the Allies all including France through Clemenc[e]au influence want and will move together to get an imperialistic peace; that Wilson really wants what history will call a just peace & a democratic peace. If he doesn't get this what will he have to show for all the sacrifice this country has made and is making. But the pressure of Tory Republicans & Bitter Enders of all shades of political opinion will be with the allies. Hence they raise the cry for unconditional surrender, ravaging and ravishing Germany—&c—&c. This sort of Hell-roaring talk about revenge catches and carries along the shallow loose thinking element [and] is capital for those who make money in prolonging the war—and is at once played up by the press. . . . Wilson has seemed to yield and has really modified some of his 14 + 4 + ( ) principles laid down by him from time to time. For instance January 8—he declared that we did not ask Germany to modify her institutions. He has given that up—and other things. . . .

"What then will become of the Democratic peace—the just peace? . . . But the fact that he is by nature a Tory—plants in him a dread of what may happen in Germany. . . . For once revolution starts in Germany there is danger that it may sweep all Europe. These are some of [the] reefs that lie close in front of the gen[er]ation who have the job of working out the results of this war to 'make the world *safe for democracy.*' "71

In discussing with Belle the terms which would contribute toward a permanent peace, he said he thought of writing an editorial "urging the President to include a condition for *peace* with Germany that she shall agree to abandon compulsory military training— . . . that she shall first submit the question of peace or war to the popular vote of the people who shall have the first right to say whether there shall be war—at least in all cases except where there has been actual invasion. . . . Of course it would be preferable to get that idea to him & have him originate [it]. He is averse to taking anything from anyone—where the public knows about it. But I know of no way to get it to him through a source that would enable him to make it his own."72

A false report of an armistice came on November 7. It was, Bob wrote, "warm and bright,—a good day for an out door celebration and Washington celebrated. About 2:30 p m the War & Navy departments turned their employees loose. The other departments followed suit. . . . It would have been interesting to know what was in the hearts of the crowd—whether they [were] celebrating victory or peace."[73]* Bob was not in the crowd, but from those who had been he heard "interesting things about the peace celebration which convulsed Washington—or so much of it as lies between and is contiguous to Pennsylvania Avenue from White House to Capitol. . . . Ev[e]ry inch of space in that quarter was packed by human beings crazy with joy. Ev[e]rybody shook hands and embraced and cheered and wept and sang It was all clean extatic [sic] joy finding expression at last. In the midst of it all a young man—a *wonderful* whistler began to whistle 'Der [sic] Wacht am Rhine.' The crowd opened and he marched along whistling the German national anthem greeted by cheers and applause. Had he attempted it two hours earlier he would have been mobbed. Peace had come and hatred seemed to have suddenly died the death. Does it not seem possible that the hatred was not real; that the war-enthusiasm was a sham; that with the *restraints off,* the thing that has been cowed and repressed found natural expression. May we not get back to the normal sooner than seemed possible and find that the *great mass* of our people were not war mad?"[74]

"The celebration was," he said, "a little premature . . . But let us hope that the all suffering masses of all the countries may be spared further slaughter I should think they would be soul sick of it."[75]

As rumors and reports flashed through the Capitol that the Kaiser had abdicated or had refused to abdicate, Bob wrote the family: "About the only thing that there does seem to be reliance in is that they are badly shaken with internal disorder. . . . It has doubtless been going on to a greater or lesser extent for 18 months. There is doubtless terrible suffering: shortage of food, clothing, coal—all the necessaries of life. There is the old hatred of the military system of compulsory service—Junker tyran[n]y—the thing because of which millions of Germans have left their fatherland in the years that

* Secretary Lansing on November 7 recorded the happenings of the day in a memorandum closing with this similar comment: "I wondered whether the rejoicing was over peace or over victory?" (*The Lansing Papers,* II, 173).

have gone by—the ruthless thing that has torn other millions from their homes in the last four years to feed the cannon in Belgium and France. . . . These are the conditions that beget revolution. The German temper[a]ment may enable them to ride out the storm. But it seems to me that there is the gravest danger of a terrible convulsion. I dread to see it and yet it may be necessary. And on top of it all we may have the shocking spectacle of the armies that have been fighting to make the world *safe* for democracy being used to *throttle* democracy, under the pretense of 'restoring order,' in Germany and *elsewhere*—as they are now being used in Russia."[76]

At one o'clock the next day the newsboys were swarming everywhere through Washington with their extras crying, "Germany swept by revolutionists." That night Bob wrote the family in California: "I wonder if the San Diego papers got out to you at La Jolla. If one can credit the dispatches the Kaiser has abdicated. . . . The Royal family is scattering in fear, Prince Henry effected his escape under cover of a red flag. The socialists are trying to form a government and the soldiers the workmen and the extreme radical element are getting control in many of the larger cities. Ev[e]ry thing would seem to be in a chaotic state.

"Verily the Bitter Enders have made a mess of it from all appearances. With what government can they make an Armistice? With what government can they conclude a peace? . . . I do not believe there is a shadow of doubt that a peace could have been concluded months ago upon terms that would have been honorable and reasonable as history will declare. It would have saved a million lives a million more from mutilation—millions of broken hearts billions upon billions of war debts and tens of billions of destruction devestation [*sic*] and waste. . . . The very thing which the Conservative statesmen of England feared has happened or is happening to Germany. The despatches say it is spreading to Austria Hungary— Schleiswig [*sic*] Holstein who can set boundaries to it now? France is in a frightful state Her war debt has passed all bounds Her young men are all killed or maimed. *Before* the war she had reached a condition where the death-rate was *fully* as *high* as the birth rate All of the disease[s] that follow at the heels of war have made her poor land the pest house of the world. The French temper[a]ment is wonderfully buoyant and elastic. Victory in expelling the armies of Germany from her soil may lift her morale to a pitch which may steady her and hold her aloof from the revolution that is apparently at her doorway—but it looks tonight as though the whole situation is critical for ev[e]ry belligerent government of Europe."[77]

In two letters written to the family at this time he said, "You can readily see that the Senate is to be the accute [*sic*] center of interest not only on reorganization but on all the important legislation which must follow in the wake of the war. It calls for poise and clearness of judgment as well as firmness and courage. Washington will be the scene of great events in the next two years. You are all members of the General Staff."[78] "We will be mighty lucky if we get out of this thing without sacrifising [*sic*] the small remnants of democratic gain we had made as the result of the last twenty years of struggle."[79]

On November 11 the President appeared before a joint session of Congress and read the terms of the armistice to an enthusiastic Congress. The applause was again led by Chief Justice White, who was there with the entire Court. The *New York Times* reported that "La Follette of Wisconsin sat silent, . . . drinking in every word that the President uttered. He joined in the handclapping—his first show of feeling—that began the demonstration over the President's declaration: 'The war thus comes to an end.' "[80]

Bob wrote that same evening briefly describing what happened and adding that the President had also informed Congress "we now had no government representing the German people with which to agree upon terms of peace. Then he submitted some rhetoric about peace and Germany having our good will—and that ended it."[81]

Bob predicted that the treaty would result in "planting the seed for a future war." He feared, as early as November 13, "that President Wilson's 1st proposition in his 14 peace declarations is already being violated. That proposition avers that there shall be: 'Open covenants of peace *openly* arrived at, &c.'

"Now right at the outset we are informed that Versailles Council 'is to be isolated'; that 'the deliberations of the Premiers Ministers & Naval and Military chiefs will be conducted amidst the quietude of a woodland dell'. . .

" 'Covenants of peace' are not to be 'open' nor are they to be *'openly arrived at'*

"It looks like the usual dark lantern methods. 'Open diplomacy' is not to be *open* at all.

"The readiness with which Wilson consented that the 'freedom of the seas' should be reserved for future consideration and that indemnities should be exacted to the limit was the first shock.

"The secrecy which is to veil all the deliberations of the peace council is another surrender."[82]

Analyzing the early reports of territorial divisions, and comparing them with the provisions of the secret treaties which had been found in the Russian archives by the Soviet Government, Bob asked in this same letter, "Doesn't it look as though we had been fighting to *enforce those secret treaties*? . . .

"And we dont hear one word of protest from Wilson or any one else.

"It looks as though about all we were going to have left is *peace* a big war debt and *Wilsons Speeches*— . . .

"But that ev[e]ry principle of democracy about which we heard so much is to be sacrificed and a peace of the rankest injustice consumated [*sic*] . . . planting the seed for a future war.

"Well let us thank God that we *have peace*."[83]

A few nights later as he stood alone in his room, Bob's thought turned to what the peace, that had finally come, meant to him and others: "When I pulled my curtain down preparatory to settling myself at my desk, I looked up at the nearly full moon and felt as if I could almost make you hear and feel me through her. You will be out on the front porch a little later feeling her wonderful spell and thinking of the absent ones so widely seperated [*sic*] And yet how favored we have been and are. We have lived with an awful fear in our hearts for our beloved boys so long that as we begin to come back toward normal life and conditions with both of them still with us and the balance of the flock well—that I want to pray or cry or sing my thankfulness for all our blessings.

"And then my heart goes out to the millions who sit in their broken, desolated homes suffering the unspeakable horrors which this wicked, brutal war has brought upon them. Peace can bring them nothing until they find the peace that passeth all understanding."[84]

CHAPTER LVI

"Real Magic in the Figures: '49 to 47'"

"As the war feeling wears away most of the old friendships will I hope be resumed," Bob had written on November 16, 1918. "There are some old timers I never can forgive I'm afraid. And not a few of them live in Madison."[1] But only three days later he learned there was one intimate relationship which could never be resumed. He telegraphed Belle of the sudden death of their classmate, Charles R. Van Hise, president of the University of Wisconsin. "Your telegram . . . was a great shock," Belle replied. "He was one of our oldest and closest friends. I am sorry this war had separated us."[2]

Van Hise had been among those who signed the university faculty petition condemning Bob and questioning his loyalty. The evening after learning of his death Bob wrote to Belle: "I would like to write to Alice [Van Hise], but I dont know as I can put together such a letter as I would really be glad to send. He of all men in Madison was the last who ought to have been willing or who could have been forced against his will to join a mob and murder the reputation of a life time friend who had pushed him into the position which had given the very power which he used to destroy that friends reputation and standing before the Country. I really dont feel resentful now—I just want to forget it. Forgive me I didn't intend to refer to it at all."[3]

That same day his friend Gilbert Roe, who, Bob wrote, was "loyalty and devotion to the last ditch, . . . a great soul directed by a great brain and heart," had returned to Washington.[4] Roe had hoped that at the meeting of the Privileges and Elections Committee, set for November 22, action would be taken on his long-pending motion to dismiss the disloyalty charges. The committee was "twisting & squirming," Bob wrote, "to find some way to dispose of my case. . . . I dont want a Scotch verdict of 'not proven.' " Ashurst, a member of the committee, "told John [Hannan] in the Cor[r]idor that the war had created some hard feelings & that the time had come now to 'forget *all* about it.' "5 It had been reported to Bob that a member of the committee had said they intended to "drop" the case. Bob commented to the family: "I dont propose to have it disposed [of] in that way—if I can help it. And I dont see how they can fail to make some sort of a *report* on it. Of course a report will bring it up in the Senate and there will doubtless be some mean speeches and a lot of newspaper reviling but I am entitled to a conviction or an acquital [*sic*] and I am going to get one or the other if I can. . . . I think there should be a showdown."6 He thought that whatever report was made, "The newspapers will have their fling at me—but they have had that all along through my life."7

As the war hysteria diminished, the atmosphere in the Senate became more cordial. The day before the committee met, Bob wrote that Senator Moses of New Hampshire came and sat beside him in the Senate saying: "We should be friends. My best friend was Senator Chandler and he was your great friend & admirer He taught me all I know about political questions and also about law."8

The day the committee was to meet, Bob had Hannan at the Capitol at half past eight to deliver to Reed, Knox, Sherman, and Dillingham copies of the printed brief Roe had presented in May, lest "they might have mislaid their copies" and as "a reminder of our view of their duty."9 The Senators who attended the meeting were Pomerene, Walsh, Reed, Vardaman, Wolcott of Delaware, Ashurst, Dillingham, Kenyon, Knox, Sherman, and Kellogg. King was in town but not present. Thompson and Fall were at home.

That night Bob wrote the family what Reed had told him about this final committee meeting on the disloyalty charges. Pomerene had declared he would make a minority report, and Reed thought "he was D—d fool enough to do it." Walsh was opposed to the proposed majority report until Bob should come "before the Committee" to make "some explanations," stating, for instance, if he "had any reliable information as to Bryan having told Wilson etc.," and "some further explanations as to certain expressions in the speech." Kellogg was inclined to vote with Pomerene and Walsh, and thought Bob should be censured; but after Knox "made a statement of the law and the rights of Senators" Reed talked to Kellogg "on the side—and Kellogg voted to dismiss."[10]

The vote was 9 to 2, and that night Bob enclosed with this same letter clippings from the Washington evening papers which carried the headlines, "LA FOLLETTE CASE ENDS," and "CHARGES AGAINST LA FOLLETTE DROPPED." Since Congress had adjourned on the twenty-first and no report could be made to the Senate until December 2, Pomerene's determination to submit a minority report left the matter still unsettled.

Although now serene about the final outcome, Bob told the family that it had "seemed an awfully long week. It is really only two months since I left you—if the weeks were months it would better accord with my feeling. This isn't life. This is just waiting and it always seems long when you wait. It is not that I have been idling. It has been work all the time—but it's—just work to clear the decks —for something more real afterward and so even the work is sort of preliminary—or 'waiting work.' The dragging sessions of the committee is but a preface to something more worth while and the work and worry of the case before the P. & E. [Privileges & Elections] Committee—is but clearing away rubbish for freer action hereafter."[11]

When "a nice little note" came from Brandeis a few days after the committee's vote to dismiss charges, Bob shared it with the family by copying it into his own manuscript letter that same evening: " 'My dear Bob: I want you to know how happy we are that the burdens which long weighed so heavily are lifting; and that you will be free to take your place of leadership in the struggle for Democracy in America. Affectionately, Louis D. Brandeis. I had a nice letter from Phil recently.' " After copying the letter, Bob added, "very dear of him. I shall write him a note of appreciation tonight." In his letter to Brandeis Bob said: "It was good of you to write me a word of cheer. The last eighteen months seem an age. Through it all—and it has been very dark at times—I have tried to keep on a straight course, always facing the same way. Democracy in America has been trampled under foot, submerged, forgotten. Her enemies have multiplied their wealth and power appallingly. She has thousands of Morgans against her now. But she calls to us as never before. I fear it will be some time before an appeal for her can get much of a hearing. All the more reason to begin forcing the issue. I never felt more fit and eager. Yours with abiding love, Bob." After quoting his note to Brandeis, Bob commented in his letter to the family, "I hope you won't think it sounds like 'a fling.' I didn't so intend it. But he suggested my taking up my 'leadership for Democracy in America.' There is nothing to lead. The forces of democracy which we had been organizing for twenty years have been scattered to the four winds by this mad stampede for democracy in Europe—led by the enemies of democracy in America. What have we left to fight with."[12]

The day the committee voted to dismiss the charges, Senator Lodge invited Bob to his office for "a little talk" which drew from Bob, Jr., the caustic comment that "It must have been an altogether new sensation to be invited to Lodge's committee room for a conference. I expect that you both found novelty in the situation."[13] As the two men walked down the corridor, Senator James A. Reed noted that Lodge had "his arm on La Follette's shoulder," and remarked cynically to another Senator, "Bob has won his case."[14] After his talk with the Massachusetts Senator, Bob wrote the family Lodge "said he realized that in the new Congress the Republicans had no 'working majority' on legislation but hoped they had majority enough to organize the Senate. . . . I listened to all he had to say and told him I'd think it over & talk to him again. So far as I have thought about my course at all—it has been that the right thing for me to do—is to vote (when the time comes next March) to make a Republican re-organization of the Senate and thereafter to do as I have always done and vote on all questions according to my convictions in an absolutely independent way."[15] As he thought of the vital problems to be dealt with in Congress, he wrote: "I find myself day by day more & more eager to lash out. I am like an old horse that has been confined in a box stall all winter. I have gotten out into the paddock. I sniff the fresh air and feel the freedom. I want to kick the bars down and go racing unrestrained over the fields. There is real danger that I might run up against the barbed wire fence—for it is *still there*."[16]

Concerned as he naturally was to have "the barbed wire fence" of the disloyalty charges cleared away, Bob's daily letters show that he did not dwell on it unduly. Most of his time and thought were given to international developments—the Peace Conference, the League of Nations, Russia—and the pressing domestic problems which must be met now that the war was ended. Commenting on the way *"our* Tories are making ready to accept a meaningless peace," he said to Bob, Jr.: "What a field it opens up for serving human interests. We must be ready. Begin storing your mind with the vital things that will constitute a real *preparedness* for this coming contest. Read Fred How[e']s book WHY WAR. Read it again and again until the facts *stick*. Read Angels [Norman Angell's] books. Get your history pat."[17] A few days later he urged him to read Professor J. Salwyn Schapiro's *Modern and Contemporary European History*, which had "27 maps—14 of which are in color."[18]

When the President had first announced he was going to the Peace Conference, Bob thought it extremely unwise: "The Allies are sure to have not only skilled diplomats but men trained to the last point on historical relations of each country to ev[e]ry other as well as on ev[e]ry feature of world trade and commerce." Wilson has "to face the problems of momentous statesmanship from this on."[19] But after thinking it over, Bob concluded, a few days later, that perhaps the President had done the right thing in deciding to go abroad: "Wilson[']s biggest job is this war and the peace in which we have been involved and why shouldn't he follow it up to a finish? That's the way its sort of working out in my mind though none of the Republicans would agree with me I suppose. I have said nothing about it so far."[20] With this view Belle wrote that she was in accord.

Once again, as on so many important issues, he and his wife had independently reached similar conclusions. From California Belle wrote that there was no doubt "the great occasion justified" Wilson's "being there in person. The test of his wisdom will be in his accomplishments. I wish he were the great man the world needs in this crisis. But it may be that no one great man is needed at this time. Perhaps as you say it is the period when the masses are to work out their own destiny."[21]

Interest in the President's address was "very keen" as the date for Congress to convene drew near. The content of his speech was a closely guarded secret. Copies were not even given to the press under the usual seal of confidence. Bob thought Wilson would give his reasons for going out of the country. It was expected, he wrote, that the President "will give assurance that he will keep Congress advised of the proceedings of the Conference—at least that he will keep the Senate Committee on Foreign relations informed of the progress of the negotiations. If he does this and makes an open fight for a just peace, disarmament and real freedom of the seas he may justify his going."[22]

The rumblings of Congress were ominous, however. Many who had supported Wilson's war policy enthusiastically were now more critical than Bob. Although the President was to sail for Europe two days after Congress met, few knew his plans. It was said some of the Cabinet had been kept in the dark, and it was known that leaders in his own party had not been taken into his confidence. Everything was shrouded in mystery. The taking over of the cables by the Administration, after the fighting had ceased, boded ill for the promised freedom of "open" discussion. The *New York Times* suggested that the President "appeared to direct the trip to France as a personal affair."[23] Among the Senators there was resentment at Wilson's failure to appoint to the Peace Conference a single member of the Senate which, under the Constitution, must ultimately ratify the Treaty of Peace.

When Wilson came before the joint session on December 2, 1918, he no longer faced the united Congress he had so often swayed by his eloquence. Neither Congress nor the members of the Supreme Court who were present leaped spontaneously to their feet in response to the President's address, which covered many domestic questions but revealed little of his plans in Europe. Bob listened attentively, but was keenly disappointed. The next day he wrote that the address was "pretty punk—poorly delivered and received," and that the President "had the gall to say: 'The allied governments have accepted the bases of peace which I outlined to Congress on the eighth of January last.' The fact that England or the Allied Govts reserved perfect freedom to take any position they please on his 'freedom of the seas' proposition was wholly ignored by him as he could not refer to it without the greatest embarrassment." Quoting a statement made during the debate by Senator Williams to the effect that "the United States would have a bigger navy than

Great Britain and that together they could *force peace* on any and all nations," Bob said, "Small nations are to be eaten up—exploited —robbed. Oh the hypocracy [*sic*] of this whole thing is simply mad[de]ning when you think of what has been done and how it has been done."[24] Later he commented that he thought the President "had the appearance of being a whipped man."[25]

The day Congress convened, Dillingham had presented the committee's majority report on Bob's case. It was not generally known that two days earlier the Vermont Senator had gone to Bob's office and submitted a copy of the report he intended to present. He said he had read the St. Paul speech through "carefully and calmly" on Thanksgiving day and "really couldn't see very much in it to criticize, much less crucify a man for." Bob refrained from telling Dillingham that he "ought to have read it 'carefully and calmly' last Thanksgiving instead of this one."[26]

As drafted and submitted to Bob by Dillingham, the report provided "that the charges preferred by the said Minnesota Commission of Public Safety be dismissed." Bob and Roe both insisted that a phrase should be added so it would read that the charges by the said Minnesota Commission of Public Safety be dismissed "for the reason that the speech in question does not justify any action by the Senate." If there was anything for the Senate to act upon, Bob "insisted on their *acting on it*—if there *was not*" he *"insisted on their saying so."* He told Dillingham he would not stand for an equivocal action, leaving it to be inferred that they were letting him off "because the war was over" or "because the Senate stood 49 to 47."[27] Dillingham agreed to amend his report as requested.

But two days later, while it was being read to the Senate by the Senate clerk, Bob noticed that "one word had been changed." As read, the charges were to be dismissed for the reason that the speech in question did not justify *further* action by the Senate. The word "further" had been substituted for the word "any." After adjournment Bob called Dillingham's attention to it. Dillingham "saw the point and said it was an inadvertence and immediately got the report and rewrote it substituting *'any'* for *'further'* and had the reporters change their notes for the Cong. Record—so it will read *right*." If the report went through that way, Bob thought it would "be an unqualified vindication" by the Senate.[28] In a letter to the family he remarked: "Of course it puts the Committee and the Senate in a nasty hole—to have dragged a victim of war hate bound and gagged—back & forth across this country, with the whole press in full cry, for fourteen months—when there was *nothing 'to justify any action by the Senate' in the case.*"[29] He was now confident that although it might "jingle along for three or four days longer," it was "coming out all right in the end." Revealing how acutely he had felt the strain of the past months, he said, "It will lend some interest to this life when I can begin to go up *against the collar.*"[30]

As soon as the Senate adjourned after the majority report had been made, Senator Hoke Smith came up to Bob in the center aisle and said, in the presence of a number of Senators: "Senator La Follette I congratulate you. There never has been a moment since this thing was brought in here that I would not have voted and fought for just such a report and I shall vote and fight for this report if any fight is necessary."[31] Bob thanked him heartily and turning to Reed, who stood near, said: "If Pomerene is to make a report I want it made. It is time to make an end of this thing."[32] A Democratic Senator was overheard to remark that Pomerene was acting like a damned fool and that if the Democrats had any influence with him he would never make a minority report. But Pomerene persistently delayed presenting his report. On the morning of December 12, when he came on the floor with two typed copies of it in his hand, Dillingham went up to him, asked to see it, and reminded him of his promise to file it that day. Pomerene declined and "again promised to file it tomorrow." Dillingham "was indignant in his polite New England way."[33]

"It makes me see red," Bob wrote his family. "All I can do is to wait and take it as it comes. But by the nine Gods there will be another day!"[34] He noticed that John Sharp Williams "had not been in the Senate for two or three days [but once for a moment]. He may be preparing a roast. But whatever befalls [,] mamma [,] I shall try to remember your wise and loving counsel, when I said good-bye, and preserve a calm and poise that will lift me above personal things."[35]

When Borah came and asked if he couldn't "go to Pomerene and shut him off from making a minority report," Bob told him "that I thought not; that P.[omerene] had prepared such a report and would file it 'sometime'; that I had been trying through Dillingham to get it on file and the matter disposed of. I thanked Borah. It was the first time he has ever spoken to *me* about the case."[30]

After almost two weeks' delay Pomerene finally submitted his report on December 14, asking that it be printed without reading.[37] About four o'clock that afternoon Bob got early proofs of the report and sent them to Reed, Dillingham, Hardwick, Vardaman, and Norris. Pomerene argued that the St. Paul speech violated the Espionage Law and that La Follette should have been indicted. Bob's secretary said that when Reed got the galley proofs and read the report he "swore till he was black in the face."[38] Pomerene was the only member of the committee who had signed the minority report. Bob commented to the family, "It is written in the first person, singular, d——d singular." He also thought the fact that Senator Thomas Walsh had decided not to sign it was "very significant and very gratifying."[39]

When the minority report was filed, Bob's first thought was that he could immediately, by his own initiative, bring up his "case" on a question of "high privilege" for final action in the Senate. But, after consulting Gilfry's *Precedents*, he found this was impossible, since the resolution merely asked for the dismissal of proceedings against him, and did not, as had been expected, refer to the Minnesota Commission of Public Safety petition requesting that the Senate unseat him. He then got Reed to consult with the Democratic floor leader and other Senators to see if an agreement could be reached to allow immediate consideration. But Pomerene blocked these efforts. It was then evident that the "case" must go over until after the holidays. Bob expressed his disappointment to the family, and added: "You know I have always been able to make the best of a thing when I have done my part as well as I could. So I have just put this aside. I will go on with my work. . . . Dont worry any more about it. *It will be all right in the end*."[40]

The "work" he specifically referred to was the pending Revenue bill, which he described as "the worst measure [,] the most technical and complicated of all the bills I have ever worked on."[41] He objected to the bill for two reasons—it did not raise enough revenue and it did not distribute the tax burden fairly. He had attended most of the committee hearings and had been particularly shocked at a revelation made by Secretary McAdoo which disclosed the way "our noble allies havent been paying their interest on our loans—

except that they have paid the interest on preceding loans out of subsequent loans. In other words we have been loaning them the money to pay the interest on what they owe us."[42] The debate on the bill began on December 10. About two weeks later Bob offered his carefully prepared minority report and substitute Revenue bill. When he brought up his substitute bill, he asked that it be printed but not read in order to save time. The work that went into preparing it is indicated by the fact that it fills thirty-eight columns of small type in the *Record*.[43] In spite of the late hour he had "good attention and quite a number of interruptions" during his two-hour speech on his substitute.[44]

Through heavier levies on high incomes and on excess war profits, his bill increased by $1,142,510,000 the amount to be raised by the Committee bill.[45] Recalling his fight for the application of similar principles of taxation in the summer of 1917, he said: "I demonstrated then the peril of raising the money to finance the war by bond issues. . . . I plead with you then to inaugurate the right kind of a plan of taxation at the beginning of this war, knowing full well, if we started out on a policy of taxing too little and borrowing too much, that it would be carried on throughout the war."[46]

"Why do you not stand up to your duty here," Bob pleaded with the Senate, "and take as much out of wealth as you take out of the blood and flesh of the people of this country? The poor do not make anything out of war. Wealth does. . . . Who ought to carry the burden of this war? Surely not the millions who were put into the ranks, who have been taken away from production, leaving their families destitute. The corporations of this country earned $10,-000,000,000 in the last year . . . in net war profit, not gross but net, over all their expenses . . . and when it comes to taxing them roundly Congress hesitates. But you did not hesitate to take not only the income of the poor family but the capital that is producing the income—the father and the sons—and putting them into the service of the government. All right, but by the God that is over us, if you want to do justice do the same thing by capital."[47]

But he got only five other votes for his substitute: Borah, Gronna, Norris, Nugent, and Vardaman. There were 54 votes against him. To the family Bob wrote: "Cummins was not present. Kenyon [of Iowa] and Johnson of Cal. sat in their seats and did not vote. Borah said to John [Hannan] who was on the floor that they were 'd—d cowards.' Lenroot voted against my substitute. I had a good substitute bill and that together with my speech rounds out and makes my record logical and consistent with the work done on the revenue bill for 1917."[48]

Two days later he wrote: "I wouldn't trade my record on financing this war for that of any other man in public life. From start to finish it is straight as a rifle barrel."[49]

Phil received his discharge from the Army on December 26. He had planned to go to his father in Washington for the holidays, as he thought it would "be a pretty lonesome Christmas for him with us all spread over the Continent."[50] But Bob had wired him to go to La Jolla and then to Madison, although it was "not a bit easy," because, as he wrote Phil, "you see if you dont go to La Jolla & come here to visit me instead I should feel that I was stealing from Mamma Bobbie & Mary."[51] In answer to an intimate letter from his son enclosing a report on his work in the Army, Bob said, "I sure am proud of the great record you have made but I knew you would do it—my boy."[52]

Phil walked in "unannounced" on the family at La Jolla. "He is the same wonderfully alive, ever thinking and ever doing lad," his mother said.[53] From his lonely study, the third night after Christmas, Bob wrote to his "Beloved Ones" at La Jolla: "I am sure that Phil is with you by this time without fail. I am so glad to have it so. If he were here we would both be mooning over the way you would miss and hunger for him. I am getting real comfort and joy out of it as I look in on you at 'Whispering Sands,'—across three thousand miles of space. There you are all close together mamma, Josie, and you blessed Kiddies. You dont see me but I'm there too, doing just what you'r[e] doing—passing round a good bear hug and real heart-hot kisses every few minutes. Phil is telling all about army life and mamma and Mary are telling all about Bobbies fight to live and Aunt Jo is telling all of the red hot things about the war hate and persecution at home. I cant even get in a word in edgewise—but I'm there heart and soul. If you had a wegie [sic] board and would only join hands you would get my messages that are flashing over the mountains and across the drifting sands of the great desert. Space and time cannot divide us. The mystic cords of love bind us close together in family communion."[54]

He shared, too, in imagination the rides they would have together in the second-hand "Saxon-six" which Belle had been convinced Bobbie needed—physically and psychologically. Bob, Jr., had responded immediately, and was soon driving the car, which gave the special exercise his leg muscles needed. "It seems almost like flying to get at the wheel after being dependent on the wheel chair," he wrote his father.[56] "Oh my boy," his father answered, "God was good to you when he picked out the woman to be your mother. She knew what was best. When I look back over the terrible months and think of the even steady way, the control, the deep insight with which she has met it all, she grows the more wonderful to me as times passes. She is the only one who never became in the least degree 'batty.' I should have worn a 'straight-jacket' [*sic*] part of the time. Let us think of her first in everything while we live. . . . Put your arms round mamma and love her for me too. She knows *whats* best and just about *when* its best."[56]

Bob spent his 1918 Christmas day quietly, dined with the La Follette "cousins," "a dear family all of them," and attended the theater for the first time since the war.[57] He had "a telegram of Christmas greetings from Rudolph Spreckels. Also a dear message from Fola. And mamma," he added mischievously, "Mr. Thomas J. Walsh—Senator from Montana sends us 'Christmas Greetings and best wishes for the New Year' Aint he *nice*?"[58]

As the last night of the year was slipping out, he recalled that it was their wedding anniversary, when, thirty-six years before, "we joined our lives to build a home and rear a family. We have been wonderfully blessed in our children and the years have given us about as much happiness as befalls mortals on this earth. No wife and mother ever gave herself more to husband and children than have you, dear heart. God bless and keep you strong and well in the years to come. . . .

"One of the hardest things about the last two years is the feeling of repression we have had to carry around with us. It is an awful strain on ones poise and control. I know it has made me a very different person to live with Sometimes I wonder if I will ever be just the same again."[59]

CHAPTER LVII

Disloyalty Charges Dismissed

"I took a little shot at the Russian target yesterday," Bob wrote Phil on January 8, just ten days before the Peace Conference was to open at Paris.[1] This brief talk "on our soldiers in Russia—what they are there for and why they are fighting the Russian people with whom we are *not at war*," was the first speech he had made in the Senate on any aspect of international affairs since his return to Washington in September.[2] Answering his protest against our intervention, Senator Swanson, later Secretary of the Navy, explained that the Allied troops, including 2,500 Americans, had been sent into Russia to prevent the use of Archangel as a German submarine base and to protect supplies which had been stored there. He charged that ever since the Bolshevik revolution, Russia had virtually been in alliance with the German Government. Bob, speaking from his knowledge of Raymond Robins' documents, replied the proof was overwhelming that from the beginning the Soviet Government had "exerted itself in every possible way to enlist the sympathy and support of the Government of the United States, to the end that it might be strong enough to resist the German Government."[3] He maintained that the kind of government the Russian people wanted was their business, not ours; that the war was over and there could no longer be any pretext that the United States soldiers on Russian soil were fighting anybody but the Russian people.

The immediate provocation for his talk was a recent newspaper report of fighting in northern Russia near Archangel by Wisconsin and Michigan troops, who had advanced "fifteen miles up the Onega River . . . driving the Bolsheviki before them."[4] For months he had been deeply concerned lest the Allies' fear of the spread of

Bolshevism in Europe, combined with pressure from reactionaries in this country, should drive us to military intervention against the Soviet Government. When the press reported on September 18, 1918, that American soldiers had landed in Russia, ostensibly to fight the Germans, Bob was distressed that the President had responded to Allied pressure and ordered our troops to Archangel, for he was convinced it would develop that their real purpose was to make war on the Bolsheviki.

Three months later, on December 12, Senator Johnson had arraigned the Administration for intervention in Russia, and Bob was glad to have the subject opened up in the Senate, although he did not agree with some things the California Senator said. On December 27 Bob had read what he thought was apparently an "inspired" article, because it coincided with a confidential prediction he had previously received. The article reported that the Allies and the United States "had agreed to send five divisions of troops into Russia at the request of 'leading Russians' to 'crush the Reds.'" He wrote the family: "It seems to me to call for *immediate and drastic action*. . . . It will be the crime of all crimes against democracy 'self-determination' and the 'consent of the governed' . . . What a mockery it makes of the message Wilson sent to the Soviet Congress of Russia when he said on the 11th of March, 1918:—'The whole heart of the United States is with the people of Russia in their attempt to free themselves forever from autocratic government and become *the masters of their own life*.'"[5]

On principle Bob would have opposed this armed intervention because he believed the people of a country had a right to determine their own form of government. But the confidential information he had received in August from Colonel Raymond Robins regarding the Russian situation made him particularly indignant at this announcement. For eleven months Robins had been in Russia with the Red Cross, and for six months he had been Commander of the American Red Cross Mission. His official position and the assistance of his able interpreter, Alexander Gumberg, gave him exceptional opportunities for securing authentic information and documents. Gumberg had served as interpreter with the United States Special Diplomatic Mission in 1917, and Robins regarded him as "the most serviceable single person in the most difficult days of the Russian situation."[6]

Robins was convinced that the new government would endure. On May 14, 1918, he had left Russia with Gumberg and returned to this country, hoping to report to the President and Colonel House in person and thus make his material available as a basis for a more constructive United States policy toward the Soviet Government. He waited in Washington for several weeks, and saw many influential people. Among others he talked with Justice Brandeis, Felix Frankfurter, Senators Norris, Smoot, Poindexter, and Johnson of California. But the combined aid of William Bullitt in trying to reach Colonel House, and that of Herbert Hoover, Senator Hollis, and William Kent in approaching Wilson did not open the door of the White House for Robins to submit his material to the President.[7]

When Robins came to Hot Springs, in August, to talk to Bob about Russia, the family shared this opportunity for firsthand information, while Bob took careful, detailed notes which he preserved. Robins had a gift for vivid narrative which held the little group under a spell. To Phil, the only absent member of the family, Belle wrote, "It is a wonderful story and you feel a *true* story he has to tell."[8] Bob thought Robins' firsthand knowledge of the Russian situation and his documentary material were valuable sources which should immediately be made public. If promptly and properly utilized, he was convinced they would help materially toward bringing about a change of the United States' policy toward Russia. But Robins thought the confidential nature of his documents precluded their public use on his own initiative.

On New Year's day, 1919, Robins arrived in Washington. Bob met him at the office, and they spent an hour together. Robins was still "not ready to come out with his material," but hoped "to be called upon to testify" before some committee "as an excuse for making public the matters which Lockhart and others gave him in confidence."[9] Bob subsequently tried unsuccessfully to bring it about through Hitchcock, who was then chairman of the Senate Foreign Relations Committee.

Later it "popped" into his head that he might draft a resolution "reciting some of the *misstatements* made in the Senate & in the press regarding the Russian matter" which would force the committee to call Robins.[10] On January 21 he wrote Robins in New York asking if he would come through with his testimony if the way were opened at Washington. Robins was in Chicago, and his wife read the letter to him over the telephone and telegraphed that her husband was willing Bob should go ahead. But at the same time another telegram was delivered to Bob, sent by Robins himself from Chicago, saying he was unwilling.[11] Therefore Bob had to drop the matter. A week later he was surprised to hear Senator Johnson quoting several of Raymond Robins' confidential documents during a speech in the Senate on January 29, denouncing intervention in Russia, but at the same time severely criticizing Lenin, Trotsky, and the Bolsheviki.[12] Bob thought that although Robins "had a right to select his own medium of communication to the Senate and the country," it was "rather a dirty deal" not to have been more frank with him about it.[13]

Replying to this letter of Bob's, Belle wrote: "It was tough treatment you got from Raymond Robins. Those jolts hurt worse than wordy tirades. But what shall we do? Shall we dissociate ourselves from everyone who disappoints us and with whom we disagree? This war has shaken the foundations and is changing the face of the earth. Tremendous and unexpected results are following[.] New issues are arising. If we would preserve our sanity, if we would not be overwhelmed with bitterness, if we are to have any chance for usefulness, must we not co-operate where we can, concentrate mind and heart on the best that can be done and keep faith in the outcome of every rightly directed effort. I am repeating this doctrine for my own benefit rather than yours. I find it very hard to convince myself any effort of individuals will avail. The forces set loose seem so beyond control. All we can do or say seems like the chatter of birds against a hurricane."[14]

Although Johnson had announced that if the Foreign Relations Committee would call for evidence on the whole Russian situation it would be forthcoming on reasonable notice, it was not until March 6, after Congress adjourned, that Robins was finally subpoenaed before another Senate committee and told his story to the public.[15] Then Bob commented, "Great isn't it that it worked out at last."[16]

The Peace Conference did not open until January 18, 1919. But Wilson sailed for Europe on December 4, arriving in Paris on December 14, where he was received with an acclaim which must have alarmed the enemies of his peace terms. The other three members of the Big Four probably sharpened their daggers as they followed his triumphal tour in England and Italy before the first formal meeting of the Supreme Council at Paris on January 12.

Throughout this period Bob commented in his daily letters to the family on the reports which came to him through the press or from individuals. He was deeply distrustful of the Allies' purposes at the peace table as represented by the Big Four. Most of the dispatches from abroad made him heartsick at the prospects for an enduring peace. Occasionally, however, something occurred which led him to hope that these reactionary forces might be compelled to yield to the pressure of an aroused public opinion in the Allied countries. He thought it encouraging when he received on December 5, the day after the President sailed, a clipping from the New York *Evening Post* giving "British Labor's Attitude" in the form of an Election Manifesto. It demanded what he believed were some of the essentials of any real peace program, including "the immediate withdrawal of allied forces from Russia." He quoted from it at length in his family letter, and noted with satisfaction that a labor party "has been formed in Chicago with a platform of 14 cracking good planks—much like the British Labor platform."[17] His own frequent talks with the returning soldiers and the reports he received about them were also heartening.[18]

But the tidings from the top men among the Allies, who would actually dominate the peace table, were disheartening to Bob. He thought the freedom of the seas a most important factor in keeping the world at peace, and "that we must fight a peace that leaves any nation with either a big army or a *big navy*."[19] Any League of Nations which would mean real international peace must, he believed, exact from each contracting nation guarantees to abolish military service and to declare or make no war, except to repel actual invasion of territory, without first submitting the question of war or no war to the qualified voters of the country. In addition, he thought it essential that no nation should have a navy or an army so formidable that either alone or in combination with other countries it could become a menace to the other nations of the League.[20]

Therefore his gorge rose when he read a London dispatch, dated December 5, which reported Winston Churchill, Secretary of State for War and a member of Lloyd George's coalition government, as saying in a speech at Dundee: "We enter the Peace Conference with the absolute determination that no limitation shall be imposed on our right to maintain our naval defense. We do not intend, no matter what arguments and appeals are addressed to us, to lend ourselves in any way to any fettering restrictions which will prevent the British Navy maintaining its well-tried and well-deserved supremacy."[21] Quoting a part of the speech in a letter to his family, Bob indignantly asked: "How many soldiers would have gone to France & how much money would have been loaned to England if B[a]lfour had made such a public statement when he was in this country seeking help? How many of our boys would this country have been willing to send over to die in France & Flanders to enable Great Britain to maintain her 'supremacy on the seas'?"[22]

From Russia the dark shadow of possible revolution stretched across Europe, distorting the vision of the Allied representatives who were to sit at the Peace Table in Paris. "They are afraid of it in England & France & Italy," Bob wrote. "That's why Lloyd George comes out . . . in favor of high indemnities. That's why Clemenceau is demanding territory and billions from Germany— they are all afraid to face high taxation to pay for the war. The rich wont stand it—and the poor cant stand it. None of them want to pay the price of war. But in the end ev[e]rybody has *to pay*. We are a long way from seeing the end of this thing yet."[23]

When it looked as if the "Bitter Enders" had pushed things so far that revolution might leave no responsible government to negotiate with in Germany, Bob wrote, "The 'have nots' outnumber the 'haves.' No wonder the ruling class of every country grows more and more alarmed. The issue of non-interference in Germany and Russia may become the big question here—and contest interest with the peace conference. . . . Verily things do work out 'in a mysterious way.' What a joke it would be if they should find that they had grabbed such a hand-full of sugar lumps that they couldn't get their big fist out of the bowl without dropping it all."[24]

As he read the handwriting on the wall from day to day, it seemed to disclose a determination on the part of the Allied peace delegates to undermine every principle for which we had ostensibly entered the war. In striking contrast he noted the unprecedented acclaim the President was receiving from the common people of France, England, and Italy wherever he appeared on his triumphal tour. Bob hoped he might be planning to use this great popular power to compel the Allies to accept some of his terms which had been the basis for the armistice. "I am getting curious about Wilson[']s course," Bob wrote. "He is putting in so much time running about making speeches. Is it not possible that he has 'discovered' that England France & Italy have the 'peace' terms all settled—settled according to the terms of the secret treaties they had made in the early months following the breaking out of the European war? You see the terms of those treaties would make Wilsons 14 peace proposals look like an ancient ruin. Is it possible that he is 'campaigning' to get the backing of the mass in the hope that they will bring pressure on the conference to the end that he may get enough out of it to save his face?

"It is vain to speculate. About all we can do is to 'mark time.' But it makes one boil within to know that the work is being done *now*—that is to determine the fate of the worlds future— of *our own future* and—we know nothing about it. What a g[h]astly thing it is that peoples—nations democracies even should be so helpless when it comes to settling matters that mean life and death to them."[25]

But when the press carried dispatches from Paris on January 16 that the Peace Conference was to be secret Bob lost hope in the outcome and commented bitterly: "Lloyd George and Clemenceau have the freedom of the seas settled to their satisfaction and now the conference have voted that the sessions shall be secret. There go points I and II of the President's '14'. . . . Our boys dead in France—the mangled thousands coming back in shiploads, the country loaded with tens of billions of debt[,] millionaires multi- plied—business still further corrupted—government debauched and all to give Wilson a holiday in Europe! ! ! If we are to get any- thing else out of it, I dont see it yet."[26]

He was convinced that while Wilson was "bowing and smiling and juggling with words, England, France and Italy" were "settling all the terms, writing down all the conditions" to which the Presi- dent would later "assent with a beautiful speech in proof of its perfect agreement with 'my fourteen propositions.' "[27]

Four days before the Peace Conference met at Paris, the long tension of the disloyalty charges which had been hanging over Bob for the sixteen months since his St. Paul speech was finally climaxed in a scene which those present in the Senate would never forget. On the night of January 15 he had written the family that if there was "no hitch" he thought his "case" would be disposed of the following day. Although prepared to speak, he intended to refrain from doing so unless it was forced upon him. Dillingham, Knox, Reed, Hardwick, Borah, Cummins, Norris, and others were also ready if there should be general debate. He added, "Ye Gods but it will be a relief to have it out of the way—I cant tell you how real a relief."[28]

At about 1:45 P.M. the next day, Senator Dillingham asked unanimous consent that the Senate proceed to consideration of the resolution he had submitted on December 2 with the majority report of the Committee on Privileges and Elections. Bob was in his seat in the front row just off the center aisle and heard the resolution and the majority report read at Dillingham's request. The resolution was phrased in precisely the form which Bob and Roe thought meant a complete vindication if passed by the Senate: "*Resolved,* That the resolutions of the Minnesota Commission of Public Safety petitioning the Senate of the United States to institute proceedings looking to the expulsion of ROBERT M. LA FOLLETTE from the Senate, because of a speech delivered by him at St. Paul, Minn., on September 20, 1917, be, and the same hereby are, dismissed for the reason that the speech in question does not justify any action by the Senate."[29]

The majority report covers thirty-one pages of the *Congressional Record*. It contains the resolutions from the Minnesota Public Safety Commission, different stenographic transcripts of the St. Paul speech, the correspondence between Pomerene and Bob, and Gilbert Roe's elaborate brief. The latter includes a statement of facts, a history of precedents, and a legal analysis of many cases previously before the Senate. As the Senate Secretary finished the majority report, Pomerene asked for the reading of the minority report, which he alone had signed, and which Bob had described as "singular, d——d singular." For an hour Bob had to listen to this argument maintaining that he had been guilty of disloyalty.

When it was ended, Dillingham stated he was willing to have a vote on the resolution without further explanation from the committee. As Pomerene rose, Bob expected a speech, but it was only to ask for an Aye and Nay vote, as Bob himself had so often done.

The vote was ordered by the Presiding Officer, but before the roll call actually started John Sharp Williams rose from his seat in the front row on the Democratic side, very near Bob, to say that he did not "quite understand what the proposition" was which was "being presented to the Senate." At the Presiding Officer's direction the resolution was again read by the Secretary. As he finished, Williams broke into one of the most scathing denunciations ever heard in the Senate.

Throughout this attack Bob sat very still, his hands on his knees, his eyes steadily fixed on the Presiding Officer directly in front of him. His deliberately controlled expression never changed. Not once did he look in the direction of the raging Senator. As the denunciation passed all bounds, Dillingham, Lodge, Knox, and Gronna, who sat beside him, urged that he take no notice of the attack. Williams walked out into the center aisle, shouting and shaking his fist, and at times peering down into Bob's face. He was not called to order by the Presiding Officer during the half- or three-quarters of an hour that he poured forth his vituperative torrent of words. But once Dillingham indignantly interrupted his distorted quotation of excerpts from the St. Paul speech to remind the excited Senator that the committee's majority report and resolution had been passed by a strictly non-partisan vote of 9 to 2, based on fourteen months' careful study of all the documents. This interruption, however, only served to drive Williams to greater extremes, and he climaxed his tirade by denouncing the St. Paul speech as "disloyal in spirit, disloyal in words, disloyal in intendment, disloyal in effect, and disloyal with a set purpose."[30]

When Williams concluded, the roll was called on the resolution to dismiss the disloyalty charges of the Minnesota Commission of Public Safety. The vote stood 50 for the resolution and 21 against it: 33 Republicans and 17 Democrats voted for it, 1 Republican and 30 Democrats against. Among the latter was Walsh of Montana. Several Senators who would have voted for it were absent. Bob himself did not vote. When the result was announced, the rigidly controlled expression he had maintained throughout Williams' speech relaxed. He "sat in his seat smiling amiably" as various Senators came over to speak to him.[31] As soon as these congratulations were over, Bob immediately went to his office and wrote out a telegram to the family. Then, responding to a call, he went over to

Senator Reed's office, where Reed told him that a wealthy Senator who had voted against Bob had said, "Damn him anyway he ought to be thrown out of the Senate he is always against money."[32] This remark, Bob thought, disclosed "the real thing behind the fight" that had been made to expel him from the Senate. Although Reed did not give the name, Bob later easily identified the Senator when he looked over the list of those who had voted against him.[33]

In a long letter to the family that night, he set down in his own hand how each individual Senator had voted, for he thought the press might not carry the roll call and he knew they would be interested. To them he also revealed then and later something of the inner ordeal his calm exterior had concealed from the public during Williams' denunciation. Belle's counsel the night he left California had helped him to endure the almost unendurable. He wrote that Williams had called him " 'liar' 'traitor'—'coward'—and made such an attack as baffles all description. . . . To have replied to it in kind would have been to be a blackguard.

"I had no thought of replying to him or noticing his speech but I did seriously think of taking the floor *after the roll call* and making my speech but Knox urged me *not* to do so. He said it would go out as a reply to Williams in the papers and would lift his speech into a position of some importance.

". . . I hope you will think I did the best thing I could under all the circumstances. But it was a pretty hard day in that it was humilliating [*sic*] to have to sit still under an attack for which a man ought to be pounded to a pulp."[34]

The next evening he wrote that friends in the gallery had told him how they marveled at "the control exercised while Williams marched across to my desk and shouted & swung his arms over me bawlirg 'he's just common clay from crown of head to soles of feet' &c &c." Bob added, "It was a great temptation when he came close but it was harder to stand afterwards—at night alone in my room—I felt as if I had been publicly horsewhipped by some fool woman. It will wear off—and I wont *forget* Belle. What you said as I waited for the Bus the night I came away is often with me."[35] A little later Bob, who had never been a "pacifist," suggested: "If after you read Williams attack you think it would be all right for me to make a brief *'reply'* outside the Senate when I meet up with him *just let me know* and I'll do it proper. You know I have no cons[ci]entious objections to overcome."[36]

Belle understood as no one else could what it had meant to him during all these months to be charged with disloyalty to the country he had loved and served throughout his life. Before receiving his detailed account, she wrote: "We were glad your 'case' was 'settled' so 'smoothly' It is probably not altogether satisfactory to you but under all the circumstances we are fortunate When we think of all the persecution that has been going on with no chance to get redress or any form of vindication, we are blessed to have escaped as we have with a *record* that stands for all time and can always be referred to in proof that you were wrongfully maligned and as- sailed[.]"[37] After his letters arrived describing Williams' attack, she added: "I know what you must have suffered. But I am sure you adopted the wisest course. . . . It has been a terrible long strain and has eaten into your heart more than any one except yourself could realize. And yet as I have said before when we consider what it has cost everyone who has stood out against war you are perhaps less martyred than most of them."[38]

For several days after the Senate adopted the resolution dismiss- ing the disloyalty charges, there were indications that Pomerene might seek reconsideration. Although Bob still had to be "on guard," his thoughts were turning to the work ahead when he wrote Phil on the night of the day the Peace Conference opened at Paris: "It took all the guts I had to sit still throughout Williams drunken attack, and then to let the vote be taken without a word.

"But everybody here who *understands* would not for the world have had me notice him. I had a speech of two hours all prepared and would have delivered it if there had been any *debate* that one could take part in. But to have taken the floor would have been to lift his filthy stuff up to a dignified level or to have answered in kind and gotten down into the dirt to do it.

"There is always another day—I don't mean—for him—but for *myself*."[39]

CHAPTER LVIII

A Filibuster to Protect Our
Natural Resources

Two days after the disloyalty charges against Bob had been dismissed, the Senate began debate on a bill which had been introduced and passed by the House at a single sitting in response to a cablegram President Wilson had sent from Rome. The President had recommended an immediate appropriation of $100,000,000 for the relief of such European peoples "outside of Germany, as may be determined upon by me from time to time as necessary."[1] When this bill came to the Senate, Senator Martin read a later cablegram from the President which stated: "Food relief is now the key to the whole European situation and to the solution of peace. Bolshevism is steadily advancing westward, has overwhelmed Poland, and is poisoning Germany. It cannot be stopped by force, but it can be stopped by food . . ."[2]

As Bob listened to the debate on this $100,000,000 bill, he was shocked to hear Martin, Hitchcock, Ashurst, Myers, Smoot, and Lodge "each straining to outdo the others to make sure not a cent should go to feed a German." In a letter to the family he poured out his burning indignation at such blindness and cruelty: "Just think of Uncle Sam handing out sandwiches to the hungry and denying a starving German child something to eat! How can they forget Grant at Appomatox—telling the rebels to take their horses back with them to till their farms and build up their homes, as he sent them back South with the benediction: 'Let us have peace.' . . . Then too the shallow scheme to 'use the food to fight Bolshevism.' No word about or understanding of the causes that underlie all the upheaval that is making Europe quake. It is the blind leading the blind. First they were going to 'shoot Bolshevism out of the damned anarchists' now they are going to offer them a 'free lunch' . . . Oh if there were a few real far seeing statesmen on the job over there. Men who could see that war has done what it must always do [—] prepare the way for another harvest of hate and bloodshed."[3]

Six days later Bob spoke extemporaneously against the bill. When he looked over the *Congressional Record,* he commented that the speech did not read smoothly but followed a pretty straight line with no digressions. Although expressed in more restrained terms than in the letter to his family, he revealed the same intensity of feeling as he argued to the Senate that food from the United States should be sent to Europe primarily to save the lives of starving peoples, not to dictate their form of government. He maintained that unless we held to this principle and also distributed it impartially we should discount and prejudice "the good work that this Government ought to be able to do as an example to the other Governments of the world."[4] Borah congratulated Bob on his speech and told him it was an important one to have contributed to the debate.[5] But the bill passed in the form the President had requested by a vote of 53 to 18,[6] and the United States went on record as ready to feed any peoples in Europe, in the discretion of the President, except the peoples of Germany, German-Austria, Bulgaria, and Turkey. Before this $100,000,000 bill was passed, the Senate had defeated an amendment to grant the American soldier of the World War sixty days' pay on demobilization.

In his letters Bob gave the family a continuous and interesting account of each day's events, the people he saw, the reports that came to him, and his own thoughts, thus keeping his "little flock" in touch with the world in which he lived. To him the time "spent in writing them" was "the best hour of all the day." It was like a "call at Whispering Sands."[7] Old friends and new appear in the pages of his letters. He wrote of each visit with keen interest— although sometimes under difficulties, as on the evening when he said he was "dividing time between this letter and an effort to get the room warm with a grate fire. Room 61°. Chester [La Follette] is a good fiddler but a dam[n] poor fireman. . . . But of course if he was a real fireman I suppose he wouldn't be much of a fiddler."[8]

Bob wrote of a "good visit" alone with his English-born friend David Thompson at his cozy "little apartment on Q Street," talking mainly about the Labor Party and the recent elections in England.[9] A Sunday, which had been "rather a lonesome day," was brightened by a call from Alice Goldmark Brandeis and Alfred Brandeis, who was visiting his brother Louis.[10] After dining at the Brandeis home a week later, he wrote that there was "just the family—Alfred Brandeis—and Elizabeth Evans . . . Elizabeth E. dressed up specially for the occasion. Alice B. very lovely. Louis is very thin—but says he's happy in his work."[11] That same day, after an Interstate Commerce Committee hearing on the railroad issue, he saw John R. Commons for the first time since Commons had signed a petition calling for Bob's expulsion from the Senate. The two men, who had been so intimate for many years, talked briefly of family matters. Bob wrote his family that Commons "shook hands with me" and "said he would call and see me, but he has not been around. He looked old and thinner than ever."[12]

St. Valentine's Day found Bob in a whimsical mood. "It was warm and bright this morning—," he wrote, "a regular spring day —a valentine day—such a day as would stir the birds to thinking of mating & nest building. When I came out of the Capitol tonight at seven o'clock I thought I was in for a long wait in the rain for a car. But lo & behold there was my good friend Senator Penrose with his Big Red Devil of a car—and 'wouldn't' I 'let him take me home.' Well I should think 'I would.' So Boise and I rode 'soide be soide' in the back seat, and it was St. Valentines day."[13]

A few days later Bob had over an hour's talk with Dr. Will Mayo, who "was just like a brother," Bob wrote. "He put me through a bit of an examination— Had me peel off in his private office and said now when the work lets up here I want you to come up and let us give you a thorough going over. He is a dear fellow just the same unspoiled genuine soul—if possible even mellower and warmer and more genial than he was eight years ago."[14] They had talked of Bob, Jr.'s, steady return to health which Mayo thought was coming along "fine."

On Bob, Jr.'s, birthday his father wrote Belle that he wondered how they were celebrating it: "I see him in your arms for the first time mamma our boy-baby. I see him as little Leather breeches— with his sweater & cap and curls—and then a chubby sturdy boy with his thick tangle of dark hair—his mother's honest eyes. I have been hunting bears with him in the Rockies again today.

And so he has been in my mind all day coming down through the years always a good pal and now a good counselor. I have been contrasting him as he is today with myself at 24. He has better book training than I had at that time. And he has a knowledge of affairs—a grasp of national and world conditions and problems and men equal to that of the men who are called the mature and profound statesmen of our time—of *today*. You will start life as a man Bobbie standing on my shoulders. You have your mothers brain my boy—the best brain in the world. With established health, what a service you can be to your community—your country and humanity! I greet you. Take one on me! Here is my check for ten."[15] Bob, Jr., wrote expressing appreciation for the birthday letter and the ten, but added: "No dad I don't start on your shoulders by a long shot. If I did I certainly would set the world on fire."[16]

His father replied: "It is a dear letter you wrote me Bobbie about what I've done. It seemed worthwhile at the time but it looks small as I turn my face to the front and see the big things waiting ahead. They will call the men & women of your generation and I know you will do your full share."[17] The "big things waiting ahead," the calls for help on many fronts, the opportunities he saw for vital public service, gave him a sense of swiftly passing time. "There are always a lot of things left over—when night comes," he wrote. "I suppose it must always be so. And when the last night comes and I go to the Land of Never Return—what an awful account of *things undone* I shall leave behind."[18] A few days later he wrote, "A week is really a lot of time out of the short end of life—when ev[e]ry tick of the clock seems to say 'hurry,' 'hurry.' "[19]

Some friends, estranged during the war, began to slip back into the rhythm of his life. But he felt that "try as you will to make it so, things and old friends are not just the same as they were. I doubt if, with me, they ever will be. It will take time—a *long* time and *new* events not related to this world-crash that has gone to the very foundation of all things human. It has changed our country our government our life. It appals me more from day to day because we are just beginning to take account of some of the consequences in detail. And the hypocracy [*sic*] of the 'holier than thou' crowd who brought it on and are now croaking about enough money to pay school teachers in the District of Columbia, or increase the pay of the poor char women in the departments are a difficult lot to associate with from day to day and *keep the peace*. Of course we have had enough experience to teach us to be philosophical and *patient*. I feel sometimes like answering with Rich[e]lieu, 'O!, Monk! Leave patience to the Saints—for I *am human*!'"[20]

One Sunday night, after returning home from work, Bob learned that Edwin Borchard of the Yale Law School was in town. He went back to his office in the Capitol, where they had a two-hour talk. Bob had a deep affection for Borchard, and thought that his long association with John Bassett Moore had "grounded him in the great fundamentals of foreign relations and given him the highest ideals." He wrote the family that Borchard quoted Moore as 'believing it utterly futile to make any impression upon the running tide of these terrible events; that a general lunacy prevails throughout the world . . . that to attempt to argue with it is but a sacrifice; that the men and their arguments will be spent and useless until the logic of events shocks the world into a receptive saner condition.' Rather a gloomy outlook for those . . . with whom time is passing— those who must speak now or never. I shall go on in the old way—if I go alone."[21]

Although the war had ended, the war legislation restricting free expression of ideas was still in force. The Espionage Law was being used to muzzle speech through a growing fear of radicalism invading this country from Europe. A week after the armistice the Department of Justice, headed by Attorney General Gregory, urged the American Protective League, an unofficial group of informers, not to relax its vigilance against activities harmful to the public morale during the discussion of peace terms. Violations of the Espionage Law must be prosecuted and further investigations instituted, the Department declared. "Whom the Gods would destroy they first make mad," Bob commented. "The elections do not appear to have taught these people anything. They are still 'mad' but more & more they will find it difficult to restrain free expression or select juries to do their bidding."[22]

Bob wrote his family that "the greatest crime of this war was the Espionage Law," and that a continued day-by-day attack should be made upon it. "Taxation, transportation, and the fraud and waste of war [were] as nothing to the destruction of free thought,"[23] and at first opportunity after the Armistice he had introduced a bill to amend it and "enlarge the right of free speech in the discussion of matters involved in the Peace Conference."[24] His bill had immediately been referred to the Judiciary Committee, which Bob described as "the tomb of the Capulets." He predicted to the family that he would "not let it rest there without creating something of a disturbance with that old gang of grave diggers" and that burying "*good* live bills wasn't going to be as peaceful an occupation in these times as tending flowers in an old-fashioned cemetary. [*sic*] At any rate there are some bills that committee wont burry [*sic*] without a wake."[25]

In preparing his bill Bob studied every brief he could get on cases involving freedom of speech. He wrote that Gilbert Roe's brief on the case of Eugene Debs, who was still held in prison under charges of having violated the Espionage Law, was exceptionally fine and "*must make its impression on the Court*—if there is anything there left to impress."[26] Bob thought that in all the cases which had been tried there was no brief which put the question up as Roe's did. It gave the Supreme Court a chance to hold the law constitutional and yet preserve freedom of assembly, speech, and press within reasonable limits. He added that he "wouldn't have the slightest hope of the Supreme Court deciding right in these cases except for the things Chief Justice White said to a certain Senator who must be nameless—about it being important that the Court should or ought to render an early decision so 'distinguishing' on these cases as to preserve the constitutional rights of freedom of speech press & assembly."[27]

At the end of "rather a dull" Sunday, Bob received from Julius Truesdell the report that Attorney General Gregory had resigned. He wrote the family that he hoped it was true, for he felt sure that Gregory had been "an evil influence" in the direction of the suppression of free speech. All of these repressive laws were, he thought, "the conception of a fifteenth century mind." The line of precedents Gregory had left would, Bob said, "be an everlasting menace to the liberties of the people of this country. The most pressing . . . need of this hour is a well organized assault upon these abominable laws and their policy of enforcement. . . . People by the thousands have been taken into custody and dragged not into court or the presence of even examining magistrates—but to the 'offices' of the District Attorneys and even the dens of the Secret Service thugs and given the third degree." Bob went on to relate to the family an authentic but "very ugly story" he had recently heard concerning the treatment of Marie Jenney Howe, wife of Frederic C. Howe, then Commissioner of Immigration of the Port of New York. She had been seized in front of her apartment in New York by the "Secret Service hounds" and not allowed to communicate with her husband or an attorney. Bob added indignantly, "I hope it is *true*—this report that Gregory has resigned."[28] *

A few weeks later a meeting in Washington "started a great row" in the Senate. On Sunday afternoon, February 2, Albert Rhys Williams and Louise Bryant, John Reed's wife, spoke at Poli's Theater in Washington. Both had recently returned from Russia, and they criticized the Wilson Administration for the failure of the United States to recognize the Soviet Union. Two days later Bob wrote his family, "The Senate frothed at the mouth today for a couple of hours" and "then passed viva voce a resolution for the famous or infamous sub. Com.[mittee] of Judiciary of the Senate to investigate the meeting . . . Guess its a good thing. It will make talk in the Senate and that will help in the long run. But just think of it—Senators taking the ground that any criticism of our government is an effort to 'overthrow' the government!" Bob noted that "The Senators from the Mountain States . . . out where they have the I.W.W. in force are the craziest of the lot . . . They are scared stiff."[29]

During the debate on the meeting, Senator King of Utah came over to Bob's seat and appealed to him to raise his voice in the Senate to stop this agitation "to bring on a *class war*." Bob replied that for twenty years he had argued that democracy had been over-thrown in this country not by the working class but by the money power; that the repression of freedom of speech was the very thing which would drive men to resort to violence to protest their wrongs; that he was in favor of "putting a soap box on every government reservation in the City and inviting everybody to state their griev-ances." In trying to persuade Bob to raise his voice in the Senate, King had told of receiving "threatening letters." Commenting on this humorously to the family, Bob said, "Seems to me I got threatening letters and mob violence in various forms[,] effigies

* Thomas W. Gregory resigned Jan. 12, 1919, effective March 4.

&c all from the dear law and order patriots. . . . Why [Elihu] Root wanted Senators 'who voted against war taken out and shot at sunrise.' Fine example of I.W.W. methods ! ! !"[30]

Four days later Bob was one of those who supported an unsuccessful effort of Borah's to suspend a Senate rule so that he might offer an amendment to the Espionage Law *"only* to the extent of *depriving the Postmaster General* of *power to exclude matter from the mails."* This revelation of Senate sentiment led Bob to write, "Men are making records these days that ought to make the framers of the Constitution open their eyes in their coffins."[31]

There was a strong movement on in the Senate to enact legislation to stop "the holding of socialist meetings in the next campaign." Bob dreaded the effect of the "recent outbreak against free speech on the Supreme Court," especially as they were "due to render a decision in the Debs case very soon."[32] When the opportunity offered a few days later, Bob made a brief, incisive speech against the repression of free public discussion. He clearly defined his own position on the issue as being willing to permit "The wildest discussion." If somebody indulged in unreasoning and violent exhortation, he said, then let him be answered. "Put an open stand on every open place in the city of Washington," and tell everybody to "say what you please." Then tell everybody else to "answer them." Error exposed could not long stand. The wholesome cure for complaint was free discussion. The point where he believed the power of the Government should be applied was where discussion was "translated into overt acts of violence." He was convinced violence would not come in this country if the freest and fullest discussion was permitted.[33] Bob found to his surprise that his "remarks" had "made some impression" on many Senators and several Members of the House who spoke to him about it during the next few days.[34]

Bob's fears that free press and free speech might be further menaced by repressive legislation seemed justified when Senator Thomas J. Walsh of Montana reported a bill from the Judiciary Committee enlarging the powers of the Postmaster General. Bob immediately got a typewritten copy and telephoned to Gilbert Roe in New York. Roe arrived at Bob's office that night to help brief an argument against the bill. Bob also conferred with Borah, who said he would oppose it.

That night when Bob got home he wrote the family he thought the bill would prohibit "carrying (and probably wearing) any thing red." He explained that it enlarged the powers of the Postmaster General to shut out of the mails anything he decided advocated violence or strikes to overthrow the Government. "No court or jury is to decide—just the Postmaster General is to determine whether the document is 'seditious,' 'treasonable,' 'preaches violence' or 'aims at the overthrow of the Government.' . . . Just think of Congress legislating on such a subject in the throes and turmoil of the last days of the session!"[35]

Walsh's "red flag bill" was only one of several measures Bob thought pernicious which were being pressed for immediate passage without proper debate in the closing hours of the Sixty-fifth Congress, which would adjourn automatically on March 4. Among these were a mass of appropriation bills, a $5,000,000,000 bond bill, a bill validating "irregular" contracts for war materials amounting to $2,000,000,000, and two long-deferred conference reports on public oil and coal lands and on water power. To protect the public interest and stop the looting of the public lands and the treasury, Bob thought a filibuster which would prevent hasty passage of these bills and force an extra session, where their iniquitous provisions could be exposed in debate and amended, was more than justified.[36]

Furthermore, discussion of the League of Nations had already begun in the Senate. It had been opened by Knox in a resolution and by Kellogg in a speech the day the President had sailed for Europe to lay his League of Nations plan before the Peace Conference.[37] The approaching adjournment of Congress necessitated Wilson's return after an absence of twelve weeks, and he was scheduled to arrive on February 24. Bob had been informed that the President had cabled an invitation to Members of the Foreign Relations Committees of both Houses to meet him at the White House when he returned and had at the same time requested them not to discuss the League of Nations until after this meeting. In a family letter Bob commented this "was going some in running things at both ends of the [Pennsylvania] Avenue," especially as Wilson himself was "discussing the subject with the American people over his private Government cable at the rate of a dozen newspaper columns a day."[38]

With all the "big things impending," Bob did not think "Wilson should be left with an absolutely free hand."[39] Bob thought it was extremely important that Congress should continue in session so that the Senate could discuss the terms of peace while the Paris Peace Conference was still in session, and before the delegates reached final agreements. Believing in open covenants openly arrived at, he thought discussion of peace terms might help to save some of Wilson's Fourteen Points which he was certain were menaced by the secret sessions in Paris.[40] Although the Senate had the constitutional right to "reject" the treaty if the terms were unacceptable, he feared that after the nations concerned had settled on the terms the Senate might find itself "pretty well tied up." The argument could then be made that rejection would necessitate the delegates all coming together again to reconsider, and this would "be urged as a reason for swallowing the thing" whether they liked it or not. Therefore the issues should be debated in the Senate while the Conference was "in session for the effect it might have on their action."[41]

For some time Bob had known that conservative Republican leaders were talking about an extra session, but he doubted if they would have "either the industry or the courage to force it."[42] None of them had approached him directly about it, however, until early in February when Lodge came to him to say "there *must* be an extra session" and that he hoped Bob's "voice would be heard on these appropriation bills." Bob replied that he had interpreted Lodge's silence and that of "our other bosses" to mean "the Republicans had quit on their extra session program." Lodge assured him this was a mistake, that he had been tied up in conference on the War Revenue bill but was free now and would be heard from. He added cautiously that although he "would have no sympathy with Russian discussion," he "might welcome anything that took up the time."[43]

But in spite of these assurances, Bob remained skeptical as to how much Lodge and the "other bosses" could be depended upon to sustain a filibuster and prevent passage of the bills he considered most pernicious. Therefore he went ahead quietly with his plan to organize a few Senators who shared his own conviction and could be counted on to help him in the final fight during the closing hours of Congress. Among the Republican "regulars" he thought there were enough Senators who, for different reasons, desired an extra session sufficiently to prolong debate for a time in a concealed filibuster even though they could not be relied on to come out into the open at the finish.

When the conference report on the Coal and Oil bill was presented to the Senate on February 20, Bob decided there was a good fighting chance to prevent its passage. During the preceding days Borah, Kenyon, Lenroot, Smoot, and others had helped "to string things out" by debate on legislation they were familiar with.[44] Only seventeen and a half days remained before Congress would automatically adjourn. Eyes were on the clock, because bills had been backing up ominously in a jam that might be hard to break. The Administration Democrats were apprehensive, and night sessions were being threatened. They seemed aware that a concealed filibuster was on. Four days later Pittman, who was chairman of the Conference Committee on the Coal and Oil bill, unexpectedly launched into a violent speech openly accusing Senators of "being in a conspiracy to filibuster it."[45] Late that afternoon, as Bob moved about the Senate floor, he sensed that the situation was set "for the Oil & Coal bill to be made the unfinished business & pushed through."[46] After consulting with Norris, Kenyon, and other Senators, he found no one who was prepared to fight the bill, and realized that he might have to undertake the brunt of it immediately.

But fortunately he was able to postpone the battle. He had learned that a new provision including Alaska in the coal-purchasing section had been introduced in conference. This fact made it possible for him to delay consideration of the bill by skillful strategy in bringing up a point of order on a recent Senate rule which sent it back to conference.[47] Thus he gained time to prepare material for a prolonged debate and to try to get "some of the other fellows" to "come in and help." Meanwhile his secretary, Hannan, and Harry Slattery, executive secretary of the National Conservation Association, were hard at work in his office on a detailed analysis of the complicated conference report which filled the better part of twelve columns in the *Congressional Record*.[48] Bob had known Slattery since 1910 when the latter had been closely associated with Gifford Pinchot in the Ballinger controversy and had also worked with Brandeis. In their frequent collaborations through the years, Bob always found Slattery "a veritable watchdog of the Nation's resources," on the people's side in every contest, and "ready to give of his time without compensation."[49]

Bob's many battles in the Senate for conservation of the natural resources of the public domain had begun in 1906, early in his first term as Senator. Therefore he was especially well equipped to lead a fight on these issues at short notice. The more he studied the conference report on the Coal and Oil bill, the worse he thought it was. As presented to the Senate, it was described as a bill "to encourage and promote the mining of coal, phosphate, oil, gas, and sodium on the public domain."[50] This sounded innocuous, but Bob was convinced that if adopted it would ultimately permit title to the public lands to pass to the great corporations[51] and end finally in monopoly control of our mineral resources. It followed the same pattern Wisconsin had gone through when he was a boy, and that pattern had "merely delivered us to monopoly."[52] He wrote the family that he believed it would be possible to show during the debate that it meant "a practical clean up of oil & coal." He added that there was a big lobby in Washington "hounding" everybody and that he had been informed by a Senator whose observation could be trusted that there had been some indications Standard Oil was behind the bill.[53]

Bob knew that Brandeis understood the situation, and he was "also *quite* sure" Secretary of the Navy Daniels, who was especially concerned about the naval oil reserves, "would like to see it beaten."[54] Bob thought it was vital to national defense that the naval oil reserves should be held in trust for the exclusive use of our Navy and not be leased to private interests. He knew the Attorney General shared his opinion of the bill because more than a year before he had gone to Gregory's office, at the latter's request, to discuss it.[55] But in spite of this, Bob expected a hard fight to defeat it because the newspaper men had reported to him that the President, who had returned from Europe on February 24, had ordered passage of both the Coal and Oil bill and the Water Power bill.[56]

After putting in most of his Sunday at the office studying the conference report, he wrote the family in California urging them to stop off at the Grand Canyon on the way home. He said: "These coal & oil vandals under their bill have the gall to write into their Conference report that they can take claims and become owners of coal mines in the Grand Canyon and the Mount Olympus monument. They have been at this thing until it has made them so sordid and degraded that they would blow up the Holy Sepulcher in their scramble for dirty money. Go and see the Grand Canyon as God made it while you can. They have a footing in Niagara—they 'got' Hetch Hetchy—and sooner or later [,] maybe very soon [,] they'll be in possession of the Grand Canyon." He added that, "If you couldn't put your finger on a single bad feature of such measures as the coal & oil and water power bills—disposing of the natural resources of the country [,] the fact that they have been held back till the closing hours of the sess:on ought [to] raise the presumption that they are too rotten to stand the light of day."[57]

The night after Bob had forced the bill back to conference on the point of order, he telephoned Senator Sherman, who agreed to help him. That same evening Slattery and Hannan went to Sherman's apartment to discuss the bill and leave material relating to it. During the few days the bill was in conference, Bob also secured promises of help from Gronna and Senator Joseph France of Maryland. He knew these three Senators could be counted on to go through to the end of the session, and he found others who were willing to help in less conspicuous ways. He wrote the family that the next nine days would be "one protracted poison-gas battle— and I fight without a mask!"[58] In this battle he had the help of Gilbert Roe, who stayed on until Congress adjourned. Throughout the next few days these two intimate friends and former law partners collaborated once more on a filibuster they believed necessary to protect the public interest.[59]

When the Coal and Oil bill came back to the Senate, Bob found that, although it had been slightly improved, the Conference Committee had kept the pernicious provision in regard to the Grand Canyon and Mount Olympus. He knew that Administration pressure could pass the bill if it came to a vote. His strategy was therefore to prevent a vote by filibustering, or if that failed, by returning it to conference again on a point of order. The Senate galleries were crowded when he began his speech against the bill on Saturday afternoon, March 1. He stood at his desk behind a huge pile of manuscript and numerous volumes of reports, from which he occasionally read.[60] The *New York Times* correspondent noted that his speech was "a remarkable combination of elements" which "held the interest of the galleries and evoked applause and laughter."[61] For nearly four hours he discussed the bill in a preliminary way that led to questions from the floor and intermittent debate. In referring to his own long fight for conservation, he mentioned his experience in 1906 with Theodore Roosevelt, who had issued the first Executive order withdrawing public lands. During the debate a sharp clash occurred with Robinson which recalled the Senator's bitter attack on Bob at the time of the Armed Ship bill filibuster in 1917.[62]

As Bob continued what a reporter termed his "spectacular discussion" which "obviously was intended to meet any endurance test," the Democratic leaders became alarmed lest his filibuster might prevent a vote on the Administration's much desired Victory Bond bill.[63] To avoid this they decided to sidetrack temporarily the Coal and Oil bill and bring up the Victory Bond bill. But Bob was sure another attempt would be made to put through the Coal and Oil bill before adjournment. Therefore he warned the Senators, "with a grim smile," that he had "much documentary evidence which he would read to the Senate if need be to hold the floor and said in so many words that he had just begun to fight."[64] At five o'clock he consented to a two-hour recess. So far his filibuster on the Coal and Oil bill had succeeded.

In consenting to a recess Bob had deliberately given the Republicans, who had previously opposed the Victory Bond bill, an opportunity to determine in caucus whether they would make an organized effort to beat it by assisting him in the filibuster. During a "stormy" caucus they decided by a vote of 14 to 11 not to join him in the filibuster. Bob recorded confidentially that two of the minority Senators, France and Sherman, were so angry they threatened "to quit the party and go in for a new deal." In a letter to his family Bob explained what he considered one of the pernicious aspects of this "bad" bond bill which "for the first time in history gives the Sec[re]t[a]ry of Treasury the right to fix the rate of interest & exempt the bonds from taxation in whole or in part as he pleases and as the banking interests demand."[65]

When the Senate met again at seven o'clock, Bob went on with his attack upon the Coal and Oil bill until the Victory Bond bill was taken up. Shortly before midnight he began a speech against the Bond bill, using the material Roe had prepared. He held the floor until nearly daylight. But as there was no organized Republican opposition, the bill passed and the Senate recessed at six forty Sunday morning until ten o'clock Monday. Bob and Roe reached home Sunday morning at seven. They slept for two hours, snatched a hasty breakfast, and returned to the office to prepare the two addresses Bob delivered that day at the memorial services for Senator Paul O. Husting and Representative James H. Davidson of Wisconsin.[66] That night he wrote his family, "I could not possibly say whether it was day before yesterday—or ages and ages ago that I last wrote you. One day has merged into another without beginning or ending. I cannot tell you the story until I have had more sleep. . . . I am standing off the Oil & Coal Bill & the water power bill. The latter has not been up yet but Bankhead is waiting his chance." Bob thought the way the Water Power bill had been amended in conference was "also a surrender of public rights."[67]

During the concluding twenty-six hours of the session, which began at ten o'clock Monday morning March 3, the $840,000,000 Deficiency Appropriation Bill was before the Senate. It had reached the Appropriation Committee only two days before. If a vote on this bill could be prevented, Bob thought it might force an extra session. But if it passed, he feared this would "enable the raiders to get away with the natural resources."[68] Senators Sherman and France shared his fear, and agreed that the filibuster must continue. The three promised to spell one another. They kept their own counsel, and waited for the other Senators to talk themselves out on the Appropriation bill until they could be sure of holding the floor to the end of the session on March 4. They knew that Pittman and Bankhead were "watching like hawks" to get up the Coal and Oil and Water Power bills.[69]

Apparently hoping to break the filibuster, Senator Martin informed the Senate that the President had told him "in two conversations, in the plainest possible English, that he had made up his mind, and it was final, that no extra session of Congress will be called under any circumstances until his return from France."[70] But this announcement did not halt the filibuster. At one thirty on the morning of March 4, Bob again took the floor. In an attack on the pernicious practice of holding back huge appropriation bills until late in the session, he said it was high time "to rebel against any power whether it comes directly from the Executive or from a congressional 'steering committee,' which attempts to coerce

Senators into playing the shameful part of automatons and blindly voting measures" without an opportunity to discuss or amend them. He declared it was the President's responsibility to call an extra session immediately. Congress should, he said, properly examine the appropriation bills at once. Furthermore, he maintained that the Senate must be in session to advise in making the treaty as provided by the Constitution. In closing his speech at five o'clock that morning, he expressed the hope that the President would "be persuaded to convene Congress in extraordinary session within the next 48 hours. There is great work for Congress to do. I trust it may be called by the Executive to perform that great public service."[71]

After Bob finished, France spoke until eight in the morning. Then Sherman held the floor to the end "against every device to get him to yield." Gronna was with them at every point, and other Republicans aided. Bob said, "They could not get France or Sherman off their guard . . . or they would have thrown the deficiency [bill] & scrambled to put the other things through."[72]

All that night Secretary of the Navy Josephus Daniels and his assistant secretary, Franklin D. Roosevelt, were at the Capitol anxiously following the filibuster because they feared legislation might be passed which would turn over the valuable oil reserves to private interests.[73] The *New York Times* reported that "The scene in the Senate Chamber during the closing hours of the long filibuster was one which will long be remembered by all who witnessed it. Democratic Senators were sitting back in their seats smiling grimly. Even the Conservative Senators were not inclined to make any expression of dismay over what had happened. They would not take seriously the statements that financial danger of far reaching consequences would ensue."[74] When the final hour of the session arrived, the President was in his room at the Capitol near the Senate Chamber. At twelve o'clock Vice President Marshall banged his gavel on "one of the most remarkable situations in the history of the Nation."[75] And then, as reported in the press and the daily *Congressional Record,* he declared the Senate "adjourned Sine Deo" (without God). In the permanent *Congressional Record* this was changed to the customary "adjourned sine die."[76]

That night the President voiced his anger in more restrained terms than he had after the Armed Ship bill filibuster. Before sailing for Paris, he told reporters that he "took it for granted that the men who have obstructed and have prevented the passage of necessary legislation are willing to assume the responsibility of the impaired efficiency of the Government and the embarrassed finances of the country during the time of my enforced absence." Ignoring the fact that Congress had been left to function alone during his previous absence in Europe, he now indicated he would not call an extra session because it was "not in the interest of the right conduct of public affairs" for Congress to sit while it was impossible for him to be in Washington. He also announced that when he came back from the Peace Conference the Covenant of the League of Nations would be so intertwined with the peace treaty that they could not be separated. "The structure of peace will not be vital without the League," he declared.[77] Commenting on this in a family letter, Bob said, "I think he is in for a stormy time when he gets back."[78]

The President's statement was interpreted as a defiant answer to the widely publicized round robin, signed by thirty-seven Republican Senators which had been presented to the Senate in the form of a resolution in the early morning hours of March 4, before Bob began his speech that day. This resolution, fathered by Lodge, ranking Republican member of the Foreign Relations Committee, declared it was the sense of the Senate that the constitution of the League of Nations in the form now proposed to the Peace Conference should not be accepted by the United States and that the proposal for a League of Nations to ensure permanent peace should be taken up after the peace terms had been settled.[79]

The round-robin declaration foreshadowed danger to the plan the President had announced on the eve of his departure for Paris. The signatures of thirty-seven Republican Senators represented enough votes to defeat a treaty "intertwined" with the League of Nations Covenant. Bob had refused to sign the round robin because he did not believe in that method of dealing with important public issues. A few days later he wrote his family: "I am going to take my stand on the League & Treaty when we get it and know what it is. Besides I think the fellows who voted for war raped the Monroe doctrine themselves & while it isn't necessary to go on raping it I dont think it lies in their mouths to make all the noise about European Entanglements. I'm going to sit in the game when I get ready and play my own hand."[80]

A Time of Waiting

Bob slept very late the morning after the successful filibuster ended on March 4, 1919, with the adjournment of Congress. That night he went with Fola and George Middleton to the Belasco Theatre to see *Adam and Eva*, a comedy his son-in-law had written with Guy Bolton. The next day Bob wrote Roe: "It did me good. I slept all that night and all the fore noon today and before God I am sleepy now. All of which shows that I am a young healthy lazy kid."[1] These intervals of extra sleep, the theater, and an occasional motion picture were the only vacation Bob allowed himself, for he felt he must prepare for the important legislation that would soon come before the Senate. He deplored Wilson's refusal to call an extra session immediately after adjournment, and wrote two editorials severely criticizing what he believed was the President's failure to carry out his constitutional responsibility in this respect.[2]

Bob's first immediate task was to read the galley proofs of his eight filibuster speeches for the permanent *Congressional Record*. After working on them for about twelve hours, he wrote his family, "I always hate a speech after I make it and dont see how I or any body else could ever have thought it even tolerable." Probably no one would look at them, he added, but "*I* may be going over them from time to time after I'm dead—and I know I should feel awfully sore about it to find some sentence awfully bad and passed [*sic*] all chance for correction."[3]

During the filibuster letters had stacked up in his office so that there was enough unanswered correspondence to keep four stenographers busy for a month. Bob wrote his family that among the many comments received was a laudatory "letter from my 'friend' Gifford Pinchot crediting me with saving the country from the conspirators for the time being at least."[4] Subsequently he read Pinchot's letter as part of an argument he made in the Senate against another coal-and-oil bill.[5] Bob often cited the debate during the final days of the March, 1919, session as proof of the concrete public service a filibuster might render. When the supply bills, which had been held up, were passed at the next session after further scrutiny and consideration, nearly a billion dollars was saved for the taxpayers.[6]

During the weeks that preceded the extra session, Bob was able to give more time to his magazine, which by March, 1919, was beginning to make its own way, and he now felt that it might become "a real family asset" as well as continue to be an influential medium for his views on public questions. "I wish I might vary my style and strike a lighter note now and then," he wrote in commenting on the length and seriousness of his editorials. "But it is a sober time in the whole world and I do not find it easy to free myself from the oppressive burden which the war has added to humanity everywhere."[7]

In another letter Bob told his family that the *Madison Democrat* was pressing for trial in the libel case, but that Crownhart and Roe wished to postpone it because they thought the situation in Madison was getting better all the time and thus increasing the possibility of a fair jury trial. Also, if the proceedings began at once, Bob knew he would have to be in Madison and thus neglect his work in Washington at a time when he ought to be preparing for the important extra session. For these reasons Bob said it had been decided that the case would be "dismissed without prejudice—that is with the right to begin it again any time within two years from the date of the libel—The two years would be up next fall . . . So I am taking about the only course I can take under all the circumstances. I know it will be galling to you all & especially to Bob, but I am not done with the Democrat yet, and I hope you wont take it too hard. . . . But I shall be prepared for anything in the way of publicity *if it comes* & so let you know as fully about it as I do. I am a patient man I can wait a little while for my innings—I have had to do that many times in my life and have managed to stand up under it until the tide set my way."[8]

On the night of March 17, as Bob sat alone in his room after dinner and dated his regular family letter, he remembered that on this anniversary of Ireland's patron saint Belle and the children had always gathered about the fireside to hear him read the Irish folk tales they all loved. "I wish I could drop in on you tonight," he wrote, "with Darby O'Gill under me arm—it bein' St. Patricks day in the *Eavenin*—and make ye acquainted wid Sleeve-Na-Mon—Anthony Sullivan's goat—the cou[p]le widout childer, King Brian Connor & the Good People. But bein only a common mortal, I havent the power of the Good People to cover long distances in a wink of yer eye. So we'll have to put it off for tonight anyway."[9]

Bob was feeling keenly the long separation from his family, but he had refrained from suggesting that Mary join him because he knew she was planning to leave La Jolla to enter the University of Wisconsin at the beginning of the second semester. Phil had written asking her to come to Madison in time to be his guest at the Junior Prom, the gayest social function of the year. She hesitated because she could not afford to buy any new clothes. But he won her consent when he wrote, "If you have two party dresses you won't need any new ones—remember *no one* here has *seen* any of your *clothes* and they will *look* new to everybody—and you are so pretty anyhow that clothes don't make much difference."[10] Before Mary left, however, an incident changed their plans.

It had been the custom to invite to the prom the United States Senators, the governor, and other high officials. But this year Bob's name was omitted. The obvious slight caused a local sensation. Mary declined to go, and Phil arranged to meet her in Chicago. "Please send Bob's silk hat," he wrote his father. "I shall want to 'dress' up for her. If it is convenient could you lend me $10.00 on next month's allowance so I can give her this little party."[11] Bob sent $15 and the hat, "so Mary will have a swell escort to all their doings in Chicago," he wrote Belle. "I am so sorry for both of the kids. To have such a nasty feeling thrust into their University life will make a lasting impression I fear. Now with me, it dont count. It is like the buzzing of a gnat after you have been having the time of your life in a den of rattlesnakes. But I hope they will forget it just as soon as the Prom is over and go right on as if the thing had never occurred. There is another day coming in all this war stuff. We have the right of it and in the end it will be the other people who will do the explaining."[12]

Phil and Mary substituted a few festive evenings in Chicago for

the Junior Prom. During the hours of visiting together, Phil persuaded Mary to give up her plan of entering the university because
he thought she would be very unhappy where there was so much
hostility toward their father. On March 25 Bob wrote in his diary,
"Mary came—great surprise and joy." That night he wrote to
Belle and Bob, Jr.: "Well, what do you think happened to me this
afternoon? I was moping away up here in my room when there
came a faint tap at the door . . . I opened the door and there *stood
Mary—my Mary*!!! Do you know what I did? I just cried!
That's what I did. I'm an old man all right . . . Ye Gods but it was
good to have my arms around her and hold her in my lap—my
baby. . . . Mary and I havent talked thing[s] over or made any
plans—yet and I dont know what she has in her head. But Washington is hers..She shall have anything she wants—and do everything she wants to do. Say, I *feel just as if I had been demobi-
lized*."[13] A few days later he pictured their life together. "We have
each of us worked all the evenings since she came . . . she in her
room and I in mine—but we run back and forth as we think of
things to say to each other. Yes indeed I like to talk over things
with Mary—she sees ev[e]rything with level eyes—and has clear
strong thinking back of it all."[14]

Bob had received a small fund for clerical help, and Mary under-
took a job in his office in addition to attending night classes at
the Corcoran School of Art. His joy in Mary's companionship
made him realize how much Bob, Jr., must miss her, and he wrote
suggesting that his son might like to continue his convalescence at
Madison whenever his mother decided to return to Washington.
Leaving the choice to his son, he said: "But I know that we can
do anything we set out to do. That's one thing we all have in us—
and it's sometimes the saving thing."[15] Bob, Jr., replied he had
decided that after his mother left he would stay on at La Jolla in
a little cottage she had found which rented for $16.50 per month.
"If I were within twelve or fifteen hours of there [Washington]
when things got hot as they will over the big problems of peace and
reconstruction [,] the temptation to go there would be too great. I
figure that the only way I can stay off the job with such big things
moving is to keep about three thousand miles between me and it.
You know that I would give anything to be there helping in my

small way but I made that mistake once and I will not make it again."[10]

During the spring Gilbert Roe, Alf Rogers, and William T. Evjue, the editor of the now successfully established *Capital Times* of Madison, came to Washington to spend a few days with Bob. "We haven't done much else but just 'visit,'" Bob wrote. "As we didn't have our knitting we smoked some so as to not seem altogether idle."[17] In another letter Bob said they went to Rock Creek Cemetery in a street car and "communed for a time with the spirit that hallows that spot where for all time St. Gaudens shrouded and hooded woman in bronze will speak her special message to each mortal who visits her. They were there to-day coming singly and in little groups to sit bowed in reverence under her spell for a little time and then go quietly and thoughtfully away. . . . We thought and talked much of you [,] mamma [,] and I am to read them to-night the beautiful thing you wrote about it."[18] Together they drove in a Ford about the Zoo, Georgetown, and Arlington, something Bob had not done for years. To him a Washington spring was "always like a miracle," and he wrote that "the soft pale green of the new spring dress—with the first pink flush of the young redbud blossoms and the white banners of the dogwood seen from Arlington in every direction is a sight never to be forgotten."[19] Bob found the days with his friends "all too short," but when they left he wrote, "Well I've had my spree and must get down to work."[20]

Bob's voluminous longhand letters to his family record his increasing apprehension regarding the secret sessions of the Peace Conference at Paris. He followed closely the official press reports, but was keenly aware that they contained only what those in authority chose to have revealed. These press dispatches and the confidential reports of friends returning from Paris were the limited sources upon which Bob necessarily had to base the opinions he expressed from day to day in his letters. His anxiety increased when he learned that the Council of Ten had been reduced to the Council of Four. This meant that the Treaty would be drafted in secret by four men: the French Premier, Clemenceau; the British Premier, Lloyd George; the Italian Premier, Orlando; and President Wilson. As Bob recalled the published terms of the secret treaties, it seemed to him that the previous commitments of three countries represented in this Council of Four would seriously menace the altruism of Wilson's Fourteen Points. Commenting on the situation in a confidential letter, Bob said: "we will see how much the Wilson doctrine as to what we were 'fighting for' will be found in the final result. I shall be a good deal surprised if it doesnt turn out to be a cold blooded, sordid 'peace' treaty dressed up in a maze of rhetorical flim flam."[21]

In response to one of Bob's letters, Belle wrote: "whatever one's attitude toward the war and our part in it, is it not the part of true statesmanship to deal with the problems as they exist? Just as I do not believe we can ever return to the old [kind] of personal competition in the business world so I think we must accept some changed conditions in the political world. . . . So it seems to me nations cannot stand *isolated* if they would or even if it is for their own particular good. Some kind of a federated world whose ideal *should be* the best good of all, is bound to come. Selfish interests are bound to do their best to dominate it. They had their part in framing our constitution which we are disposed to believe was a great document for human welfare. And it was. But we know some of the framers were almost as fearful of any real rule of the masses as the governments of to-day are now scared at Bolshevism. The proposed League of Nations may be so bad you can not support it. I am only suggesting the spirit in which I think it should be approached."[22]

Bob was fully in accord with Belle as to the need for some kind of international organization which would promote cooperation among the nations of the world. The resolution he had introduced on February 8, 1915, had been directed toward this ultimate purpose. But the reports he was receiving indicated there was nothing left in the Treaty of Wilson's Fourteen Points "that couldn't be covered with a postage stamp." These had been the basis of the armistice, and Bob expressed his profound conviction when he wrote Belle that "There can be no permanent peace based on wrong and no League can be formed strong enough to maintain such a peace."[23]

As Bob read the news dispatches from Paris toward the end of April and early in May, he thought that Wilson was "turning flip flops with a marvelous agility" in accepting inconsistent compromises on the principle of "self determination" which had been one of his Fourteen Points. On May 5, Bob wrote Belle that "The Chinese are hard hit on the deal they have gotten which practically gives the Japs control of Northern China. It was Japans price for coming in & signing up on the League & the treaty after being denied recognition as an equal. It builds up Japan to make us trouble hereafter and offends China with whom we have always professed such strong friendship."[24]

Although Bob did not know it, many of the compromises which distressed him also disturbed prominent members of the American delegation when they finally learned the terms of the treaty after it had been completed. Opinions confided to private diaries and expressed in letters written at this time reveal that General Tasker H. Bliss, Secretary of State Lansing, Herbert Hoover, and many others thought that the document framed in secret sessions was unworkable and would produce rather than prevent future wars. Lansing believed the Treaty was a document providing how the great military powers intended to divide the spoils of war and that no League could maintain a peace thus imposed and keep its character as an instrument of international justice.[25]

The Peace Treaty, which had been drafted in secret and adopted at a secret plenary session, was presented to the Germans at Versailles on May 7. From Paris that same day the President issued a call by cable for Congress to meet in extra session on May 19. The full text of the Treaty was not published in the Allied countries. But in Germany it could be purchased in a cheap edition, which also circulated in Paris, Holland, and nearby countries.[26] In the United States, however, only "an official summary" of the Treaty was given out by the Committee of Public Information. It appeared in the press on May 8. After reading part of it, Bob wrote his family that "as far as I've gone it is enough to chill the heart of the world. No one dares or has so far as I have seen to say one word publicly in sympathy for the German people who had no voice in declaring war and who had no choice but to obey their masters. The people[,] the 70 million[,] are to be ground under the heel of the conquerors. . . . How she can pay & what she will have left to pay with—but the lives of her working people God only knows."[27] When the press reported a few days later that plans were being made to compel the Germans to sign, Bob wrote: "The proposal to use the blockade to force acceptance of the Treaty . . . surpasses anything in history so far as I can now recall. 'Sign or starve men women children—all'—is going back to barbarism."[28]

Bob was also concerned at this time about the impact of the war and the peace upon economic conditions in the United States. The newspapers carried dispatches from different parts of the country reporting increasing unemployment, bread lines, strikes, and murmurings of revolt. Through his mail and talks with individuals, he learned of false arrests and brutal prosecutions in violation of proper legal procedure. He deplored the acts of violence committed by a few extremists and feared they would be made the excuse for a fresh installment of laws to repress and destroy free speech in peacetime. But he was certain that neither repression nor violence would solve the complex problems which caused the prevailing unemployment and industrial unrest. These should, he believed, have been taken up in an extra session immediately after Congress adjourned. He wrote that "While reform by the ballot is slow and discouraging, . . . in a country where every citizen has the ballot—if there is not intelligence enough to *use* it to *reform* the government would there be *intelligence enough successfully to conduct* a real democratic government—after they had established it by force?"[29] In a letter to Belle he conceded that the public was, as she had said, "suspicious of Congress and distrustful of politics generally." But he added, "the remedy does not lie in turning the government over to a one man power even [if] you had a *benevolent* despotism. And Wilson isn't a *benevolent* despot. The true remedy is in making Congress representative of the people. . . . that is always the problem of democracy. And yet it is the only way [to] restore and preserve real democracy. After all it gets back to the old issue if the people want a government of their own they must do the work of making it their own."[30]

After receiving a telegram appealing for action to stop the harsh treatment of conscientious objectors, Bob wrote his family: "I don't suppose there is anything I can do but I surely will make the trial. That is all there is to this thing we call life anyway—just doing your *best*—your *very* best to get the results. The things that are being done to the poor fellows in prison guilty only of doing what they believed to be right—is simply appalling—if the information is even an approach to the truth."[31] Bob asked a large number of Senators and Congressmen for cooperation. But only a few called him on the phone or acknowledged his appeal. Several days later he wrote: "It is quite clear that they don't want to join

in an application for their relief. Isn't it strange the difference between this country and those of Europe[?] All the Central Powers
have released their political prisoners. And last January 83 members of the British parliament came out for general amnesty for all
political prisoners." He quoted at length from an address by Lord
Hugh Cecil, British Conservative, who had spoken of the "moral
responsibility" of a government that kept "good and religious men"
in confinement "to coerce them into doing what they sincerely
think is wrong."[32] In a previous letter he had voiced a deep conviction when he wrote: "Oh if this country could have been kept
free and clean of the horrible infection of war! If just one of the
leading nations of the world could have preserved its sanity! Then
the balance of the world would have had a sane standard with
which to have tested its madness. But where ev[e]rybody is in a
frenzy there is no rational anchorage to serve as a check any-
where."[33]

In March Belle had written that Bob, Jr., had improved sufficiently so that she thought it would be safe for her to return to
Washington if his father thought it necessary or important. Bob
had replied: "You know mamma my arms will be open whenever
you feel you can come. A lot of the biggest problems will be on here
calling for the best that is in the family. I flounder along the best
I can and while I dont think I have made any serious blunders
there is no one I can council [*sic*] with—excepting as Gil [Gilbert
Roe] gets over occasionally."[34] A few days later he wrote, "The
extra session will be one of stress and excitement although it will be
profoundly interesting. Just as soon as Wilson returns the very
atmosphere here will be surcharged with high voltage currents of
deadly power. I never needed you close to me more, than I will
when the battle opens—but you must be awfully worn and fagged."[35]

After finding a smaller cottage and arranging for Bob, Jr., to
continue his convalescence alone in La Jolla, Belle left on May 6, so
that she could be in Washington before the extra session began. As
she was leaving, Bob, Jr., gave her a letter to read on the train.
"You know mother dearest just how hard it is for me to have you
go. You are so fine and wonderful . . . And yet I know how little
of my love for you I seem to express from day to day when you are
near. It's just something in my make up that makes me so for I do

love you mamma so awfully much. . . . I can never tell you just what your great fight with and for me means to me. I know something of what it has cost you mother dear. . . . And if I too should ever amount to anything it will be due to your wonderful self."[36]

Belle replied at once. "It filled my heart with joy and I have said to myself many times today that I have more than my share of happiness. You children all over appreciate me—not my love for you, but what I have been able to do for you. And Bobbie dear you quite underestimate your power of expression. *I am always conscious of your love.* . . . Dont worry about the future[.] You have the power and you will succeed when you are ready to take hold again."[37]

Phil met his mother in Chicago, and they "visited hard" for two days. In a note to Phil from the train, Belle confessed that she had only $3.50 left in her purse and added: "Really the only reason I mind being short of funds is that I wanted to make our day in Chicago more of a birthday celebration for you. But we could hardly have gotten more joy out of it if we had been millionaires, could we?"[38] While Belle was en route, Bob wrote to Bob, Jr., in La Jolla, "I have the sense of *waiting, waiting,* that subconsciously drags at the wheels of time because I know our dear mama is to come."[39] A few days later he wrote his son the story of her arrival in Washington: "How was any poor mortal 'way-down-South' in this old benighted place ever to know when Lady Belle would make her appearance. Didn't she telegraph?—Well not so-as you could notice it any. From the time she acquired her reservations—she 'efaces herself from the scenery—special'—so far as this end of the line is concerned. So I notifies old man Hannan this morning to hand me a memorandum of every train from Chicago on both lines. And this afternoon Mary and I started in to do the list for a day and a half at least. We caught her trying to slip through the gate immediately following the arrival of the first afternoon train on the B & O. She surrendered with a fight—and one on each side Mary and I escorted her to 3320-16th and we now have her securely in hand."[40]

Belle had been away for nearly a year. Three days after her arrival she wrote to Bob, Jr., and Phil, that "Daddy looked tired and 'aged' to me when I first saw him. That impression has worn off now and he seems quite well. I am in doubt whether to trust my first judgment or not. But I shall watch his state of health and let you know just what it is so far as I can determine. . . . when I said to papa that you did not seem so far away to me, he said, 'It seems a long way to me.' "[41]

CHAPTER LX

A Senate Storm over Copies
of the Treaty

The Senate was now composed of 47 Democrats and 49 Republicans, with Lodge the majority leader. As Bob had noted after the November election, there was a "real magic in the figures: '49 to 47'" which had suddenly altered his status among conservative Republican Senators. Preceding the special session he was frequently consulted in a way that revealed how important they considered his vote in the organization of the Senate.

On May 17, 1919, two days before the special session met, Bob wrote his son who was still in La Jolla, "We are going back to the 'good old days of Republican rule' with a veng[e]ance unless all signs fail."[1] Bob thought the progressive Republicans should unite to demand control of one important committee. If they did this and made a real fight, he believed they had enough votes to force the standpatters to yield, and could win important victories in shaping legislation. But a group, headed by Borah, had met and agreed, without consulting him, to try to prevent Penrose from becoming chairman of the Finance Committee by setting aside the seniority rule. Bob considered this "a sham battle" staged because they thought "a fight on poor old Penrose" would "be 'popular in the West.'"[2] Bob knew that even if they succeeded in defeating Penrose, it would mean no change in the policy of the committee because the equally reactionary Senator McCumber would then become chairman. Therefore he refused to join in this kind of a battle but told Borah that he would go the whole "sled length" if they would make a fight on principle by opposing reactionary chairmen of all important committees.[3] When the conservative Republicans sounded Bob out through Senator Lodge, who was destined by seniority rule to become chairman of the Foreign Relations Committee, Bob replied that he would fight all reactionary chairmen or none. He added with some amusement, "You're just as bad as Penrose, but you're more refined about it."[4]

Subsequently, Penrose expressed his gratitude to Bob for what Lodge had told him about Bob's refusal to join the fight against him. Bob asked, "Did Lodge tell you *all* I said?" Penrose answered, "Oh yes," and then asked what he could do for Bob, who replied that he wanted nothing. Penrose genially responded with the suggestion that "we might do something to rehabilitate you around here." Bob answered: "Damn you Penrose! You don't seem to realize that I've got a record here that I'm proud of. If I need any rehabilitation, you can leave it to me. I'll handle it." Penrose replied, "Well, you and I don't stand on the same side of things, but at least we always know where to find one another." Penrose then went to see Bob's secretary, John Hannan. After relating the incident Penrose said, "You tell me what he wants; he needn't know anything about your telling it to me. You inquire and let me know. We'll get it for him." Hannan replied, "You don't understand, Senator. He doesn't want anything and he would be offended if this was persisted in."[5] Penrose won the chairmanship of the Finance Committee in the Republican caucus fight and was accepted by a strict party vote in the Senate. Bob did not attend the caucus, but joined forty-seven other Republicans, including Borah, in voting for Penrose on the roll call.

The special session met on May 19. That evening Bob humorously described the proceedings in a letter to Bob, Jr., saying, "Well 'we' organized the Senate today appointed a committee to 'notify the President'—elected Cummins President P.[ro] T.[empore]—whose smile ran off his face from each corner of his mouth—and fairly dripped all over him . . . It was the greatest 'harmony' meeting ever stacked up. Why I,—almost but not quite unworthy to sit with the brethren in the Senate,—even I, was named *second* on the 'Committee on the Order of Business.' Just think of it! I am within *one* of the top. From which the casual observer might think I could come with[in] one of fixing the order of business— i. e. of determining *what bills* shall be taken up and the *order thereof*. Nay nay Pauline not so fast. There are seven rank reactionaries on the Committee with me and I strongly suspect they are there for a purpose. . . . I shall courteously ask to be excused. I dont want the responsibility even in a left-handed way for the business this Congress—or the Senate end of it is likely to do."[6]

Bob filed a request to remain on the Committee on Finance, Interstate Commerce, Manufactures, and Indian affairs, where he thought he could render the greatest service. He wrote his sons that he had done some work "with a view of getting the right men on the Com. of Manufactures. If I can get them on I should want to be Chairman and start some investigations on Profits & the Cost of Living. I hope it works out all right."[7] It did. He was named chairman, and the final membership included three progressive Republicans, Gronna, Kenyon and McNary, and two Democrats, Walsh of Massachusetts and James Reed, who had promised Bob to remain on the committee. After the appointments were decided, Bob wrote that "it will give us fellows a clear majority and I shall be able to run some investigations that will make the Committee on Manufactures do *real business.*"[8]

In one letter he sketched a plan of the two large rooms in the Capitol assigned to him as chairman. They were just off the Southwest Senate gallery with a view he enjoyed down Pennsylvania Avenue and across the Potomac to the Virginia hills. The day he moved in he wrote his sons, "The telephone number is Branch 43 if you should want to call me up. Its no trick at all to answer on roll call after the bell rings without hurrying at all. You see I step out of the room run down a flight of stairs walk about 15 feet and enter the Chamber on the democratic side through the door opposite to the entrance to the room of the Clerks of the Senate. It is very handy and I am going to like them very much. There are two windows in the entrance room and three in the other room which fronts towards the White House."[9]

During the early part of the special session, the debate centered chiefly on the annual appropriation bills which had been held up by the filibuster and had to be passed before the end of the fiscal year. At intervals, however, speeches were made on the Treaty and the League of Nations with which it was intertwined. Dispatches from Europe also touched off frequent discussions of its provisions during the weeks before the President returned from Paris to submit the document officially to the Senate for ratification. The discussion of foreign affairs and appropriation bills was interrupted on June 4, by a historic event which Bob described in a letter to his sons saying, "Mamma sat in the gallery all day and was rewarded as were the other fighters for suffrage and equal rights by seeing the Susan B. Anthony Amendment pass by 56 to 25—after a 70 year struggle. Six votes to spare. I started the applause *on the floor* and it swept the galleries again and again without any rebuke from the Chair[,] President Cummins presiding. All felt that it was a great victory."[10]

When the Sundry Civil Appropriation bill came up in the Senate, Bob wrote that it "cuts out the appropriation for the Tariff Commission altogether and we are going to have a round on that when it is reached tomorrow." He also noted that a fight had been made that day to cut $100,000 out of the appropriation for the Federal Trade Commission. This he interpreted as a reactionary "slap at them because a lot of fellows who love the Packers dont like the grilling the Trade Commission gave the big meat monopoly in the investigation which Heney conducted[.] They carried through their cut on the appropriation by ten majority. But we will have another vote on it in the Senate tomorrow and beat them I think. Colver Chairman of the Federal Trade Commission just called to see me about it." Bob added: "It isn't a very good record for the Republican Congress to make to open a fight on these Commissions. They have been doing good work. I suppose that is the reason they are after them."[11]

The following day Bob entered the debate on the committee's amendment to the bill which cut out the appropriation for the Tariff Commission. He had the floor off and on for about three hours. In his speech he reminded Senators of the long fight for a Tariff Commission, noted that the 1916 platforms of both parties were on record in favor of it, and urged an appropriation to continue its valuable work. He recalled that in 1909, during the debate on the Payne-Aldrich Tariff bill, Dolliver, Beveridge, and he had proposed amendments to provide for a commission which had all been voted down. But the fight made by the progressive Republicans had finally, on the night of July 8, wrested from Senators Aldrich and Hale a compromise amendment under which President Taft had appointed the Tariff Board. Bob noted, however, that when the Democrats came to power they "did a partisan and indefensible thing when they abolished it, just the same thing that this committee has done in proposing to abolish this commission, simply because it was appointed by President Wilson." He added, "I long for the time when the public service will get onto a higher plane than that of serving political parties, and come to serve the public interest instead." In urging the importance of funds to continue the present commission, he drew upon his own experience on House and Senate tariff committees which extended over some thirty years. During his plea for nonpartisan action he declared: "I undertake to say, and I say it as a Republican, that President Wilson has built up a Tariff Commission here with which no Republican has any business to find fault if he wants . . . the facts to enable him to legislate properly upon the tariff. That Tariff Commission should be left standing just as it is created."[12]

Bob described to his sons what happened when he finished his speech. "We took the vote on the Committee amendment[,] which was aimed to legislate the Commission out of office, . . . and the only votes sustaining the Committee were 2—Warren and Smoot. So the Commission is continued and it is not likely to be attacked again for a good long while—not during the life of this Congress— I am certain. We licked them good & plenty and I did my full share of it." At the end of his letter he added, "I neglected to say the Tariff Commission is composed of Prof. Taussig, Billy Kent—Culberson who worked with me on the Underwood Tariff, Costigan of Colorado and David Lewis who used to be a member of the House."[13]

During his speech Bob had also commended the work of the Federal Trade Commission and had sharply criticized the committee for reducing its appropriation by 10 per cent. Two days later the chairman, William B. Colver, wrote thanking him for his "splendid defense" and saying, "It will be our effort to justify and to deserve the things you said about us, and we shall feel that we are repaying you directly when we remain steadfast in the public service."[14]

Bob continued to comment in letters to his sons on the news that filtered through from the Peace Conference and the repercussions it stirred up in the Senate. Twelve days after the publication of the synopsis of the Treaty, a resolution was introduced by Hiram Johnson calling upon the Secretary of State to transmit the full text to the Senate. Bob thought Johnson made a good speech for the resolution when it came up in the Senate.[15] While it was still the unfinished business, the press reported that William Bullitt and five other members of the American Peace Commission had tendered resignations in protest against the Treaty.[16] Bob told his sons that they resigned "because they feel that our Government—Mr. Wilson—has surrendered to treaty terms that will give the world 'a new century of war' . . . the gutting given to the 14 points proved too much for Bullitt. When the fellows who resigned get back I hope they will tell things."[17]

A few days later Borah stated on the Senate floor that copies of the Treaty had been widely circulated in Europe, and that some copies were in the hands of certain interests in New York. Lodge confirmed this by saying that the previous day in New York he had been offered a copy to bring to Washington to show his colleagues, but that it had been withdrawn when he stated that no copy could come into his hands without being made public. He told Senators that he had "heard of four copies in existence in New York" and that apparently "the only place where it is not allowed to come is the Senate of the United States."[18] The Johnson resolution calling upon the Secretary of State to transmit the full text passed on June 6. But the Senate did not wait for action by the State Department.

Borah came into the Senate three days later with a copy of the Treaty printed in English and French which had been given to him the previous afternoon. Borah stated it had been brought to this country by Frazier Hunt and asked unanimous consent to have it printed as a Senate document. When this was refused he asked that it be printed in the *Congressional Record*.[19] That night Bob wrote his sons that "They had quite a scrap in the Senate over printing a complete copy of the Treaty in the Record . . . The Democrats tried to prevent its publication. And the general impression is that they made a mess of it. The reason they gave was that Wilson had agreed with the other members of the Big Three that it should not be made public till it was signed. You will get all the points from the papers. The Senate voted about 2 to 1— to publish it notwithstanding Wilson. So the Senate got it at last before it is signed—making Good Wilsons pledge of open Covenants openly arrived at. . . . The debate is going to grow more and more bitter over the League & Treaty as it goes on. My impression is, that Wilson & the League & Treaty are losing ground ev[e]ry day —at least it looks so from this angle."[20] The Associated Press reported that the Senate had ordered the document printed by a vote of 47 to 24 "after an epoch making fight and just after a message from President Wilson had been read saying he could not make the text of the treaty public without breaking faith with other members of the peace council."[21]

The next day Bob wrote that the Committee on Foreign Relations had summoned "J. P. Morgan *et al.* to testify as to where they got advance copies of the treaty and whether they have financial interests *especially*, involved in the League and the Treaty. Of course they will tell all about it—NOT. Borah asked me today whether I could give him any pointers to assist him in the examination. I agreed to help him any way I can . . . If he Borah will do it I am going to get him to examine them as to the extent of their private loans—prior to the time we went into the war. That will be useful information to have later on—if we can get it."[22]

In another letter Bob described how he secured modification of a resolution Knox had introduced on June 10 "to split the League & Treaty apart and consider them separately." At Knox's request it had been referred to the Committee on Foreign Relations. Bob approved considering the Treaty and the League separately, but he thought the last section of the Knox resolution "was a pledge and declaration of Gov[ernmen]t policy to the effect that the U.S. would regard *future troubles* as a grave menace to our peace and that we would take action & C." Later he told Knox that he and some other Senators could not vote for the resolution with that provision, and asked him to strike out the entire last section. Knox "agreed to do so & had Lodge make the motion in Committee striking it out = Lodge[']s motion carried by one vote," thus making it "a straight resolution to separate the Treaty from the League compact."[23] On June 17 Knox made what Bob thought was "a very good speech." In letters to his sons he said, "Its not exactly an attack on the League but is an appeal to go slow and make no mistake." He thought the speech would "incline anyone who reads it to take a little time to think over the League provisions before swallowing the document in one gulp." Bob said he had arranged to send out copies to all his lists in Wisconsin and had decided to have them go under Knox's frank because "some fellows will read it who wouldn't open it if it came to them under mine. It will help in a way to prepare the ground for some seed which I will sow later. Keep all this under your hats—as its just as well for the old stand pats to think they are being remembered by Knox himself."[24]

The day that Knox addressed the Senate, the newspapers reported the President was planning to present the case for the League of Nations to the American people in a tour which would take him to the Pacific Coast. It was also reported that Administration supporters hoped to talk the Knox resolution to death, although they denied they would filibuster.[25] The resolution never came to a vote.

Bob had publicly supported the principles expressed in Wilson's Fourteen Points address to Congress on January 8, 1918. Since the Fourteen Points had been the basis of the armistice and of Germany's agreement to negotiate peace, Bob thought the United States was in honor bound to insist that the terms of the Peace Treaty should be in accord with these proposals. But as he studied the terms which had apparently been accepted by Wilson at Paris, his criticism of the President became increasingly bitter within the family circle, and later found public expression in an editorial entitled "Wilson's Broken Pledges."[26]

One evening, after reading the newspapers, he wrote his sons: "The despatches from Paris tonight say the President insists that his 14 points are all covered in the treaty otherwise he would not be for it. I sometimes think the man has no sense of things that penetrates below the surface. With him the rhetoric of a thing is the thing itself. He is either wanting in understanding or convictions or both. Words—phrases, felicity of expression and a blind egotism has been his stock in trade."[27] Six weeks after the synopsis of the Treaty was published, Bob said in a family letter: "Everyone knows that there is scarcely an approach to the incorporation of *any* of the proposals in the Treaty which it is demanded she [Germany] sign . . . One would think that a sense of national honor, that a pride in keeping faith would make Americans with one voice insist that we make our word good. But you dont hear a peep. Outside a few radical papers like the Nation with almost no circulation there isn't a word being said. Even if ev[e]rybody is still afraid of being called pro-German if they dare to insist that we make our pledges good to German people—still one *would* think that an intelligent citizenship would demand that the peace to 'end war' should not be permitted to become a mere scramble for spoils that must inevitably sow all Europe with a hatred that makes wars in the near future an absolute certainty."[28]

Later he wrote: "The Democrats are stringing out the debate on ev[e]rything. They are counting on the Treaty being signed and then a general clamor being put up for the Senate's concurring in the treaty so that we may have 'peace.' Knowing this body as I do nothing would surprise me. There are votes enough to defeat concurrence in the League and with some to spare But that is NOW. Maybe they will *stick* but anyone who has lived with them the last two years would never put up *all* his money on them. Of course if the people were sound and outspoken on the subject these job lot statesmen could be counted on to stand hitched. But the people are thinking with their fears. They never want war again and because this is called a 'Covenant of Peace,' they think it must *make* for peace—when it binds us to fight in ev[e]ry war upon the orders of foreign governments. Not one in a thousand has ever read the League Not one in ten thousand has ever analyzed it. They are just for a 'League to stop war[.]' "[29]

Shortly before the Treaty was signed, Bob received a report about it from the confidential secretary of one of Wilson's prominent supporters. In a letter to his sons Bob said this man had just returned from Paris, where he had been "in close touch with Wilson and the Peace Commission ever since last November. I supposed he would come back running over with enthusiasm for the League & Treaty[.] He is dead against the whole thing—He says Wilson was clay in the hands of George, Clemenceau et al and that they put it all over him. Besides denouncing the Treaty he says that there are scores of matters on the side collateral to the treaty still pending and not yet definitely settled and about which the public knows nothing. That these things as they come up will make worlds of trouble He thinks the whole business should be rejected by the Senate. I think some of these great admirers of Wilsons have a belly full."[30]

The Treaty was signed on June 28, and Wilson embarked on the *George Washington* the following day. As the President sailed for home, Bob commented in a family letter: "He has signed an agreement to bind us to fight in ev[e]ry future world-war. He has entered into a treaty that is without a parallel in all history as a spoils-grabbing compact of greed and hate."[31] On July 10 the President laid the Treaty before the Senate for ratification and reported on the work of the Peace Conference. Bob was in his seat in the front row when Wilson entered the crowded Chamber. Belle was in the family gallery. The President received an enthusiastic greeting before he began his address. He discussed the Treaty in general terms, referring briefly to the difficulties encountered at the Peace Conference. Among the things that "stood in the way" of grafting "the new order of ideas on the old," he mentioned the "promises which governments had made to one another in the days when might and right were confused and the power of the victor was without restraint." But he said the "difficulties, which were many, lay in the circumstances, not often in the men." After analyzing some of these "circumstances," he declared that "A league of free nations had become a practical necessity. Examine the treaty of peace and you will find that everywhere throughout its manifold provisions its framers have felt obliged to turn to the League of Nations as an indispensable instrumentality for the maintenance of the new order it has been their purpose to set up in the world,—the world of civilized men." He admitted that the Treaty was "not exactly what we would have written," but said he thought "the compromises which were accepted as inevitable nowhere cut to the heart of any principle" and that the work of the Conference "squares, as a whole, with the principles agreed upon as the basis of the peace as well as with the practical possibilities of the international situations which had to be faced and dealt with as facts."[32]

The *New York Times* commented that "The President's address was heard with the keenest interest by his splendid audience, but it was heard in silence."[33] From the family gallery Belle had noted what happened during the early part of his speech when he said: "In one sense, no doubt, there is no need I should report to you what was attempted and done at Paris. You have been daily cognizant of what was going on there . . ."[34] When the President concluded, she left the gallery and went to Bob's office, where she wrote a letter to her sons saying: "I have just heard the President's message and am writing you before going home while my impressions are fresh. The audience was expectant and he was well received. But from the moment he said that we were cognizant of what had happened from day to day, he lost the confidence of the crowd. Then he proceeded to generalize on this false assumption and there was not one handclap throughout his address and when he finished there was not nearly the warmth in the applause that there was in his reception. From the few comments Daddy got from the floor, there was evident disappointment and not much pretence at satisfaction."[35]

As the terms of the Treaty had filtered through unofficially, Bob had freely expressed in family letters his growing indignation at what he thought was a betrayal of the principles of the Fourteen Points. He had, however, refrained from publicly stating his opinion because the President had "refused to permit the Senate to know officially the definite terms of the Treaty, with which he had decreed the League Compact should be interlocked." But after the President addressed the Senate, he challenged Wilson's evaluation in an editorial. He declared the Treaty was a document that virtually enforced the secret treaties previously entered into by the Allies, denied the principle of self-determination, surrendered the control of the seas to Great Britain, belied everyone of Wilson's most important specific pledges, and "traded off his principles— fourteen points and all,—for the League Compact . . ."[36] Later he wrote, "This League and Treaty is nothing but the old, old scheme, modified a little, to fit the times—of an alliance among the victorious governments, following a great war, by which their conquered enemies may be kept in subjugation and exploited to the uttermost."[37]

The English text of the Treaty contained 80,000 words and filled 264 quarto pages. It remained before the Foreign Relations Committee for nearly nine weeks, while extensive hearings were held. In August the committee voted unanimously to ask the President to explain the Treaty to them. The request stipulated the unprecedented conditions that the conference, if granted by the President, should not be secret and that nothing said at the meeting should be considered confidential. The President accepted and invited the committee to meet at the White House on August 19. The *New York Times* described the meeting as "an epoch making conference."[38] Stenographic reports were made of everything that was said during the three-and-a-half-hour discussion. These reports were transcribed in relays and sent to the press so that they could be published the next day in the newspapers.

Bob read with astonishment the President's replies to many of the questions asked by different Senators. Among them was an inquiry by Senator McCumber, who asked, "Do you think that if Germany had committed no act of war or no act of injustice against our citizens we would have gotten into this war?" The President replied, "I do think so." This question and reply Bob quoted in a signed editorial entitled, "The Two Wilson's."[39] To searching questions from Senators Borah and Johnson regarding the secret treaties among the Allies, the President replied that he had no knowledge of them prior to his arrival in Paris for the Peace Conference.[40] This statement shocked Bob. He knew the treaties had been published in the newspapers and he also remembered the message Steffens had brought from Kerenski to the President in June 1917. But Bob reserved his public comment on the President's answer to this question until he spoke in the Senate during the debate on the Treaty.

A few days before this conference at the White House, Senator Bristow had written Bob from the Midwest where he had been speaking for a month. At first his audiences had been "listless" when he discussed economic questions, but now he found them intensely interested. He reported that the opposition to the Treaty and the League was as pronounced "among many democrats as republicans." He wrote: "I am having great audiences. The largest I ever talked to. Even the Chautauqua teachers and preachers who were all with Wilson a month ago now are drifting away from him. Business men are as much effected [sic] by this drift as the farmers . . . Wilson's speech to Congress made no impression whatever. He will receive a cold reception on his tour is my prediction."[41]

During July, Belle had been suddenly taken ill. Her health had always been exceptionally good, but the long strain of the war years had lowered her vitality. An abscessed tooth had resulted in a systemic infection with high temperature. Bob, who could accept his own illnesses calmly, was extremely anxious about her. When the acute stage of the infection had subsided, the doctor insisted she must get away from the severe Washington heat, and Fola went with her mother to the West Virginia mountains. Bob's daily letters express his deep concern, and report his efforts to find a more satisfactory place for them, but make only incidental reference to his work in the Senate. He was alone in the large house, as Mary had gone to New York to attend art school. Aware of his anxiety Belle wrote: "It is wonderful to have Fola to rely on. She does everything with the same thoroughness that you do . . . I feel it is hard for you to be there alone but I know you will keep your strength for your work and trust you to take care of yourself."[42]

Soon after Belle left, Bob wrote her of a letter from Colonel Hannan which said: "Dear Senator and Friend I desire to express my appreciation of the uniform kindly and considerate treatment I have received during the more than sixteen years I have been your Secretary. I shall always cherish the memory of those years and that service. With each succeeding day my personal attachment to, and affection for you have grown. This not only because of your kind personal treatment of me, but because with each day I have come to have a deeper appreciation of the high ideals that govern your public service."[43] After receiving word of the colonel's resignation, Belle wrote Bob: "It is hard to imagine living in Washington without the dear man He has meant so much to all of us. His many sided nature has made him a support and comfort all these years. No one can ever take his place. Mrs. Hannan too is very dear. The change would be hard to accept if we did not hope it was to be to their advantage."[44] Belle's letter expressed the feeling of the entire family. Hannan had resigned to accept a position in New York. Several years later he became president of the Board of Control in charge of Wisconsin's charitable and penal institutions. His new position made it necessary for him to leave Washington. But the close bond and deep understanding between Bob and this friend he had first known as a brilliant young reporter never lessened.

When Hannan resigned, Bob, Jr., was on his way back from California. At Dr. Charles Mayo's suggestion he stopped off at the Mayo Clinic for a complete check-up. He reported to his father that the doctors had told him he "could go home and work his head off."[45] This verdict qualified him for the position he soon accepted as his father's secretary, thus undertaking the heavy work load Hannan had carried for so many years. Before returning to

Washington, he joined Phil at Madison, as they had planned to go on together. Phil was graduating from the University of Wisconsin, and had decided to enter the George Washington University Law School in the fall.

From Madison, Bob, Jr., wrote his father that the memory of "the war hatred" there had changed his feeling toward the city in which he had grown up. To this his father replied: "Bobbie, dont let that feeling against our home place take hold of you for a moment. It is the same crowd that always fought me. What if I had grown to hate the place because they downed me half a dozen [*sic*] times and maligned & traduced and boycotted me as they did for years? I would not let a few cheap-skates drive me away from the most beautiful place in the world—where I had made my home reared my family burried [*sic*] my dead. I whipped them . . . Eighty per cent are our real friends. They have been bound hand and foot & gagged there as they have ev[e]rywhere in this country & in the world. But *there is another day*. And where I have spent my life and done my greatest work, no set of living men shall tell me to 'move on.' "[46]

CHAPTER LXI

The Fight on the Versailles Treaty

On September 3, 1919, President Wilson left Washington to make a direct personal appeal to the Nation for ratification of the Treaty without changes. For several months the Senate debate had made it evident that his determination to keep the League Covenant intertwined with the Treaty of Peace menaced ratification, which required a two-thirds vote. The Senators who would not support it without changes needed only a majority vote to pass qualifying amendments and reservations.

A week after Wilson began his dramatic tour, Lodge presented to the Senate the majority report of the Committee on Foreign Relations which contained four proposed reservations and a number of amendments.[1] The following day, Hitchcock offered a minority report calling for ratification of the Treaty as first submitted to the Senate.[2] On September 15 it became the unfinished business while the President was still on his speaking trip urging unqualified acceptance of the Treaty. But on September 25 Wilson was suddenly stricken desperately ill and had to return to Washington. For several months he was confined to his bed and unable to see anyone except his doctors and Mrs. Wilson. During a long period after the President's tragic breakdown, those who wished ratification of the Treaty without changes had to carry on the fight without his assistance.

The opposition to the Treaty conformed to no party, factional, or sectional lines Bob had ever known during his years in the Senate. Of the fourteen Republicans who constituted the backbone of the opposition to the Treaty with or without reservations, eight were party regulars upon domestic issues: Brandegee, Fall, Knox, McCormick, Moses, Sherman, and Poindexter, formerly a Progressive.

Six were progressive Republicans or independents: Borah, France, Gronna, Johnson of California, La Follette, Norris. They had the consistent support of one Democrat, Reed. At crucial stages they also received the cooperation of a few other Democrats. Among these were Gore, Shields, Smith of Georgia, and Walsh of Massachusetts. A dozen other Republicans, headed by Lenroot, Kellogg, McNary, and McCumber, wished to cooperate with the Democrats to effect American entrance into the League provided they would agree to a few changes. In an effort to bring this about, Lenroot had a long talk with the President before he left Washington on his speaking trip. The Senator told him that the only real obstacle to ratification was Article X of the Covenant, and sought to get him to agree to a reservation relieving the United States of its obligations under this provision. But he could not win the President's consent, as Wilson thought this was the heart of the Covenant.[3]

When the first amendment came to a vote on October 2, Bob supported the attempts to obtain textual changes in the Treaty, but during the early stages of the debate they were defeated. On October 16 he made his first speech on the Treaty. The majority report of the Foreign Relations Committee as presented by Lodge had proposed an amendment that Shantung, which had been given by the Council of Four at Paris to Japan in conformity with a secret treaty with Great Britain and France, should remain with China. Bob believed that handing over Shantung to Japan was a crime which should be prevented. In urging the Senate to pass the amendment, he said: "A righteous declaration made here today will thrill the lovers of liberty in every capital on the face of the earth. It will loosen the tongues of mankind in one universal acclaim of approval. Even the allied powers can not brave the verdict of the world when once it is made articulate."[4]

Bob's personal participation in the fight on the Treaty, to which this record must necessarily be confined, has been condensed from hundreds of pages of running debate and his five carefully prepared speeches. When he delivered the first of these on October 29, there was a large attendance of Senators during his two-hour attack on the section of the Treaty setting up an International Labor Office, which the President had described as "the Magna Charter of Labor."[5] This placed Bob in direct conflict with the Administration Democrats and ranged him against Samuel Gompers, head of the

American Federation of Labor, a militant supporter of Wilson's foreign policy. Labor had been led to hope that a great improvement in its status would result from the war. Although bitterly disappointed at some omissions in the Treaty, Gompers nevertheless had obtained the Federation's endorsement for its ratification. As one of the chief spokesmen for the wage earners in Congress, Bob's attack on the labor provisions was considered so significant that the Republican Senatorial Campaign Committee distributed several hundred thousand copies of this speech.

Bob analyzed the elaborate machinery provided for drafting treaties to regulate the conditions of labor within each participating country. He said "the vice which goes to the very root of all the labor provisions of this proposed treaty is that they provide for the enactment of labor legislation by the secret and undemocratic method by which treaties are made." The Treaty, he emphasized, contained nothing even suggesting the American Constitution's Bill of Rights. No recognition was given of Labor's right to organize and to strike. There was no provision to ensure free speech, press, and assembly. These fundamental rights, proposed by the American delegate, had been refused by the commission which drafted this section. Bob noted that a provision "emancipating seamen from involuntary servitude" had also been voted down. He declared that the practical effect of this section of the Treaty would be "to crystallize the present industrial conditions and to perpetuate the wrong and injustice in the present relations existing between labor and capital."[6] Bob's amendment to strike out the labor section of the Treaty was defeated by 34 to 47, but later a reservation which accomplished virtually the same purpose was introduced by another Senator and adopted.[7]

Bob, Jr., had heard his father's speech from the Senate floor, and he wrote Mary the next day that "the comment of many Senators afterwards was very fine."[8] A few days later he wrote that his father was getting ready to go into the debate "on the Treaty and the Constitution. I do not expect that it will get any notice in the newspapers because it is rather a faux pas to mention the old worn document . . ."[9] On November 5 Bob began a long, closely knit speech in which he discussed the treaty making provisions of the Constitution. The central theme of his argument expressed Bob's profound conviction that the President had exceeded his constitutional powers in negotiating the Treaty of Versailles. He directly challenged the claim that Wilson had properly negotiated the Treaty and that the Senate should therefore ratify it without substantive change. Bob maintained that under the Constitution the President should act "with the advice and consent of the Senate" from the moment he begins to exercise his power to negotiate, because it is "too late for the advice to be effective after the treaty is made and signed and passes out of his hands and into the possession of the Senate." Many precedents were cited to support his argument, and he pointed out various specific provisions the Senate would never have tolerated had the President sought the advice and consent of the Senate before completing the Treaty. In concluding his speech on the second day, Bob said that "the iniquities of the treaty are admitted. The ratification of this treaty is not demanded upon its merits, but only because its ratification is believed by some to be the lesser of two evils."[10]

By November 6 all the proposed amendments had been defeated. Then the fight began for reservations that would define more specifically the interpretation placed by the United States upon its obligations under the different terms of the Treaty and the League. Lodge had offered fifteen reservations to be included in the resolution of ratification.[11] During the debate the controversy again centered chiefly upon Shantung, the six votes granted to Great Britain and her dependencies as against one vote to the United States, the labor provisions, and the famous Article X. Senators had learned rather incidentally during the President's conference with the Foreign Relations Committee on August 19, that Wilson had been the author of the original draft of Article X, and that it seemed to him "to constitute the very backbone of the whole covenant."[12] This particular article of the Covenant provided that "Members of the League undertake to respect and preserve as against external aggression the territorial integrity and existing political independence of all Members of the League. In case of any such aggression or in case of any threat of danger of such aggression the Council shall advise upon the means by which this obligation shall be fulfilled."[13]

As Bob studied the vast implications of this brief article of the Covenant, it became his most vital objection to the League and the intertwining of it with the Treaty. Line by line he analyzed the complicated, voluminous sections of the Versailles Treaty dealing with the proposed territorial and economic adjustments, tracing many of them directly back to the secret treaties. In a Senate speech on November 13, Bob described as a "most remarkable statement" the President's answer, during a White House Conference with the Foreign Relations Committee, when Wilson had denied having any knowledge of the secret treaties prior to the Paris Peace Conference. Bob then reminded the Senate that complete texts "had been published broadcast in November, 1917," and "in full in pamphlet form and distributed by the *New York Evening Post*. Columns upon columns on the front page of the *Post* and other great newspapers in America had carried all of the covenants of those secret treaties shortly after they were published in Russia by the Lenin government."

In answer to a question from the floor, Bob said the existence of the treaties "was not only generally known in the United States" but "it was discussed in all the parliaments of the world. . . There were more than 40 allusions to it in the British Parliament during that time. The ministry was put to answer questions respecting these secret treaties day after day, and it is a matter of record in the parliamentary debates of Great Britain that Balfour said that the President was fully informed regarding them." After noting that the President himself had stated that he had no knowledge of them until he arrived in Paris, Bob pointed out that for more than two years the press of the country and the parliaments of the world "had teemed with discussion and publication regarding the secret treaties made between the allied powers for the distribution of the territory of Europe and Asia and Africa that we are asked to ratify in the treaty which is now pending before the Senate.

"Let me say this, further, that a study of the terms of those secret treaties and of the treaty that is pending here now and of such other information as we have been able to secure with regard to other treaties shows that the work of the Paris conference, held behind closed doors at Versailles, pursued not the terms of the armistice but utterly disregarded the terms of the armistice and followed line by line the boundaries fixed in the secret treaties that had been made in 1916 and 1917.

"If he was ignorant, he was the only man connected in any way with public life in the United States who was ignorant of the terms and purposes of the secret treaties."[14]

Bob then analyzed what some of the obligations of the United States would be in maintaining the commitments embodied in the treaties of the Paris Peace Conference. As an example of the complex territorial changes this country would be obligated to enforce, he cited the Treaty with Austria which had not yet been officially submitted to the Senate, although it had been published. He reminded the Senate that on December 4, 1917, the President had said in his message to Congress, "We owe it, however, to ourselves to say that we do not wish in any way to impair or rearrange the Austro-Hungarian Empire."[15] Bob then contrasted this declaration of Wilson's with the actual provisions of the Treaty. By its terms Austria's population was reduced from 51,000,000 to 5,500,000; the territory divided into the five independent states of Austria, Hungary, Czechoslovakia, Jugoslavia, and Poland. Bob pointed out that these and other territorial changes of the Peace Conference had been made without regard to nationality, the will of subject peoples, ethnological lines, racial attractions or repulsions. The Treaty of Versailles was made, he said, "on the hard-and-fast lines of the secret treaties entered into for the purposes of the war in the period 1915 to 1918." If the United States became a member of the League, Bob said, it would assume the "obligation of standing guard over this territory, with its rivalries and hatreds and its petty and artificial governments brought into existence by the mere word of the two or three men who controlled the Paris conference."

Bob then stated that another important reason for the dismemberment of the Austro-Hungarian Empire was the control of the ancient Bagdad trade route to the East. In support of his analysis he quoted from a recent speech in which the President had said to an audience in St. Louis: "What was the old formula of Pan Germanism? From Bremen to Bagdad wasn't it? ... What lies between Bremen and Bagdad? After you get past the German territory there is Poland, there is Bohemia, which we have made into Czechoslovakia; there is Hungary, which is now divided from Austria and does not share Austria's strength; there is Roumania; there is Jugo-Slavia; there is broken Turkey; and then Persia and Bagdad. We have undertaken to say this route is closed."[16] After reading this quotation Bob said: "There you have the second cause of Austria's dismemberment and destruction. It was that the road leading to England's vast possessions in the Far East might be closed to any other country. To accomplish this purpose these petty and arbitrary States have been raised up, and we are going to underwrite their political independence and territorial integrity for the benefit of Great Britain."

Bob quoted Austin Harrison, English economist: "Europe, east of the Rhine, is to consist of lacerated and impoverished center units flanked by weak and doubtful economic units, who in turn are to remain armed, while the center units are to disarm . . . A stricken, chaotic, impoverished, and infuriated Europe must react disastrously upon the world's markets . . . must therefore still further strike at the tenuous foundations of the world's mechanism." Bob predicted "that an impoverished and infuriated Europe is also a revolutionary and a warlike Europe. And this is the Europe created by the Paris conference which we are to police."

After indicating the obligations inherent in the treaty with Austria, Bob warned the Senators that the Versailles Treaty with Germany was "only a fragment of the settlement at Paris." He reminded them that five major treaties were drafted at Paris, which were "described by President Wilson as intertwining," and that "Secretary Lansing said, the full engagements in which the United States may be involved can not be determined until we get the full texts of the treaties." Furthermore, the Senate knew nothing, Bob said, of the arrangements that were now being made from day to day by representatives of the different governments still in session at Paris. Nevertheless these unknown arrangements would, he declared, "impose obligations which we must carry out and back up with troops and money, and send soldiers to fight and die to preserve. And yet we go on complacently, ready to set our hands to a document that shall bind the people of this Government with regard to covenants about which we can know absolutely nothing. Not one of us, as a responsible lawyer dealing with a client, would do a thing of that kind any more than he would cut off his arm."

Bob concluded: "The little group of men who sat in secret conclave for months at Versailles were not peacemakers. They were war makers. They cut and slashed the map of the Old World in violation of the terms of the armistice. They patched up a new map of the Old World in consummation of the terms of the secret treaties the existence of which they had denied because they feared to expose the sordid aims and purposes for which men were sent to death by the tens of thousands daily. They betrayed China. They locked the chains on the subject peoples of Ireland, Egypt and India. They partitioned territory and traded off peoples in mockery of that sanctified formula of 14 points, and made it our Nation's shame. Then, fearing the wrath of outraged peoples, knowing that their new map would be torn to rags and tatters by the conflicting warring elements which they had bound together in wanton disregard of racial animosities, they made a league of nations to stand guard over the swag! . . .

"Senators, if we go into this thing, . . . it means greater discontent; a deeper, more menacing unrest. Mr. President, whatever course other Senators take, I shall never vote to bind my country to the monstrous undertaking which this covenant would impose."[17]

At the conclusion of Bob's speech, the Lodge reservation excluding the United States from any obligation in the territorial or political adjustments in Europe came to a vote. President Wilson had particularly denounced this reservation as a "knife thrust at the heart of the treaty." It carried by 46 to 33.[18]

After this vote a cloture motion, signed by thirty Republican Senators, was offered to limit debate.[19] Two days later it was adopted, although Bob and a number of others voted against it. Henceforth each Senator was allowed only one hour during the debate.[20] By November 18 the fifteen reservations offered by Lodge had been adopted.

The cloture rule forced Bob to condense his final speech of November 18, dealing with what he described as the "territorial plunder" granted to Great Britain and some of the other Allies, which, under the League Covenant, the United States must engage to defend.[21] To illustrate his analysis of the distribution of this territory, he had obtained three large maps which hung on the walls of the Senate Chamber during the closing hours of the debate. The territorial gains of Great Britain had been indicated on two maps of Africa and Asia in great masses of red by a fresco artist, Charles A. Whipple, who was then doing some work in the Capitol. The third map from the War College showed the naval stations controlled by Great Britain throughout the world. These maps vividly dramatized his eloquent final arraignment of the Treaty.[22] Toward the close of his speech Bob expressed his profound conviction as to the issue involved when he said: "I do not covet for this country a position in the world which history has shown would make us the object of endless jealousies and hatreds, involve us in perpetual war, and lead to the extinction of our domestic liberty. . . . we can not, without sacrificing this Republic, maintain dominion for ourselves. And, sir, we should not pledge ourselves to maintain it for another."[23]

Offers were made by Gronna and Kenyon to share their time with Bob, but the Chair ruled this could not be done. Bob therefore closed his speech at the end of a half-hour and reserved the other half that cloture allowed him until later, when he spoke on the six reservations to the League Covenant which he had previously introduced. These embodied certain specific proposals which Bob believed were essential to any effective plan for promoting international peace. The first reserved to every people "living under a government which . . . does not derive its powers from the consent of the governed, the right of revolution, or the right to alter or abolish such government." It made specific mention of Egypt, India, Ireland, and Korea. It was rejected by 49 to 24, the best vote any of his reservations received. His other resolutions provided that the United States would participate in the League only on the condition that other member nations joined in abolishing conscription; that they provide by law for a popular referendum before resort to war; that they limit expenditures for armaments; that they renounce forcible annexations and the exploitation of subject peoples in territory held under mandates from the League. These were all rejected by majorities of more than two to one.[24] But they were consistently supported by Borah, Brandegee, Capper, France, Gronna, Johnson of California, Norris, and Penrose.

The Treaty, with the reservations offered by Lodge, came to a vote on November 19. The outcome was in doubt because of uncertainty as to the position of the group of Republican Senators led by Lenroot who desired ratification and were disposed to cooperate with the Democrats provided they would agree to a few reservations. But the President intervened and determined the fate of the Treaty when he wrote a letter to the Democratic caucus saying: "I sincerely hope that the friends and supporters of the treaty will vote against the Lodge resolution of ratification. I understand that the door will probably then be open for a genuine resolution of ratification."[25] When this letter was read to the Senate, the Lenroot group refused to join the Democrats in their decision to follow the President's request and endeavor to commit the United States to the Treaty without any changes. The loss of these votes doomed the Treaty. With every Senator except Fall in his seat, the Senate by a vote of 55 to 39—7 short of the necessary two-thirds—rejected the Treaty with the Lodge reservations.[26]

Having followed Wilson's suggestion and voted to reject the Treaty, the Democrats now fought desperately to keep the door open for the President's "genuine resolution of ratification." The struggle continued until shortly before midnight. During these last hours Bob was in his seat in the front row. Senator Pomerene finally moved to refer the ratification resolution to a Committee of Conciliation. But Bob's motion to lay it on the table was carried. After further maneuvers the Treaty was rejected 38 to 53 with 4 Senators not voting.[27] A press bulletin issued by the Democratic National Committee depicted the final scene of the momentous debate and gave a hostile description of La Follette as "the general" of the Battalion of Death. It stated that "A few months ago hardly a Senator, Republican or Democrat, would speak to La Follette. In the treaty contest, however, it was this same La Follette who moved the pawns on the Senatorial opposition chess board that brought the treaty of peace to defeat."[28]

But Bob himself thought the defeat of the Treaty and the League was primarily due to Borah, Johnson, and Reed. He believed their early speeches analyzing the provisions of these intertwined Covenants had aroused a public opinion which had finally registered in the vote rejecting the Treaty.

Two days after the Treaty was rejected, Bob wrote to his friend Robert F. Paine: "This Treaty fight will be on again as soon as Congress meets. I am hoping that the milk and water fellows on the Republican side will return with a little iron in their blood. If they do, we may be able to establish a precedent which will make presidents hesitate in the future before they violate the Constitution with such contempt for its meaning."[29]

When an attempt was made during the next session to revive the Treaty, Bob was not well enough to take an active part in the ensuing five weeks' debate. Lenroot and many others thought it might have been ratified had the President been willing to accept reservations.[30] But Wilson insisted in a letter to the chairman of the

Democratic National Committee that the Treaty could not be re-written and must be taken without changes. Then, if any doubt still remained about what people of this country thought on this vital matter, he suggested it could be submitted to the voters "to give the next election the form of a great and solemn referendum." The President's letter, read at the Democratic Jackson Day Dinner in Washington, thus made acceptance of the Treaty without reservations a party issue.[31]

Bob considered his fight on the Treaty consistent with his op-position to our entry into the European War. During the debate he had offered amendments and reservations which outlined the essen-tial provisions of an international organization he would have supported. But he could not vote for the League Covenant, as presented to the Senate, because he believed it would be an instru-ment to enforce an unjust peace which could only lead to future wars.

CHAPTER LXII

A Senate Defeat and a Wisconsin Victory

While the Treaty of Versailles was still being debated in the Senate, Bob had written Belle that Senator Cummins, chairman of the Interstate Commerce Committee, had asked him to attend a conference to consider a letter received from the President regarding an advance in pay for railroad employees and an advance in railroad rates to meet the increased cost. Bob said: "The situation is critical as a strike is imminent. The cost of living is steadily mounting & the men are growing desperate[.] The unrest on account of soaring prices is general and menacing[.] Wilson is certain to discover ere long that home problems will be more pressing than world affairs."[1] When the special session had ended on November 19, 1919, with the rejection of the Treaty, it had been evident that the most imperative of these "home problems" to confront the regular session of Congress, convening on December 1, would be the disposition of the railroads which President Wilson had taken over as a war measure on December 28, 1917.

As a member of the Interstate Commerce Committee, Bob had followed closely the different plans that had been proposed for operation of the railroads. In January, 1919, William G. McAdoo, former Secretary of the Treasury and former Director General of the United States Railroad Administration, appeared before the committee to urge continued Government operation to test this method thoroughly under normal peacetime conditions. Bob thought McAdoo made "a strong statement," but as he listened to the questions asked by Cummins, Kellogg, Pomerene, and Underwood it seemed obvious that the committee would reject McAdoo's recommendations.[2] Another proposal presented by Glenn E. Plumb, counsel for the Railroad Brotherhoods, called for Government ownership operated by a private corporation with directors representing the workers, the executives, and the public. Representatives of the railroad executives and security holders had advocated returning the railroads to private operation. Months before the committee took any action, Bob wrote his sons that he would probably be the only Senator who would "stand for Government Ownership of the railroads. But it is no time to back down on that great question because it appears to have gotten a black eye at this time."[3]

Toward the end of the special session, a few days before Bob made his first speech against the Treaty of Versailles, Cummins reported a bill to the Senate which substantially adopted the recommendations made by the railroad executives. It called for the end of Government operation, the payment of large sums of money by the Government to the railroads, and the fixing of rates that would give the owners 5½ to 6 per cent upon their investments. Prepared by a subcommittee of five, it had been under consideration by the full committee during the period that Senators were engrossed in the debate on the Treaty, and had been reported without public hearings except for two brief sessions Bob had managed to secure for the railway employees to protest against an anti-strike provision. The Republican and Democratic members of the committee had united in supporting the Cummins bill.

Bob submitted to the Senate, on November 10, a seventeen-page minority report to which he could get no other signature than his own. Bob stated the bill "contains every vice which is supposed to inhere in Government ownership and none of its virtues. It has every weakness which attaches to private ownership, but none of the advantages commonly claimed for that system." He warned that guaranteeing a net profit would put a premium on extravagance for which the public would "pay in extortionate and ever-increasing transportation charges."[4]

Debate on the Cummins bill did not begin until the regular session convened on December 1. The supporters of this measure repeatedly asserted that when the Government took over the railroads they were in good condition but that even though the rolling stock had not been maintained, they had operated at a heavy loss, thus demonstrating the failure of Government control.

Bob entered the debate on December 9, challenging these assertions and analyzing the bill in five speeches delivered on five successive days, speaking in all some thirteen hours.[5] His chief opponents were Cummins and two other members of the Interstate Commerce Committee, Kellogg, a Republican, and Underwood, a Democrat. In his opening speech Bob declared the claim that the present plight of the railroads was due to Government operation was "wholly unsupported by the facts. The truth is," he said, "that the railroad system of this country had broken down prior to the war." He reminded Senators that on December 7, 1915, sixteen months before the United States entered the war, President Wilson had told Congress that "The transportation problem is exceedingly serious and pressing in this country. There has from time to time of late been reason to fear that our railroads would not much longer be able to cope with it successfully as at present equipped and coordinated."[6] Bob produced official reports to show that the Government had spent more for upkeep and equipment, carried more passengers and freight under public operation than in any previous year of railroad history, and that in the late months of 1919 the previous monthly deficits had been converted into a profit. He demonstrated that this had been done in spite of the fact that during the two years of Government operation the private owners had received a rental which Senator Cummins himself estimated was annually about "$200,000,000 more than it should be."[7] Bob contended no one could fairly claim that two years under war conditions was any test whatever and that Government operation should be continued for a "definite period long enough to give the country a complete demonstration of the success or failure of the system."[8]

In three of his speeches Bob attacked the rate provisions of the Cummins bill which he thought would tax the people of this country outrageously by guaranteeing forever a return on fictitious values of railroad securities. The bill made it mandatory for the Interstate Commerce Commission to ensure to the private owners a net profit of from $5\frac{1}{2}$ to 6 per cent. The basis for estimating what this profit should be was "the aggregate value," which meant accepting the railroads' own "book value" of their property, including billions of watered stock and the inflation values of the war years. This practically undermined the Adamson-La Follette physical-valuation law of 1913, because the Interstate Commerce Commission could not complete this valuation for several years. Bob correctly predicted that the terms of the Cummins bill would force the commission to increase railway rates to yield annually $1,500,000,000, which he estimated would mean a tax on the consumer of more than $7,000,-000,000 to be added to the already intolerably high cost of living.[9]

In his speech the next day Bob criticized the anti-strike provision of the bill, which he declared "denied labor the right to quit work in a collective body" and makes it "an offense punishable by fine and imprisonment if they cease their employment by concerted agreement." Although he deplored strikes as "wasteful," and "tragic," he believed the solution was not in the application of force or the repression of criticism of existing conditions but in establishing "such a reign of absolute social justice as would remove all occasion for strikes."[10]

On December 20, the day fixed by unanimous consent for a vote upon the Cummins bill, Bob spoke for his substitute amendment extending Government operation of the railroads for two years. Only eight Democrats and two Republicans, Norris and Gronna, joined Bob in voting for his substitute. Lenroot was among the sixty-five Senators who voted against continuing the Government operation which had been recommended by McAdoo, former Director of the Railroad Administration, and his successor, Hines.[11] When the vote was taken a little later on the Cummins bill, it passed 46 to 30. This time Lenroot joined Bob in voting against it. Late that night Congress adjourned for the Christmas holidays.

Bob was the only Senator who had spoken at length against the entire bill. Although he was unable to defeat it, he had mustered enough votes to cause some anxiety among its supporters as to what might happen when it came to the Senate again after the Conference Committee reconciled it with a similar bill sponsored by Congressman John J. Esch of Wisconsin which had previously passed the House.[12] But when the conference report finally came before the Senate as the Esch-Cummins bill, Bob was not well enough to participate in the debate and lead another fight. The Senate passed it 47 to 17. Although Bob was not present, his opposition was recorded. Lenroot's vote for the bill became an issue in the Wisconsin election. Two million railroad workers and many large farm organizations protested, but President Wilson signed the measure, and the railroads were returned to their private owners with a

Government guarantee of profits. Subsequently rates were increased. In an editorial Bob analyzed what this meant in the increased cost of food, fuel, and clothing to the breadwinner whose day's pay furnished only scanty fare for his family.[13]

During his intensive work on the railroad bill and the Versailles Treaty debates, Bob had been looking forward to having the family all under one roof for the Christmas holidays. Belle wrote Mary, who was attending art school in New York, that he seemed "to lot on your having an old fashioned party such as you had when you were all in high school." A dance was arranged for the night after Christmas, and Belle assured Mary that "we shall have plenty of room for everybody."[14] Sharing Bob's own joy in the family party, Belle had converted the attic into a temporary dormitory so that Mary and Phil could invite Miles Colean and several other friends as house guests. To complete the family circle, Fola and Mid arrived a few days before Christmas. Bob joined in the festivities and made this the kind of gay reunion he had been dreaming of and writing about during the months the family had been separated while Bob, Jr., was convalescing in California.

Early in January another guest arrived who won all their hearts.[15] Phil had known Professor Max C. Otto as an inspiring teacher of philosophy at the University of Wisconsin, but Bob and Belle had never met him until the morning he arrived for breakfast. To his diary Otto confessed the "uneasiness" he felt in his first meeting with the man he had known about for many years and often seen in action. "I have long had a kind of apologetic admiration for his fighting qualities and great admiration for his mind. Like many other people, I was repelled by what I regarded as a ruthless streak in him. I had heard him mercilessly brand men in public life, some of whom I admired. . . . I did not relish the thought of sitting next to 'Fighting Bob.' Then he came in. We shook hands and he looked at me with warm affectionate eyes, not at all the platform eyes with which I was familiar. All stiffness vanished. He won me over immediately. If 'immediately' is not quite the correct word, that is because his first gaze was searching, disconcerting.

"At any rate, my impulse after breakfast was to run up stairs and write a card to everybody I knew, and another one to the world at large, saying to them all: 'I have met Senator La Follette and I am his without reservation!' It was almost as if I had returned to my boyhood and had met my first hero.

"This impression will wear down; impressions do; yet one thing will doubtless remain, for that has passed into an intellectual judgment. The Senator is a man of warm feeling and generous sympathy. I have always recognized his extraordinary intellectual ability, but now I know that he *feels*, that there is a tender, affectionate side to him and that this drives him into action."[16]

Meditating on the "reality" of the hospitality he found in the La Follette home, Otto wrote: "All are individual persons who live here: the father, the mother, the children. There is a spontaneous, obvious appreciation of the Senator as a great man, but they all speak up, they disagree, they give advice. They seem to be doing the job as a group. Even the maid is a person. A guest is naturally himself in such a home.

"Senator La Follette is the biggest human being among men of affairs I have met on anything like a personal basis. . . . Dinner enriched my good impression of him. For one thing—and it happens that I think it to be a great thing—he listens when others speak. *How* he listens! Most men, big and little, but especially the men who 'do things' never listen. . . . This man listens with such intensity that, when he listens to you, you have a hard time remembering what you intended to say. And when he replies, you have the evidence that he heard what was said, heard, it almost seems, beyond what was said some of the things which were only thought. His own speaking is of an almost explosive directness and force, going at once to the nub of the matter, with an economy of words, with wit and not without humor."

After dinner that night Bob read some of the tales from *Darby O'Gill and the Good People* to Otto and Belle. Recording his impressions of the evening, Otto wrote: "His Irish brogue is delightful, he has an excellent sense of the dramatic, and his strong sympathetic nature easily gets into the character and the situation. I shall long remember him seated there by the mahogany table, the mellow light of the lamp falling on his strong, mobile face, introducing me to some of the most charming characters I have come upon in literature." Later, "aided and abetted by the children who had returned, he took me in hand and cross-questioned me. What did I teach? What reasons could I give for the position I held? What social justification was that for doing the job I did? His attitude was kindly, fatherly, but his intelligence was extraordinarily keen, and he was informed, strangely so, since the questions were philosophical. The sheer drive of his questioning and the relentlessness of his criticism made me feel as if I had been cut into little pieces by a big-hearted doctor, and that if I ever healed again I'd be a better man."[17] Thus did this young professor of philosophy at the University of Wisconsin, whom Bob and Belle immediately recognized as a *"great* teacher,"[18] record his first day in the home of the man, who had more than forty years earlier worked his way through the university and been profoundly influenced by another great teacher of philosophy, John Bascom.

When Congress convened in January, Bob was not feeling well enough to attend the Senate sessions. During the debates on the Versailles Treaty and the Cummins bill he had been suffering from intermittent, severe pain in his side and had decided to go to the Mayo Clinic for an examination after spending a few days in Madison. But an attack of the prevalent influenza and a severely infected tooth kept him in Washington until January 20. Two days after he left, Borah called up the house to ask that Bob be notified that the situation on the Treaty and the League was very serious. Belle and Phil decided that Borah should be told confidentially, as Gronna had been, the purpose of Bob's trip. Borah then said he thought Bob should not be troubled at present and promised to communicate with Belle "whenever he felt it was crucial and important to do so."[19]

Bob stopped off in Madison for several conferences with leading progressive Republicans and then went to the Mayo Clinic with Bob, Jr., on January 26. By February 12 the doctors had completed their examinations and agreed that a return of gallstones was the cause of Bob's pain and other symptoms. It was the opinion of Doctors Will and Charles Mayo that the removal of the gall bladder would restore him to complete health, but they did not wish to operate during the prevailing influenza epidemic. They advised Bob to return to Madison and undertake only a minimum schedule of work until conditions were more favorable at Rochester.

It happened that Governor Philipp was on the same train that Bob took when he left Rochester. They met by chance and had a brief visit. It was reported that when the governor inquired about Bob's health, he replied with a laugh: "You stalwarts don't need to think you are going to get rid of me just yet. After this operation they tell me at Rochester that I will be good for at least thirty years. You know my grandfather rode on horseback from Kentucky into Indiana when he was 115 years old. I am going to try and equal that mark."[20]

The evening after his return to Madison, Bob attended the first of many conferences relating to the organization of the progressive forces for the approaching state campaigns. The first battle was to be decided at the Presidential primary on April 6, when delegates were to be elected to the Republican National Convention scheduled to meet in Chicago on June 8. The stalwart Republicans were supporting an uninstructed delegation, headed by Governor Philipp. They did not present any platform to the voters. But the delegates who were designated as "La Follette Progressive candidates" on the ballot and in campaign leaflets pledged themselves to support a platform published in the press and widely circulated through the mails. The time was short and funds were, as usual, limited. The work had to be done by volunteers. Bob, Jr., wrote his mother of "the hectic" twenty-four hours that preceded the day when "we got all of our delegates nominated and the papers filed. It was necessary to sweat a few quarts of blood to get it done in the required time and I think we are all feeling the reaction from the strain. The eleventh [district] caused the most trouble and we watched every train up until the last minute and made it only by the skin of our teeth."[21]

The eleventh district was the one Lenroot had represented as a Member of the House. He was openly opposing the election of the La Follette progressive Republican candidates. In an open letter to George A. West, chairman of the Republican State Central Committee, Lenroot said he had been informed that placing these candidates in the field was the beginning of an organized fight to defeat him in the September primary, and he urged election of the "uninstructed" delegates, headed by Governor Philipp. Lenroot's letter was published as an advertisement in many Wisconsin newspapers preceding the Presidential primary.[22]

While Bob was working on the Wisconsin platform, telegrams began coming from Washington reporting the situation on the Versailles Treaty, which had again been placed before the Senate while he was at the Mayo Clinic. On March 8, during the debate on reservations, the President wrote Senator Hitchcock asking for ratification without changes.[23] Two days later Bob received word that Borah, Gronna, Norris, Reed, and Lodge thought he should return for the final vote, since it seemed impossible to arrange a pair. After talking with Borah on the telephone, Bob telegraphed Belle in Washington that unless a pair could be found he would come on. Bob returned in time to vote for two reservations.[24] On the final vote he joined with eleven Republicans and twenty-three Democrats in voting against ratification. The Treaty was thus rejected because it lacked seven votes of the required two-thirds majority.[25]

The day after the Senate rejected the Treaty, Representative Edward E. Browne of Wisconsin made a brief speech in the House. He declared that in the coming Presidential campaign the people would no longer be content with the generalities of former platforms but would insist upon specific declarations by all parties and candidates. After informing his colleagues that there were two sets of candidates in Wisconsin running as delegates to the Republican National Convention, he said he desired to read the brief statement of principles upon which the set of delegates "designated as 'the La Follette Republicanism ticket' stand."[26] Thus the Wisconsin platform found its way into the *Congressional Record*, where it was undoubtedly read by many who later attended the convention in Chicago.

The platform of the La Follette progressive Republican candidates for delegates to the Republican National Convention contained nineteen planks. It favored the "immediate conclusion of peace and resumption of trade with all countries." It opposed the League of Nations "as a standing menace to peace," but favored "a League for Peace, composed of all the nations of the world, provided they were mutually pledged by binding covenants, with proper guarantees, to abolish compulsory military service, and, provided further, that the several nations mutually bind themselves to a speedy disarmament, reducing the land and naval forces of each nation to the strict requirements of a purely police and patrol service." It advocated repeal of the Esch-Cummins law, the ultimate public ownership of the railroads, and gradual acquisition of stockyard terminals, large packing plants, and all other natural resources, "the private ownership of which is the basis of private monopoly." Among other planks were those advocating "a deep waterway from the Great Lakes to the sea"; "the immediate restoration of free speech, free press, peaceable assembly, and all civil rights and liberties guaranteed by the Constitution"; repeal of the Espionage and Sedition Act; abolition of injunctions in labor disputes; enactment of legislation recognizing labor and farm organizations "for the purpose of collective bargaining in industry, trade, and commerce"; such legislation as "may be needful and helpful in promoting direct cooperation and eliminating waste, speculation, and excessive profits between producer and consumer"; that taxes be levied in proportion to ability to pay and "in such a manner as will prevent such tax burdens being shifted to the backs of the poor in higher prices and increased cost of living"; that soldiers of the late war should be paid a sufficient sum to make their war wages at least equal to civilian pay, as a matter of right, not as a bonus; amendments to the Constitution to permit the direct election of Federal Judges, the extension of "the initiative and the referendum to national legislation, and the recall to Representatives in Congress and United States Senators." The candidates pledged to the people of Wisconsin that if elected as delegates to the Republican National Convention they would use their "best efforts to promote these principles and nominate candidates in sympathy with them." This platform was printed on campaign leaflets which were widely circulated throughout the State.[27]

Bob and Bob, Jr., returned from Washington to Madison on March 26. Only eleven days remained before the Presidential primary when the voters would render their verdict on this platform and the candidates pledged to support it. This election was the first test of strength since the war between the La Follette progressive Republicans and the Philipp-Lenroot faction of the party. In Washington Belle and Phil anxiously waited for the frequent reports which Bob and Bob, Jr., sent about the campaign. After receiving two letters on the same day Belle wrote: "Only one week more. It looks as though you had a cinch, but we shall *know* when the votes are counted. In spite of my faith in Charlie Crownhart's wisdom I would put all emphasis on getting the vote out—*our vote*." In another letter she said, "you have been good to write us so often and so fully about the campaign. I feel as though we were right in touch with the situation and begin to sense the strain and tension of the closing days. You have not said much about Daddy's health, but I suppose you are hardly taking notice of anything except politics until after the 6th of April. But I do hope you are getting a reasonable amount of rest Daddy dear and are keeping in mind that the most important thing after all, is being in the best possible condition for the operation." The day before the primary she received a letter from Bob, Jr., to which she replied, "I share your feeling that the 'waiting' is the hardest part of a campaign. Perhaps that is true of most of our experiences. . . . [I] wish we could wait for returns around the grate fire at Maple Bluff Farm, but we shall be there in spirit, rejoicing that we have each other whatever the result."[28]

The day after the primary, Bob, Jr., telegraphed Belle the good news of the overwhelming victory of the progressive Wisconsin platform. Twenty-two of the La Follette progressive Republican delegates had been elected. Their four delegates at large had carried the State by 50,000, and Governor Philipp had been defeated in his home city. A special dispatch from Milwaukee to the Washington *Sunday Star*, signed by J. C. Ralston, was headed by a photograph of Bob with the caption, "Holds Vote of Wisconsin in Hollow of His Hand." Ralston reported that the delegate fight was "a trial of strength between the La Follette progressive wing of the republican party and the conservative wing, headed by Gov. E. L. Philipp," and noted that La Follette delegates had carried the eleventh district "as well as Superior, Senator Lenroot's home city, though the Senator supported the Philipp uninstructed delegates."[29]

From Washington the day after the primary, Belle and Phil telegraphed Bob, "your faith in the people justified very happy here."[30] In response to letters giving more details about the election results Belle wrote: "we are all so happy for your sake papa, and for the sake of the hope it inspires now and hereafter. . . . I wish the operation was over then you could enjoy this triumph without care. . . . It is splendid that you two Bobs have had this wonderful experience together." In another letter a few days later she said: "It is wonderful papa, how you have stood the strain and what a satisfaction the result must be to you. Of course it is an epoch in all our lives. But you have suffered most and so I feel there must be a special joy and recompense to you in the upholding of your hands by the people of your state."[31]

CHAPTER LXIII

La Follette Declines a Third-Party Presidential Nomination

Bob left Madison for the Mayo Clinic on May 29, to prepare for the operation he knew must be performed. The following day Belle and Mary left Washington with Phil, driving directly to Madison to organize the household and have everything in order when Bob returned. Belle had written Bob: "We shall be waiting word from you . . . At best, ther[e] is a deal of pain and suffering, which I wish I could bear for you. Since you must go through it, the sooner it is done the sooner you will find relief. You know our hearts are with you, greatest and best of men. Hours will seem days and days weeks until we hear from you."[1]

Two days before the operation, Phil and Bob, Jr., joined their father. On the morning of June 7, two of Bob's intimate friends, Doctors Harper and Gill, were in the operating room when Dr. Will Mayo removed the gall sac and one gallstone. Bob reacted well, and Dr. Mayo predicted an early return to good health. Phil remained with his father, but Bob, Jr., went to Chicago the next evening to counsel with the Wisconsin delegation and to attend the Republican National Convention as an observer. He telegraphed his father that chaos reigned in the national situation and that there was some talk of Senator Johnson bolting.[2] The newspapers stated that Borah also threatened to bolt.

A staff correspondent for *La Follette's Magazine* noted that "men representing every form and shade of monopoly, swollen with war profits, met by night in the luxurious Blackstone Hotel and by day occupied the choice seats behind the platform in the stifling hot Coliseum, where Lodge, Smoot, Watson and [former Senator Winthrop Murray] Crane directed the tragic mum-show,—making a mockery of popular representative government."[3] Oswald Garrison Villard reported that "money was written all over the convention," and wondered "how business could be going on in Wall Street when so many of its most distinguished figures were in Chicago." To him "the one refreshing incident" in the entire Republican Convention was the presentation of the Wisconsin platform by Edward J. Gross, who had also made the minority report in 1916.[4] But the convention was in no mood for "minority reports," and "Gross was received with hisses and hoots, which grew in volume, until Chairman Lodge pounded the table and declared Gross had as good a right to a hearing as anybody else in the convention."[5] The delegates were even more hostile than in 1916. When he read the plank calling for repeal of the Esch-Cummins Law and declaring for the ultimate Government ownership of the railroads, "an angry roar" shook the rafters. "Cries of 'Throw him out!' 'Bolshevik!' 'Socialism!'" fell "like an avalanche upon Gross." This platform received the same treatment that Republican conventions had given the Wisconsin platforms in 1908, 1912, and 1916. But 11 of the 13 planks rejected in 1908 had been enacted into law; 14 of the 18 rejected in 1912 had been written into the Federal statutes, and within a few weeks a fifteenth, the extension of suffrage to women, became a provision of the Federal Constitution.[6]

During the balloting for Presidential candidates the Wisconsin delegates were "booed and hissed and jeered when 24 out of 26 voted for Robert M. La Follette from first to last."[7] Senator Warren G. Harding was nominated on the tenth ballot. The opinion of 24 members of the Wisconsin delegation was probably expressed by the staff correspondent for *La Follette's Magazine*, who wrote that Harding's nomination had been put over just as predicted months before by his campaign manager, Harry M. Daugherty. At a secret caucus, seated "at a round table in a 'smoke filled room,' a few representatives of great corporations and the manipulators at the Coliseum selected their candidate." As Lodge proposed that the convention make Harding's nomination unanimous, a roar of ayes responded. But when he called for the nays, twenty-four Wisconsin delegates leaped on their chairs, shouting a negative and serving notice that Wisconsin did "not accept the dictum of the secret caucus at the Blackstone!"[8] Calvin Coolidge was nominated for Vice President, but the Wisconsin delegation cast 24 votes for Senator Gronna and 2 for Senator Irvine L. Lenroot.[9]

The newspapers reported that the Harding victory had created great dissatisfaction among the progressive Republicans, especially in the Midwest. The *New York Times* printed a special dispatch from Chicago stating that Senator Johnson would not bolt the ticket but that La Follette might be the candidate of a third party. The next day a boxed story from the same city announced, "Senator La Follette of Wisconsin is far in the lead in a Presidential referendum vote, which is being taken among members of the 'Committee of Forty-eight,' which will hold its national convention here on July 10."[10] The founder of this committee was J. A. H. Hopkins, who had supported Theodore Roosevelt for President in 1912 and in 1916, serving as national treasurer of the Executive Committee. After Roosevelt refused the nomination in 1916, the remnants of the Progressive Party had authorized Hopkins to "turn over the assets and names" to the first political reorganization conforming to their principles.[11] Among the active members of the Committee of Forty-eight who had also supported Roosevelt were Amos Pinchot, George L. Record, and Gilson Gardner.

Hopkins and other leaders representing various groups had formally organized this committee at a conference in St. Louis in December, 1919. Its purpose was to enlist members in all the forty-eight States and to unite various progressive, independent groups for political action in 1920. To achieve this goal the leaders had carried on unofficial negotiations with representatives of the Labor Party, the Nonpartisan League, the National Farmers' Council, the World War Veterans, and other groups.[12] Hopkins and other members of the Committee of Forty-eight had also conducted an intensive organization campaign which had culminated in the calling of a Third Party Convention with delegates pledged to attend from almost every State. This convention had been scheduled to meet in Chicago on July 10, 1920, at the same time as the Labor Party Convention. The leaders of the Committee of Forty-eight hoped that the two conventions might then unite in forming a new progressive party.[13]

When the Republican Convention was over, Bob, Jr., returned to Rochester to get his father's instructions before going East to attend conferences which had been requested by the Committee of

Forty-eight and the leaders of other groups interested in forming a new third party with Bob as the Presidential candidate. In New York and Washington Bob, Jr., conferred with Hopkins, Amos Pinchot, Record, Frederic C. Howe, Edward Keating, editor of *Labor*, Warren S. Stone, grand chief engineer of the Brotherhood of Locomotive Engineers, and Philip Francis, chief editorial writer for the Hearst newspapers. John Hannan also participated in some of these discussions. Roe, Hannan, and Bob, Jr., all thought that the liberal groups tended to overestimate their strength and the feasibility of their coming together on fundamental principles.[14]

From New York Bob, Jr., returned to Rochester to report to his father. Conferences were arranged to be held at Madison before the Third Party Convention called by the Committee of Forty-eight to meet in Chicago on July 10. The delegates to this convention represented many different groups. Some were members of the Labor Party and were also delegates to its second national convention, scheduled to meet in Chicago on July 11. Previously Hopkins and Pinchot had favored Frank P. Walsh as a Presidential candidate, but about three weeks before the convention they had joined Gardner in expressing their desire to nominate La Follette.[15] They and other leaders of the Committee of Forty-eight hoped that the platform committees of both conventions would agree upon a platform which would make it possible to unite all the elements and found a powerful new third party, with La Follette as the Presidential candidate. Press comments previous to the conventions, and subsequent analyses indicate that this was the desire of the majority of the rank-and-file delegates to both conventions.[16]

On the evening of July 4, Bob and his son returned to Maple Bluff Farm. That day a statement was issued by the Committee of Forty-eight mentioning various Presidential nominees who were being considered, including La Follette, Senators Johnson and Borah, Frank P. Walsh, Governor Frazier of North Dakota, and Justice Walter Clark of North Carolina. It reported that questionnaires sent "to more than 30,000 members returned almost as many indorsements for La Follette as for all others combined."[17]

At Bob's urgent request Roe had arrived at the farm for the conferences with representatives of the Committee of Forty-eight, the Labor Party, and the Railroad Brotherhood. On July 8 Amos Pinchot and George L. Record called upon Bob, and urged that he agree to accept the nomination which it was evident would be tendered to him. Bob replied that he could give no definite answer until after both conventions had met and adopted a platform that would demonstrate there was a substantial voluntary agreement as to a program among the various groups represented. Pinchot and Record left with Bob the platform proposals they had prepared for the Committee of Forty-eight and suggested that he should have a draft made of a platform acceptable to him which could be used as a basis for discussion at the meetings of the two conventions' platform committees. After they left, Warren S. Stone arrived by appointment to talk the situation over with Bob.

The next day Robert M. Buck, a member of the Executive Committee of the Labor Party and editor of the *New Majority*, the Chicago Federation of Labor's publication, also came to see whether Bob would accept the Presidential nomination. Buck had previously discussed the matter with Bob, and this visit to the farm had been arranged in response to a letter Buck had written while Bob was still at Rochester.[18] Buck was given the same answer as Record and Pinchot. He left with Bob an elaborate draft of a platform he had · prepared, but did not request any suggestions.[19]

Buck's failure to ask for suggestions would have seemed more significant than it did that day if Bob had read an editorial in the *New Majority*, published three weeks earlier, warning delegates to the National Labor Party Convention to beware of a "third party" movement for the Presidential election.[20] It expressed a hostility toward the Committee of Forty-eight which was in striking contrast to the apparently friendly message delivered at their St. Louis Conference six months earlier by a representative of the Labor Party, Duncan McDonald.[21]

An editorial in the *New Majority* was an authoritative voice speaking for the leaders of the Labor Party. This publication had printed its first issue on January 4, 1919, and Buck's name appeared on the masthead as editor a few weeks later. Its declared purpose was to help launch the recently founded Labor Party into a nationwide political movement.[22] Later a reporter described this party as "born of hatred for the American Federation of Labor, and nurtured in wrath against its president, Samuel Gompers."[23] John Fitzpatrick, president of the Chicago Federation of Labor, and Edward Nockels, secretary, had been leading pioneers in creating the

Labor Party which had called its second national convention to meet in Chicago on July 11, 1920, to nominate candidates for President and Vice President and "to draft a platform on which to present labor candidates to the people."[24]

The convention under the auspices of the Committee of Forty-eight met at the Hotel Morrison on Saturday morning, July 10. It was called to order by the national chairman, J. A. H. Hopkins, and Allan McCurdy of New York made the keynote address to an audience of about twelve hundred people, including spectators.[25] Nine hundred delegates representing forty-three States were registered.[26] The *Chicago Daily News* noted that La Follette badges were distributed among the delegates, although "there were none in the convention who could say whether their chieftain would consent to be the standard bearer of the third party."[27]

Roe and Bob, Jr., went to Chicago to attend the two conventions as observers. They brought the platform which Bob and Roe had prepared in response to Pinchot's and Record's suggestion. It was modeled upon the Wisconsin platform recently endorsed at the election by a vote of about two to one. It also included in substance some provisions in the platform Bob had received from Buck, as well as some in the one submitted by Record and Pinchot. Later Record became chairman of the Committee of Forty-eight platform committee.

Bob considered certain conditions essential if he were to accept a nomination by the two conventions. A substantial agreement on a platform must be arrived at voluntarily among the various groups without any interference on his part. If a platform were agreed upon only because he forced it as a condition of accepting a nomination, he thought the new party would be merely a sporadic one-man affair that would be harmful to the progressive movement. He could accept the nomination only if the program voluntarily agreed upon was one that he could approve. Also, if he were to become the candidate of a new third party, the conventions must be unanimous in desiring his nomination.[28]

Roe and Bob, Jr., had left Madison in complete accord with the conditions Bob thought essential. Therefore they thought that they should remain neutral between the two conventions, and that the platform known to be acceptable to La Follette should be submitted simultaneously for discussion to the chairmen of the platform committees of both groups. Soon after they arrived in Chicago, Roe saw Buck, chairman of the Labor Party's platform committee, and made this suggestion. Buck made a definite appointment to meet Roe at the Morrison Hotel on Monday morning for this purpose.[29] The Labor Party Convention convened on Sunday morning, July 11, at Carmen's Hall with about seven hundred delegates present. The keynote speech was delivered by John Fitzpatrick, president of the Chicago Federation of Labor and the Labor Party's candidate for United States Senator.

The conservative press reported that Fitzpatrick's references to Russia and his appeal for Ireland's independence were greeted with enthusiasm.[30] Several correspondents noted the presence of William Z. Foster, the extreme left wing labor leader who had become active in the Labor Party early in 1920. One reporter observed that Foster occupied a seat "on the platform with the Fitzpatrick crowd that howls and groans whenever the name of Samuel Gompers is mentioned."[31] The *New Majority* reported that there was "prolonged cheering and vociferous applause" when Fitzpatrick said, "Oh, that the day was only near when the workers in the United States would be able to concentrate their effort and do a job such as Russia has done."[32]

Late that night William Hard, a prominent newspaper and magazine correspondent, wrote Bob an eleven-page longhand letter vividly describing the different groups represented and reporting that in the convention hall he had "felt a vitality that was deeply impressive." He said he was delighted with the platform Roe and Bob, Jr., had shown him. *"With good luck and barring accidents due to personalities which sometimes temporarily swerve great movements from their natural courses,"* he thought this platform should bring agreement from both the Labor Party and the Committee of Forty-eight which would result in unity.[33]

Earlier that same day Bob, Jr., had written his father summarizing the situation as he and Roe interpreted it during the first stages of the conferences of the conciliation committee appointed by the two conventions. They thought there was no doubt that the platform which had Bob's approval could be forced upon both conventions, but they were in accord with his judgment that this should not be done. If there was common ground for voluntary union, however, they did not wish to allow it to be prevented by a few men in each group who represented only the minority of both conventions. He wrote that Record and Pinchot were both standing pat in contending for their platform and that the left of the Labor group, which had a majority on the committee, was also standing firmly for their position. He also reported that the Labor Party had added six members to their conciliation committee, and said he had every reason to believe that Duncan McDonald, a left-wing organizer, and his group would "have most of those places." After specifying certain support that had been assured his father if he decided to accept the nomination, Bob, Jr., said, "We feel as tho we were sitting on a mine that might blow up at any minute[,] still I think it is the truth to say that I think some harmonious and satisfactory result will work out of this."[34]

On Monday, however, the prospects for a harmonious fusion of the two groups dwindled. Buck did not keep his appointment with Roe and Record to discuss the draft of a platform acceptable to La Follette. Throughout the day the two conventions held separate sessions listening to numerous speakers. Among those who addressed the Committee of Forty-eight Convention were Dr. Taraknath Das, secretary of the Friends of Freedom for India, and Eamon De Valera, who made a stirring appeal for recognition of the Irish Republic. Later speeches were made by invited delegates from the Labor Party Convention, including two left-wing laborites, Duncan McDonald and James Duncan. Meanwhile the conciliation committee of the two conventions was vainly trying to agree upon a platform and the machinery of amalgamation. Late Monday night the chairman of the joint committee, Toscan Bennett, a Labor Party delegate, reported the situation to the Labor Party Convention. After some debate and a plea by Dudley Field Malone, the convention voted to appoint a subcommittee of their platform committee to meet with a similar subcommittee from the Committee of Forty-eight. The men selected for these subcommittees had all been members of the larger conciliation committee, which had previously failed to agree.[35]

At about one o'clock Tuesday morning, the five members of the Labor Party subcommittee, headed by Buck, arrived at the Morrison Hotel to confer with the subcommittee of Forty-eight, headed by Record. The Labor group brought a complete draft of a platform that had been adopted by their entire platform committee and announced that no amendments could be accepted without referring them back. Roe, who was present as an observer, asked that the platform he had brought from Madison should be presented by Dudley Field Malone, who was a delegate to both conventions. The members of the subcommittees were told that the draft Malone presented had La Follette's approval. These two platforms and the one drafted by Record and Pinchot were read and discussed throughout the night and early morning. There was a large area of agreement among the three drafts. But when the subcommittees recessed shortly before the conventions were scheduled to convene, the Labor group was still insisting upon certain extreme provisions which the Committee of Forty-eight's representatives had previously refused to accept.[36] The *New York Times* reported that morning that a big fight had developed within the Committee of Forty-eight itself between the Eastern right wing and the Western left wing. But the dispatch also stated that "Unless arrangements are suddenly thrown out of gear, it seems a safe prediction that the Presidential candidate of the third party will be Senator La Follette."[37]

But it soon became evident that arrangements as to platform and candidates which would have been satisfactory to the majority of delegates of both conventions were being thrown out of gear. The proceedings in the conventions and in the platform conferences seem to indicate that there were many hidden maneuvers skillfully directed by a small minority with revolutionary purposes which was even then boring from within the Labor Party and trade-union groups. A few men who were apparently influential in directing strategy at this time became prominent later in the Communist Party.[38]

When the two conventions convened again on Tuesday morning, they were informed that the platform subcommittees had not reached an agreement. The delegates of the Committee of Forty-eight Convention then overrode the pleas of their Eastern leaders and voted to join the Labor Party Convention without waiting for agreement on a platform or any formal provision on procedures for an amalgamated convention. That afternoon they marched in a body from the Morrison Hotel to Carmen's Hall, where they were enthusiastically welcomed on the assumption that this was the first session of a new party permanently uniting all the groups represented by the thousand delegates on the floor.

But when they began to vote on resolutions presented by Buck, they soon learned that before their arrival at Carmen's Hall the Labor Party delegates had adopted rules of procedure which assured them overwhelming domination on contested issues.[39] A reporter observed that "Once the Forty-eight delegates were in the same hall with the Labor convention, they disappeared like drops of rain falling upon the surface of the sea. The convention became, to all intents and purposes, an enlarged Labor party convention. The Labor leaders went right on with their program as if they were just continuing the work of the day before, passing resolutions, reported by the Labor party's committee on resolutions, which the Forty-eight delegates had never seen. The Labor party simply swallowed up the Forty-eight."[40] During the evening session the convention delegates listened to speeches while marking time for the platform committees to report.

When the subcommittees met again that night at the Morrison Hotel, it was evident that although the Labor group had incorporated some suggestions from the other two platforms, they had retained their own platform substantially as it had first been drafted. They requested that a delegation go to Madison to submit it to La Follette.[41] Apparently others suggested that La Follette should be asked to break the deadlock between the subcommittees by making a direct appeal to the delegates.

At midnight Roe reported the situation to Bob by telephone. Bob's answer was recorded in a three-and-a-half-page memorandum typed on Morrison Hotel stationery by his son. Bob's position is summarized in excerpts from these pages which record him as saying: "I have had nothing to do with bringing into existence the conventions now in session in Chicago. Mr. Pinchot, Mr. Record, Mr. Hopkins and other of the Committee of 48 and Mr. Buck, Mr. Fitzpatrick, Mr. Noeckle [Nockels] and others of the Labor Party have done all the work which has resulted in the present convention. These men are my personal friends and have been for years. I would do *nothing* which would handicap or embarrass them in anyway before the convention. Even though I felt that a platform suggested by me might prevail among the delegates I should not feel justified, under any circumstances, in literally 'going over their

heads' and consenting to the presentation of my views to the convention. . . . The platform suggestions I have made have been
presented with no idea of pressing their adoption, but simply to
clear my own position and to prevent the convention from nominating me on a platform which would make it necessary for me
to decline to be a candidate. . . . If a platform of the nature I have
suggested can not be agreed upon, I should not want my name to
go to the convention." Bob also informed the committee that he
would rely upon the judgment of Roe, his son Bob, Jr., Herman
Ekern, and Basil Manly in determining whether the platform
finally agreed upon was of such a nature that he could accept the
nomination. He stated that he would be glad to receive any delegation the committee might care to send to Madison, but would prefer
that the men he had named, who were familiar with his views and
the proceedings of the convention, should speak for him.[42]

The Labor group refused to eliminate the points of difference
from their platform. Roe then told them that La Follette could not
consider a nomination on it. He also pointed out that La Follette
had always regarded a platform as a contract with the people and
that he could not be a candidate on any platform of which he did
not know the contents. The members of the two subcommittees
worked throughout the night. Malone recorded that "after a long
night of negotiation and debate," Buck declared to the joint committee: "We want Senator La Follette as our candidate just as much
as you of the Committee of Forty-eight want him, but we do not
want even Senator La Follette as much as we want our programme.
And so we now refuse to make any further concessions either to
bring about harmony between the groups or to get the Senator."[43]
Roe did not even see the final Labor Party platform. It was completed only a few minutes before it was read to the convention
by Buck.[44]

On Wednesday, the last day of the convention, the acting chairman, John Walker, announced that he had been authorized to say
Senator La Follette had refused the nomination and could not
allow his name to be considered. Lester P. Barlow, president of the
World War Veterans, immediately mounted the speakers' stand and
shouted, "There's an intriguing clique here that's trying to shut out
La Follette."[45] He declared that the Senator's platform was as progressive as any that was being written in the committee rooms,

and he then placed his name in nomination. Barlow's speech started a long demonstration which threatened to stampede the convention. An enlarged photograph of La Follette draped in the American flag suddenly appeared on the platform and a large red banner with "Bob La Follette" on it in white letters was unfurled over the gallery rail. The delegates continued cheering and shouting demands to hear La Follette's platform while the chairman vainly sought to restore order.[46] Roe was in the convention hall and reported what was happening to Bob, Jr., who was at the Morrison Hotel.

Bob, Jr., called his father on the telephone, took down his statement, dashed out for a taxi, and gave the driver a $10 tip to take him to Carmen's Hall faster than the law allowed. When he arrived, the demonstration was still going on. He rushed to the speakers' stand and read his father's message, which said: "I have just been informed that contrary to my expressed wishes my name has been placed in nomination before your convention. In view of the circumstances which have arrisen [sic] I do not consider myself avaliable [sic] and must therefore decline to run if the nomination be tendered me. I earnestly hope that my name will be withdrawn without further delay."[47]

Later a platform, signed by five members of the Labor Party subcommittee, was presented to the convention by Buck, and another platform, signed by Record, Pinchot, and Gardner of the Committee of Forty-eight subcommittee, was offered by Record. During the discussion of the two platforms a strange incident occurred which seems to have been a part of the skillfully directed hidden maneuvers. The *New York Times* reported that the La Follette men were "deeply enraged" by a statement made by C. J. France of Seattle, a Committee of Forty-eight delegate and a member of their National Executive Committee, who had represented them on their platform subcommittee.[48] France now announced to the convention that he was for the Labor Party platform and that if La Follette "couldn't stand for that we have to nominate somebody else."[49] Then mounting the rostrum, he attacked the La Follette platform and charged that the La Follette spokesman had refused to permit the Negro equality plank in the platform because it would alienate the Southern white votes.

Gardner and Roe immediately repudiated this attack and France's false statement regarding the platform. When Roe got through with what a reporter described as "a heated defense of the Wisconsin man," he called upon Buck to corroborate him. Roe ended by "assuring the convention that the statement [made to the convention by Walker] that La Follette was not available had been made upon his authority as La Follette's representative." Buck took the platform again, refused to corroborate Roe, and made a fiery speech "with an occasional interjection of mild profanity, by way of emphasis," declaring that "never again would a 'liberal' ticket hope to win. It must be a radical ticket."[50] The Labor Party platform was then passed by 308 votes to 125 votes for the Committee of Forty-eight platform signed by Record, Pinchot, and Gardner. Subsequently C. J. France became a candidate for United States Senator on this platform.[51]

After the platform was adopted, Hopkins, Pinchot, Record, Gardner, and most of the Committee of Forty-eight delegates bolted the convention and returned to the Morrison Hotel to consider future plans. Gardner reported in a confidential letter how the leaders of the committee had been outmaneuvered during the deliberately prolonged platform conferences. When it was too late for the Committee of Forty-eight Convention to nominate a Presidential candidate independently, Gardner said the leaders of the Labor group, Fitzpatrick, Buck, Toscan Bennett, and Nockels, declared quite frankly "that they did not need our people and did not want us. These leaders saw in any successful amalgamation or third party movement with La Follette as candidate an absorption of their new labor party. They felt they would be swallowed up by the white collared element. The more successful the movement, the less there would be left of them, their leadership and their party."[52] After the bolt of the delegates of the Committee of Forty-eight, the convention at Carmen's Hall adopted the new name of Farmer-Labor Party and nominated as its Presidential candidate Parley P. Christensen of Utah, who had been a delegate to both Chicago conventions.

A well known newspaper correspondent, Clinton W. Gilbert, commented that "The Labor leaders here have been bent upon creating a class party like the British Labor party. They have maneuvered themselves into control of the situation. They have taken the convention of the Forty-eight away from Mr. Pinchot, Mr. Record and their associates. They have everything except the candidate whom they wanted." The new party will be "one appealing only to working-class interests and semirevolutionary in its character."[53] During the conventions the *New York Times* had carried daily special dispatches. Their correspondent stated that within the Labor Party there had been a group "eager to set up something very like a soviet in this country and only mildly concerned with efforts to destroy Gompers which actuated the group dominated by John Fitzpatrick of Chicago." This correspondent also reported that William Z. Foster of steel-strike fame, although not a delegate to either convention, had stood "behind the scenes throughout the labor deliberations" and "had exerted a guiding influence in their every movement."[54] An Associated Press dispatch from Chicago that same day stated that "Of all the groups which joined the new party convention Tuesday only one well-organized faction is left in the Farmer-Labor ranks, and that is the former Labor Party."[55] From San Francisco Rudolph Spreckels wrote congratulating Bob on "declining the nomination of the fool hardy Convention at Chicago," and added that he could not "escape the feeling that stool pigeons in the employ of vicious interests had a hand in the shaping of the affairs of the Convention."[56]

From New York Roe wrote Bob that he thought the principles which were agreed upon in the conferences by both groups "were so fundamental and far reaching that they constituted a program fully as large and fully as advanced as any party ought to consider. . . . There is no doubt in the world that the delegates would have agreed if they had had the chance but the fact is that Buck was out to put over a trade union program and nothing else would do. This he very cleverly manipulated."[57] That same day Bob, Jr., wrote Roe from Madison: "I reported the events as best I could after the jumble of that affair. I think Dad feels that everything was handled as well as could have been in view of the fact that we did not know the labor crowd's purposes before hand. . . . As I look back on the whole affair I think the one big mistake that was made was that we got to regard the little group of fellows there in charge of the labor party as labor."[58]

The Washington correspondent of the conservative Philadelphia *Public Ledger* sent out a signed dispatch stating that "Fervent sighs of relief were heaved in both Republican and Democratic quarters today over the late news from the Chicago third-party convention.

. . . Either a La Follette or a Ford nomination, Washington politicians concede, might have thrown the presidential election into the House of Representatives under the constitutional proviso that requires a candidate to receive a majority of the electoral college."[59] The press also reported that Harding "was gratified to hear Senator La Follette had declined the nomination."[60] Later Bob received a letter from the chairman of the Republican National Committee, Will H. Hays, inviting him to participate in Harding's notification at Marion, Ohio, with the other candidates who had been placed in nomination for the Presidency at the Chicago Republican Convention.[61]

Bob did not go to Marion.

CHAPTER LXIV

A Progressive Legislative Program Assured in Wisconsin

After Bob had refused to allow his name to be considered by the convention at Chicago, the leaders of the Committee of Forty-eight continued to urge him to enter the campaign as a Presidential candidate. When the convention had voted down the platform presented by Record, many of the Committee of Forty-eight delegates had left Carmen's Hall and reconvened at the Morrison Hotel, where they decided to form a Liberal Party. While this meeting was still in session, Hopkins wrote Bob, Jr., that he understood they intended "to nominate La Follette" and "to leave the door open for the Senator to write his own platform."[1] From the East Record wrote Bob the same day suggesting that they should call another convention, not as the Committee of Forty-eight, but as a new group, with the avowed intention of nominating him.[2] A few days later Hopkins wrote Bob from the Chicago headquarters saying: "Everywhere we are being flooded with demands for your nomination . . . We are simply awaiting your consent. The second you say the word the country will light up with hope & enthusiasm."[3]

A week later Record, Pinchot, McCurdy, and James G. Blauvelt of New Jersey arrived unexpectedly from the East to urge Bob to run and to present plans for launching his candidacy. The next day Hopkins and Howard R. Williams, vice chairman of the Executive Committee of the Committee of Forty-eight, came from Chicago in accord with an appointment they had previously requested. A number of conferences were held. At Bob's request Charles H. Crownhart, Herman Ekern, Basil M. Manly, and Bob, Jr., attended these meetings. Bob's friend, James M. Pierce, editor and owner of the *Wisconsin Farmer* and other farm journals, also participated in two of the conferences.[4]

Record took a leading part in arguing for a plan to call a new convention in Chicago with the avowed purpose of nominating La Follette and a suitable running mate on a platform that had been agreed upon beforehand. He proposed that the convention should be controlled by a small group and that all opposition to this platform should be "steam rollered." Bob emphatically stated that he could not consider this proposal or any nomination that would be interpreted as indicating his candidacy had been initiated by the Committee of Forty-eight which had failed to unite the different groups at Chicago. Blauvelt, with Record's endorsement, presented a proposal that Senator La Follette "should announce his own candidacy and take his chances on finance and organization." Crownhart pointed out that without any assurance of money to finance a complete organization, the Senator was being "asked to take a jump in the dark which might not only endanger his personal standing but also might result in a political fiasco, discouraging any movement of the kind in the near future." Hopkins, Williams, and Pierce attempted to find out upon what basis Bob would consider becoming a candidate, "but any intelligent discussion was made impossible by digressions and irritations of Record and Blauvelt," who left Madison before anything had been accomplished except hours of "fruitless conversation."[5]

After they had gone, Bob talked over with Crownhart, Ekern, Manly, and Bob, Jr., the proposals made by members of the Committee of Forty-eight and decided it would be unwise to enter a campaign on any such indefinite basis. They agreed this committee might be a handicap in securing the cooperation of other progressive groups because they knew that during the Chicago conventions the ineptitude of some of its leaders had offended the representatives of several groups. In a brief talk with Hopkins and Williams, Bob indicated that he had decided not to run, but left the statement of his reasons to Crownhart, Ekern, and Manly.

That night they told Hopkins, Williams, and McCurdy that the principal reasons for Bob's decision were the late date for beginning a campaign, the lack of assurance as to a fund for organization, and the fact that no one had any firsthand information regarding the attitude of the progressive groups in the different States who must be united if an independent Presidential candidacy were to be effective in building up a new party. Hopkins and McCurdy then urged that Bob be asked to defer his final decision for two weeks and offered to place at his disposal $5,000, the minimum necessary for him to have a quick, nation-wide survey made by his own trusted friends and their agents.

After a great deal of hesitation, Bob finally agreed to undertake the survey upon certain conditions which were explicitly stated to Hopkins, Williams, and McCurdy, who accepted them with cordial approval. It was agreed that in conducting the survey Bob would incur no obligation and would be free to make whatever decision the information gathered might justify; also, that the Committee of Forty-eight should not play a conspicuous part in either the investigation or the campaign and that it should be merged into any larger movement which might be formed if he decided to become a candidate. In a long letter to Roe giving a detailed report of the conferences, Manly said: "I think you would be surprised at the Senator's physical condition. He is hard as a rock, and apparently is not fatigued, except by George Record . . . He has no desire whatever to make a campaign unless there already exists a popular demand that he should take the field and make a fight. He is anxious that every precaution be taken to ascertain the real situation throughout the country so as not to be misled by the enthusiasm of personal supporters."[6]

After Hopkins and Williams returned to Chicago, Bob started to get in touch with friends in different parts of the country to help conduct the survey. But within the next few days his plans were suddenly changed by developments which seemed to him to violate the specific conditions that had been agreed upon. Telegrams began coming in from Blauvelt, Pinchot, Gardner, and others urging the choice of George Record as the Vice Presidential candidate. Bob reported this to Ekern, who was in Chicago, and asked him to tell Hopkins emphatically that this could not be considered because Record's candidacy would introduce the Committee of Forty-eight prominently into the campaign. Other incidents occurred which led Bob to stop the survey and send a telegram to Hopkins saying, "Upon information at hand I have decided to proceed no further with the matter arranged between you Ekern Manly and Crownhart."[7]

As Bob had never at any time consented to be a candidate, he was astonished to learn the next day that a dispatch had been sent out from Detroit reporting that at a meeting of the Michigan members of the Committee of Forty-eight, now known as the Liberal Party, Howard Williams had "told of conferences with Senator La Follette, and of the Senator's final consent to run as head of the national ticket."[8] When the newspaper correspondents questioned Bob, Jr., about this dispatch, he gave out a statement to the press declaring this report "was absolutely without foundation in fact."[9]

In a letter to Roe commenting on his father's final decision, Bob, Jr., wrote: "I have been bucking as hard as I could, and still remain a member of the family, this whole proposition ever since I got back from Chicago, and am personally pleased that it has gone by the board. I do feel, however, that a wonderful opportunity has passed and regret it exceedingly, but I think it would be a task comparable to lifting one by one's boot straps to attempt anything now."[10]

In the July issue of *La Follette's Magazine,* Bob published as a signed editorial the preamble to the platform Roe had submitted through Malone to the platform subcommittees of the two conventions. Bob informed his readers that it expressed his "views on the records and platforms of the two old parties in national affairs."[11] The *New York Times* gave a column to quotations from the editorial under the headline "La Follette Flays Both 'Old' Parties."[12] A month before this editorial appeared, the Democratic Convention at San Francisco had nominated James M. Cox for President and Franklin D. Roosevelt for Vice President. Although the Senate had rejected the Treaty of Versailles in March, they had endorsed Wilson's policies and his declaration that the entrance of the United States into the League of Nations without reservations was the paramount campaign issue.

In Wisconsin the League of Nations and the Esch-Cummins Railroad Law were the most hotly debated issues throughout the primary and the election campaigns. Bob's physicians did not permit him to make any speeches until a week before the November election. Nevertheless he participated actively in efforts to reach the voters through other media. He endorsed James Thompson as a candidate for the Republican nomination for United States Senator against Lenroot and also endorsed John J. Blaine for governor. Nearly all the leading newspapers in the State except the *Capital Times* were hostile to the progressive candidates Bob endorsed. But during the primary campaign reprints of pages from the August issue of *La Follette's Magazine* containing Bob's editorial "What the Esch Cummins Law Costs the People," and a record of Lenroot's roll call votes on this law, the League of Nations, the oil-leasing bill, and other legislation were widely circulated. Bob's endorsements of Thompson and Blaine and other printed leaflets analyzing the issues were also sent out by mail or distributed at meetings.[13]

Blaine won the nomination on September 7, defeating five other candidates. His leading opponent was state Senator Roy P. Wilcox, who had introduced the resolution in the Wisconsin senate in 1918, condemning La Follette for failing "to support our government in matters vital to the winning of the war" and for utterances tending "to incite sedition among the people of our country and to injure Wisconsin's fair name before the free peoples of the world."[14] Nine progressive Republicans were also nominated for Congress. Among them were Henry Allen Cooper and Joseph D. Beck, who over-whelmingly defeated John J. Esch, the co-author of the Esch-Cummins Law. But James Thompson was again defeated by Lenroot. In analyzing the vote Bob wrote Senator Reed that Lenroot was "bone dry" and Thompson a "moderate" with the result that a third candidate, McHenry, an "ex-preacher" and an "ultra wet" had received many votes which would have gone to Thompson had there been only two candidates. Bob and many others thought that if the opposition to Lenroot had "been undivided Thompson would have been nominated by 20,000."[15] Thompson therefore decided to run as an independent candidate, and Bob again endorsed him. A month before the primary Belle wrote that Bob was going to the office every day and "seeing people all the while. He seems to be in good spirits and quite reconciled to whatever comes."[16]

As the election campaign progressed, it increased in bitterness, and Bob became an issue through his endorsement of Thompson as an independent candidate. Wisconsin's leading stalwart newspaper, the *Milwaukee Sentinel*, commented sarcastically that although

Senator La Follette was making no speeches, his pen was active.[17] Lenroot had the solid support of the Stalwarts, who then controlled the Republican State Central Committee, and also of the Progressives who had turned against Bob during the war. Herbert Hoover, Senators Kenyon and Hiram Johnson, and Gifford Pinchot came into the State to speak in behalf of Lenroot.

Bob wrote to Senators Borah, France, Reed, and David Walsh, asking them to speak on the League of Nations issue.[18] Reed was the only one who was free to come, and he addressed three meetings which were widely reported. Belle spoke before the United Women's Clubs and made a dozen speeches near Madison, "appealing to women to become interested in the issues, to register and come to the polls and vote."[19] Later she and Mrs. Blaine campaigned together for ten days, traveling across the State in a Ford car and making two or more talks each day.[20] Phil also made a number of speeches. In a letter to Roe, Bob, Jr., modestly described his strenuous weeks of campaign organization work as helping "on the edges."[21]

Bob began his brief speaking campaign in Milwaukee. The day before he arrived the *Milwaukee Sentinel* published at the top of the front page pictures of Lenroot and Harding on either side of a facsimile letter from Harding urging Wisconsin voters to return Lenroot to the Senate.[22] Until the election this letter was printed at the head of the editorial column. On the evening of October 21, Bob was greeted with tremendous enthusiasm by an audience of seven thousand that packed the large auditorium. Long before he arrived the doors had been closed and several thousand turned away. This was the first speech he had delivered outside the Senate since his extemporaneous speech at St. Paul. To avoid the possibility of being again misquoted, he read from a typescript which still preserves his own characteristic markings for emphasis. A reporter noted that he "spoke with much of his old time vigor" and that "The oratorical power which has been so potent a power in Wisconsin politics for twenty years is still in evidence."[23]

After analyzing the Esch-Cummins Law and summarizing what he believed entry into the League of Nations would mean to the American people, Bob charged that Lenroot had "*deserted the progressive ranks under fire, and now*, backed by huge campaign funds from distant states, is a candidate for reelection to the Senate. Mr. Lenroot has a *record*, and on that *record* he must be *judged*. He *cannot escape that record.*" Bob then went on to say, "You may not know where Lenroot stands *now*, but before the evening is over you are going to know *exactly where he stood* in the Senate, in the days *when* the *fate* of *this country hung in the balance* and every Senator's vote had the power to decide whether we were to remain an *independent nation* or become a *pawn* in the *shameless intrigues of foreign diplomats.*" Throughout his speech the audience followed him closely as he read the roll call of Lenroot's votes and gave the names of the Senators who voted with him and those who opposed. His review of Lenroot's record included certain war measures, the League of Nations, the Esch-Cummins Law, and the oil-leasing bill. In summing up, Bob said: "I might read you his record on practically every other great measure which has come before the Senate since he entered that body, and it would prove that he is a reactionary and a servant of special interests. On that record, I can not support Mr. Lenroot for reelection."[24]

Four days later the *Milwaukee Sentinel* printed in large type at the top of the front page an open letter to Bob from Lenroot which made headlines in newspapers throughout the State. Lenroot challenged Bob to debate with him, and charged that the speech was "filled with plain, unvarnished falsehoods deliberately made by you. In your vindictive hate of one who would not be your willing tool, you have lost all regard for truth, all sense of honor."[25] In a statement given out at Madison Bob said: "Mr. Lenroot's letter addressed to me and published in the *Milwaukee Sentinel* merits no answer. Certainly its intemperate language shows that he is incapable of presenting a fair discussion of any subject before an intelligent audience at the present time. But for the time overlooking the violence of his language, Mr. Lenroot points out no inaccuracies in my Milwaukee speech. Nor can he. My statements of fact are fully fortified by the record." A terse recapitulation of Lenroot's record on specific legislation followed. The *Milwaukee Sentinel* printed Bob's statement in small type at the bottom of the fourth page.[26]

Election day brought a nation-wide Republican landslide. In Wisconsin Harding defeated Cox by 498,576 to 113,422. Although Lenroot's name appeared on the ballot in the Republican column, he received 217,000 less in the State than Harding did.[27] Nevertheless Lenroot won the election to the Senate by 281,576 to Thompson's 235,029. Bob thought the fact that Lenroot won by only 46,547 votes showed that he "rode through on Harding's coat-tails." Since Thompson ran as an independent candidate, every citizen who cast one of the 235,029 votes for him was obliged to search for his name on the ballot and place a cross opposite it. Bob was therefore certain that these "clear-headed" voters would prove "a militant progressive army" in future contests with the stalwart faction of the Republican Party. The election of Governor Blaine and many other progressive candidates assured a progressive legislative program in Wisconsin.[28]

Four days before the election Bob was shocked to learn that his friend James M. Pierce, who had been taking an active part in the Iowa campaign against Senator Cummins, had died suddenly and unexpectedly at his home in Des Moines. For more than a quarter of a century Bob had "known and loved him."[29] The two men had first known each other when Bob drew up the articles of incorporation for the *Wisconsin Farmer*. In an editorial on Pierce's work and the influence of his three farm journals, Bob wrote: "As an editor in his young manhood Conscience pointed him the way, the hard, steep, lonely, rugged way of sacrifice and service to his fellowmen. And along that way he fought to eminence and commanding influence, where his power for lasting good will make his memory a blessed heritage to all who knew him."[30]

Pierce had written his final editorial after reading an Associated Press dispatch reporting a speech made by Dudley Field Malone in New York, on October 28, as a candidate for governor on the Farmer-Labor Party ticket.[31] Malone had publicly corroborated Bob's statement at St. Paul on September 20, 1917, that the *Lusitania* had carried ammunition and explosives on her final voyage. Malone had also declared, "I considered then, and I consider now, that the persecution of La Follette on a charge which the administration knew to be false from evidence in its own possession, was a frame-up on Senator La Follette and a fraud on the American people." Pierce quoted from Malone's speech, recalled the persistent misrepresentation of Bob's record and the belated apology of the Associated Press. He concluded his last editorial with the comment that, "No man was more maligned and more misrepresented, throughout the period of war hysteria, than Senator La Follette, and I thank heaven that belated justice is at last being done him . . . I am proud to have had the honor and privilege of standing openly with him in those dark hours, and rejoice with him in his own complete vindication . . ."[32]

CHAPTER LXV

"I'll Be Busy, Making You Be Good"

Bob returned from Madison to Washington in time to attend the opening of the third session of the Sixty-sixth Congress, December 6, 1920. By ten thirty that morning the Capitol was crowded and the Senate galleries were packed. When Vice President Marshall entered the Chamber shortly before twelve, Bob and many other Senators were in their seats. Watching the scene from the Senate floor, Bob, Jr., noted that President-elect Harding "was given an ovation as he took his seat," and that many Senators who had not seen him since his nomination "hurried over to tell him personally how happy they were over his victory and incidentally theirs.

"The prayer having been offered and the Senate called to order, Lodge introduced the customary resolutions of procedure, after which he requested that Harding be recognized for a speech. Much hand clapping followed the President-elect as he made his way to the rostrum where he spoke for ten minutes, expressing deep regret upon leaving his colleagues. Dignified and apt in choice of language, Senator Harding made a pleasing impression on all who heard him."[1] As he returned to the floor, he passed Bob's seat in the front row on the Republican side. He paused to pat him cordially on the shoulder and said, "Now, Bob, be good." Bob responded, "I'll be busy, making you be good."[2] His reply was prophetic.

During the final session of Wilson's Administration, Bob was in a strategic position because the Republican majority in the Senate was so small that by securing the cooperation of a few progressive Republicans and Democrats it was possible to block the Old Guard Republicans. Ten days after Congress convened, he halted an attempt to jam through the Poindexter bill, introduced the previous session, which made it a crime for railroad employees to strike.

It had been placed on the routine calendar under a unanimous-consent agreement, which meant that a single objection could prevent its consideration. Bob had expected to speak against it. But on December 16, when all its opponents were absent and only seven Senators were present, it was passed without a quorum call or a word of debate. A reporter noted that when Vice President Marshall announced the bill had passed, "smiles wreathed the features of Senators Poindexter, Smoot and King." When opponents of the bill learned what had happened, they rushed to the Senate Chamber. Bob, who had been at a committee meeting, returned in time to offer a motion to reconsider the vote. This stopped the bill from going to the House.[3] Subsequently Poindexter sought to put it through, but the opposition was so strong that Bob's motion to reconsider was agreed to. The bill thus went back on the calendar. It was not called up again, and therefore died at the end of the Sixty-sixth Congress.[4]

Later that same day another bill was slipped through under similar circumstances. Without calling a meeting of the Interstate Commerce Committee to consider this bill, Chairman Cummins had reported it favorably to the Senate. He had merely polled enough members of the committee to secure a majority. But Bob and another member, who might have been expected to be opposed, had not been consulted or even informed that the bill was to be reported. It provided for the extension of one year's time before Section 10 of the Clayton Anti-Trust Act should go into effect. This was the section which prevented the railroad companies from letting contracts for repair work to companies in which they had an interest or in which they held offices, except when it could be established by open bidding that such companies could perform the work more cheaply than anyone else.[5]

Two days after the Senate passed this bill, the House took similar action in response to an appeal from Representative Esch, who was still chairman of the House Committee on Interstate and Foreign Commerce, although he had been defeated for reelection by the voters of Wisconsin on the issue of the Esch-Cummins bill. The bill then went to the President, and every effort was made by its opponents to secure a veto. A brief was filed by the International Association of Machinists. Bob wrote his first letter in four years to President Wilson, giving reasons why the railroads should no longer be granted the suspension of Section 10 of the Clayton Act.[6] On December 30 the President's veto message came in. Bob, Jr., noted in his column in *La Follette's Magazine* that "it dropped like a bombshell among the members of the Interstate Commerce Committee, who, I have no doubt, were congratulating themselves on having slipped this important measure through. Since that time the veto has lain on the table, there apparently being no disposition on the part of the men who secured its passage to attempt to pass the bill over the President's veto."[7]

Throughout the final weeks of the Sixty-sixth Congress, Bob worked under great pressure, attending Senate sessions and committee hearings during the day and putting in many evenings at his office. Bob, Jr., wrote that bills were piling in "and being passed with little or no consideration."[8] Late in February, when the Winslow-Townsend bill to amend the Esch-Cummins bill came up in the Senate, Bob had his material in closely knit form, with tables and diagrams supporting his argument. The speech he delivered on two successive days was widely reported. He described the bill as even worse than the Esch-Cummins Law in the burdens it would place upon the American people because it abrogated the provisions of that law which to some degree protected the Government on the amounts to be paid to the railroads under the guaranteed-profits clause. Bob thought this bill would mean another railroad raid on the Treasury. To prevent this he offered an amendment that no money should be paid in the form of guarantees to any railroad which had paid "unreasonable and extravagant prices for supplies, equipment, repairs, . . . or unreasonable sums as salaries to its officers or directors," charging these dishonest expenditures in its accounts. It provided that the Interstate Commerce Commission should investigate and certify that the expenditures and salaries were reasonable before any Government money was paid to the railroads.[9]

The galleries were crowded during Bob's speech, and the press noted that "on one occasion following an impassioned denunciation of the measure" the applause "was promptly subdued by the Vice-President." Bob's amendment was, however, beaten by 47 to 19, and the bill was later passed by "gavel rule tactics," without a record roll call.[10]

The *New York Times* gave an unusual amount of space to his

speech in a special Sunday feature article which reproduced some of his charts. The article stated that his attack on the bill was "not marked by a conspicuous oratorical effort but consisted principally of quotations from reports, statistics and tables. . . . In outlining the inter-relationship of the financial interests Senator La Follette charged the railroads with extravagance in the matter of repair costs, and he asked leave to print in the *Record* his series of exhibits showing affiliation of the railroads with banks and supply companies, the interwoven directorates of rail and other corporations and interlocking Directors of the great banks, which headed by J. P. Morgan and Co. were pictured as controlling all the railroads. In 1920, it was set forth twenty-five men exercised the control." The author of the article stated that one of the diagrams Bob had used indicated that these twenty-five men "sat on the boards of directors of 99 class 1 railroads. They thus brought together, under a single directorship, as it were, roads operating 211,280 miles, amounting to 82% of the country's transportation system. As a matter of fact, these 25 men divide between them 193 railroad directorships."[11] Soon after Bob's speech was printed in the *Congressional Record*, former Secretary of the Treasury McAdoo wrote him from California that he thought it was "a very valuable contribution to the discussion of this important question."[12]

Bob was present on March 4, 1921, when Warren G. Harding was inaugurated President and Calvin Coolidge Vice President. At Harding's request the ceremonies were as simple as possible. Although President Wilson had not fully recovered from his long illness and could not walk without a cane, he rode with Harding from the White House to the Capitol for the last time. The traditional procedure was for the incoming and outgoing Presidents to drive to the front of the Capitol and walk up the long flight of steps together. But Wilson's strength was not equal to this ordeal, and he went to a little used entrance, out of sight of the crowd, where he had to mount only two steps before taking an elevator to the Senate floor. In the President's room he signed the bills passed during the closing hours of his Administration. After completing his final official tasks, he and Mrs. Wilson offered their congratulations to the new President and Vice President and returned to their new home in Washington. A reporter noted that although the day "taxed the President's broken physical powers greatly," he went through it "smilingly" without any hint of "regret at his retirement from high office."[13]

Harding broke a precedent by going to the crowded Senate Chamber to hear Vice President Marshall administer the oath of office to Coolidge, who spoke briefly. Harding's inauguration then took place on the east portico of the Capitol, where Chief Justice White administered the oath. The large audience that stood in front of the Capitol greeted the new President with enthusiasm and frequently applauded his brief inaugural address, which he closed by saying: "I have taken the solemn oath of office on that passage of Holy Writ wherein it is asked: 'What doth the Lord require of thee but to do justly, and to love mercy, and to walk humbly with thy God?' This I plight to God and country."[14]

The Senate returned to its Chamber, where Vice President Coolidge resumed the Chair. Bob answered the roll call, which recorded ninety-one Senators present. President Harding was notified that the Senate was ready to receive any communication he might be pleased to make. Meanwhile Senator Fall tendered his resignation as Senator, and the Senate went into executive session for twenty-five minutes. The new President revived an old precedent by appearing at an executive session and submitting in person the ten nominations to his Cabinet, reading the names one by one from a list he held in his hand. The proceedings of executive sessions do not appear in the *Congressional Record*, but a newspaper correspondent reported that the names presented by the President "were referred immediately to the committees, which had been polled in advance, and as the names were read, the chairman of each interested committee arose and gave the unanimous and favorable report of the committee for confirmation."[15] Among Harding's appointments were Harry M. Daugherty as Attorney General and Albert B. Fall as Secretary of the Interior. These two nominations made Bob particularly apprehensive about the Harding Administration. The President's adroit method of rushing through the confirmations had effectively blocked Bob's plan to oppose Fall's appointment as Secretary of the Interior.

In another secret session a few days later, however, Bob succeeded in blocking confirmation of Harding's nomination of former Representative John J. Esch of Wisconsin to the Interstate Commerce Commission to succeed Robert W. Woolley, a commissioner appointed by Wilson, who had protested against many of the railroad owners' claims and had opposed the suspension of Section 10 of the Clayton Anti-Trust Act. Bob had cited Woolley's testimony before the Interstate Commerce Committee in his arguments against the Esch-Cummins bill. He thought the President's nomination of Esch was a violation of the principle that should govern all appointments of a judicial nature. If confirmed, Esch would, Bob said, sit upon a semi-judicial body conducting an investigation and as commissioner would "pass upon the propriety of acts to which he had already given his consent as legislator."[16] When the special session adjourned on March 15, Bob's persistent opposition had forced consideration of the Esch nomination to go over until the extraordinary session of Congress which the President had called for April 11.

Between the sessions Bob left Washington to make two speeches in Wisconsin. Phil met him in Chicago, and they went together to Milwaukee, where Bob delivered an address advocating the independence of Ireland at the annual St. Patrick's day celebration of the Ancient Order of Hibernians. An audience of more than three thousand greeted Bob when he arrived at the Auditorium, where Governor Blaine introduced him. Phil wrote that "there was so much applause and cheering that it took him twenty minutes to get thru the first eight pages" and that "he had all the fire and zip which over-joyed all his friends and made his enemies fear he was going to live forever." The day after the meeting Bob and Phil went to Madison. While there he, Phil, and Judge and Mrs. Siebecker dined with Governor and Mrs. Blaine at the Executive Residence. Phil wrote his mother that "it was very pleasant and Dad was at his best."[17]

During the week that Bob was in Madison, the legislature was in session and he conferred with many men from different parts of the State. On the night of March 25, he spoke under the auspices of the People's Reconstruction League, which was holding a series of conferences in six strategic Midwestern cities preliminary to a two-day conference scheduled to meet in Washington soon after Congress convened. The Madison meeting, held in the Assembly Chamber of the capitol, was open to the public. It was the first speech Bob had made in Madison since the war. A "capacity crowd" gave him "a great ovation" when he entered. In reporting the meeting the next day, Robert S. Allen recalled that this was the chamber in which three years ago La Follette "was denounced and reproved by the legislative body of the state" and recorded that during his speech Bob said, "I wouldn't trade records with any living man on my war stand." For an hour and a half Bob discussed economic issues and warned that a program was already underway in Washington to shift the burden of taxation to those least able to bear it. Allen reported that he "recounted in his vivid manner, the influences at work in Washington. From Washington to Wisconsin and back again he took the crowd. And when he attempted to stop" they demanded, "Go on, go on, Bob."[18]

Bob was present when the extra session met on Monday, April 11. The pattern of this opening week foreshadowed the high pressure under which he was to work throughout the year. In addition to attending the regular Senate sessions and committee meetings, he had to prepare a minority report and deliver two speeches he had promised to make outside the Senate. Thursday he made a speech analyzing and condemning the Esch-Cummins Law at a meeting of more than a hundred delegates from labor, farm, and civic organizations who were attending the Washington Conference of the People's Reconstruction League.[19]

Saturday night, April 16, he acted as toastmaster and spoke on "How Wealth Dominates Legislation" at the first Congressional dinner of the People's Legislative Service which was destined to play an important part in the progressive movement during the next few years. Three hundred men and women attended this dinner at the New Ebbitt Hotel which was the "coming out party" for this non-partisan, non-lobbying service. It had been formally organized on December 17, 1920, at a meeting in Washington attended by a number of Senators, Congressmen, leaders of railroad labor organizations, representatives of farm organizations, and some fifty progressive men and women of national reputation.[20] Its avowed purpose was not only to compile facts for members of Congress to enable them to make an effective fight for the people's interest, but to analyze and inform the public on pending legislation. Bob was chairman of the Executive Committee. Basil M. Manly, who had been director of research and investigation for the Industrial Relations Board and joint chairman of the War Labor Board with Howard Taft, was its able director. The close relationship which

Bob already had with him deepened and continued throughout Bob's life. Under the title of "On Guard For the People," Manly's bulletins of the activities of the Service bearing on legislation and public affairs later became a feature in *La Follette's Magazine*. A number of individuals and organizations made financial contributions to the People's Legislative Service, but it was the great generosity of Bob's close friend W. T. Rawleigh and his enduring faith which made its continued work possible.

A week after the extra session began, the President's nomination of Esch to the Interstate Commerce Commission came up again for confirmation. While Bob was in Madison several telephone calls had been received at his office from the White House. On his return he had found a letter from the President saying that he had telephoned because he wanted to talk with Bob personally before sending in the recess appointment of Esch. The President explained that it had never occurred to him to consult Bob about the original nomination because Esch had such strong Congressional support. His conciliatory letter closed with the assurance that he wished to consult with Bob on matters of patronage, although there might be incidents growing out of the Wisconsin situation on which they could not agree.[21] Apparently it never occurred to Harding that Bob's opposition to Esch had any other basis than irritation at the President's failure to follow the customary courtesy of consulting the Senator from the same State as the man being considered for an important appointment.

When Chairman Cummins reported the President's recess appointment of Esch favorably from the Committee on Interstate Commerce, Bob submitted a minority report, although he could secure no other signature. His report protested Esch's qualifications for this position and reviewed the salient features of Esch's record in respect to railroad legislation during his long, continuous service on the House Committee on Interstate and Foreign Commerce since 1903. At Bob's request, and by unanimous consent, the injunction of secrecy was removed from the executive session proceedings on the confirmation of the nomination. Thus Bob succeeded in having the vote printed in the *Record*. The Senate confirmed Esch's nomination 52 to 3. Two Democrats joined Bob, but he was not able to persuade any Republican Senator to vote against it. After the vote was taken, Bob asked and obtained leave to print his minority report in the *Record,* which also permitted its publication in *La Follette's Magazine* and elsewhere.[22]

The Naval Expansion bill, reported but not voted on during the lame-duck session, was reintroduced. The House had appropriated about $400,000,000, which the Senate had increased to nearly $500,-000,000. This bill aimed to resume the building program adopted in 1916. It proposed to build 17 capital ships and to initiate a supplemental three-year program of 88 auxiliary craft. Bob thought this was an extravagant expenditure in peacetime, and that it was unwise to commit the Government to a program which he believed was now obsolete so far as it related to battleships. He made his first attack on the bill in a two-hour speech on May 16, and continued it at intervals during the next nine days.[23] His arguments were backed by facts he had used in his fight on the 1916 bill and a mass of material he had subsequently gathered.

Bob was convinced that the airplane and submarine had made the battleship an unreliable naval weapon. A number of young Army and Naval officers,. including General William Mitchell, had called upon him to protest against the program for spending money on capital ships to the neglect of air and submarine craft. During the war General Mitchell had been commander of the Air Service of the American Expeditionary Forces. On his return home he had openly advocated a unified air service instead of the then separate Army and Navy air forces. Bob had followed the hearings before the House Naval Affairs Committee where Mitchell had testified that capital ships had been rendered obsolete by aerial developments. During his speeches Bob offered expert testimony to show that with adequate airplanes and submarines the United States would be impregnable to offensive attack. He noted that British naval experts agreed with Admiral Sims in regarding the airplane as the important weapon of modern war and the one most useful to a country's defense.[24] Bob was thus among the first in Congress to support this opinion.

He charged that great pressure to pass this bill was coming from shipbuilders and steel manufacturers, eager to continue wartime profits and unwilling to let the Government cancel pre-war contracts. He quoted the statement of an admiral on the General Board who favored completion of the 1916 program and who had declared "that a number of our biggest concerns are practically depending upon these [contracts] . . . to tide them over until they get more work."[25] He submitted a set of tables showing the enormous increase in the profits of the United States Steel Corporation, the Midvale Company, and the Bethlehem Steel Company in the years immediately after our entry into the war. After calling attention to the scandalous transactions of the Carnegie Steel Company, exposed in the 1894 Congressional investigation, he said the Senate ought now to investigate the armor and munition companies which had large Government contracts, to ascertain their stock ownership, contracts, profits, and the combinations existing among them.[26]

The type of investigation Bob suggested in 1921 was made in 1936. It then brought out many facts which supported Bob's suspicion that there were powerful combinations of munitions companies with great financial corporations, having inter-locking directorates and close working arrangements between American munition makers and similar companies abroad; also, that such organizations as the American Security League and the Navy League had been influential in securing passage of appropriation bills.[27]

When Bob concluded his final speech against the bill on May 25, Borah brought to a vote his amendment calling for a conference of the United States, Great Britain, and Japan to limit naval armaments. This amendment had been introduced at the previous session, but it had been opposed by the Republican leaders and had died with the end of the Sixty-sixth Congress. Meanwhile a sufficiently strong public sentiment had been organized among the newly enfranchised women, the churches, and other groups to focus an effective demand on Congress for concrete action to limit armaments.

Belle had helped to organize the Women's Committee for World Disarmament, and was a member of the Executive Committee. At an open-air meeting on Christmas day, 1920, beside the Franklin Monument on Pennsylvania Avenue below Capitol Hill, she had told her audience: "We women have the power to compel disarmament. We need not plead nor beg. We have the ballot. On this issue of militarism we hold the balance of power. We propose to be practical. We propose to watch Congress. And here on this day precious to the Christian world, at the very door of the Capitol of our beloved nation, we vow to use our voices to DEFEAT those senators and representatives in Congress who stand for Militarism and War and to ELECT senators and representatives who stand for Peace and Disarmament."[28] In conducting an intensive campaign, this committee followed Bob's guidance on strategy. Meetings were initiated in many cities, including one in Washington on Easter Sunday, where Senator Borah, Representative Frear of Wisconsin, and others spoke.[29] A few days before this meeting Bob, Jr., wrote Phil: "It is very remarkable to me (you know I always see the difficulties) the results they have all ready [*sic*] accomplished in stirring other groups in the cities to take up the idea of making Easter a disarmament day and to form a permanent organization to carry on the work. It will interest you to know that Mrs. Brandeis has lent the use of her name to the group here and is very interested in what they are doing."[30]

At Bob's suggestion Belle and two other members of the committee had called upon Borah early in the new session to urge him to introduce his resolution for a disarmament conference again, and he had done so on May 4, in the form of an amendment. Although the President had opposed the amendment, the demand for a conference had become so strong that on May 25 the Senate passed it unanimously.[31] But the big Navy bill passed the Senate 54 to 17, with 25 not voting. Bob, Capper, Lenroot, Norbeck, and Norris were the only Republicans who voted against it.[32] Although defeated on this issue, Bob continued to lead a fighting minority against the legislative program of the Old Guard Republicans. Ten days after the Naval bill passed, Belle wrote Phil that "Daddy is getting in some good work in the Senate. It is wonderful how he comes back as he surely does. The load is heavy though and he comes home tired. So does Bob [, Jr.,]. Every day Daddy tells me he never had such help."[33]

Bob and many other Senators were shocked when the President submitted Secretary Mellon's request for a grant of unlimited power to take long-time bonds, with whatever rates of interest he might think best, in exchange for the demand notes of the Allied Governments. This bill thus ignored the terms of the Liberty Bond Acts. If it passed, Congress would vote away its powers to say how $11,000,000,000 of war debts should be handled. It came before the Senate Finance Committee, of which Bob was a member. Six months earlier he had learned that Great Britain was sending a special representative to discuss deferment of the interest due on its war debt. Knowing that the United States Treasury then had a $2,000,-000,000 deficit, he had promptly introduced a joint resolution forbidding the Secretaries of Treasury and State to act upon refunding the British debt without Congressional approval.[34]

Although his resolution had been successfully buried in the Finance Committee, he persisted in his effort to achieve its essential purpose. He decided that at the Senate hearings on the bill he would question Mellon as to what his program would be if the unlimited powers he had requested were granted. In a letter to Chairman Penrose, Bob suggested that Mellon should be asked to bring specific documents.[35] During the hearings Mellon was severely questioned, especially by Bob and Reed, about Treasury commitments, his attitude toward debt cancellation, and the deferment of interest or the acceptance of Germany's reparation bonds. Facts were brought out which only a few had previously known. Bob's questions indicated that he thought there were hidden undercurrents beneath what Mellon was willing to tell. Bob warned Chairman Penrose that it would "take a long time to pass any legislation on this subject, until this committee is in possession of all the facts with respect to it." Subsequently the complete file on the debt question was supplied, largely because of Bob's insistence. When the issue was raised of keeping secret all data obtained from the Treasury, Bob demanded that everything be put in the record. "This is not the money of these officials," he said, "it is the money of the people of this country and they have the right to know what is proposed to be done with it. . . I, for one, want to know just what is afoot about it."[36]

The majority of the committee voted to report the bill giving Mellon a free hand in settling the Allied debts. But Bob submitted a minority report, signed by five of the six Democratic members, among them Simmons, ranking Democratic member and former chairman. Bob stated that, "In all the history of this Nation no such sweeping powers have ever been demanded by or granted to any official in time of peace. No man has ever lived who should be intrusted with such a gigantic responsibility. . . . No man should ever be given such untrammeled control over the finances of this country and the destinies of other nations."[37]

The opposition to the bill was so strong in the Senate that Penrose did not dare bring it to a vote. The Administration had to consent to confide the refunding of debts to a commission headed by Mellon. When the bill to create this commission came before the Senate, Bob voted against it, after trying unsuccessfully to restrict its power. The commission's subsequent report, submitted in 1923, disregarded the Senate's specific instructions. Instead of twenty-five years, it extended the maturity date to sixty-two years and decreased the rate of 4 per cent to 3 per cent for ten years and 3½ per cent thereafter. A considerable part of the British debt of $4,500,-000,000 was thus canceled. Better terms were allowed her than she herself had allowed Canada and Australia. Bob pointed out that the commission had made no effort to investigate Great Britain's ability to pay. He sought to have the minutes of the commission published but was overruled.[38]

Late in July, 1921, while Mellon was still being questioned at the hearings of the Senate Finance Committee, the President sent a message to Congress proposing that further financial aid should be given to the railroads to supplement the profits that had been guaranteed under the 1920 Esch-Cummins Act.[39] A measure designed to implement the President's proposal was promptly introduced in both Houses. Known as a bill to amend the Transportation Act of 1920, it authorized the Government to sell to the War Finance Corporation, for resale, $500,000,000 of railroad securities which the Government had received in part payment of railroad indebtedness. The proceeds were to be paid to private owners of the railroads to settle what they claimed the Government owed them, without any offset of the sums they still owed it. These securities totaled about $1,359,000,000, which the Government had or would acquire under the terms of the bill.

Bob opposed it in the Senate Interstate Commerce Committee, and publicly announced his determination to fight it "inch by inch, to the dead line."[40] He thought the bill would put the Government into the business of dealing in corporate securities, "the most speculative in the world," and that it would permit the War Finance Corporation to exercise a dominating influence on the stock market. It also appeared to him to be a scheme to provide funds for the immediate cash payment of "claims" filed by the railroads against the Government, while the larger sums they owed it were to be funded in long-time obligations. When Cummins reported the bill favorably, Bob filed a minority report in which two Democrats, Pittman and Stanley, joined.[41]

The bill had the full weight of Administration support and railroad influence behind it, and the House passed it as an "emergency measure." But in the Senate the opposition became so strong that it was not brought to a vote. Bob's announced intention to offer amendments to repeal the guarantee provisions of the Esch-Cummins Law and restore the power of the state railroad commissions kept the Republican Senate leaders from bringing up the bill. Rather than risk amendment to this law, by which the railroads were profiting, they chose to let the bill die. Cummins took Bob aside one day and said, "I might as well tell you that the bill will not be brought up, and further, that nothing else will be brought up that will enable you to attack the Esch-Cummins Act."[42] By blocking this bill Bob saved the United States Treasury a round $500,000,000 slated to go to the railroads for settlement of what he considered their extravagant claims against the Government.

During hot weather which Bob, Jr., said "fries the juice right out of one even if he sits under a fan," he and Belle had been house hunting because the rent had been raised and the family could no longer afford the spacious home they had all enjoyed on Sixteenth Street. After several weeks of discouraging searching, Belle wrote Phil: "I had come to the conclusion that we might as well settle down to staying here and perhaps rent a room or two to help make up the rent. But papa said he would find something and he did."[43]

Before they left the Sixteenth Street house where the children had had so many "good times" with their friends, the youngest daughter, Mary, married Ralph G. Sucher, a young law student and newspaper correspondent who was a classmate and intimate friend of Phil's. The ceremony was performed by Dr. Ulysses G. B. Pierce, former Senate Chaplain, on June 15. It was a simple wedding. The only guests were Ann Parker, a childhood friend of Mary's, and Joe and Betty Farrington, classmates of Ralph and Phil.

Congress took a few weeks recess late in August, but Bob did not take any vacation. He worked on the Revenue bill, attended meetings of the Finance Committee, and heard Secretary Mellon present his views at the hearings regarding certain provisions of the bill. On September 21, at the first session after the recess, Penrose reported favorably the Senate bill which included Mellon's suggested amendments to the House bill. Bob thought the rates were shocking because he believed that taxes should be levied in proportion to ability to pay. Simmons submitted a minority report to which Bob added a signed statement declaring that "One single principle dominates the entire bill—to lift the burden of war costs and Government extravagances from the backs of individuals and corporations of great wealth and transfer this burden to those whose industry and productivity is essential to the Nation's prosperity. Not only are the supertaxes upon the incomes of multimillionaires cut in half and the taxes upon profiteering corporations abolished, but new loopholes are provided by which, in the future, American capitalists can more and more completely escape taxation."[44]

Opposing this bill, with Bob as leader, Simmons and a number of Democrats joined a group of Republicans known as the "agricultural bloc" in forming a powerful minority. The opening attack was launched by Bob, who pointed out a proposal to exempt from domestic taxation any American foreign trade corporation doing as much as 80 per cent of its business in foreign countries. Because of high surtaxes business was investing outside the United States, and this provision would grant these "foreign traders" complete exemption from income taxes. Bob moved to strike out this proposal because it was "a device to permit individuals and corporations of great wealth in this country to escape taxation by withdrawing their investments here and placing them abroad."[45]

In an effort to save the "foreign trader" provision, Republican leaders cited the favorable recommendations of Secretary Mellon, Secretary of Commerce Herbert Hoover, and Secretary of State Hughes. But Bob's amendment to strike it out was adopted by a vote of 35 to 30. The contest was widely reported. A correspondent commented that Penrose was deeply chagrined and declared that the situation in the Senate had become "intolerable." He sent out a hurry call for absentee Senators, but even this did not make it possible to reconsider the vote. It was predicted that the amendment would "be taken care of" when the bill went to conference.[46]

Another amendment Bob offered requiring taxpayers to list on their income-tax returns all their tax-exempt securities was also passed. Two others were rejected. A bitter running debate took place during his effort to amend the committee bill by increasing the tax scale so that the inheritance tax should be 50 per cent in excess of $30,000,000 instead of 50 per cent in excess of $100,000,000, as the bill provided. Bob read and analyzed the testimony of Secretary Mellon before the Finance Committee on September 8, in which Mellon had favored a surtax not to exceed 25 per cent. Bob also read at length from Mellon's testimony giving some dozen examples of the way taxes on wealth could be avoided. Bob's amendment was rejected 39 to 28 with 29 not voting.[47] During the seven weeks of debate Bob was constantly on the floor or in his office working on schedules. He spoke at length three times in addition to participating frequently in the debate. On all his significant amendments he asked for a roll call vote, and told the Senators that he intended "to distribute the roll calls on this bill well over the United States." He also published them in *La Follette's Magazine*.[48] The bill finally passed 38 to 24, and went to conference. Two days later Belle wrote Phil that both Bob and Bob, Jr., were extremely weary, as they had "been going to the Capitol early and getting home at twelve and one o'clock."[49]

When the tax bill came back to the Senate in the form of a conference report, several of the hard-won amendments had been eliminated so that it was substantially in line with Mellon's recommendations. The income tax on corporations had been cut, the maximum rate on estate taxes had been decreased, and the gift tax cut out. Only the Senate rate of surtaxes on large incomes and Bob's amendments in regard to foreign traders remained. A Democratic member of the conference committee, Senator Simmons, had "raised such a row" that he prevented Penrose and the Republican majority of the conferees from "taking care of it" as had been predicted. Commenting on the "foreign trader" provision of the bill, Simmons said: "The great fight that was made in behalf of that amendment was made by the Senator from Wisconsin, Mr. La Follette. I seconded him with all my power and he and members of the House and Senate and the people of the United States are to be congratulated that this amendment was saved from the slaughter prepared for it." Simmons said that on the basis of the treasury experts' estimates, the bill, without La Follette's amendment, would have been equivalent to a present to the "foreign traders" of between $200,000,000 and $300,000,000 out of the United States Treasury.

Shortly after this, Edward Keating wrote an article for *Labor* telling about the fight La Follette and Simmons had made to defeat the "foreign trader" provision. A cartoon by John M. Baer entitled "Delivering The Goods" illustrated the article. It depicted a small man labeled "The People" standing on top of the United States Treasury building, smiling and holding out his hands to La Follette, who was about to present him with a huge money bag labeled "200 Million Dollars."[50]

During the last two weeks of the debate on the tax bill, Belle had been in Wisconsin speaking with Mrs. Blaine at a series of meetings organized to aid in the disarmament campaign.[51] After the Senate passed the Borah amendment, the President had carried out its provision by calling a conference of the United States, Great Britain, and Japan, to meet in Washington. But he had added factors which Bob and others thought might complicate the situation and defeat the real purpose of the amendment, which was to achieve substantial naval disarmament. Harding had included Italy and France in the call for a conference and had also suggested that Far Eastern questions should be discussed. The *New York Times* reported that the fervent hopes of the American people for disarmament had embarrassed the Administration, and noted that Harding and Coolidge had warned against undue optimism and the expectation of great results.[52]

Bob had received confidential reports from his friend Edwin Borchard that secret international agreements were being made behind the scenes to tie up disarmament with war debts and other desired concessions.[53] He feared that these secret negotiations were undermining the conference before it met. Although he could not use this confidential information publicly, Bob warned his colleagues in a Senate speech that there was a "deep and determined conviction" in this country upon the question of disarmament and that the purpose of the resolution introduced by Borah should not "be twisted and given another meaning."[54]

The conference, popularly known as a Disarmament Conference, was officially named "The Confederation on Limitation of Armaments." Borah, who had initiated it, was deliberately ignored. The American delegates were Secretary of State Hughes, Senators Lodge, Underwood, and former Senator Elihu Root. For twelve weeks the delegates met in secret sessions at the Pan-American Building. The plenary or open sessions were held in the D.A.R. Auditorium, next door. Belle attended the open sessions and reported them for *La Follette's Magazine.*[55]

In the secret sessions Hughes' proposal to limit naval construction for ten years was soon accepted by the delegates. A ratio was agreed upon under which Japan, France, and Italy were assured three-fifths of the tonnage allowed to Great Britain and the United States, who were equal. All agreed to stop building battleships and to destroy some already built or in construction. But nothing effective was done to limit submarines, naval aircraft, or great land armies. The agreement became, as Senator Glass aptly said, "not a permanent scheme to prevent war" but "a temporary expedient to avert bankruptcy."[56]

After this agreement had been announced at the first public session, Bob described it in an editorial as "a Naval Holiday—neither more nor less."[57] The conference also adopted a "Four Power treaty" which Bob thought had "all the iniquities of the League of Nations covenant with none of the virtues claimed for that document by its advocates." He declared that under "the cloak of a world-wide sentiment for disarmament, the diplomats, representing reactionary sentiment in Great Britain, France, Japan, and the United States, have hatched in secret a treaty of alliance which morally binds this country to go to war whenever the 'rights' of either of the high contracting parties in the Pacific are 'threatened'. . . . This treaty is couched in practically the same language and avows the same purposes as the alliances which paved the way for war in 1914. . . . This treaty will no more prevent war than did the alliances consummated prior to 1914. It will provoke rather than prevent war . . ."[58]

When the conference agreements came before the Senate, Bob supported the one which limited battleships, but he spoke against the Four Power Pact. In a detailed analysis of both he reiterated his belief that "we can only serve the world and our own people while we are free to pursue our own ideals and our own ambitions in an effort to uphold freedom and democracy and the rights of the common man."[59] All the reservations he offered in the form of amendments were voted down.[60] The treaty won the necessary two-thirds to ratify by the narrow margin of 67 to 27. Borah, France, Johnson, and La Follette joined 23 Democrats in voting against it.

Norris voted for it. In a letter to a friend Bob said: "It was a great tug to have him leave us in this fight. It is the first time we have been separated on any important issue since he came to the Senate."[61]

During the brief recess between the first and second sessions, Bob had gone to Madison to be with his brother-in-law Robert Siebecker, Chief Justice of the Supreme Court, who was critically ill. His death a few weeks later was a hard blow, for they had been devoted friends ever since they were students at the university. For nearly two decades Robert Siebecker had been a leader in the pioneer work of interpreting the new laws which had made "the Wisconsin idea" famous.[62] After leaving Madison, Bob had written his sister, "I know better than most men how much more Robert deserves than can ever be said of him."[63]

Bob returned in time to take part in the final debate on the case of Senator Newberry, whose right to a seat in the Senate was being contested because of the large sum of money spent in his campaign. Bob, who in 1911 had offered the resolution to reopen the Lorimer expulsion case which led to his unseating, thought Newberry's conduct in the Michigan primary "infinitely more reprehensible and more injurious to representative government . . ." He declared the issue was "whether it is possible to buy a seat in the United States Senate for a quarter of a million to half a million dollars."[64] The Senate's decision to seat the Michigan Senator seemed to Bob to open the door to the control of elections by the unlimited use of money. Newberry resigned shortly after he was seated. But, as Bob had predicted on the Senate floor, "Newberryism" became a campaign issue. In the fall elections only two Senators were returned who had voted to confirm him.

Bob was concerned about the Administration's attitude toward the increasing encroachment of the great monopolies on the economic life of the Nation. In the spring of 1921, his apprehension had been intensified by a press report that President Harding had issued an Executive order transferring control of the naval oil reserves from the Secretary of the Navy to Secretary of the Interior Fall. He also distrusted Attorney General Daugherty because of the way he had construed the anti-trust laws in favor of mergers and monopoly practices. Therefore when Bob learned that an attempt was under way to modify the consent decree of February 28, 1920, under which the "Big Five" packers had agreed to relinquish their interest in certain unrelated lines of business, he decided to block this move. On January 16, 1922, he introduced a resolution, which was amended and adopted on February 3. It demanded a report on what steps Daugherty had taken to enforce the decree and what modifications had been proposed and considered by him. The resolution also authorized the Committee on Agriculture, of which Senator Norris was chairman, to investigate and recommend to the Senate what action it deemed "necessary and desirable."[65] This was one of the first of the numerous investigations during the Harding Administration, culminating in the famous Teapot Dome probe, which Bob subsequently initiated.

Three months earlier Bob had written his friend Robert F. Paine: "There is little encouragement to be had from the situation here. I keep pecking away as best I can but the impression one is able to make is in the aggregate very little. The tremendous majority which the Old Guard have in the Senate and House make them arrogant and relentless in putting over their program." The odds were against him in the Senate during the Harding Administration, and much of the correspondence he received at this time seemed "to indicate a discouraged and sullen attitude."[66] But letters from individuals whose judgment he valued revealed that they understood the purpose of his constant striving. From North Dakota his friend Judge Amidon wrote: "You are making a brave fight against large odds in number, but I think you are gaining ground every day. That is the way it looks to me in the press of the Northwest."[67]

This understanding of chosen friends, and Bob's own enduring faith in the American people, constantly sustained him. After visiting him in Washington, Professor Max Otto had written in his diary: "What made the deepest impression upon me is his complete faith in the common man. That faith seems so profound, strong, and dynamic, that it caused me to think of the passage in Hebrews which says, 'Of whom the world was not worthy.' I have wondered about the genuineness of the Senator's interest in 'the people,' as others have, perhaps for no other reason than that he was in politics. Did he really believe what he seemed to believe when making a political speech? I no longer have a doubt. It is his religion-basic, compelling, all-illuminating, all-directing, forever trying to express itself in word and act and forever falling short. If anything goes wrong, if the people vote for 'the system,' seem to 'sell out,' or when they turn against him in hate, it is because they are misinformed, misled. His faith stirred me to greater faith, but as it did so, I could not but wonder remembering his own bitter trials, whether such faith is justified by the fact or is a noble illusion."[68]

CHAPTER LXVI

Teapot Dome: "A Portrait in Oil"

The Harding Administration had been in office less than a year when disturbing reports began coming to Bob about the activities of the Secretary of the Interior, Albert B. Fall. When President Harding first announced Fall's appointment, Bob had feared it might lead to the private looting of the public lands with their resources of oil, coal, minerals, and timber. As Senator from New Mexico, Fall had persistently opposed conservation of these natural resources whenever measures involving them had been up in the Senate. Therefore Bob had thought this appointment so dangerous to the public interest that he had immediately started to organize a movement to prevent confirmation. But it had been rushed through the Senate before he had time to work up any effective opposition.

For years Bob had been on the alert to protect the naval oil reserves. In 1913 he became interested by chance in the initial experiments leading to the use of oil by our Navy. One day when he went for a walk he passed near the Navy Yard where experiments were being carried on in a small fenced-in area. Seeing the machines, he climbed over the fence to watch them and thus came to know some of the Navy officers who were conducting the experiments.[1]

When the policy of building all naval ships as oil burners had been adopted in 1913, the conserving of naval oil reserves became of even greater importance. As Josephus Daniels, Secretary of the Navy under President Wilson, vividly described it, "Without oil our Navy would be like painted ships upon a painted ocean."[2] Three great Western oil reserves—two in California and one in Wyoming —had been set aside by Presidential order for the Navy: the California reserves in 1912 by Taft; the Wyoming reserve, popularly

known as Teapot Dome, in 1915 by Wilson. Congress had vested
control of these reserves in the Secretary of the Navy, where it remained at the time President Harding was inaugurated. These
reserves were thus treated as storehouses to be held in trust for
future use by the Navy in the event of scarcity, high prices, or
national emergency. Throughout the Wilson Administration Secretary Daniels had zealously protected them, and Bob had repeatedly
approved his policy on the floor of the Senate.

The filibuster Bob had led in March, 1919, had protected the
naval reserves temporarily by preventing a vote on the Coal and Oil
bills. But in August the Senate Committee on Public Lands reported
another bill "to promote the mining of coal, phosphate, oil, gas, and
sodium on the public domain."[3] Study of the bill convinced Bob
that if passed as drawn it would destroy the naval reserves. One
of its provisions which he thought particularly obnoxious conferred upon the President the power to lease producing wells on oil
lands which had been reserved for the Navy's future use. When he
consulted Assistant Secretary of the Navy Franklin D. Roosevelt
and certain Navy officers and officials of the Department of Justice,
he found that they shared his opinion. The bill had the support
of the majority of both parties, with Senators Smoot, Fall, Thomas,
and Lenroot leading the debate for the Republicans and Walsh of
Montana for the Democrats. The third day of the debate Smoot
asked unanimous consent to bring the bill to a vote at the next
session of the Senate. Before the roll call began, Bob announced
that he would object "to concluding the debate at any time upon
this bill." Smoot withdrew his request. Bob then explained that he
had several amendments to offer and that he thought time should
be allowed Senators to investigate and get all the facts before en-
acting legislation of such far-reaching consequences.[4]

Three days later Bob presented fifteen amendments. On August
27 he began a series of speeches which were delivered intermittently
during six days, and included active participation in the running
debate. In these speeches and in the debate he persistently attacked
the proposed law.[5] He pointed out "jokers" in the provisions regarding the naval oil reserves, and he offered amendments designed to
protect them from the control of Standard Oil and other great
monopolistic interests. As part of his argument he read letters from
Secretary of the Navy Daniels and a letter from Assistant Secretary

of the Navy Franklin D. Roosevelt, whom he had consulted regarding the naval reserve provisions of the bill.[6]

When Bob concluded his attack upon the section granting the President power to lease the naval reserves, Smoot replied that the President and the Secretary of the Interior should be given this power in order to safeguard the wells against loss by drainage through wells outside the reserves.[7] Thomas of Colorado declared that those opposing this grant of power cast a deplorable reflection "upon the capacity and integrity of the Secretary of the Interior."[8] In attacking Bob's argument that this provision menaced the reserves, Walsh of Montana questioned the reliability of the testimony of E. B. Latham, an able geologist and oil expert Bob had quoted. Walsh maintained that this section should be passed because it would grant the President the power to protect the naval reserves from drainage by Standard Oil wells outside the reserves. In support of his argument Walsh cited the expert testimony of E. L. Doheny, whom he described as "one of the most extensive and one of the most successful oil prospectors and operators in the world." At this time Walsh believed that Doheny had no personal interest in the passage of the bill and no interest whatever in any of the property of the naval reserves which would be affected by this provision of the bill.[9] But several years later, when it was revealed that Doheny was a party to the scandalous leases this provision of the bill made possible, Walsh became the relentless prosecutor of the man whose judgment he had relied upon in voting to allow the President to lease the naval oil reserves.[10] The arguments of Walsh, Smoot, Fall, Lenroot, Thomas of Colorado, and others who spoke for the bill prevailed in the Senate. Bob's amendment to strike out the section granting the President power to lease the naval reserves was defeated 30 to 8, with 58 Senators not voting.[11] The bill passed late that evening and became a law when it was signed by President Wilson on February 25, 1920, a year before Harding became President.

Although Bob's amendment was defeated, his fight to save the naval oil reserves from leasing had attracted wide attention, and the position he had maintained on conservation of natural resources ever since he came to the Senate was well known. Naval officers, employees of the Interior Department, attorneys from the Department of Justice, newspaper men, and others interested in conservation often came to him to warn him or to consult with him about legislative strategy when they had reason to believe the public interest was in danger.

Less than three months after Harding's inauguration, Bob's apprehension regarding Fall's appointment was suddenly increased when the President issued an Executive order on May 21, 1921, transferring control of the naval oil reserves from the Secretary of the Navy to the Secretary of the Interior. It was discovered two years later that Fall had made the original draft of this order within a month after he became Secretary of the Interior and that the transfer had been put through in spite of protests from a number of naval officers. Rear Admiral Robert S. Griffin had bluntly told Secretary of the Navy Denby that if he turned the naval oil reserves over to the Interior Department "we might just as well say goodbye to our oil."[12]

At the time few were aware of what had happened. The President's order was reported inconspicuously on the inside pages of a few newspapers. Jerre Mathews, a Washington correspondent, called Bob's attention to the report of it in a seven-line story in the lower corner of the second page of the *Evening Star*.[13] To those who were aware of the significance of this Executive order it indicated a dangerous change in the naval oil reserve policy. Soon after it was issued Harry Slattery, who had worked with Bob in the 1919 fight to protect the naval oil reserves, began an active inquiry into their status. Months of quiet investigation revealed that claims upon these reserves, which had been decided against the great oil company claimants under the Wilson Administration, were being reopened by Secretary Fall and on rehearing were being decided in favor of the oil companies.[14] Also, suits to stop the Standard Oil and other companies from continuing to drill in the California reserves were being dismissed.

Slattery wrote Bob on March 15, 1922, that he had learned on reliable authority that Secretary Fall had leased a large acreage in the Elk Hills Reserve in California to a subsidiary of a company known as a Doheny company. Doheny was at that time one of the leading oil men in the United States. This particular reserve had been described by experts as best fitted for holding oil underground for future use by the Navy. Slattery also reported that the naval coal reserve in Alaska had been transferred to the Interior

Department and that it was known to be up for private leasing.[15]

Bob immediately set about gathering information in preparation for a resolution he intended to introduce. Before doing this he wished to see President Harding's Executive order of May 31, 1921 which had never been published in full and was not on file among the public records of the State Department where Executive orders were usually filed. On April 6 he wrote to Secretary of State Hughes asking for copies of the President's orders relating to naval oil and coal reserves.[16] On that same day he wrote to former Secretary of the Navy Daniels, telling him what he had learned "on reliable authority" and stating that at the first opportunity he intended to take the matter up in his own way in the Senate. He closed his letter by asking Daniels' opinion on these recent developments.[17] Within the next few weeks Bob telegraphed to a number of men in Wyoming asking them for information and opinions regarding the leasing of the Teapot Dome naval oil reserves. Among others he telegraphed was Governor Robert D. Carey of Wyoming, whose father had served with him in the House of Representatives.[18]

Secretary Hughes did not reply directly to Bob's letter but sent it to the Secretary of the Interior. On April 12 Fall responded in a long letter with enclosures of copies of the Executive orders.[19] As soon as Bob read the order transferring the naval reserves to the Interior Department, he was convinced that it was a violation of the law—an order beyond the power of the President to issue. Fall stated that it was authorized by that section of the Mineral Lands Leasing Act of February 25, 1920, which Bob had opposed so vigorously in 1919. Fall claimed that the naval oil reserves were being drained by private wells in adjacent areas and insisted that the purpose was not the sale of the naval reserve oil but the preservation of it for the Navy above ground if it could not be properly conserved within the soil. But in the eight pages of his letter Fall did not even mention leases on twenty-two wells in the Elk Hills Reserve in California, awarded to the Doheny Company on July 12, 1921, or a contract then in preparation which would be signed on April 25, giving that company a preference right to further leases in the Elk Hills Reserve.[20]

Nor did Fall mention the lease of the Teapot Dome naval oil reserve in Wyoming which he had signed on April 7 for himself as Secretary of the Interior and also for Denby as Secretary of the

Navy. This lease of the Teapot Dome reserve to Harry F. Sinclair's Company had therefore actually been signed the day after Bob had written his letter of inquiry to Secretary Hughes. Subsequently it was revealed that when rumors of this lease had begun to circulate, Denby himself had taken the precaution to sign as Secretary of the Navy. Also, that the lease had been signed in secret and then locked in Fall's desk with instructions that no information was to be given out.[21] It was estimated that under this lease oil worth hundreds of millions of dollars would be taken out by the Sinclair Company and sold. Sinclair himself estimated the property right granted him in this contract "at a greater amount than $100,-000,000."[22] Fall had sent the President a copy of his letter replying to Bob's inquiry. Harding had written his Secretary of the Interior a note saying, "I quite approve of the manner in which you responded to his inquiry."[23]

While Bob was sending out requests for information, rumors of the secret leasing of the Teapot Dome oil reserve began to circulate in Wyoming. Senator John B. Kendrick of Wyoming began to receive anxious demands for information from his constituents. His inquiries at the Department of Interior were met first with silence and later with denials. On April 15 Kendrick introduced a resolution calling upon the Secretary of the Interior and the Secretary of the Navy for specific information as to whether they were negotiating a lease of the Teapot Dome naval oil reserves with private parties and requesting them to inform the Senate of the names of all parties and the terms of all proposed contracts. The resolution was passed unanimously that same day. But Secretary of the Navy Denby and the Acting Secretary of the Interior Edward C. Finney waited until April 21 to write a letter giving the information requested.[24] Therefore Kendrick, Bob, and other Senators received their first official answer to these questions indirectly when the Interior Department issued a statement to the press on April 18 disclosing that a lease of the entire Teapot Dome reserve, comprising between six and seven thousand acres of the richest oil lands in the United States, had been executed on April 7 to Sinclair's Mammoth Oil Company, and that the Elk Hills Reserve in California was about to be leased to the Pan American Petroleum Company.[25]

Four days before this statement was given to the press, the *Wall*

Street Journal had informed its readers that Teapot Dome had been leased to Sinclair's Company and stated that it "marks one of the greatest petroleum undertakings of the age."[26] Two weeks later, in a Senate speech, Bob noted that during the interval of secrecy between the signing of the lease and the official announcement of it by the Department of the Interior, when "mystery surrounded the public's business, speculation in Sinclair oil jumped on the New York Stock Exchange in three days' trading over $30,-000,000."[27] Some stock-market speculators had known about the signing of the lease before the Senate and the general public were informed. Subsequent investigation revealed that Attorney General Harry Daugherty was among those dealing in Sinclair oil stock at this time.[28]

On April 21 Bob introduced a resolution in the Senate calling upon Secretary Fall to furnish detailed information regarding leases on all naval oil reserves. Simultaneously he inserted in the *Congressional Record* a letter he had received from former Secretary Daniels describing the persistent fight he had made, with the support of President Wilson, to protect the naval oil reserves while he had been Secretary of the Navy. In answer to Bob's request for his opinion on recent developments, Daniels said that "it would be a great wrong to lease these oil reserves. The wisest policy of conservation, as well as the Navy's efficiency in the future, depends largely upon holding these naval oil reserves intact. . . . not one acre of the naval reserve should be leased, and Congress should set a face of flint against the present exploitations."[29] When this forthright letter came from Daniels, Bob immediately telegraphed for permission to use it "in a public way," as he knew it would help toward bringing about an investigation.[30]

It was reported that Old Guard Senators were saying his resolution would not be taken up for consideration. Fall had told Poindexter, chairman of the Committee on Naval Affairs, and Smoot, chairman of the Committee on Public Lands, that the matter of the naval reserves was a very involved subject. Bob knew these two Senators were saying in the cloakroom that the whole question was a highly technical one and that he could not possibly know the facts.[31]

Bob's investigation soon convinced him that the President's transfer of the naval reserves to the Interior Department was illegal and that Fall's leases were tainted with fraud. When he sought information from certain naval officers he knew had previously been opposed to leasing the naval oil reserves, he found that they had been ordered to sea or to distant ports. Fortunately one officer he knew was still in Washington.[32] Rear Admiral Robert S. Griffin, who had opposed transferring the naval oil reserves, had been retired a few months after Harding became President. For more than eight years he had been Chief of the Bureau of Engineering of the Navy. At the suggestion of former Secretary Daniels,[33] Bob wrote the admiral asking if he would talk confidentially with Harry Slattery, who was aiding him in an investigation of the ramifications of the naval oil reserve leases.[34] Slattery called and reported to Bob that the admiral hoped an investigation might be forced and that he predicted that if they went into this thing they would find "stranger things in heaven and earth than we have dreamed of."[35] When Daniels was in Washington a few days later, he communicated with Griffin and then telephoned Bob that the admiral would be very glad to give any information within his power.[36] Later Griffin[37] and other naval officers gave important testimony at the Senate Hearings. Subsequently, in a speech in the Senate demanding Secretary Denby's resignation, Bob specifically commended the loyal services to the Nation of Admirals Griffin, Schroeder, McGowan, Captain Halligan, Commanders Richardson, Stuart, Landis, Wright, and Lieutenant Commander Shafroth, who had resisted in every honorable manner the surrender of the naval oil reserves. He said he believed the Senate should express in a proper manner its appreciation of the loyal services of these men because "it is as important to award honor to those to whom honor is due as it is to fix responsibility for every breach of trust."[38]

By Friday, April 28, Bob was certain he had enough evidence to justify a demand for a sweeping investigation. As he left his office to go to the Senate floor shortly before noon, he said: "I am going just as far as I can in the charges I make against the Interior Department. I can't prove that there has been corruption but if we get this investigation I am confident it will be shown."[39] He had revised his resolution of April 21 so that it now called for an official inquiry by the Committee on Public lands into the "entire subject of leases upon naval oil reserves," and instructed the committee "to report its findings and recommendations to the Senate."[40]

In this form it became a direct challenge to two members of the Cabinet and to the official acts of the President of the United States. When he rose in the Senate that afternoon to introduce his revised resolution, Vice President Coolidge was in the Chair and there was a good attendance of Senators. The galleries were crowded throughout his speech.

In a scathing attack on the Interior Department, he declared it was "the sluiceway" in normal peace times for a large part of the corruption to which the Government was subjected. He warned his Republican colleagues that "we can not afford to permit a record to be made here which will parallel the record of Mr. Ballinger, Secretary of the Interior under the Taft Administration." There was enough evidence already available, he said, to show that the naval reserves were being "sacrificed to private exploitation at the hands of favored interests."[41] He discussed the Teapot Dome naval reserve testimony he had gathered because it had been most recently leased by Secretary Fall. Having followed his usual painstaking method of investigation, he was able to pile up impressive testimony to show that Fall's claim was without foundation in fact. "The excuse that the naval reserve is in danger of depletion by drainage into private wells on contiguous lands" was, he declared, "as old as the date of its withdrawal. It has ever been the specious plea upon which those desiring to exploit this rich field have based their efforts to secure access to it." In answer to this claim of Fall's he read telegrams he had recently received in response to his inquiries sent to men in Wyoming. Governor Robert D. Carey, W. A. Blackmore, mayor of Casper, Wyoming; the state geologist, G. B. Morgan, and others all joined in emphatically stating that the peculiar geological structure of the Teapot Dome reserve made it impossible for contiguous wells to drain off the oil. Former Special Assistant Attorney General Robert C. Bell, who had resisted the claims of private oil companies to leases on the reserves, had telegraphed that he knew the situation relative to Teapot Dome structure on naval reserve. "To lease this field is positively criminal." Bob had had his secretary telephone Dr. David White, chief geologist of the Geological Survey, to ask whether his office had reported that Teapot Dome was being drained. Dr. White had replied: "There is no information in my office upon which

I could make any such statement. The only statements which we have are those of interested oil parties."[42]

Contrasting the courageous policy of former Secretary Daniels, who had "not supinely surrendered to these oil-grabbing corporations," Bob boldly charged that Fall had leased the public land to "pirates"[43] who would "withdraw the oil which belongs to the people and sell it back to the Government for its naval vessels at exorbitant prices." This conspiracy, he said, "not only appropriates for private gain the rich natural wealth which the Government holds in trust for the people, but it reaches out and enables the special interests behind this scheme to tighten their grip upon the farmer, the business man, and upon every person who runs a gasoline engine, and upon every family that enjoys the use of an automobile.

". . . The Ballinger-Pinchot investigation a decade ago, which broke the back of the Taft administration, did not proceed upon more damning evidence that public interests were being violated than is ready at hand at this time bearing upon the leasing of these naval oil reserves."[44] When Bob concluded, not a single Senator attempted to make a speech refuting the grave charges he had made. Poindexter merely asked that the letter, signed by Secretary of the Navy Denby and Acting Secretary of the Interior Finney, with its belated reply to Senator Kendrick's resolution, be printed in the *Congressional Record*.[45]

Soon after the Senate met the following day, a copy of the Teapot Dome lease was laid before it.[46] The lease was in direct conflict with the policy of the Government, which had been to keep a great reserve of oil for the Navy underground, and it also wholly disregarded statutes governing contracts with the United States. When Bob's resolution came to a vote early that afternoon, the Senate passed it unanimously and thus ordered the investigation which finally uncovered shocking corruption in high places as Bob had predicted.[47]

One morning soon after his resolution had been introduced, Bob arrived at his office to find unmistakable evidence that it had been broken into during the night some time after his office force had gone home.[48] Although nothing had been stolen, it was apparent that his desk and files had been thoroughly searched. Within two years Gaston B. Means, an "investigator" serving in the Bureau of Investigation of the Department of Justice, admitted that he had seen to it that La Follette's office and desk were gone through to find "Anything he had where he could be stopped in what he was doing."[49] Means, who took his orders from Jess Smith, a close friend of Attorney General Harry Daugherty's, later became a private detective for President Harding.[50]

The passage of Bob's resolution brought forth a dray load of papers from the files of the Department of the Interior. In a letter transmitting the material to the Senate, Secretary Fall wrote that he was sending "every possible paper, or scrap of paper," that could refer to the subject.[51] The sinister purpose of this phrase was revealed as soon as the papers were examined. Important documents were buried in a mass of irrelevant material, and it took months of patient research to unearth the shocking facts. Fall's intention had apparently been to swamp the committee and delay the investigation which ultimately revealed Bob had been right in believing that men in high public office had been guilty of fraud, corruption, and betrayal of public trust.

Fall had written President Harding a long report, justifying the policy of leasing the naval reserves.[52] In transmitting this report to the Senate on June 7, the President wrote that the policy adopted by the Secretary of the Navy and the Secretary of the Interior had been submitted to him and that both the policy and the subsequent acts had at all times had his "entire approval."[53] Bob was certain that Fall's report to the President was a tissue of lies. As he worked on it at his office with Harry Slattery, analyzing it line by line, the discrepancies piled up. From time to time he would remark, "Harry, we will put that under lie No. 48," the score numbers steadily mounting as they went through the report.[54]

Bob had considered carefully whether to ask for an investigation by the Naval Affairs Committee or the Public Lands Committee. As Administration Republicans had a heavy majority on the former, he finally framed his resolution to provide that the Public Lands Committee should conduct the investigation. Although he thought Smoot, Lenroot, and some others might be hostile, the membership included Norris of Nebraska, Ladd of North Dakota, Norbeck of South Dakota, Republicans, and Kendrick and Walsh of Montana, Democrats. Bob knew Walsh was an able constitutional lawyer, and he had absolute confidence in his integrity. The two men had often differed on important questions, and Walsh had been one of the twenty-one Senators who had voted against dismissing the charges petitioning Bob's expulsion from the Senate. But Bob joined Kendrick in urging Walsh to take the leadership in investigating the naval oil leases, and the Montana Senator later became the militant prosecutor of the committee. Bob turned over all the evidence he had gathered, and continued to cooperate actively with Walsh throughout the long investigation which ultimately exposed the corruption of Cabinet officers and others. On the floor of the Senate in 1928, Walsh referred to the oil investigation he had carried on "in conjunction with Senator La Follette."[55]

Bob knew that in conducting the investigation, Walsh would be blocked in every possible way by Fall and Denby. Therefore, as soon as his resolution passed he began to devise means to uncover leads and information which would help Walsh and the Public Lands Committee in discovering the hidden ramifications of the corruption he was convinced existed. Bob and Gilbert Roe decided that one effective instrument for this purpose would be an investigation into the high cost of gasoline and petroleum products, conducted by the Committee on Manufactures of which Bob was chairman. Their judgment proved correct.[56] The rapid increase in the price of gasoline, in spite of the decrease in the price of crude oil, had caused enough protest to lead to the introduction in the Senate of resolutions calling for an inquiry. But these had been referred to a committee where they had been quietly buried. For some time Roe had been gathering information from individual retail dealers which convinced him and Bob that an investigation would bring forth striking proof of the way monopolistic control of a great natural resource manipulated prices and robbed the average consumer. Since so many people used gasoline and petroleum products, they correctly anticipated this would stimulate public interest and thus aid the investigation of the naval oil reserve leases.[57]

Two weeks after the Senate had authorized an investigation of the naval oil leases, a resolution providing for an investigation of the price of crude oil and gasoline by the Committee on Manufactures passed the Senate. Sufficient cooperation had been secured from Democratic Senators to overcome the opposition of Smoot and other Administration Senators. The resolution was introduced by

Senator McKellar and supported in the debate that ensued by Senator Joe Robinson.[58] Two days later Bob introduced a resolution amending the one introduced by McKellar, extending its scope, providing funds, and giving the committee authority to subpoena witnesses. In this form the resolution was considered and passed on June 5.[59] A subcommittee was appointed with Bob as chairman, and Gilbert Roe was employed as counsel. They immediately began to gather the essential information which involved securing detailed reports from some 360 oil companies and the examination of the officers of 19 leading companies from every section of the country and every branch of the industry. Several of the principal men involved in leasing the naval oil reserves were summoned to testify before Bob's committee. Among those questioned were Henry M. Blackmer of Colorado, Harry F. Sinclair of New Jersey, and Colonel Robert W. Stewart of Indiana. Through skillful examination of these witnesses, Roe uncovered leads as to their activities which were passed on to Walsh and materially helped to uncover the trails of corruption leading to high places. For many months the two committees were carrying on their investigations simultaneously.[60]

Bob published in *La Follette's Magazine* a part of the speech he made in the Senate when he introduced his resolution demanding an investigation of the naval oil reserves. For that same issue he also wrote an editorial, entitled "A Portrait In Oil," excoriating the Harding Administration and declaring that the "damning circumstances which surrounded the leasing of the rich oil reserves held in trust for the people call for an examination of the whole case of the most sweeping character. . . . The time has come when the Executive branch of this Government must enforce the plain letter of the law and check monopoly, or it must turn the people over bodily into the hands of exploiters grown impudent and ruthlessly aggressive through long years of wanton violation of the law.

"The people have it within their power to get relief. . . .

"It is the people's government. President and Congress are answerable to the people. Assume nothing. Investigate carefully. Get the truth and then act. You have the power. You have the responsibility."[61]

The investigation of the naval oil reserve leases finally revealed that $100,000 in cash had been transported from New York to Washington in a "little black bag" by Edward L. Doheny's son and presented to Secretary of the Interior Fall. This transaction, which Edward L. Doheny described to the Senate investigating committee as "a loan," had been put through two days after he had proposed to Fall that a lease be granted him on certain wells in the California Elk Hills Naval Reserve.[62] It was also revealed that thereafter, by a series of contracts and leases, Doheny had obtained from Fall leases to the entire Elk Hills Reserve of 30,000 acres, estimated to contain 250,000,000 barrels of oil, from which Doheny expected to get $100,000,000 profit.[63] The essential steps in this transaction had all been secretly taken before the Senate adopted Bob's resolution under which the investigation had been made. Subsequently it was also discovered, as Bob had suspected, that Sinclair had made contributions to Fall. Five weeks after the execution of the Teapot Dome leases, Fall's son-in-law received $233,000 in Liberty Bonds from Sinclair which were turned over to Fall's account in various banks.[64]

As the investigations made these facts known, the naval reserve oil leases, valued at not less than half a billion dollars, were denounced in the Senate as fraudulent.[65] The contracts and leases made to Doheny were eventually voided by the courts as having been "consummated by conspiracy, corruption, fraud."[66] The Sinclair lease of Teapot Dome was held to have been made "fraudulently by means of collusion and conspiracy."[67] Fall was branded by the United States Supreme Court as a "faithless public officer."[68] Fall was later convicted of taking a bribe, but another jury acquitted Doheny of the charge of giving it. Fall was sentenced to serve one year in jail and pay a fine of $100,000. This was the first time in United States history that a Cabinet officer had ever served a term in prison.[69] Sinclair served nine months in jail for contempt of the Senate and for attempting to "shadow" the jury in the Fall-Sinclair conspiracy trial.[70]

Several years later former Secretary Daniels said in a letter to Phil La Follette, "As you know, your father and I were devoted friends and I shall never forget the obligation the country owes him with reference to the Naval oil reserves, along with his other contributions during his long and distinguished career."[71]

CHAPTER LXVII

"There Are Those Who Love You"

Although Bob's third term was expiring and he knew he would shortly face a hard primary campaign, the Senate situation made it difficult to go to Wisconsin. He had introduced, and the Senate had adopted without opposition, a resolution requesting Daugherty and the Federal Trade Commission to inform the Senate what they had done to protect the public interest in the proposed merger of seven of the largest iron and steel corporations.[1] As the last vestige of competition in steel seemed about to be smothered, he had urged immediate action. He feared that unless the merger were stopped before completion, it might not be possible to do anything because of a 1920 Supreme Court 5 to 4 decision.[2] Upon a charge that the United States Steel Corporation and its subsidiaries were an unlawful combination in restraint of trade, the Court had then held that a corporation's mere size was not an offense.[3] Bob had described the decision at the time as "the epitaph of the Sherman Anti-trust law."[4] During this post-war period the Supreme Court had also handed down numerous decisions declaring Acts of Congress and of state legislatures unconstitutional.

When the Executive Committee of the A.F. of L. invited Bob to speak on June 14, 1922, at its annual convention in Cincinnati, Bob accepted. The Supreme Court had recently handed down two significant 5 to 4 decisions. In one case it held that the Federal Child Labor Law was unconstitutional, in the other that labor unions were subject to the anti-trust laws and liable for damages caused in labor disputes.[5] Bob thought the Federal Courts had exceeded their powers and decided that discussion of this issue was salutary and timely.

Bob was enthusiastically greeted when he appeared upon the

platform. Among the delegates who led the applause was his friend Andrew Furuseth, who sat in the first row directly in front of the speaker's stand. In his introduction President Gompers said Bob had a record of "unbroken advocacy and defense of the rights of the people," and referred to him as the author of the Seamen's Act.[6] Before Bob began his prepared address, he said: "You have accorded to me more praise and achievement than is my due. I am not the author of the Seamen's law. . . . I wish I might claim it all as mine. To Andrew Furuseth, more than any other living man, is due the credit of that piece of legislation."[7]

Bob's review of the Supreme Court's increasing use of the veto over Acts of Congress was fortified with extensive citations. He said he could find no constitutional sanction for this right. The framers of that document had rejected the theory of a "paramount judiciary," and the courts had assumed the power "by usurpation." Bob quoted Thomas Jefferson as having foreseen that "the germ of dissolution of our Federal Government is in the judiciary—the irresponsible body working like gravity, by day and by night, gaining a little today and gaining a little tomorrow, and advancing its noiseless step like a thief over the field of jurisdiction until all shall be usurped."

Bob declared that by "a process of gradual encroachments, uncertain and timid at first, but now confident and aggressive," the Court had become the actual ruler of the people, a sovereign power composed of nine men, who hold that role by Presidential appointment. Bob alluded to Harding's appointment to the Court of former President Taft, who had been repudiated by the voters on his record as President, and yet had been placed where he could help annul the Child Labor Law and hold labor unions subject to the Anti-Trust Law. As "hoots, jeers and hisses greeted the name of Chief Justice Taft," Bob said he was not criticizing the present Court's personnel, but the fact that any body of men, not chosen by the people, could have such supreme power over them.[8]

Bob then presented to the convention what he believed would be an effective instrument to check this growing usurpation of power. He proposed that the power of Federal judges should be restricted by a constitutional amendment so unequivocal that no court could twist its meaning. No inferior court should pass upon the constitutionality of an Act of Congress. The Supreme Court alone should have that power, subject to the right of Congress to nullify the Court's decision by reenacting the law. This proposed amendment would give Congress, as the legitimate lawmaking body, power over a judicial interpretation of legislation similar to the power it had over a Presidential veto.

The *New York Times* reported that during Bob's attack on what he described as " 'the judicial oligarchy,' the delegates stood on chairs, pounded on tables and shouted at the top of their voices . . . time and again he was interrupted by shouts of agreement."[9] As he concluded, he received an ovation. One delegate offered a resolution endorsing Bob's proposal, and at a subsequent session the Federation called upon Congress to submit it as a constitutional amendment.

Disjointed fragments of the speech were reported in the press and drew forth sharp personal attacks. Dr. Nicholas Murray Butler, who had bitterly assailed Bob during the war, publicly rebuked him in a speech before the New Jersey State Bar Association for his "revolutionary program." He charged Bob with preaching doctrines that were anti-American and inimical to liberty and justice. "Let him," Butler said, "put on the livery which he should wear and take both name and uniform of a destructionist and a revolutionary. Let him stop boring from within and be compelled to attack America openly from without."[10]

Butler's criticism was printed in the *Congressional Record* at the request of Senator Edge of New Jersey, who two days later repeated and enlarged upon Butler's attack.[11] Bob rose to reply to Edge, but the chair recognized Kellogg of Minnesota, who proceeded to arraign La Follette's speech as "subversive of our representative government, the liberties of the people, and the guaranties of the Bill of Rights."[12] When Kellogg concluded, Bob took the floor. He assailed Butler and commented caustically upon Edge's violation of Senate custom in having Butler's attack printed in the *Record* without giving him notice or having his Cincinnati speech printed along with the attack.

"Up to the present hour," he said, "the address that I made before the American Federation of Labor has been printed nowhere and yet Senators seizing upon the opportunity to prejudice the American public with respect to that address, have taken the floor here and assailed it. . . . I am going to put the speech into the

Record." Bob then read the entire address he had delivered at Cincinnati.[13]

In the Wisconsin campaign those who were trying to prevent Bob's reelection made the most of these attacks on his speech. Since Bob had openly opposed the Harding policies, harassed the Interior Department as well as the Attorney General, the Republican National Committee and Federal officeholders were lined up solidly against him. But he had earlier written Crownhart that he expected "to make this one of the most thorough campaigns" of his life.[14]

The Republican opposition to Bob had been at work within the State for over a year. Early in 1921 Lenroot had helped organize a "United Progressive Republican League." In August a committee of forty-four, consisting of two men and two women from each Congressional district, had been formed to defeat all La Follette progressive candidates in the primary. A state-wide organization was set up, and all Republicans were invited to enroll as "sane progressives." Lenroot had unsuccessfully sought to have Bob read out of the Republican Party on the charge that he was not loyal to it. As the primary approached, his opposition became more bitter.[15] He had been given all the State's senatorial patronage, and the Republican National Committee had even been asked to recommend postmasters in districts of progressive Republican Congressmen identified with Bob. Federal patronage had thus stimulated the growth of the "sane Progressive" movement.

Early in June nearly a thousand delegates representing the "sane Progressives" met at a convention in Milwaukee to draft a platform and name candidates. Among them were some pioneer progressive Republicans like Senator Otto Bosshard, who had turned against Bob during the war. As keynote speaker Bosshard declared "this convention and its candidates have a right to condemn and are justified in keeping alive the war record of Senator La Follette and giving the people of our State the opportunity of declaring upon it."[16] The platform, including an attack on Bob's course in the war, was unanimously and enthusiastically adopted. A full primary ticket was named, with William A. Ganfield, president of Carroll College, to run against Bob. The delegates went home to perfect a thorough organization for one of the bitterest campaigns in the State's history.

On June 17 the Socialist Party held its state convention in Milwaukee and nominated a complete state ticket, except a candidate for United States Senator. After bitter debate a resolution was adopted commending Bob's war record, but declaring that refraining from nominating a candidate against him was not intended as an endorsement of his position on other issues. It also condemned him for "still clinging to the Republican Party" after it had "kicked him out of three successive conventions."[17] Although Bob had not been consulted about this left-handed endorsement, the hostile press described him throughout the campaign as the "Socialist candidate."

Bob, Jr., was in Wisconsin at this time organizing his father's campaign. Late in May Bob had written that he was sending "a humdinger for a platform" which should be called "A Declaration of Principles."[18] Belle, who had collaborated with Bob and others in drafting it, wrote, "Personally—that means speaking for myself—I very much like the inseparable relationship of the National and State issues in our platform. It seems to me their *unity* will be a great source of strength and enthusiasm. I believe the people will like it. They will feel that they are fighting one great cause."[19]

Bob was held in Washington until July 15 by the tariff debate and the investigation he and Roe had been conducting into the high price of gasoline and petroleum products. He arrived in Madison to open the Chautauqua program on Sunday to an audience of five thousand with his lecture on Hamlet. The next day he began his campaign with a speech at the Auditorium in Milwaukee, where he had an audience of "more than five thousand men and women who cheered wildly."[20] His long and carefully prepared address dealt mainly with state and national issues. But in discussing his support of the bonus bill, then before Congress, he touched upon his opposition to the war. In response to a challenging question, he paused, walked to the edge of the platform, and, after a hush, told the audience that he had been urged not to discuss the war. But he wanted to say that he was proud of his war record and that he would not change it with that of any man in the United States. The audience gave him an ovation.[21]

After his Milwaukee meeting the hostile newspapers predicted that he would discuss this part of his record only in districts predominantly German. But everywhere he spoke he briefly reviewed the events leading up to the war and gave his reasons for opposing the declaration of war. In every section of the State the reaction was the same regardless of whether the national backgrounds were Scandinavian, French, Belgian, or New England. The opposition speakers and press soon dropped this line of attack and tried another. The *Milwaukee Journal* published what it described as a "digest" of Bob's "erratic" record.[22] The argument that he was a "mere voice of protest in the Senate" became the dominant charge of the campaign.

This attack was answered by nationally known men and women who knew Bob's work in Congress. Senators Norris, Borah, McNary, Caraway, Simmons, Walsh of Massachusetts, as well as former Senators Clapp, Bristow, and Sherman, publicly endorsed Bob's record and urged his reelection. "The historian who writes the story of the last quarter of a century," said William Allen White, "will have to go to La Follette and his work many times if history tells the truth about the major currents of American life in this era. . . . His is not the courage of the man who tears down, but the courageous wisdom of the builder. . . . No other living American has impressed himself so deeply upon the life and thought and institutions of America." Julia Lathrop, the first chief of the Children's Bureau, wrote: "His work proves that he is inspired by a profound belief in the progress of our country under constitutional forms toward the better social order of which we all have occasional glimpses, while his vision is sure and constant." Roscoe Pound, then dean of the Harvard Law School, said: "Even Senator La Follette's enemies must concede if they are commonly honest, that he is one of the great figures in contemporary public life. . . . Senator La Follette has stood consistently and courageously for the right as he saw it through good report and bad, and has not changed his convictions with each change of political fashion." Chief Justice Walter Clark of the North Carolina Supreme Court wrote that, "Above all men of my time he is the representative of the great common people of this country in the United States Senate."[23] Progressive speakers read these endorsements at their meetings throughout the State.

Meantime Bob was making a six weeks' campaign, which covered practically every county. Phil was speaking in southern Wisconsin. Bob, Jr., was managing his father's campaign and that of the entire state ticket from the headquarters in Madison where he received reports on all the meetings. Bob traveled by automobile, making two or three speeches a day, in all the larger cities and small towns. This was his first intensive campaign since 1916. Bob, Jr., wrote: "Dad's meetings are one ovation after another. He has never had such meetings in his life."[24]

It was apparent by midnight, on September 5, that Bob was renominated by a landslide. Day by day his lead increased until finally he had 362,445 votes to 139,327 for Dr. Ganfield. He carried all but one of the 71 counties, and he lost that traditionally stalwart county by only 481 out of 7,785 votes cast. The Associated Press reported that he won by the greatest majority that any candidate had ever polled at a Wisconsin primary. All the progressive Republican candidates for Congress save one had been nominated, as well as the candidates on the state ticket, headed by Governor Blaine and including Herman Ekern for attorney general. Both branches of the legislature also appeared to be progressive. The press throughout the country interpreted the victory as significant, and it evoked wide editorial comment. Some predicted that he would be "the strongest factor in the next Presidential election."[26] Former Secretary Josephus Daniels' newspaper the Raleigh *News and Observer* said that "his success under all the circumstances is the most remarkable exhibition of personal power in American politics in the present decade."[26] In a full syndicated report Paul Anderson wrote, "Never in his career was he more completely at odds with the party leaders in the primary . . . and never before, in all that career, has he received such an overwhelming endorsement from the people of the State."[27] In writing of the Wisconsin result to Fola and Mid, who had just returned after two years in Europe, Belle said: "Daddy is quite well and deep down happy . . . There is a general feeling that the Primary settled everything and that there is no need of an election campaign. Daddy thinks there should be a speaking campaign and he expects to go out."[28]

Bob returned to Washington for the closing weeks of the session. When he entered the Chamber, he was warmly greeted by his colleagues, who flocked about his desk. Senator Watson, regular Republican, told Bob he had expected him to win, but had not looked for such a complete victory.[29] Bob voted to override Harding's veto of the bonus bill[30] and against the Fordney-McCumber tariff bill,[31] which he had denounced in two speeches in July,[32] as far exceeding the Payne-Aldrich Act of 1909 in its concessions to favored interests. The Senate adjourned on September 22, after an eighteen-month session. Bob returned to open his campaign at La Crosse on October 19, and spoke frequently during the next ten days.

Before the election Bob spoke in two other States. In Minnesota Henrik Shipstead was a candidate against Senator Kellogg. Shipstead had twice been a candidate for governor and had the support of the rank and file of the Nonpartisan League. But opposition to him among the leaders, who were involved in a factional fight, made his chances of election seem slim. At the suggestion of Andrew Furuseth, Shipstead had gone to Madison to ask Bob's support.[33] This was the first time the two had met, and it proved to be the beginning of a close friendship. Bob had also been urged to speak in North Dakota for Lynn J. Frazier, who had defeated the reactionary Senator McCumber in the Republican primary, but was having a hard fight for election against the combined Republican and Democratic conservatives. After two days in North Dakota, Bob, accompanied by Phil, went to Minnesota on November 1. At Mankato he was denied the use of the armory by a member of the National Guard, because of his "war record."[34] He spoke at a theater instead. State Republican Chairman Charles R. Adams hailed him as the "high priest of radicalism."[35] This phrase was featured in the St. Paul and Minneapolis newspapers, which were supporting Kellogg, who was attacking Bob's war record.

At Minneapolis Bob addressed one of the largest audiences the Minneapolis Armory ever held, with about three thousand waiting outside to hear Phil and others speak. The tariff was his chief theme, and he did not discuss the war. The *Minneapolis Morning Tribune* commented that, "He left that subject strangely alone."[36] The next night another large audience heard him in the St. Paul Auditorium, where he had made the speech in 1917 that led to the attempt to expel him from the Senate. When he arrived at the Auditorium, he found the streets for blocks around filled from curb to curb with crowds seeking admission. The *Minneapolis Morning Tribune*, one of Kellogg's strongest supporters, estimated the audience at 12,500.[37]

"Every nook and corner was occupied before the speakers arrived," the Madison *Capital Times* reported. "Workmen, with their dinner pails, stopped on their way to their homes and remained until the meeting was over at 11 o'clock. Outside a crowd of 10,000 surged impatiently for hours, vainly seeking a chance to get into the hall. Two blocks away another meeting was scheduled for a small hall seating about 2,500. Minneapolis and St. Paul had been plastered with posters advertising addresses by Senator Frank B. Kellogg and Governor Preus. Senator Kellogg, who led the fight in the Senate, to drive . . . La Follette from public life, suffered the humiliation, in his home city, of seeing thousands flock to do honor to 'Fighting Bob' . . ."[38]

Facing the immense audience, Bob made what Phil, and others, who had often heard him in political campaigns, described as one of his most effective speeches. The newspapers had predicted he would discuss the war. But his only reference to his 1917 St. Paul speech was to declare: "All that I said at that time has been demonstrated to be true. Not one word . . . will I ever need to retract or to modify in the slightest degree. If the theme I discussed were an issue in this campaign I would glory in discussing it."[39] He went on to talk of the struggle for democracy in the United States, and the way it was menaced by the power of great financial and industrial interests. He read the roll call to show how Kellogg had voted on various bills, and referred to his previous record as attorney for the Steel and Harvester trusts before he entered the Senate. "The best that can be said of him," Bob said, "is that he has served these powerful trusts just as well in the Senate as he served them in the courts."

Bob then uttered the most bitter arraignment he ever made of a political opponent. Although free from actual physical infirmity, Kellogg walked with a pronounced stoop. As Bob completed the last roll call, he remarked: "God Almighty through nature writes men's characters on their faces and in their forms. Your Senator has bowed obsequiously to wealth and to corporations' orders and to his masters until God Almighty has given him a hump on his back—crouching, cringing, un-American, unmanly."[40] It was probably the only time in years of campaigning that Bob referred to the personal appearance of an antagonist. To Belle, who deplored the incident, as did many of his friends, it seemed unworthy and out of character.

In the election three days later, Shipstead won in a campaign that had "started with all the signs of proving a walk over" for Senator Kellogg.[41] With this election Shipstead began his service of four terms in the Senate. In Wisconsin Bob carried every county, winning by the largest majority ever given to a candidate in that State. His total vote was 279,484 to 78,029 for his Democratic opponent, Mrs. Ben Hooper. Soon after Bob's victory his son-in-law, George Middleton, reminded him that during the war he had prophesied, "I may not live to see my own vindication: but you will." Bob smiled and said: "Yes, Mid. The circle is complete: all the rest is velvet."[42]

Throughout the country the elections went against the Harding Administration. The *New York Times* reported that Washington "was dazed by the big reversal," since no one seemed to expect it "could follow so soon after the Republican tidal wave of 1920." The seven million majority then given Harding had "been wiped out. The demonstration of disapproval of the Administration was unmistakable."[43] On March 4, 1923, when the new Senators and Representatives would take office, the Republican majority would be reduced in the Senate to 11 and to 17 in the House. This meant that in the Sixty-eighth Congress the progressive Republican group would hold the balance of power. The newly elected Senators, Shipstead, Frazier, Brookhart, and Howell, would add decisive votes on many issues to the veteran group which included La Follette, Norris, Borah, Johnson, and Ladd. A similar progressive group would hold the balance in the House. In spite of the strong anti-Republican trend, progressive Republicans had been elected in all States in which they had won nominations, except Indiana, where a Democrat defeated Beveridge. The Progressives had not held such power since 1911, during the Taft Administration.

Bob's overwhelming victory placed him in a position where the press was again referring to him as the national progressive leader.[44] In a special Sunday article summarizing the election results, the *New York Times* commented: "There is no overlooking the fact that Senator La Follette, standing alone, will be the most powerful legislative factor in the next Congress. He is recognized as the leader of the radical-progressives and will be followed by five or six new Senators. His influence, potent in the Senate, will be even greater in the House, for there he has eleven members from Wisconsin, who will follow him. To-day La Follette is stronger than at any other time in his career."[45]

A few days after Harding knew the election results, he hastily called a special session of Congress to meet November 20, 1922. He hoped this maneuver would make it possible to rush certain legislation through the Sixty-seventh Congress while it was still controlled by a large Republican majority. Ostensibly the special session was summoned to pass the ship-subsidy bill. It would authorize the sale to private companies of hundreds of vessels acquired by the Government during the war at a cost of over $3,000,000,000 and grant a large annual subsidy to the purchasers for ten years. The vessels would be sold at a time when ships glutted the market. The Shipping Board had operated these ships at a loss, and had been charged with favoring the great private shipping companies. It was supporting the ship-subsidy bill. At a previous session Bob had sought unsuccessfully to have a Senate investigation of the Board. He maintained that the annual deficits were due to the policy of the Board, which was hostile to either Government-operated or Government-owned vessels. In a Senate speech he had presented evidence to show that the Board was controlled by British interests and that our foreign commerce was at the mercy of our most important business competitor. He had also charged that the labor policy of the Board was driving American seamen from American ships by breaking down the provisions of the La Follette Seamen's Act.[46] The ship-subsidy bill had been condemned by many labor and farm organizations and had been an issue in the recent midwestern election campaigns.

Bob also had reason to believe that the Administration was planning to transfer the National forests from the Department of Agriculture and Forestry to the Department of the Interior and also to merge the railroads into a few gigantic systems and give the Labor Board power to prevent strikes. He knew that during the previous sessions of the Sixty-seventh Congress the progressive Republicans and Democrats had disagreed with the policies of their party leaders. Although these Progressives had been in harmony as to their general aims and purposes, he was aware that "the necessary elements" had not previously been present "for the formation of an aggressive group, united upon a program of positive action." But Bob interpreted the election as "a mandate which could not be ignored," and he thought the announced policies of the Administration made immediate action imperative.[47]

Bob took action a few days after his return to Washington. On November 18, as chairman of the People's Legislative Service, he and Representative George Huddleston as vice chairman joined in issuing a call for a conference to meet in Washington on December 1 and 2, to discuss a definite plan for the cooperation of Progressives in Congress and throughout the country. The call, sent to each individual on the large and imposing list, was headlined in the national press. Its political implications aroused much speculation. Newspaper correspondents sought a group interview, which Bob granted, contrary to his custom. All asked whether this conference implied a third party. Bob replied that such a thing might, of course, come about "whenever a party of progressives amalgamated all the progressive elements of the country." He was reported as saying that a third party "will not be formed by a set of men passing a resolution. Eventually there will be a line of cleavage between those calling themselves conservatives and the progressives. You cannot hurry this, but the Harding administration may be able to hasten it. In my judgment, this movement has gone forward very considerably in the past few years." When questioned further Bob added: "I'm not chasing will-o'-the-wisps at this time. I'm a bit near sighted when it comes to looking for new parties. My interest lies at the present time in transplanting into results the lessons of the election just over."[48]

The conference opened on December 1, in the room of the Committee on Agriculture and Forestry of which Norris was chairman. The first day only Members of Congress were present, and they discussed the legislative program on which they could unite. Bob, who called the meeting to order, made it clear that the "chief and sole object" of the conference was "to map out thoroughly constructive legislative action which will produce the quickest and best results, regardless of party ties." Bob's nomination of Norris as chairman was unanimously approved. Among the thirteen Senators and Senators-elect present were nine Republicans, three Democrats, and one Farmer Labor. The group included Borah,

Brookhart, Capper, France, Frazier, Ladd, McNary, Owen, Sheppard, Shipstead, and Wheeler. Senators Ashurst, Dill, and Howell also expressed warm approval of the purpose of the conference. More than twenty-three Members of the House came, and fourteen others wired support, including La Guardia, who attended the afternoon session.

Bob offered a resolution which was unanimously adopted. It stated that the purpose of the conference was to cooperate, regardless of party, "to drive special privilege out of control of government and restore it to the people." Special committees composed of Senators and Representatives were created to work with men of affairs and experts to prepare and submit to the group plans for dealing with agriculture, labor, railroads, shipping, natural resources, credits, taxation; a nation-wide campaign for direct, open primaries for all elective offices, including the Presidency, effective Federal and state corrupt-practices acts, as well as Constitutional amendments providing for the abolition of the Electoral College, and the earlier meeting of newly elected Congresses, which Norris formulated in his "Lame Duck" amendment. An advisory committee of both parties was promptly selected.

"So business-like were the proceedings of the conference," wrote Manly, "and so complete was the harmony among those present that this conference, which it had been predicted by the reactionary press, would break up in a row, concluded its business by three o'clock in the afternoon, and adjourned to go to work immediately to carry out the fundamental objects laid down in the resolution."[49]

The next day, in the Assembly Room of the City Club, two hundred influential men and women met with these progressive Senators and Representatives. Bob called the meeting to order and gave a brief summary of the action taken the previous day. Among the speakers who addressed this session were Norris, Brookhart, Senators-elect Frazier and Wheeler, Samuel Gompers, W. T. Rawleigh, Governor Blaine, and Representative Frear. The audience had come from all parts of the country. Many were official representatives of large organizations numbering thousands of members. The *New York Times* reported that "Despite the injection of radical ideas, the prime movers were able to hold the conference well within the limits of progressive national and state legislation," and noted that La Follette, who "appeared to have the cordial support of all present, helped by his opening speech to keep the conference from wandering all over the field of radical reform."⁵⁰ The action taken at the previous session was endorsed.

In the evening a banquet was given in honor of the newly elected progressive Senators and Representatives. Edward Keating served as toastmaster, and paid tribute to all that Basil Manly, director of the People's Legislative Service, had done to make the conference a success. In introducing him Keating said, "I want you to know him for what he is—one of the most modest of men, but one of the great constructive forces in public life." When Keating introduced Bob as the "undisputed leader of the Progressive movement," the audience "rose en masse to pay a stormy welcome." Keating observed that there were "tears in his eyes" as Bob responded to the toast with a brief, informal talk that was soon touched with a whimsical humor.⁵¹ Over four hundred heard the speeches. One by Samuel Untermeyer was widely reported. In it he attacked Attorney General Daugherty, declaring he was "conspicuously unfit" for his office and was appointed "solely on the basis of personal friendship and political service for President Harding."⁵² The tenor of all the speeches foreshadowed the difficulties ahead for the Administration. The *New York Times* stated that "the group will be a powerful factor in the next Congress is generally conceded."⁵³

The President had appeared personally before a joint session of Congress to advocate passage of the ship-subsidy Bill. It passed the House and was introduced in the Senate on December 9. Bob opened the attack on it the following week, before packed galleries, with many Senators of both parties on the floor. This was his first speech in the Senate since the conference at which this bill had been condemned. He spoke four hours, analyzing each section of the bill. After assaying the election results, he criticized the President's effort to have the bill passed by a Congress in which the Administration's majority had been repudiated by the voters. He noted that the bill had been put through the House by the small majority of only 24 votes and that at least 70 who voted for it were "lame duck" representatives who had been defeated at the November elections. Bob then warned the President that the majority in the next Congress would oppose Administration policies.⁵⁴

After Bob's speech the Administration leaders made many futile efforts to bring the bill to a vote. It was set aside several times and was threatened by a filibuster. After a stormy three months it was finally withdrawn by its sponsor shortly before the Sixty-seventh Congress ended. This was a severe defeat for Harding and Administration Senators who could not overcome the opposition to the bill which the progressive conference in Washington had helped to organize so effectively in December.

An hour before the Sixty-seventh Congress adjourned *sine die* on March 4, 1923, Bob and Roe completed and secured the signatures of all five committee members to the report on the hearings in the investigation of the price of gasoline and petroleum products. Although many days of tedious work still remained in preparing the statistical tables for final printing, Roe wrote his wife, "My God what a relief."[55] After adjournment Bob stayed on in Washington for many weeks to write his editorials, clear up his correspondence, and attend to other work that had accumulated. He had to decline many invitations to speak in different parts of the country. These included requests from Chautauquas which had excluded him from their programs during the war. Dr. Marbury had insisted that he must take a rest, and he reluctantly promised to follow the doctor's orders.

While Bob and Belle were still in Washington, Phil and Isabel Bacon were married in Chicago on April 14, and returned to Madison to make their home at Maple Bluff Farm during the summer. Although no formal announcement had ever been made, they had been engaged for many months. Isabel had visited Bob and Belle in Washington, and they had been very happy about the engagement. Phil and Isabel had met in Madison while she was a student at the university. After graduating with honors in 1920, she had taken a position in New York City, where she was active in social work. At the time of their marriage Phil had already entered the law firm of La Follette and Rogers, of which his father was the senior partner. The newspapers predicted that he would be a candidate for district attorney of Dane County, which was the first public office his father ever held.[56]

Phil had been in close touch with Governor Blaine, and had been keeping his father informed of the developments in the Wisconsin legislature, where a fight was brewing over certain phases of the tax bill. The conflict became so serious that it was feared the entire progressive program might be jeopardized. Ekern and others wrote begging Bob, Jr., to come to Madison and help, as everyone recognized how successful he had been in organizing the election campaign. Ekern admitted that the situation was so difficult that "it was an awful thing to put Bob [Jr.,] up against."[57] Bob, Jr., responded to the appeal because he and Phil both felt it was the only way to keep their father out of the legislative "turmoil" at Madison.

This situation in the Wisconsin legislature made it impossible for Bob, Jr., to attend the meetings in Chicago at which his father presided on May 25 and 26. Bob, as chairman of the Committee on Transportation created by the Washington progressive conference in December, had called this two-day conference in Chicago. The *New York Times* described it as "the first concerted movement to insure proper representation of the public interest in the valuation proceedings before the Interstate Commerce Commission and the Courts."[58] Invitations had been sent to many railroad authorities, Members of Congress, governors, and other public officials. A permanent organization was formed and designated as the National Conference on Valuation of American Railroads. Bob was elected national chairman to preside over an executive committee of six officers. This committee was instructed to present to the Interstate Commerce Commission a formal demand that it "comply fully with the requirements of the Valuation Act, particularly in regard to reporting original cost."[59] Donald Richberg was selected as legal counsel, and during the next ten years appeared before the Interstate Commerce Commission and the Courts to resist excessive valuation of railroad property and public-utility property. The theory of original cost and prudent investment as the proper basis for railroad valuation which Bob had long advocated was accepted by Government agencies many years later.

After the Chicago conference Bob joined Belle at the Battle Creek Sanitarium on May 27. His friend Rawleigh had finally succeeded in persuading him to take a vacation there. He had generously insisted that both Bob and Belle should be his guests at the sanitarium during whatever period of rest the doctors advised. Bob followed the regime faithfully and took all the tests. He wrote Rawleigh: "If there are any unexplored places in my interior geography they are not to be found on their anatomical charts. We are giving ourselves to this one thing for which we came and I am confident already, at the end of ten days—that it will add substantially to my working capacity. It is another of the many things for which I shall be everlastingly grateful to you my dear friend."[60]

Although Bob was at Battle Creek for a rest, he kept in touch with the situation in the Wisconsin legislature, about which he was deeply concerned. On June 5, Bob, Jr., wrote his father, "we are dealing in personalities not principles, and this constant jockeying for position has tried my patience to the limit but after three weeks of effort, which at times seems fruitless, I can say that I am still on good terms with all the parties to the controversy."[61] He was soon able to tell his father that the favored bill had passed the Assembly. His father wrote, "Your reports upon the tax situation in the legislature have given me great comfort far and away beyond what the passage of a good tax bill means to our legislative record. But above all that in its *personal* significance *to me*, is the *fact* that you have been able to go into a perfectly chaotic condition there, after the bickering and backbiting had reached the knifing stage and bring out a bill & put it through the Assembly with an overwhelming majority is the *highest* test of *generalship* in a bitter conflict of ideas and ambitions. It is simply great. . . . Individuals disappoint us in this life when you put them to the final test. That is nobody's fault—not even their own fault. Men have to be tested before anyone *can* know them—indeed before *they know themselves*."[62]

Ten days later an appeal came to Bob from Shipstead for help in an unexpected campaign in Minnesota which it was hard for him to resist. The death of the reactionary Republican Senator, Knute Nelson, had created a vacancy in the Senate which meant it might be possible to capture another seat for the progressive group. The regular Republican candidate was J. A. O. Preus. The Farmer-Labor group had nominated Magnus Johnson. Bob was alert to the national importance of electing Johnson. He had previously written Bob, Jr.: "It will give us a *sure* balance of power in the Senate without a question. It would make Minnesota pretty safe for 1924. That would go a long way towards a solid Northwest, which is the key-stone on the arch of Progressive power for the future. It is a *national* battle and it is vital to make no mistake." It would "give

us the key to all legislative possibilities, because it will put us in a
position to speak the last word on organization [of the Senate].
I[t] means stage center for two years with all the chances to do
real big things in ev[e]ry way."[63]

Bob gave out a statement urging Johnson's election which was
widely circulated.[64] The regular Republicans were also aware of
the national significance of the contest, and "a lot of standpatters"
began to go to Minnesota to help defeat Johnson. This brought
appeals to Bob to come into the State and speak for Johnson as he
had for Shipstead. It was hard to refuse these pleas. Bob's letters
reveal the conflict they caused, which he described as "such a
conscientious tugging from within." At first he tentatively planned
to go to Minnesota with Phil, but his physicians urged him to
remain at Battle Creek. Phil went, however, and Bob asked other
speakers to join him in what the press described as "Wisconsin's
flying squadron." Phil put in four days of speaking. On July 16
Johnson defeated Preus by 95,000. The press generally interpreted
the election as a test of strength between Harding and La Follette.
It added another Senator to the progressive bloc in the next Congress. Senator Moses and other Republican leaders thought the
election indicated the possibility of revolt in other States.[65] So
did Bob.

During the campaign the reactionary press had ridiculed Magnus
Johnson as "a dirt farmer" unqualified to serve in the Senate. In a
letter congratulating him on his election, Rawleigh recorded the
background of his friendship with Bob and of his own service in
the progressive movement as a legislator and mayor in Illinois. "I
have known and been watching Senator La Follette ever since I
was a boy on the farm in southern Wisconsin, when my father predicted that the Senator would become one of our greatest statesmen. I have been a student of the Senator's work ever since then
and as I have never known him to compromise where questions of
principle were involved, I have grown to love and admire him
more than any man I have ever known."[66]

While Bob and Belle were still at Battle Creek, Rawleigh had
persuaded them to take a trip to Europe and allow him to defray
the expenses. During their absence he was planning with Dante
Pierce and others to organize and finance preliminary moves toward

a possible 1924 progressive Presidential campaign. In the fall of 1919, before going to Europe, Rawleigh had placed a fund of $25,000 at Bob's disposal in the event he needed it for a 1920 campaign.[67] Now he was offering to do much more. From Battle Creek Bob wrote Rawleigh: "We must sit down together and take stock of the whole situation before we go through with some of the plans you are making with such a free and all too generous hand. . . . You must go only so far as will keep results within reach, which are adequate and worthy of what you are doing from the standpoint of permanent gain to public service—not so much for individual success as for the upbuilding of progressive democracy.

"I know you have assured me again and again, that this is exactly what you have in mind, and it is in this spirit that we have accepted all you have done and are doing.

"But my more than friend I feel since being here that we must see each other soon, very soon and have a heart to heart again."[68]

In the middle of July the doctors consented to his going provided he avoided public receptions, banquets, speechmaking and anything that interfered with building up his reserve. While at Battle Creek, Bob had received a letter from one of his colleagues which he especially treasured. It expressed the warm personal affection which many felt for him even though they differed politically. Senator George H. Moses of New Hampshire, one of the conservative Republican leaders, wrote that he had heard of Bob's being at the sanitarium, "but whether because you are sick or because you are only going through a prize-fighter's preliminary, I did not learn. In any event I hope your course of treatment is doing you no end of good and that you will come back to Washington in December in superior condition. As Webster said of Dartmouth College: 'There are those who love you.' "[69]

CHAPTER LXVIII

To Europe to Learn

Bob said he was going abroad "to learn." He wished to see for himself, as far as possible, just what the situation was so that he could form his own judgment "on a basis of personal knowledge," and not have to rely entirely on picking his "way through the maze of inspired propaganda with which Congress is flooded."[1] Bob, Belle, and Bob, Jr., arrived in New York the day before their ship was to sail. They dined with Fola and Mid, and later in the evening Robert Morss Lovett called by previous appointment. Bob told Lovett that he was one of several men who were being considered for the presidency of the University of Wisconsin, and discussed the possibility with him tentatively. Bob noted in his diary that night that "All present *were most favorably impressed with Lovett.*"[2] On August 1, 1923, Bob, Belle, Bob, Jr., Basil Manly and his wife, Mollie, sailed from New York on the *George Washington* for the trip they had planned together. Before sailing Bob had written Rawleigh: "I shall be indebted all the days of my life to you for this opportunity to go abroad. It comes, I believe, at a time in my life when I shall reap the largest benefit from it, and I want you to know that I appreciate it from the bottom of my heart."[3]

The third day out, at about six in the morning, the room steward knocked on Bob's stateroom door to inform him of the sudden death of President Harding. As the senior Senator on shipboard Bob was asked to preside at the memorial service. Other Senators and Representatives also participated. Belle and Bob, Jr., prepared a statement about the service which Bob secured Captain Cunningham's consent to sign and radio to Mrs. Harding with an expression of sympathy.

During the trip there was some high wind for about twenty-four hours, but Bob, who had always been a poor sailor, was not seasick. He found the *George Washington* as steady as its namesake, and thought that Captain H. A. Cunningham and every member of his staff "were men who could not be surpassed in any respect on the seven seas." As the *George Washington* was owned by the United States Lines, Bob was interested in their relations with the Shipping Board. He recorded: "We went over the ship from engine room to the Captains quarters. We could find nothing but order and cleanliness in every cranny and quarter of the great ship. The men were provided with excellent bill of fare—the kitchens & dining quarters and sleeping compartments were first class in ev[e]ry respect—no dust—no dirt—no vermine The hospital and operating room were models—good light air perfect ventilation."[4] Bob talked with the crew, and Belle kept a memorandum of wages and working conditions.[5] He closely questioned Captain Cunningham and Chief Engineer W. Hodgkiss as to existing administrative practices under the Shipping Board which might lessen the effectiveness of the great fleet of merchant vessels which the Government had built up during the war. The data thus obtained reinforced his conviction that the United States could profitably operate a strong merchant marine if "put under the control of loyal and experienced Americans" who would "checkmate the sabotage of private owners and British interests."[6]

Bob's arrival at Plymouth on August 9 was reported in the London *Times*, which had previously carried a long article about his growing national importance as the leader of a possible third party in the coming election.[7] A telegram from Ramsay MacDonald expressed regret that he could not be at Plymouth to welcome Bob, and asked if there was any chance of seeing him in Scotland.[8] When they arrived in London many newspapers requested interviews. Bob, Jr., had charge of his father's program, and Belle wrote that he was "kept busy whenever we are in our rooms answering the telephone . . . The London papers seem quite as eager as our own correspondents. Bob, Jr., is very courteous and patient—tells them all that his father has come to observe and learn . . . that he is here to acquire information that will be helpful in his work and must devote himself to seeing the people who can best serve this purpose."[9]

They spent four busy days at the Hyde Park Hotel, although

some individuals to whom Bob sent letters were away on vacation. Cordial replies were received from the Princess Bibesco, daughter of Herbert Asquith, and from Mrs. H. G. Wells, who both asked Bob to visit them.[10] Harold Laski, whom Felix Frankfurter had especially wished him to meet, began a long letter from Belgium by stating, "I need not say that to any radical you are one of the few Americans for whom real veneration is possible."[11] Among those Bob saw were Norman Angell and J. M. Keynes, whose books he had read with such interest; H. Hamilton Fyfe, editor of the London *Daily Herald*, the labor newspaper; Raymond Unwin, Mr. and Mrs. Pethick-Lawrence, Lees-Smith, Labour M.P. and also professor at the University of London; and Sydney Arnold, secretary to Ramsay MacDonald, leader of the opposition in the House of Commons and soon to become Prime Minister.

One afternoon they called at the Labour Party headquarters, where there was discussion of the American political situation. Bob suggested the advisability of having some means of regular correspondence between groups in England and the United States. The idea was "heart[i]ly received."[12] He found that both liberals and conservatives hoped Great Britain and the United States would unite in dealing with European problems, especially those created at that time by France's policy on reparations and the seizure of the Ruhr to obtain her quotas of coal and money from its mines, railways, and factories. Certain British leaders, believing France was acting illegally and gravely endangering Europe's peace, hoped the United States might assume the principal financial and military responsibility in enforcing the Versailles Treaty.[13]

Belle shared in many of these interviews. She felt no apology for their necessarily rapid visits to the historic shrines of London and elsewhere. "Why not take a panoramic view of the wonders of the world if you have not time to see them in detail? When we are riding on a fast train we do not scorn to take a fleeting glance at the landscape, do we?" Among her cherished memories was the famous old grapevine at Hampton Court bearing luscious purple fruit as though still in the prime of life. "I should rather have missed seeing Windsor Castle."[14] It recalled the venerable grapevine over the porch of their Wisconsin home. They stopped at Windsor, Warwick, and Kenilworth castles and Stratford-on-Avon. Belle wrote Mary that "Daddy regretted not having more time at Shakespear's house,

but he got a great deal out of it and it was a source of profound
satisfaction to him to have visited this spot on which his imagination has dwelt since boyhood." In Manchester, Belle wrote of
seeing "a fine statue of John Bright which thrilled me. Next to
Lincoln I love Bright."[15]

She wrote her impressions for *La Follette's Magazine*, which led
the *New York Times* to comment later editorially that if the Senator's "experiences and his mood have been even a quarter as
pleasant and gracious as those of Mrs. La Follette, who is writing
in his magazine on 'Seeing Europe With Senator La Follette,' he
has been having a mighty good time . . . She had been fitting herself
for the voyage for years. She had studied. She was ready to enjoy it.
. . . Mrs. La Follette has an open mind, a cheerful spirit. She puts
to shame that not innumerous tribe of posing melancholiacs who
seem to be saying, 'Well, here I am in Venice. The more fool I.
When I was home I was in a better place.' "[16]

Belle wrote Mary about the two days they spent at Torkington
Lodge with Sir John and Lady Barlow, who "is as beautiful, dainty
and alive and as constantly busy hand and brain as when we last
saw her." She arranged for them to visit Marple Hall, a property
which had belonged to the same family for over three hundred
years. The present owner, John Henry Bradshaw Isherwood, slept in
the same bed Oliver Cromwell had slept in when the Marple Hall
owner of that time had been one of Cromwell's supporters. At Bob's
request Mr. Isherwood wrote an article about his home for *La
Follette's Magazine*.[17] They met C. P. Scott, editor of the influential
Manchester Guardian, which he had owned for fifty years. Belle
wrote Mary that "He is 72 but rides to and from his office every
day on a bicycle. You should have seen daddy's surprise when he
took hold of Mr. Scott's arm. They had a good laugh comparing
muscle. Mr. Scott made the tea himself and at the same time discussed world events—not overconfidently, but with a familiarity and
grasp that made us feel his power and authority. . . . Lady Barlow
told us he could have sold [the *Manchester Guardian*] almost any
time for unlimited sums. He told us that he had two sons, who
by the way are following in his footsteps found it much more fun
to run a newspaper for the public interest than for profit. And he
whispered in Daddy's ear as he was leaving that the way to make

a success of his magazine was to put back into it all that came out of it."[18]

While in Manchester, Bob, Manly, and Bob, Jr., visited the different departments of the English cooperative wholesale society, popularly known as the CWS. They met the members of the board of directors, Scotch and North of England men, looking "less like reformers than a group of Wall Street brokers," but, underneath, "deeply appreciative of the broad humanitarian significance of their great cooperative."[19] With its factories, plantations, and farms scattered over the world and a banking turnover of more than three billion dollars in 1920, it was "a truly big business, but it belongs to the people, and its profits are being used to lower their cost of living, not to pile up huge fortunes for a few individuals." His study of this and other cooperatives abroad led Bob to decide that he would devote a large part of his time and energy "during the coming years to fostering the development of co-operation in the United States, because I see in this movement an opportunity for great good for the common man and a means of escape from the operation of the monopolies and combinations which are slowly but surely throttling the economic life of America."[20]

They arrived on August 19 at the Hotel Continental in Berlin. Except for one sight-seeing trip they spent their time with people. They dined with the American Ambassador, Mr. Houghton, who made every effort to supply consular reports of conditions all over Germany, met the new Prime Minister, Stresemann, various members of the Reichstag, heads of labor organizations, editors, and businessmen. Belle wrote that Bob was "getting pretty tired and today he started in with a cold which worried me, but he felt much better after taking a rest this afternoon."[21]

During his visit he conferred with Baron Mahlzer, expert on Russia, Herr Sorger, director of Krupps, and Dr. Luther, Minister of Food Control and Agriculture, later Minister of Foreign Affairs and Hitler's Ambassador to the United States. Bob collected data on the food supply, for, after years of undernourishment, the people's strength was sapped and disease was taking a terrible toll. He visited hospitals and children's feeding stations and saw sights that intensified his bitter resentment against the Versailles Treaty, which, he felt, had inflicted unnecessary suffering on the war's helpless victims. The German Republic had been created "in good faith" and had been sustained "by the people with patience and fortitude." He thought that the first care of those "who believed in self-government and democracy" should be to see that food be speedily sent before starvation "drives Germany's hard-working, intelligent, disciplined 60,-000,000 citizens to either the extremes of communism or anarchism."[22]

Bob had been assured by the representatives of the Soviet Government in London that every consideration would be given him to study conditions in Russia. On August 30 they left Berlin for Petrograd. Steffens and Jo Davidson had been invited to join them, and the party of seven took a small boat at Stettin expecting to sail directly to Petrograd. But when the ship put in at Revel to discharge cargo, they decided to go by train to save time. Manly recorded that they "were supposed to be in a sleeping car but there were no mattresses or sheets, just two shelves which let down and thus, with two seats provided four bunks in each compartment on which anyone could lie down that wanted to and cover up with all the coats he could borrow from other members of the party."[23]

Bob noted in his diary that they were met at the station by S. Asnis, who "said he represented Mr. [Gregory] Weinstein, head of the Petrograd Branch of the Foreign Office of the Soviet Govt. Asnis escorted us to the Europa Hotel where we registered as pay guests. The hotel is owned and controled [sic] by the Government as are all hotels. But I informed Asnis that I could not be entertained by anybody but would pay regular rates. Asnis lunched with us and then left us to ourselves. It was understood that he would call for me at 5 P.M. and take me to the Foreign Office to see Weinstein.

"This he did and I requested Davidson and Steffens to accompany me. Manly Bob and others had gone out to see the city.

"I had a very interesting interview with Weinstein who formerly edited a Socialist paper in the U.S. As I understood he was deported during the war.

"I informed him that I wanted to get the truth as to the Soviet Government and the condition of the people socially economically and politically; that I would be glad to have any assistance he could give me; that I wanted to see the seamy side as well as the outside of their government, the bad as well as the good; that I wanted the privilege of taking with me during my stay such persons as I wished besides my party; that I had letters of introduction to American citizens who resided in Russia understood their language and had been connected with the American Relief Association. He said that was perfectly agreeable to the Government for whom he was acting. He had a program of places for me to visit: the port, the Chamber of Commerce, the bank &c and that he would detail Mr. Asnis to accompany me. I made my own selections from his program and then told him I wished to see the inside of their Communist system of conducting business such as factories and that I wanted the privilege of looking into them as fully as possible. He said he would be glad to have me do so.

"We talked for a couple of hours. I asked the size of their Army & was informed that it was in round numbers six hundred and fifty thousand.

"I asked if the Soviet Government permitted a free expression of opposition to its policies, its practices and administration of affairs generally—either through opposition newspapers or otherwise. He answered very frankly that it did not tolerate either criticism or opposition of any sort.

"I asked if he did not think their government would stand much better with the other governments of the world if they would discontinue their propaganda for the overthrow of other governments and attend to the business of conducting their own government? And I suggested that I believed in the American Democracy and that I thought it was our business to cure its evils and so perfect it that its example would appeal to all mankind but that I believed it wrong to try to force our form of government upon others and that I thought the Soviet Government was making a great mistake in pursuing that course.

"He did not take issue with me and said that their propaganda for world revolution was not now active.

"Weinstein is an earnest intelligent man and was courteous and direct with me throughout our interview—and during our stay in Petrograd he was at great pains to aid and assist in my investigation along the lines which I prefered [sic] to pursue.

"Neither he nor any other representative of the Soviet Government either in Petrograd, Moscow or on the way in and out of Russia withheld any information from me which I requested or attempted to divert me from any line of investigation which I pursued or sought to pursue.

"My interview with Weinstein lasted a couple of hours."[24]

The president of the Chamber of Commerce took them about the port, up the Neva, and to the Chamber, where they saw exhibits illustrating the Soviet Government's accomplishments and future plans. They saw several factories and visited the living quarters of the workers. As far as Bob was able to learn, the workers seemed happy under the conditions in their plants. He was impressed with the improvement in health education and with the day nurseries provided for the children of mothers working in the textile mills. Manly noted that "Senator La Follette with an interpreter dropped behind the management guides and interviewed a small group of women workers."[25]

From Petrograd they went to Moscow on what Steffens described as "a perfect train of Pullmans, with every comfort, in cleanliness and on time."[26] At the station they were met by Anna Louise Strong and Nuorteva, who had called upon Bob in Washington in 1919. Bob, Belle, and Bob, Jr., were taken to the "Guest House," which was "a half palace & half museum" that had been confiscated by the Government during the revolution. Bob noted that they had "sumptuous" apartments and that from their windows they looked out on "the palace & other Government buildings within the Kremlin walls."[27]

Bob had looked forward to this trip to Russia with keen interest because he "believed that she was destined to play a large, if not a dominant, part in the international development of the next ten years." Before leaving Berlin he had stated, "World peace is impossible without Russian cooperation."[28] While in Russia he was "afforded every opportunity to investigate, unhampered and unconducted," except as he "requested guidance." No interview that he sought with any official of the Soviet Government or the Communist Party was denied him. During his stay he dined with Tchitcherin, Minister of Foreign Affairs, and spent four hours with him. He had a conference with Rykoff, who was the acting Premier during Lenin's absence because of illness. He talked with Lunacharsky, Minister of Education; Krassin, Minister of Foreign Trade, and many other important leaders.[29]

Bob was especially interested in the current "all Russian exposition" which he thought gave "evidence of the constructive energies of the Soviet Government" and was "like a huge picture of all Russia spread out before the eyes."[30] They found Moscow "a thriving, busy city." Bob, Jr., wrote that "The new economic policy, adopted by the government which permits trading by individuals as well as the government trusts has revived business, and one leaves Moscow with the distinct impression that Russia is on the up grade in dead earnest."[31].

Through his own interpreters Bob talked with individuals who dared to tell him that they deplored the suppression of free speech, free press, and the conditions that resulted from this lack of freedom. One of the men who trusted him to an amazing degree was then a prominent official in the Government.[32] It seemed to Bob that "in their eagerness to carry out the Marxian theory, the leaders of the Soviet Government had sacrificed the cardinal principles of democracy." An outstanding fact to him was that there were 150,000,000 people in Russia of whom between 80 and 90 per cent were peasants, and that the elections were "completely controlled by the Communist Party, numbering less than 400,000." This inevitably led Bob to conclude: "If I were a citizen of Russia I should resist this communistic dictatorship as vigorously as I have endeavored to resist the encroachment upon our democratic institutions in America. I hold that government by one class, denying to other classes the right to participate, is tyranny."[33]

Bob and Steffens were not in accord about Russia. Steffens later recorded his interpretation of why they differed. "That journey brought out the difference between an American liberal, called at home a radical, and a real radical. Senator La Follette was very friendly to the Russians, who liked him well, but he deplored their excesses, both in the terror and in the lengths to which they had gone to change the foundations of life and government. I heard him tell the Russians that they need not have gone so far. . . ."[34] In a letter to his brother-in-law, Steffens said Bob "was against them; 'Marx is not the way to do it,' he said. And he really believes he is on the way. But what he and Mrs. La Follette said merely was that they did not want our civilization to be destroyed in order to correct its evils."[35]

Steffens and Davidson remained in Moscow when Bob and his party left for Warsaw, where they spent a day sight-seeing. Belle wrote her daughter that it was a relief to be in a place "in which we do not feel obliged to study the conditions."[36] En route from Warsaw to Vienna, Bob, Jr., wrote Rawleigh that "Every day this trip grows more interesting and profitable to each one of us. Dad is gathering information which will be of invaluable service to him in his work in the Senate and the campaign to come."[37] When they arrived in Vienna, they were surprised and delighted to find that Suzanne La Follette was staying at the Hotel Bristol, where they had reservations. For three days she acted as their guide. They visited the art museum, the emperor's palace at Schönbrunn, and heard Jeritza sing *Carmen*. Belle took advantage of this period of comparative "rest" to write up her impressions of Russia.[38] Bob "saw only a few leaders in Vienna and got some light on the situation but did not make hard work of it," although he filled a small scratch pad with notes.[39]

The difficulty of getting hotel rooms limited their time in Venice. But Belle wrote Mary that "our day in Venice was quite perfect. We rejoice that we came and wish we might stay."[40] Bob was awake at daylight on the morning their train was due to reach Rome. As always, he was interested in the way of man with the earth. He noted that every inch of soil was used. "Workers out in their fields at 6:30 AM White oxen the standard team. We are running South down a wide valley now probably sixty to 80 miles from Rome. One large lake with Castle (old) overlooking it. This valley is irrigated. The soil looks old and tired. But the orchards and vines look good & vigorous."[41] They spent four days in Rome sightseeing. They drove along the Appian Way, visited the Coliseum in the moonlight, went to Tivoli and all the places Bob and Belle had read about and longed to see ever since their university days.

"It has been wonderful to be here even for this short time," Belle wrote. "Daddy has enjoyed it very much. We saw Mussolini. He has a strong personality."[42]

While in Rome, Bob and his party were given window seats to watch the funeral procession of a prominent Fascist. Mussolini, usually cheered at each public appearance, walked erect, with eyes straight ahead and a studied avoidance of any appeal for applause. "What an actor," Bob remarked. This was further impressed upon him when they called upon Mussolini by appointment and walked to his desk in the rear of the long room where he waited to receive them. Through an interpreter Bob questioned the Dictator about freedom of the press in Italy. Mussolini replied that it was necessary to control the press until such time as democratic ideals could be realized. Mussolini's replies to the questions Bob persistently asked seemed to echo the responses that Bob had received in Russia. He kept bringing Mussolini back to the question of freedom of the press and freedom of speech, but the Dictator wanted to talk about how the Italian trains were now running on time.[43]

Bob had no more sympathy with Italian fascism than with Russian communism. To a "Jeffersonian Democrat," as Steffens called him, both were equally offensive.

They left Rome on September 23, passing through the Tyrolean Alps by daylight and arriving in Munich the next night. Bob and Belle went for a walk before breakfast and noted that there were "book stores and art shops everywhere." But upon the walls in the office of the Continental Hotel they saw "some threatening cartoons on the Ruhr situation" and there was "a regiment of soldiers drilling in the street."[44] Hitler had already become the popular idol of a movement to separate Bavaria from the Reich. He had organized his "storm troops" and was calling for revolution. Bob had a day in the old town of Nuremberg, where they visited the churches, the home of Albrecht Dürer, the home of Hans Sachs, and the house where Goethe lived when he wrote *Faust*. From Frankfurt the American consul general, Frederick Dumont, drove them to Wiesbaden, which was within the French-occupied territory. The next morning they took a boat down the winding Rhine to Cologne, where Belle and Mrs. Manly remained while Bob, his son, and Manly went to Essen for three days.[45]

Through Bob's letters, from Dr. Luther, Governor von Winterfeldt, president of the German Red Cross, and others, they met the leading industrialists. James H. Causey, an American banker whom Bob had known for many years, was especially kind and helpful. Causey had been cooperating with the Red Cross in getting food into the Ruhr for the German people. A small scratch pad of Bob's personal notes reveals his thirst for facts.[46] He went to the Ruhr to see the actual conditions under the French occupation, and to find out as much as he could about France's purpose "in seizing and holding this area in violation of the Versailles treaty."[47]

They started out in a Ford, the only private car then permitted in Essen. Under Causey's guidance the party drove about the most concentrated industrial district in the world. Within its twenty square miles lived 5,000,000 people, controlled by 40,000 French troops. In almost the only letter Bob wrote during the trip he told his sister Josephine that, "In the Ruhr—in and about Essen—where we visited a number of towns—the suffering is unspeakable. France is as merciless and unfeeling as the rack and the thumb-screw."[48] From the Ruhr all returned to Berlin for a few days, where the food shortage and currency inflation had increased the distress. "I don't see how Germany holds out," Belle wrote. "But there seems a sort of endurance and faith that if they keep on working, they will see better times after a while."[49]

Bob and his party left Berlin on the morning of October 5, and rode all day to Copenhagen, where they stayed three days. Bob, Jr., wrote, "This lush little country seems like the anteroom to Paradise after the want and fear in Germany[;] one almost begrudges the people their too red cheeks."[50] They did some sight-seeing, drove to Elsinore, "and stood on the platform where Hamlet's ghost walked."[51] Bob spent most of his time studying the cooperatives. In a country of some 3,000,000 there were 5,000 cooperatives, with an annual turnover of $27,000,000. He compared the forty cents out of every dollar paid by the consumer that the American farmer received for his product, with the eighty cents received by the Danish farmer. In fifty years the country had evolved from miser-able poverty to general comfort. He was especially interested in the fact that thousands of farmers supported their families on tiny farms of no more than eight acres, some of which he visited.[52]

From Copenhagen they went via Holland to Paris, arriving the night of October 10. Davidson met them at the station and took them to the Hotel de Crillon, where they had a suite looking out over the Place de la Concorde. After making a duty call at the American Embassy, they went to Waldo Peirce's studio to see a portrait he had painted of Fola when she was in Paris. That same day they visited Jo Davidson's studio. Bob was so impressed with his work that he consented to pose for him. While they were in Paris, Jo completed a bust which they all thought excellent. During one of the sittings Suzanne La Follette was at the studio. When she said to Jo, "I think you're going to have a very fine portrait there," he sighed and replied, "you should have seen it before I started it. It was wonderful then."[53] Subsequently Davidson did the full-length statue of Bob which is in the Nation's Capitol. Bob talked with many people, including lawyers, economists, businessmen, and labor leaders. At his request a complete diagram was made for him of the numerous French political parties.

The day after they arrived in Paris, Belle wrote Fola that her father was not free from a cold contracted in Berlin and that at times he had a recurrence of pain "such as he had before going to Battle Creek. He has walked and climbed stairs more than I ever thought he could do without any bad effect. But this pain has come on sometimes at night, waking him up out of his sleep. When it passes off he feels quite all right again."[54]

Bob, Jr., also wrote Fola and Mid that his father's heart had been "kicking up didos the last week . . . It may be only a passing thing but you know *our* rule, to tell everything good or bad, so I am letting you know. What I would give to live here as you did for a year and let politics go its way without me."[55]

Bob was forced, by doctor's advice, to cancel his return to London and the plans Causey and Manly had made. It meant foregoing seeing many he had hoped to meet: General Smuts, Sir Horace Plunkett, Sir Edgar Speyer, Ramsay MacDonald, Raymond Unwin, J. L. Garvin, editor of the *Observer,* and liberal members of Parliament, including Colonel Wedgwood. He had already declined requests of the English-Speaking Union to discuss at Albert Hall the policy of France in the Ruhr.

A lifetime of reading had prepared him for Europe, and it stirred his imagination. He had lingered lovingly over the relics at Stratford-on-Avon, Elsinore, and Kenilworth. In Paris he had sought out the grave of Victor Hugo. "It was wrong," he told Mary, "that Belle and I did not go to Europe thirty years earlier. Everyone should go to Europe and go in youth."[56]

The beauty of Paris fascinated him, and he regretted leaving it so soon. One morning Davidson came upon Bob as he stood alone in front of the Hotel de Crillon looking out over the Place de la Concorde. Tears were in his eyes. Responding to Davidson's unexpected greeting, he said, "It is a crime to have waited so many years to see all this beauty."[57]

Later in October, Bob, Belle, and Bob, Jr., sailed from Cherbourg on the *George Washington,* where they met the Manlys, who had embarked at Southampton. During the voyage home Bob jotted down in his notebook a brief summary of his view of the European situation. "Democracy is now being crucified in Europe," he wrote.

"In Russia it has been crushed by the Communist oligarchy. In Italy it has been destroyed by Missoulini [*sic*] and his Fascist groups. In Austria it has been put in pawn to the Allied money lenders. In Germany the democracy established with enlightened constitution is being ground between the upper and nether mill stones of Communism and Monarchism[.]

"The greatest contribution that America can make to Europe and the world is to restore and perfect her democratic institutions and traditions, so that they will stand as a beacon lighting the way to all the peoples[.] . . . There are evils in our own democracy. No one knows it better than I do. But the cure lies in the application of genuine republican principles."[58]

When the *George Washington* arrived at Portland, on November 2, Bob gave out a statement which included an appeal to send food to starving children in Germany, and a warning that the hunger there was a menace to the whole world.[59] In one of a series of articles published after his return, Bob predicted that what had happened in Italy and Russia might happen in Germany, where conflicting groups were "simultaneously striving to tear down the republic and erect in its place a dictatorship, resting not on the will of the people, but upon force of arms."[60] He declared in his concluding article that until the infamous Treaty of Versailles and its sister treaties "have been completely wiped out and replaced by enlightened understanding among the European nations, there will be no peace upon the Continent or in the world, and all the pettifogging conferences, councils and world courts will not prevent or seriously retard the new world war that is now rapidly developing from the seeds of malice, hatred and revenge that were sown at Versailles."[61]

CHAPTER LXIX

"The Ripe Issue of Events"

While Bob and Belle were abroad, Mary had supervised the moving of their furniture to another house, at 2112 Wyoming Avenue, which they had rented from Bob's cousin, William La Follette, who had returned to his home in Pullman, Washington.

A week after Bob's return he wrote a friend that he could not express how much the trip abroad had meant. "It was the biggest experience of my life and I hope that I've done enough work on it to make the benefit lasting."[1] During the voyage home he, Basil and Mollie Manly, Bob, Jr., and Belle had assembled the lengthy reports and the notes each had made of their impressions. This material formed the basis for the six articles Bob had contracted to write for the Sunday edition of the Hearst newspapers. While Bob was writing them, he had a recurrence of the chest pain he had suffered in Paris. A check-up by Dr. Marbury and Dr. Lee, a heart specialist, brought the report that although there was some enlargement of the aorta, he was "in pretty good shape." They said he "must cut down on his work" and rest. They put him to bed and prescribed a definite regime. Both doctors thought that if he followed their instructions he would "be able to resume his duties when the Senate meets."[2] The first of the articles on which Bob had been working was scheduled to appear on November 25. Belle, Bob, Jr., and Manly assisted him in completing it. In spite of his illness each article made the dead line, including an extra one which ended the series on January 6, 1924. Each was limited to two thousand words for which Bob received $500 an article. They were widely quoted in other newspapers and were subsequently reprinted in *La Follette's Magazine*. The manager of the Hearst newspapers, Bradford Merrill, wrote him that, "Your European articles gave us the greatest satisfaction."[3] Bob expressed his own appreciation for "the complete freedom of expression, both as to the subject matter and the titles of the articles, which has been accorded me."[4]

After his physicians advised Bob that he must take a rest, Bob, Jr., wrote Norris a strictly confidential letter saying that "In view of the important situation developing with respect to the organization of the next Congress, and particularly with regard to the Senate, I believe that it is my duty, in all fairness to you and the progressive cause, in which we are all so interested, to inform you that my Father is confined to his bed by order of Doctor Charles Marbury. And that the present prospect is that he will not be able to take part in the conferences preliminary to the opening of Congress. His condition is in no wise critical but rather one requiring rest and complete freedom from care and responsibility." Bob, Jr., also suggested that he hoped Norris would not hesitate to call upon him and Manly "at any time for conferences or other service."[5]

Soon after this the press reported that Cummins would again have the support of the regular Republicans for the chairmanship of the Interstate Commerce Committee. A few days before Congress met, Bob wrote a confidential letter to Senators Norris, Ladd, Frazier, Brookhart, Shipstead, and Magnus Johnson outlining a plan to promote progressive legislation by overhauling the entire committee set-up. He suggested they "concentrate Progressive strength" on two important committees which dealt with economic questions and thus "insure the drafting and reporting of bills that had teeth in them."[6]

Bob was not present when Congress convened on December 3. Although he had steadily improved, his physicians had advised him not to return to the Senate until after the holidays. Bob, Jr., wrote the family that "This is worrying him greatly especially because the progressives on the Senate side do not show the fight he wants them to. They naturally defer to Norris with Dad out of the picture and George is tired and philosophical about everything. He is inclined to let every opportunity go by without being ready with some plan of action. You can understand how that worries dad . . . I am spending all my time and energy trying to screw these porgressive [*sic*] Senators up to some aggressive action. Without success so far."[7]

It was evident that, as predicted after the elections, the progressive bloc held the balance of power in both Senate and House. Two days after Congress convened, President Coolidge wrote Bob the customary cordial letter regarding patronage in Wisconsin. This seemed to indicate that the press had been accurately informed when it predicted the Harding ban would be lifted. A week after the President delivered his message to Congress on December 6, Bob released two statements in Washington which were published as signed editorials in his magazine. The first was a sharp criticism of Coolidge's message, which he said was "an able, concise and frank presentation of the stand-pat, reactionary theory of government."[8] Bob's other statement declared the Progressives demanded a right to introduce constructive legislation and "to have that legislation fairly considered and reported to the Senate and the House, there to be voted up or down in the presence of the American people, by a record vote. No honest man will deny that the present committee system of Congress has been employed by predatory privilege, seeking new laws and evading old ones, as a vicious obstacle to decent, orderly representative government."[9] The *New York Times* commented that in issuing these two statements Senator La Follette had resumed "active command of his forces in the Senate and House of Representatives."[10]

The next day Bob released another statement attacking the renomination of Cummins as chairman of the Interstate Commerce Committee, which Lodge had reported to the Senate on December 10. Bob declared that in Congress and during the campaign the Progressives had fought the Esch-Cummins Law and they regarded the election results as "a clear mandate from the people" to repeal it. He charged that Cummins had used his chairmanship to prevent any amendment of this repudiated law and stated that to reelect him as chairman would "sanction a continuation of this policy of secret committee control to bury legislation which the people demand." Bob also said that the election of Senator Ellison Smith, a Democrat who had opposed the Esch-Cummins Law, would be "a clear cut" victory for the insurgent forces.[11]

The deadlock on the chairmanship continued through a dozen roll calls. The Progressives gave complimentary votes to Bob and Couzens. Without their support the Administration Republicans did not have enough votes to elect Cummins, and the Democrats were unable to elect their candidate, Ellison Smith of South Carolina.

The result was that Congress recessed, on December 20, for the holidays without electing a chairman.

Bob returned to the Senate on January 3, 1924, to take the oath of office which had been delayed by his illness in December. The newspapers noted that "he was warmly welcomed by Senators on both sides of the aisle" and that Senator Moses was among the first to greet him.[12] A little leather booklet was given to him which had been signed by thirty-one members of Congress. The engraved dedication read, "With your many friends the nation over, we rejoice in your return to good health and active participation in the fight for Progressive legislation."[13] The *New York Times* reported that he immediately "resumed active command."[14] A correspondent noted that on January 9 he directed the move which broke the stalemate on the effort to reelect Cummins to the Interstate Commerce Committee. After the second ballot that day, Bob conferred for a moment with Senators Brookhart, Frazier, Ladd, Magnus Johnson, and Shipstead. Then on the next ballot, which was the thirty-second since Cummins had been nominated, Bob switched his vote from Couzens, and the five Senators joined him in voting for Ellison D. Smith, thus electing the Democratic Senator, who had opposed the Esch-Cummins Law, by one vote more than was necessary.[15] In an editorial Bob described this as a "clear-cut victory" for the Progressives and gave credit to Senator Wheeler, a progressive Democrat, who had initially objected to the election of Cummins when his confirmation as chairman had been sought without a record vote.[16]

During January Bob introduced a series of bills and resolutions as a part of his legislative program. The first was to amend the Esch-Cummins Law and the Railroad Valuation Act to require the Interstate Commerce Commission to fix railroad rates on the basis of operating expense plus the cost of actual capital invested.[17] The next day the press quoted him as having stated that these amendments would "for the first time in the history of Federal legislation provide for a scientific method of fixing railroad rates." The railway executives promptly declared they would fight the bill on the ground that it was confiscatory.[18] Bob's only reply was to introduce additional resolutions to require the commission to reduce freight rates on farm products,[19] to investigate the settlement of all claims arising out of Federal control of the railroads and to report its findings and recommendations to the Senate.[20] Other proposals were to recognize the independence of the Philippines[21] and to provide seamen on American vessels a continuous discharge book.[22] A combination of the reactionary elements of both parties prevented these bills and resolutions from coming before the Senate for consideration. But Bob was more successful with several resolutions relating to the Teapot Dome investigation. On February 7 he reintroduced his 1922 resolution to investigate naval oil reserves, in order to continue the authority of the Public Lands Committee to hold hearings, since Fall had declined to answer its questions on the ground that the committee's right to act had expired with the end of the Sixty-seventh Congress.[23] The next day Bob moved to investigate the claims of the Honolulu Consolidated Company to lands within one of the California oil reserves, including the reversal of Fall's earlier decision against the company.[24] A week later he presented another resolution directing the Secretary of the Interior to send to the Senate information, including all Executive orders and other papers concerning the transfer of the naval coal reserves in the Territory of Alaska from the Navy Department to the Interior, and the proposed leases of said reserves.[25] He also introduced a resolution calling for a national inquiry into the baking industry.[26] His oil resolutions were all passed.

During the early part of the winter the committee which had been investigating the naval oil-reserve leases made during the Harding Administration had established corruption and dishonesty. Late in January the Senate unanimously called upon President Coolidge to annul the leases and to appoint special counsel, thus excluding Attorney General Daugherty.[27] Fall had resigned nearly a year before, but Secretary of the Navy Denby was still in office. A resolution calling upon Coolidge to ask for Denby's resignation had been introduced by a Democratic Senator, Joseph T. Robinson.[28] During two weeks of debate the Administration Senators had defended Denby. But the opponents had broadened their attack to include evidence of abuse of power and corruption in other Departments, including: the sale of surplus war supplies; fraud and larceny in the Shipping Board transactions; sinister activities in the Department of Justice under Attorney General Daugherty; graft in the Veterans' Bureau under Colonel Forbes; scandals of prohibition enforcement; delays in settling tax cases and hundreds of millions in refunds to large taxpayers.

In the closing hours of the debate Bob took the floor. Practically every seat on the Democratic side was occupied. "On the Republican side all the newer Senators were in their seats, and this included the regulars as well as the progressives. Only the Old Guard members like Lodge and Smoot were absent. Not a vacant seat was to be seen in the press galleries and many correspondents were standing."[29] At the beginning of his speech Bob paid tribute to Walsh of Montana for his fearless conduct of the oil-reserve investigation and to the naval officers who had courageously opposed transfer of the reserves from the Navy to the Interior Department. And again, as in 1922, he expressed his appreciation of the contribution made by Harry Slattery, who had aided him in gathering information.

In his attack on Denby's record Bob said that the Senate was not "dealing with an exceptional case of official corruption, or discussing the fate of a single Cabinet officer." This case was, he said, only "the latest of a series of organized raids upon the Public Treasury and the public domain." He declared that every public official involved and every individual involved in the oil scandals must "bear the responsibility for his own acts." Fall "must not be made the scapegoat so that others may be allowed to evade responsibility for what they have done." Denby, who knew Fall's "consistent opposition to and contempt for all conservation legislation," must be held to "strict responsibility and accountability." Attorney General Daugherty, who had "never raised a hand to protect the public interest in these matters," was also responsible. President Coolidge must also "bear his full measure of responsibility" because he had been aware of the policy of both Denby and Fall "long before the present investigation." Bob reminded Senators that "When I introduced Senate resolution 282, authorizing and directing the investigation which the Committee on Public Lands is now conducting into the subject of leases upon naval oil reserves, the Vice President, now the President, was then in the chair. This was on April 21, 1922. When that resolution was called up for discussion and the whole subject thoroughly gone into on April 28, 1922, the Vice President, Mr. Coolidge, now the President, was then in the chair and heard the discussion. At that time the revelations were foreshadowed which have since been publicly made." Bob also declared that responsibility must be borne by the political party whose managers "connive at the looting of the public and seek to excuse the misconduct of members of its party in high official position. . . . I say it with shame and mortification, but it is unfortunately true, that the political party of which I am a member, as represented by those in control of the machinery of the party, has played as sorry a part in this investigation as it did in the Ballinger investigation." But he added: "Democratic administrations are not by any means free from like offenses. The records of the Interior Department and the Department of Justice as well as other departments have their dark pages written under Democratic rule since I have been in public life in Washington. . . . There should be no politics on an issue like the present one."[30]

A well-known newspaper correspondent who had "watched him carefully" during his speech wrote that "His face had lost some of its old color. His voice had not quite the angry power it used to have, but still it was a strong voice; perhaps a little pleasanter to listen to because somewhat mellowed. He read his speech, which was unusual, but I noticed that his hand was steady as he held the manuscript. . . . He was more moderate than of old. Success and power, for he is now the most powerful single factor in the Senate, and perhaps, too, advancing in years, have mellowed him."[31]

The Senate adopted the resolution 51 to 25, and a week later Denby resigned. On March 1 Bob defied Senate custom and the Old Guard Republicans by nominating Senator Brookhart from the floor for the chairmanship of the special committee to investigate Attorney General Daugherty. In a brief speech he cited precedents for his unusual action and condemned the customary procedure which permitted a few men to determine the fate of legislation by their control of the make-up of committees.[32] The Senate elected Brookhart. Bob pointed out in an editorial that if the choice had been left to the reactionary Republican leaders the special committee would have been appointed by the President pro tempore "after careful selection in a secret conference."[33]

A week later Bob contracted a respiratory infection with temperature and a bad cough. Dr. Marbury advised him to go to bed. He reluctantly obeyed orders but kept closely in touch with the Senate situation through his son. Two weeks later he wrote Rawleigh that he "was confident that he would be back in harness shortly" and able to go on with his work for many years to come "if I will simply give myself the care and attention at this time that I would insist on if it were Bob, Jr., who were ill instead of myself."[34] Just as he seemed to be convalescing and was planning to go away for a brief rest before returning to the Senate, the infection suddenly flared up and developed into bronchial pneumonia. For several days he was so seriously ill that Fola and Mid came on to Washington. The press report that he had pneumonia and that Dr. Marbury had called two other physicians in consultation brought anxious inquiries from friends. He recuperated rapidly, however, and when the newspapers reported his improvement, Elizabeth Evans wrote Belle expressing her happiness at the good news and saying: "He has never consented to use prudence before. But perhaps even he can learn. Life—and a near look at death, should be a teacher."[35]

Before Bob was taken ill, he had collaborated with friends in Washington and Wisconsin on a platform to be submitted to the Wisconsin voters on April 1. When it was given out at Madison on March 17, by Senator Henry A. Huber, the *New York Times* interpreted the dispatch as meaning that La Follette would head a third-party movement, and even went so far as to state that Vice Presidential candidates were being sought and that Louis Brandeis and Josephus Daniels were among those mentioned.[36] The fact was that at this time Bob had not decided whether he himself would be a candidate. The day that the platform was published he had written his friend Rawleigh that if he became a candidate, he would make these twelve planks his platform.[37] At the primary on April 1, the platform was overwhelmingly adopted and twenty-eight progressive Republican delegates were elected to the Republican National Convention to be held in Cleveland in June. Bob's name did not appear as a Presidential candidate on the Wisconsin ballot, and he formally withdrew it in Michigan, Montana, and North Dakota. Nevertheless, in North Dakota, in a three-cornered race with Coolidge and Hiram Johnson avowed candidates, nearly one-half of the State's delegation was instructed for La Follette, although the voters had to paste his name on the ballot. In Wisconsin more voters had written in his name than had voted for Coolidge, whose name appeared on the ballot. The New York *World* commented editorially that, "La Follette . . . is the only man now on the political horizon who can lead hosts in an independent pilgrimage."[38]

A special article to the *New York Times* a few days after the primary stated that "Amid many rumors the actual position of Senator La Follette on the third party movement is of importance." The author had interviewed someone he described as "admittedly among the best informed men in Washington." This man must have been close to Bob, for he accurately stated that the Senator had not reached a decision and that it would depend upon the action of the Republican and Democratic conventions. "If one or both of these conventions should put real Progressive candidates before the country . . . Senator La Follette would, of course, decline to enter the race. . . . If he runs, it will be as an 'independent Progressive.' Make no mistake about this." The author of the article then recalled that in a talk with newspaper men some time ago the Senator had said: "Independent movements and third parties cannot be built by a few leaders sitting around a table. They are the ripe issue of events, and they must come from the people."[39]

This interview correctly expressed the opinion Bob had long held, and it was in substance what he had repeatedly said to the representatives of a number of different organizations who had been urging him to run. But newspaper speculation as to whether he would be a candidate in the 1924 campaign had been stimulated by the public endorsements he had received during the winter and spring from various groups and individuals.[40] Bob thought in 1924, as he had in 1920, that any final decision as to his candidacy should be based upon definite knowledge as to the sentiment among the active progressive men and women in the different States. Therefore in January he had decided that such a survey should be made and that if they desired to undertake the work, petitions should be circulated for placing La Follette's name on the ballot as an independent candidate in the event that the Republican and Democratic conventions nominated reactionary candidates.

This project was similar to the independent candidacy plan which had been considered at the 1920 conferences after Bob had declined to become the candidate of the Farmer Labor Party Convention in Chicago. After the 1923 elections in Minnesota and Michigan, he had again discussed this plan with his family and intimate friends. Toward the end of January, 1924, he talked it over with Herman Ekern, Manly, and Julius A. Truesdell, who was now on his office staff. At Bob's request Manly summarized the main points of the plan in a rough outline which Bob sent on to Phil and Bob, Jr., who were both in Madison at this time. The plan proposed that a committee of five, including W. T. Rawleigh, Dante Pierce, and John F. Sinclair of Minnesota, be created to sponsor the initial move in finding a "key man" in each State to form another committee of five which should include "at least one woman." Each state committee was to organize city and county committees. It was contemplated that if Bob became a candidate, these committees would be the basis for a campaign organization. Phil was to be in charge of an office in Madison "through which everything can be managed, records preserved, etc."[41] Later, after receiving reports on the work his son was doing in seeing "key men" in the Northwestern States, Bob wrote, "Phil—dear boy I know how much you are sacrifising [sic] in all you are doing—for your Dad. It is a great load you are carrying and I marvel that you are doing your work like a veteran-campaigner[.] Whatever befalls we are going to make some history within the next year. It is impossible to gauge the public mind on the present national situation."[42]

On May 5 Bob and Belle went to Atlantic City. From Galen Hall he wrote the family that they were "delightfully located" on the fourth floor, facing the ocean with its breezes pouring in at their windows. Each day they took long rides on the boardwalk in a wheel chair, napped for several hours, and read. When they left Washington, Bob had vainly begged his son to come with them for a few days' vacation. But the morning after their arrival he read the *New York Times* and the *Washington Post* reports of the fight in the House on the Railroad Labor Board bill and in the Senate on the tax bill, and wrote Bob, Jr.: "I imagine you were kept pretty much on the job watching the combat on two fronts and keeping our forces steady under the rapid fire of a desperate enemy. I am so glad you did not heed my begging and were where you could be, as I know you were, of great help in both Houses."[43] Although Bob had been reluctant to leave Washington, he accepted his absence from the Senate with good grace, and arranged with Bob,

Jr., to have his vote paired or recorded on important measures. Thus he supported the tax bill, with the provisions by the progressive Senators, and it was announced in the Senate that if present he would have joined the majority in voting to override the President's veto of the soldiers' adjusted compensation bill.

Characteristically, Bob turned his convalescence into a holiday for himself and others by inviting Fola and the Roe family to visit him. While Fola was there, Bob, Jr., came from Washington to urge his father to take some action that would prevent his nomination by the delegates to a Farmer-Labor-Progressive Convention which had been called to meet in St. Paul on June 17. The Communists had been invited to participate, and Bob, Jr., thought their purpose was to capture the convention and undermine the progressive movement. The national publication of the Railroad Brotherhoods, edited by Edward Keating, had already warned its members to stay away from the St. Paul convention because "A small but very active band of communists is in control of the arrangements." This same editorial had informed its readers that the Conference for Progressive Political Action, scheduled to meet in Cleveland on July 4, would be "a thoroughly representative gathering and authorized to speak for large groups of organized farmers and industrial workers."[44] Several Farmer-Labor meetings which were sending delegates to the St. Paul convention had already endorsed Bob for President. Bob, Jr., urged his father to write an open letter to Attorney General Herman Ekern stating his position on the Communist issue and thus prevent any possibility of his nomination. Fola, who was present during these discussions at this time and later, wrote Mid, "They feel the extreme left wing are going to try to capture this meeting under cover of endorsing Dad, some such move as was carried out by the Farmer-Labor party in Chicago several years ago."[45]

When Bob, Jr., returned to Washington, he found that William Mahoney of St. Paul, a member of the Farmer-Labor Party who was chairman of the Arrangements Committee of the convention, had come to Washington a second time to try to find out whether Bob intended to be a Presidential candidate. Bob, Jr., and Manly met with Shipstead and Magnus Johnson and listened to Mahoney, who went into "a long oratorical recital of the details leading up to the calling of their convention. He endeavored to slur over the invitation extended to the Communists," but Manly "pinned him down on this pretty hard." At the end of the conference Bob, Jr., said he could make no statement as to his father's position on the St. Paul convention. Shipstead "told Mahoney in plain English" that La Follette was "the leader of the progressives in this country," that he intended to follow that leadership and thought "it was the duty of every other real progressive to do the same thing."[46]

After his visit to Atlantic City, Bob, Jr., had drafted a letter for his father to consider sending to Attorney General Herman Ekern. He submitted this letter to Roe and Manly and talked over the entire political situation with them. The three men were unanimous in their opinion as to what Bob should do with respect to the St. Paul convention. Before leaving for Wisconsin to attend a meeting of the State Central Committee, Bob, Jr., wrote his father that Roe was coming to Atlantic City and would report on their conference and bring the letter to Ekern. In a postscript Bob, Jr., modestly added: "Bas [Manly] is revising my letter to Herman[.] I did not want you to think the credit is mine."[47]

When Roe brought the letter to Atlantic City, Bob discussed with him whether it might not be wiser to have the warning regarding the June 17 St. Paul convention come from someone other than a potential Presidential candidate. After Roe left, Bob wrote an eight-page longhand letter to his son-in-law Ralph Sucher which was to be shared with Manly and Bob, Jr.[48] Late the next afternoon Bob, Jr., wrote his father from Washington that he had "spent about five hours with Bas [Manly] and Ralph going over the political situation generally, but particularly with regard to your letter to Ralph." After telling his father that they still thought the warning in regard to the June 17 convention should come from him, Bob, Jr., analyzed the alternatives and pointed out why he thought statements by others would not be effective.[49]

After receiving this letter and talking the matter over with Belle and Manly, who came to Atlantic City for a day, Bob decided to publish his letter to Herman Ekern. It was dated May 26, and Bob, Jr., gave it to the newspaper correspondents for release in the noon edition of the press on May 28. He wrote his father that "From the way in which the newspaper boys have taken the statement I think it will have good publicity. During the day such men as Bill Hard, Gilson Gardner and Bill Powell have dropped in and

I have asked them to read it. They are unanimous in praising it as a splendid statement of your position and are enormously relieved that you have done it."[50] Bob's letter to Ekern was carried by the leading newspapers throughout the country and had a powerful impact on the St. Paul Farmer-Labor-Progressive Convention. In subsequent elections, as the Communist issue became increasingly im-

BATTLING BOB'S DOUBLE WALLOP
By John M. Baer in *Labor*, June 7, 1924.

portant, it was frequently cited and quoted. In 1948 the Washington *Sunday Star* published it in full under the heading "LA FOLLETTE MINCED NO WORDS in BRUSHING OFF THE REDS," and suggested that the formula of this letter should be used by Henry A. Wallace, then a Presidential candidate under a Progressive Party label, to repudiate the unanimous endorsement given him by the American branch of the Communist Party at its national convention.[51]

Bob's four-page letter to Herman Ekern, dated May 26, 1924, read in part as follows: "I have your letter of May 17th saying that many of my friends in Wisconsin are anxious to know my attitude toward the 'Farmer-Labor-Progressive Convention' called to meet at St. Paul, June 17th.

"I should not feel it incumbent upon me to declare my attitude except that my name is being used by the promoters of that Convention in such a way as to convey the impression that it has my approval and as a result some of my friends in different parts of the country contemplate attending the St. Paul Convention. Because of these facts, I feel it my duty to state my view frankly.

"I have no doubt that very many of those who have participated in bringing about the St. Paul Convention have been actuated by the purest desire to promote genuine political and economic progress.

"Nevertheless, in my judgment, the June 17 convention will not command the support of the farmers, the workers, or other progressives because those who have had charge of the arrangements for this convention have committed the fatal error of making the Communists an integral part of their organization.

"The Communists have admittedly entered into this political movement not for the purpose of curing, by means of the ballot, the evils which afflict the American people, but only to divide and confuse the Progressive movement and create a condition of chaos favorable to their ultimate aims. Their real purpose is to establish by revolutionary action a dictatorship of the proletariat, which is absolutely repugnant to democratic ideals and to all American aspirations. . . .

"This is shown by an official statement of the Central Executive Committee of the Workers Party of America [printed in the *Daily Worker*, March 31, 1924], as follows:

"The policy which we adopt in Minnesota will be a precedent for the whole Party in relation to the National Farmer-Labor Party when that organization is finally crystallized. It is therefore important that we adopt the correct Communist policy in Minnesota as a guide to our whole Party for its *work inside of the Farmer-Labor Party throughout the country*. . . .

"The Workers Party prides itself in being a Communist Party; that means, that *it considers its work to build up and lead the forces which will bring*

about a proletarian revolution in the United States and establish a Soviet
form of government and the Dictatorship of the Proletariat.
                                    "CENTRAL EXECUTIVE COMMITTEE,
                                    "C. E. RUTHENBERG, *Secretary*.

"Progressives inclined to attend the June 17 Convention should
also consider the statement, published in 'The Daily Worker' of
May 16, 1924 by the Central Executive Committee of the Workers
Party of America over the signatures of William Z. Foster, Chairman, and C. E. Ruthenberg, Executive Secretary:

"In order to settle the question of whether the Farmer-Labor United Front
was a policy that a communist Party such as the Workers Party should put
into effect and in support of which it should throw all its strength, the Central
Executive Committee of the Workers Party submitted this question to the
Communist International (Moscow), with which it is affiliated as a fraternal
organization.
"The view of the Communist International on this question is expressed in
the following cablegram:
"Communist International considers June 17 Convention momentous importance for Workers Party. Urges C. E. C. not to slacken activities preparation June 17. Utilize every available force to make St. Paul Convention great
representative gathering labor and left wing.
                    "EXECUTIVE COMMITTEE, COMMUNIST INTERNATIONAL.

"The Communist organization in America, thus acting under
orders from the Communist International at Moscow, will not only
participate in the St. Paul Convention on June 17, but has already
secured a strategic position in the direction of that Convention. . . .
Reliable information shows that a very large number of Communist
delegates will be present at St. Paul with duly authorized cre-
dentials.

"Reposing complete confidence in the soundness of the deliberate judgment of the American people, I have no apprehension
that the Communist Party can ever command any considerable
support in this country. I do not question their right, under the
Constitution, to submit their issues to the people, but I most emphatically protest against their being admitted into the councils of
any body of progressive voters. . . .

"Not only are the Communists the mortal enemies of the progressive movement and democratic ideals, but, under the cloak of
such extremists, the reactionary interests find the best opportunity

to plant their spies and provocatory agents for the purpose of con-
fusing and destroying true progressive movements.

"I have devoted many years of my life to an effort to solve the
problems which confront the American people by the ballot and not
by force. I believe that the people through the ballot can completely control their government in every branch and compel it to
serve them effectively. I have fought steadfastly to achieve this
end, and I shall not abandon this fight as long as I may live. I
believe, therefore, that all progressives should refuse to participate
in any movement which makes common cause with any Communist
organization. . . ."[52]

Later, when the Farmer-Labor-Progressive Convention met in
St. Paul, the press reported that "Any one doubting the influence
of Robert Marion La Follette in so-called progressive circles had
only to visit the Auditorium today to become thoroughly convinced.
Wisconsin's 'Fighting Bob' put a decided crimp in William Mahoney's third party show. There wasn't as much left as a fair-sized
side show when the time came to get the proceedings under way."[53]
Row after row of seats reserved for different States were vacant,
and the attendance had dwindled to fewer than 400 when the gavel
fell and Mahoney called the convention to order. As Bob had
predicted in his letter to Ekern, the proceedings were dominated
by the Communists under the leadership of William Z. Foster and
C. E. Ruthenberg. Foster and others who had played influential
but concealed roles in preventing agreement on a progressive platform at the 1920 Chicago conventions were now openly working to
put through the Communist program as directed by the Executive
Committee of the Communist International in their cablegram from
Moscow. On the second day Ruthenberg took the platform to attack
La Follette and his record.[54] Among those who joined in denouncing La Follette was Duncan McDonald, who had been active in
the 1920 Labor Party Convention at Chicago. After being elected
vice chairman of the St. Paul convention, McDonald attacked
La Follette by saying: "If the man who frowned on this gathering
has gone over to the crowd that plundered the public domain at
Teapot Dome and acted as bootleggers down in Washington, then
it is our right to return the compliment. If he calls us reds then by
God he is 'yellow.' "[55] The delegates cheered, and what was left of

the St. Paul Farmer-Labor-Progressive Convention nominated Duncan McDonald as its Presidential candidate.

Shortly after Bob's letter to Ekern was published, he received a brief penciled note from William J. Bryan congratulating him upon the skill with which he had disarmed the reactionaries by advising his friends to avoid political association with the Communists. Bryan said he feared that since the reactionaries were in such complete control of the Republican Party, Bob could accomplish little in the convention except to make a record as he had in 1904 when the Roosevelt convention turned down by 7 to 1 his platform plank for the popular election of United States Senators. Bryan added that he thought the threat of Bob's candidacy would strengthen the Progressives in the Democratic convention and closed his note with a wish for strength to Bob's arm.[56] In thanking Bryan for his "word of encouragement," Bob said: "I am in complete agreement with you concerning the reactionary control of the Cleveland [Republican] Convention. . . . If you care to do so, I will be pleased to have your judgment as to the probable outcome at New York. You know of course that anything you may care to say concerning it will be regarded as entirely confidential."[57]

When Bob returned to the Senate on May 31, the *New York Times* reported that he "was in his best fighting trim" and that on arriving at his office in the Capitol soon after 10:00 A.M., he "got to work on the telephone rallying the Progressive and radical forces. As a result there was a strong showing of Progressives and anti-Administration forces at the Interstate Commerce Committee meeting, where the Howell-Barkley bill was under consideration." Three hours after Bob's arrival, the committee voted 10 to 3 "to report favorably" this bill "which would do away with the Railroad Labor Board." The press also noted that this was "one of La Follette's pet measures" and that Senator Cummins, former chairman of the committee, who had been "one of the authors of the act which established the Railroad Labor Board, voted with the majority."[58]

A few days later Belle wrote Phil that his father had returned to the Senate Saturday and had been "at his post since including one night session. He looks very tired when he comes home but is standing the strain better than I had expected . . . Daddy has been the center of the stage both in the Senate and the Press Gallery. Just now I judge he occupies more space in the Eastern than the Western papers. The news value of every move he makes seems to cause them to play it up—and almost forget to berate him as heretofore[.] That will come later I presume."⁵⁹

Before the Senate adjourned, Bob introduced a resolution providing for a special committee of five Senators to investigate the sources and expenditures of funds in the 1924 Presidential and Vice Presidential campaigns. It included an inquiry into the money spent to defeat candidates as well as that contributed to elect them. This was a new feature in the investigation of campaign expenditures, and some newspapers interpreted it "as referring to his own prospective candidacy." The resolution, which also provided that the committee should be elected by the Senate, was passed unanimously by a viva voce vote.⁶⁰ The five Senators nominated were Borah, Jones of Washington, Shipstead, Caraway, and Bayard. The *Milwaukee Journal* reported: "It was viewed generally as the strongest committee that has ever been named for this purpose. There was general amusement as Senator Lodge read the names proposed, for thereby he preserved the appearance of having chosen them, but there was not a member of the Old Guard on the list and the La Follette authorship was so evident it could not be mistaken."⁶¹

Bob also tried to put through another resolution before adjournment. In March the House had passed by a large majority a joint resolution to appropriate $10,000,000 to purchase food in the United States to be distributed to starving women and children in Germany. The resolution had been held in the Senate Foreign Relations Committee until June 3, when it was rejected. Bob gave notice that same day that he would move to discharge the committee and thus bring it to the floor for debate.⁶² Three days later he called it up and delivered a forty-minute speech at a night session of the Senate on June 6. In urging passage of the relief-fund resolution, he described the conditions he had seen in Germany, the shortage of food and milk for children, the spread of disease and death due to slow starvation. With deep concern for the survival of the new German Government struggling to maintain itself out of the wreckage of a defeated monarchy, he pleaded for the help, understanding, and human kindness needed to maintain the institutions of a democracy in the new republic.

During the heat of debate opponents of the relief measure had insinuated that the motives of its advocates were not humanitarian but political and directed toward courting the German-American vote in the coming election. Bob protested against these innuendoes, declaring that after nearly forty years of public service he could honestly say: "wherever my convictions have led me, I have gone forth, even though alone, to defend those convictions. In peace and in war, with all that it might bring upon my head, I have stood by what I believed to be right, and in pressing for a vote upon this resolution I am simply pursuing the course which I have followed all my life.

"The war is five years behind us. Let us set our faces to the new day and accept the conditions which must make for the peace of the world and for the restoration of Germany to her just place in the family of nations. Above all things, as American Senators, as representatives of the chivalry and generous impulse of the people of this country, let us, I appeal to you, refuse to invoke the war spirit against starving women and children."

He recalled the spirit in which Grant had made terms to Lee who had come to surrender at Appomattox: " 'Take your horses and your mules. Let the starving Confederate soldiers come for their rations to the commissary of the winning troops. Let us have peace. . . .' We have to live in the world with the German people who are kin to millions of people of the United States. They represent one of the great powers of Europe, and Europe can never recover industrially and economically until Germany is restored. We can help to restore the international amity which must precede peace and stability by passing the pending resolution."[63]

Later that night Bob's motion to discharge the Foreign Relations Committee from further consideration of the House relief resolution was rejected by 53 to 25, Eastern and Southern Senators, Republican and Democratic, voting together to defeat it.[64] The following day Congress adjourned in time for the Republican Members to take a special train for the national convention at Cleveland. Bob decided not to go to Wisconsin, but to stay in Washington to await "the ripe issue of events."

CHAPTER LXX

The Nomination of La Follette
and Wheeler

On the eve of the 1924 Republican National Convention at Cleveland, former Secretary of the Navy Josephus Daniels described it as "already cut and dried" and "done up in moth balls to prevent injury." In a signed article Daniels said, "Today La Follette is the Sphinx, the pivotal man in politics. Only a few years ago the Republicans refused him recognition and he seemed down and out. It is among the possibilities that La Follette can turn the tables and put those 'down and out' who wanted to kick him downstairs a few years ago. Stranger things have happened."[1]

When Bob, Jr., left Washington on the night of June 7 to attend the Republican Convention, he carried a letter from his father to Governor Blaine, who headed the Wisconsin delegation. Twenty-eight out of Wisconsin's twenty-nine delegates had been instructed to vote for La Follette. After they arrived in Cleveland a caucus was held, and Blaine read the letter from Bob requesting them not to present his name, but to offer as a minority report the Wisconsin platform which the voters had approved.[2] The caucus also passed eight resolutions to be presented to the Resolutions Committee in addition to the platform.

The eight resolutions were given to the press and received wide publicity. The following day Governor Blaine presented them at the open hearings of the Resolutions Committee, where they were received with mingled cheers and hisses. They included two resolutions condemning Harry M. Daugherty and Albert B. Fall for their gross betrayal of public trust and debarring them from any future position of trust or honor in the gift of the Republican Party. An-

1107

other resolution recommended Senators Borah, Brookhart, Couzens, Howell, and Norris for special services and cited La Follette "for his signal service in bringing about an investigation of the corrupt leasing of Teapot Dome and other naval oil reserves." Representative Cooper presented the Wisconsin platform in the executive session of the committee. It was voted down, and he notified them he would present it to the convention as a minority report. On the floor of the convention a hostile atmosphere surrounded the Wisconsin delegation. The nomination of Coolidge was a foregone conclusion. When his name was mentioned, a demonstration started with delegates marching about the auditorium, but the Wisconsin delegates refused to join. A correspondent noted that the La Follette men "sat coolly, steadily in their seats," not heeding the shouts, "Stand up, Wisconsin! Stand up!" until the band played "The Star-Spangled Banner." They stood at attention through the anthem and then quietly resumed their seats.[3]

This tension furnished the background for the appearance of Henry Allen Cooper, the dean of the Wisconsin delegation in Congress. The convention had granted him ten minutes to present the Wisconsin platform as a minority report. A newspaper correspondent wrote that from the rear of the platform "a tall, elderly man, bald head fringed with white hair, strong rugged face rimmed with a snowy beard, moved in deliberate dignity to the front of the stage and stood, head proudly erect. . . . no one knew what that crowd would do . . . Most of them had no use for his views, but half at least were demanding that he be heard, and giving him a cheer, so he began with applause, warm and hearty, rising equally with hisses and boos."[4] In a brief speech before reading the platform, Cooper reminded the delegates that Wisconsin had submitted a minority platform in 1908 and that, as he read it, every plank had been greeted by calls of "kick him out," "take it to Denver," and "socialistic." He recalled that since 1908 thirty-one planks had been presented by Wisconsin and that they had all been hissed, but that now all but one was the law of the land, and one, the direct election of Senators, was in the Constitution. When Cooper left the speaker's stand, he was given an ovation. Bob, Jr., telegraphed his father that "Cooper was magnificent wish you could have seen him handle most hostile crowd we have ever faced spoke ten minutes then read every line of platform."[5] Calvin Coolidge and Charles

Dawes were nominated. But the Republican Convention had served to carry the progressive Wisconsin platform by press and radio throughout the United States.

The Democratic Convention began its protracted sessions in New York on June 24. Bob had previously written Bryan that he would be pleased to have his judgment confidentially on the probable outcome, and he kept in close touch with the proceedings through Bob, Jr., who was in New York.[6] Bob hoped to postpone any public statement regarding his own candidacy until he knew whether the Democrats would nominate a progressive or a reactionary candidate. But a deadlock developed, and no one seemed able to predict when it would end. On July 3, while the deadlock was still on, representatives of the La Follette For President Committee, including Chairman W. T. Rawleigh, Zona Gale, Gilbert Roe, and others, called upon Bob at his home. They brought a box containing petitions asking him to become a candidate. Over two hundred thousand signatures had been gathered by volunteers after less than a month's work. More were coming in at the rate of ten thousand a day. Zona Gale described the arrival of the committee with the petitions. "It looked like any other box, three feet long and two feet wide. The taxi-driver swung the box down from his seat and carried it into 2112 Wyoming Avenue, Washington, and deposited it in the passage. The box looked as if it might contain files of dusty reports.

"But they were not dusty. They had come fresh from nearly a quarter of a million hands. The list of the occupations of those hands was in the box, and every industry, every profession—cowboy, ice-man, inventor, the classified and the unclassified—the roll of the people. From across miles, from down in the earth and from the sea appeals for a new leadership met in the box in the passage.

"The little committee that had brought the petitions went up the stairs to a book-lined room. Senator La Follette was there and Mrs. La Follette and Bob, Jr., and two friends of years. When Chairman W. T. Rawleigh of the La Follette For President Committee rose to speak for the others, the Senator also rose—there was no other formality. But in the speaker's voice was the fine formality of feeling—so deep that it was like still other words. Chairman Rawleigh was speaking to the friend of his Wisconsin boyhood, the literal log-cabin friend, of whom his father had said: 'Watch that boy; we're going to hear from him.' . . .

"It came to those who watched . . . [that if La Follette's] principles and his personality can reach the people undistorted, the people
will follow him. Now he was saying:

" 'I am more moved by this than by any incident of my life. Yet
I know that this is no personal tribute. The principles for which
we are standing together are greater than any person or any party.
When you call for an independent progressive movement, I know
that you are right. The two old parties have betrayed the people.
. . . I see nothing in either of their platforms on which to build a
hope for tomorrow . . . and they have ignored the supreme issue,
involving all others: the encroachment of the powerful few upon
the rights of the many. . . . This great power has come between the
people and their government. . . . We must meet our problem or else
lay it upon our children. My friends, from my heart I give you my
thanks for your trust in me. I shall answer you and the emergency
committee together tomorrow, in Cleveland. Whatever happens the
cornerstone of a new structure has been laid.' "[7]

That night Bob received a telegram from the chairman of the
National Committee of the Conference for Progressive Political
Action, William H. Johnston, asking him to become the Presidential
candidate of the progressive forces and requesting a message giving
his "views on the present political situation."[8] Although the Democratic Convention was still deadlocked, it seemed evident after
seventy-odd ballots that a progressive Democrat would not be nominated. The C.P.P.A. Convention was scheduled to convene in
Cleveland the next day. Bob knew that many of the delegates in
the different groups wished to form a third party with full tickets
for all offices in the 1924 campaign. He was opposed to this because
it would inevitably mean three-cornered contests which would endanger the election of Progressives to Congress. In a letter written
in May he had warned that a third-party fight would jeopardize
"the election of ev[e]ry progressive Senator & Representative in
Congress candidates in 1924—the men who now hold the balance
of power in both houses and into whose hands will be committed
the issue if the Presidency is thrown into the House of Rep.
[resentatives] there to be settled in 1924."[9] He decided to announce
his candidacy as an independent and to make the announcement
before he was nominated by the C.P.P.A. Convention. Bob had
spent many years building up the group of progressive Republican

and progressive Democratic Representatives in both Houses of Congress through his Chautauqua and other speaking campaigns and the roll call column in *La Follette's Magazine*. He thought the 1924 fight against the two old parties should be made through independent candidacies for the offices of President and Vice President. Bob had great hopes that his independent candidacy would lead to the fusing of the progressive elements in the different groups and parties and that this might later bring about the formation of a new party.[10]

When Bob, Jr., left Washington, on July 3, to attend the C.P.P.A. Convention in Cleveland, he took with him a document which his father wished him to read to the delegates. It was subsequently widely distributed in booklet form under the title "Statement and Platform of Robert M. La Follette Independent Candidate for President of The United States." The opening speech of the convention was made on the morning of July 4 by Chairman William H. Johnston, president of the International Association of Machinists. In a brief talk Edward Keating asked for contributions. Straw hats were passed, and the collection netted over $2,300, enough to defray the expenses of the convention. The *New York Times* reported that more than a thousand delegates were present and that about nine thousand others attended the opening session.[11] Many of the delegates represented different organizations. Among these were the Railroad Brotherhoods, various labor, farm, and cooperative groups, some church organizations, the Association for the Advancement of Colored People, the Committee of Forty-eight, progressive Republicans and Democrats from Wisconsin and other States, and representatives of various women's organizations who were participating for the first time as voters in a national election throughout the United States. Political clubs of some colleges had sent accredited delegates, and there were undergraduates from Columbia University, Barnard, Dartmouth, Harvard, Vassar, Yale, and Union Theological Seminary. The credentials committee had scrutinized the delegates so carefully that the roll call was delayed for a day.[12] No known Communists were admitted, and those who had been conspicuously identified with the recent St. Paul convention were rigorously excluded. But outside the hall representatives of William Z. Foster's Communist forces denounced the meeting "as the worst reactionary political convention held that year."[13]

The convention was held in the same auditorium where the Republicans had recently nominated Coolidge. Many newspaper correspondents contrasted the two meetings. Nearly all noted the amazing fact that a band had not been hired, and commented on the spontaneous enthusiasm in response to the speeches. The *New York Herald Tribune* observed how young the delegates were, estimating that the majority were under forty.[14] In a dispatch to the New York *Evening Post*, Clinton Gilbert said, "There is little organization and no machine, but there is a sort of self-imposed discipline."[15] The special correspondent for the *New York Times* thought "a more complete cross section of American life was never assembled in one hall," and said that "One of the striking aspects of the gathering and its demonstrations was the fact that there was no artificial staging of the demonstrations. None of them lasted more than two or three minutes, but they came one right after the other, at every mention of Mr. La Follette and the principles for which he stands."[16]

Among those on the floor of the auditorium were Bob's two sons. Shortly before five o'clock Bob, Jr., went to the speakers' stand. The audience rose and cheered when Chairman Johnston introduced him as "a chip off the old block." As Bob, Jr., read his father's statement and platform, a reporter thought he "lived up to the picture. He had his father's mannerisms—the wave of the hand, the nod of the head and the smile. Again and again the reading of the message was interrupted by the wild applause of more than a thousand delegates and the many other thousands who were in the galleries."[17]

In "a strong, earnest voice" Bob, Jr., read his father's statement containing his analysis of the issues of the 1924 campaign, the announcement that he was a candidate, and the program he intended to put into effect if elected. After analyzing the specific issues on which both old parties had failed to represent the best interests of all classes of the American people, Bob declared in this document: "I stand for an honest realignment in American politics, confident that the people in November will take such action as will insure the creation of a new party in which all Progressives may unite. I would not, however, accept a nomination or an election to the Presidency if doing so meant for Progressive Senators and Representatives and Progressive state governments, the defeat which would inevitably result from the placing of complete third party tickets in the field at the present time. . . . Permanent political parties have been born in this country after, and not before national campaigns, and they have come from the people, not from the proclamations of individual leaders. . . . If the hour is at hand for the birth of a new political party, the American people next November will register their will and their united purpose by a vote of such magnitude that a new political party will be inevitable. . . . I shall submit my name as an Independent Progressive candidate for President, together with the names of duly qualified candidates for electors, for filing on the ballots in every state in the Union. My appeal will be addressed to every class of the people in every section of the country. I am a candidate upon the basis of my public record as a member of the House of Representatives, as Governor of Wisconsin, and as a member of the United States Senate. I shall stand upon that record exactly as it is written, and shall give my support only to such progressive principles as are in harmony with it."[18]

When Bob, Jr., "concluded the reading of his father's message, delegates on the floor and the visitors in the galleries jumped to their feet in a sincere and enthusiastic tribute to the one man they are ready to follow. And Senator La Follette came very near being nominated by acclamation twenty-four hours in advance of the time set for the ceremony."[19] During the night recess, a bitter contest developed in the organization committee. The Socialist delegates, Morris Hillquit and Victor Berger, insisted that a national third party be formed immediately with a complete ticket. They refused to yield until Bob, Jr., was sent for and told them definitely that his father would run as an independent but would not become the candidate of a third party with complete tickets in the field at this time.[20]

The next day Bob's candidacy was endorsed by acclamation. A reporter who watched the demonstration said, "There was no camouflage; no artificiality about it."[21] Bob's brief platform of a thousand words was read by Herman Ekern, and unanimously adopted. The National Committee was authorized to cooperate with the La Follette For President Committee in naming a candidate for Vice President. It was also directed to take charge of the campaign and, if the November election results warranted, to call a convention in early 1925 for the formal launching of a new party.[22]

During the two days of the conference speeches were made by a number of delegates. Senator Frazier explained that the farmers were not present in greater numbers because "they were broke and couldn't pay railroad fare." Morris Hillquit spoke for the Socialists. Mabel C. Costigan presented a program of legislation the women hoped to achieve under progressive leadership; Harriot Stanton Blatch recalled Bob's early support of woman suffrage when it was unpopular; George Lefkovitch, head of the Farmer-Labor Party, pledged his group's support; William Pickens, a Yale graduate, who was one of the Negro delegates, declared the group he represented had been deceived by both old parties and were ready for independent action. Special tributes were paid by the poet Edwin Markham, Senator Shipstead, Representative John M. Nelson, Andrew Furuseth, president of the Seamen's Union, and W. T. Rawleigh. Fiorello La Guardia, then a Republican member of Congress from New York, won cheers by his epigram, "I would rather be right than regular."[23]

Bob, Jr., and Phil were deeply moved by Peter Witt, a disciple of Tom Johnson's, who said in closing his eloquent speech: "I have not much faith in political parties, but the hope lies in what happened yesterday. . . . For forty years Robert M. La Follette has stood four-square to all the winds that blow . . . And it has been the inspiration of a great woman . . . that made Bob La Follette possible. With her help, this man has faced the withering flame of persecution, the cruel lash of slander, and he has stood like a lion, the captain of his own soul, fighting for a better chance for the children yet to come."[24]

Bob made no statement to the press. The day after his nomination Belle wrote Elizabeth Evans that he "was deeply gratified and ready to accept the responsibility of launching the movement. So far his health has not suffered from the added strain. He has gained in strength right along."[25] Previously Gilbert Roe had written Bob, "If it is possible to secure harmonious action of all the forces which desire to support you, your election is quite possible, indeed probable but at all events you will have brought into existence a political party which would advance the policies you labored so hard for long after you and all the rest of us have passed out of the picture."[26] This word from his most intimate friend expressed his own hope. After John W. Davis and Charles Bryan were finally chosen on the 103rd ballot, Belle wrote Phil that his father thought "everything happened about as well as could be over in New York."[27]

The Socialist Party Convention formally endorsed Bob on July 7. Debs had advised this unusual course, and later wrote the New York Socialist leaders that while not fully in accord with the Convention of the Conference For Progressive Political Action, the party need not blush for supporting La Follette, who "all his life had stood up like a man for the right according to his light; he has been shamefully maligned, ostracized and persecuted by the predatory powers of the plutocracy yet his bitterest foe had never dared to question his personal integrity or his political rectitude."[28]

Rumors had been prevalent that a progressive Democrat would be selected as the Vice Presidential candidate to run with Bob. Numerous names had been suggested. Bob's initial hope had been that Justice Louis D. Brandeis might accept the nomination. Bob had never personally discussed it with him, but he had requested Gilson Gardner to call upon Brandeis at his summer home in Chatham to inquire whether or not he would accept. Brandeis refused. Alice Brandeis wrote Belle that "Mr. Gardner will have brought you Louis' decision. My great—indeed only regret is that Louis should not be standing shoulder to shoulder with Bob in the fight. But he will help, I feel sure in his own way when the opportunity offers. It is a thrilling & great moment & full of hope. You both will meet it with all the strength, devotion & courage that is in you and 'it will help build the future' for a darkened & discouraged world. With unfailing love from us both, Alice."[29]

Belle's reaction to this decision was expressed in a letter to Elizabeth Evans. "This campaign is such a tremendous undertaking and all our resources appeared so puny relatively that I could not see how we could cope with it further than to get the names on the ballots in all the states and see what would happen. They are encouraged to believe, however that they will have quite a respectable campaign fund. It is beautiful—the way many are eager to help. Some of those in charge say things are moving *too well*.

They fear they will reach the peak too early. This optimism and the widespread appeal to have Louis' name on the ballot seemed to justify at least putting the matter before him[.] It would have been a great adventure but it could hardly be expected that Louis would make it. With Bob it is the logic of his life[.] With Louis it would be stepping into a new field. Even if playing the game made him President it might not be worth while."[30] Later Alice Brandeis came out for Bob, and wrote an article supporting his record and policy on foreign affairs.[31]

A week after the Democratic Convention had nominated Davis, the press reported that Senator Burton K. Wheeler had declared that "when the Democratic party goes to Wall Street for its candidate I must refuse to go with it."[32] Bob first met Wheeler in December, 1922, when the young Democratic Senator-elect came to Washington to attend the Progressive Conference. Bob had previously known of Wheeler's courageous record in the legislature and as United States District Attorney in Montana. At their first meeting he had been drawn to the young man, and for two years they had cooperated on legislation in the Senate. It was upon Bob's unusual motion from the floor to elect a special committee to investigate Attorney General Daugherty and corruption in the Department of Justice that Wheeler became a member of this committee. Bob thought Wheeler had displayed great ability and absolute fearlessness in the conduct of the investigation. From the beginning of the inquiry Wheeler had been subjected to espionage, personal vilification, and open and secret threats against his life. Wheeler acccepted and was promptly endorsed by the Executive Committee. His letter of acceptance included a blistering attack on both old parties.[33]

After the Cleveland convention pledges of support came to Bob from many sections of the country. Among the groups that were organized was the Committee of One Hundred, of which Oswald Garrison Villard was chairman. This committee was composed of prominent men and women previously identified with various bipartisan or nonpartisan civic reform movements in New York City. They pledged their support in a telegram to Bob saying: "Without this action of yours millions of your fellow citizens would have been compelled to abstain from the polls or to choose once more between two corrupt and decadent political parties now separated by no distinction of principle whatsoever . . . We believe that the time has come for a new deal . . . to put an end to the period of black reaction of wholesale corruption leading into the cabinet room itself of the sale of governmental favors and of administration in the interests of the privileged classes. We are profoundly moved by your willingness to lead in that great struggle."[34]

His election was urged by five thousand clergymen of various denominations East and West,[35] as well as two hundred educators, for "having stood consistently for public weal against special privilege."[36] Among these was Professor John Dewey, who said in a statement: "Senator La Follette is the outstanding figure in American public life who applies the thoroughly scientific method to public problems. He never proceeds with regard to any issue until he has made himself master of the situation. He digs to the bottom of it and gets all the facts. He never appears in action without all the information and statistics that are to be had. That is what makes his proposals realistic and sound."[37] Among the many individual endorsements that Bob received from people he had never known personally was a long letter from Helen Keller saying that for years she had followed his public efforts "with approval and admiration." She wrote, "I am for you because you have held fast to the three elements of human liberty, free speech, a free press and freedom of assemblage. . . . You stand for an enlightened world policy, for international cooperation and amity."[38]

An organization was formed of more than seventy women from different parts of the United States under the chairmanship of Mrs. Mabel Costigan. The Executive Committee of sixteen included: Jane Addams, Alice Stone Blackwell, Harriot Stanton Blatch, Mary Dreier, Zona Gale, Mrs. Norman Hapgood, Elizabeth G. Evans, Florence Kelley, Mrs. William Kent, Freda Kirchwey, Mrs. Fremont Older, Rose Schneiderman, Ellen Scripps, and Bertha Poole Weyl. An article by Zoe Beckley listed many women in the organization with brief quotations summarizing their reasons for supporting La Follette.[39]

The press gave wide publicity to the unusual action of the Executive Committee of the American Federation of Labor in endorsing the independent candidacies of La Follette and Wheeler. The committee stated that this unique exception to its previous policy was due to the fact that "Mr. La Follette and Mr. Wheeler have throughout their whole political careers stood steadfast in the defense of the rights and interest of the wage-earners and farmers."[40] The New York *World* commented that "It is not claimed that the Federation support will deliver the labor vote solidly, but it makes possible for the [La Follette] leaders to go ahead with their annealing process as between farmer and labor strength."[41] Later, when the A.F. of L. issued a nation-wide appeal to trade unions for needed funds, the *New York Herald Tribune* noted that "in no preceding campaign in the history of the country had there been a parallel to this call to arms by the American Federation Leadership."[42] The Railroad Brotherhoods' official publication *Labor*, edited by Edward Keating, subsequently issued a "victory edition" of 2,500,000, which was sent out in behalf of La Follette and Wheeler.[43]

The Scripps-Howard newspapers endorsed Bob. Through their NEA news service they also syndicated a series of short articles which Bob assisted Lowell Mellett in preparing. These articles were based upon *La Follette's Autobiography* up to 1912, and included brief summaries of his record during the ensuing years.[44]

In the 1924 campaign Bob followed the same nonpartisan policy he had previously maintained in his personal endorsements of candidates for Congress. Furthermore, these did not depend upon their attitude toward his own Presidential candidacy. He supported the men he believed would strengthen the progressive position on legislation in the next sessions of Congress. Among the candidates he endorsed for the Senate were Frazier, Ladd, Shipstead, Brookhart, Floyd Olson, Couzens, David Walsh of Massachusetts, and Thomas J. Walsh of Montana. When Borah was renominated by the state convention in Idaho, his campaign manager appealed to Bob because he feared an independent candidate might enter the contest and defeat Borah. To prevent this three-cornered contest, Bob sent a telegram for publication saying, "Although Senator Borah and I have not always agreed upon issues he is outstanding progressive figure and should receive the wholehearted support of Progressives in Idaho."[45] The Idaho Progressives nominated him on their ticket. Commenting on this support Borah said, "I have no words adequate to express my appreciation, my deep sense of obligation, for this expression of commendation and confidence." Later the press reported that Borah had endorsed

Coolidge and stated he would fight for progressive principles "inside the party."[46] When Bob learned that Norris was hesitating about being a candidate for reelection, he urged him to run. Norris finally changed his mind and entered the Republican primary. Bob then sent messages to Nebraska saying that Norris' reelection to the Senate was of paramount importance regardless of his attitude toward the La Follette-Wheeler Presidential candidacies. Norris refused to endorse the Coolidge-Dawes ticket and announced he would continue to pursue an independent course if reelected. Borah and Norris were both returned to the Senate. Bob's intervention had helped in avoiding a split in the progressive forces similar to that which had defeated Senator Bristow by a narrow margin.

While Phil was still out on an organizing trip, Bob wrote Wheeler saying: "My son Phil has just been through South Dakota, Montana, Idaho, and Washington, and today is in Colorado. In each of the states he has visited, he has secured a very fine agreement. . . . These arrangements have been made on the basis that the *state* manager in charge of our campaign shall not take part in state, local or congressional candidacies. Phil made it very clear that he could not speak for you or for me, but did guarantee that the state managers would not get mixed up in any local fights. I think this is sound and must be the policy adopted everywhere."[47]

The La Follette-Wheeler platform had made no specific declaration regarding Prohibition or the Ku Klux Klan. A prominent prohibitionist, Clarence True Wilson, had assailed Bob as "the only wet candidate" for the Presidency. Bob himself had stated in an open letter to Mrs. Edward Costigan that as long as the Volstead Act remained upon the statute books "it should be enforced for rich and poor alike, without hypocrisy or favoritism."[48] The Klan had been active in many Western and Southern States. Whether or not it should be condemned by name had been an issue in the Democratic Convention. As the Klan was bitterly opposing the Catholic Church and had a large membership among farmer and labor groups, the question was considered political dynamite. On August 6 Robert P. Scripps requested Bob to state his position.[49] In an answer written for publication, Bob denounced the masked order. "Anyone familiar with my record, especially in my own state, knows I have always stood without reservation against any discrimination between races, classes and creeds. I hold that every citizen is entitled to the full exercise of his constitutional rights. I am unalterably opposed to the evident purposes of the secret organization known as the Ku Klux Klan, as disclosed by its public acts. . . . It has within its own body the seeds of its death."[50]

Bob was also urged to make a statement on the race question to assure support of the Negro voters. When Charles Ervin brought this suggestion to him at his office, he indignantly answered: "I have no right to make pledges to the colored man which I know if elected I could not carry out. And I must assume when I make a pledge that I expect to be elected." Ervin recalls that Bob then took from his bookcase a volume containing his speech made in the House in 1889 during a debate on whether a Negro named Smalls had been elected Representative from a South Carolina district.[51] It was a plea for fair treatment for the Negro. "Here," Bob said, "are my sentiments with regard to the race question. This was made when I had no idea of ever running for the office of President. . . . Just as I stood then, I stand now. But I will make no new statement on this issue just to get votes."[52]

The Republicans soon recognized that their greatest menace lay in the ticket headed by La Follette and Wheeler, which endangered their hold on the Western States. The aggressive campaign waged against Bob soon descended to personal abuse. It included many phases, from charges of anti-Semitism by Louis Marshall[53] to that of his being an "infidel."[54] After Bob repudiated the Klan, the Imperial Wizard declared the Klan neutral between Coolidge and Davis, but said it would throw its strength against La Follette, "the arch enemy of the nation."[55] It was also reported that the Klan tried to intimidate La Follette supporters by threatening and blacklisting those who were subscribers to *La Follette's Magazine*.[56] Governor Stokes of New Jersey warned that La Follette's "lack of loyalty and his utterances during the war should not be forgotten."[57] Senator Smoot, who praised Coolidge and Davis as "worthy nominees," expressed his "unbounded faith" that the American people would not give power "to the man who should have been in the penitentiary for his actions and utterances during the war."[58] Fifty-three of Theodore Roosevelt's followers, some of whom had never forgiven Bob for his refusal to support the colonel in 1912, also joined in denouncing La Follette by saying his candidacy was "based on radicalism" and quoting Roosevelt's statement that he was "a most sinister enemy of democracy." Among those who signed were James R. Garfield, Frank Knox, Raymond Robins, E. A. Van Valkenburg, and Chester Rowell.[59] This attack was immediately repudiated by La Guardia, Wheeler, Harold Ickes, Gilson Gardner, and Roe. And later forty-two former Roosevelt supporters signed a public statement endorsing La Follette and Wheeler.[60] Among these were Jane Addams, Francis J. Heney, Mr. and Mrs. Fremont Older, Amos Pinchot, and George L. Record.[61]

Added to the personal attacks made by the Theodore Roosevelt group were those of the resentful Klan, Communist William Z. Foster, Presidential candidate of the Workers Party, and a series of over one hundred speeches by the Republican Vice Presidential candidate, Charles Dawes, in a tour of the country extending over fifteen thousand miles. In his acceptance speech at Evanston the Chicago banker struck the note he harped upon throughout the campaign. He described La Follette as "leading an army of extreme radicalism. . . . massed behind an aggressive personality, a heterogeneous collection of those opposing the existing order of things, the greatest section of which, the socialists, flies the red flag."[62] Other speakers and the hostile Republican newspapers followed Dawes' lead in attacking Bob, whom he later described as "this master demagogue."[63] The slogan "Coolidge or Chaos" became the Republican chant.

Late in August Belle wrote her friend Elizabeth Evans that Lincoln Steffens had said the "American people may feel the impulse to support Bob. But the least little thing will stampede them. Some banker will pass the word that a vote for La Follette will be a vote wasted and they will chuck Bob and vote for Coolidge. Perhaps they are just feeling the *impulse* now and will be stampeded before election."[64]

But while headlines were being made in newspapers and encouraging personal responses were coming to Bob, the problems of launching a campaign for an independent Presidential candidate that confronted the men and women of the various La Follette-Wheeler headquarters would have overwhelmed less dedicated volunteer workers. The actual campaign machinery had to be formulated, a working staff set up, speakers found and routed, meetings advertised, publicity and press releases prepared, regional control over radio and motion pictures established, funds raised to meet all expenses, differing state election laws searched for and interpreted. In selecting "key men" political experience often had to be sacrificed in favor of loyalty.

Bob, Jr., pictured the immediate situation that confronted the campaign managers, which the old established parties did not have to meet: "No party positions on the forty-eight Presidential ballots were awaiting the simple process of selection of electors through party committees or platform conventions. Instead there were forty-eight different provisions for independent or new party electors, each one designed to make the process of obtaining a place for an independent ticket difficult if not impossible."[65] In some States it was necessary to get court decisions or rulings from attorney generals.[66]

These were only a few of the many problems that harassed Congressman John M. Nelson as national campaign manager of headquarters in Chicago, Donald Richberg, a member of the Executive Committee and legal advisor; Gilbert Roe, regional director in the East; and Rudolph Spreckels, Western regional director. They kept in touch with Bob, Jr., the national vice chairman, who constantly consulted with his father in Washington.

"Almost before we could open our headquarters in Chicago," Bob Jr., related, "the filing date in Nevada loomed upon us. Ten percent, or three thousand signatures, were required to place our ticket on the ballot. Not even the name of a man to write to in the State was in our possession. We wired to Rudolph Spreckels in California, and seven days before the last day of filing his representatives arrived in Reno. On the fourth day with the able assistance of volunteer workers he had secured four thousand signatures and on the seventh day he had secured six thousand eight hundred, or in round figures, one-fifth of the voters in that sparsely settled state."[67]

Attempts were made to intimidate progressive voters and also to deceive them by the misuse of the La Follette name and the progressive designation on the ballot. In some States unfriendly election officials delayed court appeals to prevent the La Follette-Wheeler electors from getting on the ticket. In California, for example, the law regarding placing independent electors on the ballot was so ambiguously worded that the question early arose whether the courts would allow the La Follette-Wheeler electors a place in the inde-

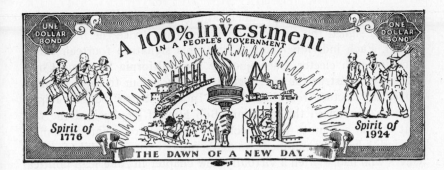

ONE DOLLAR BOND

A 100% Investment
IN A PEOPLE'S GOVERNMENT

Spirit of 1776

Spirit of 1924

THE DAWN OF A NEW DAY

ONE DOLLAR BOND

HON. W. T. RAWLEIGH, Chairman
MANUFACTURER,
FREEPORT, ILL.

DANTE M. PIERCE, Vice Chairman
PUBLISHER, PIERCE'S FARM WEEKLIES,
DES MOINES, IOWA

JULIUS KESPOHL,
MERCHANT,
QUINCY, ILL.

DONALD RICHBERG,
ATTORNEY AT LAW,
CHICAGO, ILL.

R. F. KOENIG, Treasurer,
DIRECTOR SECOND NAT'L BANK
FREEPORT, ILL.

"The Will of the People Shall be the Law of the Land"

LA FOLLETTE
FOR PRESIDENT
COMMITTEE

HEADQUARTERS
AUDITORIUM HOTEL
CHICAGO, ILL.

ALAN BOGUE
ATTORNEY AT LAW
PARKER, S. D.

MISS ZONA GALE,
AUTHOR,
PORTAGE, WIS.

JAMES H. McGILL,
MANUFACTURER
VALPARAISO, IND.

HARRY SAUTHOFF,
Secretary

August 30, 1924.

Hon. Robert M. LaFollette,
Senate Office Building,
Washington, D. C.

My Dear Senator:-

    The Illinois State LaFollette-Wheeler Campaign Committee, as a method of raising finances in this state, has devised a bond issue which will be known as "Emancipation Bonds". These bonds are in denominations of $1.00 and $5.00 for sale to individuals, and in larger denominations up to $1,000.00 for lodges and large contributors.

    We have just received the first consignment from the printer this morning and I have the honor to present to you, with the compliments of the Illinois State Committee, Bond No. 1, Series A.

    We are convinced that this will prove the most satisfactory method of raising money in this state. Our forces are being organized to intelligently and systematically handle their sale, and I am convinced that the Progressive people of this state will make large investments in Emancipation Bonds during the next sixty days.

Sincerely yours,

State Chairman.

CJM-FB

"The Supreme Issue Is the Encroachment of the Powerful Few upon the Rights of the Many" pendent column. Although uncertain as to the court ruling, fifty thousand signed the petitions on Labor Day, twice the number required. Each individual had to write his signature fourteen times, once for each elector. Subsequently the California Supreme Court refused to construe the law liberally and by a four to three decision barred the electors from the ballot as Independents.[68] Senator Hiram Johnson denounced this decision. Bob himself emphasized the fact that it was a four to three decision, and declared that "one man, one individual, has nullified the deliberately expressed will of 50,000 voters who had written a virtually new chapter in American political initiative . . ."[69]

The California Socialists promptly offered their ballot as a refuge. The offer was accepted, although Rudolph Spreckels, Western regional director, and other leading La Follette supporters thought the decision unwise.[70] The Republicans made effective use of the fact in their charges of La Follette's "radicalism." In many other States the Socialists rendered valuable assistance through their experienced workers in helping to get the signatures required by law to place electors for independent Presidential candidates on the ballots.

Financing the campaign was a constant problem. The contributions from the labor unions fell far below expectations. The major part of the financial support came from individuals in small sums, mainly dollar bills. For these each contributor received a bronze campaign button bearing in relief the heads of La Follette and Wheeler, designed by Gutzon Borglum. A plan of selling bonds, known as "Emancipation Bonds," was devised. Frequently small admission charges to campaign meetings were made, and collections were always taken. Such funds as the national and state headquarters had grew slowly, and the situation was frequently desperate. Devoted campaign workers dug into their own pockets time and time again. At great personal sacrifice Gilbert Roe gave his entire time to the campaign, temporarily abandoning his law office except for instructions to his secretary. In late August Belle summed up the situation when she wrote Phil, "They are tragically short of help and the finances are harassing everyone."[71]

Notwithstanding all these complications, in less than two months the La Follette-Wheeler electoral tickets were placed on the ballot in practically all the States. In relating this, Bob, Jr., commented that "an organization constructed over night was able with the help of volunteer workers in every state to accomplish the feat which experienced politicians said was impossible."[72] Belle wrote Phil that his father was "glad of his opportunity and keeps it uppermost in his mind. Whatever the obstacles and difficulties he will say 'I never would have believed we could accomplish so much.' "[73]

In September Bob shared in pioneering with the new "moving pictures that talked," briefly stating his position as a Presidential candidate. Similar films were made of Coolidge and of Davis by the De Forest Phonofilm. These three pictures were released in one program that was shown throughout the country. This was the first time that the voices and moving pictures of rival candidates had ever been shown together.[74]

For some time Bob had been much interested in the potentialities of radio as a medium for presenting public issues to the voters, and he wished to try it in this campaign. Although the initial outlay of $3,500 for the telephone service on a single speech seemed a heavy tax on their meager funds, Bob finally decided to open his campaign with a radio address. Broadcasting of speeches at meetings was not a novelty in 1924. But Bob's speech was the first political address ever delivered exclusively over the radio without a visible audience. It was thus "a unique experiment in American politics."[75] Aware of its importance, Bob carefully rehearsed his reading. While he sat alone at the microphone in the stuffy padded studio, Bob, Jr., stood by the loudspeaker outside and with prearranged signals, which could be seen through the glass panels, indicated how the voice was coming over.

On one of the hottest afternoons of a typical Washington summer, Bob spoke for thirty-five minutes to a Labor Day audience throughout the country, estimated at several millions, since receivers were set up at large public meetings. In a rapid survey of the various abuses he had persistently attacked, Bob pledged himself to be guided by but one purpose in this campaign: to tell the American people exactly what had been going on in Washington during the eighteen years of his Senate service. He outlined briefly what he would do if elected. In closing he said: "Our faith is in democracy. Upon that faith we enter this contest, ready to meet falsehood with truth, to confront the claims of privilege with the demands of justice, to restore the government to the American people and to establish economic freedom throughout the land."[76]

Bob commented later that his radio talk had been a far cry from his "first political speech back in the eighties to a very sparse crowd at Sun Prairie, as a candidate for District Attorney of Dane County" and that if he had then predicted he would see the time when he could speak to them from Washington, without using a wire, "They would have had me locked up." It naturally seemed strange to one used to handling an audience: "But after a moment or two I could see that audience just as well as any I ever addressed before in my life. . . . I thought of friends in Wisconsin who I knew would be listening, and farmers out in the Northwest and laboring men attending their picnics and Labor Day meetings." And he added with a chuckle, "Of course I do not flatter myself that the whole country paused while I delivered that speech; but I will say that I never had a more respectful hearing or fewer interruptions."[77]

CHAPTER LXXI

Bob's 1924 Presidential Campaign

Bob left Washington with Bob, Jr., on September 18, to open his speaking campaign at Madison Square Garden in New York City. Before he appeared that night, short speeches had been made by Harriot Stanton Blatch, Fiorello La Guardia, Norman Thomas, the Socialist candidate for governor, and Matthew Woll, vice president of the A.F. of L. Bob, Gilbert and Netha Roe, Bob, Jr., and George Middleton drove to Madison Square Garden together, arriving shortly before it was time for him to speak. Bob was escorted to the main door by the reception committee and entered the vast auditorium while John Haynes Holmes was still speaking. A reporter noted that as Bob walked briskly toward the platform, he was "wildly greeted" by a crowd that was said to be "one of the largest that had ever attended a political gathering in the Garden."[1]

The cheering continued for ten minutes, and after Bob was introduced by Arthur Garfield Hays, the state chairman, it continued for another five minutes until Bob finally checked it by pointing repeatedly to his watch and the microphone. Because a speaker had to keep directly in front of the instrument, and Bob was known to have a propensity for moving about the platform, an enclosing rail had been built about it within which he was told he "must stay." This was the first time Bob had ever been placed under the rigid mechanical limitations of reading a speech from manuscript to "visible and invisible audiences" at the same time. It was estimated that seven thousand heard him through amplifiers in the park outside. Among those who listened from different parts of the country was his daughter Fola, who wrote him from Nantucket Island: "It is amazing the way your voice registers on the radio. I had the sense of space being absolutely an[ni]hilated, and much of the time I could not realize that you were not actually inside the machine from which the voice came."[2]

The press reported that the audience "cheered the Wisconsin Senator to the echo" as he presented the progressive program.[3] He gave a reasoned discussion of the gradual encroachment of the Supreme Court's power upon the Constitution and the sovereignty of the people by declaring the Acts of Congress unconstitutional, as in the recent Child Labor legislation. To halt this usurpation of power he proposed that by a constitutional amendment Congress be granted the power to override a Supreme Court decision that a law was unconstitutional by again passing that law. His New York audience received this proposal with the same enthusiasm that had greeted it when Bob first presented it to the A.F. of L. Convention in Cincinnati on June 14, 1922. The New York *World* described it as "a vigorous speech, full of fighting language and conceived with the flair of controversial utterance which is characteristic of La Follette."[4] The *New York Times* reported that "about half of the audience had paid admission fees ranging from $2.50 to 55 cents. Of the 14,000 seats some 7,000 had been placed on sale while the others were free." An aggregate of between $12,000 and $13,000 was thus contributed toward the progressive campaign fund and the expenses of this meeting which included payment of $1,295 for the radio broadcast.[5]

On Sunday, September 21, Bob again came to New York with Bob, Jr., for another meeting. From the center of the city he rode in an automobile "escorted by a motor cycle squad with screeching horns" which "whisked him at full speed through halted traffic, to the awaiting thousands at the Yankee Stadium."[6] As guest of the Steuben Society he was driven around the ball field and "received an enthusiastic reception from the audience, which numbered about 18,000." In accord with the tradition of their meetings, impressive group chorals by a thousand members of the German singing societies honored him. In his address Bob emphasized the important contribution that the American citizens of German heritage had made to the development of the United States, and praised their loyal support of the country during the war, when under stress of the prevailing hysteria many had suffered "heart-breaking humiliation."[7]

After a visit the next day to the New York headquarters, 25 West

43rd Street, to greet nearly one hundred men and women volunteer workers, Bob returned to Washington to prepare for his speaking trip. This was scheduled to begin early in October and to cover twenty States. The progressive campaign was already proceeding, along the lines previously indicated, with color and enthusiasm in spite of handicaps. Press releases,[8] prepared largely by Ernest Gruening, director of publicity, were being widely distributed from Washington Headquarters, where Bob, Jr., was in charge. Senator Wheeler had already started on a nationwide tour which in thirty days was to take him to twenty cities in fourteen States.[9]

On September 28 Belle spoke at Mountain Lake Park, Maryland, before beginning an extensive tour which Gilbert Roe had arranged in New York, New Jersey, Pennsylvania, and Connecticut.[10] As she was the first woman who had ever taken the stump for her husband's Presidential candidacy, this meeting was widely reported. "I am not going to talk technical politics," she said. "I am going to talk to you neighbor to neighbor, friend to friend. I want especially to speak to you women . . . to talk things over with you, get your views, answer your questions and see if we can't mutually understand and agree."[11] A few days later "the distaff side of the La Follette party" addressed a capacity meeting in Town Hall, New York, at which Harriot Stanton Blatch presided. Belle received "an enthusiastic reception." Again speaking intimately, she told of the long fight she and Bob had shared together. "He never advocates a reform that experience has not shown is needed. . . . In all these years his opponents have tried to frighten the people with the bugaboo that he was too radical, that his platform was a menace, and that something terrible would happen if he was elected again. But the people kept right on electing him." She admitted she was more radical and that he was "almost old fashioned in his worship of our institutions."[12]

Zoe Beckley, in a special Sunday article, wrote that "On the platform she looks taller than she really is. Her quiet, cultured speaking voice takes on a ringing tone that carries to the backmost rows. She uses much gesture and a smile of winning sweetness . . . and carries herself with grace and sprightliness. Her hair is graying blond, parted, waved and done in a simple knot behind. Her eyes are blue and kind and understanding, her features small, her mouth particularly attractive and there is a hint of dimple in her chin. . . . She and Senator La Follette look amazingly alike: people often speak of it. Mrs. La Follette laughs and says it is because they've lived so long together . . ."[13]

Upon Belle's return to Washington, she wrote: "Daddy seemed fine when he left last night. The doctors gave him a good bill of health."[14] Accompanying him, in his special car "Manhattan," which was hooked to the regular night train for Rochester, were a large group of newspaper men, Dr. John Colver, a throat specialist; Bob, Jr., and a few friends. These included Basil Manly and Frederic C. Howe, who prepared the groundwork for Bob's speeches, while Sam Evans handled the daily press releases from the car. A series of general topics had been mapped out and the material assembled, centering on one subject for each evening's address. After the draft for the speech was discussed, it was worked over with Bob, and the final mimeographs prepared for release, often just under the wire.

Mindful, however, of his St. Paul experience, Bob determined to prevent misquotation and to have, in addition, stenographic reports of what he actually said. These transcripts differ from the formal press releases given to local newspapers and the special writers traveling with him. The transcripts show his friendly give and take with his audiences, who always called him "Bob," his quick retorts and humor which colored his impromptu recollections of the places where he had so frequently spoken.[15]

The Baltimore *Sun* stated that when the train started out, there was not enough money in sight to "make certain a pilgrimage beyond St. Louis. This money is expected, but is not in hand now. The source from which it is expected is the masses to be met between here and St. Louis. Collections will go to the general fund and half to the local management."[16] A careful record has been preserved of the receipts of each meeting from admissions, collections, and bond sales.[17]

Bob "was given an ovation" when he arrived on the platform of Convention Hall in Rochester, New York, to interpret his platform and outline what he would recommend to Congress if elected President.[18] Bob, Jr., telegraphed his mother after the speech: "Biggest meeting ever held here. 4800 jammed the hall and filled the aisles. 3000 outside. Doors locked at seven thirty. Dad talked hour twenty minutes. Stood it well. He is in good spirits. Love."[19]

The next night Bob spoke in Scranton, Pennsylvania, where "three thousand people jammed the hall" and the police had to close the doors at seven forty-five. An overflow crowd of five hundred waited outside to hear him after his forty-minute speech to the main meeting.[20] It was here that Bob made his charges about a Republican "slush fund" which became one of the most widely reported issues of the campaign. Someone had sent him an original copy of a letter signed by Joseph R. Grundy, president of the Pennsylvania Manufacturers Association. This letter was addressed to "Citizens of Pennsylvania," and was being sent out by the Ways and Means Committee of the National Republican Committee of Pennsylvania. After informing his audience of these facts, Bob read the letter, dramatizing its contents by pausing to make ironic comments which repeatedly evoked laughter and applause. Frequently he reminded his listeners that the letter's scathing denunciations of his supporters referred to them. The audience listened intently as he read that Mr. Grundy had said: "We are confronted by the possibilities of a violent social and industrial revolution. We have in La Follette and Wheeler, a Lenine and Trotsky with a formidable band of followers made up of the vicious, ignorant and discontented element, openly organized for battle." Bob looked up from the letter, paused and, pointing to the audience, said: "Aren't you ashamed of yourselves? This means you. You are vicious, says Mr. Grundy. You are ignorant, says Mr. Grundy."[21]

Bob then read to his audience a recent *New York Times* special dispatch from Washington revealing how Republican campaign funds were to be collected and used. This dispatch reported that "Last week hurried conferences on the subject of finances as well as organization were held by the party leaders here and in New York. Chairman Butler conferred with E. T. Stotesbury, the Philadelphia partner of Morgan and Co., and plans were immediately set afoot in Pennsylvania by W. L. Mellon of Pittsburgh and Joseph R. Grundy of Philadelphia to raise $600,000 in that state for use elsewhere."[22] Bob pointed out that the Grundy letter combined with the *New York Times* dispatch gave the key to what would be done with a huge fund "to be collected in the Eastern States." According to press reports, Bob said that "auxiliary headquarters were to be opened in some city west of Chicago to direct the expenditure of this fund." Bob presented other letters and reports to the audience to support his declaration that Calvin Coolidge would be the beneficiary of this huge corruption fund to buy the election.

Then he read a telegram he had sent that day to Senator Borah, chairman of the Special Committee on Campaign Expenditures, demanding "immediate action to halt this outrageous conspiracy." Bob explained that this demand was based upon his own resolution calling for the creation of this committee which he had had the foresight to introduce in the Senate before Congress adjourned.[23]

When Borah had previously outlined the committee's work, he had stated "we do not contemplate holding hearings until late in the campaign unless there is a development of facts which would warrant such an undertaking."[24] Bob's telegram galvanized the committee into immediate action. Borah called the committee to meet in Chicago on October 15, and requested the chairman of each party's national committee to "report all facts touching upon campaign contributors, both as to contributions and amounts available to committee."[25]

Bob's speech at Scranton was reported on the front pages of leading newspapers throughout the country. The chairman of the Republican National Committee, William Butler, denied these "slushfund" charges, and questioned the source of the progressive funds. Bob promptly repeated his charges in a statement given out from Hoboken, where he was spending the day in the special car at the Lackawanna Yards, awaiting his evening meeting at Newark, New Jersey. After breakfast with Bob, Jr., Phil, Fola, and Mid, he made a series of action pictures for the Fox Movietone News.[26] That evening they all went with him to Laurel Gardens in Newark, where a capacity audience of some 2,300 people greeted him. The press reported that nearly all of them had "paid a dollar each," and it was estimated that 6,000 had tried to get into the hall but had to attend the overflow meeting in the open. When Bob went on the platform for his speech, he was received "with enthusiasm by a standing cheering audience."[27] He recalled the twenty-one speeches he had made in New Jersey in 1908 when he had "helped to retire" the reactionary Senator Dryden. After endorsing Chairman George L. Record, who was the progressive candidate for Senator, Bob attacked both old parties as "vest pocket" possessions of certain dominant economic interests.

By hard traveling Bob reached Michigan the next evening. The *Detroit News* reported that he had "one of the most enthusiastic political meetings in the history of Detroit."[28] It was "estimated nearly 7,500 heard the address at Arena Gardens, most of whom paid $1 for the opportunity, the supply of fifty-cent seats having been exhausted early. In addition a tin-plate collection is understood to have produced about $1,000."[29] Bob suggested that at least half the seats at all future meetings were to be free. Bob endorsed Senator Couzens, and spoke extemporaneously for half an hour before he took up his manuscript to analyze the power of monopoly and to renew his slush-fund charges. On October 10, at Music Hall in Cincinnati, he discussed secret diplomacy and the issue of ridding the world of the causes of war before a "tumultuous enthusiastic crowd."[30] He declared that he was "not an advocate of peace at any price" and that he would "repel the aggressive acts of any Power that attempted to seize our territory or imperil our national life or institutions.[31] Bob, Jr., wired his mother: "Largest meeting ever held in Cincinnati. Five thousand in hall. Five thousand outside heard speech through amplifiers. Spoke fifty-five minutes. In great form. Feeling fit now. Love"[32]

In Chicago they were met at the station "by a crowd of more than 4,000 shouting men and women who packed Michigan Avenue."[33] In an open car, with Bob, Jr., beside him "through streets manned with uncounted thousands of shouting partisans," Bob "led a parade that looked like a regal procession."[34] He stood acknowledging the cheers along the crowded boulevards en route to headquarters at the Morrison Hotel. After greeting the staff, he said, "I'm feeling fit as a fiddle, 69 years young, and have never had such a wonderful tour in my life."[35] That night, at the huge 35th Street Armory, an audience of 10,000 men and women greeted him "with extraordinary enthusiasm," while thousands more listened to the address on the outside.[36]

He was introduced by Jane Addams, head of Hull House, who had sat on the platform at his Chicago meeting on January 3, 1912. After thanking Miss Addams for her "more than gracious introduction to this audience," Bob spoke on the growth of "economic oligarchy," the concentration of wealth, and the abuse of financial power. He explained that he read from manuscript because his speech had to be furnished to the reporters in advance if the "dozen or fifteen Knights of the Press" traveling with him were to get it to the people. "They have been very gracious and exceedingly fair in presenting to the public what I have had to say. I know they will pardon me if I say that there was a time when my name was not permitted to appear in the public print. It was not the fault of the writers—the orders came from way back somewhere. But a new day has come. I am the spokesman not only for myself, but I speak for the millions of people who will cast their ballots on the 4th of November."[37]

Bob, Jr., wired his mother: "Chicago reception and parade great success. Meeting of eight thousand with three thousand outside hearing from amplifiers. Dad in great form. Talked one hour and five minutes. Great reception from crowd. Many visitors today but he stood it well . . . Hope your meetings good. Love"[38]

After Bob's Chicago meeting Frank Kent wired his Baltimore paper, which was supporting Davis, that "no such electric meeting as he held here last night would be possible for either of the two other candidates. Beyond compare, this flaming old man and his two attractive sons present the one dramatic, colorful spectacle of the campaign and the fight they make surpasses in ardor anything of which the others are capable."[39]

At the close of Bob's first week of strenuous campaigning, a number of the special correspondents who had traveled with Bob wrote evaluations of the trip for their home papers. John W. Owens reported to the Baltimore *Sun* that "The effect of last week's appearance after appearance before great cheering crowds far from wearing down the vitality of a man nearing 70 years, has been a tonic to him. After a week of sleeping cars, he is in better condition than any of the men of half his age who are with him. . . . The tour, taking it all in all, is a marvellous performance. This old man, charging entrenched enemies with the furious abandon of a romantic young cavalier, and the throngs of men and women massing in city after city to hear him, and gladly to give mites of money to aid him, what has there been in politics in years that is comparable?"[40]

To meet the difficult problem of financing the special car, Bob had asked his friend and former secretary John J. Hannan to join him in Chicago and take charge of raising the money for it during the remainder of the trip. When Hannan arrived, only $288.51 remained on hand, and the special car could not leave until he personally borrowed $600 to buy railroad tickets and pay other expenses.[41] Through his skillful management money was collected at the meetings to carry on from one city to the next. Hannan would go before the audiences and frankly say: "The National Committee is strapped. We are travelling on the country. We want to get to the next town."[42] And they got there somehow.

Bob adhered to a strict program. He attended no receptions or social affairs. He made few speeches from the rear platform of the car. During the morning he stayed in his "little box-stall" as he called it, working on his evening address. He did not go to the meeting until it was time for him to speak. After the appeal for funds, Phil, who was then twenty-seven, would talk to the enormous crowds until his father came. Sometimes after Bob arrived at the auditorium he would stand in the background, where the audience could not see him, listening to his son and insisting upon delaying his appearance because Phil was "going so well."[43] Phil also addressed the overflow meetings. A newspaper correspondent wrote that "in his campus garb of blue coat and grey flannel trousers, this blue-eyed, smiling chap looks hardly old enough to vote. But how he can talk."[44] When Phil was speaking in a nearby town, Bob, Jr., sometimes talked to the outside crowds, although he usually sat on the platform behind his father. Occasionally he would hand his father a brief note admonishing him to "Watch your time" or "Take it easy." As each had the gift of pantomime, there was frequently an amusing by-play between the two.

During the second week of the campaign it was estimated that in his five meetings Bob spoke to over 30,000 people, exclusive of his radio audiences. Before his Kansas City meeting at which Frank Walsh presided, Bob told of an hour's ride he had had with Senator "Jim" Reed, who "is just about the gamest fighter, for what he believes, that there is in public service today. . . . You may not always agree with a public servant, but, my friends, if he be fearless, if he be honest in his convictions you cannot afford to swap him for some spineless contriver with public affairs."[45] Bob discussed the plight of the farmers, resulting from the rise of trusts, high tariffs, and control of the railroads by the dominant banking groups through their interlocking directorates. Hannan reported "meeting enthusiastic."[46]

His audience included a radio hook-up covering Oklahoma, Kansas, and Missouri. When some one shouted to him to speak louder, Bob replied: "Well, my friend, it is a question between you and this radio . . . I have been advised . . . that if I bellow too loudly the radio doesn't get it . . . I have got to shoot right at this thing. What I like when I am speaking to an audience is freedom; I like the freedom of the stage; I like the freedom that comes from not being tied down to a miserable manuscript."[47] He could, in fact, never get used to sticking close to the "mike." Once his radio hearers were startled to hear him say, "I wish I had some straps to put my feet in."

In St. Louis, on October 14, the day started with a parade. In the evening, before an audience of 10,000, Bob discussed foreign relations and how great financial interests had brought about a change in American foreign policy, as it had been defined by Washington and Jefferson. He told his audience that a great St. Louis newspaper was broadcasting this address but that his speech in Des Moines the next day would not be broadcast because the Bankers Life Insurance Company which owned the station had refused him "the right accorded to others in like position."[48]

In Iowa the next day Bob was on familiar ground. Along the way farmers gathered at the little country stations to greet him. When the train stopped to pick up Senator Brookhart, Bob made one of his few speeches from the rear platform of the car. Crowds met him at the station in Des Moines, where he spoke that evening, before 9,000 people, on the deflation of the farmers. The press reported that this was the largest gathering that had ever attended a political meeting in this city.[49] Bob recalled his many visits to Iowa in "campaign after campaign, Chautauqua season after Chautauqua season, in almost every hamlet, village and city." He endorsed Brookhart, and expressed his deep affection for Senator Jonathan Dolliver, who had campaigned for him in Wisconsin in 1910, when Bob was ill, and for James M. Pierce, publisher of the Iowa *Homestead*.[50]

At Minneapolis the next evening Bob spoke to a capacity audience which overflowed into another large meeting outside. John F. Sinclair presided. Brief speeches were made by Floyd B. Olson and Senator Magnus Johnson before Bob was introduced by John Lind, a former Democratic governor of Minnesota who was supporting Bob. In presenting him Lind said: "It gives me great pleasure to introduce an old friend of mine. I challenge any man to put a finger on a single spot in the record of this man which doesn't become an

American citizen."[51] During his speech Bob read his famous roll call on Coolidge's record before and after he became President. He did this in answer to a recent assertion by Secretary of State Hughes that "the issue of this campaign is the election of Calvin Coolidge." Bob declared that the "supreme issue is to break the control of the Private Monopoly System over the Government."[52]

A letter from Mrs. Lorena K. Fairbank to her sister, Netha Roe, tells of calling on Bob in his special car the next evening before his meeting in Sioux Falls, South Dakota. From the time Bob arrived the car had been standing in the railroad yards beneath a blazing sun. Mrs. Fairbank wrote: "It was a very hot night and he was having his supper alone in his compartment in his shirt and suspenders and looked so frazzled that I couldn't believe he was equal to the speech which was two hours later. But he seemed a different person on the platform."[53] On this hot night 5,000 people had crowded into the city coliseum, leaving a thousand or more outside.[54]

The *Sioux Falls Press* reported that "This audience had travelled from far and near to see Robert M. La Follette, one of the dominant and romantic figures in American history and politics . . . the man who had been much maligned and much praised, who to some spelled freedom and to others spelled chaos. . . . When he walked into the light last night the audience saw first a magnificent head of waving white hair crowning a massive head and softening a square resolute face filled with weary lines. La Follette is a small man in stature but his face and hair and fairly broad shoulders give him an air of bigness that belies reality. His eyes were blue and almost hidden by narrowed lids. These eyes emitted sparks of light and with them he watched his audience closely, alert to its responsiveness and ready to respond instantly when anyone would call out to him with a good natured remark."[55]

The next day he and Phil lunched with Mrs. Fairbank, and they "deposited Mr. La Follette on the davenport and closed the door on him. He seemed to fall asleep instantly. Phil telephoned from coast to coast and in between . . . I read Mr. La F. what you had written about Mrs. La Follette's talk at Town Hall and it pleased him very much."[56] It was the first respite since starting on the trip. They stayed at the Fairbank home until it was time to leave for Omaha, where Bob endorsed Senator Norris, urged repeal of the

Esch-Cummins Law, and discussed his own railroad program before more than 10,000 people with thousands "turned away."[57] Bob told his audience that the railroad interests were determined to preserve the special privileges they had acquired under the Esch-Cummins Law and were actively engaged in an effort to elect "either Calvin Coolidge or John W. Davis, and they don't give a whoop which." To illustrate the tactics they were using, he read one of the dozens of orders that had come into his hands from friendly railroad employees. He read an order issued by a superintendent of the Chicago, Rock Island & Pacific to "All Agents, Roundhouse Foremen Section Foremen" which suggested that they form either Coolidge or Davis political clubs at each station, with the roundhouse foremen or the section foremen as chairmen. The order also requested that as soon as the clubs were formed, the names of the chairmen, secretary, and treasurer and the number of men who had joined should be sent to the superintendent, as it was "desired that we put forth our efforts to support either Mr. Coolidge or Mr. Davis." Pointing out that these foremen were "the men who hire and fire employees," Bob declared, "When I am elected President, as I shall be, this kind of coercion, this invasion of the fundamental rights of American citizens is going to stop."[58]

Hannan reported that at this Omaha meeting "The seat sale was $1,639.00 but the expenses, among which were $900 for amplifiers, and the broadcasting of the speech, totaled $1514.70, leaving only $124.50 as the net from the meeting, to which was added $887.00 the amount of the collection, making a total net of $901.30."[59] Of this total only $450 went toward the expenses of the car, as the balance was allocated to the local campaign fund.

During his trip Bob kept in touch with Wheeler, who was also traveling in a private car financed by collections and ticket sales. Throughout his Western tour Wheeler had large, enthusiastic audiences. When Bob telephoned to him in California, Wheeler reported that he had talked to 12,000 people at the Los Angeles Bowl, and that they had contributed $7,500 toward the progressive campaign expenses.[60] A master of ironic criticism and vigorous invective, the tall, handsome Montana Senator attacked Davis as the "Democratic Wall Street candidate," and denounced Dawes for his banking connections and his association with former Senator Lorimer. After six weeks of campaigning, Wheeler stated, "I have daily issued a challenge to the men of all parties in my audience to name a single national administration in American history that was as venal, as corrupt, and as careless of the rights of American citizens as that of the past three and one-half years."[61] Much press comment was evoked by his effective dramatic questioning, directed, as a prosecuting attorney, at an empty chair he placed on the platform, in which Coolidge was supposed to be a witness. Drawing on his intimate knowledge of the Teapot Dome and Daugherty scandals, Wheeler hurled question after question, paused in the ensuing silence to liken it to the President's persistent silence on the charges of corruption in the Republican Administration.[62] After traveling and speaking with Wheeler for a week, Oswald Garrison Villard had written Bob: "He is doing extremely good work, quiet, modest and unassuming yet dramatic to a remarkable degree by his simple straightforward narrative of Teapot Dome and the Daugherty scandals. I have never seen audiences more fascinated, or that listened more closely and attentively."[63]

Wheeler was in Wichita, Kansas, when Bob telegraphed his decision to turn East.[64] Several reasons had prompted this change in Bob's plans. His family and friends thought he should not undertake the hard travel involved in the long trip West. It had been freely predicted that he would carry a dozen Western States. Nevertheless Bob was for continuing his campaign to the coast because he thought his meetings would assure the majorities necessary in each State if his Presidential Electors were to win. After much discussion he was finally persuaded that turning East would dramatically emphasize that the progressive aim was to win the election and not merely to throw the decision into the House of Representatives. Also, there was little money in the till, and the railroad travel of the Western trip would have been a heavy expense.

The progressive funds were small in contrast to the enormous sums that were being collected and spent by the Republican National Committee. From day to day this was being revealed at the hearings before the Borah Committee, which were extensively reported in the newspapers. After the committee had received the requested financial statements from the different chairmen of the National Campaign Committees, Frank Walsh, as La Follette's representative, had submitted six Grundy letters and other material. These documents supported Bob's charges at Scranton as to the way funds were being solicited in the East for transfer to other States. Walsh also informed the committee that Samuel Untermeyer would be associated with him. At Bob's specific request certain men had been subpoenaed to appear before the committee. From the time Bob turned East to the end of his speaking campaign, the hearings of the Borah Committee continued in Chicago and Washington, as a parade of political personalities, investment bankers, and industrial leaders took the stand.[65] As Bob read the extensive, detailed press reports of the hearings from day to day, he thought an important record was being made of the concealed use of money to influence public opinion.

At one of the hearings George Barr Baker, publicity director of the National Republican Campaign Committee, admitted that a large part of the reported $437,000 expenditure had been for "debunking La Follette." This propaganda included supplying to more than 3,000 Republican and "independent" newspapers, for reproduction without cost and without revealing their source, 6,000 "boiler plate" mats of "canned" editorials and articles, many of which had been prepared by his committee.[66] W. W. Atterbury, vice president and later president of the Pennsylvania Railroad, defended the printing upon the back of its dining-car menus attacks on La Follette's position regarding Government ownership of railroads.[67] Cyrus H. K. Curtis, publisher of the Philadelphia *Public Ledger* and the New York *Evening Post,* which printed vicious cartoons of the progressive leaders, also used his *Saturday Evening Post* to oppose La Follette. Although the final committee report states that Curtis made only a $1,000 cash donation to the Republican campaign, he readily admitted at the hearing that he had spent as an additional "contribution" $71,247 for newspaper "ads" in nearly every large city to assure a wide reading of the articles condemning La Follette.[68] One advertisement of an article by Samuel G. Blythe cost $40,221. This article called La Follette the candidate of the "Reds, the Pinks, the Blues and the Yellows."[69]

Although Bob had publicly repudiated the Communists in his open letter to Herman Ekern on May 26, the Republican publicity campaign persistently tried to represent him as their ally. Articles had frequently appeared in the *National Republican,* previously the official organ of the Republican National Committee, designating the progressive movement as "bolshevistic" and "red," and declaring that "it stands for confiscation of property and destruction of the Constitution."[70] The *New York Times* reported another effort to "Link La Follette With Russian Reds" made in a speech by former Congressman Martin Littleton delivered before the American Defense Society, which had been so active in efforts to expel La Follette from the Senate during the war.[71] Another attack came from T. V. O'Connor, chairman of the Shipping Board, which Bob had severely criticized on the Senate floor. O'Connor in a public statement challenged anyone with "absolute authority" to deny that "a large amount of money had been sent from Russia through Mexico to aid the campaign of Senator La Follette."[72] When O'Connor was questioned about this statement before the Borah Committee, he answered, "I believe it in my own heart, though I have no way to prove it."[73]

In Bob's speeches and statements to the press, he drove home the truth of the charges he had made regarding the Republican campaign funds by citing the testimony as it was revealed piecemeal in the newspaper reports of the committee hearings. Grundy testified that he himself gave $7,500, and admitted that $365,000 had already been raised in Pennsylvania, with a total of $600,000 expected because he had asked for contributions from 70,000 people "outside of the Pittsburgh area."[74] Grundy also stated that there was still a possibility that La Follette might "muster enough votes to defeat the Republicans."[75] When the report of the Borah Committee was finally submitted to Congress after election, it substantiated a statement that Frank Walsh filed with the committee regarding the Republican campaign funds. In his analysis Walsh declared that "Of the individuals making these large contributions, more than 92 per cent are found listed in the financial manuals and directories as officers or directors in large industrial and financial corporations" and that "75 per cent of the total sum reported has been contributed by officers or directors of corporations."[76]

Of the Republican contributors specifically named in the Borah Committee's report, more than a thousand were listed as giving between $1,000 and $5,000 each, while over a hundred gave more. More than a hundred Democrats reported contributions of $1,000 or over. The progressive campaign fund had only one contributor, W. T. Rawleigh, who gave over $5,000. John M. Nelson, national manager of the Chicago headquarters, testified that Rawleigh had written that "I could rely upon him for assistance up to $40,000."[77] One other contribution of $5,000 was received. This was from Irene Richter, who gave it in memory of her mother, Mrs. Samuel Untermyer.[78] Less than a half dozen people gave between $1,000 and $2,500. It was estimated that more than half of Bob's modest fund had been made up by contributions of less than $100 and that 32 per cent came from ticket and bond sales and collections at meetings. Subsequently this was authoritatively said to be "A record of *small gifts* which has never been equalled by either of the major parties."[79] The final totals as listed in the Borah report, which differ slightly from the official records filed with the Clerk of the House, were: Republicans, $4,360,478.82; Democrats, $821,037.00; Progressives, $221,977.58. These figures, as Walsh pointed out, did not approximate the total sums actually contributed to the Republican and Democratic campaign funds because they did not include the large amounts collected by the two major parties through their various state, county, and city organizations.[80] Nor did it include the large sums spent in the Republican campaign by individuals and groups for propaganda through paid advertisements.

Bob closed the third week of his tour at Syracuse, New York, where he analyzed the powerful financial forces which he charged controlled both old parties. From Syracuse he went to Aiken, Maryland, where his car was shunted to a secluded spot on the banks of the Susquehanna River so that he could rest over the week end before starting on another strenuous week of speaking in Eastern cities.

As Bob passed through Philadelphia, he had released to the newspapers a telegram he sent from there to the Democratic Senator Thomas J. Walsh which said: "I trust that the Progressives of Montana will unite in their support of your candidacy for re-election to the United States Senate. We have not been in agreement on many matters and measures, but your signal service in prosecuting the Teapot Dome investigation transcends all other issues in this campaign in Montana . . . I urge all Progressives in Montana to join in rolling up a majority for you in the election that will be an admonition to wrong doers and an encouragement to every public servant in the full performance of his duty."[81]

During his brief "rest" at Aiken, Bob worked in his "little box-stall" on the special car. The initial publication of income-tax returns had brought forth indignant protests from Wall Street. Bob wrote out a statement for the press in which he hailed it "as a complete justification of the long fight made by the Progressives to open tax returns to public inspection."[82]

The newspapers estimated that Bob spoke to over 60,000 people at the six meetings during the last week of the campaign. At Baltimore, on October 27, he spoke in the Fifth Regiment Armory, where he had heard Bryan address the 1912 Democratic Convention. The *Baltimore News* reported Bob had an audience of 12,000, "one of the largest political crowds ever assembled in Maryland, . . . it was the first big political gathering that had an admission fee and general collection."[83] In his speech that night Bob vigorously attacked the powerful influence on legislation as exercised by certain political-economic organizations, typified by the Sugar Trust.

On the way to his next meeting in Brooklyn, Bob stopped off to see Belle, who had been ill for a week at the Brevoort Hotel in New York. It was a great comfort to see him and to have firsthand news of his trip. She had followed the reports of his speeches in the *New York Times* while convalescing from a severe cold with high temperature which had forced her to cancel her meeting on October 20. On short notice Fola had read her mother's speech to an audience of 2,000 at Cooper Union, where it was received with "an ovation."[84] From then until the end of the campaign, Fola continued to fill her mother's engagements in this same way. Belle's speech appealing for Bob's election on his record was the last one made in the campaign by a member of his family. During the campaign many articles and interviews had been published about the close relationship of the La Follette family.

In one interview Belle had said: "I have loved my life. I have been fortunate, marvellously lucky in having all these years a companion. True companionship is the greatest thing in the world. We have been through everything, my husband and I, bad times and good times, disappointments, illness, poverty, hard work, the struggle for principle, the climb to success. But when you have a companion to count upon through thick and thin, it's all easy. We two have kept together because—well, because our minds and our hearts matched."[85]

When Bob spoke at the Clermont Avenue Rink in Brooklyn, all of the 4,500 seats were filled, and nearly half of those present had contributed "from 50 cents to $2.50 for section reservations."[86] One correspondent reported that he had "one of the most enthusiastic welcomes that had ever been given a candidate in Brooklyn."[87] The *Brooklyn Daily Eagle* commented editorially that "He is beyond all doubt a unique figure in the public life of America."[88] Before his speech, dealing with the corrupt "rule of oil and gold," Bob was deeply moved when Commander Warren Shaw Fisher of the United War Veterans gave him a gold medal "in recognition of his services to his country, his people and the war veterans." The *New York Times* reported there were tears in his eyes as he "uttered his thanks haltingly and nearly broke down several times before concluding the brief remarks that prefaced his prepared address." When he concluded his speech, "he was instantly caught in a maelstrom of enthusiastic supporters who crowded and crushed one another to reach him. It required efforts of two policemen, his son Robert, and his son-in-law George Middleton to escort the Presidential candidate out of the crush."[89]

The next night in Schenectady, New York, home of the General Electric Company, "fully 3,000 people jammed the State Theatre and gave him a warm greeting" while an unseen radio audience joined in listening to his discussion of public ownership and the development of public utilities.[90] In Boston, where he spoke for the first time in his life, he endorsed Senator David I. Walsh for reelection. When he attacked the imperialistic policies of both the old parties in Latin America, a Boston newspaper noted that "a tumultuous roar of welcome greeted America's foremost apostle of revolt."[91] His speech was broadcast throughout New England. The *Boston Evening Transcript* reported that he "held a friendly audience of more than 9,000 people in Mechanics Hall in the hollow of his hand as he pleaded his cause."[92] After the speech Bob, Jr., wired his mother to join them in Cleveland and added, "Boston meeting great."[93]

From Boston Bob turned westward again. It was Halloween night when he drove from the special car to the Carnegie Music Hall in Pittsburgh. He recalled to his large audience that many years before he had not been allowed to continue his speech in that same hall because he had insisted upon reading the roll call votes of one of the Pennsylvania Senators. Then he went on to discuss the power which Secretary of the Treasury Andrew Mellon had and his influence on Government policies. In analyzing where power actually resided, Bob said: "Andrew Mellon is today the real President of the United States. Calvin Coolidge is merely the man who occupies the White House."[94] Bob's speech was broadcast, and as former Senator Joseph L. Bristow listened in from his home in Fairfax, Virginia, he thought it must be a wonderful meeting. Before election he wrote Bob: "How I would like to have been there. You are a wonder. How you can stand such a physical strain is a marvell [*sic*]. The result in England makes me apprehensive but am hoping for the best. But regardless of the results Tuesday you have started something worth while that will last long after we are gone. Good luck and with prayers for success."[95]

"It's a great show, this La Follette campaign," Paul Anderson wrote at this time. "The spectacle of a man nearly seventy years old with little organization and no money of his own, relying largely for assistance upon his two youthful sons setting out to lick both the great national parties, is alone sufficient to command respect. Realize that this forlorn charge has been carried out with such savage power, such superb skill and resourcefulness, and that it has frightened the rich ruling party into a state of nightmare; add the picture of vast, clamorous crowds fighting for a chance to pay admission, and you have a drama powerful enough to thrill almost any community . . . with the exception, as Mr. Grundy's celebrated letter ran, 'of the Pittsburgh district.' "[96]

From Pittsburgh Bob went to Cleveland. When he had been endorsed by the convention there on July 5, he had promised to close his campaign with a speech in that same auditorium. In the morning, on a clear, beautiful day, he visited the Public Square and, before a crowd of ten thousand people, placed a wreath at the foot of Tom Johnson's monument. After the ceremony Bob, Jr., telegraphed his mother and also Fola, because she had known Johnson better than any others of the family.[97]

In the evening, before 20,000 people who were "swept away in a frenzy almost religious,"[98] while thousands stood outside, in presenting Bob, Peter Witt said: "Senator La Follette, I shall not introduce you to this audience but, rather, I shall introduce the audience to you . . . these are the men and the women who have graduated from the university of Tom L. Johnson. They are his friends and your friends. . . . Through him, this magnificent audience knows you, Senator La Follette, and they have watched your career. . . . there was one sentiment above all the rest, that was left in the memories of those men who were privileged to be associated with him, and today those . . . words were on the ribbon that bound the wreath that you laid upon the bronze figure that commemorates the nine years of wonderful service by Tom L. Johnson, and these people before me say to you, as you said to him : 'Fight on, brave heart, fight on.' "[99] They were the words Bob had wired Johnson in 1909 after his defeat for a fourth term as mayor of Cleveland.

Bob could hardly speak as he faced what he felt was "the greatest audience representing the true American spirit that ever assembled in the United States."[100] Even when the place was hushed, it took time to control his emotion. He spoke of what the "precious heritage of liberty" had cost in the past and what those present must pay to preserve it. In every great crisis in the life of this Republic, the spirit "that this is the people's government" had "been invoked to save it." He reminded them of those who, only four months before, had come to that same auditorium and who had petitioned him to lead the movement to that end. "I thank God that I did accept," he added. "For no matter what may be the outcome of this election, no matter what may be my fate in the years that are to come, I shall forever rejoice that I had a part in this great campaign to restore government to the people."[101]

With an expression of his abiding faith in the American people, Bob spoke his last words from a public platform. To his unseen audience he whispered into the microphone a special good night, "God be with you all."[102]

Quitting his special car at Chicago, Bob took the train to Madison. In a reminiscent mood he pointed out landmarks associated with his early campaigns for office in the State he dearly loved. He smiled, too, as the train passed his old home on Wilson Street where he and Belle had shared so many fortunes and their four children were born. At the Madison Station over 3,000 friends and supporters met him, as a surprise, to cheer and escort him to the capitol, from whose steps he said a few words of appreciation, adding that whatever the result of the election, "Providence willing, I believe I shall last long enough to see the nation freed from its economic slavery and the government returned to the people."[103] Deeply moved by the reception, he recalled that forty-five years before, when a student at the university, he had been escorted from the station to celebrate his winning of the Inter-State Oratorical Contest.

He was driven in Governor Blaine's car to Maple Bluff Farm, where he rested quietly until evening, when he called on Alice Van Hise, the ailing widow of Charles R. Van Hise, who, until the war, had been among the closest friends Bob and Belle had. "I must tell you how truly pleased mother was at your visit," her daughter wrote him. "Thank you a thousand times for snatching a moment out of your busy life for her."[104] Bob cast his vote on election day with Bob, Jr., Phil, and Isabel. That night he heard the returns at the Capitol with them and a group of friends. Belle was not there because she had remained in Washington to be with Mary, who was expecting the birth of her first child. As the returns came in, it was soon evident that although he might have what was a large vote for an independent candidate throughout the country, Wisconsin was the only State in which his Presidential electors would win. Phil had been elected district attorney of Dane County, the first office to which Bob had himself been elected in 1880. An editorial writer, who was present during the evening, later wrote: "and what of Senator La Follette? The average man, even in younger years, would falter. This man will not. He had always seemed personally stronger in defeat than in victory. When the returns poured in Tuesday night this staunch old warrior was at his best. Men about him, devoted friends and admirers, winced. There were moist eyes in the group. But Senator La Follette's shoulders were a little higher, his smile a little surer than ever."[105]

Bob was silent as he rode home. Those with him expressed their bitterness over the result, especially at Labor's obvious failure to rally its full support to him. The Senator rebuked them for their "lack of understanding," saying, "Those pay checks are all that stand between starvation for those workers and their families. You are asking too much of them."[106]

CHAPTER LXXII

"We Have Just Begun to Fight"

The day after the election Bob received a telegram from William B. Colver, who, as editor in chief of the Scripps Howard newspapers, had followed the campaign closely and had joined the special car at intervals during the trip. Colver's message read: "With love and appreciation and joyful anticipation of many more honorable battles in your company[.] Dont let anybody tell you it wasnt worth while nor that the net result is not a great gain in the public service[.] We who know the odds against which you fought know how well you fought and that the real victory is yours[.]"[1] This and other messages which came to Bob by telegraph and telephone found expression in the statement he issued that same day saying: "The election of Calvin Coolidge by a landslide is apparent from the returns now in. . . . The Progressives will not be dismayed by this result. We have just begun to fight. There is no compromise on the fundamental issues for which we stand. The loss of this one battle in the age-long struggle of the masses against the privileged few is but an incident."[2]

The official election returns gave Coolidge 15,718,783; Davis 8,378,962; La Follette 4,822,319. Bob received the second highest vote in the eleven States of California, Idaho, Iowa, Minnesota, Montana, Nevada, North Dakota, Oregon, South Dakota, Washington, and Wyoming. Subsequent analysis showed that although his Presidential Electors had won only Wisconsin, he had received the largest popular vote ever given to the candidate of an independent movement at its first appearance in a national campaign. One out of every six votes cast for President had been for La Follette.

The day after the election Dante M. Pierce came to the farm

and found that Bob was not depressed or embittered by the result but "looked upon it as merely another skirmish lost."[3] Bob began making plans at once to organize the progressive votes for the next campaign. He conferred with progressive leaders and had a questionnaire sent out from his office to the state chairmen of the La Follette-Wheeler campaign committees suggesting that they keep their organizations together for future action. In an editorial entitled "Forward Progressives for Campaign of 1926," Bob shared with his readers the reports he had received on how the "economic thumbscrews were twisted down upon the farmer, the wage earner and the independent business man" during the final days of the recent campaign. "Notices were posted in the shops that only the foremen need report for work on the Wednesday after election unless Coolidge was elected. The farmers were quietly informed by their bankers that there would be no extension of mortgages unless Coolidge was elected. The merchants whispered to the housewives that prices would advance and that no credit could be had unless Coolidge was elected. Business men were given fat orders subject to cancellation if Coolidge was not elected." Under such pressure as this, Bob said, "the wonder is not that so many millions were intimidated and voted for Coolidge, but that so many millions stood by their convictions and voted the Independent ticket. . . . The priceless heritage of our free institutions is not to be yielded up because one battle with the enemy of progressive democracy has been lost. . . . The Progressives will close ranks for the next battle."[4]

Throughout November Bob and Bob, Jr., stayed at the farm with Phil and Isabel. Belle remained in Washington awaiting the arrival of Mary's baby. Six days after the election she wrote, "It was good to hear from you last night and be assured you were all well. . . . This morning I called up Mrs. Wheeler. She was cheerful. She felt they had done what it seemed right to do and had no regrets. . . . Most every one agrees with the diagnosis as to fear. The part it played. I have thought many times of Lincoln Steffens' prophecy."[5] The day after this letter was written Bob received a telephone message that brought him deep and enduring joy. Mary's baby was born on November 11, and his parents named him Robert La Follette Sucher.

Bob was still in Madison on November 28, when a Republican

Caucus was held in Washington which was attended by thirty-four Senators, seventeen being absent. The press reported that, with the approval of President Coolidge, the caucus had adopted by a viva voce vote a resolution that La Follette, Brookhart, Frazier, and Ladd "be not invited to future Republican conferences, and be not named to fill any Republican vacancies on Senate committees." The *New York Times* stated that Senator Edge of New Jersey "was in the forefront of the movement to eject Senator La Follette" from the party councils.[6] The next morning the *Washington Herald* carried a headline across the front page declaring, "ATTACK ON LA FOLLETTE SPLITS G.O.P." Bob refused to make any public comment on the action of the caucus. But it was denounced by Borah, Norris, and several other Senators who had not attended the meeting. Norris stated that he had been assured in advance that no punitive action would be taken.[7]

Two days before Congress convened, Bob and Bob, Jr., left Madison for Washington. The press reported that when the Senate met on December 1, "All the radicals were on hand. Senator La Follette was among the first to enter the chamber and he walked straight to his old seat on the aisle in the front row on the Republican side. Senators Brookhart, Ladd and Frazier came in a moment later and took their old seats on the Republican side. They looked entirely at home and there was no indication of objection on the part of the Old Guard. Senator La Follette received a warm welcome. Senator Moses of New Hampshire, a stand-patter and one of the Senators who voted him out of the party, was especially cordial. He put his arms around the Wisconsin veteran and whispered earnestly to him."[8] Another correspondent, Frank R. Kent, wrote that Senator La Follette "bore himself more as a conqueror than as one of the conquered. . . . There was a buoyant and light-hearted lilt in his voice. When the session ended he was the center of an animated group of Senators, who jested with him. He gave every evidence of enjoyment and exchanged repartee with a zest that could not have been assumed."[9] When the Senate adjourned, a newspaper correspondent asked Bob how he felt about his exclusion from the Republican councils. He replied: "I have not attended any Republican caucuses for twenty years, so being deprived of invitations in the future will not matter much. As for my committee assignments, if I were removed from all committees I would still find plenty of work to do in the Senate."[10]

That night Bob confided to his diary: "At Senate at 12 noon. Full attendance Was surprisingly well received Ev[e]rybody cordial many coming to my desk to greet me. I tried to be the good sport & think I succeeded fairly well judged by comment of press & friends."[11] Later he wrote his sister that "It was not easy to face the old gang with the election just over and ev[e]ry state lost except Wisconsin. But I sailed in my head up & all smiles You [may] be sure I would not give any outward evidence of the taste in my mouth."[12]

During the night following the first day's Senate session, Bob had a recurrence of a severe cough he had contracted in Madison while going about the farm on a rainy afternoon with a tree expert. A sudden high temperature indicated he had an attack of the prevailing influenza. The doctor ordered him to bed to avoid a possible recurrence of pneumonia. Although distressed at being away from the Senate, he obeyed orders and was well enough to record in his diary on December 11, "Feeling stronger this morning . . . I went with Belle & Bob to see Mary & her baby. Mary looking well & very beautiful. Her face shows the change—indescribable but divine —that goes with motherhood. The boy, blessings on him! He fills the heart and hopes—a beautiful head & a certain look that speaks for the things to come. God give him a long and useful life."[13]

The next day a conference was held in Washington in which Bob was keenly interested. More than forty members of the National Committee of the Conference for Progressive Political Action met in response to the call of Chairman William H. Johnston. Although Bob did not attend, he received detailed reports from Bob, Jr., and Manly. At the beginning of the session a representative of the Railroad Brotherhoods announced their organizations would participate in no further conferences, thus declaring they were opposed to participation in a new party as a group. After their representatives withdrew, it was agreed that, in accord with the mandate from the Cleveland C.P.P.A. Convention, a conference should be held on February 21 and 22, in Chicago, to decide whether steps should be taken toward forming a new party.[14] That night, after talking with his son, Bob noted in his diary: "R[ailwa]y groups repudiated agreement made at Cleveland July 4 & declined to join in calling convention to consider perman[en]t organizat[ion] of new party. They were beaten in comt. meeting by 39 to 13—after which they took no further part."[15]

Before the Christmas holiday Bob returned to the Senate, but soon contracted another cold. He wrote Rawleigh that "The doctor says I must get away very soon & build up my resistance against taking cold ev[e]ry time the door is opened . . . he assures me that if I will get into the Florida sun & sand and bake the remnants of the pneumonia out of me I will come back stronger than I have been in years." Bob suggested that Rawleigh and Mrs. Rawleigh join him and Belle in Florida and urged his friend, whom he called "my more than brother," to remember "that you have only so many heart-beats left. Ev[e]ry day you drive the engine over time shortens life. Stop the good old machine and give it some rest. You and Mrs. Rawleigh have ev[e]rything to live for and both of you should begin to think now and plan to *extend this precious life as long as possible*."[16] In a letter telling his sister of his plans, Bob said: "The prices in Florida with all the doctors bills I have accumulated stagger me But if I can get strong again I'll be able to earn some good money during the new year—which is just at hand."[17]

On January 14 Bob and Belle left Washington for Fort Lauderdale, Florida. When they arrived, their friend Mrs. Glenn Plumb was at the train to meet them, as were the mayor and several photographers. The following day she took them to Las Olas Inn on the beach two miles from town. Originally built as a hunting lodge, it had once belonged to Senator Tom Watson. Situated in the midst of tall coconut palms, Australian pines, and red-leaved almond trees, the inn faced the ocean on the east and the bay on the west. The place was quiet, the food good, and the prices reasonable. Belle wrote that the rooms had doors and windows opening on the verandas and were "practically sleeping porches. The finish is rustic and the furniture commonplace. But there is just that much less temptation to stay indoors."[18]

When the weather was fair Bob spent his days in the open, taking sun baths regularly. He wrote that he "slept under a blanket at night with windows & doors open & the sea breez[e] blowing right through the room & across the bed but no sign of taking cold."

He especially enjoyed the thought that Belle was also "getting great good out of it." She was "up early—in the ocean and then out for a walk twice a day along the beach."[19] Sometimes Bob and Belle walked or sat together watching the ocean from the nearby public park. In a letter telling Mr. Rawleigh about Bob, Belle said, "for pure unalloyed satisfaction I have never known him to get so much out of anything as he is getting out of this stay in Florida. The climate and location and surroundings suit his needs exactly. He spends hours each day baking in the sun. And his health seems to respond to the treatment accordingly. His cough has left him entirely. His appetite is good and he has gained in strength and endurance although he does not appear to have gained weight."[20]

While in Florida Bob kept in touch with the Washington and Wisconsin situations through Bob, Jr., and Phil. Although Belle had her typewriter with her, Bob wrote many long letters in his own clear script, often making carbon copies which have been preserved in his files. Some of these expressed the deep concern they both felt about the selection of a president for the University of Wisconsin to succeed Van Hise, who had died in 1918. From the time they were students under President Bascom, the university had seemed to them the most important public institution in Wisconsin. They hoped that a man of vision and courage would be chosen who was qualified by endowment and experience to carry on Bascom's ideal of a state university.

The qualifications they had always considered most essential had been concisely expressed when Bob answered an inquiry about the appointment of a professor as president of another university by saying in a confidential letter: "My opinion is that he is able but is lacking in strength of character—in high moral courage. If this be true then he is wanting in the very first essential of a University president. The greatest work of a university is to *build character*. It takes the raw youth of the state in the formation period, when the mental and moral fiber is most pliable. It should give the youth back to the state—a citizen, well grounded in scholarship; but *above and before all else*—a citizen in whom the upbuilding and *development of character* has been the *first consideration* of those who have controlled his university life. I believe that a university president should have the broadest scholarship, possess executive ability and tact,—but *more than all else*, that he should be a *great moral and spiritual power,* strong enough to make that *the dominant influence in the university over which he presides.*"[21]

During 1923 and 1924 several of the University of Wisconsin regents had consulted Bob, and he had made confidential inquiries as to the qualifications of some men who might be available. Also in 1923, at Governor Blaine's request, Bob had talked informally with Robert Morss Lovett of the University of Chicago, who had impressed him very favorably.[22] Subsequently Bob had urged that those authorized to select a president should talk with Lovett and also personally investigate his qualifications as a scholar and administrator.

Early in 1924 the regents had appointed a nominating committee of five to investigate the availability of men for the presidency. From time to time Bob had been informed about different men the committee members had seen, but many months passed without any official report being made to the regents. In January, 1925, before Bob left for Florida, one regent had written that, although he had no official knowledge, the press dispatches had stated "the plan was to elect a new president at the meeting on January 21st." He asked Bob to tell him, either confidentially or with permission to communicate to others in sympathy with liberalism, whom out of his long experience and nation-wide acquaintance he would recommend.[23]

In replying to this letter Bob did not recommend any specific individual but urged that final action should not be taken on the same day that the committee reported to the regents. He gave his reasons for fearing that hasty action might mean the selection of an inadequate or reactionary man, and frankly expressed his opinion as to what had happened to the university in recent years. He said that the selection of a president was "of the utmost importance, not only for Wisconsin, but for the entire country. There was a time when the University of Wisconsin was the outstanding figure in the educational world. She was the model for academic freedom and democracy in education.

"Under the deadly influences which came with the war, and the evils attending the Philipp administrations, she became a veritable hot-bed for the hatching out and spreading of ideas hostile to the old democratic spirit which had prevailed at the University from the days of President John Bascom down. Every member of her

1924

Gilbert E. Roe and Bob, Jr., at La Follette and Wheeler campaign headquarters in New York

Chicago Daily News

1924 Presidential campaign
"Fighting Bob," independent Presidential candidate, arriving in Chicago with his
son Bob, Jr.

Bob arriving in Madison on November
2, 1924

Bob speaking from the steps of the Wisconsin State Capitol, November 2, 1924

Kollar, Paris. Permission Jo Davidson Estate.

Statue of Robert M. La Follette by Jo Davidson, unveiled in Statuary Hall of the Capitol at Washington, 1929

faculty known as a liberal or progressive in his beliefs has been quietly discriminated against or openly persecuted.

"Some of us have spent a lifetime in making the government of Wisconsin stand before all the world for liberty and equality, and today the men who control the University openly teach hostility to everything the State of Wisconsin represents before all the world. . . .

"It is vital that a broad, liberal-minded man with bedrock ideas of democracy in education should be selected. Our University is a *state University*. It belongs to the people of Wisconsin. The state was not made for the university. The university was established to serve the state. . . . Now is the time of greatest crisis for the University, and through the influence of the University for the state. The man chosen as President will, whether he be right or wrong, be President for the next ten years. In that time the University will have become deeply rooted in reaction or she will be established as the great exponent of all that is progressive in higher education."[24]

When the regents met on January 21, they unanimously approved the appointment of Dean Roscoe Pound of the Harvard Law School, who was proposed by the nominating committee.[25] Phil telephoned the decision to Bob, Jr., who telegraphed his father. A few days later Bob, Jr., wrote his mother and father saying he had received confidential messages that Pound was still wavering, although a definite announcement of his acceptance had appeared in the press.[26] To this Belle replied that Bob thought, with the board of regents as now constituted, "Pound is the best we can get so we hope he may accept." Later, when Pound refused the presidency, she wrote, "The University situation makes the heart ache."[27] Subsequently Bob learned that after Pound declined, Lovett asked to have his name withdrawn as a candidate.[28]

During the three weeks preceding the C.P.P.A. Conference at Chicago, Bob and Bob, Jr., exchanged almost daily letters and telegrams regarding what action should be taken before the meeting. They agreed that the only effective way to organize a new progressive party was on the basis of individual membership with the States as the units of organization. They hoped that the Chicago conference would decide to call state meetings during the summer to select delegates to a convention to be held for that avowed purpose in the fall. But they were aware that the Socialists and some other delegates were determined the conference should immediately form a new party based upon group membership along Marxian class lines.

Before leaving Washington, Bob had written his sister that he was hopeful an agreement could be reached at Chicago "for going ahead on the right basis. We receive a very large mail from over the whole country which is most encouraging. I am not for a class party—or a party composed [of] organized labor & organized farmers & organized socialists—or any other form of group organization. Where such a party is attempted there must inevitably be organized strife for class or group control. I think the citizen should be the unit for any political organization & I hope such a party can be formed on principles which will appeal to ev[e]ry American citizen who believes in a government *of the people by and for the people*. I cannot go into any new party movement upon any other basis."[29]

As the date of the Chicago conference drew near, Bob, Jr., started out on what he described as "a swing to get as many strong people [as possible] committed to our plan and agreed to go to the conference to put it over."[30] After talking with Roe and many other people in New York, Bob, Jr., thought the conference would probably be dominated by the Socialist delegates who were determined to form an American Labor Party "on the spot" along class lines that would appeal to the more radical trade unionists. Therefore he and Roe were convinced that Bob and the Progressives who desired his leadership would have to break with the Socialists. Bob, Jr., wrote his father that "To take any other course at Chicago will throw us into the hands of the Socialists in my judgment which is a thing we cannot afford, nor have we any right to do so because while our objective, namely a better political system and a more just economic situation may be the same, they have entirely different ideas as to how these reforms should be accomplished."[31] A telegram from his father said, "Think it will be helpful rather than harmful if conference divided early and S[ocialists] form labor party leaving real progressives to form new progressive party."[32]

While Bob, Jr., was carrying the responsibility of all these different conferences, his mother wrote from Florida: "You have been wonderfully patient Bob and I admire the way you hold to the proposition in spite of all the discouragement. It is the spirit of Daddy all over again."[33] Two days before Bob, Jr., left to attend the Chicago conference as an observer, he wrote his father: "I dread very much to have to carry alone the responsibility connected with my representing you at Chicago. It is a burden greater than any one man should be asked to carry but under the circumstances I see no other way out and I trust you will be lenient in your judgment concerning the manner in which I shall meet the many difficulties and situations which will arise during the deliberations of the conference."[34] When he arrived at his hotel in Chicago, Bob, Jr., found a telegram from his father saying, "Absolute confidence in your judgment and ability to meet all requirements tactfully and wisely. All love."[35]

Bob, Jr., communicated his father's views on the formation of a progressive party to the delegates through personal talks with certain leaders and a brief statement which appeared in the newspapers on the morning of the conference.[36] About three hundred delegates met on February 21 at the Lexington Hotel, with William H. Johnston presiding. Bob, Jr., heard the Socialists, led by Eugene Debs and Morris Hillquit, urge the immediate formation of a third party. In the late afternoon the conference adjourned without taking any action, and the C.P.P.A. thus officially ended its existence.

That evening the Socialists and others met in the same room and passed a resolution declaring a new party formed. After long debate as to what the basis of representation should be in a new party, the question was referred to a committee of seven which made a divided report the next day. The Socialists brought in a minority report for group representation. The majority report recommended that Chairman Johnston should appoint a committee to call meetings in the respective States to select delegates to a national convention. This was the La Follette plan as it had been presented to the leaders by his son. The majority report was adopted by 94 to 63. Bob, Jr., telegraphed his father that the issue really was upon the question of a broad progressive party. "All feel we have made the best of a bad mess and are in shape to go ahead."[37]

Bob thought his son had carried the heavy burden of deciding everything alone at Chicago like a veteran.[38] A week after the conference Bob wrote Manly from Florida: "We surely have ev[e]ry reason to be happy over the Chicago event. There was ev[e]ry chance to get smashed up in the affair and it seems to me that there was not a point lost in the game from start to finish. It was fine that Mollie [Manly] and Mrs. Costigan could be on the ground to block a lot of bad work and aid so effectively in pulling off the result." He also discussed tactical procedure in forming a new party and expressed his concern about protecting the Senators and Representatives in Wisconsin and other States who would be up for reelection in 1926, when the new movement might not be strong enough to enable some of them to win on a progressive ticket. "Wisconsin is of first importance[.] Leaving myself and other officials out of consideration for we must pass sooner or later—the state must be protected as the very citadel of democracy [.] It will take years to make another Wisconsin. And indeed I have often thought that the way to National redemption lies along state by state occupation and conquest until we have enough states for a national base of commanding proportions so I am always finding myself planted on the proposition that *I will not sacrifice Wisconsin.*"[39]

Bob planned to call a conference of a few representatives from each of the States which then constituted "the real seat of power of this progressive movement." In asking Rudolph Spreckels to participate, he wrote: "It is not within the power of any group of men and women, however worthy and good intentioned, to 'wish' a political party of national importance into being. But I believe the call is upon those who were responsible for the progressive vote, five million strong . . . to make our survey, and . . . to meet our obligations as they shall appear after well-considered and deliberative counsel."[40]

The day after the Chicago conference, Republican Senators held a caucus in Washington to work out a slate of committee assignments before the new Congress convened in special session immediately after Coolidge's inauguration on March 4. Through the press Bob learned that the Administration leaders had announced they intended to deprive him and the three Republican Senators who had supported his Presidential candidacy of the assignments to which the time-honored rule of seniority entitled them.[41] Long service had given Bob high rank on his committees, and he was in line for the chairmanship of the Interstate Commerce Committee. The day after the caucus Senator James E. Watson, a reactionary Republican from Indiana who was chairman of the powerful Committee on Committees, wrote Bob that he had been instructed "to inquire of you whether or not you desire to have your committee assignments made by the Democratic or the Republican Committee."[42] As Bob had been elected on the Republican ticket, he considered this question "a piece of damned impudence" and did not reply to the letter. Watson sent similar inquiries to Senators Brookhart, Frazier, and Ladd.

Bob hoped that these three Senators would act with him in refusing to put themselves in the hands of either the Republican or Democratic caucuses and then later taking the question of committee assignments to the Senate floor. He was therefore disappointed when he read the press reports indicating that in replying to Watson they had "placed their cases in the hands of the Rep.[ublican] highbinders." Bob thought that the resolution on committees would probably not come before the Senate until the regular session in the fall, and wrote Manly that he might fight out his own case on the Senate floor "if the Dem[ocrat]s & enough soft shell progressives agree to stand by me to make it worth while." But he expressed doubt about what the Democrats might do under Senator Robinson as floor leader. If there was no chance for a winning fight, he intended to make "a hot speech and tell them to go to hades with their Committee assignments."[43]

But the Committee on Committees moved more swiftly than Bob had anticipated. Before the special session met, the press reported that some Democrats thought that in demoting La Follette and his supporters the regular Republicans were making a serious tactical error which would bring dividends to the Democratic Party in the 1926 elections.[44] This was interpreted to mean that in the organization of the new Congress the Democrats would not cooperate with the progressive Republicans as in 1924, when Bob had aided in the fight to oust Cummins by electing Ellison D. Smith, a Democrat who had opposed the Esch-Cummins Law.[45] On March 6, two days after Coolidge was sworn in for the second time, Senator Robinson, as floor leader, told a conference of Democratic Senators they should "refrain from participation in clashes among Republicans concerning committee assignments." In a more vigorously partisan statement he declared, "All Republicans look alike to us, and none of them look good to us."[46]

The morning after Robinson's instructions to the Democratic conference, the Republican Caucus ratified its slate of committee assignments for the Sixty-ninth Congress. That afternoon Chairman Watson sought to have the Senate approve them en bloc by unanimous
consent. Borah and Norris, who had not attended the caucus, blocked
this move. The carefully prepared slate proposed to remove Bob
from the chairmanship of the Committee on Manufactures, which he
had held since 1921, and placed him at the foot of the Committees
on Finance, Indian Affairs, and Interstate Commerce on which he
had served for many sessions.[47]

During the debate with Watson, which made front-page headlines
in the Sunday newspapers, Borah warned his party colleagues that
they would regret their proposed action against these Senators who
had been elected from Republican States by Republicans who shared
their views. After sharply questioning Watson's right to decide what
should be the test of party loyalty, Borah declared that "there are
men sitting in this Chamber to-day whose seats will be imperiled in
1926 if this program shall go through . . . These are times, as I have
said, of wide difference of view as to what constitutes Republicanism,
and I am deeply thankful under present conditions that it is so."[48]

When the debate was resumed on Monday, Norris led the fight
for five hours. He pointed out that the report submitted by Watson
"names himself chairman of perhaps the most important committee
in the Senate, and in order to do it he has to take some other Senator who has served here longer than he has and demote him." Before
concluding his protest, Norris declared that during the campaign no
candidate in the Middle West would have dared to say to his constituents, "If I am elected to the Senate of the United States, right
after I take my oath of office, one of the first things I shall do will
be to put the Senator from Indiana [Mr. Watson] in the chairmanship of the great railroad committee, in preference to the Senator
from Mr. Wisconsin [Mr. La Follette]."[49] When the vote was finally
taken, the Senate approved the committee assignments precisely as
Watson reported them by a vote of 65 to 11. Only three Democratic
Senators, Blease, Walsh of Montana, and Wheeler, had violated
their floor leader's instructions and voted with the progressive Republicans.

Bob had expected to remain in Florida until April, but his plans
were suddenly changed when he received messages from Senators

Reed and Norris urging him to return at once to help prevent the confirmation of Charles Beecher Warren as Attorney General. When the President first nominated Warren, the People's Legislative Service began digging into his record, and exposed his close connection with the Sugar Trust, which had long been notorious in its violation of the Sherman Anti-Trust Law.[50] To many Senators Warren's record seemed to disqualify him for this post. If he became Attorney General, he would have to decide whether corporations with which he had been actively associated for years should be prosecuted. To prevent Warren's confirmation, Norris and other progressive Republicans had joined in a fight led by Walsh of Montana and Reed of Missouri. On March 10, by a roll call vote of 41 to 39, the Senate for the first time in over fifty years refused to confirm a Presidential nomination to the Cabinet.

But two days later Coolidge surprised everyone by refusing to accept this decision and resubmitting Warren's nomination to the Senate. The margin against Warren had been so close that Reed, Norris, and other Senators thought Bob's vote would be needed.[51] Therefore Bob and Belle left Florida as soon as they could get train reservations. Arriving in Washington on Sunday, March 15, Bob learned that the Senate had agreed to vote on the Warren nomination not later than two thirty Monday with the understanding that no Senator should speak more than thirty minutes. The Sunday newspapers reported that anger had flared up in the Senate late Saturday afternoon when two Senators read press dispatches from the floor, in advance of publication, stating the President had announced at the White House that if Warren was not confirmed he would give him a recess appointment after the Senate adjourned.[52] Bob thought this threatened violation of an important constitutional provision was a dangerous precedent. The argument of Warren's supporters that the President had a right to "name his official family" seemed to him the same argument that had led to the confirmation of Fall, Denby, and Daugherty in the Harding Administration.[53]

Long before the Senate convened on Monday morning, the galleries were packed, and long lines extended out into the corridors. A stormy session was expected. It was known that Senators on both sides "had been marshalled, some coming from sick beds and others having been summoned from great distances to cast their votes in the history-making struggle between the White House and the Senate."[54]

Bob did not answer the roll call when the Senate met at ten thirty because he was still working on a five-minute speech protesting against the Warren nomination and Coolidge's threat to override the constitutional provision that the President shall appoint high officers of the Government "with the advice and consent of the Senate." It was completed and typed while the fiery debate was on. But before Bob went to the floor, Senator Walsh of Montana came to Bob's office in the Capitol and persuaded him to let the Senate proceed to vote without delivering his speech.[55] Bob entered the Chamber after the roll call began. As he took his seat in the first row directly in front of Vice President Dawes, a ripple of applause started in the galleries which was quickly checked. When the roll call concluded, it was announced that the Senate had "refused to advise and consent" to the nomination of Warren by a vote of 46 to 39. In analyzing the roll call by party designations, the Associated Press and other news services listed Bob among the ten Republicans who had joined the Democrats in opposing Warren. But the *New York Times* followed the Republican Caucus line by placing the names of La Follette, Brookhart, Frazier, and Ladd in a separate column entitled "Radicals." Unaware that Bob had refrained from speaking at Walsh's request, this newspaper reported that "The La Follettites, all against Warren, kept aloof from the discussion."[56]

In the five-minute speech Bob had expected to deliver, he tersely expressed his interpretation of his oath as a Senator to support and defend the Constitution in strictly maintaining the provisions for separation of powers explicitly granted to the judicial, executive, and legislative branches of the Government. It was his profound conviction that this separation of powers was essential to the preservation of democracy. If he had spoken before the vote was taken on the Warren nomination, he would have reminded Senators that "During the last campaign speakers were heard throughout the length and breadth of the land proclaiming the necessity of preserving inviolate the Constitution of the United States. . . . Today we see those who most loudly mouthed their worship of the Constitution engaged in an attempt to disregard, to override one of its most explicit and fundamental provisions. . . .

"The Constitution provides that the President 'shall appoint' the officers of the government 'with the advice and consent of the Senate.' President Coolidge now threatens to appoint Charles B. Warren, Attorney General without the consent and against the will of the Senate. . . . [This] is no mere partisan conflict in which Senators are free to follow the dictates of their party leaders. It is a crisis in the life of the nation. If a President may thus with impunity violate one of the provisions of the Constitution, he may violate all of them. If he may override the Constitution in defiance of the Senate on this one occasion to appoint some unfit favorite to office, he may override it upon every occasion. He may make and consummate treaties without your consent. He may create new offices and order money paid out of the Treasury without your appropriation. He may declare war and plunge the United States into bloody conflict without your action and against your will. . . .

"The issue is joined. It is democracy against dictatorship. It is the Constitution of the United States against the whim of Calvin Coolidge."[57]

After the Senate's second refusal to confirm Warren, the President carried out his threat to override an adverse decision and again offered him the appointment. Warren declined. Coolidge then appointed another Attorney General "with the advice and consent of the Senate." In a signed editorial Bob denounced the initial choice of Warren and the President's declared purpose to override an explicit provision of the Constitution.[58]

The special session adjourned on March 18. As Congress would not convene until December, Bob looked forward to a summer free from the intense pressure of Senate sessions and committee work. He began at once to plan for conferences with one or two men from a dozen or fifteen of the leading progressive States to discuss the formation of a new party along the lines laid down at the Chicago conference. Aware of the hard work that was ahead, Bob, Jr., who was "tired to the bone," accepted an invitation to go abroad with a friend for a brief vacation. On March 30 Bob noted in his diary, "Cold & spitting snow— . . . Baby Bob here most of day. Growing and becoming playful. Fine little fellow. Will be a great joy to us all. Bob, Jr., making ready to sail Saturday. It will be awful lonesome, but splendid thing for him. And the lad is entitled to ev[e]rything. He is so good to us—and indeed to ev[e]rybody." On the night of

April 1, Bob recorded that "At 2 p.m. I met General (now Col. [William] Mitchell) for conference on his fight against battleships & for airplanes—as great economy—and preparation for defense rather than aggression. He is demoted and ordered to Texas as punishment for his advocacy of his belief in re obsolesence [*sic*] of battleships and value of air-planes He will be trying politics in Wis[consin] in a few years I predict. At three p.m. had fine talk with John Nelson—Bob & Bas [Manly] present. Johns work as he explains it in House & for election of progressive members all right. He expressed willingness to co-operate in any way with me in the progressive movement. His whole attitude is admirable."[59]

The following afternoon Bob, Jr., left for New York to have a day there with Fola before sailing. That night Bob confessed to his diary: "It was a pull to see him go though we were all for it. . . . I have to struggle to keep from being sentimental about it. I am awfully dependent on the lad—and feel guilty at taking so much out of his life to keep me company as the years come on me. It is the most pronounced symptom I note of their advance." The next day Bob leafed through his notes on their 1923 trip to Berlin to see if he could find anything that might be helpful to his son. That night he noted in his diary: "Bright & beautiful this morning here in Washington. It will I hope be the same in New York tomorrow so that the lad begins his trip in the bright sun-shine." On Saturday Bob, Jr., telephoned from New York, and that night his father wrote, "It was good for us to have word with him befor[e] he sails. I shall be busy for the next week getting off material for the Magazine[.] Work is good medicine for lots of our ills & will help over the beginning of our lon[e]someness at Bobs absence."[60]

Bob was still working on his editorials a few days later when Gilbert and Netha Roe and their two young daughters, Janet and Gwyneth, arrived for a visit he had been counting on to "make the house lively & full of good cheer." He laid aside his work for the Easter holiday and planned to "go in for a good time" during their visit. When he learned that Janet and Gwyneth wished to go to Mount Vernon, he offered to be their guide, and insisted the trip must be made by boat, as this was the only proper approach for a first visit to George Washington's home. On a fine, clear day when there happened to be few tourists, he and Belle shared with the Roe family the serene beauty of Mount Vernon as they had so often done with their own children. While Bob was standing at one end of the long veranda looking out on the magnificent view of the Potomac in which he always delighted, a group of high-school students from New York State recognized him. They ventured to ask if he would be willing to be photographed with the group and explained that they had recently been studying his work with keen interest. Bob was touched by their interest, and responded with a spontaneous little talk which the principal of the Watkins Glen high school re-membered vividly many years later.[61]

Soon after this trip to Mount Vernon, Bob wrote Rawleigh out-lining his plans for the summer and fall. During the period before Congress convened, he hoped to visit a dozen or fifteen of the strong-est progressive States, making one speech in each State and conferring the next day with as many progressive leaders as could be brought together. An alternative or supplementary part of his plan was to invite one or more leaders from these States for a conference at Madison. He also told Rawleigh that he expected "to dictate—in the rough—the material bringing my autobiography from 1912 to date."[62] In an inscription prepared for autographed copies of his *Autobiography*, Bob had expressed the purpose of his desire to com-plete the record of his life when he wrote, "It is my hope that this story, of such public service as I have been able to render Wisconsin and the country, may aid to enlist others to give the best that is in them to the cause of human rights and true democracy."[63]

On April 30 Bob wrote Phil that they were planning to return to Madison early in June, and outlined in detail the things which ought to be done at the farm. Phil and Isen had spent the previous summer at the farm, and he had enjoyed their companionship after the elec-tion. In expressing his disappointment at their decision to remain in town, he said, "It seems to me a mistake for you not to go back to the farm for the Summer. . . . But quite apart from the sentiment involved, I am sorry to see you merge yourself so wholly in your professional work. It is all very well for you to think that it is only a temporary thing you are doing this going to office nights and Sun-days. How much I would give if I could make over that part of my life. It is very wrong and in the long run I am sure that it is wasteful of the best that is in one. Moreover its tendency is very narrowing in its effect on the cultural side of the individual besides being mighty hard on home life."[64]

The day after this letter was written, Bob noted in his diary that he had a "Very bad nigh[t] last night. Great difficulty in breathing Coughed all night. All this imposed great labor on heart & I was forced to use quantities of N.[itro] g.[lycerin] all night. Belle called Marbury & Dr. Randolph They came about 10."[65] This severe bronchial cough had developed suddenly during the evening of the day Bob had been to see his dentist. But it soon yielded to treatment, and he took up his work again. When Belle chided him for sitting so long at his desk, he would answer, "I enjoy writing for the magazine; it never tires me."[66]

When Bob told his family that he intended to take several children to see Ringling's circus on the afternoon of May 15, Mary pleaded with him to give up this plan. He yielded reluctantly on condition that Mary would go with him and Belle that evening to a motion picture in the neighborhood. When Mary arrived at the house, he spoke to her of the sudden death of General Nelson A. Miles that afternoon at the circus just after the completion of the opening pageant. "I can understand what happened," Bob said. "The old soldier heard the band playing and the bugles blowing. It stirred him and quickened his pulse." Bob tapped his left side and added with a smile, "You were right about my going to the circus." At the theater he had an attack of pain, but it yielded quickly to the medicine the doctors had prescribed, and he was in good spirits throughout the evening.[67]

On Sunday afternoon, May 17, Bob drove with Belle, Mary, Ralph, and the baby for several hours through Potomac Park and Rock Creek Park. It was a clear day with brilliant sunshine. As always, Bob delighted in the beauty of a Washington spring and found a special pleasure in watching the families with children enjoying their holiday in the public parks. "Life is good," he said to Mary. Shortly after they started out, Bob had left the car for a few moments to buy a little camera, and they stopped in Rock Creek Park to take some photographs. At sunset they returned home. As Bob closed the door of the car, he lingered a moment, smiled at Mary, and said, "We had a good time, didn't we?"[68]

Later in the evening, while he and Belle were sitting out on the lawn, Bob suddenly complained of feeling chilly and went to his room. During the early morning hours he wakened with a severe chill and acute, shooting pains in his heart. Not wishing to disturb Belle, he wrapped himself in blankets and sat close to the radiator, trying to get warm. This exertion, when he should have remained absolutely quiet in bed, added to the strain on his heart.

After Dr. Marbury and the heart specialist, Dr. Lee, had made a careful examination, Belle wrote Phil and Fola that Dr. Lee said their father must remain in bed for a month. "This lying in bed for a period of time compensates, according to Dr. Lee, for any sacrifice it calls for in the way of being out of door or in the sun or taking drives. He believes Daddy can rest this way and restore the heart tissue and build a reserve on which to take up work again—the extent of course to be determined by his condition. Dr. Marbury acquiesces. I have not talked to Daddy but he is always reasonable. The attack which was so slow to yield to control was a shock and a warning he must heed. I am sure he will adjust himself to the doctors decision. And we must all unite in making it easy for him."[69]

Each day he enjoyed Mary's visits, and frequently asked to have the baby brought to his room. As he watched his grandson playing on his bed, he said to his daughter: "See how he reaches for things beyond his grasp. That will always be true—and it is right and good to have it so."[70] Belle thought it a blessing that Bob could enjoy this baby "with all his deep sense of the meaning of such experiences in life."[71]

In letters to her "dear Ones" Belle gave the doctors' reports and recounted the little happenings which mean so much in times of illness. She wrote how helpful Grace Lynch and Rachel Young were. "We rely on Grace for almost everything. She has been with us so long and knows all phases of the various sides of life and she has a wonderful heart and brain." Belle reported that on the third evening after Bob was taken ill he asked for a book and read until one o'clock. He gave Grace Lynch a list of detective stories to be sent from the Library of Congress. When he had been in bed a week, Dr. Marbury and Dr. Randolph said all the specific symptoms were good and they were both confident he would recover.[72]

Bob had been looking forward to his son's return from Europe, and on the day the ship was due in New York he wakened feeling so well that he insisted upon shaving himself. That afternoon he had another attack of pain. Although it was less severe than the previous one, Dr. Marbury thought it best to have a night nurse. The next day Belle wrote that Bob, Jr.'s, "coming did us all a lot of good. It did not seem to tax Daddy's strength to visit with him."[73] Bob was interested in hearing about his son's trip, and they had good talks together.

On June 3 Bob, Jr., wrote Phil and Isen that "Drs. Lee and Marbury both feel that our dear Daddie has lost ground in the last 48 hours."[74] On June 13 Bob's blood pressure went up to 140, the highest since he had been ill, and Dr. Marbury thought he did not seem so well. That morning a letter came from Phil saying Isen would stop off in Washington June 16, on her way to New York. Bob was delighted at the prospect of her visit. Bob, Jr., thinking it would be a natural way for his brother to see his father, suggested that it would be nice if Phil came with Isen. But his father said that as he planned to be home so soon, he did not think Phil ought to spend the money for the trip. On Sunday, June 14, Bob enjoyed the flowers and messages friends sent for his seventieth birthday. That day Bob., Jr., wrote his brother: "Mother bears up well under the strain, although I fear that she is much worn. I find it difficult to get her to leave the house at all even though I am there."[75] Phil surprised his father and the family by arriving with Isen on June 16. That day Bob, Jr., wrote Gilbert Roe that the situation was becoming very serious, "and although we have not given up hope, it is about all we have left."[76] But Bob had a good night's rest, and the next morning, when Fola and Mid arrived, his condition seemed to have improved, and the doctors were still hopeful of recovery. At noon that day Bob, Jr., gave a statement to the press that "though the condition of Senator La Follette is somewhat more serious than before, he is holding his own and the physicians hold every hope for his ultimate recovery."[77] Each day Bob seemed "to pick up in strength and be so like himself for an hour or two with all his keen wit and quickness of mind" that neither Belle nor his physicians could believe until the last day that he was not going to get well.[78] One evening when he was alone with Bob, Jr., and feeling in a philosophical mood, he said to his son: "I am at peace with all the world, but there is a lot of work I still could do. I don't know how the people will feel toward me, but I shall take to the grave my love for them which has sustained me through life."[79]

On June 18, at eight o'clock in the morning, Bob had a severe heart attack which marked a sudden turn in the wrong direction. Dr. Marbury came at once, and later called the family into the room where they remained until Bob left them at one twenty-one in the afternoon.

In a letter to her father's and mother's friend Elizabeth Evans, Fola wrote: "We were all in Daddy's room when the end came. Mother seated by his bed, holding his hand; speaking to him, pouring out the love and devotion of a lifetime in the last long farewell; all hesitation gone from her speech; her voice clear and sweet— telling him her vision of the nobility and beauty of his life and work. If he heard it was with other senses than those that he had used through the years, for as far as nurses and doctors could tell he was 'unconscious' just at the end. But we heard—we who were gathered about—and we can never forget. And if he could have heard, there has not been and never can be any tribute which would so deeply have satisfied his mind and heart. His passing was mysteriously peaceful for one who had stood so long on the battle line. Never have I seen so slight a demarcation in the transition from life to death. And yet within an hour of the final silence he had spoken quite naturally and simply, had shortly before evoked a smile by one of his inimitable little jests. Within two hours of his death he had taken half a glass of milk, raised it to his lips with his own hand, and had said it was 'good.' His body was strong and he was in complete command of his physical coordinations: his mind was clear and his spirit serene to the last moment of consciousness. But his heart was tired and refused to carry on. He went to sleep, and we shall not hear his voice again—strangely that was the thought that came to each one of us when dear Dr. Marbury looked up and signed to us that all our yearning and love could do no more for him. The transition was so gentle and untroubled that, though he had his hand on Daddy's pulse, Dr. Marbury could not be certain it had come until he listened with the stethoscope. We kissed his brow in silence and turned to mother—and she gave us of her strength speaking of how Daddy had loved life and found it good. And from this thought it seemed as if everything flowed. Through all the hours and days that followed each one gathered strength and courage from the other. There was an almost mysterious accord as to how everything should be done. Each detail was met as if Mother's thought had shaped our minds before she spoke. We have done and do what we can for her, but it all seems so little and inadequate compared with what she gives us."[80]

Bob had always disliked the garb of mourning, and none of his family wore black on the afternoon of June 19, when they followed the simple gray casket as it was carried from the house. There was no ceremony in Washington, but thousands gathered at the Union Station and stood silently as the casket was lifted into the same special car that he had traveled in during his 1924 speaking campaign. Trainmen in the yards dropped their tools and bowed their heads as the train passed bearing his body on the final trip home from the Nation's Capital where he had lived and worked for so many years. Traveling in the special car with Belle were her four children, her sons-in-law, George Middleton and Ralph Sucher, Gilbert Roe, Basil Manly, and Grace Lynch. On the same train were Senators Wheeler, Lenroot, and other members of the Congressional delegation. During that afternoon and night and the next morning, as the train passed through towns and villages, crowds gathered to pay a last tribute. Farmers stopped work in the fields and bowed their heads. "At every railroad center or yard where stops were made crowds of workers gathered with bare heads to pay homage to their fallen leader."[81]

Outside Chicago Herman Ekern, W. T. Rawleigh, and Alfred T. Rogers joined Bob's family. At the station thousands who had welcomed him in 1924 waited to say farewell, unaware that in the railroad yards outside the city the car bearing his body home had been transferred to a special train for the journey to Madison. "Along the wayside stations as the train rolled into the rich green land of his home state, men and women sorrowfully watched the funeral car. In Janesville hundreds gathered in tribute to him. In Madison there were thousands at the station." Between long lines of silent men, women, and children the casket was borne to the governor's room in the capitol. That night a correspondent who had been on the train wrote, "Fighting Bob, On His Shield, Home At Last."[82] Throughout the night state soldiers in civilian dress and members of the legislature stood guard.

From the hour of his death messages had been coming to Belle and her children, including many from his Senate colleagues and one from President Coolidge. Those in distant lands joined with men and women in his own country in tribute to the enduring meaning of his life and their sense of loss at his passing. The Wisconsin legislature passed a joint resolution commemorating his life and work. This was immediately followed by a law providing that a statue of him should be placed in Statuary Hall of the national Capitol. The regents of the university commended his lifelong service to the university and to the cause of education in the State. Hundreds of graduates were in Madison for the Commencement ceremonies, and the Alumni Association unanimously passed a long resolution which closed with the words: "While the sweet graciousness of his winning, noble person is lost to us, his spirit prevails. His influence for high and upright conduct in public service pervades the life of the state as that of no other man has ever done."[83] The day after his death the faculty of the university passed a resolution expressing sympathy and "their sincere admiration for his heroic life, for his mighty contributions to a nobler public service, and to the cause of education."[84]

On Sunday morning the casket, draped in the United States flag, was placed in the east rotunda of the capitol. Flowers with messages from individuals and organizations throughout the country were banked behind the balustrades of the main balcony. Mingled with formal wreaths and sprays of lilies and roses were blossoms from home gardens, and wild flowers. At the head of the casket was a floral tribute from the Chicago Teachers' Federation. Another wreath had also been placed beside the casket at Belle's request. It was from Plutarco Elías Calles, President of Mexico, sent as a tribute to La Follette's efforts to preserve peace between the United States and Mexico. During the morning intimate friends who had worked with him through the years came to say farewell. At twelve o'clock the doors were opened to the thousands who had been traveling along the congested highways of the State and arriving in Madison since dawn. A slowly moving line of men, women, and children began passing the casket in double file to look upon his face for the last time. Young men and women in cap and gown, students from India, Japan, and South America mingled with men and women who had known him as boy and youth in paying tribute to the life that had begun seventy years earlier in a log cabin.

Throughout the afternoon, from farms, towns, villages, and cities in Wisconsin and other States, trains and automobiles brought men, women, and children who joined the long lines that extended around the square and moved steadily up the steps leading into the capitol. When the doors were closed at eight o'clock, many had not been able to enter, although it was estimated fifty thousand people had passed his bier. On Monday morning the highways leading into Madison were choked with traffic. Before the doors of the capitol were opened, the long lines had formed again, and the sorrowing pilgrimage continued until they were closed to permit the final preparation for the funeral ceremony. By proclamation of the mayor the banks and stores were closed, and the university suspended the graduation program until after the funeral.

When the services began, every available space on the balconies, stairways, and ground floor was filled, and thousands listened from the park outside as the seventy-five voices of the Mozart Club and the Madison Maennerchor joined in singing "Nearer, My God, to Thee." After Dr. A. E. Haydon of the University of Chicago Divinity School had read selections from several poems and the Book of Job, the chorus sang "Abide with Me." These were two hymns which Bob's mother had often sung, and he had selected them for her funeral service.

Standing beside the casket, Dr. Haydon read his brief but moving tribute in which he said: "We shall remember him as the embattled prophet of the new democracy, a democracy directed by intelligence and organized to guarantee an opportunity for full and beautiful life to every child of man. His voice was the voice of humanism in politics. . . . We shall remember him as one who in a cynical age loved and kept his faith in humble men and women. He was always ready to trust the people, if you could give them the facts. It is not an accident that he should have stressed investigation, that he should have made the discovery of facts central and fundamental, that statistics could upon his lips become eloquence; but it was his human heart which kept him close to the life problems of the folk. . . .

"We shall remember him as a leader of dauntless courage . . . forsaken even by those for whom he was giving his life. Almost alone, he held his vision true . . . he kept his faith in us. That love which bound him to his people and to his neighbors still supported him; he trusted us yet. It is almost heart-breaking to think that we

could have left him alone. But he won; he lived to see his friends—
his people who he was sure would understand when they knew—
give him vindication at the last. . . .

"We must say farewell, but we shall always remember him. We
may do more. We may give him earthly immortality in our lives. The
old enemies against which he fought still are in the field; the causes
which he championed still call for battling, heroic hearts. The future
democracy of which he dreamed still is to win . . . And here, here in
his presence still, we may with bowed heads and quiet courage,
dedicate ourselves to that sublime and splendid task. We say farewell, but we shall always remember him."

At a sign from Dr. Haydon, thousands of voices rose in the song
"America." As the anthem swelled through the corridors of the capitol, it was taken up by the multitudes massed in the grounds outside.
As the song ended, there was an instant of silence, and then Dr.
Haydon's brief benediction: "To be true to the vision of him, to
stand in the full blaze of the open day, searching, finding, and ready
to die in the path of the ideal—this we pray may be our opportunity,
this may we give in loyalty to our memory of him."[85]

The chimes in the steeple of Grace Episcopal Church played "Lead,
Kindly Light" as friends bore the casket down the steps between
rows of distinguished men and on "through a great circle of labor
men whose small badges were the only mark of uniformity to be
seen except the white ribbons of the ushers."[86] Belle, her children,
and Bob's sister followed slowly through the crowds lined on either
side to the waiting automobiles. Then the three-mile journey to the
cemetery began. Headed by the Congressional delegation, state officers, and members of the legislature, the funeral procession "wound
interminably along the streets of his town, from the Capitol to Forest
Hill, between the mass of the workers, marching in the dust and
heat, or standing with uncovered heads. Not a drum or a gun or a
uniform. Not a soldier as such. Only the people and their flowers
and the sound of bells, not tolling, but chiming out old hymns—
'Abide With Me,' 'Lead, Kindly Light,' "[87]

Long before the funeral procession arrived at Forest Hill Cemetery, thousands had gathered about the La Follette family lot. At the
grave beneath an ancient oak tree, Dr. Haydon read a brief service
before the casket was lowered to rest in the earth of the State he had
loved and served.

Among the papers found in his desk in the Capitol at Washington after Belle and Bob, Jr., returned, was a small piece of scratch paper on which he had written in pencil shortly before his last illness these words:

I would be remembered as one who in the worlds darkest hour kept a clean conscience and stood to the end for the ideals of American Democracy

Epilogue

On June 20, 1926, memorial services were held in the United States Senate in memory of Robert M. La Follette. Addresses were delivered on his life, character, and services by Senators Irvine L. Lenroot of Wisconsin, Joseph T. Robinson of Arkansas, Henrik Shipstead of Minnesota, Thomas J. Walsh of Montana, Lynn J. Frazier of North Dakota, Bert M. Fernald of Maine, Hiram W. Johnson of California, Furnifold M. Simmons of North Carolina, George H. Moses of New Hampshire, Clarence C. Dill of Washington, William E. Borah of Idaho, Burton K. Wheeler of Montana, James A. Reed of Missouri, and George W. Norris of Nebraska.

In the House of Representatives memorial services were held on February 20, 1927, in memory of Robert M. La Follette. Addresses were delivered by Representatives John M. Nelson of Wisconsin, Henry R. Rathbone of Illinois, Edward E. Browne of Wisconsin, Fiorello H. La Guardia of New York, George J. Schneider of Wisconsin, Joseph D. Beck of Wisconsin, Edgar Howard of Nebraska, Hubert H. Peavey of Wisconsin, O. J. Kvale of Minnesota, Victor L. Berger of Wisconsin, James H. Sinclair of North Dakota, John C. Shafer of Wisconsin, Florian Lampert of Wisconsin, Edward Voigt of Wisconsin, George Huddleston of Alabama, James A. Frear of Wisconsin, Henry Allen Cooper of Wisconsin, James O'Connor of Louisiana, John Morrow of New Mexico, and Oscar E. Keller of Minnesota.[1]

On June 24, 1925, the people of Wisconsin had conferred upon Robert M. La Follette the highest honor within the gift of the State. Acting through the legislature, by a unanimous vote of both branches and under unanimous consent, they had provided that in commemoration of his services to the State and the Nation a statue of him should be placed in Statuary Hall, the former Hall of the House of Representatives in the national Capitol.[2]

Nearly forty years earlier, Wisconsin had chosen Father Jacques Marquette as the first of its residents to be thus honored under an Act of Congress passed on July 2, 1864, authorizing each State to provide and furnish statues of two deceased residents of historic renown to be placed in the old Hall of the House of Representatives in the Capitol at Washington.[3]

In 1929 when the marble statue of Robert M. La Follette was completed by Jo Davidson, it was accepted by the Senate and the House of Representatives in the name of the Nation. At the unveiling on April 25, 1929, his son Robert M. La Follette, Jr., who had been elected to fill his father's unexpired term, presided. In a brief address his son Philip F. La Follette expressed the profound gratitude of the family to the people of Wisconsin. The statue was unveiled by his grandson Robert La Follette Sucher and Marion Montana Wheeler, daughter of Senator and Mrs. Burton K. Wheeler. The statue was presented by Senator John J. Blaine of Wisconsin on behalf of the State. Addresses were delivered by Dr. A. Eustace Haydon of the University of Chicago, Charles H. Crownhart, Associate Justice of the Supreme Court of Wisconsin, Gilbert E. Roe of New York City, Victor A. Olander, Secretary-Treasurer, International Seamen's Union of America, Mrs. Mabel Cory Costigan of Denver, Colorado, Edward Keating, editor of *Labor,* and Claude G. Bowers of New York City.

The following poem by Edgar Lee Masters is included in the printed volume of the proceedings in the Congress and in Statuary Hall:

ROBERT M. LA FOLLETTE

Neither the wind that changes; nor the tide
That brings the sailor home; nor the summer's sun
That scatters clouds, have ever swifter run
Their course than did that passion which belied
This Hampden of America, and with pride
Of violence scourged; yet seeing our countryman
Fallen in death, reversed what it had done,
And honored him in this Hall by the side
Of those famed niches for his figure hewed
Out of the rock, as even his soul was urged.
He is our Milton, and the high and far
Cliff of our light-house, where the waters spewed
Weed drift and slime—by the same waters purged
Clean for the midday and the evening star![4]

Notes

Chapter XLVI
(Pages 731–748)

[1] Lincoln Steffens to R. M. L., March 26, 1917, LFP.
[2] Gustav A. Lake, Harvard Law School, to R. M. L., April 7, 1917, is typical of many letters in files of LFP.
[3] *Record*, 65th Cong., 1st Sess., Vol. 55, p. 746, April 17, 1917.
[4] *Ibid.*, p. 1362, April 27, 1917.
[5] *New York Times*, April 19, 1917.
[6] *Ibid.*, April 26, 1917.
[7] *Record*, 65th Cong., 1st Sess., Vol. 55, p. 2166, May 12, 1917.
[8] *Ibid.*, p. 3144, May 31, 1917.
[9] *New York Times*, April 17, 1917; Joseph P. Tumulty to Woodrow Wilson, April 12, 1917, Tumulty Papers.
[10] *Record*, 65th Cong., 1st Sess., Vol. 55, pp. 1119-1123, April 25, 1917; p. 960, April 23, 1917.
[11] *Ibid.*, pp. 907-908, April 21, 1917.
[12] *Ibid.*, p. 1153, April 26, 1917.
[13] *Ibid.*, p. 995, April 24, 1917.
[14] *Ibid.*, pp. 1354-1364, April 27, 1917.
[15] B. C. L. to Phil and Mary, April 29, 1917, LFP.
[16] *Record*, 65th Cong., 1st Sess., Vol. 55, pp. 1354-1355, April 27, 1917.
[17] *Ibid.*, pp. 1355-1357, April 27, 1917.
[18] *Ibid.*, p. 1358, April 27, 1917.
[19] *Ibid.*, p. 1364, April 27, 1917.
[20] Arthur Garfield Hays to author, July 17, 1917, LFP.
[21] *Record*, 65th Cong., 1st Sess., Vol. 55, p. 1478, April 28, 1917.
[22] B. C. L. to Phil and Mary, May 1, 1917, LFP.
[23] *Record*, 65th Cong., 1st Sess., Vol. 55, pp. 1616-1620, 1624, May 1, 1917.
[24] B. C. L. to Phil and Mary, May 1, 1917, LFP.
[25] *Record*, 65th Cong., 1st Sess., Vol. 55, p. 2457, May 17, 1917.
[26] *New York Times*, May 19, 1917.
[27] *Record*, 65th Cong., 1st Sess., Vol. 55, p. 5368, July 21, 1917.

[28] *Martin* v. *Mott,* 12 Wheaton 19, 29 (1827).

[29] Selective Draft Law Cases, 245 U.S. 366, decided Jan. 7, 1918; *Cox* v. *Wood,* 247 U.S. 3, decided March 6, 1918.

[30] *Record,* 65th Cong., 1st Sess., Vol. 55, p. 5369, July 21, 1917.

[31] R. M. L. to Gilbert E. Roe, June 16, 1917, LFP.

[32] *Idem* to Josephine La Follette Siebecker, June 19, 1917, LFP.

[33] *Idem* to B. C. L., Phil, and Mary, June 23, 1917, LFP.

[34] *Idem* to Gilbert E. Roe, June 16, 1917, LFP.

[35] *La Follette's Magazine,* June, 1917, p. 3.

[36] R. M. L., Jr., to B. C. L., Phil, and Mary, June 9, 1917, LFP.

[37] R. M. L. to B. C. L., Phil, and Mary, June 7, 1917, LFP.

[38] *Idem* to Gilbert E. Roe, July 17, 1917, LFP.

[39] Agnes Smedley to Mrs. Gilbert E. Roe, Feb. 22, 1930.

[40] *Record,* 65th Cong., 1st Sess., Vol. 55, p. 103, April 2, 1917; *Boston Herald,* April 3, 1917; *Oregon Daily Journal,* April 3, 1917; *Boston Evening Transcript,* April 3, 1917.

[41] F. M. Simmons, *Simmons, Statesman of the New South* (Duke University Press, 1936), p. 63.

[42] R. M. L. to Gilbert E. Roe, June 2, 1917, LFP.

[43] *Idem* to B. C. L., Phil, and Mary, June 7, 1917, LFP.

[44] *Idem* to B. C. L., Phil, and Mary, July 2, 1917, LFP.

[45] R. M. L., Jr., to author, July 14, 1945, LFP. Senator Gore recalled overhearing this conversation but did not remember who the two Senators were. Thomas P. Gore to author, April 12, 1938, LFP.

[46] *Oregon Daily Journal,* Aug. 2, 1917.

[47] *Collier's Weekly,* Aug. 4, 1917.

[48] *Record,* 65th Cong., 1st Sess., Vol. 55, pp. 5827-5828, Aug. 6, 1917.

[49] *Evening Star,* Washington, D.C., Aug. 14, 1917.

[50] Suzanne La Follette, diary entry, Aug. 14, 1917, LFP.

[51] R. M. L. to B. C. L., Phil, and Mary, Aug. 28, 1917, LFP.

[52] R. M. L., Jr., to author, July 14, 1945.

[53] *Record,* 65th Cong., 1st Sess., Vol. 55, pp. 6201-6202, Aug. 21, 1917.

[54] *Ibid.*

[55] *Ibid.,* p. 6209, Aug. 21, 1917.

[56] Aug. 21, 1917.

[57] *Record,* 65th Cong., 1st Sess., Vol. 55, p. 6243, Aug. 22, 1917.

[58] *Ibid.,* pp. 6244-6248; 6250-6251, Aug. 22, 1917.

[59] *Oregon Daily Journal,* Aug. 23, 1917; R. M. L. to B. C. L., Phil, and Mary, Aug. 22, 1917, LFP.

[60] *Record,* 65th Cong., 1st Sess., Vol. 55, p. 6270, p. 6273, Aug. 23, 1917.

[61] *Ibid.,* p. 6273, Aug. 23, 1917.

[62] *Ibid.,* p. 6288, Aug. 23, 1917.

[63] *Ibid.,* pp. 6432-6433, Aug. 29, 1917.

[64] *Ibid.,* p. 6435, Aug. 29, 1917.

[65] *New York Times,* Aug. 30, 1917.

[66] *Record,* 65th Cong., 1st Sess., Vol. 55, pp. 6479-6480, Aug. 31, 1917.

[67] *Ibid.*, p. 6503, Sept. 1, 1917.

[68] *Ibid.*, pp. 6503-6519, Sept. 1, 1917.

[69] R. M. L., Jr., to B. C. L., Phil, and Mary, Sept. 2, 1917, LFP.

[70] *Record*, 65th Cong., 1st Sess., Vol. 55, pp. 6526-6529, Sept. 3, 1917.

[71] *Ibid.*, pp. 6542, 6549, Sept. 3, 1917; pp. 6560-6561, Sept. 4, 1917.

[72] R. M. L., Jr., to B. C. L., Sept. 4, 1917, LFP.

[73] *New York Times*, Sept. 6, 1917.

[74] *Oregon Daily Journal*, Sept. 6, 1917.

[75] *Record*, 65th Cong., 1st Sess., Vol. 55, pp. 6853-6854, Sept. 10, 1917.

[76] *Ibid.*, p. 6858, Sept. 10, 1917.

[77] *Ibid.*, p. 6879, Sept. 10, 1917.

[78] *Ibid.*, p. 6886, Sept. 10, 1917.

[79] *World*, New York, Dec. 17, 1917.

[80] *La Follette's Magazine*, editorial, Sept., 1917, p. 2.

[81] *Salina Journal*, Sept. 14, 1917, reprinted in pamphlet entitled "Bristow's Editorials That Caused Such a Stir in Kansas," LFP.

[82] *La Follette's Magazine*, Dec., 1917, p. 2.

[83] *Record*, 65th Cong., 2nd Sess., Vol. 56, pp. 7114-7115, May 27, 1918.

[84] *La Follette's Magazine*, June, 1918, pp. 1, 2.

[85] R. M. L., Jr., to author, March, 1939, LFP.

[86] *Record*, 65th Cong., 1st Sess., Vol. 55, p. 6732, Sept. 7, 1917.

[87] *Ibid.*, p. 6741, Sept. 7, 1917.

[88] *Ibid.*, p. 6856, Sept. 10, 1917.

[89] B. C. L. to R. M. L., Sept. 5, 1917, LFP.

[90] *Record*, 77th Cong., 2nd Sess., Vol. 88, Part 4, p. 4746, June 1, 1942; pp. 4863-4869, June 4, 1942; pp. 4989-4995, June 8, 1942.

Chapter XLVII
(Pages 749–760)

[1] R. M. L. to B. C. L., Phil, and Mary, June 23, 1917, LFP.

[2] *Record*, 65th Cong., 1st Sess., Vol. 55, p. 1364, April 27, 1917. See also *Foreign Relations*, 1918, Russia, I, 39-40.

[3] *New York Times*, May 17, 1917.

[4] *Foreign Relations*, 1918, Russia, I, 79-80.

[5] *New York Times*, May 24, 1917.

[6] R. M. L. to Gilbert E. Roe, June 2, 1917, LFP; *World*, New York, signed dispatch by Louis Seibold, June 2, 1917.

[7] Ray Stannard Baker, *Woodrow Wilson*, VII, 91.

[8] Charles Seymour, *The Intimate Papers of Colonel House*, III, 139.

[9] *Springfield Daily Republican*, May 31, 1917.

[10] *Chicago Herald*, May 28, 1917; *Unity*, Vol. 79, No. 14, p. 212, May 31, 1917; *Chicago Daily Tribune*, May 28, 1917.

[11] *Chicago Herald*, May 29, 1917.

[12] *Unity*, Vol. LXXIX, No. 15, pp. 229-231, June 7, 1917.

[13] *Ibid.*, No. 22, pp. 344-350, July 26, 1917; No. 25, p. 399, Aug. 16, 1917.

[14] *Minneapolis Morning Tribune*, Aug. 29, 1917.

[15] Louis P. Lochner to Woodrow Wilson, Aug. 28, 1917, with attached memorandum by Woodrow Wilson, Wilson Papers.

[16] Woodrow Wilson to Albert S. Burleson, Aug. 7, 1917, Wilson Papers.

[17] *The Autobiography of Lincoln Steffens*, Vol. II, pp. 745-746.

[18] R. M. L., Jr., to Phil, June 27, 1917, LFP.

[19] Typewritten memorandum made by R. M. L., Jr., after talk with Lincoln Steffens, June 25, 1917, LFP.

[20] *The Autobiography of Lincoln Steffens*, II, 764-765; Lincoln Steffens to E. M. House, June 20, 1917, *Letters of Lincoln Steffens*, I, 399; recollection of R. M. L., Jr., and author.

[21] *The Autobiography of Lincoln Steffens*, II, 770-772.

[22] Grace Lynch to author, Aug. 8, 1939, LFP.

[23] R. M. L., Jr., to author.

[24] *Foreign Relations*, 1917, Supplement 2, I, 139-140.

[25] *New York Times*, July 27, 1917.

[26] *Record*, 65th Cong., 1st Sess., Vol. 55, pp. 5495-5496, July 26, 1917.

[27] July 28, 1917.

[28] *Minneapolis Journal*, July 12, 1917.

[29] R. M. L. to B. C. L., Phil, and Mary, July 27, 1917, LFP.

[30] *Record*, 65th Cong., 1st Sess., Vol. 55, p. 5691, Aug. 2, 1917.

[31] Robert Lansing to Woodrow Wilson, June 3, 1917; Executive Office Diary, June 4, 1917, Wilson Papers.

[32] R. M. L. to B. C. L., Phil, and Mary, Aug. 4, 1917, LFP.

[33] *Record*, 65th Cong., 1st Sess., Vol. 55, p. 5956, Aug. 11, 1917.

[34] *Ibid.*, p. 5957, Aug. 11, 1917.

[35] Aug. 14, 1917.

[36] *Oregon Daily Journal*, Aug. 14, 1917.

[37] Aug. 17, 1917.

[38] B. C. L. to R. M. L., Aug. 11, 1917, LFP.

[39] *New York Times*, Aug. 12, 1917.

[40] *Ibid.*, Aug. 13, 1917.

[41] Suzanne La Follette diary entry, Aug. 14, 1917, LFP.

[42] Allan Nevins, *Henry White: Thirty Years of American Diplomacy* (New York, Harper & Brothers, 1930), pp. 341-346; Ray Stannard Baker, *Woodrow Wilson*, VII, 224.

[43] *Record*, 65th Cong., 1st Sess., Vol. 55, p. 6039, Aug. 15, 1917.

[44] *Ibid.*, p. 6040, Aug. 15, 1917.

[45] *New York Times*, Aug. 7, 1917.

[46] Aug. 17, 1917.

[47] *Springfield Daily Republican*, Aug. 16, 1917.

[48] *Foreign Relations*, 1917, Supplement 2, I, 162-164.

[49] Aug. 18, 1917.

[50] *War Memoirs of David Lloyd George*, IV, 2062.

[51] Ray Stannard Baker, *op. cit.*, VII, 241; Seymour, *op. cit.*, III, 165.

[52] *Foreign Relations,* 1917, Supplement 2, I, 177-179.
[53] *Record,* 65th Cong., 1st Sess., Vol. 55, p. 7882, Oct. 6, 1917.
[54] *New York Times,* Aug. 12, 1917.
[55] Aug. 13, 1917.
[56] *New York Times,* Aug. 16, 1917.
[57] *Minneapolis Morning Tribune,* Sept. 7, 1917.
[58] Lincoln Steffens to R. M. L., Aug. 17, 1917, LFP.

Chapter XLVIII
(Pages 761–778)

[1] *Record,* 59th Cong., 1st Sess., Vol. 40, pp. 7832-7833, June 5, 1906.
[2] R. M. L., Jr., to Phil and Mary, Sept. 20, 1917, LFP.
[3] *Idem* to B. C. L., Phil, and Mary, Sept. 25, 1917, LFP.
[4] Robert M. La Follette, "My Own Story," Part 5, *Washington Daily News,* Sept. 23, 1924.
[5] Senator Lynn J. Frazier to author, Feb. 1, 1939, LFP.
[6] *Speech of Senator Robert M. La Follette, September 20, 1917, Hearings Before the Committee on Privileges and Elections United States Senate,* 65th Cong., 2nd Sess., Part 2, pp. 90-91, May 21, 1918.
[7] *Ibid.,* pp. 91-92, May 21, 1918.
[8] *Ibid.,* pp. 92-93, May 21, 1918.
[9] *Ibid.,* pp. 94-95, May 21, 1918.
[10] *Ibid.,* p. 98, May 21, 1918.
[11] Senator Lynn J. Frazier to author, Feb. 1, 1939, LFP.
[12] R. M. L., Jr., to B. C. L., Phil, and Mary, Sept. 25, 1917, LFP.
[13] *Speech of Senator Robert M. La Follette, September 20, 1917, Hearings Before the Committee on Privileges and Elections United States Senate,* 65th Cong., 2nd Sess., Part 2, p. 94.
[14] Frederick Roy Martin to Atlee Pomerene, May 23, 1918.
[15] *St. Paul Pioneer Press,* Sept. 21, 1917. The *Milwaukee Journal,* September 21, also quoted R. M. L. as saying we had grievances.
[16] Sept. 22, 1917.
[17] *Post-Intelligencer,* Seattle, Wash., Sept. 26, 1917, signed editorial by Scott C. Bone.
[18] *Morning Tribune,* Minneapolis, Sept. 22, 1917; *St. Paul Pioneer Press,* Sept. 22, 1917.
[19] Copy of testimony of A. C. Townley, before Minnesota Public Safety Commission, LFP.
[20] *New York Times,* Sept. 26, 1917.
[21] United Press dispatch, *News Bee,* Toledo, Ohio, Sept. 29, 1917.
[22] James Manahan to Gilbert E. Roe, Nov. 20, 1917, LFP.
[23] *Hearings before Special Committee of the House of Representatives,* 65th Cong., 3rd Sess., on H. Res. 469 and H. Res. 476 *to Investigate The*

National Security League, 1918–1919, p. 411; also pp. 398 and 520 *in re* Theodore Roosevelt's trips under auspices of the National Security League.

[24] *Ibid.,* No. 1173, March 3, 1919, pp. 15-16.

[25] *North American,* Philadelphia, Sept. 28, 1917.

[26] *Kansas City Star,* Sept. 24, 1917.

[27] *Chicago Daily Tribune,* September 27, 1917.

[28] *North American,* Philadelphia, Sept. 28, 1917.

[29] *Ibid.,* Sept. 29, 1917.

[30] *St. Paul Pioneer Press,* Sept. 29, 1917.

[31] Theodore Roosevelt to Henry Cabot Lodge, Oct. 4, 1917, TR Papers.

[32] *New York Times,* Sept. 27, 1917.

[33] *Ibid.,* Oct. 14, 1917.

[34] Fola to R. M. L., Jr., Sept. 28, 1917, LFP.

[35] *New York Times,* Sept. 28, 1917.

[36] H. J. Hahn to author, June 22, 1938, LFP.

[37] *News-Bee,* Toledo, Ohio, Sept. 24, 1917.

[38] H. J. Hahn to author, June 22, 1938, LFP.

[39] *News-Bee,* Toledo, Ohio, Sept. 24, 1917.

[40] B. C. L. to Netha Roe, Sept. 24, 1917.

[41] R. M. L., Jr., to B. C. L., Phil, and Mary, Sept. 25, 1917, LFP.

[42] *New York Times,* Sept. 24, 1917; *St. Paul Free Press,* Sept. 24, 1917. Dispatch from Toledo, Sept. 23.

[43] *St. Paul Pioneer Press,* Sept. 24, 1917.

[44] Letter from Frederick Roy Martin, assistant general manager, Associated Press, to Senator Atlee Pomerene, May 23, printed in *Hearings Before the Committee on Privileges and Elections, United States Senate,* 65th Cong., 2nd Sess., Part 2, p. 160, May 22, 1918.

[45] *La Follette's Magazine,* Nov., 1917, p. 6.

[46] Oswald Garrison Villard, *Prophets True and False* (New York, A. A. Knopf, 1928), p. 192; Oswald Garrison Villard to author, Dec. 30, 1937, LFP.

[47] *Record,* 65th Cong., 1st Sess., Vol. 55, p. 7305, Sept. 21, 1917.

[48] *New York Times,* September 28, 1917.

[49] R. M. L. to B. C. L., Phil, and Mary, Sept. 27, 1917, LFP. See also *Washington Post,* Sept. 28, 1917.

[50] *New York Times,* Sept. 23, 1917.

[51] *Washington Post,* Sept. 30, 1917.

[52] R. M. L. to B. C. L., Phil, and Mary, Sept. 27, 1917, LFP.

[53] *Record,* 65th Cong., 1st Sess., Vol. 55, p. 7491, Sept. 29, 1917.

[54] *Oregon Daily Journal,* Sept. 29, 1917.

[55] *Ibid.*

[56] R. M. L. to B. C. L., Sept. 29, 1917, LFP.

[57] *Record,* 65th Cong., 1st Sess., Vol. 55, pp. 7632-7633, Oct. 2, 1917.

[58] Suzanne La Follette diary entry, Oct. 2, 1917, LFP.

[59] *Sun,* Baltimore, Oct. 5, 1917, dispatch from Columbus, Ohio, dated Oct. 4.

[60] *Madison Democrat,* Oct. 4, 1917; *Wisconsin State Journal,* Oct. 4, 1917.

[61] Oct. 4, 1917.

[62] *North American,* Philadelphia, Oct. 6, 1917.
[63] Mrs. Louis D. Brandeis to B. C. L., Oct. 4, 1917, LFP.

Chapter XLIX
(Pages 779–791)

[1] *The Lansing Papers,* II, 48; Robert Lansing Diary (Desk), Oct. 3, 1917, Robert Lansing Papers (hereafter cited as Lansing Papers).
[2] *Nebraska State Journal,* Oct. 4, 1917.
[3] *MINUTES Committee on Privileges and Elections. United States Senate,* Oct. 3, 1917, Records of the United States Senate, Committee on Privileges and Elections, 65th Cong., re La Follette Investigation, National Archives.
[4] B. C. L. to Phil and Mary, Oct. 4, 1917, LFP. Suzanne La Follette Diary, Oct. 3, 1917, LFP.
[5] Grace Lynch to author.
[6] Julius A. Truesdell to R. M. L., Oct. 3, 1917, LFP.
[7] *The Lansing Papers,* II, 48; Robert Lansing Diary (Desk), Oct. 3, 1917, Lansing Papers.
[8] *MINUTES Committee on Privileges and Elections. United States Senate,* Oct. 4, 1917, Records of the United States Senate, Committee on Privileges and Elections, 65th Cong., re La Follette Investigation, National Archives.
[9] Executive Office Diary, Oct. 4, 1917, Wilson Papers.
[10] B. C. L. to Phil and Mary, Oct. 4, 1917, LFP.
[11] Nicholas Gunderson, Sept. 11, 1950, to author, LFP. Gunderson was principal, Rib Lake Schools, 1902–1907; superintendent of schools, Prairie du Chien, 1909–1921; Sparta, 1921–1935.
[12] *Sun,* Baltimore, Oct. 5, 1917.
[13] *New York Tribune,* Oct. 6, 1917.
[14] *MINUTES Committee on Privileges and Elections. United States Senate,* Oct. 5, 1917, Records of the United States Senate, Committee on Privileges and Elections, 65th Cong., re La Follette Investigation, National Archives. See also Atlee Pomerene to Thomas J. Walsh, Oct. 6, 1917, Thomas J. Walsh Papers (hereafter cited as Walsh Papers).
[15] *Record,* 65th Cong., 1st Sess., Vol. 55, p. 7817, Oct. 5, 1917.
[16] Atlee Pomerene to R. M. L., Oct. 5, 1917, LFP.
[17] R. M. L. to Atlee Pomerene, Oct. 5, 1917, Records of United States Senate, 65th Cong., Committee on Privileges and Elections, re La Follette Investigation, National Archives.
[18] *New York Tribune,* Oct. 6, 1917.
[19] John J. Hannan to author; George Middleton to author.
[20] *Record,* 65th Cong., 1st Sess., Vol. 55, p. 7798, Oct. 4, 1917.
[21] *Evening Star,* Washington, D.C., Oct. 5, 1917; *Morning Oregonian,* Portland, Oct. 5, 1917.
[22] *New York Times,* Oct. 6, 1917; *World,* New York, Oct. 6, 1917.

[23] Records of United States Senate, 65th Cong., Committee on Privileges and Elections, re La Follette Investigation, National Archives.

[24] *Sunday Boston Herald,* Oct. 7, 1917.

[25] B. C. L. to Phil and Mary, Oct. 7, 1917, LFP.

[26] *Record,* 65th Cong., 1st Sess., Vol. 55, p. 7878, Oct. 6, 1917. Clipping with LFP.

[27] Judge Charles F. Amidon to R. M. L., Oct. 2, 1917, LFP; *Record,* 65th Cong., 1st Sess., Vol. 55, p. 7878, Oct. 6, 1917.

[28] *Record,* 65th Cong., 1st Sess., Vol. 55, p. 7878, Oct. 6, 1917.

[29] *Ibid.,* p. 7879, Oct. 6, 1917.

[30] *Ibid.,* pp. 7879-7881, Oct. 6, 1917.

[31] Speech by Secretary of Treasury McAdoo before West Virginia Bankers' Association, Sept. 21, 1917, quoted by R. M. L., *Record,* 65th Cong., 1st Sess., Vol. 55, p. 7880, Oct. 6, 1917.

[32] *Record,* 65th Cong., 1st Sess., Vol. 55, p. 7880, Oct. 6, 1917.

[33] *Ibid.,* p. 7881, Oct. 6, 1917.

[34] *Ibid.,* p. 7882, Oct. 6, 1917.

[35] *Ibid.,* pp. 7883-7886, Oct. 6, 1917.

[36] B. C. L. to Phil and Mary, Oct. 7, 1917, LFP.

[37] R. M. L., Jr., to author.

[38] *Record,* 65th Cong., 1st Sess., Vol. 55, pp. 7886-7888, Oct. 6, 1917.

[39] *Oregon Sunday Journal,* Oct. 7, 1917.

[40] *Record,* 65th Cong., 1st Sess., Vol. 55, pp. 7888-7893, Oct. 6, 1917.

[41] *Ibid.,* p. 7893, Oct. 6, 1917.

[42] *Oregon Sunday Journal,* Oct. 7, 1917.

[43] *Record,* 65th Cong., 1st Sess., Vol. 55, p. 7894, Oct. 6, 1917; *Speech of Senator Robert M. La Follette, Hearings before a Subcommittee of the Committee on Privileges and Elections, United States Senate,* 65th Cong., 1st Sess., Part I, pp. 12, 20.

[44] *Daily Congressional Record,* 65th Cong., 1st Sess., Vol. 55, p. 8643, Oct. 6, 1917.

[45] *Idem.*

[46] *Record,* 65th Cong., 1st Sess., Vol. 55, p. 7895, Oct. 6, 1917.

[47] *Springfield Sunday Republican,* Oct. 7, 1917.

[48] *Sunday Boston Herald,* Oct. 7, 1917.

[49] R. M. L., Jr., to author.

[50] *Idem* to Phil and Mary, Oct. 6, 1917, LFP.

Chapter L
(Pages 792–816)

[1] B. C. L. to Phil and Mary, Oct. 7, 1917, LFP.

[2] *Sunday Herald,* Boston, Oct. 7, 1917. See also *Springfield Sunday Republican,* Oct. 7, 1917; *Washington Post,* Oct. 7, 1917.

[3] Henry Cabot Lodge to Theodore Roosevelt, Oct. 12, 1917, TR Papers.

[4] Theodore Roosevelt to Henry Cabot Lodge, Oct. 24, 1917, TR Papers.

[5] Memorandum from President Wilson to Joseph P. Tumulty, Oct. 12, 1917, attached to telegram from State Council of Defense, Oct. 9, 1917, Wilson Papers.

[6] Merle Curti and Vernon Carstensen, *The University of Wisconsin* (Madison, University of Wisconsin Press, 1949), II, 20-21; Horace M. Kallen, "Politics, Profits and Patriotism in Wisconsin," the *Nation*, Vol. 106, pp. 257-259, March 7, 1918.

[7] *Wisconsin State Journal*, Oct. 10, 1917.

[8] Magnus Swenson to Woodrow Wilson, Oct. 10, 1917, Wilson Papers; Magnus Swenson to Atlee Pomerene, Oct. 10, 1917, Records of the United States Senate, Committee on Privileges and Elections, 65th Cong., re La Follette Investigation, National Archives.

[9] John M. Olin to Atlee Pomerene, Oct. 9, 1917, Records of the United States Senate, Committee on Privileges and Elections, 65th Cong., re La Follette Investigation, National Archives.

[10] *Wisconsin State Journal*, articles by John M. Olin, September 14, Oct. 8, 1917.

[11] *MINUTES Subcommittee of Committee on Privileges and Elections, United States Senate*, Oct. 8, 1917, Records of the United States Senate, Committee on Privileges and Elections, 65th Cong., re La Follette Investigation, National Archives.

[12] Robert Lansing Diary (Desk), Oct. 9, 1917, Lansing Papers.

[13] Atlee Pomerene to Robert Lansing, Oct. 9, 1917, *The Lansing Papers*, II, 49-51.

[14] Executive Office Diary, Oct. 9, 1917, Wilson Papers.

[15] *New York Times*, Oct. 10, 1917.

[16] Oct. 10, 1917, signed by Albert W. Fox. See also *Sun*, New York, Oct. 10, 1917.

[17] B. C. L. to Mary [Oct. 11, 1917], LFP.

[18] R. M. L. to Atlee Pomerene, Oct. 11, 1917, Records of the United States Senate, Committee on Privileges and Elections, 65th Cong., re La Follette Investigation, National Archives.

[19] *Evening Post*, New York, Oct. 11, 1917.

[20] *New York Times*, May 24, 1918.

[21] Oct. 11, 1917.

[22] Oct. 12, 1917.

[23] *New York Times*, Sept. 22, 1917, Vol. LXVII . . . No. 21, 791, p. 3, c. 8; *New York Times*, Sept. 22, 1917, Vol. LXVII . . . No. 21, 791. . . . , p. 11, c. 4.

[24] Atlee Pomerene to R. M. L., Oct. 12, 1917, LFP. See also *MINUTES Subcommittee of Committee on Privileges and Elections, United States Senate*, Oct. 11, 1917, Records of the United States Senate, Committee on Privileges and Elections, 65th Cong., re La Follette Investigation, National Archives.

[25] R. M. L. to Atlee Pomerene, Oct. 13, 1917, Records of the United States

Senate, Committee on Privileges and Elections, 65th Cong., re La Follette Investigation, National Archives.

[26] *Washington Times,* Oct. 13, 1917.

[27] *The Lansing Papers,* II, 52, footnote, states, "Enclosure not printed"; for Summary of the Manifest, see I, 435.

[28] Atlee Pomerene to R. M. L., Oct. 15, 1917, LFP.

[29] *Washington Times,* Oct. 16, 1917.

[30] *Speech of Senator Robert M. La Follette, Hearings Before a Subcommittee of The Committee on Privileges and Elections, United States Senate,* 65th Cong., 1st Sess., Part I, p. 25.

[31] Suzanne La Follette Diary, Oct. 19, 1917, LFP.

[32] R. M. L. to Atlee Pomerene, Oct. 16, 1917, Records of the United States Senate, Committee on Privileges and Elections, 65th Cong., re La Follette Investigation, National Archives.

[33] *Washington Times,* Oct. 16, 1917.

[34] Atlee Pomerene to Robert Lansing, Oct. 16, 1917, *The Lansing Papers,* II, 53-55.

[35] Robert Lansing Diary (Desk) entry, Oct. 17, 1917.

[36] Atlee Pomerene to R. M. L., Oct. 17, 1917, LFP.

[37] *Record,* 65th Cong., 1st Sess., Vol. 55, p. 6721, Sept. 7, 1917, for statement made by R. M. L. from which sentences were quoted in the *Sun* and *New York Tribune.*

[38] New York, Oct. 18, 1917, special unsigned dispatch. See also *New York Tribune,* Oct. 18, 1917.

[39] Typewritten statement in LFP, undated, released Oct. 21, 1917; excerpts printed in many newspapers.

[40] R. M. L. to Amos Pinchot, Dec. 5, 1917, LFP; Amos Pinchot to R. M. L., Dec. 3, 1917; also, many letters in LFP and other collections.

[41] Typewritten statement in LFP, undated, released Oct. 21, 1917.

[42] New York, Oct. 22, 1917.

[43] *Madison Democrat,* Oct. 24, 1917.

[44] Grace Lynch to author.

[45] *Nonpartisan Leader,* Oct. 4, 1917; *Evening Mail,* New York, letter from Oliver S. Morris (undated) to Edward A. Rumely, clipping with LFP.

[46] James Manahan to R. M. L., Oct. 24, 1917, LFP.

[47] R. M. L. to James Manahan, Nov. 15, 1917, LFP.

[48] *Minneapolis Morning Tribune,* Sept. 26, 1917.

[49] James Manahan to R. M. L., Nov. 20, 1917, LFP; *idem* to Gilbert E. Roe, Nov. 20, 1917, LFP.

[50] R. M. L., Jr., to Phil and Mary, Oct. 10, 1917, LFP.

[51] *Wisconsin State Journal,* Nov. 16, 1917.

[52] *Minneapolis Evening Tribune,* Nov. 17, 1917.

[53] *The Public Papers of Woodrow Wilson, War and Peace; Presidential Messages, Addresses, and Public Papers (1917–1924),* V, 127. See also *New York Times,* Nov. 17, 1917.

[54] *Helena Independent,* Nov. 7, 1917.

[55] J. H. Stevens to R. M. L., Nov. 15, 1917, LFP.

[50] Gilbert E. Roe to R. M. L., March 14, 1918, LFP; *idem* to John J. Hannan, April 23, 1918, LFP; recollection of Netha Roe.

[57] "Inquiries La Follette Examination," p. 3, Walsh Papers.

[58] Typescript: Questions submitted by the Senate Committee on Privileges and Elections in the Matter of St. Paul speech of Senator La Follette, Sept. 20, 1917; by Senator Pomerene, Oct. 9, 1917; by Senator Walsh, Oct. 11, 1917, Walsh Papers.

[59] *New York Times,* May 10, 1915.

[60] Dudley Field Malone to the editor of the *Nation,* Dec. 15, 1922, the *Nation,* Vol. CXVI, pp. 15-16; Netha Roe to author.

[61] Recollection of author; *Daily Globe-Democrat,* St. Louis, Oct. 29, 1920; the *Nation,* Vol. CXVI, pp. 15-16, Jan. 3, 1923; letter from Dudley Field Malone to editor of the *Nation,* Dec. 15, 1922.

[62] Carbon copy of report of Collector of the Port of New York (Dudley Field Malone) to the Secretary of the Treasury (William G. McAdoo), June 4, 1915, and signed copies of affidavits, LFP. This report, with summary of *Lusitania* manifest, was subsequently published in *The Lansing Papers,* I, 428-436; also in Carlton Savage's *Policy of The United States Toward Maritime Commerce in War,* II, 332-340.

[63] Gilbert E. Roe to Dudley Field Malone, Nov. 14, 1917, LFP.

[64] *Milwaukee Journal,* Nov. 9, 1917; *Wisconsin State Journal,* Nov. 9, 1917.

[65] *Madison Democrat,* Jan. 13, 1918.

[66] July 22, 1917; *Record,* 65th Cong., 1st Sess., Vol. 55, pp. 5368-5369, 5372, July 21, 1917; R. M. L. to B. C. L., Phil and Mary, July 27, 1917, LFP.

[67] *Testimony of Richard Lloyd Jones in Examination in Superior Court of Dane County,* pp. 344-347, LFP.

[68] Richard T. Ely to Albert Shaw, Jan. 29, 1918; *idem* to Theodore Roosevelt, Jan. 29, 1918, Richard T. Ely Papers.

[69] Woodrow Wilson to Richard Lloyd Jones, April 16, 1917; March 26, 1918; Wilson Papers. See also *Capital Times,* May 12, 1940.

[70] James R. Mock and Cedric Larson, *Words That Won the War* (Princeton University Press, 1939), pp. 110, 145.

[71] *Testimony of Richard Lloyd Jones in Examination in Superior Court of Dane County,* pp. 269-286, LFP.

[72] *Wisconsin State Journal,* Dec. 6, 1917.

[73] Magnus Swenson to Woodrow Wilson, Dec. 3, 1917, Wilson Papers.

[74] Charles H. Crownhart to R. M. L., with clipping, Nov. 14, 1917, LFP. See also *Wisconsin State Journal,* Nov. 13, 14, 1917.

[75] *New York Tribune,* Nov. 11, 1917.

[76] *New York Times,* June 10, 1915.

[77] *Record,* 65th Cong., 1st Sess., Vol. 55, p. 231, April 4, 1917.

[78] R. M. L. to B. C. L., Phil, and Mary, Sept. 27, 1917, LFP.

[79] Suzanne La Follette Diary, Oct. 3, 1917, LFP; Robert Lansing Diary (Desk), Oct. 3, 1917, Lansing Papers.

[80] Julius A. Truesdell to R. M. L., Oct. 3, 1917, LFP.

[81] Direct Examination of Julius Truesdell [1917], LFP.

[82] Julius A. Truesdell to author, July 18, 1937; substance of Truesdell's statement submitted to W. J. Dwyer and corroborated by him, July 23, 1937, LFP.

[83] Direct examination of Julius A. Truesdell [1917], LFP.

[84] Affidavit of Judge John M. Becker, Dec. 21, 1917, LFP.

[85] Gilbert E. Roe to James H. Garrison, Nov. 15, 1917, LFP.

[86] Typescript of questions prepared by Gilbert E. Roe in 1917, LFP.

[87] *New York Times*, Nov. 24, 1917.

[88] Ray Stannard Baker, *Woodrow Wilson*, VII, 372.

[89] *Milwaukee Sentinel*, Nov. 24, 1917.

[90] *New York Times*, Nov. 26, 1917.

[91] Robert Lansing to Atlee Pomerene, Nov. 20, 1917, *The Lansing Papers*, II, 60.

[92] Atlee Pomerene to R. M. L., Nov. 26, 1917, LFP.

[93] R. M. L. to Atlee Pomerene, Nov. 27, 1917, LFP.

[94] Atlee Pomerene to R. M. L., Nov. 30, 1917, LFP.

[95] *Idem*, Dec. 1, 1917, with notation in manuscript of R. M. L.: "Recd 4 P.M. Saturday, Dec. 1," LFP.

[96] B. C. L. to Phil and Mary, Dec. 2, 1917, LFP.

[97] R. M. L. to Atlee Pomerene, Dec. 3, 1917, LFP.

[98] *Idem* to William H. King, Philander C. Knox, James A. Reed, Lawrence Y. Sherman, William H. Thompson, James K. Vardaman, Josiah O. Wolcott, Dec. 4, 1917, LFP.

[99] Atlee Pomerene to R. M. L., Dec. 6, 1917, LFP; John J. Hannan to Gilbert E. Roe, Dec. 12, 1917, LFP; R. M. L. to Gilbert E. Roe, Dec. 21, 1917, LFP.

[100] George W. Norris to author, Feb. 15, 1939, LFP.

[101] Dudley Field Malone, speech, Oct. 28, 1920, reported in *Daily Globe-Democrat*, Oct. 29, 1920.

[102] James A. Reed to author, April 28, 1938, LFP.

[103] R. M. L., Jr., to Phil and Mary, Dec. 5, 12, 1917, LFP.

Chapter LI
(Pages 817–831)

[1] *Madison Democrat*, Dec. 5, 1917.

[2] Stephen Gwynn, *The Letters and Friendships of Sir Cecil Spring-Rice*, II, 417.

[3] *Record*, 65th Cong., 2nd Sess., Vol. 56, pp. 18-21, Dec. 4, 1917.

[4] *New York Times*, Dec. 5, 1917.

[5] Gwynn, *op. cit.*, II, 417; Ray Stannard Baker, *Woodrow Wilson*, VII, 390.

[6] *New York Times*, Dec. 5, 1917.

[7] *Record*, 65th Cong., 2nd Sess., Vol. 56, p. 18, Dec. 4, 1917.

Notes   1189

⁸ Typescript of R. M. L.'s undelivered speech opposing declaration of war against Austria-Hungary, pp. 8-9, LFP.
⁹ Dec. 4, 1917.
¹⁰ *Washington Post*, Dec. 5, 1917.
¹¹ Typescript of R. M. L.'s undelivered speech opposing declaration of war against Austria-Hungary, LFP.
¹² Recollection of author.
¹³ *Foreign Relations*, 1917, Supplement 2, Vol. I, 327.
¹⁴ *Evening Star*, Washington, D.C., Nov. 30, 1917; *New York Times*, Dec. 2, 1917, Sec. I, p. 1; *New York Tribune*, Dec. 1, 1917.
¹⁵ B. C. L. to Phil and Mary, Dec. 8, 1917, LFP.
¹⁶ *Idem; Record*, 65th Cong., 2nd Sess., Vol. 56, pp. 66-67, Dec. 7, 1917.
¹⁷ *Record*, 65th Cong., 2nd Sess., Vol. 56, p. 68, Dec. 7, 1917.
¹⁸ B. C. L. to Phil and Mary, Dec. 8, 1917, LFP.
¹⁹ *New York Times*, Dec. 8, 1917; *New York Tribune*, Dec. 8, 1917; *Des Moines Register*, Dec. 8, 1917; *Springfield Daily Republican*, Dec. 8, 1917.
²⁰ *Wisconsin State Journal*, Dec. 6, 7, 1917.
²¹ *Life*, Vol. 70, pp. 1000, 1002, 1020, Dec. 13, 1917.
²² R. M. L., Jr., to Gilbert E. Roe, Dec. 12, 1917, LFP.
²³ Gilbert E. Roe to R. M. L., Dec. 19, 1917, LFP.
²⁴ R. M. L. to Gilbert E. Roe, Dec. 21, 1917, LFP.
²⁵ *Wisconsin State Journal*, Dec. 18, 1917.
²⁶ John I. Newell to R. M. L., Dec. 24, 1917, LFP.
²⁷ *Life*, Vol. 70, cover, Dec. 13, 1917.
²⁸ *Ibid.*, Vol. 71, p. 72, Jan. 10, 1918.
²⁹ William Bross Lloyd to R. M. L., Jan. 15, 1918, with clipping, LFP; R. M. L. to William Bross Lloyd, Jan. 23, 1918, LFP.
³⁰ *Wisconsin State Journal*, Dec. 13, 1917.
³¹ Phil to B. C. L. and R. M. L., Jr., Dec. 12, 1917, LFP.
³² Charles H. Crownhart to R. M. L., Dec. 22, 1917, LFP.
³³ Gilbert E. Roe to Alfred T. Rogers, Jan. 11, 1918, LFP.
³⁴ Charles H. Crownhart to R. M. L., Dec. 29, 1917, LFP.
³⁵ R. M. L. to Charles H. Crownhart, Jan. 7 [4], 1918, LFP.
³⁶ Charles H. Crownhart to R. M. L., Oct. 29, Nov. 9, 28, Dec. 6, 1917, with enclosure of list, LFP.
³⁷ Edward E. Browne to Charles H. Crownhart, Nov. 1 [Dec. 1], 1917, LFP.
³⁸ Charles H. Crownhart to R. M. L., Dec. 16, 1917, with clipping from *Milwaukee Sentinel*, Dec. 14, 1917, dispatch from Waco, Texas, signed by staff correspondent, Fred Sheasby, LFP. See also R. M. L. to James M. Pierce, Jan. 12, 1918, LFP.
³⁹ Charles H. Crownhart to R. M. L., Dec. 29, 1917, LFP; Fred L. Holmes to R. M. L., Dec. 13, 1917, with enclosure of circular letter signed La Follette's Magazine, dated Dec. 12, 1917, LFP.
⁴⁰ *Wisconsin State Journal*, Dec. 17, 1917.

[41] Charles H. Crownhart to R. M. L., Dec. 22, 1917, LFP.

[42] *Idem*, Dec. 29, 1917, LFP.

[43] W. N. Parker to R. M. L., Dec. 29, 1917, LFP.

[44] *Wisconsin State Journal*, Feb. 16, 1918; *Madison Democrat*, Feb. 17, 1918; Charles H. Crownhart to Gilbert E. Roe, Feb. 19, 1918, LFP.

[45] R. M. L. to B. C. L. and R. M. L., Jr., Nov. 13, 1918, LFP.

[46] Charles H. Crownhart to Gilbert E. Roe, Feb. 19, 1918, LFP. See also *State of Wisconsin, Supplement to the Assembly Journal,* Special Session, March 6, 1918, p. 157, speech delivered by William T. Evjue.

[47] Gilbert E. Roe to Charles H. Crownhart, Feb. 22, 1918, LFP.

[48] Contemporary copy of letter from the State Journal Printing Company to Robert M. La Follette Co., Nov. 8, 1917, LFP.

[49] Charles H. Crownhart to R. M. L., Dec. 16, 1917, LFP.

[50] *Wisconsin State Journal*, Dec. 29, 1917.

[51] B. C. L. to Josephine La Follette Siebecker, Jan. 3, 1918, LFP.

[52] James C. Kerwin to R. M. L., Dec. 17, 1917, LFP.

[53] R. M. L. to James C. Kerwin, Jan. 5, 1918, LFP.

Chapter LII
(Pages 832–853)

[1] *Record*, 65th Cong., 2nd Sess., Vol. 56, p. 620, Jan. 5, 1918. A few of these letters from Vigilantes have been preserved in Records of the United States Senate, Committee on Privileges and Elections, 65th Cong., re La Follette Investigation, National Archives.

[2] *Outlook*, Vol. 119, No. 2, pp. 67-69, May 8, 1918.

[3] *Touchstone*, Vol. II, No. 1, pp. 91-93, 112, October, 1917, article by Hermann Hagedorn.

[4] *Outlook*, Vol. 119, No. 2, pp. 67-69, May 8, 1918. See also *Touchstone,* Vol. II, No. 1, pp. 91-93, 112.

[5] Charles Hanson Towne, *So Far So Good* (New York, Julian Messner, Inc., 1945), p. 182.

[6] *Washington Post*, Jan. 6, 1918; *New York Tribune*, Jan. 6, 1918.

[7] *New York Times*, Oct. 21, 1917. See also George Creel to Woodrow Wilson, Nov. 3, 1917, Wilson Papers.

[8] Clipping from the *New York Times*, Oct. 21, 1917, of article by Rupert Hughes, sent to R. M. L. in envelope postmarked "New York, Dec. 1, 1917," LFP.

[9] *New York Tribune*, Jan. 6, 1918.

[10] *Saturday Evening Post*, Vol. 190, No. 32, pp. 3-5, 38, 41-42, Feb. 9, 1918.

[11] Irvin S. Cobb to George Middleton, Aug. 25, 1933, LFP. See also George Middleton, *These Things Are Mine*, p. 175.

[12] Nov. 27, Dec. 5, 1917.

[13] Letterhead of American Defense Society, Inc., containing resolution

passed Oct. 31, 1917, calling for special session of Congress to declare war on Austria, LFP.

[14] *Record*, 60th Cong., 1st Sess., Vol. 42, pp. 3436-3447, March 17, 1908.

[15] Clipping from *New York Herald*, Jan. 6, 1918, LFP. See also *Brief presented by the American Defense Society In the Matter of the Inquiry into Certain Conduct and Utterances of Robert M. La Follette, a member of the Senate*, Records of the United States Senate, 65th Congress, Committee on Privileges and Elections, re La Follette Investigation, National Archives.

[16] Gilbert E. Roe to R. M. L., Dec. 4, 1917, LFP; *idem* to B. C. L., Dec. 5, 1917, LFP; *New York Times*, Nov. 27, Dec. 5, 1917.

[17] *Des Moines Register*, Jan. 9, 1918; *Washington Post*, Jan. 9, 1918.

[18] R. M. L. to Atlee Pomerene, James A. Reed, Jan. 8, 1918, carbon copies; the one to Pomerene is marked "not sent" in manuscript of Gilbert E. Roe. See also R. M. L. to Josiah O. Wolcott, Jan. 9, 1918, ribbon copy, LFP.

[19] Charles Seymour, *The Intimate Papers of Colonel House*, III, 338-339, 343. Ray Stannard Baker, *Woodrow Wilson*, VII, 417, 452, 454.

[20] Seymour, *op. cit.*, III, 317. See also Ray Stannard Baker, *op. cit.*, VII, 417.

[21] *War Memoirs of David Lloyd George*, V, 2515ff.; *The Times*, London, Dec. 20, 21, 1917; Seymour, *op. cit.*, III, 338, 340.

[22] Typed report, dated Nov. 21, 1917, by William C. Huntington, U.S. Commercial Attaché at Petrograd, enclosure with letter from Charles R. Crane to Joseph P. Tumulty, Jan. 3, 1918, Wilson Papers; Ray Stannard Baker, *op. cit.*, VII, 450.

[23] *Foreign Relations*, 1917, Supplement 2, Vol. I, 493.

[24] *Foreign Relations*, 1918, Russia, I, 405-408.

[25] Ray Stannard Baker, *op. cit.*, VII, 417. See also Seymour, *op. cit.*, III, 317.

[26] *Washington Times*, Jan. 8, 1918.

[27] *Record*, 65th Cong., 2nd Sess., Vol. 56, pp. 680-681, Jan. 8, 1918.

[28] *La Follette's Magazine*, Jan. 1918, p. 4.

[29] R. M. L., Jr., to Phil, Jan. 8, 1918, LFP.

[30] B. C. L. to Phil and Mary, Jan. 9, 1918, LFP.

[31] *La Follette's Magazine*, Jan. 1918, p. 1.

[32] R. M. L. to James M. Pierce, Jan. 12, 1918, LFP.

[33] *Madison Democrat*, Jan. 15, 1918, LFP.

[34] M. C. Otto to Charles R. Van Hise, Jan. 16, 1918.

[35] Charles R. Van Hise to M. C. Otto, Jan. 18, 1918. See also Merle Curti and Vernon Carstensen, *The University of Wisconsin*, II, 115, and footnote 88.

[36] Charles H. Crownhart to R. M. L., Jan. 16, 1918, LFP.

[37] *Wisconsin State Journal*, Jan. 16, 1918; *Madison Democrat*, Jan. 17, 1918.

[38] Telegram and letter dated respectively Oct. 2 and 3, 1917, Records

of United States Senate, 65th Cong., Committee on Privileges and Elections, re La Follette Investigation, National Archives.

[39] *Wisconsin State Journal,* Oct. 4, 1917.

[40] *Ibid.,* Oct. 21, 1917.

[41] *Milwaukee Journal,* Nov. 3, 1917.

[42] Resolution adopted October 4, Records of United States Senate, 65th Cong., Committee on Privileges and Elections, re La Follette Investigation, National Archives.

[43] Ernest F. Rice, secretary, University of Wisconsin Club of Philadelphia, to R. M. L., Dec. 17, 1917, LFP; *Public Ledger,* Philadelphia, Dec. 16, 1917; *Wisconsin Alumni Magazine,* Vol. 19, No. 2, p. 35, December, 1917.

[44] Nov. 17, 1917; *Wisconsin Alumni Magazine,* Vol. 19, No. 3, p. 71, January, 1918.

[45] *Wisconsin Alumni Magazine,* Vol. 19, No. 2, pp. 33-35, December, 1917.

[46] *Chicago Daily Tribune,* Sept. 26, 27, 1917.

[47] *Wisconsin Alumni Magazine,* Vol. 19, No. 2, pp. 34-37, December, 1917.

[48] Robert S. Crawford, secretary, Wisconsin Alumni Association, to Woodrow Wilson, Jan. 3, 1918, Wilson Papers.

[49] *Wisconsin Alumni Magazine,* Vol. 19, No. 2, pp. 36-38, December, 1917.

[50] *Wisconsin State Journal,* Nov. 27, 1917; *Helena Independent,* Nov. 26, 1917.

[51] Original document, Library of State Historical Society of Wisconsin; photostat, LFP.

[52] Richard T. Ely, *Ground Under Our Feet,* pp. 217-218; Edward A. Ross, *Seventy Years of It* (New York, D. Appleton-Century Company, 1936), p. 293.

[53] Confidential statement to author, December, 1948.

[54] Horace M. Kallen to author, July 3, 1949, with enclosure of draft of letter to Charles R. Van Hise, copy with LFP.

[55] M. C. Otto to author, April 1, 1949, LFP.

[56] A. R. Hohlfeld to Charles R. Van Hise, Jan. 17, 1918.

[57] Frederic L. Paxson, William A. Scott, George C. Sellery, to R. M. L. with enclosure of copy of protest and typed list of 399 signatures, Feb. 2, 1918, LFP.

[58] Richard T. Ely, *op. cit.,* p. 216.

[59] *Ibid.,* p. 217.

[60] M. C. Otto to author, April 18, 1940, LFP.

[61] *State of Wisconsin Senate Journal,* 56th Sess., pp. 86-87, Jan. 19, 1923.

[62] R. M. L. to Henry A. Huber, Feb. 9, 1923, LFP. This letter is printed in *State of Wisconsin Senate Journal,* 56th Sess., p. 429, March 7, 1923.

[63] *New York Times,* March 17, 1923.

[64] *State of Wisconsin Senate Journal,* 56th Sess., pp. 417-418, 428-429, March 6, 7, 1923; *State of Wisconsin Assembly Journal,* 56th Sess., p. 420, March 8, 1923.

[65] B. C. L. to Phil, Jan. 18 [19], 1918, LFP.

Chapter LIII
(Pages 854–873)

[1] R. M. L., Jr., to Phil, Jan. 16, 1918, LFP.
[2] "The Week In Washington," by R. M. L., Jr., mailed Jan. 15, 1918, LFP; George Creel to R. M. L., Jr., Jan. 25, 1918, with enclosure from Arthur E. Bestor, to George Creel, Jan. 25, 1918, LFP; R. M. L., Jr., to George Creel, Jan. 26, 29, 1918, LFP.
[3] B. C. L. to Fola and Phil, Jan. 29, 1918, LFP; recollection of author.
[4] R. M. L. to Alfred T. Rogers, Feb. 1, 1918, LFP.
[5] Gilbert E. Roe to Charles H. Crownhart, Feb. 6, 1918, LFP.
[6] Charles H. Crownhart to R. M. L., Jan. 31, 1918, LFP.
[7] M. B. Allison to Senate Committee on Elections and Privileges [*sic*], Jan. 19, 1918, Records of United States Senate, 65th Cong., Committee on Privileges and Elections, re La Follette Investigation, National Archives.
[8] Emerson Ela to Joseph P. Tumulty, Jan. 22, 1918, with attached memorandum Woodrow Wilson to Joseph P. Tumulty, Jan. 28, 1918, Wilson Papers.
[9] Gilbert E. Roe to R. M. L., Jan. 21, 1918, LFP.
[10] *World,* Jan. 21, 1918.
[11] *Milwaukee Journal,* Feb. 5, 1918; *Milwaukee Sentinel,* Feb. 5, 1918; *Madison Democrat,* Feb. 5, 1918.
[12] *Washington Post,* Feb. 6, 1918.
[13] John J. Hannan to Gilbert E. Roe, Feb. 6, 1918, LFP. The minutes of the February 5 committee meeting were not among those preserved in the National Archives.
[14] B. C. L. to Fola and Phil, Feb. 8, 1918, LFP; nurse's chart, Feb. 7, 8, 1918, LFP.
[15] *New York Times,* Oct. 23, 1917.
[16] Woodrow Wilson to Thomas R. Marshall, March 15, 1918, in Ray Stannard Baker, *Woodrow Wilson,* VIII, 30; also, memorandum Joseph P. Tumulty to Woodrow Wilson, attached to telegram from Joseph E. Davies to Joseph P. Tumulty, Oct. 27, 1917, Joseph P. Tumulty Papers (hereafter cited as Tumulty Papers).
[17] *La Follette's Magazine,* Nov. 1917, p. 1.
[18] *Milwaukee Journal,* Feb. 19, 1918; *Wisconsin State Journal,* Feb. 23, 1918; *Madison Democrat,* Feb. 23, 1918.
[19] Feb. 19, 1918. See also *Milwaukee Sentinel,* Feb. 21, 1918.
[20] *Madison Democrat,* Feb. 27, 1918.
[21] *Wisconsin State Journal,* Feb. 25, 1918.
[22] *Milwaukee Journal,* Feb. 28, 1918.
[23] *Ibid.,* Feb. 27, 1918.
[24] *Madison Democrat,* Feb. 20, 21, 22, 1918. See also *State of Wisconsin Supplement To The Senate Journal,* pp. 3-5, Feb. 23, 1918.

[25] Phil to B. C. L., Feb. 22, 1918; B. C. L. to Phil, Feb. 22, 1918; recollection of author.

[26] *State of Wisconsin, Supplement To The Senate Journal*, pp. 5-26, Feb. 23, 1918.

[27] *Ibid.*, Special Sess., pp. 26-96, Feb. 25, 1918.

[28] *Milwaukee Sentinel*, Feb. 26, 1918.

[29] R. M. L. to Gilbert E. Roe, Feb. 25, 1918, LFP.

[30] *Sun*, March 4, 1918.

[31] *Milwaukee Journal*, March 2, 1918.

[32] *Ibid.*, March 1, 1918.

[33] *Ibid.*

[34] *Milwaukee Journal*, March 2, 1918.

[35] *Ibid.*

[36] *World*, March 4, 1918.

[37] Phil to B. C. L., March 4, 1918, LFP.

[38] *Wisconsin State Journal*, March 5, 1918.

[39] March 6, 1918.

[40] *Washington Post*, March 5, 1918; *New York Times*, March 5, 1918; *Sun*, New York, March 5, 1918; *Chicago Daily Tribune*, March 5, 1918; *St. Paul Pioneer Press*, March 5, 1918, A.P. dispatch.

[41] The *Sun*, New York, March 5, 1918.

[42] Henry Cabot Lodge to Theodore Roosevelt, March 5, 1918, TR Papers.

[43] Theodore Roosevelt to Francis E. McGovern, March 8, 1918, TR Papers.

[44] Francis E. McGovern to Theodore Roosevelt, March 8, 1918, TR Papers.

[45] *Wisconsin State Journal*, March 6, 1918; *Capital Times*, March 6, 1918; *Kansas City Star*, March 6, 1918; *Chicago Herald, New York Times, World*, New York, *Sun*, New York, March 7, 1918.

[46] *State of Wisconsin Supplement To The Assembly Journal*, Special Sess., p. 160, March 6, 1918. See also *Madison Democrat*, March 7, 1918.

[47] *State of Wisconsin Supplement To The Assembly Journal*, Special Sess., pp. 154-165, March 6, 1918.

[48] March 7, 1918.

[49] *Wisconsin State Journal, Milwaukee Sentinel, Milwaukee Journal, Madison Democrat*, March 9, 1918.

[50] *Milwaukee Sentinel, Wisconsin State Journal, Madison Democrat*, March 9, 1918.

[51] *Milwaukee Journal, Wisconsin State Journal*, March 12, 1918.

[52] John J. Hannan to R. M. L., March 9, 10, 1918, with enclosure of draft of Thompson's statement, LFP.

[53] March 12, 1918.

[54] John J. Hannan to R. M. L., March 11, 1918, LFP.

[55] March 13, 1918.

[56] *Milwaukee Sentinel*, March 16, 1918.

[57] *Milwaukee Journal*, March 27, 1918.

[58] March 16, 1918. See also *New York Times*, March 13, 1918; *World,* March 13, 1918.

[59] John J. Hannan to R. M. L., March 8, 1918, LFP; Fred L. Holmes to R. M. L., March 11, 1918, LFP.

[60] Fred L. Holmes to R. M. L., March 13, 1918, LFP.

[61] *St. Paul Pioneer Press,* March 15, 1918.

[62] *Ohio State Journal,* March 17, 1918.

[63] March 18, 1918.

[64] R. M. L. to "Dear Friend," March 13, 1918, LFP.

[65] John J. Hannan to R. M. L., March 20, 1918, LFP.

[66] March 20, 1918.

[67] *Madison Democrat,* March 27, 1918.

[68] March 21, 1918.

[69] B. C. L. to Phil, March 20, 1918.

[70] *Milwaukee Journal,* March 30, 31, 1918; *Springfield Daily Republican,* April 4, 1918; *Madison Democrat,* March 30, 1918.

[71] *Kansas City Star,* March 31, 1918; *World,* New York, March 31, 1918.

[72] *La Follette's Magazine,* March, 1918, p. 2.

[73] Woodrow Wilson to Thomas R. Marshall, March 15, 1918, in Ray Stannard Baker, *op. cit.,* VIII, 30.

[74] Woodrow Wilson to Joseph E. Davies, March 18, 1918, in Ray Stannard Baker, *op. cit.,* VIII, 34. See also *Milwaukee Journal,* March 20, 1918.

[75] *Kansas City Star,* March 21, 1918; *Milwaukee Sentinel,* March 24, 26, 1918; *Wisconsin State Journal,* March 29, 1918; *Madison Democrat,* March 29, 1918.

[76] *Milwaukee Journal,* March 27, 1918.

[77] *Record,* 64th Cong., 2nd Sess., Vol. 54, p. 4692, March 1, 1917.

[78] *Madison Democrat,* March 29, 1918.

[79] *Indianapolis News,* March 27, 1918.

[80] *Record,* 65th Cong., 2nd Sess., Vol. 56, pp. 4133-4137, March 27, 1918.

[81] *Ibid.,* pp. 4137-4139, March 27, 1918.

[82] *Ibid.,* p. 4196, March 28, 1918.

[83] *New York Times, New York Tribune, World,* New York; *Boston Herald, Springfield Daily Republican,* Mass.; *Minneapolis Morning Tribune,* March 29, 1918.

[84] John Sharp Williams Papers (hereafter cited as Williams Papers), March and April, 1918.

[85] L. D. Ratliff to John Sharp Williams, March 29, 1918, Williams Papers.

[86] Emmett G. Blair to John Sharp Williams, March 29, 1918; John Sharp Williams to Emmett G. Blair, March 30, 1918, Williams Papers.

[87] John Sharp Williams to John W. Kerr, April 2, 1918, Williams Papers.

[88] John Sharp Williams to Theodore Roosevelt, April 1, 1918, Williams Papers.

[89] March 29, 1918.

[90] March 29, 1918.

[91] March 31, 1918.

[92] *Madison Democrat,* March 30, 1918.
[93] *La Follette's Magazine,* April, 1918, p. 2.
[94] B. C. L. to Phil, April 3, 1918, LFP.
[95] Charles H. Crownhart to R. M. L., April 3, 1918, LFP.

Chapter LIV
(Pages 874–886)

[1] B. C. L. to Phil, April 3, 15, 1918, LFP. Also, Philip F. Fox to R. M. L., April 8, 1918, LFP; recollection of author.

[2] John Sharp Williams to Theodore Roosevelt, April 1, 1918, Williams Papers.

[3] Theodore Roosevelt to John Sharp Williams, April 8, 1918, TR Papers.

[4] John Sharp Williams to Theodore Roosevelt, April 20, 1918, Williams Papers.

[5] Theodore Roosevelt to John Sharp Williams, April 26, 1918, Williams Papers.

[6] *MEMORANDUM OF CONVERSATION BETWEEN POMERENE AND COL. JOHN HANNAN, THURSDAY, April 18th, at 12:30 P.M., Senator Pomerene seeking the Colonel out,* LFP.

[7] Gilbert E. Roe to John J. Hannan, April 18, 1918, LFP.

[8] John J. Hannan to Atlee Pomerene, April 19, 1918, LFP.

[9] Gilbert E. Roe to John J. Hannan, April 23, 1918, LFP.

[10] *Idem* to Atlee Pomerene, April 24, 1918, LFP; John J. Hannan to Atlee Pomerene, April 26, 1918, LFP.

[11] John J. Hannan to Gilbert E. Roe, May 6, 10, 1918, LFP.

[12] Gilbert E. Roe to Atlee Pomerene, May 9, 1918, LFP; R. M. L. to Atlee Pomerene, May 10, 1918, LFP.

[13] John J. Hannan to Gilbert E. Roe, 4:45 P.M., May 11, 1918, LFP; *idem,* May 11, 1918, LFP.

[14] Gilbert E. Roe to Atlee Pomerene, May 13, 1918, LFP.

[15] R. M. L. to Gilbert E. Roe, May 14, 1918, LFP.

[16] MINUTES *Committee on Privileges and Elections United States Senate,* May 15, 1918, Records of the United States Senate Committee on Privileges and Elections, 65th Cong., re La Follette Investigation, National Archives.

[17] James K. Vardaman to James A. Reed, undated carbon, LFP.

[18] R. M. L. to Phil, May 18, 1918, LFP.

[19] *Sun,* New York, May 22, 1918.

[20] *Milwaukee Sentinel, St. Paul Pioneer Press,* May 18, 1918.

[21] *Speech of Senator Robert M. La Follette Hearings Before The Committee On Privileges And Elections, United States Senate,* 65th Cong., 2nd Sess., Part 2, pp. 47-48.

[22] *Ibid.,* pp. 99-100, 126-127.

[23] *Speech of Senator Robert M. La Follette Memorandum of Information Submitted To The Committee On Privileges And Elections United States Senate,* 65th Cong., 2nd Sess., pp. 1-3.

[24] R. M. L. to Phil, May 21 [22], 1918, LFP. Also, recollection of author.

[25] *New York Times, Sun,* New York; *New York Tribune, Springfield Daily Republican,* Mass.; *St. Paul Pioneer Press, Minneapolis Journal, Des Moines Register,* May 22, 1918.

[26] *Speech of Senator Robert M. La Follette Hearings Before the Committee on Privileges and Elections United States Senate,* 65th Cong., 2nd Sess., Part 2, pp. 104, 146-147.

[27] *Ibid.,* p. 110.

[28] *Ibid.,* p. 124.

[29] *Ibid.,* pp. 144-146.

[30] R. M. L. to Phil, May 21 [22], 1918, LFP.

[31] B. C. L. to Netha Roe, envelope postmarked May 23, 1918, LFP.

[32] John J. Hannan to Gilbert E. Roe, May 27, 1918, LFP.

[33] Recollection of author.

[34] R. M. L. to Phil, May 26, 1918, LFP.

[35] B. C. L. to Phil, May 26, 1918, LFP.

[36] P. D. Craig, American secretary, Defense Society, to Atlee Pomerene, May 22, 1918, Records of the United States Senate, Committee on Privileges and Elections, 65th Cong., re La Follette Investigation, National Archives.

[37] *New York Times,* Dec. 5, 1917; *New York Herald,* Jan. 6, 1918.

[38] *Speech of Senator Robert M. La Follette Hearings Before the Committee on Privileges and Elections, United States Senate,* 65th Cong., 2nd Sess., Part 2, pp. 35, 84, 88, 102. See also *New York Times, New York Tribune,* May 22, 23, 1918; *St. Paul Pioneer Press,* May 22, 1918; *Sun,* New York; *Evening Post,* New York, May 23, 1918.

[39] *La Follette's Magazine,* Nov., 1917, p. 6.

[40] Laura Thompson to author.

[41] R. M. L. to Gilbert E. Roe, May 27, 1918, LFP.

[42] *Idem* to Atlee Pomerene, Oct. 11, 1918, Records of the United States Senate, Committee on Privileges and Elections, 65th Cong., re La Follette Investigation, National Archives.

[43] *Evening Post,* New York, October 11, 1917. See also *Ohio State Journal,* October 12, 1917, Associated Press dispatch from Washington, D. C.

[44] *New York Times, Chicago Daily Tribune, Sun,* New York, Oct. 12, 1917; *Washington Times,* Oct. 11, 1917.

[45] Frederick Roy Martin to Atlee Pomerene, May 23, 1918, Committee on Privileges and Elections, 65th Cong., re La Follette Investigation, National Archives.

[46] *Speech of Senator Robert M. La Follette Hearings Before The Committee On Privileges And Elections,* 65th Cong., 2nd Sess., Part 2, p. 160. See also pp. 160-161 for telegrams from Atlee Pomerene to Frederick Roy Martin, May 24, 1918; the Associated Press to Atlee Pomerene, undated; Atlee Pomerene to the Associated Press, May 28, 1918.

[47] *Evening Post,* New York, May 24, 1918.

[48] *La Follette's Magazine,* June, 1918, p. 3.

[49] R. M. L. to Gilbert E. Roe, May 27, 1918, LFP; B. C. L. to Phil, May 26, 1918, LFP.

[50] Gilbert E. Roe to John J. Hannan, May 24, 1918, LFP; *idem* to R. M. L., May 25, 1918, LFP.

[51] John J. Hannan to Gilbert E. Roe, June 18, 1918, LFP.

[52] *Idem.*

[53] *Idem.* Many years later Cochran said, after reading this letter, that Hannan had correctly recorded the substance of their talk. Negley D. Cochran to author, Feb. 1, 1938, LFP.

[54] Gilbert E. Roe to R. M. L., May 25, 28, 29, 1918, LFP.

[55] R. M. L. to Gilbert E. Roe, May 30, 1918, LFP.

[56] *Reply Brief In Behalf Of Senator Robert M. La Follette,* Gilbert E. Roe, Attorney for Senator Robert M. La Follette, pp. 2, 21, LFP. See also *New York Tribune,* June 7, 1918; *New York Times,* June 7, 1918.

[57] *Speech of Senator Robert M. La Follette Hearings Before The Committee On Privileges And Elections, United States Senate,* 65th Cong., 2nd Sess., Part 2.

[58] With LFP.

[59] R. M. L. to Atlee Pomerene, carbon of letter dated July 3, 1918, and various drafts of this letter made on different dates with revisions in manuscript of R. M. L., B. C. L., John J. Hannan, and Gilbert E. Roe, LFP.

[60] This letter is not with the Committee on Privileges and Elections papers in the National Archives. The only correspondence between Pomerene and R. M. L. and his representatives that is preserved there is the exchange of letters between Pomerene and R. M. L. which was published in the printed Hearings, Part I, pp. 20-27, Part II, pp. 63-64.

Chapter LV
(Pages 887–908)

[1] R. M. L. to Alfred T. Rogers, Jan. 2, 1918, LFP.

[2] R. M. L. to Alfred T. Rogers, Jan. 2, 1918, LFP.

[3] Alfred T. Rogers to R. M. L., June 27, 1918, with enclosure of H. W. Adams to Alfred T. Rogers, June 22, 1918; Alfred T. Rogers to R. M. L., July 9, 1918, LFP.

[4] Phil to R. M. L. and B. C. L., May 24, 1918, LFP.

[5] R. M. L. to Phil, May 26, 1918, LFP.

[6] Phil to R. M. L., June 6, 1918, LFP.

[7] Recollection of author.

[8] Phil to Bob, Jr., July 13, 1918, LFP.

[9] Fola to Phil, July 31, 1918, LFP.

[10] Recollection of author.

[11] B. C. L. to Mary, July 21, 1918, LFP.

[12] *Idem* to Phil, Aug. 12, 1918, LFP.

[13] *Idem* to R. M. L., Sept. 12, 1918, LFP.

[14] John J. Hannan to R. M. L., Sept. 23, 1918, LFP.

[15] R. M. L. to B. C. L., Oct. 22, 1918, LFP.

[16] *Idem* to B. C. L., R. M. L., Jr., and Mary, Dec. 11, 1918, LFP.
[17] *New York Times,* Sept. 27, 1918.
[18] Oct. 1, 1918.
[19] *New York Times,* June 14, 25, 1918; Ray Stannard Baker, *Woodrow Wilson,* VIII, 199, 230-231.
[20] *Record,* 65th Cong., 2nd Sess., Vol. 56, p. 10929, Sept. 30, 1918.
[21] *Chicago Daily Tribune,* Oct. 2, 1919.
[22] *Record,* 65th Cong., 2nd Sess., Vol. 56, p. 10976, Oct. 1, 1918.
[23] R. M. L. to B. C. L., R. M. L., Jr., and Mary, Oct. 6, 1918, LFP.
[24] *Idem.*
[25] *Idem.*
[26] R. M. L. to Phil, Oct. 11, 1918, LFP.
[27] *Idem* to B. C. L., R. M. L., Jr., and Mary, Oct. 25, 1918, LFP.
[28] *Idem.*
[29] R. M. L. to B. C. L., R. M. L., Jr., and Mary, Oct. 8, 1918, LFP.
[30] *Idem,* Oct. 20, 1918, LFP.
[31] *Idem,* Oct. 28, 1918, LFP.
[32] *Idem,* Nov. 6, 1918, LFP.
[33] *Idem,* Nov. 2, 1918, LFP.
[34] R. M. L. to Mary, Oct. 14, 1918, LFP.
[35] William Kent to R. M. L., Oct. 17, 1918, LFP.
[36] B. C. L. to R. M. L., Fola, Mid, and Phil, Oct. 27, 1918, LFP.
[37] R. M. L. to B. C. L., R. M. L., Jr., and Mary, Oct. 25, 1918, LFP.
[38] *Idem,* Nov. 1, 1918, LFP.
[39] *La Follette's Magazine,* Oct. 1918, pp. 6-7, published the text of the German note of Oct. 6; Lansing's reply of Oct. 9; Germany's note of Oct. 12; Lansing's reply of Oct. 14; Germany's note of Oct. 21, 1918.
[40] R. M. L. to B. C. L., R. M. L., Jr., and Mary, Oct. 6, 1918, LFP. Justice Clarke's speech was subsequently printed in the *Congressional Record,* Vol. 47, pp. 2344-2347, Jan. 30, 1919.
[41] R. M. L. to B. C. L., R. M. L., Jr., and Mary, Oct. 8, 1918, LFP.
[42] *Idem,* Oct. 19, 1918, LFP.
[43] *Idem,* Oct. 23, 1918, LFP.
[44] R. M. L. to Phil, Oct. 24, 1918, LFP.
[45] *Idem* to B. C. L., R. M. L., Jr., and Mary, Oct. 25, 1918, LFP.
[46] *Idem,* Oct. 15, 1918, LFP.
[47] *Idem,* Oct. 26, 1918, LFP.
[48] *Idem,* Oct. 15, 1918, LFP.
[49] *Idem.*
[50] R. M. L. to B. C. L., R. M. L., Jr., and Mary, Oct. 29, 1918, LFP.
[51] *Idem.*
[52] *New York Times,* Oct. 26, 1918.
[53] R. M. L. to B. C. L., R. M. L., Jr., and Mary, Oct. 25, 1918, LFP.
[54] *Idem,* Oct. 26, 1918, LFP. Bob quoted from memory. The italics were his own. The *New York Times,* Oct. 26, 1918, reported Wilson had said: "This is no time either for divided counsels or for divided leadership. Unity

of command is as necessary now in civil action as it is upon the field of battle."

[55] R. M. L. to B. C. L., R. M. L., Jr., and Mary, Oct. 28, 1918, LFP.
[56] *Idem,* Nov. 1, 1918, LFP.
[57] *Idem,* Nov. 2, 1918, LFP.
[58] *Idem,* Nov. 6, 1918, LFP.
[59] *Idem,* Nov. 7, 1918, LFP.
[60] *Idem,* Nov. 6, 1918, LFP.
[61] Senator Thomas P. Gore to author, April 12, 1938, LFP.
[62] R. M. L. to B. C. L., R. M. L., Jr., and Mary, Nov. 8, 1918, LFP.
[63] *Idem* to Phil, Nov. 9, 1918, LFP.
[64] Nov. 9, 1918.
[65] *Ibid.*
[66] R. M. L. to B. C. L., R. M. L., Jr., and Mary, Nov. 11, 1918, LFP.
[67] *Idem,* Nov. 1, 1918, LFP.
[68] *Official Statements of War Aims and Peace Proposals,* December, 1916, to November, 1918 (Washington, D.C., Carnegie Endowment, 1921), pp. 456-457.
[69] Charles Seymour, *The Intimate Papers of Colonel House,* IV, 168. Stephen Bonsal, *Unfinished Business* (Garden City, N. Y., Doubleday, Doran and Company, 1944), p. 2.
[70] R. M. L. to B. C. L., R. M. L., Jr., and Mary, Nov. 6, 1918, LFP. The *Washington Herald,* Nov. 5, 1918, apologized for issuing this "Extra."
[71] R. M. L. to Phil, Nov. 5, 1918, LFP.
[72] *Idem,* to B. C. L., R. M. L., Jr., and Mary, Nov. 5, 1918, LFP.
[73] *Idem,* Nov 7, 1918, LFP.
[74] *Idem,* Nov. 10, 1918, LFP.
[75] *Idem,* Nov. 7, 1918, LFP.
[76] *Idem,* Nov. 9, 1918, LFP.
[77] *Idem,* Nov. 10, 1918, LFP.
[78] *Idem,* Nov. 9, 1918, LFP.
[79] *Idem,* Nov. 17, 1918, LFP.
[80] Nov. 12, 1918.
[81] R. M. L. to B. C. L., R. M. L., Jr., and Mary, Nov. 11, 1918, LFP.
[82] *Idem,* Nov. 13, 1918, LFP.
[83] *Idem.*
[84] R. M. L. to B. C. L., R. M. L., Jr., and Mary, Nov. 15, 1918, LFP.

Chapter LVI
(Pages 909–920)

[1] R. M. L. to B. C. L., R. M. L., Jr., and Mary, Nov. 16, 1918, LFP.
[2] B. C. L. to R. M. L., Nov. 20, 1918, LFP.
[3] R. M. L. to B. C. L., R. M. L., Jr., and Mary, Nov. 20, 1918, LFP.
[4] *Idem,* Dec. 11, 1918, LFP.

[5] *Idem,* Nov. 18, 1918, LFP.
[6] *Idem,* Nov. 21, 1918, LFP.
[7] R. M. L. to Phil, Nov. 25, 1918, LFP.
[8] *Idem* to B. C. L., R. M. L., Jr., and Mary, Nov. 21, 1918, LFP.
[9] *Idem,* Nov. 22, 1918, LFP.
[10] *Idem.* See also *MINUTES Committee on Privileges and Elections, United States Senate,* Nov. 22, 1918, Records of the United States Senate Committee on Privileges and Elections, 65th Cong., re La Follette Investigation, National Archives.
[11] R. M. L. to B. C. L., R. M. L., Jr. and Mary, Nov. 23, 1918, LFP.
[12] *Idem,* Nov. 27, 1918, LFP.
[13] R. M. L., Jr., to R. M. L., Nov. 29, 1918, LFP.
[14] Senator James A. Reed to author, April 12, 1938, LFP.
[15] R. M. L. to B. C. L., R. M. L., Jr., and Mary, Nov. 23, 1918, LFP.
[16] *Idem,* Nov. 26, 1918, LFP.
[17] *Idem,* Nov. 26, 1918, LFP.
[18] *Idem,* Nov. 29, 1918, LFP.
[19] *Idem,* Nov. 28, 1918, LFP.
[20] *Idem,* Dec. 5, 1918, LFP.
[21] B. C. L. to R. M. L., Dec. 16, 1918, LFP.
[22] R. M. L. to B. C. L., R. M. L., Jr., and Mary, Dec. 1, 1918, LFP.
[23] Dec. 1, 1918.
[24] R. M. L. to B. C. L., R. M. L., Jr., and Mary, Dec. 3, 1918, LFP.
[25] *Idem,* Dec. 10, 1918, LFP.
[26] *Idem,* Nov. 30, 1918, LFP.
[27] *Idem.*
[28] R. M. L. to B. C. L., R. M. L., Jr., and Mary, Dec. 2, 1918, LFP. For report as finally passed, see *Record,* 65th Cong., 3rd Sess., Vol. 57, p. 1525, Jan. 16, 1919.
[29] R. M. L. to B. C. L., R. M. L., Jr., and Mary, Nov. 30, 1918, LFP.
[30] *Idem,* Dec. 2, 1918, LFP.
[31] *Idem.*
[32] *Idem.*
[33] R. M. L. to B. C. L., R. M. L., Jr., and Mary, Dec. 12, 1918, LFP.
[34] *Idem.*
[35] R. M. L. to B. C. L., R. M. L., Jr., and Mary, Dec. 11, 1918, LFP.
[36] *Idem,* Dec. 12, 1918, LFP.
[37] *Record,* 65th Cong., 3rd Sess., Vol. 57, p. 440, Dec. 14, 1918.
[38] R. M. L. to B. C. L., R. M. L., Jr., and Mary, Dec. 14, 1918, LFP.
[39] *Idem,* Dec. 13, 1918, LFP.
[40] *Idem,* Dec. 17, 1918, LFP.
[41] *Idem,* Dec. 18, 1918, LFP.
[42] *Idem,* Dec. 4, 1918, LFP.
[43] *Record,* 65th Cong., 3rd Sess., Vol. 57, pp. 799-818, Dec. 23, 1918.
[44] R. M. L. to B. C. L., R. M. L., Jr., and Mary, Dec. 24, 1918, LFP.
[45] *Record,* 65th Cong., 3rd Sess., Vol. 57, p. 830, Dec. 23, 1918.

⁴⁶ *Ibid.*, p. 819, Dec. 23, 1918.

⁴⁷ *Ibid.*, p. 823, Dec. 23, 1918.

⁴⁸ R. M. L. to B. C. L., R. M. L., Jr., and Mary, Dec. 24, 1918, LFP.

⁴⁹ *Idem*, Dec. 26, 1918, LFP.

⁵⁰ Phil to B. C. L., Dec. 13, 1918, LFP.

⁵¹ R. M. L. to Phil, Dec. 19, 1918, LFP.

⁵² *Idem* to B. C. L., R. M. L., Jr., Phil, and Mary, Dec. 31, 1918, LFP.

⁵³ B. C. L. to R. M. L., Dec. 30, 1918, LFP.

⁵⁴ R. M. L. to B. C. L., R. M. L., Jr., Phil, and Mary, Dec. 28, 1918, LFP.

⁵⁵ R. M. L., Jr., to R. M. L., Dec. 5, 1918, LFP.

⁵⁶ R. M. L. to B. C. L., R. M. L., Jr., and Mary, Dec. 12, 1918, LFP.

⁵⁷ *Idem*, Jan. 12, 1919, LFP.

⁵⁸ *Idem*, Dec. 25, 1918, LFP.

⁵⁹ *Idem*, Dec. 31, 1918, LFP.

Chapter LVII
(Pages 921–931)

¹ R. M. L. to Phil, Jan. 8, 1919, LFP. *Record*, 65th Cong., 3rd Sess., Vol. 57, pp. 1102-1103, Jan. 7, 1919.

² *Idem* to B. C. L., R. M. L., Jr., and Mary, Jan. 7, 1919, LFP.

³ *Record*, 65th Cong., 3rd Sess., Vol. 57, pp. 1102-1103, Jan. 7, 1919.

⁴ *New York Times*, Jan. 2, 1919.

⁵ R. M. L. to B. C. L., R. M. L., Jr., and Mary, Dec. 27, 1918, LFP. Bob was quoting from memory. Wilson's exact phrasing was: "The whole heart of the people of the United States is with the people of Russia in the attempt to free themselves forever from autocratic government and become masters of their own life." *Foreign Relations*, 1918, Russia, I, 395.

⁶ *Brewing and Liquor Interests and German and Bolshevik Propaganda*, Report and Hearings of the Subcommittee on the Judiciary, U.S. Senate, 66th Cong., 1st Sess., Vol. 3, pp. 887-888, March 7, 1919.

⁷ R. M. L. manuscript notes of Raymond Robins' talk at Hot Springs, Va., Aug., 1918, LFP. See also *Record*, 65th Cong., 3rd Sess., Vol. 57, p. 2265, Jan. 29, 1919.

⁸ B. C. L. to Phil, Aug. 20, 1918, LFP.

⁹ R. M. L. to B. C. L., R. M. L., Jr., Phil, and Mary, Jan. 1, 1919, LFP.

¹⁰ *Idem*, Jan. 29, 1919, LFP.

¹¹ Fola to R. M. L., Jan. 7, 23, 1919, and recollection of author; R. M. L. to B. C. L., R. M. L., Jr., and Mary, Jan. 22, 1919; R. M. L. to Fola, Jan. 26, 1919, LFP.

¹² *Record*, 65th Cong., 3rd Sess., Vol. 57, pp. 2261-2270, Jan. 29, 1919.

¹³ R. M. L. to B. C. L., R. M. L., Jr., and Mary, Jan. 29, 1919, LFP.

¹⁴ B. C. L. to R. M. L., Feb. 6, 1919, LFP.

¹⁵ *Brewing and Liquor Interests and German and Bolshevik Propaganda*,

Report and Hearings before Subcommittee on the Judiciary, U.S. Senate, 66th Cong., 1st Sess., Vol. 3, pp. 763-856, 857-896, 1007-1032, March 6, 7, 10, 1919.

[16] R. M. L. to B. C. L., and R. M. L., Jr., March 6, 1919, LFP.
[17] *Idem* to B. C. L., R. M. L., Jr., and Mary, Dec. 5, 1918, LFP.
[18] *Idem*, Jan. 10, 1919, LFP.
[19] *Idem*, Dec. 4, 1918, LFP.
[20] *La Follette's Magazine,* December, 1918, p. 1, editorial, "A Real League of Peace."
[21] *New York Times,* Dec. 6, 1918.
[22] R. M. L. to B. C. L., R. M. L., Jr., and Mary, Dec. 6, 1918, LFP.
[23] *Idem*, Jan. 6, 1919, LFP.
[24] R. M. L. to B. C. L., R. M. L., Jr., Phil, and Mary, Dec. 28, 1918, LFP.
[25] *Idem* to B. C. L., R. M. L., Jr., and Mary, Jan. 9, 1919, LFP.
[26] *Idem*, Jan. 16, 1919, LFP.
[27] *Idem*, Jan. 3, 1919, LFP.
[28] *Idem*, Jan. 15, 1919, LFP.
[29] *Record,* 65th Cong., 3rd Sess., Vol. 57, p. 1525, Jan. 16, 1919.
[30] *Ibid.,* p. 1526, Jan. 16, 1919.
[31] *New York Times,* Jan. 17, 1919.
[32] R. M. L. to B. C. L., R. M. L., Jr., and Mary, Jan. 16, 1919, LFP.
[33] *Idem* to Phil, Jan. 18, 1919, LFP.
[34] *Idem* to B. C. L., R. M. L., Jr., and Mary, Jan. 16, 1919, LFP .
[35] *Idem*, Jan. 17, 1919, LFP.
[36] *Idem*, Jan. 20, 1919, LFP.
[37] B. C. L. to R. M. L., Jan. 21, 1919, LFP.
[38] *Idem*, Jan. 26, 1919, LFP.
[39] R. M. L. to Phil, Jan. 18, 1919, LFP.

Chapter LVIII
(Pages 932–948)

[1] 65th Cong., 3rd Sess., House of Representatives Document No. 1640. See also *The Public Papers of Woodrow Wilson,* V, 366.
[2] *Record,* 65th Cong., 3rd Sess., Vol. 57, p. 1656, Jan. 18, 1919.
[3] R. M. L. to B. C. L., R. M. L., Jr., and Mary, Jan. 18, 1919, LFP.
[4] *Record,* 65th Cong., 3rd Sess., Vol. 57, p. 1984, Jan. 24, 1919.
[5] R. M. L. to B. C. L., R. M. L., Jr., and Mary, Jan. 29, 1919, LFP.
[6] *Record,* 65th Cong., 3rd Sess., Vol. 57, p. 1996, Jan. 24, 1919.
[7] R. M. L. to B. C. L., R. M. L., Jr., and Mary, Feb. 4, 1919, LFP.
[8] *Idem*, Feb. 3, 1919, LFP.
[9] *Idem*, Feb. 1, 1919, LFP.
[10] *Idem*, Feb. 2, 1919, LFP.
[11] *Idem*, Feb. 11, 1919, LFP.
[12] *Idem*, Feb. 13, 1919, LFP.
[13] *Idem*, Feb. 14, 1919, LFP.

[14] *Idem,* Feb. 17, 1919, LFP.

[15] *Idem,* Feb. 6, 1919, LFP.

[16] R. M. L., Jr., to R. M. L., Feb. 12, 1919, LFP.

[17] R. M. L. to B. C. L., R. M. L., Jr., and Mary, Feb. 19, 1919, LFP.

[18] *Idem,* Jan. 26, 1919, LFP.

[19] *Idem,* Feb. 15, 1919, LFP.

[20] *Idem,* Feb. 10, 1919, LFP.

[21] *Idem,* Dec. 29, 1918, LFP.

[22] *Idem,* Nov. 26, 1918, LFP.

[23] *Idem,* Jan. 11, 1919, LFP.

[24] *Idem,* Dec. 6, 1918, LFP.

[25] *Idem,* December, 1918, LFP. See also *Record,* 65th Cong., 3rd Sess., Vol. 57, p. 171, Dec. 6, 1918.

[26] R. M. L. to B. C. L., R. M. L., Jr., and Mary, Jan. 28, 1919, LFP.

[27] *Idem,* Jan. 27, 1919, LFP.

[28] *Idem,* Jan. 12, 1919, LFP.

[29] *Idem,* Feb. 4, 1919, LFP.

[30] *Idem.*

[31] *Idem,* Feb. 8, 1919, LFP.

[32] *Idem,* Feb. 16, 1919, LFP.

[33] *Record,* 65th Cong., 3rd Sess., Vol. 57, p. 3856, Feb. 20, 1919.

[34] R. M. L. to B. C. L., R. M. L., Jr., and Mary, Feb. 23, 1919, LFP.

[35] *Idem,* Feb. 24, 1919, LFP. This bill, known as "the red flag bill," was opposed by Norris and France and prevented from coming to a vote. See *Record,* 65th Cong., 3rd Sess., Vol. 57, p. 4561, Feb. 28, 1919.

[36] R. M. L. to B. C. L., R. M. L., Jr., and Mary, Feb. 24, 1919, LFP.

[37] *Record,* 65th Cong., 3rd Sess., Vol. 57, p. 23, Dec. 3, 1918; Knox Resolution; p. 73, Kellogg speech, Dec. 4, 1918.

[38] R. M. L. to B. C. L., R. M. L., Jr., and Mary, Feb. 15, 1919, LFP.

[39] *Idem,* Feb. 7, 1919, LFP.

[40] *Idem,* Jan. 16, 1919; also other letters of January and February, 1919, to family, and author's recollection.

[41] R. M. L. to Phil, Nov. 25, 1918, LFP.

[42] *Idem* to B. C. L., R. M. L., Jr., and Mary, Feb. 2, 1919, LFP.

[43] *Idem,* Feb. 3, 1919, LFP.

[44] *Idem,* Feb. 17, 1919, LFP.

[45] *Idem,* Feb. 22, 1919, LFP.

[46] *Idem.*

[47] *Record,* 65th Cong., 3rd Sess., Vol. 57, pp. 4044-4048, Feb. 22, 1919; R. M. L. to B. C. L., R. M. L., Jr., and Mary, Feb. 22, 1919, LFP.

[48] R. M. L. to B. C. L., R. M. L., Jr., and Mary, Feb. 22, 1919, LFP.

[49] *Record,* 68th Cong., 1st Sess., Vol. 65, p. 2231, Feb. 11, 1924.

[50] *Ibid,* 65th Cong., 3rd Sess., Vol. 57, p. 3639, Feb. 18, 1919.

[51] *Ibid.,* p. 4980, March 4, 1919.

[52] *Ibid,* p. 4713, March 1, 1919.

[53] R. M. L. to B. C. L., R. M. L., Jr., and Mary, Feb. 21, 22, 1919.

[54] *Idem*, Feb. 23, 1919, LFP.

[55] *Record*, 65th Cong., 3rd Sess., Vol. 57, p. 4715, March 1, 1919.

[56] R. M. L. to B. C. L., R. M. L., Jr., and Mary, Feb. 26, 1919, LFP.

[57] *Idem*, Feb. 24, 1919, LFP.

[58] *Idem*, Feb. 23, 1919, LFP.

[59] *Idem*, March 4, 1919, LFP.

[60] *North American*, Philadelphia, March 2, 1919.

[61] *New York Times*, March 2, 1919.

[62] *Chicago Daily Tribune*, March 2, 1919.

[63] *North American*, Philadelphia, March 2, 1919.

[64] *New York Times*, March 2, 1919.

[65] R. M. L. to B. C. L., R. M. L., Jr., and Mary, March 4, 1919, LFP.

[66] *Record*, 65th Cong., 3rd Sess., Vol. 57, pp. 4811-4812, 4816, March 3, 1919.

[67] R. M. L. to B. C. L., R. M. L., Jr., and Mary, March 2, 1919, LFP.

[68] *Idem*, March 4, 1919, LFP.

[69] *La Follette's Magazine*, March, April, 1919.

[70] *Record*, 65th Cong., 3rd Sess., Vol. 57, p. 4894, March 3, 1919.

[71] *Ibid.*, pp. 4980-4990, March 4, 1919. See also R. M. L. to B. C. L., R. M. L., Jr., and Mary, March 4, 1919, LFP.

[72] *Record*, 65th Cong., 3rd Sess., Vol. 57, pp. 4999-5021, March 4, 1919.

[73] Josephus Daniels to R. M. L., April 18, 1922, copy with LFP; *Record*, 67th Cong., 2nd Sess., Vol. 62, p. 5792, April 21, 1922.

[74] *New York Times*, March 5, 1919.

[75] *Ibid.*

[76] *Daily Congressional Record*, 65th Cong., 3rd Sess., Vol. 57, p. 5203, March 4, 1919; *Record*, 65th Cong., 3rd Sess., Vol. 57, p. 5021, March 4, 1919.

[77] *New York Times*, March 5, 1919.

[78] R. M. L. to B. C. L., R. M. L., Jr., and Mary, March 5, 1919, LFP.

[79] *New York Times*, March 5, 1919; *Record*, 65th Cong., 3rd Sess., Vol. 57, p. 4974, March 4, 1919.

[80] R. M. L. to B. C. L., R. M. L., Jr., and Mary, March 10, 1919, LFP.

Chapter LIX
(Pages 949–959)

[1] R. M. L. to Gilbert E. Roe, March 6, 1919, LFP.

[2] *La Follette's Magazine*, March, 1919, pp. 33-35; April, 1919, pp. 53-54, 59-60.

[3] R. M. L. to B. C. L., R. M. L., Jr., and Mary, March 14, 1919, LFP; *idem* to B. C. L., R. M. L., Jr., April 17, 1919, LFP.

[4] *Idem* to B. C. L., and R. M. L., Jr., March 21, 1919, LFP.

[5] *Record*, 66th Cong., 1st Sess., Vol. 58, p. 4750, Sept. 3, 1919.

[6] *La Follette's Magazine*, July, 1919, pp. 103, 114; *Record*, 66th Cong., 1st Sess., Vol. 58, pp. 4760-4761, Sept. 3, 1919.

[7] R. M. L. to B. C. L. and R. M. L., Jr., April 22, 1919, LFP.

[8] R. M. L. to B. C. L., R. M. L., Jr., and Mary, March 12, 1919, LFP. Stipulation by attorneys on both sides was filed on March 14, 1919, and signed by Judge E. Ray Stevens.

[9] R. M. L. to B. C. L., R. M. L., Jr., March 17, 1919, LFP.

[10] Phil to Mary, Feb. 8, 1919, LFP.

[11] *Idem* to R. M. L., March 13, 1919, LFP.

[12] R. M. L. to B. C. L. and R. M. L., Jr., March 16, 1919, LFP.

[13] *Idem*, March 25, 1919, LFP.

[14] *Idem*, April 2, 1919, LFP.

[15] *Idem*, April 2, 1919, LFP.

[16] R. M. L., Jr., to R. M. L., March 30, 1919, LFP.

[17] R. M. L. to B. C. L. and R. M. L., Jr., April 24, 1919, LFP.

[18] Reprinted in Memorial edition *La Follette's Magazine*, Nov. 7, 1931. See also George Middleton, *These Things Are Mine*, p. 97.

[19] R. M. L. to B. C. L. and R. M. L., Jr., April 27, 1919, LFP.

[20] *Idem*, April 28, 1919, LFP.

[21] *Idem*, March 30, 1919, LFP.

[22] B. C. L. to R. M. L., April 16, 1919, LFP.

[23] R. M. L. to B. C. L. and R. M. L., Jr., April 21, May 4, 1919, LFP.

[24] *Idem*, May 3, 5, 1919, LFP.

[25] Frederick Palmer, *Bliss: Peacemaker. The Life and Letters of Tasker H. Bliss* (New York, Dodd, Mead & Company, 1934), pp. 387-388, 391, 395, 397-399; Herbert Hoover, *The Memoirs of Herbert Hoover: Years of Adventure 1874–1920* (New York, The Macmillan Company, 1952), pp. 461-468; Robert Lansing, Confidential Memoranda, Vol. IV, entry May 5, 1919, Lansing Papers; *Sun*, New York, May 24, 1919.

[26] Charles Seymour, *The Intimate Papers of Colonel House*, IV, 472; the *Nation*, Vol. 108, p. 899, June 7, 1919.

[27] R. M. L. to R. M. L., Jr., May 10, 1919, LFP.

[28] *Idem*, May 14, 1919, LFP.

[29] R. M. L. to B. C. L. and R. M. L., Jr., April 7, 1919, LFP.

[30] *Idem*, April 14, 1919, LFP. See also B. C. L. to R. M. L., April 5, 1919, LFP.

[31] R. M. L. to B. C. L. and R. M. L., Jr., April 29, 1919, LFP.

[32] *Idem*, May 1, 1919, LFP.

[33] *Idem*, April 17, 1919, LFP.

[34] *Idem*, March 23, 1919, LFP.

[35] *Idem*, March 29, 1919, LFP.

[36] R. M. L., Jr., to B. C. L., May 6, 1919, LFP.

[37] B. C. L. to R. M. L., Jr., May 8, 1919, LFP.

[38] *Idem* to Phil, May 12, 1919, LFP.

[39] R. M. L. to R. M. L., Jr., May 11, 1919, LFP.

[40] *Idem*, May 12, 1919, LFP.

[41] B. C. L. to R. M. L., Jr., and Phil, May 15, 1919, LFP.

Chapter LX
(Pages 960–973)

[1] R. M. L. to R. M. L., Jr., May 17, 1919, LFP.
[2] *Idem* to B. C. L., R. M. L., Jr., and Mary, Nov. 27, 1918, LFP.
[3] John J. Hannan to author, March 17, 1938, LFP.
[4] Suzanne La Follette to author, April, 1936, LFP.
[5] *Idem*. See also John J. Hannan to author, March 17, 1938, LFP.
[6] R. M. L. to R. M. L., Jr., May 19, 1919, LFP.
[7] *Idem*, May 17, 1919, LFP.
[8] R. M. L. to R. M. L., Jr., and Phil, May 27, 1919, LFP.
[9] *Idem*, May 26, June 4, 1919, LFP.
[10] *Idem*, June 4, 1919, LFP.
[11] *Idem*, June 27, 1919, LFP.
[12] *Record*, 66th Cong., 1st Sess., Vol. 58, pp. 1964-1965, 1967, 1973, June 28, 1917.
[13] R. M. L. to R. M. L., Jr., and Phil, June 29, 1919, LFP.
[14] William B. Colver to R. M. L., June 30, 1919, LFP.
[15] R. M. L. to R. M. L., Jr., and Phil, May 23, 1919, LFP; *Record*, 66th Cong., 1st Sess., Vol. 58, pp. 157-159, May 23, 1919.
[16] *Sun*, New York, May 24, 1919. See also Robert Lansing, Confidential Memoranda, Vol. IV, entry May 19, 1919, Lansing Papers.
[17] R. M. L. to R. M. L., Jr., and Phil, May 27, 1919, LFP.
[18] *Record*, 66th Cong., 1st Sess., Vol. 58, p. 558, June 3, 1919.
[19] *Ibid.*, p. 781, June 9, 1919.
[20] R. M. L. to R. M. L., Jr., and Phil, June 9, 1919, LFP.
[21] *Detroit Journal*, June 10, 1919.
[22] R. M. L. to R. M. L., Jr., and Phil, June 10, 1919, LFP.
[23] *Idem*, June 12, 1919, LFP.
[24] *Idem*, June 17, 22, 27, 1919, LFP.
[25] *New York Times*, June 17, 1919.
[26] *La Follette's Magazine*, July, 1919, pp. 101-102.
[27] R. M. L. to R. M. L., Jr., and Phil, June 6, 1919, LFP.
[28] *Idem*, June 15, 1919, LFP.
[29] *Idem*, June 21, 1919, LFP.
[30] *Idem*, June 27, 1919, LFP.
[31] *Idem*, June 29, 1919, LFP.
[32] *Record*, 66th Cong., 1st Sess., Vol. 58, pp. 2337-2339, July 10, 1919.
[33] *New York Times*, July 11, 1919.
[34] *Record*, 66th Cong., 1st Sess., Vol. 58, p. 2336, July 10, 1919.
[35] B. C. L. to R. M. L., Jr., and Phil, July 10, 1919, LFP.
[36] *La Follette's Magazine*, July, 1919, pp. 101-102.
[37] *Ibid.*, Sept. 1919, p. 134.
[38] *New York Times*, Aug. 15, 20, 1919.
[39] *La Follette's Magazine*, September, 1919, pp. 135-136. See also *Treaty*

Of Peace With Germany Hearings Before The Committee On Foreign Relations United States Senate, 66th Cong., 1st Sess., p. 536.

[40] *Treaty Of Peace With Germany Hearings Before The Committee On Foreign Relations United States Senate,* 66th Cong., 1st Sess., pp. 517-518, 524-526.

[41] Joseph L. Bristow to R. M. L., Aug. 16, 1919, LFP.

[42] B. C. L. to R. M. L., July 23, 1919, LFP.

[43] John J. Hannan to R. M. L., July 22, 1919, LFP.

[44] B. C. L. to R. M. L., Aug. 9, 1919, LFP.

[45] R. M. L. to B. C. L. and Fola, July 29, 1919, LFP.

[46] R. M. L. to R. M. L., Jr., Aug. 6, 1919, LFP.

Chapter LXI
(Pages 974–984)

[1] *Record,* 66th Cong., 1st Sess., Vol. 58, pp. 5112-5139, Sept. 10, 1919.

[2] *Ibid.,* pp. 5213-5215, Sept. 11, 1919.

[3] Irvine L. Lenroot, "The Opportunity at San Francisco," *Sunday Star,* Washington, D.C., March 4, 1945.

[4] *Record,* 66th Cong., 1st Sess., Vol. 58, pp. 7011-7012, Oct. 16, 1919.

[5] *Ibid.,* p. 4999, Sept. 8, 1919.

[6] *Ibid.,* pp. 7671-7677, Oct. 29, 1919.

[7] *Ibid.,* p. 7969, Nov. 5, 1919, vote on La Follette amendment; *ibid.,* p. 8730, Nov. 18, 1919, vote on McCumber reservation.

[8] R. M. L., Jr., to Mary, October 30, 1919, LFP.

[9] *Idem,* Nov. 4, 1919, LFP.

[10] *Record,* 66th Cong., 1st Sess., Vol. 58, pp. 8001-8010, Nov. 5, 6, 1919.

[11] *Ibid.,* pp. 8022-8023, Nov. 6, 1919.

[12] *Treaty Of Peace With Germany, Hearings before The Committee On Foreign Relations, United States Senate,* 66th Cong., 1st Sess., 1919, pp. 502-505.

[13] *Record,* 66th Cong., 1st Sess., Vol. 58, p. 2342, July 10, 1919.

[14] *Ibid.,* pp. 8428-8429, Nov. 13, 1919.

[15] *Ibid.,* 65th Cong., 2nd Sess., Vol. 56, p. 19, Dec. 4, 1917, for quotation from President's message.

[16] *Ibid.,* 66th Cong., 1st Sess., Vol. 58, p. 5004, Sept. 8, 1919, for President's speech, delivered at Hotel Statler in St. Louis, Sept. 5, 1919.

[17] *Ibid.,* pp. 8427-8433, Nov. 13, 1919.

[18] *Ibid.,* p. 8437, Nov. 13, 1919.

[19] *Ibid.,* p. 8437, Nov. 13, 1919.

[20] *Ibid.,* p. 8555, Nov. 15, 1919.

[21] *Ibid.,* pp. 8719-8729, Nov. 18, 1919. See also *La Follette's Magazine,* December, 1919, pp. 184-190. Maps were reproduced with the speech in both of the publications cited.

[22] Emma Wold to author.

[23] *Record,* 66th Cong., 1st Sess., Vol. 58, pp. 8727-8728, Nov. 18, 1919.

[24] *Ibid.,* pp. 8748-8753, Nov. 18, 1919.

[25] *Ibid.,* p. 8768, Nov. 19, 1919.

[26] *Ibid.,* p. 8786, Nov. 19, 1919.

[27] *Ibid.,* p. 8803, Nov. 19, 1919.

[28] *La Follette's Magazine,* January, 1920, p. 14.

[29] R. M. L. to Robert F. Paine, Nov. 21, 1919, LFP.

[30] Irvine L. Lenroot, "The Opportunity at San Francisco," *Sunday Star,* Washington, D.C., March 4, 1945. Also Irvine L. Lenroot to author.

[31] Woodrow Wilson to Homer S. Cummings, Jan. 8, 1920; *Record,* 66th Cong., 2nd Sess., Vol. 59, p. 1249, Jan. 9, 1920.

Chapter LXII
(Pages 985–995)

[1] R. M. L. to B. C. L. and Fola [Aug. 2, 1919], LFP.

[2] *Idem* to B. C. L., R. M. L., Jr., and Mary, Jan. 3, 1919, LFP.

[3] *Idem* to R. M. L., Jr., and Phil, May 23, 1919, LFP.

[4] *Government Control of Railroads,* Minority Report, Committee on Interstate Commerce, Nov. 10, 1919, 66th Cong., 1st Sess., Report 304, Part 2, pp. 10, 11.

[5] *Record,* 66th Cong., 2nd Sess., Vol. 59, pp. 502-529, speeches delivered Dec. 9, 10, 11, 12, 13, 1919.

[6] *Ibid.,* p. 502, Dec. 9, 1919.

[7] *Ibid.,* p. 136, Dec. 4, 1919; Vol. 59, Appendix, p. 8761, Dec. 20, 1919.

[8] *Record,* 66th Cong., 2nd Sess., Vol. 59, pp. 527-528, Dec. 13, 1919.

[9] *Ibid.,* pp. 507-521, speeches of Dec. 10, 11, 12, 13, 1919. See also *La Follette's Magazine,* December, 1919, pp. 181-183, August, 1920, pp. 113-115, October, 1920, pp. 145-147, 150.

[10] *Record,* 66th Cong., 2nd Sess., Vol. 59, pp. 524-527, Dec. 13, 1919.

[11] *Ibid.,* p. 903, Dec. 19, 1919; p. 951, Appendix, pp. 8746-8761, Dec. 20, 1919.

[12] Phil to R. M. L., Feb. 22, 1920, LFP.

[13] *La Follette's Magazine,* August, 1920, p. 115.

[14] B. C. L. to Mary, Nov. 29, Dec. 5, 1919, LFP.

[15] *Idem* to Fola and Mary, Jan. 8, 1920, LFP.

[16] M. C. Otto Diary, January, 1920, copy of this excerpt with LFP.

[17] *Ibid.,* copy of this excerpt with LFP.

[18] B. C. L. to Fola and Mary, Jan. 8, 1920, LFP.

[19] *Idem* to R. M. L. and R. M. L., Jr., Jan. 22, 1920, LFP.

[20] *Capital Times,* Feb. 14, 1920.

[21] R. M. L., Jr., to B. C. L., March 8, 1920, LFP.

[22] *Wisconsin State Journal,* April 5, 1920.

[23] Woodrow Wilson to Gilbert M. Hitchcock, March 8, 1920; *Record,* 66th Cong., 2nd Sess., Vol. 59, p. 4051, March 9, 1920.

[24] *Record,* 66th Cong., 2nd Sess., Vol. 59, pp. 4333, 4532, 4536, March 15, 18, 1920.

[25] *Ibid.,* p. 4599, March 19, 1920.

[26] *Ibid.,* pp. 4665-4666, March 20, 1920.

[27] *Ibid.,* pp. 4665-4666, March 20, 1920. See also *La Follette's Magazine,* March, 1920, p. 36; campaign leaflet, LFP.

[28] B. C. L. to R. M. L., R. M. L., Jr., Fola, and Mary, March 30, April 2, 5, 1920, LFP.

[29] *Sunday Star,* Washington, D.C., April 11, 1920.

[30] B. C. L. and Phil to R. M. L., April 7, 1920, LFP.

[31] *Idem* to R. M. L., April 9, 14, 1920, LFP.

Chapter LXIII
(Pages 996–1010)

[1] B. C. L. to R. M. L., April 17, 1920, LFP.

[2] R. M. L. to Phil, June 10, 1920, LFP.

[3] *La Follette's Magazine,* July, 1920, p. 106.

[4] *Nation,* Vol. 110, p. 820, June 19, 1920.

[5] *New York Times,* June 11, 1920.

[6] *La Follette's Magazine,* July, 1920, pp. 102-103.

[7] *Nation,* Vol. 110, p. 821, June 19, 1920.

[8] *La Follette's Magazine,* July, 1920, pp. 102, 106.

[9] *New York Times,* June 13, 1920.

[10] *Ibid.,* June 14, 15, 1920.

[11] Kenneth C. MacKay, *The Progressive Movement of 1924* (New York, Columbia University Press, 1947), pp. 56-57; *La Follette's Magazine,* January, 1920, p. 6.

[12] J. A. H. Hopkins to the Members of the Executive Committee, Feb. 19, 1920, Amos Pinchot Papers; Amos Pinchot to Frederick M. Kerby, Feb. 25, 1920, Amos Pinchot Papers.

[13] *Facts About the Chicago Convention,* printed leaflet, Amos Pinchot Papers.

[14] R. M. L., Jr., to R. M. L., June 21, 1920, LFP; *idem* to Phil, June 22, 23, 24, 25, 1920, LFP; George L. Record to R. M. L., June 25, 1920, LFP; Amos Pinchot to R. M. L., June 25, 1920, LFP.

[15] George L. Record to R. M. L., June 25, 1920, LFP; Amos Pinchot to R. M. L., June 25, 1920, LFP.

[16] *New York Times,* June 15, July 5, 13, 1920; *Chicago Herald and Examiner,* July 11, 1920; *Minneapolis Journal,* July 12, 1920; *Chicago Evening Post,* July 15, 1920; *Labor,* July 24, 1920; *Nonpartisan Leader,* Aug. 9, 1920; *Socialist Review,* Vol. IX, No. 4, Sept., 1920, pp. 134-136, "The Farmer Labor Party's Birth," by Arthur Warner.

[17] *New York Times,* July 5, 1920.

[18] Robert M. Buck to R. M. L., June 30, 1920, LFP.

[19] Gilbert E. Roe, "The Third Party Convention. Why Senator La Follette Declined the Nomination," unpublished MS, LFP; R. M. L., Jr., to author, June 23, 1951; *Chicago Herald and Examiner*, July 11, 1920.

[20] June 19, 1920, p. 4.

[21] *Facts*, National Conference Number Issued By Committee of 48, St. Louis, Dec. 12, 1919, Vol. 1, No. 4, Amos Pinchot Papers.

[22] *New Majority*, Jan. 3, 1920, p. 4.

[23] *New York Times*, July 13, 1920.

[24] *New Majority*, May 8, 1920, p. 2.

[25] *Toledo News-Bee*, July 10, 1920.

[26] *Facts About the Chicago Convention*, printed leaflet, Amos Pinchot Papers.

[27] *Chicago Daily News*, July 10, 1920.

[28] Gilbert E. Roe, "Third Party Convention," unpublished MS, LFP.

[29] *Ibid.*; Gilbert E. Roe to Amos Pinchot, July 10, 1920, Amos Pinchot Papers; *idem* to R. M. L., July 16, 1920, LFP; R. M. L., Jr., to author.

[30] *Seattle Times*, July 12, 1920, A.P. dispatch; *New York Times*, July 12, 1920; *Ohio State Journal*, July 12, 1920, A.P. dispatch.

[31] *Sun and New York Herald*, July 14, 1920.

[32] *New Majority*, July 17, 1920, p. 6.

[33] William Hard to R. M. L., July 11, 1920, LFP.

[34] R. M. L., Jr., to R. M. L. [July 11, 1920], LFP.

[35] Gilbert E. Roe, "The Third Party Convention," unpublished MS, LFP.

[36] *Ibid.*

[37] *New York Times*, July 13, 1920.

[38] William Z. Foster, *From Bryan to Stalin* (New York, International Publishers, 1937), pp. 140, 163, 179-181, 274.

[39] *New York Times*, July 14, 1920; *New Majority*, July 24, 1920, p. 2; *Nonpartisan Leader*, Aug. 9, 1920, pp. 5-6.

[40] *Chicago Evening Post*, July 14, 1920, report signed by Clinton W. Gilbert.

[41] Gilbert E. Roe, "The Third Party Convention," unpublished MS, LFP; *Toledo News-Bee*, July 14, 1920.

[42] Memorandum of Conversation with Senator La Follette at 12 midnight; Statement from Senator La Follette taken over the long distance at 1 P.M. today, LFP.

[43] The *Freeman*, July 28, 1920, pp. 467-468, "The Birth of the Third Party," by Dudley Field Malone. See also Dudley Field Malone to R. M. L., July 23, 1920, LFP.

[44] Gilbert E. Roe, "The Third Party Convention," unpublished MS, LFP.

[45] *New York Times*, July 15, 1920.

[46] *New York Times*, July 15, 1920; *New Majority*, July 24, 1920, p. 2; *Wisconsin State Journal*, July 14, 1920.

[47] "Statement from Senator La Follette taken over the long distance telephone at 11:45," LFP. Also, R. M. L., Jr., to author.

[48] July 15, 1920.

[49] *Post Intelligencer*, Seattle, July 15, 1920.

[50] *New York Times,* July 15, 1920.
[51] *New Majority,* Oct. 9, 1920.
[52] Gilson Gardner to Robert P. Scripps, July 19, 1920, Amos Pinchot Papers.
[53] *Chicago Evening Post,* July 14, 1920.
[54] *New York Times,* July 16, 1920.
[55] *St. Louis Post-Dispatch,* July 16, 1920.
[56] Rudolph Spreckels to R. M. L., July 15, 1920, LFP.
[57] Gilbert E. Roe to R. M. L., July 16, 1920, LFP.
[58] R. M. L., Jr., to Gilbert E. Roe, July 16, 1920, LFP.
[59] *Public Ledger, Philadelphia,* July 16, 1920.
[60] *Chicago Daily Tribune,* July 15, 1920.
[61] Will H. Hays to R. M. L., July 16, 1920, LFP.

Chapter LXIV
(Pages 1011–1019)

[1] J. A. H. Hopkins to R. M. L., Jr., July 16, 1920, LFP.
[2] George L. Record to R. M. L., July 16, 1920, LFP.
[3] J. A. H. Hopkins to R. M. L., July 19, 1920, LFP.
[4] In addition to specific citations, the narrative of these conferences is based upon the following sources: A thirteen-page typescript entitled *MEMORANDUM* CONFERENCE AT MADISON, WISCONSIN, July 25 to 27, by Basil Manly, Aug. 2, 1920, LFP; a four-page memorandum by Charles H. Crownhart, made early in August, 1920, after reading Manly's *MEMORANDUM,* LFP; R. M. L., Jr., to author.
[5] Basil M. Manly to Gilbert E. Roe, July 28, 1920, LFP.
[6] *Idem.*
[7] R. M. L. to J. A. H. Hopkins, July 30, 1920, LFP. See also James G. Blauvelt to R. M. L., July 28, 1920, LFP; *idem* to Amos Pinchot, July 28, 1920, Amos Pinchot Papers; Amos Pinchot to James G. Blauvelt, July 30, 1920, Amos Pinchot Papers; Allen McCurdy to Amos Pinchot, letter, July 30: telegram, July 30, 1920, Amos Pinchot Papers; typed memorandum of R. M. L., Jr., "Substance of long distance conference with J. A. H. Hopkins, July 31, 1920, at about 10 o'clock A.M.," LFP; typed memorandum of R. M. L., Jr., "Long distance conference with Herman Ekern, Chicago, Illinois, July 31, 1920, at about 10:30 A.M.," LFP; R. M. L., Jr., to Gilbert E. Roe, Aug. 2, 1920, LFP.
[8] *Detroit Journal,* July 31, 1920. See also *Cleveland News,* July 31, 1920.
[9] R. M. L., Jr., to Basil M. Manly, July 31, Aug. 2, 1920, LFP. See also Basil M. Manly to R. M. L., Jr., July 31, 1920, LFP.
[10] R. M. L., Jr., to Gilbert E. Roe, Aug. 2, 1920, LFP.
[11] *La Follette's Magazine,* July, 1920, pp. 97-98.
[12] *New York Times,* July 23, 1920.
[13] 1920 campaign leaflets, LFP.

[14] *State of Wisconsin Supplement to The Senate Journal,* Special Sess., pp. 26-96, Feb. 25, 1918.

[15] R. M. L. to James A. Reed, Oct. 2, 8, 1920, LFP.

[16] B. C. L. to Mary, Oct. 5, 1920, LFP.

[17] *Milwaukee Sentinel,* Oct. 12, 1920.

[18] R. M. L. to James A. Reed, Oct. 6, 1920, LFP; *idem* to Joseph I. France, Oct. 9, 1920, LFP; *idem* to David I. Walsh, Oct. 9, 1920, LFP; *idem* to William E. Borah, Oct. 2, 1920, LFP.

[19] *La Follette's Magazine,* Nov. 1920, p. 168.

[20] B. C. L. to Mary, Oct. 20, 1920.

[21] R. M. L., Jr., to Gilbert E. Roe, Aug. 21, 1920, LFP.

[22] Oct. 20, 1920.

[23] *Milwaukee Journal,* Oct. 22, 1920.

[24] Typescript of speech delivered by R. M. L. at Milwaukee, Oct. 21, 1920, LFP.

[25] Oct. 25, 1920. See also *Wisconsin State Journal,* Oct. 25, 1920.

[26] Oct. 27, 1920. See also *Milwaukee Journal,* Oct. 26, 1920.

[27] *Wisconsin Blue Book,* 1921, pp. 164, 209.

[28] *La Follette's Magazine,* Nov., 1920, p. 162.

[29] R. M. L. to Dante M. Pierce, Nov. 2, 1920, LFP.

[30] *La Follette's Magazine,* November, 1920, p. 162.

[31] *Des Moines Register,* Oct. 29, 1920; Albert O. Barton to R. M. L., Nov. 5, 1920, LFP.

[32] *Wisconsin Farmer,* Nov. 4, 1920, p. 2, clipping with letter from Albert O. Barton to R. M. L., Nov. 5, 1920, LFP. See also *La Follette's Magazine,* November 1920, p. 163.

Chapter LXV

(Pages 1020–1040)

[1] *La Follette's Magazine,* December, 1920, p. 179, "Fact and Fable from Washington," by R. M. L., Jr.

[2] Grace Lynch to author.

[3] *Record,* 66th Cong., 3rd Sess., Vol. 60, p. 409, Dec. 16, 1920; *La Follette's Magazine,* Jan., 1921, p. 7, "Fact and Fable from Washington," by R. M. L., Jr.; *Washington Post,* Dec. 17, 1920; *Labor,* Dec. 25, 1920; *Des Moines Register,* Dec. 17, 1920.

[4] *Record,* 66th Cong., 3rd Sess., Vol. 60, pp. 568-569, Dec. 20, 1920; p. 1675, Jan. 19, 1921.

[5] *La Follette's Magazine,* January, 1921, pp. 3, 5, "Fact and Fable from Washington," by R. M. L., Jr.; *Record,* 66th Cong., 3rd Sess., Vol. 60, p. 411, Dec. 16, 1921.

[6] R. M. L. to Woodrow Wilson, Dec. 22, 1920, Wilson Papers; MS draft with LFP.

[7] *La Follette's Magazine,* January, 1921, p. 7, "Fact and Fable from Washington," by R. M. L., Jr.

[8] R. M. L., Jr., to Phil, Feb. 26, 1921, LFP.

[9] *Record,* 66th Cong., 3rd Sess., Vol. 60, p. 3599, Feb. 21, 1921; Appendix, pp. 4602-4665, Feb. 21, 22, 1921.

[10] *Record,* 66th Cong., 3rd Sess., Vol. 60, p. 3599, Feb. 22, 1921. See also *New York Times,* Feb. 23, 1921; *La Follette's Magazine,* March, 1921, pp. 34-35.

[11] *New York Times,* Mar. 27, 1921, Special Feature Section 8.

[12] William G. McAdoo to R. M. L., April 2, 1921, LFP.

[13] Edith Bolling Wilson, *My Memoir,* pp. 318-319, copyright, 1939, used by permission of the publishers, The Bobbs-Merrill Company, Inc. See also *Detroit Free Press,* Mar. 5, 1921.

[14] *Record,* 67th Cong., Special Session of Senate, LXI, 6, Mar. 4, 1921.

[15] *Milwaukee Journal,* Mar. 4, 1921.

[16] *La Follette's Magazine,* April, 1921, pp. 50-51. See also *Wisconsin State Journal,* Mar. 12, 1921; *New York Times,* Mar. 13, 1921; *Wisconsin Farmer,* editorial by Dante M. Pierce, printed in *La Follette's Magazine,* April, 1921, p. 62.

[17] Phil to B. C. L. and R. M. L., Jr., Mar. 24, 1921, LFP.

[18] *Wisconsin State Journal,* Mar. 26, 1921.

[19] *Labor,* April 23, 1921.

[20] *Sunday Star,* Washington, April 17, 1921; *Labor,* April 23, 1921; *La Follette's Magazine,* May, 1921, p. 67.

[21] Warren G. Harding to R. M. L., Mar. 28, 1921, LFP.

[22] *Record,* 67th Cong., 1st Sess., Vol. 61, pp. 405-406, April 18, 1921; *La Follette's Magazine,* April, 1921, pp. 50-51; *Labor,* April 23, 1921.

[23] *Record,* 67th Cong., 1st Sess., Vol. 61, pp. 1731-1757, speeches delivered, May 16, 17, 23, 25, 1921.

[24] *Ibid.,* p. 1739, May 25, 1921.

[25] *Ibid.,* p. 1743, May 23, 1921.

[26] *Ibid.,* p. 1748, May 23, 1921; *New York Times,* May 24, 1921; *Violation of Armor Contracts,* Report and Evidence submitted by the Committee on Naval Affairs (House of Representatives). By order 55th Congress, 2nd Sess., Report No. 1468, Washington, 1894.

[27] Part 3 of Report No. 944 of the Special Committee on Investigation of Munition Industry. U.S. Senate, 73rd Congress, Washington, 1936.

[28] *La Follette's Magazine,* January, 1921, p. 10.

[29] *Ibid.,* May, 1921, pp. 68-69.

[30] R. M. L., Jr., to Phil, Mar. 23, 1921, LFP.

[31] *New York Times,* April 19, May 4, 5, 1921; *Record,* 67th Cong., 1st Sess., Vol. 61, p. 1758, May 25, 1921.

[32] *Record,* 67th Cong., 1st Sess., Vol. 61, p. 1971, June 1, 1921; *La Follette's Magazine,* June, 1921, p. 83.

[33] B. C. L. to Phil, June 10, 1921, LFP.

[34] *Record,* 66th Cong., 3rd Sess., Vol. 60, p. 1341, Jan. 13, 1921.

[35] R. M. L. to Boies Penrose, July 13, 1921, LFP.

[36] *Refunding of Obligations of Foreign Governments*, Hearing before the Committee on Finance, U.S. Senate, 67th Cong., 1st Sess., pp. 69-70, July 18, 1921.

[37] *Ibid.*, Report from the Senate Committee on Finance, 67th Cong., 1st Sess., Report No. 264, Part 2, pp. 1-2. See also *Record*, 67th Cong., 1st Sess., Vol. 61, p. 5316, Aug. 21, 1921.

[38] *Refunding of Obligations of Foreign Governments*, Hearings before the Committee on Finance, U. S. Senate, 67th Cong., 4th Sess., Feb. 10, 1923.

[39] *Record*, 67th Cong., 1st Sess., Vol. 61, pp. 4298-4299, July 26, 1921.

[40] *New York Times*, Aug. 2, 1921.

[41] *Record*, 67th Cong., 1st Sess., Vol. 61, pp. 5606-5608, Aug. 24, 1921.

[42] Robert M. La Follette, "My Own Story," *Washington Daily News*, Sept. 25, 1924.

[43] R. M. L., Jr., to Phil, July 4, 1921, LFP; B. C. L. to Phil, July 14, 1921, LFP.

[44] *Internal Revenue Bill of 1921*, Minority Views, Committee on Finance, U.S. Senate, 67th Cong., 1st Sess., Report 275, Part 2. See also *New York Times*, Oct. 6, 1921.

[45] *Record*, 67th Cong., 1st Sess., Vol. 61, p. 5868, Sept. 29, 1921. See also *New York Times*, Sept. 30, 1921; *La Follette's Magazine*, October, 1921, p. 146.

[46] *New York Times*, Oct. 22, 1921.

[47] *Record*, 67th Cong., 1st Sess., Vol. 61, pp. 7365-7374, Nov. 5, 1921.

[48] *Ibid.*, pp. 7522-7523, Nov. 7, 1921. See also *La Follette's Magazine*, Dec., 1921, p. 185.

[49] B. C. L. to Phil, Nov. 9, 1921, LFP.

[50] Dec. 3, 1921, p. 4, article by Raymond Lonergan (Edward Keating). See also *La Follette's Magazine*, December, 1921, pp. 184, 187.

[51] *La Follette's Magazine*, Nov., 1921, p. 170.

[52] Oct. 13, 1921.

[53] Edwin Borchard to R. M. L., Sept. 8, 22, Oct. 6, Nov. 3, 21, Dec. 1, 19, 1921, LFP.

[54] *Record*, 67th Cong., 1st Sess., Vol. 61, p. 5870, Sept. 29, 1921. See also *La Follette's Magazine*, September, 1921, p. 138.

[55] February, 1922, pp. 28-29.

[56] *Record*, 67th Cong., 2nd Sess., Vol. 62, p. 4326, Mar. 23, 1922.

[57] *La Follette's Magazine*, November, 1921, p. 161.

[58] *Ibid.*, December, 1921, pp. 177-178.

[59] *Record*, 67th Cong., 2nd Sess., Vol. 62, pp. 4227-4235, Mar. 22, 1922.

[60] *Ibid.*, p. 4335, Mar. 23, 1922.

[61] R. M. L. to O. J. Schuster, April 1, 1922, LFP.

[62] *La Follette's Magazine*, January, 1923, pp. 10, 14.

[63] R. M. L. to Josephine La Follette Siebecker, Jan. 11, 1922, LFP.

[64] *Record*, 67th Cong., 2nd Sess., Vol. 62, Appendix, p. 13550, Jan. 12, 1922.

[65] *Record*, 67th Cong., 2nd Sess., Vol. 62, p. 1182, Jan. 16, 1922; p. 2107, Feb. 3, 1922.

[66] R. M. L. to Robert F. Paine, Oct. 19, 1921, LFP.

[67] Charles F. Amidon to R. M. L., Oct. 8, 1921, LFP.

[68] Diary of M. C. Otto, entry January, 1920, copy with LFP.

Chapter LXVI
(Pages 1041–1054)

[1] Recollection of Harry Slattery, Feb. 13, 1932, LFP.

[2] R. M. L. to Josephus Daniels, April 6, 1922, quotes from address delivered by Daniels to American Society of Engineers in Washington, D.C., Dec. 18, 1920, LFP.

[3] S. 2775, *Record*, 66th Cong., 1st Sess., Vol. 58, pp. 3886, 4054-4057, Aug. 15, 20, 1919.

[4] *Record*, 66th Cong., 1st Sess., Vol. 58, pp. 4251-4252, Aug. 23, 1919.

[5] *Ibid.*, pp. 4417, 4444, 4506, 4585-4592, 4619-4623, 4732-4761, 4770-4774, 4784-4785, Aug. 27, 28, 29, 30, Sept. 2, 3, 1919. Two of La Follette's speeches, with the interruptions they evoked, were printed in the *Record* several days after they were delivered. His speech of August 27 seems to have been omitted.

[6] *Ibid.*, pp. 4759-4760, speech delivered Aug. 29, printed Sept. 3, 1919.

[7] *Ibid.*, p. 4446, Aug. 28, 1919.

[8] *Ibid.*, p. 4449, Aug. 28, 1919.

[9] *Ibid.*, p. 4770, Sept. 3, 1919.

[10] *Leases Upon Naval Oil Reserves*, Hearings before the Committee on Public Lands and Surveys, U.S. Senate, 68th Cong., 1st Sess., 3 vols., 1924.

[11] *Record*, 66th Cong., 1st Sess., Vol. 58, p. 4772, Sept. 3, 1919.

[12] *Leases Upon Naval Oil Reserves*, Hearings before the Committee on Public Lands and Surveys, U.S. Senate, Oct. 26, 1923, p. 348.

[13] Jerre Mathews to author, March, 1939, LFP; *Evening Star,* Washington, D.C., June 2, 1921.

[14] One of these outstanding claims was that of the Honolulu Consolidated Oil Company in one of the California reserves. This claim had been denied during the Wilson Administration. It was reopened on Nov. 18, 1921, and leases were granted the company on Feb. 11, 1922. R. M. La Follette asked for an investigation, which was agreed to (S. Res. 151, agreed to Feb. 8, 1924, *Record*, 68th Cong., 1st Sess., Vol. 65, p. 2072). See Supreme Court Reports for what eventually happened to this case.

[15] Harry Slattery to R. M. L., Mar. 15, 1922, copy with LFP.

[16] R. M. L. to Charles Evans Hughes [April 6, 1922], LFP. See also Albert B. Fall to R. M. L., April 12, 1922, LFP.

[17] R. M. L. to Josephus Daniels, April 6, 1922, LFP.

[18] R. M. L. to Gov. Robert D. Carey, April 22, 1922, LFP.

[19] Albert B. Fall to R. M. L., April 12, 1922, LFP.

[20] *Leases Upon Naval Oil Reserves,* Hearings before the Committee on Public Lands and Surveys, U.S. Senate, Oct. 24, 1923, pp. 296, 560.

[21] *Ibid.,* Feb. 14, 1924, pp. 2244-2247.

[22] *The High Cost of Gasoline and Other Petroleum Products,* Hearings before a Subcommittee of the Committee on Manufactures, U.S. Senate, 67th Cong., Jan. 18, 1923, p. 701.

[23] Warren G. Harding to Albert B. Fall, April 26, 1922, *Leases Upon Naval Oil Reserves,* Hearings before Committee on Public Lands and Surveys, Oct. 24, 1923, p. 267.

[24] *Record,* 67th Cong., 2nd Sess., Vol. 62, pp. 6048-6049, April 28, 1922.

[25] *New York Times,* April 19, 1922.

[26] *Wall Street Journal,* April 14, 1922.

[27] *Record,* 67th Cong., 2nd Sess., Vol. 62, p. 6043, April 28, 1922.

[28] *Leases Upon Naval Oil Reserves,* Hearings before the Committee on Public Lands and Surveys, U.S. Senate, Mar. 18, 1924, p. 2755.

[29] Josephus Daniels to R. M. L., April 18, 1922, *Record,* 67th Cong., 2nd Sess., Vol. 62, p. 5792, April 21, 1922.

[30] R. M. L. to Josephus Daniels, April 20, 1922, LFP.

[31] Recollection of Harry Slattery, Feb. 12, 1932, LFP.

[32] *Idem,* Feb. 13, 1932, LFP.

[33] Josephus Daniels to R. M. L., April 15, 1922, LFP.

[34] R. M. L. to Robert S. Griffin, April 19, 1922, LFP.

[35] Recollection of Harry Slattery, Feb. 12, 1932, LFP.

[36] Josephus Daniels to R. M. L., April 25, 1922, LFP.

[37] *Leases Upon Naval Oil Reserves,* Hearings before the Committee on Public Lands and Surveys, U.S. Senate, Oct. 26, 1923, pp. 347-356.

[38] *Record,* 68th Cong., 1st Sess., Vol. 65, p. 2231, Feb. 11, 1924.

[39] Interview with Harry Slattery, Feb. 12, 1932, p. 16, LFP.

[40] *Record,* 67th Cong., 2nd Sess., Vol. 62, p. 6041, April 28, 1922.

[41] *Ibid.,* pp. 6041-6043, April 28, 1922.

[42] *Ibid.,* p. 6044, April 28, 1922.

[43] *Ibid.,* p. 6045, April 28, 1922.

[44] *Ibid.,* p. 6047, April 28, 1922.

[45] *Ibid.,* p. 6048, April 28, 1922.

[46] *Ibid.,* p. 6097, April 29, 1922.

[47] *Ibid.,* pp. 6096-6097, April 29, 1922. See also Resolution 282, passed by a vote of 58 to 0. R. M. L. had asked for the yeas and nays. Thirty-eight Senators were recorded as not voting. Sixty-three Senators had answered to the roll call earlier in the day.

[48] R. M. L., Jr., to author.

[49] *Investigation of the Hon. Harry M. Daugherty, formerly Attorney General of the United States, Hearings before the Select Committee on Investigation of the Attorney General,* 1924, p. 89.

[50] M. R. Werner, *Privileged Characters* (New York, Robert M. McBride & Company, 1935), pp. 160-165.

[51] Albert B. Fall to Reed Smoot, June 7, 1922, *Leases Upon Naval Oil*

Reserves, Hearings before the Committee on Public Lands and Surveys, U.S. Senate, April 15, 1924, p. 3142.

[52] *Leases Upon Naval Oil Reserves,* Hearings before the Committee on Public Lands and Surveys, U.S. Senate, Oct. 22, 1923, pp. 27-53.

[53] *Ibid.,* p. 25; also, *Record,* 67th Cong., 2nd Sess., Vol. 62, p. 8398, June 8, 1922.

[54] Recollection of Harry Slattery, Feb. 12, 1932, LFP.

[55] *Record,* 70th Cong., 1st Sess., Vol. 69, p. 4978, Mar. 19, 1928.

[56] Burton K. Wheeler to author, December, 1946.

[57] Netha Roe to author.

[58] *Record,* 67th Cong., 2nd Sess., Vol. 62, p. 6867, pp. 6893-6894, May 13, 1922 (S. Res. 292).

[59] *Ibid.,* p. 6932, May 15, 1922; p. 8140, June 5, 1922 (S. Res. 295).

[60] *The High Cost of Gasoline and Other Petroleum Products,* Hearings before the Committee on Manufactures, U.S. Senate, 67th Cong., 2nd and 4th Sess., 2 vols., 1922, 1923.

[61] *La Follette's Magazine,* May, 1922, p. 66.

[62] *Leases Upon Naval Oil Reserves,* Hearings before the Committee on Public Lands and Surveys, U.S. Senate, Jan. 21, 1924, p. 1772; Feb. 1, 1924, p. 1914.

[63] *Ibid.,* Dec. 3, 1923, pp. 1003-1013.

[64] *Ibid.,* Jan. 4, 1928, pp. 52-55.

[65] *Record,* 68th Cong., 1st Sess., Vol. 65, pp. 1728-1729, Jan. 31, 1924.

[66] *Pan American Petroleum Co.* v. *United States,* 273 U.S. 456, 509, Feb. 28, 1927.

[67] *Mammoth Oil Co.* v. *United States,* 275 U.S. 13, 53, Oct. 10, 1927.

[68] *Ibid.*

[69] Werner, *op. cit.,* p. 190.

[70] *Ibid.,* pp. 160-165.

[71] Josephus Daniels to Phil La Follette, Aug. 6, 1935, copy of excerpt with LFP.

Chapter LXVII
(Pages 1055–1073)

[1] *Record,* 67th Cong., 2nd Sess., Vol. 62, p. 6482, May 8, 1922.

[2] *Ibid.,* pp. 6782-6786, May 10, 1922.

[3] *United States* v. *United States Steel Corporation,* 251 U.S. 417, Mar. 1, 1920.

[4] *La Follette's Magazine,* March, 1920, p. 33.

[5] *Bailey* v. *The Drexel Furniture Co.,* 259 U.S. 20, May 15, 1922; *United Mine Workers of America* v. *Coronado Coal Co.,* 259 U.S. 344, June 5, 1922.

[6] *Cincinnati Enquirer,* June 15, 1922.

[7] *Record,* 67th Cong., 2nd Sess., Vol. 62, p. 9076, June 21, 1922.

[8] *New York Times,* June 15, 1922.
[9] *Ibid.*
[10] *Record,* 67th Cong., 2nd Sess., Vol. 62, pp. 8931-8932, June 19, 1922.
[11] *Ibid.,* pp. 9071-9073, June 21, 1922.
[12] *Ibid.,* p. 9073, June 21, 1922.
[13] *Ibid.,* pp. 9075-9082, June 21, 1922.
[14] R. M. L. to Charles H. Crownhart, Nov. 18, 1921.
[15] *New York Times,* Jan. 3, 1922.
[16] *Milwaukee Journal,* June 1, 1922.
[17] *Ibid.,* June 18, 1922.
[18] R. M. L. to R. M. L., Jr., May 25, 1922, LFP.
[19] B. C. L. to "Dear Ones," June 5, 1922, LFP.
[20] *Milwaukee Journal,* July 18, 1922.
[21] *La Follette's Magazine,* July, 1922, pp. 100-104.
[22] Aug. 23, 1922.
[23] *The La Follette-Wheeler Campaign Text Book* (1924), pp. 133-134 (some quotations previously published in 1922).
[24] R. M. L., Jr., to Ralph G. Sucher, July 27, 1922, LFP.
[25] *St. Louis Post-Dispatch* in the *Literary Digest,* Sept. 23, 1922.
[26] In the *Literary Digest,* Sept. 23, 1922, p. 12.
[27] *St. Louis Post-Dispatch,* Sept. 17, 1922.
[28] B. C. L. to Fola and Mid, Oct. 2, 1922, LFP.
[29] *Wisconsin State Journal,* Sept. 18, 1922.
[30] *Record,* 67th Cong., 2nd Sess., Vol. 62, p. 12907, Sept. 19, 1922.
[31] *Ibid.,* p. 12999, Sept. 20, 1922.
[32] *Ibid.,* pp. 10054-10063, July 8, 1922; pp. 10074-10086, July 9, 1922.
[33] Henrik Shipstead to author.
[34] *New York Times,* Nov. 2, 1922.
[35] *Minneapolis Journal,* Nov. 1, 1922.
[36] Nov. 3, 1922.
[37] Nov. 4, 1922.
[38] Clipping, LFP.
[39] *Minneapolis Morning Tribune,* Nov. 4, 1922.
[40] *St. Paul Pioneer Press,* Nov. 4, 1922.
[41] *New York Times,* Nov. 5, 1922.
[42] George Middleton, *These Things Are Mine,* p. 173.
[43] Nov. 9, 1922.
[44] *New Republic,* Dec. 20, 1922, pp. 87-89; *Review of Reviews,* Oct. 1922, pp. 397-399.
[45] Nov. 19, 1922.
[46] *Record,* 67th Cong., 1st Sess., Vol. 61, pp. 4237-4244, July 25, 1921.
[47] *La Follette's Magazine,* Nov., 1922, p. 1.
[48] *New York Times,* Nov. 19, 1922.
[49] *La Follette's Magazine,* December, 1922, pp. 183-184.
[50] Dec. 3, 1922.
[51] *Labor,* Dec. 9, 1922, p. 2.

[52] *Sunday Oregonian,* Dec. 3, 1922.

[53] Dec. 3, 1922.

[54] *New York Times,* Dec. 16, 1922; *Record,* 67th Cong., 4th Sess., Vol. 63, pp. 508-518, Dec. 15, 1922.

[55] Gilbert E. Roe to Netha Roe, Mar. 4, 1923, LFP.

[56] *Wisconsin State Journal,* April 14, 15, 1923.

[57] R. M. L. to W. T. Rawleigh, June 16, 1923, LFP.

[58] May 7, 1923. See also *La Follette's Magazine,* May, 1923, p. 67.

[59] *La Follette's Magazine,* June, 1923, p. 85.

[60] R. M. L. to W. T. Rawleigh, June 5, 1923, LFP.

[61] R. M. L., Jr., to R. M. L., June 5, 1923, LFP.

[62] R. M. L. to R. M. L., Jr., June 15, 1923, LFP.

[63] *Idem.*

[64] *New York Times,* July 2, 1923.

[65] *Ibid.,* July 21, 1923.

[66] W. T. Rawleigh to Magnus Johnson, July 29, 1923, LFP.

[67] *Idem* to R. M. L., Oct. 29, 31, 1919, LFP.

[68] R. M. L. to W. T. Rawleigh, June 24, 1923, LFP.

[69] George H. Moses to R. M. L., June 18, 1923, LFP.

Chapter LXVIII
(Pages 1074–1087)

[1] *La Follette's Magazine,* December, 1923, p. 180. See also *Washington Herald,* Nov. 25, 1923.

[2] R. M. L. Diary entry, LFP.

[3] R. M. L. to W. T. Rawleigh, July 31, 1923, LFP.

[4] R. M. L. Diary entry, LFP.

[5] *La Follette's Magazine,* October, 1923, p. 152.

[6] Basil M. Manly MS, LFP.

[7] *The Times,* London, July 27, Aug. 10, 1923.

[8] Ramsay MacDonald to R. M. L., Aug. 8, 1923, LFP.

[9] B. C. L. to Mary, Aug. 10, 1923, LFP.

[10] Elizabeth Bibesco to R. M. L., Jr., Aug. 26, 1923, LFP; Catherine Wells to R. M. L., Aug. 15, 1923, LFP.

[11] Harold J. Laski to R. M. L., Aug. 12, 1923, LFP.

[12] R. M. L., Jr., Diary, Aug. 11-12, 1923, LFP.

[13] Basil M. Manly MS, pp. 3-5, LFP.

[14] *La Follette's Magazine,* October, 1923, pp. 152-153.

[15] B. C. L. to Mary, Oct. 15, 1923.

[16] Oct. 28, 1923.

[17] B. C. L. to Mary, Aug. 21, 1923, LFP; *La Follette's Magazine,* January, 1924, pp. 7-10.

[18] B. C. L. to Mary, Oct. 21, 1923, LFP.

[19] Basil M. Manly MS, p. 7, LFP.

20 *Washington Herald,* Dec. 23, 1923. See also *La Follette's Magazine,* February, 1924, pp. 26-28.

21 B. C. L. to Mary, Aug. 21, 1923, LFP.

22 *Washington Herald,* Nov. 25, 1923. See also *La Follette's Magazine,* November, 1923, pp. 164-166.

23 Basil M. Manly MS, p. 18, LFP.

24 R. M. L. Diary, entry Sept. 4, 1923.

25 Basil M. Manly MS, p. 21, LFP.

26 *The Letters of Lincoln Steffens,* II, 625.

27 R. M. L. Diary, Sept. 7, 1923, LFP.

28 *New York Times,* Aug. 21, 1923.

29 *Washington Herald,* Dec. 16, 1923. See also *La Follette's Magazine,* January, 1924, p. 5; R. M. L., Jr., to W. T. Rawleigh, Sept. 14, 1923, LFP.

30 *Washington Herald,* Dec. 16, 1923. See also *La Follette's Magazine,* January, 1924, p. 5.

31 R. M. L., Jr., to W. T. Rawleigh, Sept. 15, 1923, LFP.

32 *Idem* to author.

33 *Washington Herald,* Dec. 16, 1923. See also *La Follette's Magazine,* January, 1924, p. 5.

34 *The Autobiography of Lincoln Steffens,* II, 806.

35 *The Letters of Lincoln Steffens,* II, 631.

36 B. C. L. to Mary, Sept. 13, 1923, LFP.

37 R. M. L., Jr., to W. T. Rawleigh, Sept. 14, 1923, LFP.

38 *La Follette's Magazine,* December, 1923, pp. 184-186.

39 B. C. L. to Mary, Sept. 19, 1923, LFP.

40 *Idem.*

41 R. M. L. Diary entry, Sept. 20, 1923, LFP.

42 B. C. L. to Mary, Sept. 23, 1923, LFP.

43 R. M. L., Jr., to author.

44 B. C. L. to Mary, Sept. 25, 1923, LFP.

45 *La Follette's Magazine,* January, 1924, pp. 11-12.

46 LFP.

47 *Washington Herald,* Dec. 9, 1923. See also *La Follette's Magazine,* January, 1924, pp. 4-6.

48 R. M. L. to Josephine La Follette Siebecker, Oct. 6, 1923, LFP.

49 B. C. L. to Mary, Oct. 2, 1923, LFP.

50 R. M. L., Jr., to Fola, Oct. 7, 1923, LFP.

51 B. C. L. to John Ernest Roe, Oct. 8, 1923, copy with LFP.

52 *Washington Herald,* Dec. 23, 1923; *La Follette's Magazine,* February, 1924, p. 26.

53 Recollection of Suzanne La Follette, Dec. 3, 1941, LFP.

54 B. C. L. to Fola, Oct. 11, 1923, LFP.

55 R. M. L., Jr., to Fola and Mid, Oct. 11, 1923, LFP.

56 Mary to author.

57 Jo Davidson to author.

58 R. M. L. notebook, LFP.

⁵⁹ *New York Times,* Nov. 3, 1923.
⁶⁰ *Washington Herald,* Nov. 25, 1923. See also *La Follette's Magazine,* December, 1923, pp. 180-181, 187.
⁶¹ *Washington Herald,* Jan. 6, 1924. See also *La Follette's Magazine,* March, 1924, pp. 41, 45.

Chapter LXIX
(Pages 1088–1106)

¹ R. M. L. to Alfred T. Rogers, Nov. 9, 1923, LFP.
² R. M. L., Jr., to Phil and Isen (Isabel) Nov. 12, 1923, LFP.
³ Bradford Merrill to R. M. L., Dec. 29, 1923, LFP.
⁴ R. M. L. to Bradford Merrill, Dec. 28, 1923, LFP.
⁵ R. M. L., Jr., to George W. Norris, Nov. 19, 1923, LFP.
⁶ R. M. L. to George W. Norris, Edwin F. Ladd, Smith W. Brookhart, Lynn J. Frazier, Henrik Shipstead, Magnus Johnson, Nov. 30, 1923, LFP.
⁷ R. M. L., Jr., to "Dear Ones," Dec. 4, 1923, LFP.
⁸ *La Follette's Magazine,* December, 1923, p. 175.
⁹ *Ibid.,* p. 178.
¹⁰ Dec. 15, 1923.
¹¹ *New York Times,* Dec. 16, 1923.
¹² *Ibid.,* Jan. 4, 1924.
¹³ LFP.
¹⁴ Jan. 4, 1924.
¹⁵ *New York Times,* Jan. 10, 1924; *Record,* 68th Cong., 1st Sess., Vol. 65, p. 747, Jan. 9, 1924.
¹⁶ *La Follette's Magazine,* February, 1924, p. 18.
¹⁷ *Record,* 68th Cong., 1st Sess., Vol. 65, p. 774, Jan. 10, 1924.
¹⁸ *New York Times,* Jan. 11, 12, 1924.
¹⁹ *Record,* 68th Cong., 1st Sess., Vol. 65, p. 981, Jan. 15, 1924.
²⁰ *Ibid,* p. 1555, Jan. 28, 1924.
²¹ *Ibid.,* p. 920, Jan. 13, 1924.
²² *Ibid.,* p. 1367, Jan. 25, 1924.
²³ *Ibid.,* pp. 1972-1973, Feb. 7, 1924.
²⁴ *Ibid.,* p. 2072, Feb. 8, 1924.
²⁵ *Ibid.,* p. 2481, Feb. 15, 1924.
²⁶ *Ibid.,* p. 2541, Feb. 16, 1924.
²⁷ *Ibid.,* p. 1728, Jan. 31, 1924.
²⁸ *Ibid.,* p. 1547, Jan. 28, 1924.
²⁹ Clinton W. Gilbert, *You Takes Your Choice* (New York, G. P. Putnam's Sons, 1924), p. 104.
³⁰ *Record,* 68th Cong., 1st Sess., Vol. 65, pp. 2232-2234, Feb. 11, 1924.
³¹ Gilbert, *op. cit.,* pp. 104-105.
³² *Record,* 68th Cong., 1st Sess., Vol. 65, pp. 3410-3411, March 1, 1924.
³³ *La Follette's Magazine,* March, 1924, p. 33.

[34] R. M. L. to W. T. Rawleigh, March 19, 1924, LFP.

[35] Elizabeth G. Evans to B. C. L., April 1, 1924, LFP.

[36] March 18, 1924.

[37] R. M. L. to W. T. Rawleigh, March 19, 1924, LFP.

[38] March 22, 1924.

[39] April 6, 1924, Sect. 9, "How La Follette Stands On Leading A Third Party."

[40] *New York Times,* Dec. 4, 5, 30, 1923; *ibid.,* Jan. 18, 25, Feb. 24, 27, 28, 29, March 2, 6, 16, 18, 24, 1924.

[41] R. M. L. to R. M. L., Jr., and Phil, Jan. 20, 1924, with enclosures, LFP.

[42] *Idem* to Phil, May 7, 1924, LFP.

[43] R. M. L. to R. M. L., Jr., May 6, 1924, LFP.

[44] *Labor,* April 5, 1924.

[45] Fola to Mid, May 26, 1924, LFP.

[46] R. M. L., Jr., to R. M. L., May 14, 1924, LFP.

[47] *Idem.*

[48] R. M. L. to Ralph G. Sucher, May 19, 1924, LFP.

[49] R. M. L., Jr., to R. M. L., May 20, 1924, 5:00 P.M., LFP.

[50] *Idem,* May 27, 1924, LFP.

[51] *Sunday Star,* Washington, Sept. 5, 1948.

[52] R. M. L. to Herman L. Ekern, May 26, 1924, press release, LFP.

[53] *St. Paul Dispatch,* June 17, 1924.

[54] *Ibid.,* June 18, 1924; *St. Paul Pioneer Press,* June 18, 20, 1924; William Z. Foster, "The Communists and the La Follette Movement of 1924," *political affairs,* Vol. XXXI, No. 2, pp. 21-31, February, 1952.

[55] *St. Paul Pioneer Press,* June 18, 1924.

[56] William J. Bryan to R. M. L., June 2, 1924, LFP.

[57] R. M. L. to William J. Bryan, June 6, 1924, LFP.

[58] June 1, 1924.

[59] B. C. L. to Phil and Isabel, June 4, 1924, LFP.

[60] *Record,* 68th Cong., 1st Sess., Vol. 65, p. 10652, June 5, 1924; *ibid.,* p. 11139, June 7, 1924.

[61] June 8, 1924.

[62] *Record,* 68th Cong., 1st Sess., Vol. 65, p. 10287, June 3, 1924.

[63] *Ibid.,* pp. 10985-10986, June 6, 1924.

[64] *Ibid.,* pp. 10993-10994, June 6, 1924.

Chapter LXX
(Pages 1107–1126)

[1] *New York American,* June 8, 1924.

[2] R. M. L. to John J. Blaine, June 7, 1924, LFP.

[3] *New York Times,* June 10, 11, 1924.

[4] *Sun,* Baltimore, June 12, 1924.

[5] R. M. L., Jr., to R. M. L., June 11, 1924.

[6] R. M. L. to William J. Bryan, June 6, 1924, LFP; R. M. L., Jr., to author.

[7] Zona Gale to the editor of the *Nation*, July 10, 1924, published in the *Nation*, July 23, 1924, Vol. 119, p. 96. See also Address to Hon. Robert M. La Follette on behalf of The La Follette For President Committee, delivered by W. T. Rawleigh, July 3, 1924, LFP.

[8] *New York Times*, July 4, 1924.

[9] R. M. L. to Ralph G. Sucher, May 19, 1924, LFP.

[10] R. M. L., Jr., to author.

[11] *New York Times*, July 5, 1924.

[12] Kenneth MacKay, *The Progressive Movement of 1924*, pp. 110-111; *Proceedings*, C.P.P.A. Convention, II, 168ff.; M. G. Johnston Papers.

[13] *New York Times*, July 6, 1924. See also *World*, New York, July 6, 1924. See also Jay Lovestone, *The La Follette Illusion as Revealed in An Analysis of the Political Role of Senator Robert M. La Follette* (Chicago, Literature Department Workers Party of America, 1924).

[14] July 4, 1924.

[15] July 5, 1924.

[16] July 5, 1924.

[17] *New York Times*, July 5, 1924.

[18] *Statement And Platform of Robert M. La Follette Independent Progressive Candidate for President of the United States*, presented on July 4, 1924, to the Progressive Conference at Cleveland, Ohio, by R. M. L., Jr., LFP.

[19] *New York Times*, July 5, 1924.

[20] *Ibid.*, July 6, 1924.

[21] *Ibid.*

[22] *La Follette's Magazine*, July, 1924, pp. 104-105.

[23] *Labor*, July 12, 1924. See also *La Follette's Magazine*, July, 1924, pp. 101-103, 109.

[24] *Labor*, July 12, 1924. See also *La Follette's Magazine*, July, 1924, p. 103.

[25] B. C. L. to Elizabeth Evans, July 6, 1924, LFP.

[26] Gilbert E. Roe to R. M. L., June 17, 1924, LFP.

[27] B. C. L. to Phil, Isen, and Mary, July 11, 1924, LFP.

[28] *New York Times*, July 17, 1924.

[29] Alice Brandeis to B. C. L., July 16, 1924, LFP.

[30] B. C. L. to Elizabeth G. Evans, July 21, 1924, LFP.

[31] *La Follette's Magazine*, October, 1924, p. 146; *New York Times*, Oct. 15, 1924.

[32] *New York Times*, July 17, 1924.

[33] *Ibid.*, July 21, 1924; *La Follette's Magazine*, August, 1924, pp. 124-125.

[34] Oswald Garrison Villard to R. M. L., July 20, 1924, LFP. Those who signed this telegram were: John B. Andrews, Katherine Anthony, Mary Austin, A. A. Berle, Jr., Mrs. Karl Bitter, Franz Boas, W. E. Burghardt DuBois, Rev. Edmund B. Chaffee, Dr. L. Pierce Clark, Mrs. Albert De Silver, Katherine Dreier, Theodore Dreiser, Dr. Will Durant, John Lovejoy Elliott, Morris L. Ernst, Payson Irwin, Alvin Johnson, Bishop Paul Jones, Paul

Kellogg, Paul Kennedy, Freda Kirchwey, Mrs. Mary Knoblauch, Dr. Herman Kudelich, Isabel Lamonte, Ellen La Motte, Margaret Lane, Mrs. Henry Goddard Leach, Henry R. Linville, Owen R. Lovejoy, Robert Morss Lovett, Rev. George Mackay, Darwin J. Meserole, Dr. Henry Neumann, Mrs. Gordon Norrie, William F. Ogburn, Leroy Peterson, Eleanor M. Phelps, Amos Pinchot, Mrs. S. Pollitzer, George Pratt, Charles Fleischer, Mrs. Simeon Ford, Lewis Gannett, Mrs. Anna Vankirk Geller, Hermann Habicht, Bolton Hall, Norman Hapgood, Arthur Garfield Hays, Sidney Hillman, Morris Hillquit, John Haynes Holmes, Frederic C. Howe, J. A. H. Hopkins, B. W. Huebsch, Gilbert E. Roe, Margaret Sanger, George Soule, Mrs. P. G. Stone, Frank Tannenbaum, Norman Thomas, Carl Van Doren, Thorstein Veblen, Mrs. Henry Villard, Oswald Garrison Villard, Mrs. Oswald Garrison Villard, Rabbi F. Max Weis, Mrs. Bertha Poole Weyl, Mrs. John Jay White, Jesse Lynch Williams, Margaret Wycherly.

[35] *New York Times,* Oct. 26, 1924.

[36] *Ibid.,* Oct. 22, 1924.

[37] *Ibid.,* Oct. 23, 1924.

[38] Helen Keller to R. M. L., *La Follette's Magazine,* August, 1924, pp. 121, 125.

[39] *La Follette's Magazine,* October, 1924, pp. 156-157, 160.

[40] Executive Committee Report of A.F. of L. sent to R. M. L. by Samuel Gompers, Aug. 4, 1924, LFP.

[41] Aug. 4, 1924.

[42] Sept. 4, 1924.

[43] LFP.

[44] Robert M. La Follette, "My Own Story," *Washington Daily News,* clippings with LFP.

[45] R. M. L. to H. F. Samuel, Aug. 7, 1924, LFP.

[46] *New York Times,* Oct. 7, 8, 1924.

[47] R. M. L. to Burton K. Wheeler, Aug. 6, 1924, LFP.

[48] *Idem* to Mrs. Edward Costigan, Aug. 11, 1924, LFP.

[49] Robert P. Scripps to R. M. L., Aug. 1, 1924, LFP.

[50] R. M. L. to Robert P. Scripps, Aug. 5, 1924, LFP.

[51] *Record,* 50th Cong., 2nd Sess., Vol. 20, Feb. 13, 1889, pp. 1866-1871.

[52] Charles Ervin to author, Oct. 19, 1943, LFP.

[53] Gilbert E. Roe to Mercer G. Johnston, Oct. 31, 1924, LFP.

[54] Arthur E. Holder to K. M. Erickson, Aug. 12, 1924, LFP.

[55] *New York Times,* Aug. 23, 1924.

[56] C. A. Brothers to William H. Johnston, LFP.

[57] *New York Times,* July 30, 1924.

[58] *Salt Lake Tribune,* July 10, 1924.

[59] *New York Times,* Sept. 15, 1924.

[60] *Ibid.,* Sept. 16, 1924.

[61] *Ibid.,* Oct. 24, 1924.

[62] *Milwaukee Sentinel,* Aug. 20, 1924.

[63] *Ibid.,* Sept. 12, 1924.

⁶⁴ B. C. L. to Elizabeth G. Evans, Aug. 24, 1924, LFP.
⁶⁵ R. M. L., Jr., MS of speech delivered in New York, Sept. 15, 1924, LFP.
⁶⁶ Gilbert E. Roe to James Frear, Sept. 4, 1924, LFP.
⁶⁷ R. M. L., Jr., MS of speech delivered in New York, Sept. 15, 1924, LFP.
⁶⁸ *New York Times,* Sept. 25, 1924.
⁶⁹ *Ibid.,* Sept. 26, 1924.
⁷⁰ Rudolph Spreckels to R. M. L., July 11 and Sept. 10, 1924, LFP.
⁷¹ B. C. L. to Phil and Isen, Aug. 25, 1924, LFP.
⁷² R. M. L., Jr.'s speech in New York, Sept. 15, 1924, LFP.
⁷³ B. C. L. to Phil and Isen, Aug. 24, 1924, LFP.
⁷⁴ *New York Times,* Sept. 19, 1924.
⁷⁵ *New York Evening Journal,* Sept. 2, 1924.
⁷⁶ *La Follette's Magazine,* September, 1924, pp. 133-135.
⁷⁷ *Capital Times,* Madison, Wis., Sept. 29, 1924, signed dispatch by Robert B. Black.

Chapter LXXI
(Pages 1127–1147)

¹ *New York Times,* Sept. 19, 1924.
² Fola to R. M. L., Oct. 1, 1924, LFP.
³ *New York Times,* Sept. 19, 1924.
⁴ Sept. 19, 1924.
⁵ *New York Times,* Sept. 19, 1924.
⁶ George Middleton, *These Things Are Mine,* p. 294.
⁷ *New York Times,* Sept. 22, 1924.
⁸ LFP.
⁹ Wheeler itinerary, LFP.
¹⁰ B. C. L. speaking itinerary, LFP.
¹¹ *New York Times,* Oct. 19, 1924.
¹² *Ibid.,* Oct. 1, 1924.
¹³ *Ibid.,* Oct. 19, 1924.
¹⁴ B. C. L. to Fola, Oct. 6, 1924, LFP.
¹⁵ LFP.
¹⁶ Oct. 6, 1924.
¹⁷ Journal of Receipts & Division of same and Expenses, LFP.
¹⁸ *Democrat and Chronicle,* Rochester, Oct. 7, 1924.
¹⁹ R. M. L., Jr., to B. C. L., Oct. 6, 1924, LFP.
²⁰ *Idem,* Oct. 8, 1924, LFP.
²¹ Stenographic Report, Oct. 7, 1924, pp. 6-11, LFP. See also Special Committee on Campaign Expenditures, Oct. 18, 1924, pp. 186-187, National Archives, Legislative Division, Washington, D.C.
²² *New York Times,* Oct. 6, 1924.
²³ Stenographic Report, Oct. 7, 1924, LFP.
²⁴ *New York Times,* Sept. 21, 1924.

[25] *New York Times,* Oct. 16, 1924.

[26] Films are preserved in the Fox Library, 11th Avenue and 53rd St., New York City.

[27] *Newark Evening News,* Oct. 9, 1924.

[28] Oct. 10, 1924.

[29] *Detroit Free Press,* Oct. 10, 1924.

[30] *Commercial Tribune,* Cincinnati, Oct. 11, 1924.

[31] *Cincinnati Enquirer,* Oct. 11, 1924.

[32] R. M. L., Jr., to B. C. L., Oct. 11, 1924, LFP.

[33] *Chicago Daily News,* Oct. 11, 1924.

[34] *St. Louis Post-Dispatch,* Oct. 11, 1924.

[35] *New York Times,* Oct. 13, 1924.

[36] *Chicago Daily News,* Oct. 13, 1924.

[37] Stenographic Report, Oct. 11, 1924, p. 7, LFP.

[38] R. M. L., Jr., to B. C. L., Oct. 13, 1924, LFP.

[39] *Sun,* Baltimore, Oct. 13, 1924.

[40] *Ibid.*

[41] Journal of Receipts & Division of same and Expenses.

[42] *Pittsburgh Gazette Times,* Nov. 1, 1924.

[43] Recollection of George Middleton.

[44] *St. Louis Post-Dispatch,* Nov. 1, 1924.

[45] Stenographic Report, Oct. 13, 1924, p. 1, LFP.

[46] John J. Hannan to W. T. Rawleigh, Oct. 13, 1924, LFP.

[47] Stenographic Report, Oct. 13, 1924, pp. 1-2, LFP.

[48] *Ibid.,* Oct. 14, 1924, p. 1, LFP. See also Jeannette P. Nichols to Roy F. Nichols, from Des Moines, Iowa, Oct. 14, 1924, copy of excerpt with LFP.

[49] *New York Times,* Oct. 16, 1924.

[50] Stenographic Report, Oct. 15, 1924, pp. 1-2, LFP; *Des Moines Register,* Oct. 16, 1924; Press Release, No. 20, LFP.

[51] *Minneapolis Morning Tribune,* Oct. 17, 1924.

[52] Stenographic Report, Oct. 16, 1924, LFP.

[53] Lorena King Fairbank to Netha Roe, Oct. 23, 1924, LFP.

[54] Stenographic Report, Oct. 17, 1924, p. 1, LFP; *Sun,* Baltimore, Aug. 18, 1946, article by John W. Owens.

[55] *Sioux Falls Press,* Oct. 18, 1924.

[56] Lorena King Fairbank to Netha Roe, Oct. 23, 1924, LFP.

[57] *Morning World-Herald,* Omaha, Oct. 21, 1924.

[58] Stenographic Report, Oct. 20, 1924, pp. 6-10, LFP. Typescript of one of the orders issued by Superintendent of Chicago, Rock Island & Pacific Railway, Circular No. 137, Oct. 15, 1924, LFP.

[59] John J. Hannan to W. T. Rawleigh, Oct. 21, 1924, LFP.

[60] *New York Times,* Oct. 15, 1924.

[61] Press Release No. 119, Oct. 22, 1924, LFP.

[62] *New York Times,* Nov. 2, 1924.

[63] Oswald Garrison Villard to R. M. L., Sept. 13, 1924, LFP.

[64] R. M. L. to Burton K. Wheeler, Oct. 17, 1924, LFP.

65 Special Committee on Campaign Expenditures, Oct. 16, 17, 18, 1924, p. 165ff., National Archives.

66 Special Committee on Campaign Expenditures, pp. 126, 149, 150, National Archives.

67 *New York Times,* Oct. 25, 1924.

68 *Ibid.,* Oct. 29, 1924.

69 *Saturday Evening Post,* Oct. 18, 1924.

70 Special Committee on Campaign Expenditures, p. 237, National Archives.

71 Oct. 23, 1924.

72 *New York Times,* Oct. 16, 1924.

73 *Ibid.,* Oct. 23, 1924.

74 Special Committee on Campaign Expenditures, pp. 89, 95, 111, 189, National Archives.

75 *New York Times,* Oct. 23, 1924.

76 Special Committee on Campaign Expenditures, Report No. 1110, 68th Cong., 2nd Sess., Feb. 3 (calendar day, Feb. 12), 1925.

77 Special Committee on Campaign Expenditures, p. 61, National Archives.

78 Irene Richter to R. M. L., Oct. 6, 1924, LFP.

79 Louise Overacker, *Money in Elections* (New York, The Macmillan Company, 1932), p. 110. See also James K. Pollock, Jr., *Party Campaign Funds* (New York, Alfred A. Knopf, 1926).

80 Memorandum in Frank P. Walsh Papers cited by Kenneth C. Mackay in *The Progressive Movement in 1924,* p. 185. See also R. M. L. to William E. Borah, Jan. 14, 1925, LFP.

81 R. M. L. to Thomas J. Walsh, Oct. 25, 1924, LFP. See also *New York Times,* Oct. 26, 1924.

82 *New York Times,* Oct. 26, 1924.

83 Oct. 28, 1924.

84 *Brooklyn Daily Eagle,* Oct. 21, 1924.

85 *New York American,* Oct. 12, 1924, I, 11-13.

86 *Brooklyn Daily Eagle,* Oct. 29, 1924.

87 *New York Evening Journal,* Oct. 29, 1924.

88 Oct. 29, 1924.

89 Oct. 29, 1924.

90 *New York Times,* Oct. 30, 1924.

91 *Boston Daily Globe,* Oct. 31, 1924.

92 Oct. 31, 1924.

93 R. M. L., Jr., to B. C. L., Oct. 31, 1924, LFP.

94 Stenographic Report, Oct. 31, 1924, LFP.

95 Joseph L. Bristow to R. M. L., Nov. 1, 1924, LFP.

96 *St. Louis Post-Dispatch,* Nov. 1, 1924.

97 R. M. L., Jr., to B. C. L., Nov. 1, 1924, LFP; *idem* to Fola, Nov. 1, 1924, LFP.

98 *Cleveland Plain Dealer,* Nov. 2, 1924.

99 Stenographic Report of Peter Witt's Introduction, Nov. 1, 1924.

100 Stenographic Report of R. M. L.'s speech, Nov. 1, 1924.

[101] *Ibid.*, p. 3.
[102] *Cleveland Plain Dealer*, Nov. 2, 1924.
[103] Stenographic Report, Nov. 1, 1924, p. 3, LFP.
[104] Janet Van Hise to R. M. L., Nov. 5, 1924, LFP.
[105] *Wisconsin State Journal*, Nov. 6, 1924.
[106] Isabel B. La Follette to George Middleton, May 29, 1940, LFP.

Chapter LXXII
(Pages 1148–1174)

[1] William B. Colver to R. M. L., Nov. 5, 1924, LFP.
[2] *Wisconsin State Journal*, Nov. 5, 1924. See also *New York Times*, Nov. 6, 1924.
[3] *La Follette's Magazine*, July, 1925, p. 113.
[4] *Ibid.*, November, 1924, p. 165.
[5] B. C. L. to R. M. L., R. M. L., Jr., Phil, and Isabel, Monday, Nov. 12 [10], 1924, LFP.
[6] Nov. 30, 1924.
[7] Nov. 29, 1924. See also *Idaho Daily Statesman*, Nov. 29, 1924.
[8] *New York Times*, Dec. 2, 1924.
[9] *Sun*, Baltimore, Dec. 3, 1924.
[10] *Washington Herald*, Dec. 2, 1924.
[11] R. M. L. Diary, Dec. 1, 1924, LFP.
[12] R. M. L. to Josephine La Follette Siebecker, Dec. 27, 1924, LFP.
[13] R. M. L. Diary, Dec. 11, 1924, LFP.
[14] R. M. L., Jr., to W. T. Rawleigh, Dec. 29, 1924, LFP.
[15] R. M. L. Diary, Dec. 12, 1924, LFP.
[16] R. M. L. to W. T. Rawleigh, Dec. 26, 1924, LFP.
[17] *Idem* to Josephine La Follette Siebecker, Dec. 27, 1924, LFP.
[18] *La Follette's Magazine*, April, 1925, pp. 58-59.
[19] R. M. L. to Josephine La Follette Siebecker, Jan. 22, 1925, LFP.
[20] B. C. L. to W. T. Rawleigh, Feb. 24, 1925, LFP.
[21] R. M. L. to A. B. Butler, July 14, 1923, LFP.
[22] R. M. L. Diary [August], 1923, LFP.
[23] John C. Schmidtmann to R. M. L., Jan. 6, 1925, LFP.
[24] R. M. L. to John C. Schmidtmann, Jan. 13, 1925, LFP.
[25] Merle Curti and Vernon Carstensen, *The University of Wisconsin*, II, 157-158.
[26] R. M. L., Jr., to R. M. L. and B. C. L., Jan. 25, 26, 1925, LFP.
[27] B. C. L. to R. M. L., Jr., Jan. 30, Feb. 11, 1925, LFP.
[28] Robert Morss Lovett to Herman L. Ekern, Feb. 19, 1925, copy, LFP; Robert Morss Lovett, *All Our Years* (New York, The Viking Press, 1948), pp. 196-197.
[29] R. M. L. to Josephine La Follette Siebecker, Dec. 27, 1925, LFP.
[30] R. M. L., Jr., to R. M. L. and B. C. L., Jan. 29, 1925, LFP.

[31] R. M. L., Jr., Feb. 17, 1925, letter and telegram, LFP.

[32] R. M. L. to R. M. L., Jr., Feb. 18, 1925, LFP.

[33] B. C. L. to "Loved Ones," Feb. 11, 1925, LFP.

[34] R. M. L., Jr., to R. M. L. and B. C. L., Feb. 17, 1925, LFP.

[35] R. M. L. to R. M. L., Jr., Feb. 19, 1925, LFP.

[36] R. M. L., Jr., to R. M. L., Feb. 18, 19, 21, 1925, LFP; *Chicago Daily News*, Feb. 21, 1925; *New York Times,* Feb. 21, 1925; *Chicago Herald and Examiner,* Feb. 22, 1925.

[37] R. M. L., Jr., to R. M. L., two telegrams, Feb. 22, 1925, LFP. See also *New York Times,* Feb. 23, 1925; *Wisconsin State Journal,* Feb. 23, 1925.

[38] R. M. L. to Ralph and Mary, Feb. 27, 1925, LFP.

[39] *Idem* to Basil M. Manly, Feb. 28, 1925, photostat, LFP.

[40] R. M. L. to Rudolph Spreckels, March 25, 1925, LFP.

[41] *New York Times,* Feb. 14, 21, 1925.

[42] James E. Watson to R. M. L., Feb. 24, 1925, LFP.

[43] R. M. L. to Basil M. Manly, Feb. 28, 1925, LFP.

[44] *New York Times,* Feb. 21, 1925.

[45] *Ibid.,* Jan. 10, 1924.

[46] *Evening Star,* Washington, D.C., March 6, 9, 1925. See also *Record,* 69th Cong., Special Sess., Vol. 67, p. 62, March 9, 1925.

[47] *Record,* 69th Cong., Special Sess., Vol. 67, p. 42, March 9, 1925.

[48] *Ibid.,* p. 16, March 7, 1925.

[49] *Ibid.,* pp. 63, 65, March 9, 1925.

[50] *La Follette's Magazine,* April, 1925, p. 52.

[51] James A. Reed to R. M. L., March 12, 1925, LFP; R. M. L., Jr., to R. M. L., March 12, 13, 1925, LFP; Ralph G. Sucher to R. M. L., March 12, 1925, LFP.

[52] *Sunday Star,* Washington, D.C., March 15, 1925; *New York Times,* March 15, 1925; *Record,* 69th Cong., Special Sess., Vol. 67, p. 244, March 14, 1925.

[53] *La Follette's Magazine,* April, 1925, p. 49. See also *La Follette's Magazine,* June, 1929, pp. 81-83, article by Robert M. La Follette, Jr., entitled "Secrecy Rules of the United States Senate"; *ibid.,* July, 1929, p. 98, article by *idem* entitled "The Doors of the Senate Swing Ajar."

[54] *Helena Daily Independent,* A.P. dispatch, March 17, 1925.

[55] R. M. L., Jr., to author; Grace Lynch to author.

[56] March 17, 1925.

[57] Typescript of speech prepared by R. M. L., but not delivered during debate March 16, 1925, LFP.

[58] *La Follette's Magazine,* April, 1925, p. 49.

[59] R. M. L. Diary, March 30, April 1, 1925, LFP.

[60] *Ibid.,* April 2, 3, 4, 1925, LFP.

[61] Netha Roe to author.

[62] R. M. L. to W. T. Rawleigh, April 17, 1925, LFP.

[63] Draft of inscription for enclosure with letter from R. M. L. to Fred L. Holmes, March 1, 1925, LFP.

[64] R. M. L. to Phil and Isen, April 30, 1925, LFP.

[65] R. M. L. Diary, May 1, 1925, LFP.

[66] *La Follette's Magazine*, Memorial Edition, July, 1925, p. 98.

[67] Recollection of Mary La Follette.

[68] *Idem.*

[69] B. C. L. to Fola, Phil, and the Roe family, May 19, 1925, LFP.

[70] Recollection of Mary La Follette.

[71] B. C. L. to Mary, Aug. 18, 1925, LFP.

[72] B. C. L. to "Dear Ones," May 21, 23, 25, 1925, LFP.

[73] *Idem* to "Loved Ones," May 27, 1925, LFP.

[74] R. M. L., Jr., to Phil and Isen, June 3, 1925, LFP.

[75] *Idem*, June 14, 1925, LFP.

[76] R. M. L., Jr., to Gilbert E. Roe, June 16, 1925, LFP.

[77] *Chicago Daily Tribune*, June 18, 1925, LFP.

[78] B. C. L. to Elizabeth G. Evans, July 12, 1925, LFP.

[79] R. M. L., Jr., to author.

[80] Fola to Elizabeth G. Evans, Sept. 7, 1925, LFP.

[81] *Washington Daily News*, June 20, 1925.

[82] *Chicago Sunday Tribune*, June 21, 1925.

[83] *La Follette's Magazine*, Memorial Edition, July, 1925; Calvin Coolidge to B. C. L., June 18, 1925, LFP.

[84] *Resolutions of the University of Wisconsin on the death of Robert Marion La Follette*; E. A. Birge to B. C. L. Aug. 13, 1925, LFP. See also *Wisconsin State Journal*, June 21, 1925.

[85] *La Follette's Magazine*, Memorial Edition, July, 1925.

[86] Julia Lathrop to Laura Thompson, June 23, 1925, copy with LFP.

[87] *La Follette's Magazine*, Memorial Edition, July, 1925, p. 113, article by Zona Gale entitled "La Follette Planned for the Government of Tomorrow."

EPILOGUE

(Pages 1175–1176)

[1] *Robert M. La Follette: Memorial Addresses Delivered in the Senate and House of Representatives of the United States in Memory of Robert M. La Follette, Late a Senator from Wisconsin, Sixty-Ninth Congress, Proceedings in the Senate, June 20, 1926; Proceedings in the House, Feb. 20, 1927*, 69th Cong., 1st Sess., Senate Document No. 157 (Washington, D.C., United States Government Printing Office, 1927).

[2] *La Follette's Magazine*, Memorial Edition, July, 1925, p. 115.

[3] United States Statutes at Large, Vol. 13, p. 347, July 2, 1864.

[4] *Acceptance and Unveiling of the Statue of Robert Marion La Follette Presented by the State of Wisconsin Proceedings in the Congress and in Statuary Hall United States Capitol*, 71st Cong., 1st Sess., Senate Document No. 4 (Washington, D.C., United States Government Printing Office, 1929). See also *La Follette's Magazine*, May, 1929, article by Basil Manly entitled "Unveil Statue to Senator La Follette"; *La Follette's Magazine*, June, 1929, pp. 94-95.

Bibliography

Manuscripts

Ray Stannard Baker Papers, Library of Congress.
Louis D. Brandeis Papers. Selected correspondence relating to R. M. L. consulted by courtesy of Louis D. Brandeis and Alice Goldmark Brandeis.
William Jennings Bryan Papers, Library of Congress.
Moses E. Clapp Papers, in possession of Mrs. Harvey Clapp.
Thomas W. Gregory Papers, Library of Congress.
Mercer Green Johnston Papers, Library of Congress.
William Kent Papers, Yale University Library.
La Follette Papers, Library of Congress and State Historical Society, Madison, Wisconsin.
Suzanne La Follette Diary.
Robert Lansing Papers, Library of Congress.
Basil M. Manly Diary of European trip with R. M. L. in 1923.
George W. Norris, correspondence relating to World War I, courtesy of Senator Norris.
Amos Pinchot Papers, Library of Congress.
Records of the United States Senate, Committee on Privileges and Elections, 65th Cong., re La Follette Investigation, National Archives.
Gilbert E. Roe Papers. This collection is with La Follette Papers, Library of Congress.
Theodore Roosevelt Papers, Library of Congress.
Joseph P. Tumulty Papers, Washington, D.C.
Thomas J. Walsh Papers, Library of Congress.
John Sharp Williams Papers, Library of Congress.
Woodrow Wilson Papers, Library of Congress.

Personal Interviews

Ray Stannard Baker
Dr. Frederick J. Bates
Bessie Beatty
Senator William E. Borah
Professor Edwin Borchard

Senator Joseph L. Bristow
Alice Goldmark Brandeis
Justice Louis D. Brandeis
Percy E. Budlong (Official Reporter of Debates United States Senate)
Mrs. Harvey Clapp
Negley D. Cochran
Walter D. Corrigan
Charles R. Crane
John C. Crockett (Chief Clerk of the Senate)
William J. Dwyer
Herman L. Ekern
Charles Ervin
Elizabeth Glendower Evans
Senator Lynn J. Frazer
Mrs. Gilson Gardner
Senator Thomas P. Gore
Mrs. Asle J. Gronna
Mrs. Lynn Haines
Edwin A. Halsey (Secretary of the Senate)
John J. Hannan
Senator Thomas W. Hardwick
Edward Keating
John A. Kingsbury
Representative Michael Joseph Kirwan
William Kittle
Mrs. William Kittle
Chester La Follette
Mary La Follette
Philip F. La Follette
Senator Robert M. La Follette, Jr.
Suzanne La Follette
Judge Irvine L. Lenroot
Louis P. Lochner
Representative Louis Ludlow
Senator Ernest Lundeen
Grace Lynch (Clerk to Senator R. M. La Follette)
Basil M. Manly
Jerry A. Mathews
Professor Charles E. Merriam
George Middleton
Representative John M. Nelson
Senator George W. Norris
John S. Phillips
Amos Pinchot
Walter Pollock
James E. Pope
Senator James A. Reed

Mrs. Gilbert E. Roe
Walter S. Rogers
Representative Harry Sauthoff
Senator Henrik Shipstead
John F. Sinclair
Dean Frank H. Sommer
Julius A. Truesdell
Joseph P. Tumulty
Oswald Garrison Villard
Judson Welliver
Senator Burton K. Wheeler
Major General Walter K. Wilson

Public Documents
(U.S. Govt. Print. Off.)

U.S. *Congress.* Congressional record. Proceedings and debates of the 49th, 50th and 51st Congress. Washington, 1885-1891.

———. Congressional record. Proceedings and debates of the 59th-69th Congress. Washington, 1906-1925.

U.S. *Congress. House. Committee on Appropriations.* Relief of European peoples outside of Germany. Letter from the Secretary of the Treasury, transmitting a cablegram from the President of the United States and the tentative draft of a bill appropriating $100,000,000 for the relief of European peoples outside of Germany. Washington, 1919. (65th Cong., 3d sess. House. Doc. 1640)

U.S. *Congress. House. Special committee to Investigate the National Security League.* Investigation of National Security League. Report. To accompany H. res. 469. Washington, 1919. (65th Cong., 3d sess. House. Rept. 1173)

U.S. *Congress. Senate. Committee on Finance.* Hearings 67th Cong., 1st sess., on H. R. 8245, An Act to reduce and equalize Taxation, to amend and simplify the Revenue Act of 1918, and for other purposes, Sept. 1–Oct. 1921. Washington, 1921. Confidential print for use of Members of the Senate.

———. . . . . Internal revenue bill of 1921. Report. To accompany H. R. 8245. Washington, 1921. (67th Cong., 1st sess. Senate. Rept. 275) "Views of a minority" signed: Robert M. La Follette.

U.S. *Congress. Senate. Committee on Finance.* Refunding of obligations of foreign governments. Hearings 67th Cong., 1st sess., on S. 2135. Washington, 1921.

———. Refunding of obligations of foreign governments. Report. To accompany S. 2135. Washington, 1921. (67th Cong., 1st sess. Senate. Report 264) "Minority report" signed Robert M. La Follette, et al.

————. Refunding of obligations of foreign governments. Hearings . . . 67th Cong., 4th sess. on H. R. 14254 . . . Washington, 1923.

U.S. *Congress. Senate. Committee on Foreign Relations.* Treaty of peace with Germany. Hearings . . . 66th Cong., 1st sess. Washington, 1919. (66th Cong., 1st sess. Senate. Doc. 106)

U.S. *Congress. Senate. Committee on Interstate Commerce.* Government control of railroads. Report. To accompany S. 3288. Washington, 1919. (66th Cong., 1st sess. Senate. Rept. 304) Part 2, "Minority report" submitted by Mr. La Follette. Ordered printed November 10, 1919.

U.S. *Congress. Senate. Committee on Manufacturers.* The high cost of gasoline and other petroleum products. Hearings before a subcommittee . . . 67th Cong., 2d and 4th sess. Washington, 1923. Robert M. La Follette, chairman.

————. High cost of gasoline and other petroleum products. . . . Report. Pursuant to S. res. 295. Washington, 1923. (67th Cong., 4th sess. Senate. Rept. 1263) Submitted by Mr. La Follette.

U.S. *Congress. House. Committee on Naval Affairs.* Violations of armor contracts. Report and evidence submitted to the committee. . . . Washington, 1894. (55th Cong., 2d sess. House. Report 1468)

U.S. *Congress. Senate. Committee on Privileges and Elections.* Minutes. Records of the U.S. Senate Committee on Privileges and Elections, 65th Congress re La Follette investigation. National Archives.

————. Minutes of the subcommittee. Records of the U.S. Senate, 65th Congress, re La Follette investigation. National Archives.

————. Senator from Wisconsin. Report to accompany S. Res. 360. 2 pts. (65th Cong., 3d sess. Senate. Report 614)

————. Senator Robert M. La Follette. Letter from the Secretary of the Minnesota Commission of Public Safety to Senator Frank B. Kellogg, transmitting a copy of a resolution passed at a meeting of the Commission held on Sept. 25, 1917, together with a stenographic report of the speech of Senator Robert M. La Follette. Washington, 1917. (65th Cong., 1st sess.)

————. Speech of Senator Robert M. La Follette. Hearings before a subcommittee, 65th Cong., 1st-2d sess., on the resolutions from the Minnesota Commission of Public Safety petitioning for proceedings looking to the expulsion of Senator Robert M. La Follette, on account of a speech delivered before the Nonpartisan League, at St. Paul, Minn., on September 20, 1917 . . . Washington, 1917-18.

————. Speech of Senator Robert M. La Follette. Memorandum of information submitted to the Committee, 65th Cong., 2d sess., relative to the resolutions from the Minnesota Commission of Public Safety, petitioning for proceedings looking to the expulsion of Senator Robert M. La Follette, on account of a speech delivered before the Nonpartisan League, at St. Paul, Minn., on September 20, 1917 . . . Washington, 1918. Printed for the use of the Committee on Privileges and Elections. During the Hearings, Senator Atlee Pomerene stated that the Memorandum had been prepared by the Department of Justice at the request of a member of the Committee.

U.S. *Congress. Senate. Committee on Public Lands and Surveys.* Leases upon naval oil reserves. Hearings . . . 68th Cong., 1st sess. Washington, 1924.

U.S. *Congress. Senate. Committee on the Judiciary.* Brewing and liquor interests and German and Bolshevik propaganda. Report and hearings before the subcommittee . . . Washington, 1919. (66th Cong., 1st sess. Senate. Doc. 62)

――――. Maintenance of a lobby to influence legislation. Hearings before a subcommittee, 63d Cong., 1st–2d sess., under S. Res. 92, instructing the Committee on the judiciary to investigate the charge that a lobby is maintained to influence legislation pending in the Senate . . . Washington, 1913-14.

U.S. *Congress. Senate. Select committee on Investigation of the Attorney General.* Investigation of the Attorney General. Hearings, 68th Cong., 1st sess., pursuant to S. Res. 157, directing a committee to investigate the failure of the Attorney General to prosecute or defend certain criminal and civil actions, wherein the government is interested . . . Washington, 1924.

U.S. *Congress. Senate. Special committee to Investigate the munitions industry.* Munitions industry. Reports of the Special committee, pursuant to S. Res. 206 (73d Congress) a resolution to make certain investigations concerning the manufacture and sale of arms and other war munitions . . . Washington, 1935-36. (74th Cong., 1st–2d sess. Senate. Rept. 944)

U.S. *Congress. Senate. Special Committee on Campaign Expenditures.* Campaign expenditures. Report pursuant to S. Res. 246. Washington, 1925. 68th Cong., 2d sess. Senate. Rept. 1100)

U.S. *Congress. Senate. Special Committee to Investigate Campaign Expenditures.* Hearings . . . 68th Cong., 1st sess. Unpublished and incomplete stenographic report in National Archives.

U.S. *Dept of State.* Foreign relations of the United States. Diplomatic papers. Washington, 1914-1919.

U.S. *69th Cong., 1925-1927.* Robert M. La Follette. Memorial addresses delivered in the Senate and House of representatives of the United States in memory of Robert M. La Follette, late a senator from Wisconsin. 69th Cong. Proceedings in the Senate. June 20, 1926. Proceedings in the House. February 20, 1927. Washington, 1927. (69th Cong., 1st sess. Senate. Doc. 157)

U.S. *71st Cong., 1st sess., 1929.* Acceptance and unveiling of the statue of Robert Marion La Follette. Presented by the state of Wisconsin. Proceedings in the Congress and in Statuary hall, United States Capitol. Washington, 1929. (71st Cong., 1st sess. Senate. Doc. 4)

Related Documents

American Defense Society.
Brief presented in the matter of the inquiry into certain conduct and utterances of Robert M. La Follette, a member of the Senate. Records of the U.S. Senate, 65th Cong., re the La Follette investigation. National Archives.

Roe, Gilbert E.
Brief in behalf of Senator Robert M. La Follette. [Presented to] the Senate of the United States Committee on Privileges and Elections in the matter of the investigation by the Senate of the charge made by the Minnesota Commission of Public Safety that on the 20th date of September 1917, Senator Robert M. La Follette made an address of "a disloyal and seditious nature" at a public meeting before a large audience at St. Paul, Minnesota. [New York, N.Y., 1917.]

Roe, Gilbert E.
Reply brief in behalf of Senator Robert M. La Follette. [New York, N.Y., 1917.]

State of Wisconsin Publications

Wisconsin. *Legislature. Senate.*   Journal, Madison, 1901-1925
Wisconsin. *Legislature. Assembly.*   Journal, Madison, 1901-1925
Wisconsin Blue Book, Madison, 1885-1891; 1901-1925

Books

Aaron, Daniel, *Men of Good Hope* (New York, Oxford University Press, 1951).
Abbott, Lawrence F., *Impressions of Theodore Roosevelt* (Garden City, New York, Doubleday, Page & Company, 1919).
Allen, Philip Loring, *America's Awakening: the Triumph of Righteousness in High Places* (New York, Fleming H. Revell Company, 1906).
Angell, Norman, *America and the New World-State* (New York, G. P. Putnam's Sons, 1915).
———, *The Great Illusion* (New York, G. P. Putnam's Sons, 1910).
Arnett, Alex Mathews, *Claude Kitchin and the Wilson War Policies* (Boston, Mass., Little, Brown and Company, 1937).
Axtel, Silas Blake, *A Symposium on Andrew Furuseth* (New Bedford, Mass., The Darwin Press, 1949).

Ayer, N. W. & Sons, *American Newspaper Annual and Directory* (Philadelphia, Pa.).

Babson, Roger W., *Actions and Reactions: An Autobiography* (New York, Harper and Brothers, 1935).

Bailey, Thomas A., *Woodrow Wilson and the Lost Peace* (New York, The Macmillan Company, 1944).

Baker, Ray Stannard, *American Chronicle: The Autobiography of Ray Stannard Baker* (New York, Charles Scribner's Sons, 1945).

——, *Woodrow Wilson and the World Settlement* (Garden City, New York, 3 vols., Doubleday, Page & Company, 1922).

——, *Woodrow Wilson, Life and Letters* (Garden City, New York, Doubleday, Page & Company, Vols. 1–8, 1927–39).

Bartlett, Vernon, *Behind the Scenes at the Peace Conference* (London, G. Allen & Unwin Limited, 1919).

Barton, Albert O., *La Follette's Winning of Wisconsin* (Des Moines, Iowa, The Homestead Company, 1924).

——, *The Story of Primrose* (Madison, Wis., Taylor and Gleason, 1895).

Bascom, John, *Things Learned by Living* (New York, G. P. Putnam's Sons, 1913).

Bassett, John Spencer, *A Short History of the United States* (New York, The Macmillan Company, 1933, 1934, 1939).

Beard, Charles A., *A Foreign Policy for America* (New York, Alfred A. Knopf, 1940).

——, *The American Spirit: A Study of the Idea of Civilization in the United States* (New York, The Macmillan Company, 1942).

Bernstorff, Johann H. A. von, *The Memoirs of Count Bernstorff* (New York, Random House, 1936).

Binkley, W. E., *American Political Parties* (New York, Alfred A. Knopf, 1945).

Birdsall, Paul, *Versailles Twenty Years After* (New York, Reynal and Hitchcock, 1941).

Bishop, Joseph Bucklin, *Theodore Roosevelt and His Time* (New York, Charles Scribner's Sons, 1920).

Blum, John M., *Joe Tumulty and the Wilson Era* (Boston, Houghton Mifflin Company, 1951).

Bonsal, Stephen, *Unfinished Business* (Garden City, New York, Doubleday, Doran and Company, Inc., 1944).

Borchard, Edwin B., *The Diplomatic Protection of Citizens Abroad* (New York, The Banks Law Publishing Company, 1915).

——, and William P. Lage, *Neutrality for the United States* (New Haven, Conn., Yale University Press, 1937).

Bowers, Claude G., *Beveridge and the Progressive Era* (Cambridge, Mass., Houghton Mifflin Company, 1932).

Brandeis, Louis D., *Business—A Profession* (Boston, Small Maynard & Company, 1924).

——, *Other People's Money* (New York, Frederick H. Stokes, 1934).

Brandes, Georg, *The World at War* (New York, The Macmillan Company, 1917).

Britt, George, *Forty Years—Forty Millions: The Career of Frank A. Munsey* (New York, Farrar and Rinehart, 1935).

Brooks, Aubrey L., *Walter Clark, Fighting Judge* (Chapel Hill, N.C., The University of North Carolina Press, 1944).

Bryan, William Jennings, *A Tale of Two Conventions* (New York, Funk & Wagnalls Company, 1912).

——, and Mary Baird Bryan, *The Memoirs of William Jennings Bryan* (Philadelphia, Pa., The John C. Winston Company, 1925).

Buck, Solon Justus, *The Granger Movement* (Cambridge, Mass., Harvard University Press, 1913).

Bullitt, William C., *The Bullitt Mission to Russia* (New York, B. W. Huebsch, 1919).

Burdette, Franklin L., *Filibustering in the Senate* (Princeton, N.J., Princeton University Press, 1940).

Butt, Archibald W., *The Letters of Archie Butt* (Garden City, New York, Doubleday, Page and Company, 1924).

——, *Taft and Roosevelt* (Garden City, New York, Doubleday, Doran & Company, Inc., 1930).

Carr, Ezra, *The Patrons of Husbandry on the Pacific Coast* (San Francisco, Calif., A. L. Bancroft and Company, 1875).

Case, Victoria, and Robert Ormond Case, *We Called It Culture* (Garden City, New York, Doubleday and Company, Inc., 1948).

Chamberlain, John, *Farewell to Reform* (New York, Liveright, 1932).

Chase, Mary Ellen, *A Goodly Fellowship* (New York, The Macmillan Company, 1939).

Clapp, Edwin J., *Economic Aspects of the War; Neutral Rights, Belligerent Claims and American Commerce in the Years 1914–1915* (New Haven, Conn., Yale University Press, 1915).

Cochran, Negley D., *E. W. Scripps* (New York, Harcourt, Brace and Company, 1933).

Commons, John R., *Myself* (New York, The Macmillan Company, 1934).

Coolidge, Calvin, *The Autobiography of Calvin Coolidge* (New York, Cosmopolitan Book Corporation, 1929).

Costigan, Edward P., *Papers of Edward P. Costigan Relating to the Progressive Movement in Colorado, 1902–1917*, ed. Colin B. Goodykoontz (Boulder, Colo., University of Colorado, 1941).

Creel, George, *Rebel at Large: Recollections of Fifty Crowded Years* (New York, G. P. Putnam's Sons, 1947).

Croly, Herbert D., *The Promise of American Life* (New York, The Macmillan Company, 1912).

Curti, Merle E., *Peace or War: The American Struggle 1636–1936* (New York, W. W. Norton and Company, 1936).

——, *Bryan and World Peace* (Northampton, Mass., from Smith College Studies in History, 1931).

——, and Vernon Carstensen, *The University of Wisconsin* (Madison, Wis., University of Wisconsin Press, 2 vols., 1949).

Curtis, Francis, *The Republican Party* (New York, G. P. Putnam's Sons, 2 vols., 1904).

Daniels, Josephus, *The Wilson Era, Years of Peace, 1910–1917* (Chapel Hill, N.C., The University of North Carolina Press, 1944).

——, *The Wilson Era, Years of War and After, 1917–1923* (Chapel Hill, N.C., The University of North Carolina Press, 1946).

Davis, Oscar K., *Released for Publication* (Boston, Mass., Houghton Mifflin Company, 1925).

Democratic Textbook, 1916.

Dewey, Davis Rich, *Financial History of the United States* (New York, Longmans, Green and Company, 1936).

Dillon, Emile J., *The Peace Conference* (London, Hutchinson and Company, 1919).

Duffy, Herbert S., *William Howard Taft* (New York, Minton, Balch and Company, 1930).

Edwards, Everett E., *American Agriculture: The First 300 Years, The Year Book of Agriculture 1940* (Washington, D.C., 1940).

Ely, Richard T., *Ground Under Our Feet: An Autobiography* (New York, The Macmillan Company, 1938).

Fallows, Alice K., *Everybody's Bishop* (New York, J. H. Sears and Company, 1927).

Faulkner, Harold U., *From Versailles to the New Deal* (New Haven, Conn., Yale University Press, 1950).

Fitzpatrick, Edward, *McCarthy of Wisconsin* (New York, Columbia University Press, 1944).

Foster, William Z., *From Bryan to Stalin* (New York, International Publishers, 1937).

Frear, James A., *Forty Years of Progressive Public Service* (Washington, D.C., The Associated Writers, 1937).

Gardner, Gilson, *Lusty Scripps* (New York, The Vanguard Press, 1932).

Gauvreau, Emile H., and Lester Cohen, *Billy Mitchell* (New York, E. P. Dutton and Company, Inc., 1942).

Gerard, James W., *My Four Years in Germany* (New York, George H. Doran Company, 1917).

Gilbert, Clinton W., *"You Takes Your Choice"* (New York, G. P. Putnam's Sons, 1924).

Gjerset, Knut, *Norwegian Sailors in American Waters* (Northfield, Minn., Norwegian American Historical Association, 1933).

Goldman, Eric F., *Rendezvous With Destiny* (New York, Alfred A. Knopf, 1952).

Grattan, C. Hartley, *Why We Fought* (New York, Vanguard Press, 1929).

Gray, James, *Pine, Stream and Prairie: Wisconsin and Minnesota in Profile* (New York, Alfred A. Knopf, 1945).

Green, William R., *The Theory and Practice of Modern Taxation* (New York, Commerce Clearing House, Inc., 1938).

Grenard, Fernand, *La Révolution Russe* (Paris, Colin Armand).

Grey, Edward, Viscount of Fallodon, *Twenty-Five Years* (New York, Frederick A. Stokes Company, 1937).

Gwynn, Stephen L., *The Letters and Friendships of Sir Cecil Spring-Rice* (London, Constable and Company, 1929).

Hagedorn, Hermann, *Leonard Wood* (New York, Harper and Brothers, 2 vols., 1931).

Haines, Lynn, *The Senate from 1907 to 1912* (Washington, D.C., The National Capital Press, 1912).

———, *Your Congress* (Washington, D.C., The National Voters' League, 1915).

———, and Dora B. Haines, *The Lindberghs* (New York, The Vanguard Press, 1931).

Hallinan, Charles T., *American Investments in Europe* (London, Europa Publishing Company, Limited, 1927).

Hansen, Harry, *The Adventures of the Fourteen Points* (New York, The Century Company, 1919).

Hapgood, Norman, *The Advancing Hour* (New York, Boni and Liveright, 1920).

Haugen, Nils P., *Pioneer and Political Reminiscences* (Madison, Wis., The State Historical Society of Wisconsin).

Haynes, George Henry, *The Senate of the United States* (Boston, Mass., Houghton Mifflin Company, 1938).

Hays, Arthur G., *City Lawyer* (New York, Simon and Schuster, 1942).

Heaton, John L., *Cobb of "The World"* (New York, E. P. Dutton and Company, 1924).

Hechler, Kenneth W., *Insurgency Personalities and Politics of the Taft Era* (New York, Columbia University Press, 1940).

Hendrick, Burton J., *Life and Letters of Walter H. Page* (New York, Doubleday, Page and Company, 3 vols., 1922, 1923, 1926).

Hibben, Paxton, *The Peerless Leader* (New York, Farrar and Rinehart, Inc., 1929).

Hicks, John D., *The Populist Revolt* (Minneapolis, Minn., The University of Minnesota Press, 1931).

Hosford, Hester E., *The Forerunners of Woodrow Wilson* (East Orange, N.J., East Orange Record Print, 1914).

House, Edward M., and Charles Seymour, *What Really Happened at Paris* (New York, Charles Scribner's Sons, 1921).

Houston, David F., *Eight Years with Wilson's Cabinet, 1913–1920* (Garden City, Doubleday, Page & Company, 2 vols. 1926).

Howe, Frederic C., *Wisconsin: An Experiment in Democracy* (New York, Charles Scribner's Sons, 1912).

———, *The Confessions of a Reformer* (New York, Charles Scribner's Sons, 1925).

Howland, Harold, *Theodore Roosevelt and His Times: A Chronicle of the Progressive Movement* (New Haven, Conn., Yale University Press, 1921).

Jessup, Philip C., *Elihu Root* (New York, Dodd, Mead and Company, 2 vols., 1938).

Johnson, Claudius O., *Borah of Idaho* (New York, Longmans, Green and Company, 1936).

Johnson, Tom L., *My Story*, ed. Elizabeth J. Hauser (New York, B. W. Huebsch, 1911).

Josephson, Matthew, *The President Makers* (New York, Harcourt, Brace and Company, 1940).

Kavanagh, Herminie Templeton, *Darby O'Gill and the Good People* (New York, McClure, Phillip and Company, 1903).

Kent, Elizabeth Thacher, *William Kent, Independent* (Kentfield, Calif., no publisher, 1950).

Kerensky, Alexander F., *The Catastrophe* (New York, D. Appleton and Company, 1927).

———, *The Prelude to Bolshevism* (New York, Dodd, Mead and Co., 1919).

Keynes, John Maynard, *The Economic Consequences of the Peace* (New York, Harcourt, Brace and Company, 1920).

La Follette, John Henton, *History of the La Follette Family in America*, ed. Will La Follette (Ottumwa, Iowa, Charles F. Lang, 1898).

La Follette, Robert M., *La Follette's Autobiography: A Personal Narrative of Political Experiences* (Madison, Wis., La Follette Company, 1913).

———, *My Own Story* (articles in newspapers, syndicated serial, 1924).

La Follette-Wheeler Campaign Textbook, 1924.

Lane, Franklin K., *The Letters of Franklin K. Lane*, ed. Anne Wintermute Lane and Louise Herrick Wall (Boston, Mass., Houghton Mifflin Company, 1922).

Lansing, Robert, *The Peace Negotiations* (Boston, Mass., Houghton Mifflin Company, 1921).

———, *The Big Four and Others of the Peace Conference* (Boston, Mass., Houghton Mifflin Company, 1921).

———, *War Memoirs* (Indianapolis, Ind., The Bobbs-Merrill Company, 1935).

Lawrence, David, *The True Story of Woodrow Wilson* (New York, George H. Doran Company, 1924).

Lief, Alfred, *Brandeis: The Personal History of an American Ideal* (New York, Stackpole Sons, 1936).

———, *Democracy's Norris* (New York, Stackpole Sons, 1939).

Lloyd George, David, *War Memoirs of David Lloyd George* (London, Ivor Nicholson & Watson, 6 vols., 1933–1936).

———, *The Truth About the Peace Treaties* (London, V. Gollancz, Ltd., 1938).

———, *Memoirs of the Peace Conference* (New Haven, Conn., Yale University Press, 1939).

Lochner, Louis P., *La Conference des neutres pour une mediation continue* (Stockholm, A. B. Thule, 1916).

Lodge, Henry Cabot, *The Senate and the League of Nations* (New York, Charles Scribner's Sons, 1925).

———, *Selections from the Correspondence of Theodore Roosevelt and*

Henry Cabot Lodge, 1884–1918 (New York, Charles Scribner's Sons, 2 vols., 1925).

Longworth, Alice Roosevelt, *Crowded Hours* (New York, Charles Scribner's Sons, 1933).

Lovejoy, Allen F., *La Follette and the Establishment of the Direct Primary in Wisconsin, 1890–1904* (New Haven, Conn., Yale University Press, 1941).

Lovett, Robert Morss, *All Our Years* (New York, The Viking Press, 1948).

McAdoo, Eleanor Wilson, *The Woodrow Wilsons* (New York, The Macmillan Company, 1937).

McAdoo, William G., *Crowded Years* (Boston, Mass., Houghton Mifflin Company, 1931).

McCaleb, Walter F., *Theodore Roosevelt* (New York, A. & C. Boni, 1931).

McCarthy, Charles, *The Wisconsin Idea* (New York, The Macmillan Company, 1912).

MacKay, Kenneth C., *The Progressive Movement of 1924* (New York, Columbia University Press, 1947).

MacKaye, Percy, *The Scarecrow* (New York, The Macmillan Company, 1908).

McKinley, William, *Speeches and Addresses* (New York, Doubleday and McClure Company, 1900).

Manahan, James, *Trials of a Lawyer: Autobiography by James Manahan* (privately printed).

Mason, Alpheus T., *Brandeis and the Modern State* (Washington, D.C., National Home Library Foundation, 1936).

———, *The Brandeis Way: A Case Study in the Workings of Democracy* (Princeton, N. J., Princeton University Press, 1938).

———, *Bureaucracy Convicts Itself: The Ballinger-Pinchot Controversy of 1910* (New York, The Viking Press, 1941).

Merriam, Charles E., and Louise Overacker, *Primary Elections* (Chicago, Ill., University of Chicago Press, 1928).

Meyer, Ernst C., *Nominating Systems: Direct Primaries Versus Conventions in the United States* (Madison, Wis., published by author, 1902).

Middleton, George, *These Things Are Mine* (New York, The Macmillan Company, 1947).

Millis, Walter, *Road to War* (Boston, Mass., Houghton Mifflin Company, 1935).

Mock, James R., and Cedric Larsen, *Words That Won the War* (Princeton, N. J., Princeton University Press, 1939).

Morel, Edmund D., *The Secret History of a Great Betrayal* (London, "Foreign Affairs," 1922).

Mowry, George E., *The California Progressives* (Los Angeles, Calif., University of California Press, 1951).

———, *Theodore Roosevelt and the Progressive Movement* (Madison, Wis., The University of Wisconsin Press, 1946).

Neuberger, Richard L., and Stephen B. Kahn, *Integrity: The Life of George W. Norris* (New York, The Vanguard Press, 1937).

Nevins, Allan, *Henry White: Thirty Years of American Diplomacy* (New York, Harper and Brothers, 1930).
———, *Grover Cleveland: A Study in Courage* (New York, Dodd, Mead and Company, 1932).
———, *John D. Rockefeller* (New York, Charles Scribner's Sons, 2 vols., 1940).
Nicolson, Harold, *Peacemaking, 1919* (New York, Harcourt, Brace and Company, 1939).
Noble, Ransom E., Jr., *New Jersey Progressivism Before Wilson* (Princeton, N. J., Princeton University Press, 1946).
Norris, George W., *Fighting Liberal: The Autobiography of George W. Norris* (New York, The Macmillan Company, 1945).
Nye, Russell B., *Midwestern Progressive Politics: A Historical Study of Its Origins and Development, 1870–1950* (Lansing, Mich., Michigan State College Press, 1951).
Official German Documents Relating to the World War (New York, Oxford University Press, 1923).
Official Statements of War Aims and Peace Proposals, December 1916 to November 1918 (Washington, D.C., Carnegie Endowment for International Peace, 1921).
Older, Freemont, *My Own Story* (New York, The Macmillan Company, 1926).
Osborn, George C., *John Sharp Williams* (Baton Rouge, Louisiana State University Press, 1943).
Overacker, Louise, *Money in Elections* (New York, The Macmillan Company, 1932).
———, *The Presidential Primary* (New York, The Macmillan Company, 1926).
Palmer, Frederick, *Newton D. Baker: America at War* (New York, Dodd, Mead and Company, 1931).
———, *Bliss, Peacemaker: The Life and Letters of Tasker H. Bliss* (New York, Dodd, Mead and Company, 1934).
Petersen, Walter J., *Marine Labor Union Leadership* (San Francisco, Calif., Employment Service Bureau, 1925).
Peterson, Harold C., *Propaganda for War: The Campaign Against American Neutrality, 1914–1917* (Norman, Okla., University of Oklahoma Press, 1939).
Philipp, Emanuel L., assisted by Edgar T. Wheelock, *Political Reform In Wisconsin* (Milwaukee, Wis., E. L. Philipp, 1910).
Pinchot, Amos, *Facts About the Chicago Convention, 1920* (printed pamphlet).
Pinchot, Gifford, *The Fight for Conservation* (New York, Doubleday, Page and Company, 1910).
———, *Breaking New Ground* (New York, Harcourt, Brace and Company, 1947).
Platt, Chester C., *What La Follette's State Is Doing* (Iowa City, Iowa, The State Historical Society of Iowa, 1918).

Prather, Charles E., comp. and ed., *Winning Orations of the Inter-State Oratorical Contests and Biographies of Contestants* (Topeka, Kan., 1891).

Pringle, Henry F., *Theodore Roosevelt: A Biography* (New York, Harcourt, Brace and Company, 1931).

———, *The Life and Times of William Howard Taft* (New York, Farrar and Rinehart, 2 vols., 1939).

Proceedings of the Academy of Political Science (1915).

Pusey, Merlo J., *Charles Evans Hughes* (New York, The Macmillan Company, 2 vols., 1951).

Pyre, J. F. A., *Wisconsin* (New York, Oxford University Press, 1920).

Raney, William F., *Wisconsin, A Story of Progress* (New York, Prentice-Hall, 1940).

Rhodes, James F., *The McKinley and Roosevelt Administrations, 1897–1909* (New York, The Macmillan Company, 1923).

Richardson, Leon B., *William E. Chandler: Republican* (New York, Dodd, Mead and Company, 1940).

Riddell, George Allardice, Baron, *Lord Riddell's Intimate Diary of the Peace Conference and After, 1918–1923* (London, Victor Gollancz Limited, 1933).

Ripley, William Z., *Railroads: Rates and Regulations* (New York, Longmans, Green and Company, 1912).

Robinson, Edgar E., *The Evolution of American Political Parties* (New York, Harcourt, Brace and Company, 1924).

Robinson, William A., *Thomas B. Reed, Parliamentarian* (New York, Dodd, Mead and Company, 1930).

Roe, Gilbert E., *Our Judicial Oligarchy,* with Introduction by Robert M. La Follette (New York, B. W. Huebsch, 1912).

———, *In Memoriam Robert M. La Follette,* address before Dane County Bar Association, March 30, 1929 (Madison, Wis., Democrat Printing Company).

Roosevelt, Theodore, *The Works of Theodore Roosevelt,* National Edition (New York, Charles Scribner's Sons, 1926).

———, *An Autobiography* (New York, The Macmillan Company, 1916).

———, *Selections from the Correspondence of Theodore Roosevelt and Henry Cabot Lodge 1884–1918* (New York, Charles Scribner's Sons, 1925).

Ross, Edward Alsworth, *Seventy Years of It: An Autobiography* (New York, D. Appleton-Century Company, 1936).

Saloutos, Theodore, and John D. Hicks, *Agricultural Discontent in the Middle West, 1900–1939* (Madison, Wis., University of Wisconsin Press, 1951).

Savage, Carlton, *Policy of the United States Toward Maritime Commerce in War* (Washington, D.C., United States Government Printing Office, 1936).

Schapiro, Jacob S., *Modern and Contemporary European History* (New York, Houghton Mifflin Company, 1918).

Scott, James B., *A Survey of International Relations Between the United States and Germany, 1914–1917* (New York, Oxford University Press, 1917).

———, *Diplomatic Correspondence Between the United States and Germany, August 1, 1914–April 6, 1917* (New York, Oxford University Press, 1918).

Seldes, George, *Freedom of the Press* (Indianapolis, Ind., Dobbs-Merrill Company, 1935).

Short History of the International Seaman's Union (Law Department of I.S.U., 1934).

Seymour, Charles, *The Intimate Papers of Colonel House* (Boston, Mass., Houghton Mifflin Company, 4 vols., 1926, 1928).

Simmons, Furnifold M., comp. and ed. by J. Fred Rippy, *F. M. Simmons, Statesman of the New South: Memoirs and Addresses* (Durham, N.C., Duke University Press, 1936).

Smith, Arthur D. H., *Mr. House of Texas* (New York, Funk and Wagnalls Company, 1940).

Smith, James A., *The Spirit of American Government: A Study of the Constitution: Its Origin, Influence and Relation to Democracy* (New York, The Macmillan Company, 1907).

Squiers, James D., *British Propaganda at Home and in the United States from 1914 to 1917* (Cambridge, Mass., Harvard University Press, 1935).

Steffens, Lincoln, *The Shame of the Cities* (New York, McClure, Phillips and Company, 1904).

———, *The Struggle for Self-Government* (New York, McClure, Phillips and Company, 1906).

———, *The Autobiography of Lincoln Steffens* (New York, Harcourt, Brace and Company, 2 vols., 1931).

———, *The Letters of Lincoln Steffens*, ed. with Introductory Notes by Ella Winter and Granville Hicks, with a Memorandum by Carl Sandburg (New York, Harcourt, Brace and Company, 2 vols., 1938).

Stephenson, Isaac, *Recollections of a Long Life* (Chicago, Ill., privately printed, 1915).

Stephenson, Nathaniel W., *Nelson W. Aldrich: A Leader in American Politics* (New York, Charles Scribner's Sons, 1930).

Stirn, Ernest W., *An Annotated Bibliography of Robert M. La Follette* (Chicago, Ill., University of Chicago Press, 1937).

Stoddard, Henry L., *As I Knew Them* (New York, Harper and Brothers, 1927).

Sullivan, Mark, *Our Times* (New York, Charles Scribner's Sons, 4 vols., 1926–32).

Taney, Chief Justice Roger B., *Thoughts on the Conscription Law of the U. States—Rough Draft Requiring Revision* (an undelivered opinion), MS. in his own handwriting at New York City Public Library.

Tansill, Charles C., *America Goes to War* (Boston, Mass., Little, Brown and Company, 1938).

Tarbell, Ida M., *The Life of Abraham Lincoln* (New York, The Doubleday and McClure Company, 1900).

———, *The History of the Standard Oil Company* (New York, McClure, Phillips and Company, 1904).

Taylor, Paul S., *The Sailors' Union of the Pacific* (New York, The Ronald Press Company, 1923).

Temperley, Harold W. V., *A History of the Peace Conference of Paris* (London, H. Frowde and Hodder and Stoughton, 6 vols., 1920–24).

Thompson, J. David, *The Amendment of the Federal Constitution*, monograph, *Proceedings of the Academy of Political Science,* Vol. III, January, 1913.

The Times Documentary History of the War (London, Printing House Square, Vol. 4, 1917).

Torelle, Ellen, comp., *The Political Philosophy of Robert M. La Follette* (Madison, Wis., La Follette Publishing Company, 1920).

Towne, Charles H., *So Far, So Good* (New York, Julian Messner, Inc., 1945).

Tumulty, Joseph P., *Woodrow Wilson As I Know Him* (New York, Doubleday, Page and Company, 1921).

Turnbull, George S., *History of Oregon Newspapers* (Portland, Ore., Binsfords and Mort, 1939).

Turner, Frederick J., *The Frontier in American History* (New York, Henry Holt and Company, 1920).

Vagts, Alfred, *Deutschland und Die Vereinigten Staaten in Der Weltpolitik* (New York, The Macmillan Company, 2 vols., 1935).

Villard, Oswald G., *Fighting Years* (New York, Harcourt, Brace and Company, 1939).

Voter's Handbook (1902).

Warren, Louis A., *The Lincoln and La Follette Families in Pioneer Drama* (Madison, Wis., reprinted from the *Wisconsin Magazine of History,* 1929).

Watson, James E., *As I Knew Them* (Indianapolis, Ind., The Bobbs-Merrill Company, 1936).

Werner, M. R., *Privileged Characters* (New York, Robert M. McBride and Company, 1935).

Weyl, Walter E., *The New Democracy* (New York, The Macmillan Company, 1912).

White, William Allen, *Politics: The Citizen's Business* (New York, The Macmillan Company, 1924).

———, *Calvin Coolidge* (New York, The Macmillan Company, 1926).

———, *Woodrow Wilson: The Man, His Times and His Task* (Boston, Mass., Houghton Mifflin Company, 1929).

Wight, William W., *Henry Clay Payne* (Milwaukee, Wis., Burdick and Allen, 1907).

Wilson, Edith Bolling, *My Memoir* (Indianapolis, Ind., The Bobbs-Merrill Company, 1939).

Wilson, Woodrow, *Constitutional Government in the United States* (New York, The Columbia University Press, 1911).

———, *The New Freedom* (Garden City, New York, Doubleday, Page and Company, 1918).

———, *The Public Papers of Woodrow Wilson 1917–1924,* ed. Ray Stannard Baker and William E. Dodd (New York, Harper and Brothers, 6 vols., 1925–27).

Winning Orations of the Inter-State Oratorical Contests and Biographies of Contestants, comp. and ed. Charles Edgar Prather (Topeka, Kan., 1891).
Wise, Jennings C., *Woodrow Wilson: A Disciple of Revolution* (New York, The Paisley Press, Inc., 1938).

Periodicals

(Among the many periodicals and newspapers consulted, only those which were either cited or quoted in text are here included.)

American Federationist
American Historical Review
American Journal of International Law
American Magazine
Collier's Weekly
Commoner
Current History
Everybody's Magazine
Facts (by Committee of '48)
Forum
Four Lights
Freeman
Hampton's Magazine
Harper's Magazine
Harper's Weekly
Hearst's International Magazine
Independent
Labor (previously, *Railroad Democracy*)
Ladies' Home Journal
La Follette's Magazine (1909–1929) (including Memorial Edition for Robert M. La Follette, July, 1925).
Life (Note: Not the present magazine of same title).
Literary Digest
Munsey's Magazine
Nation
National Magazine
New Majority
New Republic
New York Times Magazine
Nonpartisan Leader (formerly, *National Leader*)
Outlook
Palimpsest (Iowa State Historical Society)
Pearson's Magazine
Political Science Quarterly

Progressive (Memorial Edition for Belle Case La Follette, November 7, 1931, edited by Fred L. Holmes and Fola La Follette).
Saturday Evening Post
Socialist Review
Survey
Touchstone
Twentieth Century Magazine
Unity
University Press (Wisconsin)
Wisconsin Alumni Magazine
Wisconsin Farmer
Woman Citizen
Woman's Journal
World's Work

Newspapers

Age-Herald, Birmingham, Ala.
Argus, Rock Island, Ill.
Ashtabula Beacon Record
Atlanta Journal
N. W. Ayer & Sons, *American Newspaper Annual and Directory*
Beloit Free Press (1879)
Boston Journal
Boston Sunday Globe
Boston Transcript
Brooklyn Daily Eagle
Bulletin, San Francisco
Capital Times, Madison, Wis.
Capitol News, Washington, D.C.
Chicago Daily Tribune
Chicago Evening Post
Chicago Herald
Chicago Times
Chippewa Falls Independent
Christian Science Monitor, Boston
Cincinnati Times-Star
Cleveland Plain Dealer
Colorado Springs Gazette
Commercial Tribune, Cincinnati
Daily Argus Leader, Sioux Falls, S.D.
Daily Globe-Democrat, St. Louis, Mo.
Daily Inter-Ocean, Chicago
Daily Union, Salina, Kan.

Day Book, Chicago
Democrat and Chronicle, Rochester, N.Y.
Detroit Free Press
Detroit Journal
Detroit News
Dispatch, Moline, Ill.
Dodgeville Chronicle (1886)
Emporia Daily Gazette
Enquirer, Cincinnati
Evening Crescent, Appleton, Wis.
Evening Mail, New York
Evening Post, New York
Evening Star, Washington, D.C.
Fargo Forum, Fargo, N.D.
Gazette, Hutchinson, Kan.
Globe, Toronto, Canada
Globe and Commercial Advertiser, New York
Globe-Gazette, Mason City, Iowa
Grand Rapids Herald
Hawk-Eye, Burlington, Iowa
Herald, Boston
Idaho Daily Statesman
Indianapolis News
Jefferson County Union, Wisconsin
Johnstown Democrat, Pennsylvania
Kansas City Journal
Kansas City Star
Madison Democrat, Wisconsin
Mail and Empire, Toronto, Canada
Milwaukee Daily News
Milwaukee Free Press
Milwaukee Journal
Milwaukee Sentinel
Minneapolis Journal
Minneapolis Sunday Tribune
Morning World-Herald, Omaha
Nashville American
Nebraska State Journal
Newark Evening News
New Haven Evening Register
News and Observer, Raleigh, N.C.
News-Bee, Toledo
New York American
New York Evening Journal
New York Herald
New York Times
New York Tribune

North American, Philadelphia
Ohio State Journal
Omaha Daily News
Oshkosh Northwestern
Philadelphia Inquirer
Pittsburgh Gazette-Times
Pittsburgh Post
Portland Oregonian
Post-Intelligencer, Seattle, Wash.
Press, New York
Public Ledger, Philadelphia
Quincy Journal, Illinois
Record-Herald, Chicago
Register and Leader, Des Moines
Rocky Mountain News
St. Paul Dispatch
St. Paul Pioneer Press
Salina Journal, Kansas
San Francisco Call
San Francisco Examiner
Seattle Daily Times
Sioux Falls Press
Spokesman-Review, Spokane
Springfield Daily Republican, Massachusetts
Sun, Baltimore
Sun, New York
Telegram, Winnipeg, Canada
Wall Street Journal
Washington Daily News
Washington Herald
Washington Post
Washington Times
Whitewater Register, Whitewater, Wis.
Wisconsin State Journal, Madison, Wis.
Witness and Canadian Homestead, Montreal, Canada
World, New York
World-Herald, Omaha

Unpublished Manuscripts

Barr, William M., *George Lawrence Record,* Master's essay, Columbia University, 1936.
Crownhart, Charles H. *Memorandum,* August, 1920.

Goldstein, Milton W., *The La Follette Movement in Wisconsin,* Washington University, St. Louis, Mo., 1936.

Isaacs, William, *Hiram Johnson—A Political Study,* Master's essay, Columbia University, 1932.

Katz, Isaac, *Gifford Pinchot—Progressive,* Master's essay, Columbia University, 1932.

McCue, Claire Francis, *Taft, Roosevelt Break,* Master's essay, Columbia University, 1932.

McGuiness, Mary F., *George W. Norris, Senator from Nebraska 1913–1921,* Master's essay, Columbia University, 1932.

Manly, Basil M., *Memorandum Conference at Madison,* July 25–27, 1920.

———, Diary of European Trip with R. M. L., 1923.

Morgan, Charles E., *Political Philosophy of William Allen White,* Master's essay, Columbia University, 1931.

Page, William Tyler, Pair Clerk to the House Minority.

Pinchot, Amos, *The Progressive Party.*

Ridderhof, Emily E., *Thomas J. Walsh,* Master's essay, Columbia University, 1934.

Roe, Gilbert E., *The Third Party Convention* [1920], *Why Senator La Follette Declined the Nomination.*

Sayre, Wallace S., *Robert M. La Follette: A Study in Political Methods,* Doctor's thesis, New York University, New York, 1930.

Studer, N., *The La Follette 1924 Campaign in Greater New York,* Master's essay, Columbia University, 1934.

Index

The following abbreviations have been used in this Index: RML for Robert Marion La Follette, Sr.; BCL for his wife, Belle Case La Follette; TR for Theodore Roosevelt; and WW for Woodrow Wilson.